A PEOPLE CALLED CUMBERLAND PRESBYTERIANS

# A People Called

# Cumberland Presbyterians

*Vol. II*

BEN M. BARRUS
*Professor of History, Bethel College*

MILTON L. BAUGHN
*Professor of History, Florence State University*

THOMAS H. CAMPBELL
*Professor of New Testament and Dean,
Memphis Theological Seminary*

Foreword by
C. RAY DOBBINS

Introduction and Chapter 16 by
HUBERT W. MORROW

*Wipf & Stock*
PUBLISHERS
*Eugene, Oregon*

Wipf and Stock Publishers
199 West 8th Avenue, Suite 3
Eugene, Oregon 97401

A People Called Cumberland Presbyterians
A History of the Cumberland Presbyterian Church
By Barrus, Ben M., Baughn, Milton L., and Campbell, Thomas H.
Copyright©1972 Cumberland Presbyterian Church
ISBN: 1-57910-100-3
Publication date 2/5/1998
Previously published by Frontier Press, 1972

# TABLE OF CONTENTS

*Volume I*

# TABLE OF CONTENTS

*Volume II*

PART III: THE CUMBERLAND PRESBYTERIAN CHURCH IN THE TWENTIETH CENTURY, 1901-1970

Chapters 17-24, Thomas H. Campbell

# FOREWORD

The first history of the Cumberland Presbyterian Church was published in 1835, twenty-five years after the new denomination had come into being. Written by the Rev. James Smith, it was appended to a general history of the Christian Church which Smith "compiled from various authors." The entire work was published under the interesting and engaging title *History of the Christian Church from Its Origin to the Present Time, Compiled from Various Authors, Including a History of the Cumberland Presbyterian Church, Drawn from Authentic Documents.* Smith had set this new religious movement on the American frontier in the context of the entire Christian Church.

A little more than half a century elapsed before the appearance of another book entitled *History of the Cumberland Presbyterian Church,* by the Rev. B. W. McDonnold, in 1888. A unique work, written in a warm, personal style, the book was largely without documentation and was often obviously drawn from personal recollections and from conversations with eyewitnesses. McDonnold's book (to which several other writers contributed topical portions, with his consent) enjoyed widespread popularity and remained for many decades the authoritative history of the Church.

In the twentieth century, with McDonnold's book out of print, the Rev. Thomas H. Campbell published in 1944 a new work entitled *Studies in Cumberland Presbyterian History.* A rewritten and somewhat abbreviated version of this book appeared in 1965 under the title *Good News on the Frontier; A History of the Cumberland Presbyterian Church.*

This present volume has grown out of two felt needs. First, no comprehensive history of the Cumberland Presbyterian Church is now in print, nor has the twentieth century period in the life of the Church been adequately covered in any previously published work. Second, every ongoing community needs periodically to come to grips with its history. Just as each person must establish his own identity, so each generation in a historical community must discover who it is. From the time of the Old Testament prophets, the Covenant Community has frequently recounted its history, not in order to glorify the past, but in order to understand its nature and mission in the present.

The first action which was taken in relation to the publication of this book was a directive by the General Assembly of the Church in 1957 to its Historical Committee. The Assembly had acted in response to recommendations concerning a new history from its retiring Moderator, the Rev. Hubert W. Morrow, and from the Historical Committee, then consisting of the Rev. H. Shaw Scates, W. A. Smith, and Thomas H. Campbell. The original hope was that the book would be available by 1960, the sesquicentennial of the Church, a hope that was not realized.

In 1958 the Historical Committee recommended to the General Assembly that an Editorial Board be created to plan and supervise the writing of the history, consisting of the Rev. Raymon Burroughs, the Rev. C. Ray Dobbins, Robert Corlew, the Rev. Charles E. Zapp, and Hubert W. Morrow, who later was named chairman. Robert Corlew resigned from the Board in the early stages of the planning of the project. Louis Adams, who was appointed to succeed him, served only a short time before his death in 1964, and Charles E. Zapp died in 1966. The Editorial Board which completed the project included Burroughs, Dobbins, and Morrow from the original membership, and W. A. Smith and Jimmie J. McKinley.

Early in its planning the Board projected a history which would be divided into three periods, each of which would be written by a separate author. The writer chosen for the early period was the Rev. Ben M. Barrus, now professor of history, Bethel College, McKenzie, Tennessee; Milton L. Baughn, now professor of history, Florence State University, Florence, Alabama, was secured as writer for the middle period; and Thomas H. Campbell, now professor of New Testament and dean of Memphis Theological Seminary, Memphis, Tennessee, was selected for the modern period. Two variations from this scheme have been made: Chapter 7 in the early period was written by Campbell, and Chapter 16 in the middle period was written by Hubert W. Morrow, now Hannibal Seagle Professor of Bible and Philosophy and chairman of the Division of Religion and Philosophy at Bethel College.

For the most part the writers have done their work while carrying on the full duties of their regular jobs. Early in the project, an interested donor provided a gift of $1,500 which was used for expenses of the Editorial Board and for travel and secretarial help for the writers. Later a fund established with the Board of Finance of the Cumberland Presbyterian Church by Mr. and Mrs. Dwight McDonald of Knoxville, Tennessee, in honor of the late Fines Ewing Keene, an elder in the First Cumberland Presbyterian Church, Knoxville, and father of Mrs. McDonald, assured the publication of the book.

Final editing of the manuscript and the determination of the format of the volume have been done by Jimmie J. McKinley, Hubert W. Morrow, and C. Ray Dobbins. The Rev. Alfred Bennett and W. T. Franklin, members of the Historical Committee of the Cumberland Presbyterian Church, read the manuscript and offered valuable comments. The title was suggested by Raymon Burroughs.

# FOREWORD

Persons who have given valuable help in financial and publishing details include Eugene Warren, executive secretary of the Board of Finance; the Rev. Harold Davis, executive secretary of the Board of Publication and Christian Education of the Cumberland Presbyterian Church; and William E. Phalan, manager, and Garvis Frazier of Frontier Press. Many other persons contributed to the project, including librarians, typists, members of the authors' and editors' families, and persons who simply were interested in the history of the Cumberland Presbyterian Church.

Whereas previous histories of the Church were written entirely or largely by single authors, this volume is the result of a team effort. It is offered to its readers with the hope that it will fill the gap that exists among contemporary works in American church history concerning the origin and development of the Cumberland Presbyterian Church.

C. Ray Dobbins

Memphis, Tennessee
April 21, 1971

# INTRODUCTION

On the bleak, wintry evening of February 3, 1810, Samuel McAdow gazed intently through his cabin window as three men on horseback approached his cabin. Finis Ewing, Samuel King, and Ewing's cousin, Ephraim McLean, had ridden over eighty miles from Logan County, Kentucky, to Dickson County, Tennessee. The three horsemen were chilled by the frigid weather, but they were spurred onward by the determination to solicit McAdow's assistance in an action they felt compelled to take.

When McAdow recognized the men, he pondered carefully their intentions as they approached his isolated cabin. He recalled the past five years. These three men represented five years of turmoil, ecclesiastical controversies, alienations, and disaffections in the Presbyterian Church in Tennessee and Kentucky. When the Synod of Kentucky, in 1805, suspended a number of ordained ministers, licentiates, candidates, and exhorters of Cumberland Presbytery in an effort to settle the problems, some of the suspended members had organized into a Council until the differences between them and the synod could be resolved by the General Assembly of the Presbyterian Church.

After the trouble began in 1805, the middle-aged McAdow, who had no desire to enter into the conflict, moved with his new bride (his third wife) into seclusion in Dickson County, Tennessee, in 1806. Now, these three men, somewhat younger than himself, were seeking him out for some purpose. Intuitively, he knew what they wanted, but the thought of conflict was still distasteful to him. Why couldn't they capitulate and follow James McGready, William Hodge, and others who had submitted to the dictates of the synod and the General Assembly? Why should they be heroes of the presbytery and prolong the controversy? What specifically did they have in mind? What did they want him to do?

McAdow greeted the visitors and welcomed them to the protection of his house. The impetuous Ewing came directly to the point. The presbyterian form of government required three ordained ministers to constitute a presbytery. They saw no solution of the problem with the synod short of complete capitulation to what they regarded as illegal demands. They were now determined to organize an independent presbytery and they needed a third member. Ewing indicated that he was ready to constitute a presbytery with two members, if necessary, but he hoped McAdow would join in the action. The first action he had in mind for the presbytery was the ordination of Ephraim

McLean. Ewing felt the urgency to act because the Council had agreed that if reconciliation with the church proved impossible, it would be dissolved in March 1810, and the recalcitrant members would submit to the synod. This he did not intend to do.

Recalling previous conversations with McAdow, Ewing said, "Brother McAdow, we know that when the trouble began five years ago, you moved away from the arena of conflict. We have no hard feelings toward you, and we have come to ask you now to take a stand on the matter. Join with us in forming an independent presbytery that the work of the Council may not be lost."

McAdow attempted to hide some feeling of guilt about the matter. "Well," he replied, "this is a serious step which you are considering. I will have to think about it." There was a silence. McAdow continued, "I will have to think and pray about it. You wait here while I go off alone for a time. I'll let you know. If it is the will of the Lord, I will do it."

Ewing was impatient. King wondered why his brother-in-law, William McGee, had not consented to join them. This would have solved the problem. Ewing and King were agreed that if McAdow would not join them, they would constitute a presbytery and ordain McLean. However, King was still bothered by the obvious constitutional problem.

Time stretched on. Finally McAdow returned, and from the look on his face they knew he had decided to join them. They could confirm what was later said of him, that "he came in with a most cheerful and heavenly countenance and informed them he was ready to constitute the Presbytery, that God had heard and answered the doubtful question." [1] The three, Ewing, King, and McAdow, constituted Cumberland Presbytery immediately and proceeded to ordain Ephraim McLean. The new presbytery, with four members, would hold its first meeting in March 1810. In the meantime, in order to make clear the reason for their actions, Ewing, King, and McAdow published a statement which set forth the basis of their covenant with each other:

In Dixon county Tennessee State, at the Rev. Samuel M'Adow's this 4th day of February, 1810.

We Samuel M'Adow, Finis Ewing, and Samuel King, regularly ordained ministers, in the presbyterian church against whom, no charge, either of immorality, or Heresy has ever been exhibited, before any of the church Judicatures. Having waited in vain more than four years, in the mean time, petitioning the general assembly for a redress of grievances, and a restoration of our violated rights, have, and do hereby agree, and determine, to constitute into a presbytery, known by the name of the Cumberland presbytery. On the following conditions (to wit) all candidates for the ministry, who may hereafter be licensed by this presbytery; and all the licentiates, or probationers who may hereafter be ordained by this presbytery; shall be required before such licensure, and ordination, to receive, and adopt the confession and discipline of the presbyterian church, except the idea of fatality, that seems to be taught under the mysterious doctrine of predestination. It is to be understood, however, that such as can clearly receive the confession, without an exception, shall not be required to make any. Moreover, all licentiates, before they are set apart to the whole work of the ministry (or ordained) shall be required to undergo an examination, on English Grammar, Geography, Astronomy, natural & moral philosophy, and church history. The presbytery may also require an examination on all, or any part, of the above branches of literature, before licensure if they deem it expedient.[2]

It was thus that the Cumberland Presbyterian Church had its beginning, in a log house in Dickson County, Tennessee, in 1810. Though the dialogue in this account is an imaginative reconstruction, it contains a core of historical fact. The Cumberland Presbyterian Church was a frontier movement. Born of the Great Revival of 1800 in Kentucky and Tennessee, it rode the crest of the population movement westward, growing up with the young nation whose democratic ideals it reflected. This book is about the origin and development of the Cumberland Presbyterian Church.

The beginning of a historical movement is seldom abrupt. Its roots usually reach back into previous periods and developments. It was so with the Cumberland Presbyterian Church. Therefore, the history of this religious movement is begun with an examination of its roots in early American Presbyterianism. The Cumberland Presbyterian Church was born in the midst of controversies, and it is to these controversies and their resolution that Part I of this book is devoted.

After the formation of the independent Cumberland Presbytery in 1810, efforts were made to effect a reconciliation with the parent church. During the next three years the presbytery showed remarkable growth, and in 1813, apparently with hope of reconciliation abandoned, Cumberland Presbytery was divided into three presbyteries and these constituted into Cumberland Synod. It was then that the fledgling Church embarked on its mission to frontier America.

Part II of this history tells the story of circuit-riding Cumberland Presbyterian ministers who moved steadily with the frontier, planting churches in communities as they went. As the Church grew in membership and resources its missionary activities were augmented by the development of institutional activities in such areas as publication of religious literature and education. It weathered the division of the nation in the Civil War and was able immediately after the war to resume its ministry as a united church. As a result of growing dissatisfaction with its limited revision of the Westminster Confession, in 1883 the Church adopted a new, radically rewritten

# INTRODUCTION

Confession of Faith. In the following year the Cumberland Presbyterian Church was accepted into membership of the World Alliance of Presbyterian and Reformed Churches, attaining for the first time a full recognition in the family of churches out of which it came.

In the last three decades of the nineteenth century the Cumberland Presbyterian Church exhibited a lively interest in the possibility of union with other Protestant denominations. This interest bore fruit in 1906 in what proved to be an ill-fated union with the Presbyterian Church, U.S.A. Though the union was officially consummated, it was only partially successful. The denomination was fragmented with a portion withdrawing to perpetuate the Cumberland Presbyterian Church.

Part III of this history tells the story of this unhappy episode and the efforts that were expended in rebuilding. By the mid-twentieth century the Church had moved beyond most of the bitterness and heartaches that followed 1906. A new searching began for a positive mission. Preoccupation with self-perpetuation was no longer sufficient to command the interest and energies of Cumberland Presbyterians. For some, at least, a new interest in the Church's history provided a perspective in which to discover who it is and what it is about in the world.

HUBERT W. MORROW

McKenzie, Tennessee
April 21, 1971

xiii

# PART I

*Background and Formation*

*of the*

*Cumberland Presbyterian Church*

*Through 1829*

The formation of the Cumberland Presbyterian Church in 1810 is described in the following chapters as a convergence of factors—theological, organizational, sociological, and personal. Both from the standpoint of causal connections and interpretation, it is highly important that the Cumberland Presbyterian Church be seen in the context of the history of American Presbyterianism. Chapters 1-4 present this background. Chapter 5 gives an account of the organization of the Church. Chapter 6 interprets this event in light of its background. Chapter 7 begins the story of the growth and development of the new Church.

# 1

## BORN IN CONTROVERSY:

## EARLY AMERICAN PRESBYTERIANISM

*The early history of the Presbyterian church in this country is involved in no little controversy.*

William B. Sprague

The history of American Presbyterianism in general, and Cumberland Presbyterianism in particular, can be understood only by studying the origins of American Presbyterianism during the seventeenth century and its conflicts during the eighteenth century. In its origin, American Presbyterianism was characterized by conflicting points of view. A nineteenth century Presbyterian historian, William B. Sprague, correctly asserted that "the early history of the Presbyterian church in this country is involved in no little controversy." [1] "Commingled in it . . . we find the elements of English dissent, Irish fervor, Scotch persistence, and Huguenot devotion." [2] A thorough consideration of the history of American Presbyterianism must take into account many and diverse sources.

One important factor contributing to the origin and character of American Presbyterianism is revealed in the creedal development of the Congregationalist synods of New England in which the importance of the eldership was endorsed as a means of saving the theocratic state. When the "holy experiment" began to disintegrate, New England Congregationalism was forced to a more centralized church government with an increasingly presbyterial character.

3

During the first half of the seventeenth century, the New England Way had been attacked by Roger Williams and Anne Hutchinson. Williams, an avowed Separatist at the time, preferred to serve as pastor in Plymouth, instead of Boston, because the church in the latter was not clearly separated from the Church of England. His criticism of enforced conformity and the right of the King of England to issue a charter involving lands belonging to the Indians led to his trial and banishment in 1635. Williams had come to New England "loosing wild foxes with fire brands to ravage the snug fields of the Presbyterian Utopia." [3] He fled to Rhode Island and founded Providence on land purchased from the Indians.

Mrs. Hutchinson had dared to question the oligarchy of the Massachusetts Bay Colony. In March 1638, she was excommunicated from the church. John Winthrop, governor of the Bay Colony, recorded the verdict of the inquisitional proceedings: "After much time and many arguments had been spent to bring her to see her sin, but all in vain, the church with one consent, cast her out." [4] Following Williams, she found refuge in Rhode Island.

As the attack continued against the New England Way, Presbyterianism gradually emerged. A large number of Presbyterians had settled in New England. Cotton Mather reported that at least 4,000 Presbyterians had been among the 21,000 Puritans who landed in New England between 1620 and 1640.[5]

In 1646, a group of dissenters presented a remonstrance to the magistrates of Boston in an effort to abolish the law limiting the franchise to church members. They expressed a desire to gain the civil liberty that Presbyterians and Congregationalists were enjoying in England following the overthrow of the episcopal hierarchy in 1642. The dissenters were led by a Presbyterian Puritan, Robert Childs, who was arrested later as he prepared to sail for England. In his possession was found a petition to the House of Commons, requesting a royal governor to enforce the freedom of Englishmen, and asking for a legal recognition of Presbyterianism.

The opposition to the holy experiment in New England gained momentum by the debates between the Independents and the Presbyterians in the Westminster Assembly in England.[6] The New Englanders found it necessary to distinguish their church polity from Independence or Separatism on the left and from Presbyterianism on the right. The criticisms were met in 1648 by a consensus known as the Cambridge Platform. The synod at Cambridge was convened by the General Court of Massachusetts. Out of a possible twenty-nine churches, twenty-eight participated in formulating the first platform of American Congregationalism.[7] The Cambridge Synod adopted the Westminster Confession of Faith and a Congregational polity based upon the ideas of Robert Browne, Henry Barrowe, and Henry Jacob.

The Cambridge Platform asserted that synods are "not necessary to the Being" of a church; yet at times, they are "necessary to the Well-being of Churches." With the shift of authority in the local church from the congregation to pastor and elders—even though the pastor's and elders' authority did not extend beyond their local church—the wedge was inserted which would give more authority to church officers along presbyterial lines.

In theory, a synod or presbytery could exercise no authority over congregations: synods like Cambridge were to limit their authority simply to an advisory capacity. No congregation had to accept the advice of a synod. In actuality, a synod had greater power. The Cambridge Synod did not merely offer advice; it adopted a Confession of Faith which included a Form of Government and Rules of Discipline. The civil magistrate had power "to debate and determine controversies of Faith and Cases of Conscience." The magistrates, referred to as "nursing Fathers," could take the role of a presbytery or synod in administering discipline.[8]

The New England Way received a devastating blow in 1662. The early Congregationalists insisted upon a regenerated church membership, with full church membership being conditioned upon a public testimony of personal religious experience. The Cambridge Platform had allowed for children of the Covenant of Grace to become members by being baptized at birth. When many of the second generation came of age, they failed to make a profession of a personal religious experience; therefore, they were not considered as full communicants of the church, and they could not partake of the Lord's Supper. The second generation not only considered themselves full members by virtue of their parents' covenantal relationship, but they requested baptism for *their* children. The church was in a dilemma.

Had the churches yielded to this demand, the great majority of the third generation of church members, no doubt, would have been unregenerated. Had the church not yielded at all, and insisted that even the second generation should be excluded from the church unless they professed regeneration, the churches would have lost many of their younger and most influential members.[9]

The Cambridge Synod had dealt with the problem in 1648 but had refused to make a decision. A group of ministers met in Boston in 1657 and reached a compromise which was confirmed by a Massachusetts synod in 1662.[10] The compromise, known as the Half-Way Covenant, defined baptized children of covenant parents as being "half-way" in the covenant, and their children, in turn, by reason of their grandparents' relation to the covenant, were entitled to baptism. That is, the second generation, if they qualified by living an upright life and by "solemnly owning the covenant before the church," could present their children for baptism.[11] They were simply "half-way" members.

As half-way members, they could not participate in the Lord's Supper, nor could they exercise the franchise. Since authority of the theocracy rested on the close identification of the church and the civil power, the restriction of the franchise only to church members had important political implications. The Half-Way Covenant also affected the nature of the New England church. "By lowering the conditions of membership to the 'half-way covenant,' New England Congregationalism chose the 'presbyterian way' and ceased to be in any real sense a 'gathered church.' "[12]

The only barrier left against full participation by half-way members in the life of the church was the Lord's Supper. The removal of this final barrier was expressed in the organization of the Brattle Street Church in 1698 by a group of wealthy and independent businessmen who wanted a church free from the current controversies. Benjamin Colman, a Presbyterian minister ordained in London, accepted a call to the church as pastor. The Brattle Street Church did not require a conversion experience for membership, children of professing parents could be baptized, the Lord's Supper would be given to qualified persons as determined by the preacher, and *all* baptized persons could vote in calling a new minister.

Although the Brattle Street Church action represented a shift from the individual's profession of salvation to the minister's prerogative in determining who could participate in the communion service, a justifiable rationale was needed for freely allowing noncovenanters to come to the communion table. This was supplied by Solomon Stoddard, pastor of the Northampton church. Stoddard maintained that the Lord's Supper was open to all "visible saints." Visible saints included all who "make a serious profession of true religion together with those that do descend from them, til rejected of God." Even those who know themselves to be in a "natural condition" must participate in the Supper, because "as no man may neglect prayer, or hearing the word, because he cannot do it in faith, so he may not neglect the Lord's Supper."[13] The definition of the New England ecclesiastico-political community was rendered meaningless by allowing participation in the Lord's Supper by those not included in the covenant.

In an effort to defend the Holy Commonwealth, plans were made to save the crumbling Puritan theology. For fifty years (1648-1698), the theocratic state defended itself by stressing the proper church government. In the effort to curb the change in New England, the emphasis was again placed on ecclesiastical polity. In 1691, Increase Mather had attempted an agreement between the New England clergy and the Presbyterians. By 1700, associations of ministers were begun under the leadership of Stoddard. Five years later, an attempt to make the ministerial associations a part of the Massachusetts ecclesiastical structure failed to materialize.

The use of ministerial associations gained a foothold in Connecticut. The clergy approved a platform at Saybrook in 1708, which included three documents: the *Heads of Agreement,* a plan of union adopted by Congregationalists and Presbyterians in London in 1691; the *Savoy Confession,* as adopted by Massachusetts in 1680; and a group of *Articles,* based on the *Massachusetts Proposals* of 1705. The *Articles* provided for semipresbyterian judicatories called "consociations" for the purpose of exercising ecclesiastical discipline, ordination of ministers, and installation and dismissal of pastors. Delegates from the various associations were to meet as a General Association at least once a year.[14] As the consociations moved the Puritans a step closer to the Presbyterians—many of whom were among the New England Puritans—the "children of the holy experiment found it impossible to maintain the faith without the recognition of a power beyond the congregation."[15]

The Saybrook platform was accepted generally throughout Connecticut. The consociations began to function more and more like presbyteries, with the result that Connecticut Congregationalism developed a closer affinity with the Presbyterianism of the middle colonies than with the Congregationalism of Massachusetts. This trend was expressed at a later date in a declaration passed by the Hartford North Association, in 1799:

> The constitution of the churches of Connecticut . . . adopted at the earliest period of the settlement of this state is not Congregational, but contains the essentials of the Church of Scotland or of the Presbyterian Church in America . . . though sometimes indeed the associated churches of Connecticut are loosely and vaguely, though improperly, termed Congregational.[16]

In addition to the development in New England of a "Congregationalized Presbyterianism" or a "Presbyterianized Congregationalism,"[17] there was a distinct Presbyterian endeavor in progress. Elements of Presbyterianism were evident in New England during the seventeenth century. Churches at Newbury and Hingham, Massachusetts, had Presbyterian pastors as early as 1634. Other ministers with Presbyterian views left England and settled in Connecticut.

Because of the conflict occurring in England between the Independents (Congregationalists) and the Presbyterians, things were made intolerable for the New England Presbyterians by the Congregationalists who sought to prevent a similar movement in America. New England Puritans moved from Massachusetts and Connecticut and established churches on Long Island, in Westchester County, New York, and in East Jersey. Most of these churches were Congregational and were served by New England Puritans. Historians differ as to the number of churches established, the number that were or became Presbyterian, and the identity of the first permanent Presbyterian church.[18] The name and location of the first Presbyterian church in New England is not as important as the type of Presbyterianism that evolved from the New England Puritan influence in New York and New Jersey.

Small groups of Presbyterians were scattered throughout the colonies. Unlike other churches, they were not concentrated in one particular area. From 1660, when Charles II of England abolished the Presbyterian Church and reestablished episcopacy in its place, the harassed Presbyterians sought refuge in America. Settlements were made in Virginia, Maryland, and the Carolinas, chiefly in the frontier regions. On the Eastern Shore of Maryland and Virginia, several congregations, composed of Scotch, Scotch-Irish, and English Puritans, were established.

Presbyterians, consisting of Scots and Scotch-Irish, fled to South Carolina to escape persecution after the Battle of Bothwell in 1684. A premature attempt to form a presbytery in 1698 by Archibald Strobo, Francis Boreland, and Alexander Shields failed because of Episcopalian opposition. The Scots were more successful in New Jersey, especially at Woodbridge, where two pastors and over one hundred other persons settled in 1685. In Philadelphia, Jedediah Andrews became pastor of the only Presbyterian church established in Pennsylvania before 1705.

Another important group of Presbyterians, the Huguenots, came to America after the revocation of the Edict of Nantes in 1685. The French refugees settled in South Carolina with the Scots and the Scotch-Irish. Another group of Huguenots organized a church in Boston in 1686, and others settled in the vicinity of New York.

Obviously, American Presbyterianism of the seventeenth century derived its character from many sources. This fact was candidly asserted by Francis Alison, a Presbyterian leader, who wrote to Great Britain for financial assistance in 1760. After reviewing the background of Presbyterianism in the colonies, especially in Pennsylvania, he said:

That Pensylvania [sic], a Province Distinguished for civil and religious Liberty has been peopled with numbers from England, Scotland, Ireland, Wales, Sweden, Germany, and Holland and some French refugees. That those in general who held a parity among all Gospel Ministers (the Dutch excepted) united and formed Churches after the Presbyterian Plan, both in this and the neighbouring Provinces of New York, New Jersey, Maryland, etc. and at length their ministers agreed to hold a Synodical Meeting once a Year in the City of Philadelphia.[19]

Before the end of the seventeenth century, the Presbyterian Church had made little progress. This was partly a result of the restrictions placed upon dissenters by the established churches in Virginia, the Carolinas, New York, and New England. But even with the difficulties caused by the established churches, the eighteenth century was one in which the Presbyterian Church made rapid gains. By the time of the organization of the General Assembly in 1789, American Presbyterianism was the faith of the largest denominational group in the middle colonies.

The growth of American Presbyterianism in the eighteenth century was a result of (1) the influence of Francis Makemie; (2) the organization of a presbytery in 1706 and a synod in 1716; and (3) the Ulster-Scotch migration to America.

The scattered Presbyterian elements needed a leader to organize them into a more cohesive body. At this critical juncture Francis Makemie, a Presbyterian minister, arrived in America in 1683, at the age of twenty-five. Born in Ireland, educated at Glasgow University, and ordained by the Presbytery of Laggan in 1681, Makemie came in response to an appeal from a number of families from northern Ireland who had settled in Maryland and Virginia and who were in need of a minister in their new home.

Makemie did not establish himself at any one place, preferring to travel throughout the colonies along the coast. He refused to accept a salary for his missionary labors, except for occasional voluntary offerings. He financed his work by becoming a merchant and by marrying Naomi, the daughter of a rich merchant, William Anderson. At the death of his father-in-law in 1698, Makemie inherited 1,000 acres of land and another mercantile business to add to his own. As he carried on his business in the Chesapeake Bay area and Barbados, he preached and established new churches,[20] including five in Maryland.

Makemie was constantly traveling. His journeys carried him to Barbados in the years 1696-1698; he visited London in 1704, where he secured enough money from the United Brethren, an association of Presbyterian and Congregationalist preachers, to finance two missionaries for two years in the colonies. He returned to America with two Presbyterians, John Hampton and George McNish.

After Makemie's return to America with his two associates, he began to organize the scattered Presbyterian congregations into one body. Seven ministers responded to Makemie's plan to organize a presbytery in America. In the spring of 1706, the first presbytery was constituted at Philadelphia. Makemie served as its first moderator.[21]

En route to New England after the meeting in Philadelphia, Makemie and Hampton were arrested by Lord Cornbury, governor of New York, for preaching without a license. Cornbury insisted that Makemie's license from Virginia was invalid in New York, according to the Act of Toleration of 1689. He demanded that Makemie give bond and security for his "good behaviour, and also bond and security to preach no more in my government." Makemie replied, "If your lordship requires it, we will give security for our behaviour; but to give bond and security to preach no more in your excellency's government, if invited and desired by any people, we neither can nor dare do."

"Then you must go to Gaol," replied the governor.[22]

Makemie and Hampton were declared innocent by the jury and released; nevertheless, they had to pay a fine of about $400. This incident had two immediate results. It led to the investigation and removal of Cornbury, and the notoriety of the trial made Makemie and Presbyterianism more popular with the people. Cornbury wrote to England about the affair with Makemie and the trouble the Presbyterian had caused as a "strolling preacher":[23]

. . . I hope I have done nothing in this matter but what I was obliged in duty to do, especially since I think it is very plain by the Act of Toleration it was not intended to tolerate or allow strolling preachers. . . . So I entreat your lordship's protection against this malicious man, who is well known in Virginia and Maryland to be a disturber of peace and quiet of all places he comes into. He is a Jack-of-all-trades; he is a preacher, a doctor of physik, a merchant, an attorney, a counsellor-at-law, and, which is worst of all, a disturber of governments.[24]

Makemie is referred to as "the Father of American Presbyterianism," and his greatest fame rests in giving the necessary leadership in the organization of the Presbyterian Church in America.

The second factor conducive to the rapid growth of the Presbyterian Church was the constitution of a presbytery in 1706 and a synod in 1716. When the new Presbytery of Philadelphia was organized in 1706,[25] three ministers attended: Makemie, Hampton, and Jedediah Andrews.

At the next meeting of the presbytery, in March 1707, five ministers and four elders answered the roll call.

As early as 1707, the new presbytery began a program of missionary activity by passing a resolution that "every minister of the Presbytery supply neighboring desolate places where a minister is wanting, and opportunity of doing good offers."[26] By 1710, a shortage of ministers to fill the calls for ministerial supplies prompted the presbytery to seek ministers and financial aid from London, the Presbytery of Dublin, and the Synod of Glasgow. Only a few ministers were added before the first synod, the Synod of Philadelphia, was organized in 1716.

The composition of the first synod reveals a group with mixed backgrounds.[27] Five of the members came from New England, six from Scotland, six from Ireland, and two from Wales. The heterogeneous nature of colonial Presbyterianism contributed to the schism of 1741-1758 by creating differences of opinion regarding subscription to a creed and revivalistic methods. The division confederated the New Englanders and liberal Scotch-Irish against the conservative Scots and Scotch-Irish. The controversies precipitated by these two groups with their different views on Presbyterianism, and the subsequent settlement of their differences, molded a distinctive American Presbyterianism.

The third factor in the growth of American Presbyterianism was the immigration of the Scotch-Irish to America from the Ulster plantation in Ireland. When James I followed Elizabeth I on the English throne, he completed her plans to establish colonies in Ireland. Jesuit missionaries attempted to excite the Irish lords into a rebellion to free themselves from the authority of England, and when King James heard of the plan he put an immediate end to the revolt, confiscated about 400,000 acres of land, annexed most of Ulster to the English crown, and colonized Ulster with Scotch and English Protestants. The land was divided into estates and leased to members of the English ruling class. By 1641 about 100,000 Scots and 20,000 English had settled in Ulster. Since most of the settlers were Scots, a large segment of Roman Catholic Ireland became a center of Presbyterianism.[28]

FRANCIS MAKEMIE
(1658-1708)

This statue of the "founding father" of Presbyterianism in America stands above a doorway at the Witherspoon Building, in Philadelphia, Pennsylvania, location of the Office of the General Assembly of the United Presbyterian Church in the U. S. A.

With the death of Oliver Cromwell and the reestablishment of the monarchy and the Anglican Church, Ulster soon began to feel the power of Charles II. The prelates removed sixty-one Presbyterian ministers between 1665 and 1688, but upon the overthrow of ardently Catholic James II in the "Glorious Revolution" in 1688, William and Mary issued the Act of Toleration, freeing Presbyterians in Ireland and Scotland from the oppressive measures of England. William adhered to a policy of leniency and moderation after his wife's death, and by 1702, when Anne, her sister, succeeded him on the throne, 120 churches had organized nine presbyteries, three synods, and a General Synod that met annually. Fifteen years later, 140 churches existed with a membership of 200,000.[29]

A trickle of Scotch-Irish had migrated to the colonies during the seventeenth century. The beginning of the Scotch-Irish migration to America may be dated as early as 1649 when they responded to the offer of Lord Baltimore to give 3,000 acres of land for every thirty persons brought in by adventurers and planters. This early group settled on the Eastern Shore of Maryland.[30] It was not until the second decade of the eighteenth century that a steady stream of Ulster Scots began to flow to the colonies.[31]

In the same year, a minister in Ireland wrote to a friend in Scotland: There is likely to be a great desolation in the northern parts of the kingdom by the removal of several of our brethren to the American plantation. No less than six ministers have demitted their congregations, and great numbers of their people go with them; so that we are daily alarmed with both ministers and people going off.[32]

From 1725 to 1768, it is estimated that from 3,000 to 6,000 persons left Ulster and Scotland every year for the shores of America.[33] James Logan, secretary for the Province of Pennsylvania, wrote to John Penn in 1729:

It now looks as if Ireland or the Inhabitants of it were to be transplanted hither. Last week I think no less than 6 ships arrived at New Castle and this place [Philadelphia], and they are every 2 or 3 days when the wind serves dropping in loaded with passengers, and therefore we may easily believe there are some grounds for the common apprehension of the people that if some speedy Method be not taken, they will soon make themselves Proprietors of the Province.[34]

Again, in 1730, Logan expressed his fears that the Scotch-Irish were taking lands in disregard of Indian or proprietorial rights. The Scotch-Irish replied that "the Proprietory and his agents had solicited for colonists and . . . they came accordingly." [35]

After 400,000 persons died in Ireland during the famine of 1740-1741, an estimated 12,000 left Ulster annually.[36] By 1750, the Scotch-Irish represented about 25 per cent of the total population of Pennsylvania.[37]

A number of causes led to the great migration. The English began to oppress the Scots in Ulster by imposing economic hardships and religious suppression. A law was passed to prevent the importation of foodstuffs, such as meat and dairy products, from England, and the Woolen Act of 1699 ruined the Irish woolen industry. Leases for landholders, which had been set low enough by James I to attract settlers, were increased as much as 200 per cent. Presbyterians were not allowed to hold civil office unless they would receive the Anglican sacrament, and Presbyterian ministers were forbidden to perform wedding ceremonies.[38]

Because they entered America through Delaware Bay and Chesapeake Bay, the earliest Scotch-Irish immigrants settled in Philadelphia, Lewes, and New Castle; by the middle of the eighteenth century, however, the search for land carried them to the Susquehanna River, southward through the Virginia Valley, into the back country of North Carolina, and as far south as Georgia.

Presbyterianism became the strongest religious force in the frontier areas, and by the time of the American Revolution, over 200,000 Ulstermen had entered the colonies. New presbyteries were organized in rapid succession: Donegal in 1732, East Jersey in 1733, Lewes in 1735, New York and New Brunswick in 1738, Abington in 1751, and Hanover in 1755.

The Scotch-Irish, or Ulster Scots, should be distinguished from other inhabitants of both Scotland and Ireland.

In three important aspects of life the Ulster . . . was recognizably different from his cousins in Scotland: social distinctions had changed their character; his loyalties were now centered in Ulster rather than in Scotland; and his religion had subtly hardened.[39]

Although they lived among the Irish, the Ulster people refused to mix with the Irish either socially or religiously. The Ulster Scot had a distinct personality of his own. He was earnest in his religion and viewed life with a determined seriousness. A rigid Presbyterianism, buttressed by the Scriptures and the Westminster Confession of Faith, determined his way of life. He kept "the commandment of God and every other thing he [could] get his hands on." [40] After a week of hard labor, he might become drowsy on a "warm Sabbath afternoon, but an Arminian squint or a heretical suggestion in a sermon would rouse him like a pistol shot." [41]

The Ulster Scot usually refused to entertain any view contrary to his own. John W. Dinsmore, a historian of the Scotch-Irish, declares that the Scotch-Irish thought of themselves as being governed by "principle and conscience when in fact it is only prejudice and stubbornness," and many of their alienations are due to this racial characteristic. He says,

If the Presbyterian Jew did not openly curse the Presbyterian Samaritan in his synagogue, he at least unsparingly denounced him, and warned his flock against his perilous wiles and pernicious delusions. This was in keeping with the temperament of the people.[42]

The Ulster Scot was firm in principle, narrow-minded, stubborn and resolute, persistent and unwavering, "as tenacious of his own rights as he was blind often to the rights of others, acquisitive yet self-sacrificing, but most of all fearless, confident of his own power, determined to have and to hold."[43]

Another group of Presbyterians, the Highland Scots, settled in North Carolina after 1747.[44] For the past century, it has been assumed by historians that the Highlanders left Scotland as political exiles.[45] More recent studies, however, find the causes of emigration to have been the agricultural changes brought about by such factors as high rents and new agricultural methods, the breakdown of the clan system, and the rapid population increase.[46] The Highland Scots were virtually a distinct nationality from the Ulstermen or the Scotch-Irish, who had migrated from the Lowlands of Scotland. The Scotch-Irish settlements were along the Eno and Haw rivers in western North Carolina and in the central Appalachians; the Highlanders from Scotland settled in the coastal regions of North Carolina, the Cape Fear Valley, the Mohawk and upper Hudson valleys in New York, the Altamaha Valley in Georgia, Pictou in Nova Scotia, and Prince Edward Island. The Scotch-Irish were frontiersmen; the Scots were farmers and merchants. The Scotch-Irish participated on the side of the colonies in the struggle for independence; the Scots, with few exceptions, were Loyalists.[47]

The leadership of Francis Makemie, the organization of a presbytery and a synod, and the Ulster migration worked together for the spread and growth of American Presbyterianism. The synod was important for two reasons. First, it provided a structure of smaller judicatories which could render more effective supervision of the churches. Before 1717, the vast extent of the single presbytery caused many ministers to absent themselves from the yearly meetings. A commentary on this situation is offered in the 1710 records: "The Presbytery met today, though yesterday was appointed, because the members had not come together before this day."[48] Secondly, the organization of the church occurred at the beginning of the Scotch-Irish migration. As the mighty wave of Ulster peoples flowed into the unoccupied regions of the Great Valley of Pennsylvania, the new synod had the necessary organization to conduct missionary work among the people and to establish new churches as the frontier made its westward advance.

# 2

## THE RIGHT TO DISSENT

*I think subscription to any human Composure as the Test of our Orthodoxy, is to make it the standard of our Faith; and thereby to give it the Honour only due to the Word of God.*

Jonathan Dickinson

Ecclesiastical structure and the influx of the Scotch-Irish not only contributed to the rapid growth of Presbyterianism; it also led to troubles within the church. In 1721, the Synod of Philadelphia adopted an overture introduced by George Gillespie:

> As we have been for many years in the exercise of Presbyterian government and Church discipline, as exercised by the Presbyterians in the best reformed Churches, as far as the nature and constitution of this country will allow, our opinion is, that if any brother have any overture to offer to be formed into an act by the Synod, for the better carrying on in the matters of our government and discipline, that he may bring it in against next Synod.[1]

Such an ambiguous declaration has caused historians to study the motives of Gillespie. One year prior to his overture, Gillespie had opposed the lenient disciplinary decision of the synod against Robert Cross. Cross had been found guilty of fornication. As a result, the synod forbade him to preach for "four Sabbaths."[2] When the synod refused Gillespie's request for a review of the Cross case in 1721, he introduced his vague overture. It appears that Gillespie was inserting a wedge to open the door at a future synod for introducing an overture asking for a more stringent discipline. Since the European churches were in the midst of subscription controversies, a logical conclusion would be that Gillespie had in mind to introduce sub-scription to the Westminster Confession of Faith at the next synod.

Jonathan Dickinson led the New England group in opposition to the Gillespie overture; they withdrew their protest at the next synod, however, and in an effort to preserve harmony, they submitted four articles for adoption:

1. We freely grant that there is full executive power of church government in presbyteries and synods, and that they may authoritatively in the name of Christ use the keys of church discipline to all proper intents and purposes, and that the keys of the church are committed to the church officers and to them only.
2. We also grant that the mere circumstantials of church discipline, such as the time, place, and mode of carrying on, in the government of the church, belong to ecclesiastical judicatories to determine as occasions occur, conformable to the general rules in the word of God, that require all things to be done decently and in order. And if these things are called *acts,* we will take no offence at the word, *provided that these acts be not imposed on such, as conscientiously dissent* from them [Italics not in the original].
3. We also grant that synods may compose directories and recommend them to all their members, respecting all the parts of discipline; provided that all subordinate judicatories may decline from such directories, when they conscientiously think they have just reason to do so.
4. We freely allow that appeals may be made from all inferior to superior judicatories, and that they have power to consider and determine such appeals.[3]

The compromise offered by the four articles allowed harmony to reign for another two years. In Ireland, meanwhile, a series of synodical decisions fanned the flame of the subscription controversy, which led to a renewal of the conflict in America. In 1723, the Irish Synod resolved that the declaration of the Articles of Faith in scriptural language only, which had been allowed in the Pacific Articles,[4] would no longer be accepted as the proof of a person's orthodoxy. The Irish Synod, gaining more confidence in 1725, resolved to suspend any minister who reproached the synod for requiring subscription. In addition, the synod declared that ministers would not be allowed to vote if they believed the judicatories to be "consultative" meetings rather than judicatories having direct authority from Christ. When the non-subscribers opposed these measures, they were excluded from the synod.

The deliberations of the Irish caused the New Castle Presbytery in America to adopt subscription in 1724. All candidates were required to sign a subscription formula: "I do own the Westminster Confession as the Confession of my faith."[5] John Thomson, of Lewes, in New Castle Presbytery, introduced the following resolution at the 1727 meeting of synod:

Now the expedient which I would humbly propose you may take is as follows: *First,* that our Synod, as an ecclesiastical judicature of Christ, clothed with ministerial authority to act in concert in behalf of truth and opposition to error, would do something of this kind at such a juncture, when error seems to grow so fast, that unless we be well fortified, it is like to swallow us up. *Secondly,* that in pursuance hereof, the Synod would, by an act of its own, publicly and authoritatively adopt the Westminster Confession of Faith, Catechisms, &c., for the public confession of our faith, as we are a particular organized church. *Thirdly,* that further the Synod would make an act to oblige every candidate for the ministry, to subscribe, or otherwise acknowledge *coram presbyterio,* the said confession as theirs, &c. and to promise not to preach or teach contrary to it. *Fourthly,* to oblige every actual minister coming among us to do the like. *Fifthly,* to enact, that if any minister within our bounds shall take upon him to teach or preach any thing contrary to any of the said articles, unless, first, he propose the said point to the Presbytery or Synod to be by them discussed, he shall be censured so and so. *Sixthly,* let the Synod recommend it to all their members, and members of their flocks, to entertain the truth in love, to be zealous and fruitful, and to be earnest with God by prayer, to preserve their vine from being spoiled by those deluding foxes; which if the Synod shall see cause to do, I hope it may, through the divine blessing, prevent in a great measure, if not altogether, our being deluded with the damnable errors of our times; but if not, I am afraid we may be at least infected with the errors which so much prevail elsewhere.[6]

The synod postponed a decision on the Thomson overture until 1729 when it could be called to convene as a "full" synod.[7]

Thomson has three important ideas imbedded within his overture. First, it is significant that he, a Scotch-Irishman, would state that the American church was entirely independent of the Scotch, Scotch-Irish, and English Presbyterian churches. Secondly, his statement reveals that no confessional statement had been adopted since the inception of organized Presbyterianism in America. Finally, the purpose of subscription, for Thomson, had to do with doctrinal errors; whereas Gillespie, who had inaugurated the move for subscription, was concerned with moral reform in conduct and discipline.[8]

Thomson's views were opposed by Dickinson. On April 10, 1729, he published *Remarks Upon a Discourse Entitled An Overture Presented to the Reverend Synod of Dissenting Ministers Sitting in Philadelphia, in the Month of September, 1728.*[9] In reply to Thomson's assertion that subscription to a creed would act as a wall against the intrusion of error, Dickinson maintained that the best defense would be a thorough examination of candidates on experimental religion, the imposition of discipline, and the preaching of the whole counsel of God. To exclude nonsubscribers from the ministry, Dickinson pointed out, is to make the Confession, rather than the Bible, the standard of the church.

Three days before Dickinson published his *Remarks,* Jedediah Andrews wrote to Benjamin Colman describing the existence of two distinct parties in the synod. Andrews claimed that the Scots and Scotch-Irish were in favor of requiring subscription to the Westminster Confession of Faith as a condition of membership in the synod. The members with a New England background agreed to making the Westminster Confession the standard of the Presbyterian Church, but they would not agree to making the Confession a test of orthodoxy and the basis for ministerial communion. Andrews confessed that "all the Scotch are on one side, and all the English and Welsh on the other, to a man." [10]

The tension between the New England and the Scotch-Irish factions in American Presbyterianism had existed from the very beginning of the synod in 1717; it was to continue throughout the eighteenth and nineteenth centuries. This tension had roots in their different backgrounds. The Scots and Scotch-Irish always had a hatred for "old" England, and this was no doubt reflected in their attitude toward the "new" England. Scots and Scotch-Irish who settled in New England suffered the scorn of the New Englanders, many being forced to leave with their congregations in search of more tolerant settlements.

On the other hand, the New Englanders had cause for alarm. In the colonies, the Anglicans were controlled by the Bishop of London, the Dutch Reformed Church was governed by the Classis of Amsterdam, and the Roman Catholics were answerable to Rome. Thomson had pointed out in his overture the disadvantage of having no superior judicatory to impose measures to prevent errors and heresy. Did this mean that the Scots and Scotch-Irish would follow other churches in the colonies and place themselves under a superior judicatory—the General Assembly of Scotland or the Irish Synod? Dickinson and other New England clergy may well have considered such a prospect. But both parties feared a schism, and the Adopting Act of 1729 seemed to be the answer for both segments of the synod. [11] Influenced by Dickinson, the body adopted the compromise measure unanimously.

The Adopting Act was in two parts. The morning session of the synod adopted a general statement giving a precise definition to subscription. The Adopting Act disclaimed any authority for the synod to control the conscience; nevertheless, the synod agreed that all ministers "shall declare their agreement in, and approbation of, the Confession of Faith . . . as being in all the essential and necessary articles, good forms of sound words and systems of Christian doctrine." If any minister or candidate should have any "scruple with respect to any article or articles of said Confession . . . he shall, at the time of making said declaration, declare his sentiments to the

presbytery or synod." If the presbytery or synod "shall judge his scruple . . .
to be only about articles not essential and necessary in doctrine, worship,
or government," he will be admitted to the ministry. The afternoon session
afforded the members an opportunity to discuss their scruples. Agreement
was reached on every item except those regarding the civil magistrate and
his relation to the church.[12]

The Adopting Act established two important concepts. First, some doctrines in the Westminster Confession were essential and necessary; others
were not. Second, since the essential and necessary articles would be variously
interpreted by different judicatories, the same judicatory which hears the
scruples of a particular person will make the decision of whether the scruples
are contrary or in agreement to the essential and necessary articles. The
Adopting Act embodied many ideas of Jonathan Dickinson, and it had a
close affinity to the Irish Pacific Articles of 1720.[13]

A feeling of optimism was evident after the acceptance of the Adopting
Act. The Rev. Ebenezer Pemberton wrote to a fellow minister in Boston:

Reverend Sir—When I had the pleasure of seeing you at Boston last
Summer, I was expressing my fears that the subscription controversy would
be the cause of a great disturbance and division in our Synod. But I have
now the satisfaction of acquainting you that Providence had been better to
us than our fears. The storm is blown over, and the debate is peaceably and
satisfactorily ended. . . .[14]

The peace was like the eye of a hurricane. The calm was brief. The full
fury of the storm made a wreck of the synod.

The peace afforded by the Adopting Act held the synod together until the
Presbyterian Church divided in 1741. From the time of the Adopting Act
until the schism three groups of Presbyterians became distinguishable. The
conservative party were Scots and Scotch-Irish who preferred to retain the
ecclesiastical system of Ireland and Scotland. The second group led by
William Tennent and his sons were also Scotch-Irish, but they were liberal
in their attitude toward subscription to the Westminster Confession and
they contended that candidates for the ministry could be educated at the
"Log College" instead of a New England university or one of the schools in
Ireland or Scotland. The third party, comprising the presbyteries of Long
Island and East Jersey, were of New England Puritan background. They
took the lead in the formulation of the Adopting Act with its liberal view
of subscription. When the schism of 1741-1758 began, the second and third
groups united to form the New Side Synod of New York.[15]

To understand the conflict between the Old Side and New Side parties
and to comprehend how the same issues were involved in the division within

the Synod of Kentucky during the Revival of 1800, it is necessary to study in detail the events which took place within the Synod of Philadelphia after the passage of the Adopting Act in 1729. The Adopting Act was a compromise settlement of a seven-year controversy between a Scotch-Irish group who demanded subscription by ministers to the Westminster symbols, and a New England group, led by Jonathan Dickinson, who stressed his belief that the Bible was the only sufficient standard.

Another group, composed of Scotch-Irish, who agreed with Dickinson's views began to form around William Tennent. When Tennent joined the Synod of Philadelphia in 1718, he came from Ireland—but not from the Presbyterian Church. He was a Puritan Anglican, and he had been educated at the University of Edinburgh in Scotland. (Tennent appeared before the Synod of Philadelphia and gave his reasons for "dissenting from the Established Church in Ireland." His reasons were sustained. He disagreed with the Episcopal church government, the autocratic power of the Bishops at their yearly visitations, pluralities of benefices, the practice of Arminian doctrines, and "besides," he said, "I could not be satisfied with their ceremonial way of worship.")[16] This mixed background helps to explain his liberal views toward subscription, and his party's alliance in 1745 with the New England ministers of the Presbytery of New York to form the Synod of New York.

William Tennent settled at Neshaminy, near Philadelphia, in 1726.[17] Realizing the immediate need for additional ministers as the Scotch-Irish poured into Pennsylvania, he began to educate young ministers in his own home. By 1733, his three sons—Gilbert, William, Jr., and John—and Samuel Blair had completed their Log College course and had been admitted to the Synod of Philadelphia.

Of all the Tennents, Gilbert, the eldest son of William, played the most prominent role in the Great Awakening. After serving in the New Castle church for one year, he accepted a call to the church at New Brunswick, New Jersey, in 1727. At New Brunswick, he became acquainted with Theodorus Jacobus Frelinghuysen, a minister in the Dutch Reformed Church. A revival in 1727 in the Raritan Valley of New Jersey under Frelinghuysen is usually referred to as the first movement in what became known as the Great Awakening. The Presbyterian phase of the Awakening began with the preaching of Gilbert Tennent.

Gilbert Tennent's ministry at New Brunswick was not successful as measured by the criterion of the number of conversions. His lack of results cast him into a despondent mood:

I began to feel very much distressed about my want of success; for I knew not for half a year or more after I came to New Brunswick, that any person was converted by my laboring. . . .

During a serious illness, he reflected on his ministry, realizing that he had been spending too much time "conversing with trifles." After Frelinghuysen sent him a letter of encouragement, Tennent prayed to God to be granted at least another eighteen months, for he was "determined to endeavor to promote his kingdom with all [his] might at all adventures." [18]

Gilbert Tennent became the leader of the Presbyterian phase of the Great Awakening. He and his brothers preached the doctrine taken over from the English Puritans that no one could be converted without passing through an experience of realizing that he was not a Christian. Revival fires were kindled by the preaching of John Tennent in 1732 at Freehold, New Jersey. After one year at Freehold, John died, and William, Jr., continued the work. Other ministers joined the Tennents in the revival movement. Eleazer Wales, a Yale graduate, settled at Kingston in 1735 and gave support to the Tennents. John Cross led an outstanding revival at Baskingridge in 1735-1736. Samuel Blair, another graduate of the Log College, settled first at Shrewsbury in 1733, then moved to Fagg's Manor and established a Log College in 1740. In 1738, the five ministers named above were instrumental in having the Presbytery of New Brunswick erected, giving the revival party a base of operations to ordain their own men as they completed their studies at the Log College.

George Whitefield, upon his arrival in America, said: "It happens very providentially that Mr. Tennent and his brethren are appointed to be a Presbytery by the Synod, so that they intend breeding up gracious youth and sending them out from time to time into our Lord's vineyard." [19]

The apparent success of Tennent's party was frustrated by the conservatives who were enjoying a majority in the synod. With determination and zeal, mingled with a confidence gained from the increasing number of Scotch-Irish ministers, the conservatives voted a series of enactments to strangle the Log College and to restrict or stamp out the revival movement. The decisions of the synod for the next several years not only precipitated the schism of 1741-1758, but the issues involved also gave to American Presbyterianism its distinctive character. In 1736, a committee of seven conservatives brought in an overture to abrogate the liberal subscription policy embodied in the Adopting Act of 1729:

The Synod doth declare, that the Synod have adopted and still do adhere to the Westminster Confession, Catechisms, and Directory, without the least variation or alteration, and without any regard to said distinctions.

And we hope and desire, that this our Synodical declaration and explication may satisfy all our people as to our firm attachment to our good old received doctrines contained in said confession, without the least variation or alteration.[20]

The year 1738 was important in several respects for the Presbyterian Church. The presbyteries of New Brunswick and New York were constituted, and the synod passed two acts designed to curtail the revival movement. One enactment prohibited ministers of one presbytery from preaching within the bounds of another presbytery without permission from both of the presbyteries involved. The other act prohibited any presbytery from licensing a candidate for the ministry who could not furnish a diploma from a European or New England university, unless the candidate first be subjected to an examination by a synodical commission. These two acts were bold attempts to close the Log College and to strangle the revival.[21]

The propagators of the revival endeavored to justify their actions by resorting to the Four Articles of Jonathan Dickinson, adopted by the synod in 1722. The allowance in the articles for conscientious objections to synodical acts gave the revival ministers grounds to claim a legal right not to be bound by the recent restrictions.

The restrictions passed by the conservatives involved several issues which established a line of demarcation between the conservatives and the liberals. First, the conservatives opposed the revival methods and the practice of itinerant preaching. Second, they favored strict subscription to the Westminster Confession of Faith. Third, they objected to candidates being educated at the Log College, with its emphasis on revivalism and personal piety, rather than at European and New England colleges. Finally, they believed that the synod had the right to pass on the qualification of a candidate for the ministry before his licensure or ordination.[22]

The Presbytery of New Brunswick disregarded the attempt of the synod to traduce the Log College and proceeded to grant licenses without the synodical examination. At its first meeting, the new presbytery licensed John Rowland, a Log College alumnus. The conservative party, being a majority in the synod, declared the licensure of Rowland illegal.

The attitude of the Log College men toward the synod's avowed right to reexamine or preexamine licentiates involved a deeper struggle than simply the fact of educational qualifications. It involved the whole meaning of ecclesiastical authority and the interpretation of the Adopting Act.

William Tennent refused to present Rowland and other candidates of New Brunswick Presbytery for reexamination.[23] The revival members of the synod felt that the progress of the work would be seriously impeded if the candidates had to attend college in New England or "old" England. They viewed the action of the synod as an attempt to close the Log College and inconsistent with the rights of presbyteries to judge of the qualifications of their own members and candidates. Both groups were equally obdurate in their attitude toward ministerial education. The historian Charles A. Hodge passes over this phase of the controversy with a rather conciliatory attitude:

Whatever unworthy motive may, on either side, have mingled with better feelings, there is not a doubt that the majority were influenced in the adoption of the rule in question, by a sincere desire to secure an adequately educated ministry, and the minority by an equally conscientious belief, that the operation of the rule would be inimical to the progress of religion in the church.[24]

A definite cleavage nevertheless was evident among the Presbyterians as the New Jersey revival grew in intensity. The conservatives, who were in the majority and controlled the church, attempted to curb the advance of the revival by restricting the revival ministers to one locality and removing their source of evangelistic ministers, the Log College.[25] Gilbert Tennent cried out at one of the meetings that the synod sought "to prevent [his] father's school from training gracious men for the ministry." [26]

The conservative efforts to silence the revivalists were hampered by the arrival of George Whitefield in America and the alliance of the Presbytery of New York with the Presbytery of New Brunswick. Before Whitefield arrived in November 1739, the spiritual awakenings resulting from the work of Frelinghuysen, Jonathan Edwards, and the Tennents were confined to separate geographical areas. After Whitefield's journey throughout the colonies from Georgia to New England in 1740, the separate revivals were considered as one immense spiritual awakening—the Great Awakening. He was opposed by Charles Chauncy and Jonathan Mayhew, two New Englanders, and the conservative Presbyterians, but he was welcomed by the New Brunswick and New York presbyteries. "No public figure of the eighteenth century was more highly praised on the one hand and more vilified and denounced on the other than George Whitefield," says the historian William W. Sweet.[27] Ola Winslow attributes Whitefield's success to his sincerity:

Colossally egotistical, intellectually shallow and lazy, he was unimpeachably sincere. He believed what he preached. Therein lay his power.[28]

Although Whitefield's contribution to the religious life of America is debatable, his importance to the liberal Presbyterians was of real value. He brought together into one party those who favored the revival: the Log College men of New Brunswick Presbytery and the New England men of the Presbytery of New York, including Jonathan Dickinson, Aaron Burr, Ebenezer Pemberton, and Joseph Webb.

The subscriptionist-antirevival party was opposed to Whitefield's violation of the 1738 act of synod relating to the restrictions of preachers from preaching outside the bounds of a given presbytery without the permission of the presbytery visited. Revival preachers accompanied Whitefield on his itinerary. Samuel Blair broke the synodical rule when he accepted an invitation to preach at the pastorless church of Nottingham in Donegal Presbytery. Only one preaching service had been conducted at the Nottingham church during the previous four months. Donegal Presbytery demanded that New Castle Presbytery discipline Blair. Gilbert Tennent knew that the antirevival group commanded a majority in New Castle Presbytery and that Blair would be at their mercy; therefore, when he also received an invitation from the Nottingham people, he lowered the bars of restraint.

On March 8, 1740, he preached his famous sermon: "The Danger of an Unconverted Ministry."[29] Tennent referred to the orthodox as an "ungodly ministry," as "catapillars" who "labour to devour every green thing." Unconverted ministers are unable to convert others because they have "no Experience of a special Work of the Holy Ghost," and "they have not the Courage, or Honesty, to thrust the Nail of Terror into sleeping Souls."[30] Effective results from preaching of ungodly ministers is against all logic:

Is a blind man fit to be a Guide in a very dangerous Way? Is a dead Man fit to bring others to life? a mad Man fit to cast out Devils? a Rebel, an Enemy to GOD, fit to be sent on an Embassy of Peace, to bring Rebels into a State of Friendship with GOD? a Captive bound in the Massy Chains of Darkness and Guilt, a proper Person to set others at Liberty? a Leper, or one that has Plague-sores upon him, fit to be a good Physician? Is an ignorant Rustick, that has never been at Sea in his Life, fit to be a Pilot, to keep Vessels from being dashed to Pieces upon Rocks and Sand-banks? Isn't an unconverted Minister like a Man who would learn others to swim, before he had learn'd it himself, and so is drowned in the Act, and dies like a Fool?

Tennent believed the situation could be remedied by having candidates for the ministry attend private schools, "under the Care of skilful and experienced Christians; in which those only should be admitted, who upon strict Examination have . . . the plain Evidences of experimental Religion."[31] In conclusion, Tennent admonished his listeners: "If the Ministry of natural men be as it has been represented; Then it is both lawful and expedient to go from them to hear Godly Persons."[32]

The die was cast. When the synod met in May 1740, it rejected the protest of the Tennents against the avowed right of the synod to examine "such persons as have had a private education." Another protest was issued. The synod repealed the law against itinerant preaching, but it merely modified the law relating to synodical examinations. It agreed that the presbytery had the right to ordain ministers, but the synod had the right to judge of the qualifications of its *own* members.[33] This meant that regardless of the number of men ordained by New Brunswick Presbytery, the conservatives would still be in control of the synod.

Plans were advanced to heal the wounds caused by the question of examinations. Dickinson proposed arbitration by members from Scotland, Ireland,

London, or Boston. Gilbert Tennent refused to negotiate. He believed that "one party would have said the issue was the revival controversy; the other would have said it was concerning an educated ministry." [34]

The schism which divided the Presbyterian Church into the Old Side and New Side factions began in 1741. As the breach between the parties grew wider, the Old Side party determined to settle the whole matter in a summary manner by introducing into the synod a lengthy and extremely severe protest.[35] The authors of the protest declared themselves "grieved at our very hearts with the dreadful divisions, distractions, and convulsions, which all of a sudden have seized this infant church," and charged that the New Brunswick Presbytery and their associates "were the direct cause thereof, by their unwearied, unscriptural, anti-presbyterial, uncharitable, divisive practices," which they pursued "with such barefaced arrogance and boldness." [36]

The protestors declared that no minister or elder should be allowed to sit in synod who had not subscribed to the Westminster Confession as promulgated by the synod of 1736. The signers of the protest also stated they would not recognize the legality of anything transacted by the New Brunswick ministers until they had given satisfaction to the synod. The New Brunswick ministers were declared guilty of seven charges: (1) the concept that the presbytery, rather than the synod, has immediate jurisdiction over ministers; (2) the ordination of men "in contempt of said act of Synod"; (3) the invasion of churches without the permission of the presbytery in which the church is located; (4) the rash judgments pronounced by Gilbert Tennent in his sermon on "an Unconverted Ministry"; (5) the efforts of the revivalists to persuade church members not to attend churches which are pastored by "graceless" ministers; (6) the preaching of the terrors of the law, which is contrary to the Word of God, and causing people "to cry out in a hideous manner, and fall down in convulsion-like fits"; and (7) that all true Christians know of the time and manner of their conversion. Union with such ministers, continued the protest, would be "absurd and Monstrous."

The signers of the protest were adamant in their position, declaring that "whatsoever shall be done, voted or transacted by them contrary to our judgment, shall be of no force or obligation to us, being done or acted by a judicatory, consisting in part of members who have no authority to act with us in ecclesiastical matters." [37]

The propriety of the revival preachers' invasion of other ministers' churches must certainly be questioned, but the "Protest" of their opponents was made without allowing the accused party a trial. The power of majority rule forced the minority to withdraw.

During the poignant proceedings of the synod in 1741, the entire Presbytery of New York was absent; the following year they made their appearance, led by Jonathan Dickinson. Dickinson, the elected moderator, proposed a conference to heal the breach, but the problem relative to the selection of judges caused an impasse. The excluded members insisted on omitting all who signed the "Protest," a move which would give the power of decision into the hands of New York Presbytery. The protesting ministers refused to allow either the ejected ministers or the absentees of the previous year to be judges.[38] This would eliminate those from New Brunswick and New York presbyteries.

Realizing that their attempt for reconsideration would be ineffectual, the New York members entered a protest, declaring the whole matter to be illegal, unprecedented, and "contrary to the rules of the Gospel, and subversive of our excellent constitution"; moreover, they declared that "the excluded members ought to be owned and esteemed as members of the Synod, until they are excluded by a regular and impartial process against them, according to the methods prescribed in Sacred Scripture, and practised by the churches of the Presbyterian persuasion." [39]

The controversy continued for another year. Dickinson opened the 1743 synod with a sermon on the text: "Now I beseech you brethren, by the name of our Lord Jesus Christ, that ye all speak the same thing, and that there be no divisions among you; but that ye be perfectly joined together in the same mind and in the same judgments." [40] Dickinson led the movement for reconciliation of the synod and the Presbytery of New Brunswick. Dickinson and his fellow-members of New York Presbytery acknowledged that the ejected members had erred in several respects. They could by no means justify the intrusion of preaching in churches other than their own or the judgments pronounced upon the spiritual condition of ministers of unimpeached standing in the church.

They believed, however, that the members of the New Brunswick group were right in the immediate conflict, that they had been excluded without the process of the legal trial. A paper was presented which would allow for another synod to be erected so that all members of the Presbyterian Church could freely become members of the synod of their choice. The ejected members refused to hear terms of reconciliation, however, until the "Protest" would be removed. The synod would not yield on this point.[41]

Upon the rejection of the proposals of the Presbytery of New York, another paper was presented in the name of Jonathan Dickinson:

As I look upon myself to be a member of the Synod of Philadelphia, and have a continued right to sit and act in the same as such, so I look upon the New Brunswick Presbytery, and those other brethren that adhere to them, and are therefore shut out of the Synod on that account, to be truly members of this Synod as myself, or any others whatsoever, and have a just claim to sit and act with us. I cannot, therefore, at present see my way clear to sit and act as though we were the Synod of Philadelphia, while the New Brunswick Presbytery, and the other members with them, are kept out of the Synod in the manner they are now.[42]

The New York members were absent when the synod met in 1744.[43] Efforts were made to settle the differences; when these failed, the Presbytery of New York united with the two presbyteries into which the former Presbytery of New Brunswick had grown. On September 17, 1745, the Synod of New York was constituted at the Elizabethtown, New Jersey, church, whose pastor, Jonathan Dickinson, was the first moderator of the new synod.[44] The new synod adopted the Westmister Confession as interpreted by the Adopting Act of 1729. To avoid a recurrence of the "Protestation" of 1741, the new synod agreed that charges against ministers must be placed according to regular disciplinary process. To prevent conflict on ecclesiastical authority, it was agreed that whenever the minority could not conscientiously submit to the decision of the majority, the minority should peaceably withdraw.[45]

Thus the Synod of New York stood for the evangelism of the Revival, for liberty in the Gospel, for reasonable authority, for an open door to Christians, for peace and unity in the church. It was a new day in American Presbyterianism when the Synod of New York with this spirit was founded.[46]

During the period of schism (1746-1758), the Old Side party declined in strength as the number of its ministers dropped from twenty-seven to twenty-three. The New Side party, however, grew rapidly by using the revival

GILBERT TENNENT
(1703-1764)

SAMUEL DAVIES
(1723-1761)

method of evangelism and by engaging in a vigorous missionary campaign. One of the most successful missionary efforts was the planting of New Side Presbyterianism in Virginia.

New Side Presbyterianism was carried into Virginia by ministers sent out by the Presbytery of New Brunswick. William Robinson was sent to western and central parts of Virginia and Carolina in 1743. Meanwhile, a spontaneous revival was developing in the region of Hanover. Samuel Morris, a wealthy planter, had acquired a copy of Martin Luther's *Galatians*. He was so moved by the writings of the German reformer that he invited friends into his home to listen as he read from the commentary on Galatians. Later, a Scotsman gave Morris a volume of Whitefield's sermons. While Morris read, "the concern of some was so passionate and violent that they could not avoid crying out, weeping bitterly." [47]

Morris and his friends were charged with breaking the law because they absented themselves from the services of the established church. When asked by the court to give reason for their absence and to state the denomination to which they belonged, they remembered Luther's writings and designated themselves as Lutherans.

The self-styled Lutherans led by Morris had no preacher, but they had heard of Robinson's preaching tour. Robinson was invited to preach to them on his return trip. When he arrived at Morris's "Reading House," on July 6, 1743, large crowds were waiting to hear him preach. His preaching met with "agreeable surprise and astonishment."

Many that came through curiosity, were pricked to the heart; and but few in the numerous assemblies . . . appeared unaffected. They returned alarmed with apprehensions of their dangerous condition, convinced of their former entire ignorance of religion, and anxiously inquiring *what they must do to be saved* [Italics in the original].[48]

When they learned that Robinson belonged to the Presbyterian Church, they dropped the appellation of Lutheran, called themselves Presbyterians, and joined the Presbytery of New Castle.

After spending four days at Hanover, Robinson returned to New Jersey, and the people he had influenced came under the care of the New Side Presbyterians. They received regular visits from Gilbert Tennent, Samuel Finley, William Tennent, Jr., Samuel Blair, and George Whitefield. Finally, Samuel Davies was sent to supply Hanover for six weeks in 1747.

Davies's work was hampered by the hostility of the Anglican Church. He considered a call to a church in Delaware, but after 150 people of Hanover signed a petition for him to accept a call to their congregation he decided to remain in Virginia. He traveled to Williamsburg to obtain a license to preach and was quite surprised to receive one. He returned to Hanover in 1748 and brought with him another young minister, John Rodgers.

The governor of Virginia continually gave Davies and Rodgers trouble, a factor which undoubtedly contributed to Davies's struggle for religious toleration. In 1755, the Presbytery of Hanover was constituted with six ministers. Four years later, Davies left Hanover to become the president of the College of New Jersey. He died two years after returning to New Jersey.[49]

The reunion in 1758 of the Old Side and New Side was consummated chiefly through the efforts of Gilbert Tennent, who had at one time preached the sermon on "The Danger of an Unconverted Ministry." In 1748, he preached a sermon on brotherly love in the city of Philadelphia. The following year, he preached his famous sermon, later published, *Irenicum,* in which he sought to minimize the differences between the Old Side and the New Side parties.[50] Proposals for union by the Synod of New York to the Synod of Philadelphia were made in the same year.[51] The Synod of Philadelphia disavowed the "Protest" that had prevented reconciliation in the past.

The schism ended in 1758 and the two synods organized the new Synod of New York and Philadelphia. (During the years 1745-1758, the Synod of New York grew from twenty-two members to seventy-four; the Synod of Philadelphia decreased from twenty-seven to twenty-three.) It held its first meeting in Philadelphia on May 22, 1758, with Gilbert Tennent as the first moderator. The Old Side and New Side were now joined together again, but it was union rather than unity. During the last half of the eighteenth century, the tension between the two groups never ceased to exist.[52]

Although Presbyterianism in America had made some progress in the seventeenth century, a distinct American Presbyterianism had its beginning at the formation of the first presbytery in 1706. The seven ministers who were instrumental in constituting the first presbytery were of different backgrounds. Francis Makemie, its first moderator, was Scotch-Irish. When Makemie went to England in 1704 to obtain funds from the United Brethren to support two ministers for a period of two years in the colonies, he returned to America with two graduates of the University of Glasgow: John Hampton, a Scotch-Irishman, and George McNish, a Scot.

Three of the seven ministers were from New England. Jedediah Andrews, the son of New England Presbyterians, was pastor of the Philadelphia church. John Wilson was pastor of the church at New Castle, and Nathaniel Taylor, the third New Englander, ministered at Patuxent, Maryland. The seventh member was Samuel Davis, a Scotch-Irish merchant-preacher, of Lewes, Delaware. He never took an active role in American Presbyterianism.

McNish accepted a pastorate at Jamaica, Long Island; Hampton settled at Snowhill, Maryland.[53]

Of the six active members of the new presbytery, Andrews, Wilson, and

Taylor had New England backgrounds, and they served congregations with mixed backgrounds. Makemie, McNish, and Hampton represented Scotch and Scotch-Irish elements. Makemie maintained a close relationship with the clergy in England and New England; McNish and Hampton served churches comprised of Scots, Scotch-Irish, and Huguenots. The new church was to follow this mixed pattern.[54]

The Scotch-Irish, who migrated to America in such large numbers during the first half of the eighteenth century, settled in western Pennsylvania, Maryland, the Virginia Valley, and the Carolinas. Presbyterian churches in Philadelphia, Delaware, and central New Jersey consisted of congregations with mixed backgrounds. The New England influence accounts for the Presbyterian churches in New York and northern and southern New Jersey.[55]

Although the Scotch-Irish outnumbered the New Englanders, the New England ministers furnished the leadership of the church during the eighteenth century. Jonathan Dickinson, a New Englander, provided the leadership in effecting the compromise in the Adopting Act of 1729, which allowed a minister to object to some features of the Westminster Confession, if his scruples did not affect the "essential and necessary" doctrines of the Confession. The Scotch-Irish, in 1736, were able to muster a majority in the synod, and they immediately abrogated the compromise and adopted the Confession "without the least variation or alteration." [56] When the Presbyterian Church divided in 1745, the New England group sided with the Log College men and organized the Synod of New York. The new synod accepted the Adopting Act of 1729, and when the two synods reunited in 1758, the Adopting Act was included in their constitution.[57]

The New England ministers also influenced the acceptance of the principle that the basic authority of the church rested in the presbyteries rather than the synods. During the Great Awakening the issue of synodical authority arose because of the bitter controversies over the revival, the disciplining of immoral ministers, the educational qualifications of ministers, and whether or not the synod—or a synodical commission—had the right to reexamine ministers after they had been licensed and ordained by a presbytery.

The Scotch-Irish, led by John Thomson, favored synodical control. The New England ministers and the Log College men (many of whom were Scotch-Irish) favored presbyterial control. The New England and the Log College ministers organized the Synod of New York after the schism of 1745 and adopted a form of government based on the principle that the basic authority of the church rested in the presbyteries. When the two synods reunited in 1758, this presbyterial authority was written into the reunion platform. Upon the establishment of the General Assembly in 1788, the same principle became a part of the government of the Presbyterian Church.

The Presbyterian churches in Scotland and Ireland had their highest authority vested in the General Assembly or General Synod, which in turn would
delegate power to the presbyteries.

Throughout the eighteenth century, however, the New England men and
the Log College men had refused to consider the Presbyterianism of Scotland
and Ireland as normative. They had insisted upon their right to develope a
Presbyterianism suited to their situation and expressive of the heritage of
all the many Reformed groups which made up the Presbyterian Church in
their highly mixed areas. The Presbyterianism which they developed was,
therefore, a decentralized system which left the ultimate authority in the
hands of the presbyteries. The authority of the Synods and of the General
Assembly was determined and granted by the presbyteries.[58]

This basic shift of authority from synods to presbyteries had important
consequences. The Presbyterian Church acquired a distinctive character; it
was a product of America, an indigenous organization, rather than a transplanted segment of the Scotch or Scotch-Irish churches.[59] The issue of
synodical versus presbyterial authority was central in the conflict between the
Synod of Kentucky and the Cumberland Presbytery during the Revival of
1800, the conflict which resulted in the forming of the Cumberland Presbyterian Church.

The New Side influence of the New England and Log College men,
rather than that of the Old Side Scots and Scotch-Irish, shaped the character
of American Presbyterianism. The two schools or views of Presbyterianism
which developed during the eighteenth century were still a reality as the century closed. The controversies from 1721 to 1758 brought the principal
differences into focus.

The liberal or progressive view of the New Side was shared by the New
England and Log College men; the conservative view of the Old Side was
upheld by the Scots and Scotch-Irish. The two groups were at opposite poles
on a number of issues: subscription, the locus of ecclesiastical authority,
educational qualifications, Calvinistic doctrine, the use of revivals as a method
or technique for evangelism, and the nature of the "call" to the ministry.

The distinctive character of American Presbyterianism exemplified in
the first General Assembly in 1788 was essentially New Side; the Old
Side tradition was still in evidence, however, especially in the frontier regions.
In Tennessee and Kentucky, the Old Side ministers formed a majority.
The issues involved in the Presbyterian conflict during the eighteenth century
were again the source of strife and schism when the New Side clergy
moved to Kentucky and Tennessee and commanded a majority in only one
presbytery, Cumberland.

# 3

## PRESBYTERIANISM ON THE FRONTIER:

## A NEW AWAKENING

*Although many saints in these congregations . . . have been
savingly converted . . . yet all that work is only a few drops before
a mighty rain, when compared with the wonders of Almighty Grace,
that took place in the year 1800.*

James McGready

The westward movement of the Presbyterians began within the bounds of
the Presbytery of New Castle. The town of New Castle on the Delaware
became the most important port of entry for Presbyterians from Ireland as
they moved to the West looking for cheap land. By 1734 ministers had
crossed the Susquehanna, which had been the western boundary of settlement. The movement of the frontier soon extended to the Allegheny River,
and settlers began to create a new society in the area which extended from
"the falls of the rivers of the South Atlantic colonies on the one side and
the Allegheny Mountains on the other."[1] Even the Alleghenies were con-
quered as the immigrants from Ireland pushed the frontier westward. They
reasoned that "it is against the laws of God and nature that so much land
should be idle while so many Christians wanted it to labor on and to raise
their bread."[2]

The Presbyterian Church felt responsible for the new settlements of
Scotch-Irish. In 1732 the western part of the Presbytery of New Castle was
erected into the Presbytery of Donegal to provide ministers as far as the

foothills of the Allegheny Mountains.[3] The need for additional ministers to meet the needs caused by the influx of the Scotch-Irish and the rapid growth of churches during the Great Awakening became one of the causes for the division of the church into the New Side and Old Side parties.[4]

While the Old Side and the New Side Presbyterians were agreeing in 1758 to terms of peace and a reunion, the French and the British were engaged in the French and Indian War (1756-1763). The French, who claimed the Ohio Valley, were defeated, and the territory west of the Alleghenies was joined to the British Empire. King George III issued the Proclamation of 1763 forbidding further settlement in the trans-Allegheny lands until plans could be discussed in England for the most advantageous way to use the newly acquired territory. The colonists opposed the proclamation, and during the next five years, about 30,000 settlers crossed the mountains.

In 1774, Parliament passed the Quebec Act which gave the entire trans-Allegheny region to Quebec. Since this Act indicated that the purpose of England was to use the western region for fur trading instead of to open it for settlement, the English colonists interpreted the Act as another part of the anticolonial legislation passed the same year.

The Presbyterian Church formed its plans to send missionaries into the new territory. In 1763, the Synod of New York and Philadelphia sent Charles Beatty and John Brainerd as missionaries to the frontier settlements, to "Preach to the distressed frontier inhabitants, and to report their distresses, and to let us know when new congregations are forming, and what is necessary to promote the gospel among them, and that they inform us what opportunities there may be of preaching the gospel to the Indian nations in that neighborhood." [5]

This first attempt to visit the frontier was hindered by the Indian uprisings under Pontiac and Guyasuta; but, three years later, Beatty and George Duffield traveled among the settlers, preached at Fort Pitt, and carried their mission to the Delaware Indians, 130 miles beyond Fort Pitt.[6] The missionaries reported to the synod that they "had found on the frontiers numbers of people earnestly desirous of forming themselves into congregations . . . but in circumstances exceedingly distressing and necessitous from the late calamities of war in these parts." [7]

Other missionaries were sent out by Donegal Presbytery during the next several years. James Finley went over the Alleghenies for two months in 1771;[8] the following year, the presbytery was ordered to send either John Craighead or John King to "Monongahela, and places adjacent, to supply as long as they conveniently can." [9]

The most notable missionaries to visit the settlers west of the mountains were David McClure and Levi Frisbee, who crossed the mountains in August

1772. After establishing themselves at Pittsburgh, they searched in vain for a settled minister west of the mountains. The settlers "expressed an earnest desire that they should preach to them." On their return trip, McClure and Frisbee discussed the plight and needs of the settlers. "Truly," said McClure, "the people here in this country are as sheep scattered upon the mountains without a shepherd. May the good Lord raise up and send forth faithful laborers into this part of His vineyard." [10] McClure's prayer was answered. Four men settled permanently in western Pennsylvania; later, they organized themselves into the Presbytery of Redstone.[11]

The first of the four ministers to settle west of the mountains was James Power, who arrived in 1776. After establishing preaching stations at Laurel Hill, Mount Pleasant, Sewickley, Tyrone, and Unity, he settled as permanent pastor of the Mount Pleasant and Sewickley congregations in 1779.[12]

The second minister to settle west of the Alleghenies was John McMillan. After making a tour of the western settlements in 1775, he returned the following year to accept a call from the Pigeon Creek and Chartiers churches. McMillan's ministry in western Pennsylvania for over sixty years earned him the title of "the Apostle of the West." [13]

The third minister to help organize Redstone Presbytery was Thaddeus Dod, from Mendham, New Jersey. In 1778, after being on the field for one year, he organized and became pastor of the Upper Ten Mile and the Lower Ten Mile churches.[14]

The final member of "the four horsemen of Old Redstone" was Joseph Smith, who became pastor at Buffalo and Cross Creek in 1779. In September 1781, just one month before the British surrender at Yorktown brought the American Revolution to an end, McMillan, Power, and Dod organized the Presbytery of Redstone in McMillan's church at Pigeon Creek. The Indian menace prevented Joseph Smith from attending the first meeting of the new presbytery. The danger of Indian attack did not cease until General Anthony Wayne's victory at Fallen Timbers in 1794.[15]

Two attempts to hold the second meeting of the Presbytery of Redstone failed; the third attempt proved successful. On October 15, 1782, the presbytery convened at Dunlap's Creek.[16] At this meeting, James Dunlap was added as the fifth member of Redstone Presbytery.[17] John Clark was added in 1783 and James Finley in 1785, increasing the membership to seven.[18] These "honored seven" were all graduates of Princeton College. During the next four years, no new additions were made; but during the next five years (1788-1793), twelve men came forward as candidates for the ministry. The increase was a result of men receiving their training from the seven Princeton men. Not one of the last twelve was a graduate of Princeton.

One of the twelve was James McGready, under whose ministry the Great

Revival began in Kentucky.[20] Although Redstone Presbytery did not extend south any farther than the Ohio Valley, its New Side influence was carried into Virginia and North Carolina, and then into Kentucky and Tennessee.

While the Presbyterians were moving into the Ohio Valley, ministers from Virginia and North Carolina moved to the new settlements in Kentucky and Tennessee. Settlers from western Virginia had established a community on the Watauga River by 1769. During the next ten years Daniel Boone led a group of pioneers into the area of the present city of Nashville.[21]

David Rice was the first Presbyterian minister to settle in Kentucky. After serving for thirteen years as a member of Hanover Presbytery in Virginia, he left his pastorate at the Peaks of Otter Church in southwest Virginia and moved to Kentucky in 1783.[22] The following year, Adam Rankin left Virginia to take charge of a church in Lexington.[23] In 1785, Rice and Rankin, with the assistance of two visiting ministers, examined and ordained James Crawford and Terah Templin as evangelists.[24] This permitted the organization of a new presbytery. Accordingly, Transylvania Presbytery was constituted in Danville in October 1786. It included "the district of Kentucky and the settlements upon the Cumberland River." [25]

Samuel Doak was the first Presbyterian minister to become permanently established in Tennessee. After teaching at Hampden-Sydney College, Doak loaded his books on "an 'old flea-bitten' grey horse . . . crossed the Alleghenies, and came down along blazed trails to the Holston settlements," arriving in 1778.[26] Five years later, he established Martin Academy, a Log College, which became Washington College in 1795.[27]

Samuel Carrick left Virginia for Tennessee in 1793. He settled as pastor in Knoxville, where he established Blount College. Because of financial difficulties, Blount College surrendered its resources to the new state school, East Tennessee College, in 1807. This became the foundation for East Tennessee University, which later became the University of Tennessee.[28]

Thomas Craighead became the first Presbyterian minister to visit the Nashville area. Craighead left North Carolina in 1783. After spending some time in Logan County, Kentucky, he journeyed to Nashville, and in 1785 he became the first president of the newly organized Davidson Academy.[29]

The clergymen who followed the pioneers and settlers to the West were faced with an enormous task. Religion was at a low ebb, marked by a general worldliness and desecration of the Sabbath. "The closing years of the eighteenth century show the lowest low-water mark of the lowest ebbtide of spiritual life in the history of the American church," wrote Leonard W. Bacon, the historian.[30] When David Rice first visited Kentucky in 1783, he was appalled at the state of religion. "After I had been here several weeks," he declared:

. . . I found scarcely one man and a few women who supported a credible profession of religion. Some were grossly ignorant of the first principles of religion. Some were given to quarrelling and fighting, some to profane swearing, some to intemperance, and perhaps most of them totally negligent of the forms of religion in their own houses.

The ministers were not much better. According to Rice they were "men of some information, and held sound principles but did not appear to possess much of the spirit of the Gospel." [31]

Robert Davidson, a historian of the Presbyterian Church, supports Rice's evaluation:

That this picture is not overcharged, must appear from the melancholy fact, gathered from an inspection of the records, that nearly half the entire number of preachers were, at one time or other, subjected to church censures more or less severe; several being cut off for heresy or schism, two deposed for intemperance, one suspended for licentiousness, several rebuked for wrangling, and others for other improprieties unbecoming the gravity or dignity of the clerical character. . . .[32]

In a Pastoral Letter in 1789, the General Assembly confessed that it "perceived with pain and fearful apprehension" that the "corruption of the public morals" was in proportion to the continuing declension in religion. "Profaneness, pride, luxury, injustice, intemperance, lewdness, and every species of debauchery and loose indulgence abound." The General Assembly feared "that the eternal God has a controversy with our nation, and is about to visit us in his sore displeasures." [33] A spirit of avarice hindered efforts to preach and to convert.[34]

The low moral condition of the frontier inhabitants may be accounted for by their isolated and monotonous existence and their limited sources of entertainment. Boredom was alleviated by drinking hard liquor at every social occasion, and brutal fighting was often a by-product of overindulgence.[35] As a result, "the drinking of whiskey, the fighting, and the swearing were accompanied by repellent conditions of living. . . . Social relations were loose and undisciplined." [36]

Another factor contributing to irreligion in the West was the greed for land. Bishop Francis Asbury, of the Methodist Church, during a trip in Tennessee, wrote in his diary of the frontier conditions: "When I reflect that not one in a hundred came here to get religion; but rather to get plenty of good land, I think it will be well if some or many do not eventually lose their souls." [37] In other aspects, the spiritual desert of the frontier differed little from that prevailing in the East. The intellectual climate of the closing decades of the eighteenth century made its contribution.

The demoralization of army life, the fury of political factions, the catchpenny materialist morality of Franklin, the philosophic deism of men like Jefferson, and the popular ribaldry of Tom Paine, had wrought, together with other untoward influences, to bring about a condition of things which to the eye of little faith seemed almost desperate.[38]

The time was ripe for a religious awakening. Into the region of the West came a revitalizing force—the Presbyterian minister James McGready.[39]

The revival which broke out on the frontier was a continuing movement from about 1798 to 1810. East of the Alleghenies, sporadic outbursts occurred prior to 1800. During the years 1787-1789, a revival movement began in Hampden-Sydney College and spread rapidly to Liberty Hall and throughout the Presbyterian Church in the South. But there was no sustained movement of a spiritual awakening until after the revival in the West had begun under James McGready. When the revival in the West reached its peak in the years 1801 to 1803, its influence began to be felt in western Pennsylvania, New England, and the Carolinas.

The revival in western Pennsylvania began under the leadership of Elisha Macurdy in November 1802. The phenomenon of the falling exercise gave to it the name of the "Falling-work Revival." Joseph Badger, a Presbyterian minister, delivered a sermon to a large assembly in September 1803. As he preached, "many cried out and fell in perfectly helpless condition. . . . Hundreds fell and cried out, yet order and decency were preserved in a remarkable manner." [40]

In North Carolina the awakening began in 1801 under the preaching of William Paisley, who succeeded McGready as pastor of the Hawfields and Cross-Roads churches.[41] Occasional awakenings had occurred before 1801,[42] but at a camp meeting at Hawfields the spirit of the movement of the West prevailed:

It was a solemn moment and pregnant with most glorious results. A man by the name of Hodge happened to be there who had seen something of the work in the West and he, rising slowly from his seat, said in a calm and earnest voice, "Stand still and see the salvation of God." A wave of emotion swept over the congregation. Sobs, moans, and cries arose from every part of the church. Many were struck down, or thrown into a state of helplessness if not of insensibility. . . . It was like the day of Pentecost and none were careless or indifferent.[43]

The movement spread throughout North Carolina as thousands began to attend "general meetings" at which Presbyterian, Baptist, and Methodist preachers labored together.[44]

The revival movement in Connecticut began soon after Timothy Dwight became president of Yale College. Scattered manifestations of revivals had been reported during the latter half of the eighteenth century, but the first widespread movement occurred during the years after 1800. In 1800, the General Association could state that

The reports of the members of the Association happily evince the state of religion and of our churches to be more encouraging than at any preceding period, for many years past; especially in regard to the awakening and renewing influences in the hearts of sinners in various places; the purity of the work, and the harmony which is generally prevalent in our churches.[45]

Yale College experienced a great revival in 1802, resulting in the conversion of about one-third of its 230 students. The revival movement in Connecticut oscillated, with the revivals lasting for a year or two, followed by a downward trend for about four years. After 1802, the revivals reached their peaks in 1807-1808, 1812, 1815-1816, 1820-1821, and 1825-1826. Unlike the revival in the West, no physical exercises were in evidence, nor was the camp meeting used in the Connecticut revival.[46]

The revival in the West began in Logan County, Kentucky, in the churches of James McGready. McGready was born of Scotch-Irish parents in Pennsylvania in 1763 and moved with his family to Guilford County, North Carolina, when quite young. He confessed to living a puritan life, with daily private prayer, from the age of seven.[47] An uncle influenced him to study for the ministry, and at the age of seventeen he returned to Pennsylvania to study at the Joseph Smith Academy.

One day he overheard a conversation between his landlord and a neighbor

MARKER NEAR SITE OF
RED RIVER CHURCH

This roadside sign commemorates a place of continuing historical interest in Logan County, Kentucky, near Adairville. The Red River Church Memorial Association rebuilt the church in 1959, making use of the original foundation.

in which McGready was described as having "not a spark" of religion. When his indignation had subsided, he made a careful self-analysis of his personal religion. He reasoned that he knew the principles of religion; he had put those principles to work by studying Scripture and remaining separated from the worldly things of life; nevertheless, he still lacked something. He lacked an experimental acquaintance with what he professed to believe and practice.

This deficiency was remedied in 1786 when McGready experienced conversion at a sacramental meeting near the Monongahela River. After he became satisfied with achieving the correct inner feeling, McGready used this as the criterion for soul salvation in his ministry.[48] He preached the "New Birth," emphasizing a spiritual experience at a definite time and place.[49] McGready's ministry was to have a far-reaching influence upon his colaborers in North Carolina and Kentucky.[50]

McGready left the Smith Academy and attended a school established by John McMillan in western Pennsylvania. Redstone Presbytery licensed McGready to preach in August 1788. The following year he returned to North Carolina. On his return trip he visited John Blair Smith at Hampden-Sydney College in Virginia. Smith was engaged in revivalistic activities at this time, and it is very probable that McGready learned some of the techniques of revivals as he witnessed the manifestations of the revival in progress.

When McGready returned to North Carolina, his preaching initiated a revival; at the same time, it aroused a great deal of opposition to his hard preaching against sin and hypocrisy. His homiletic technique attracted the attention of some, such as Barton Stone, who described McGready as a man with

. . . small piercing eyes. His coarse, tremulous voice excited in me the idea of something unearthly. His gestures were *sui generis,* the perfect reverse of elegance. Everything appeared by him forgotten but the salvation of souls. Such earnestness, such zeal, such powerful persuasion . . . I had never witnessed.[51]

A number of his converts entered the ministry and migrated to Kentucky. The faction that opposed McGready wrote him a letter in blood, demanding that he leave the country "on pain of his life." Weighing wisdom against valor, and giving heed to the former, he accepted a call to the Gasper River, Red River, and Muddy River churches in Logan County, Kentucky.

After McGready received the letter in blood, he and his congregation assembled at Stony Creek the next Sunday to find that vandals had destroyed the furniture in the meetinghouse and had burned the pulpit. Without a pulpit, but with determination, he led the congregation he had served for nearly a decade in singing one of Isaac Watts's hymns, "Will God Forever Cast Us Off." The hymn includes these verses:

> Lift up thy feet and march in haste,
> Aloud our ruin calls;
> See what a wide and fearful waste
> Is made within thy walls.
>
> How are the seats of worship broke!
> They tear thy buildings down,
> And he that deals the heaviest stroke
> Procures the chief renown.
>
> With flames they threaten to destroy
> Thy children in their nest;
> Come let us burn at once, they cry,
> The temple and the priest.

For his sermon, McGready preached from the very appropriate text: "O Jerusalem, Jerusalem, thou that killest the prophets and stonest them that are sent unto thee, how often would I have gathered thy children together, even as a hen gathereth her chickens under her wings, and ye would not. Behold, your house is left unto you desolate" (Matthew 23:37-38).[52]

McGready arrived in Kentucky in 1796 and found the situation somewhat better than in North Carolina. There was no opposition; the people were simply indifferent to spiritual matters. The presence of murderers, horse thieves, and highway robbers earned Logan County the nickname of "Rogues' Harbor." McGready began his ministry in the West by asking his congregation to sign a covenant based on the promises of Jesus Christ:

None ever went to Christ when on earth, with the case of their friends, that were denied, and, although the days of his humiliation are ended, yet, for the encouragement of his people, he has left it on record, that where two or three agree upon earth to ask in prayer, it shall be done. Again, *whatsoever you shall ask the Father in my name, that will I do, that the Father may be glorified in the Son.* With these promises before us, we feel encouraged to unite in supplication to a prayer-hearing God for the outpouring of his Spirit, that his people may be quickened and comforted, and that our children, and sinners generally, may be converted. Therefore, we bind ourselves to observe the third Saturday of each month, for one year, as a day of fasting and prayer for the conversion of sinners in Logan County, and throughout the world. We also engage to spend one half hour every Saturday evening, beginning at the setting of the sun, and one half hour every Sabbath morning, from the rising of the sun, pleading with God to revive his work.[53]

Within a year a revival of religion was in progress; within three years the revival had spread throughout Kentucky and most of Tennessee. The revival began in May 1797, in the Gasper River Church. This first awakening was followed by another period of spiritual deadness. During the summer of 1798, the revival broke out again at a sacramental meeting in the Gasper River Church. In July 1799, the power of God was manifested at the Red River Church during another sacramental meeting. In August, the same manifestation occurred at Gasper River, and in September, the movement spread to the Muddy River Church during another sacramental meeting. It has been noted that the spiritual outbreaks were nearly always preceded by a sacramental meeting.[54]

During the next decade, when difficulties developed between Kentucky Synod and Cumberland Presbytery, McGready took his stand with the revival party; however, he submitted to the demands of the synod and became once more a member in good standing with the Presbyterian Church in 1809. Shortly after this, he left Logan County and lived in Henderson County, Kentucky, until his death in February 1817.[55] Before he died, McGready is supposed to have told his congregation: "Brethren, when I am dead and gone, the Cumberland Presbyterians will come among you and occupy this field; go with them, they are the people of God." The majority of his congregation later became a part of the Cumberland Presbyterian Church.[56]

The revival experienced in McGready's congregations gradually increased until it reached its height during the sacramental services at the Red River Church in June 1800. McGready's description of the awakening gives reason for calling it the Revival of 1800:

Although many saints in these congregations . . . have been savingly converted . . . yet all that work is only a few drops before a mighty rain, when compared with the wonders of Almighty Grace, that took place in the year 1800.[57]

McGready, aided by William Hodge, John Rankin, William McGee, and John McGee, a Methodist, preached to about 500 persons who attended the four-day meeting at Red River. The emotional tenor increased with each service. On Sunday, some fell to the floor crying, "What must I do to be saved?" The next day, at the final service, John McGee went through the congregation, "shouting and exhorting with all possible ecstasy and energy," until "the floor was covered by the slain."[58]

Reports of the Red River meeting caused considerable excitement. When it was announced that the next sacramental meeting was scheduled for the Gasper River Church in July, people came from as far away as one hundred miles to attend this first planned camp meeting.[59] The church could not accommodate the crowds. People came with provisions for the four-day meet-

ing. Some set up makeshift tents; others slept in the open wagons.[60] The
camp meeting was born of necessity to provide adequate means of ministering
to frontier inhabitants who traveled great distances to attend the open-air
services.

After the Gasper River camp meeting the contagion of enthusiasm spread
with amazing rapidity.

The laborer quitted his task; Age snatched his crutch; Youth forgot his
pastime; the plough was left in the furrow; . . . business of all kinds was
suspended; dwelling houses were deserted; whole neighborhoods were emptied; bold hunters and sober matrons, young women and maidens, and little
children, flocked to the common center of attraction; every difficulty was
surmounted, every risk ventured, to be present at the camp-meeting.[61]

McGready and his fellow laborers in the camp meetings departed from
the traditional Presbyterian concept of election and preached a modified
form of Calvinism. Instead of the elect being known only to God, McGready
insisted that a person could know the time when and the place where he
experienced conversion.[62]

McGready's sermons are typical of the frontier preaching: Man is under
God's condemnation because of the fall of Adam. He must be regenerated;
he must experience a new birth.[63]

In that awful day [of judgment] . . . the question brethren, will not
be, were you a Presbyterian—a Seceder—a Covenanter—a Baptist—or a
Methodist; but, did you experience a new birth?

McGready invoked the "sinner to flee the wrath, to come without delay." [64]
The wrath of God condemned the sinner to a real hell in which "all the
pains and torments that ever were endured by all the human bodies which
ever existed in earth . . . would not bear the same comparison to the
torments in hell." Besides his preaching on the temperature and torments
of hell, McGready cried out against the social sins of "Sabbath breaking,
cursing, balls, parties, horse-racing, gambling, the attitudes of anger, malice,
revenge, and a bitter unforgiving temper." [65] He even attacked the use of
hard liquor, the accepted and widely used beverage of the frontier.[66] Deists,
especially those of high social and political position, were described as "half-
read fops, who never made the Bible their study." [67] The "fierceness of his
invectives" and the "hideousness of his visage and thunder of his tone"
proved to be the right combination of ingredients as evidenced by the
spiritual awakenings which burst forth sporadically in his congregations.[68]

Barton Stone, pastor of the Cane Ridge and Concord Presbyterian
churches, visited the camp meeting at McGready's church in 1800. When
Stone returned to his churches in eastern Kentucky, he described the revival

in Logan County to his congregations. Stone, who had been influenced by McGready, used the same approach to his people by proclaiming the necessity of immediate conversion. The effect paralleled that of the revival in Logan County. People fell as though dead, displaying paleness, trembling, and anxiety.[69]

The movement spread "like fire in dry stubble driven by a strong wind." [70] In June, about 4,000 attended a meeting at the Concord Church. A visitor described the scene as "awful and solemn":

It was performed in a thick grove. . . . Candles were furnished by the congregation. The night was still and calm. Add to that exhortations, prayers, singing, the cries of the distressed on account of sin; the rejoicing of those that were delivered from sin's bondage, and brought to enjoy the liberty that is in Christ Jesus; all going on at the same time.[71]

The success at Concord led to the preparation of a "great meeting" in August at Cane Ridge. Estimates by Barton Stone, Peter Cartwright, and others of the attendance at Cane Ridge have ranged upward from 12,000 to a possible 30,000. The figure of 20,000 is mentioned in four accounts.[72] In any case, Cane Ridge is supposed to have been the colossus of all camp meetings, and several months earlier an estimated 20,000 gathered at Cabin Creek Union, 10,000 at Indian Creek, 8,000 at Point Pleasant, and 6,000 at Lexington.[73] These numbers are the more impressive when it is realized that there were not more than about a quarter of a million people in Kentucky in 1800.[74]

Regardless of the number in attendance, the Cane Ridge meeting would have been famous because of the confusion that ran rampant during the four-day sacramental season:

Some [were] bursting forth into loud ejaculations of prayer; others flying to their careless friends, with tears of compassion; . . . some struck with terror, and hastening through the crowds to make their escape, or pulling away their relations; others . . . fainting and swooning away.[75]

Eighteen Presbyterian ministers were present.[76] Denominational boundaries were cast aside as Baptists and Methodists joined in preaching to the crowds; sometimes as many as seven preachers were exhorting simultaneously.

A sense of awesomeness permeated the meeting, creating a mood of solemnity, but the prevailing mood was often shattered with exhilarated shouts which could be heard for miles. The flickering torchlights cast grotesque shadows in every direction. "One sabbath night," said an eyewitness, "I saw 100 candles burning at once and I saw, I suppose, 100 persons at once on the ground, crying for mercy, of all ages from 8 to 60 years." Laymen related their experience to private groups with as many as 300 testifying at one time. Hymns were chanted, prayers offered, impassioned appeals made, during which time sobs, shouts, groans, and cries for mercy could be heard on every hand. The preaching, the "Amens," the "Hallelujahs" combined to sound like the "roar of Niagara." [77]

Out of the intense excitement generated by the camp meeting the strange phenomenon of bodily agitations gave additional testimony to the unusual religious awakening. The bodily agitations were not peculiar to the Second Great Awakening: they had been in evidence during the Great Awakening of the 1740s. Samuel Blair said they occurred in his congregation while he was preaching in 1744:

> Under the sermon there was a visible appearance of much soul concern. . . . Many times the impressions were very great and general; several would be overcome and fainting, others deeply sobbing. . . . And sometimes the soul-exercises of some (though comparatively but very few), would so far effect their bodies as to occasion some strange, unusual bodily motions.[78]

Jonathan Edwards, the leader of the Great Awakening in New England, did not favor the extravagances; however, he claimed the work might be divine in spite of the visible emotional aspects. Edwards reasoned that true religion had to do with the affections, and since lively affections inevitably affect the body, "if there be a very powerful influence of the Spirit of God in a mixed multitude, it will cause in some way or other a great visible commotion." [79]

When the New Side and the Old Side parties of the Presbyterian Church healed their thirteen-year division in 1758, the New Side party demanded as one of the conditions for reunion that when sinners are made aware of the ability of Christ to redeem them, and when they rejoice in God, it is to be acknowledged as a work of God, and "even though it should be attended with unusual bodily commotions . . . we desire to rejoice in and thank God for them." [80]

During the Great Revival in the West, the exercises took a number of definite forms. The "falling exercise" was the most common manifestation. Although it was first reported in the Gasper River meeting in 1800, the number "struck down" reached its height at Cane Ridge. Even those who opposed the revival were affected. Some sought to escape the emotional influence, but they were "struck down as they fled." [81] The falling exercise was no respecter of persons or age. It affected those "from 8 years and upwards; male and female; rich and poor; the blacks; and of every denomination." [82] Most of those who fell displayed similar physical reactions.

> Some feel the approaching symptoms by being under deep convictions; then the heart swells, their nerves relax, and in an instant they become

motionless and speechless, but generally retain their senses. It comes upon
others like an electric shock . . . closes quick into the heart, which swells,
like to burst. The body relaxes and falls motionless; the hands and feet
become cold, and yet the pulse is as formerly. . . . They will continue in
that state from one hour to 24. . . . They often continue in that state
many days.[83]

The number that fell astonished even the preachers. When Stone had
visited Logan County, he reported that "many, very many, fell down as men
slain in battle." [84] One of the preachers at the Cane Ridge meeting
declared:

At one time I saw at least five hundred swept down in a moment, as if
a battery of a thousand guns had been opened upon them; and then immediately followed shrieks and shouts that rent the very heavens. My hair
rose upon my head, my whole frame trembled, the blood ran cold in my
veins, and I fled for the woods.[85]

The falling exercise became so common that nobody was disturbed as
the fallen were "collected together and laid out in order . . . which like so
many dead corpses, covered a considerable part of the floor." [86] The number
"struck down" became the criterion of a successful meeting. A traveler
through Kentucky reported the typical results of various meetings:

At Mr. Camble's meeting house—a number became affected. . . . On
Cabin creek . . . about sixty persons were struck down. . . . Next Sabbath,
on Fleming creek . . . about 100 persons were struck down. . . . At Concord . . . a number were struck down . . . about 150. . . . At Point Pleasant
. . . 250 were struck down. . . . At Indian Creek . . . 800 struck. . . .
At Kainridge [Cane Ridge] . . . 300 were struck.[87]

Scriptural support was offered for the falling exercise. Preaching in Pennsylvania in 1803, Joseph Badger noted that many "fell" while he was
preaching. He related this to examples in Scripture; when fire from heaven
consumed Elijah's sacrificial offering, Israel "fell on their faces." Also, on
the Damascus road, Paul heard Jesus Christ speak to him, and he "fell to
the ground." [88]

Perhaps the most spectacular of the exercises was the "jerks," which
caused a person to bounce around like a ball with head, limbs, and trunk
shaking "as if they must fly asunder." Sometimes the person would move the
head so violently that the "features of the face could not be distinguished." [89]
Jacob Young, a Methodist preacher, reported that women at home would
be affected with the jerks so unexpectedly that they would fling their cups
up to shatter against the ceiling.[90] All classes of society were susceptible to
the jerks:

Saints and sinners, men and women, learned and ignorant, strong and feeble, all felt the effects of this strange exercise. Sometimes at the close of a discourse hundreds were to be seen jerking at the same time. Persons were affected by it when travelling on the highway, or when at their usual occupation at home.[91]

The neuromuscular exercises took a number of other forms such as barking, dancing, and singing. Davidson, in his history of the Presbyterian Church in Kentucky, attributed the unusual physical manifestations to "the influence of the Imagination upon the Nervous System, originally stimulated by earnest hortatory preaching, venting itself in vehement ebullitions of Animal Excitement, and easily propagated by the natural operation of the laws of Sympathy." [92] No better conclusion has been offered by contemporary historians.

Some reports of the exercises were undoubtedly used to cast ridicule upon the revival; and some commentators, like Peter Cartwright, were prone to amplify what actually happened; nevertheless, the testimonies of travelers and opposers to the revival testify to the genuineness of the bodily agitations. Furthermore, the same exercises attended revivals in widely separated areas such as Kentucky, Tennessee, Pennsylvania, and North Carolina.[93]

Not all aspects of the revival and the camp meeting were as sensational, extravagant, and emotional as envisioned by the critics. Camp meetings afforded the isolated farmers and townspeople a temporary escape from their accustomed practical and mundane existence which accompanied a crude physical life in a sparsely settled country. The camp meetings provided them with a mystical sense of communion with God and their fellowmen.

A familiar subject for the critics of the revival was the immoral activity during the revivals, especially at the camp meeting. The critics are not without evidence for their accusations. In the early, unsupervised meetings, something had to yield when thousands of both sexes were brought together in a highly emotionally charged environment, when the preachers fanned the flames of passion and hell as local vendors supplied the firewater. James B. Finley observed that "all matter of wickedness was going on" during the Cane Ridge meeting. "Men furious with the effect of the maddening bowl would outrage all decency by their conduct." [94]

John Lyle, a Presbyterian preacher who opposed the revival and led the movement against the revival members of Cumberland Presbytery, attended the Cane Ridge meeting. Later, he noted in his *Diary*: "Becca Bell—who often fell, is now with child to a wicked trifling school master of the name of Brown. . . . Raglin's daughter seemed careless. . . . Kitty Cummings got careless. . . . Polly Moffitt was with child to Petty and died miserably in child bed." [95]

Barbs at the moral tone of the camp meeting are usually aimed at the early gatherings such as Cane Ridge; however, the services were soon brought under close supervision, suspicious characters and dealers in the "maddening bowl" excluded, and the camp meetings were so organized as to separate the sexes in sleeping arrangements.[96]

The use of revivalism as a method or technique for evangelism and missions had both negative and positive results. It was effective for reaching a large part of the unchurched, who numbered 90 per cent of the population at the time of the revival in the West; but the emphasis of revivalism resulted in a superficial piety which required periodic galvanizing.[97]

The advocates of the revival also received criticism from those who feared the breakdown of the traditional doctrines and standards of the church. The free will of man was stressed by proclaiming a "whosoever-will" gospel. Placing the emphasis on man's initiative in conversion was viewed as Pelagianism, a heresy condemned by the church in the fifth century.

The structure of Calvinism, for example, had been weakened point by point from New England Puritanism through Jonathan Edwards, Joseph Bellamy, Samuel Hopkins, Timothy Dwight, and others who caused the terminology to be changed from "Calvinism" to "Edwardianism" because of the emphasis on free will of man and their criticism of election and predestination.[98]

Other critics questioned the value of revivals and camp meetings because the sufficiency of the regular or settled ministry was undermined. The itinerant evangelists were created into heroes at the cost of losing the intellectual leadership of the "shepherd of the flock." [99]

Some of the critics sympathized with the revival technique, but they voiced their disapproval of the excesses, especially the physical phenomena. David Rice, the first Presbyterian minister to settle in Kentucky, endorsed the revival when he addressed Kentucky Synod in 1803:

A considerable number of persons appear to me to be greatly reformed in their morals. This is undoubtedly the case within the sphere of my particular acquaintance. Yea, some neighborhoods, noted for their vicious and profligate manners are now as much noted for their piety and good order. Drunkards, profane swearers, liars, quarrelsome persons, etc., are remarkably reformed.[100]

Five years later, Rice confessed that there had been "a revival of the spirit and power of Christianity amongst us . . . but we have sadly mismanaged it; we have dashed it down, and broken it to pieces." [101]

John Lyle recorded in his *Diary* that he was not hostile to the revival in the West in its early stages;[102] but later he vigorously opposed the revival because he felt the results were not "the effects of a Divine impulse," but rather "the evidence of human infirmity." [103]

The records of the Presbyterian Church, as expressed through the General Assembly, provide a commentary on the slow change of attitude toward the revival in Kentucky and Tennessee. In 1801, the Assembly declared: "On the borders of Kentucky and Tennessee, the influence of the Spirit of God seems to have been manifested in a very extraordinary manner." The following year, the Assembly expressed its sentiment toward the revival: "Doubtful as the nature of the revival there first appeared . . . the Assembly do exceedingly rejoice . . . that its author is God, and its effects highly desireable." In 1803, the Assembly was less complimentary of the effects when it received reports of the "bodily agitations," but it confessed that there was "increasing evidence that it is indeed the work of God." A year later, the Assembly praised the influence and spread of the revival, and although it agreed that "it is not incredible" that some conversions should react violently on the nervous system, it warned the ministers in revival areas against inciting the people into emotional outbursts. By 1805, the supreme judicatory, while still favoring the revival, began to discountenance the bodily affections:

Whilst there is satisfactory evidence to believe that there has been a great and glorious work of God carried on throughout . . . the South and West, it is proper to observe that in general this has been accompanied with very uncommon and extraordinary effects on the body. There appears also reason to believe that in certain places some instances of these bodily affections have been of such a nature, and proceeded to such lengths as greatly tended to impede the progress and to tarnish the glory of what, in its first stages, was so highly promising.

By 1806 the high point of the revival had passed. The Assembly referred to the "late glorious revival" and expressed sentiment against what seemed to be "extravagant and indecent outrages against Christian decorum." [104]

The above testimonies indicate that there was opposition to the revivalistic methods; nevertheless, many who opposed the emotional outbursts were favorable to the revival itself. Others were amazed at the moral change on the frontier after the revival fires were ignited. George A. Baxter, president of Washington College in Virginia, wrote of a personal visit to Kentucky at the height of the revival:

I found Kentucky the most moral place I had ever been in. . . . Upon the whole, I think the revival in Kentucky among the most extraordinary that have ever visited the Church of Christ; and all things considered, it was peculiarly adapted to the circumstances of the country with which it came.[105]

The revival in the West reveals a movement that brought forth both good and bad results. As the historian Ezra H. Gillett points out, "Infidelity was laid prostrate; but churches were rent in sunder. The deadness and the lethargy of religion were broken up; but Stoneites, Shakers, and the Cumberland schism sprang up out of the chaos." [106]

The final and most reliable criterion of the effect of the revival must be the increase of church membership in the first decade of the nineteenth century. Between 1800 and 1803, the Baptists in Kentucky increased by 10,000. In two years the Methodists added over 6,000. The Presbyterians reported in 1803 that "thousands" had embraced the gospel; however, the Presbyterian increase was largely erased by the great numbers lost to the "Stoneites," the Shakers, and the Cumberland Presbyterians during the first decades of the nineteenth century. [107]

The increase in the churches led to an immediate need for additional preachers. The Methodists and Baptists had no problem with their circuit riders and farmer-preachers, but the Presbyterians, with their strong emphasis on a classical education, were unable to meet the demands of the frontier. As early as 1801, the General Assembly had recognized the problem:

The settlements on the frontier appear very desirous to have the gospel preached amongst them . . . and churches are rapidly forming, which will soon need settled pastors. [108]

Filling this need was the first in a series of events which led to the suspension of the revival members of Cumberland Presbytery in December 1805 and the subsequent organization of an independent Cumberland Presbytery in 1810.

# 4

## PRESSURE FOR MINISTERS:

## A GROWING DISPUTE

*We do not say that a liberal education is absolutely essential to a man's usefulness in the ministry of the gospel; but reason and experience both demonstrate its high importance and utility.*

General Assembly of the Presbyterian Church, 1804

Frontier churches found it difficult to secure enough ministers with the educational qualifications required by the Presbyterian Church to meet the demands of the rapidly growing frontier church. As early as 1792, Transylvania Presbytery had protested that the proposal of the General Assembly to require three years of study in divinity previous to the licensure of candidates "would be no means suit the taste of our country & of our churches in the remote parts of the United States." [1]

People who had participated in the camp meetings went home enthusiastic to spread the good news. As a result of the rapid growth in the number of churches, the need for more ordained ministers was keenly felt. Not more than one-third of the churches had regular preaching services; consequently, Transylvania Presbytery, at its meeting in October 1801, at the Muddy River Church, licensed four men, Finis Ewing, Alexander Anderson, Samuel King, and Ephraim McLean, as exhorters and catechizers. [2]

The use of readers and exhorters had been provided for in the First Book of Discipline adopted by the first General Assembly of the Church of Scotland in 1560. [3] The provision for readers and exhorters resulted from the lack of qualified ministers to fill vacant churches. The title of "exhorter" was given to a reader who had become proficient in explaining the Scriptures he read. The use of readers had a twofold purpose: it provided for scriptural instruction where no regular minister was available, and it was a means of training young aspirants to the ministry until Scottish universities could develop into more adequate training institutions for theological students. According to the Book of Discipline, a reader could progress beyond the office of exhorter and become a candidate for the ministry:

> For the Kirkis quhair no ministers can be haid presentlie, must be appointed the most apt men, that distinctly can read the Common Prayeris and the Scriptures . . . in process of tyme he that is but ane Reader may attain to the further gree, and . . . may be permitted to minister the sacraments.[4]

When the universities began to supply the needed preachers, the offices of reader and exhorter fell into disuse. They were officially abolished in the Church of Scotland by the General Assembly in 1581.[5]

In 1796, Transylvania Presbytery had sanctioned the use of exhorters, with careful instructions to regulate their activities. Exhorters could not exhort more often than once every two weeks, and they had to limit their exhortation to forty-five minutes.[6] The use of exhorters on the western frontier during the Revival of 1800 was prompted by a situation not dissimilar to that of the Scottish church in the sixteenth century. Transylvania Presbytery was influenced in its decision to use exhorters by David Rice, who had surveyed the effects of the revival movement and had seen the need for additional workers to supply the many empty churches. Rice, following the example of the early church in Scotland, recommended that gifted young men be chosen from the laity and licensed to exhort, even though they lacked a classical education.[7]

In addition to the Scottish precedent, the licensing of men who lacked a classical education was an example of the "extraordinary cases" provided for in the *Form of Government* of the Presbyterian Church which recommended that

> The candidate be required to produce a diploma of bachelor or master of arts from some college or university: or at least, authentic testimonials of his having gone through a regular course of learning. . . . That the most effectual measures may be taken to guard against admission of insufficient men into the sacred office, it is recommended, that no candidate, *except in* extraordinary cases, be licensed . . . [Italics not in the original].[8]

The frontier revival prompted the leaders of the revival to appeal to the reference "except in extraordinary cases," in order to meet an immediate situation.

In April 1802, at the spring meeting of Transylvania Presbytery, Alexander Anderson was received as a candidate for the ministry by a one-vote majority; Samuel King, Finis Ewing, and Ephraim McLean failed to be received, also by a one-vote majority. In October, several churches petitioned the presbytery to license the same four men to preach the gospel. The presbytery responded by licensing Anderson, King, and Ewing. To support its decision, Transylvania Presbytery declared that they had "after mature deliberation considered this matter as coming under the view of that extraordinary exception in the book of discipline, examined them on their experimental acquaintance with religion, the evidence of their call to the ministry & examined them upon their knowledge in divinity; in which trials pby. received satisfaction & licensed them to preach the gospel." [9]

Five members of the presbytery submitted a signed remonstrance to the relaxing of the requirements. The objectors included Thomas Craighead, James Balch, and Samuel Donnell, ministers, and two elders: Daniel McGoodwin and John Hannah. They claimed that the trials of Ewing, King, and Anderson "consisted only in one short sermon & an examination on experimental religion & divinity, being destitute of classical learning, & they discovered no extraordinary talents as to justify such measures." [10]

One week later, on October 15, 1802, the Synod of Kentucky was constituted at Lexington. It divided Transylvania Presbytery into two presbyteries, Transylvania and Cumberland. [11] Cumberland Presbytery, encompassing the Green River and Cumberland countries, included ten ordained ministers. Five of the ministers—James McGready, William Hodge, William McGee, John Rankin, and Samuel McAdow—favored the revival; five others—Thomas Craighead, Terah Templin, John Bowman, Samuel Donnell, and James Balch—either opposed the revival or refused to sanction it. The five revival ministers had been fellow members of Orange Presbytery in North Carolina before going to Kentucky and Tennessee. [12]

At the first meeting of Cumberland Presbytery in April 1803, at the Ridge meetinghouse, James Haw, who had been received into Transylvania Presbytery the previous October from the Republican Methodist Church, was recognized as a regular member of Cumberland Presbytery. [13] Haw's reception into Cumberland Presbytery gave the revival party a majority of one. From this date until the suspension of all the revival members by the Synod of Kentucky in December 1805, the records of Cumberland Presbytery reveal the definite formation of two opposing parties, the revival and the antirevival.

The first session of Cumberland Presbytery ratified the decisions of Transylvania Presbytery in licensing and ordaining the preachers who were transferred to Cumberland Presbytery as a result of the presbyterial division. In addition to receiving James Haw, it received Finis Ewing, Samuel King,

Alexander Anderson, John Hodge, and William Dickey as licensed probationers, and it recognized Lawrence Rolleson, Robert Bell, and James Farr
as licensed exhorters. Hugh Kirkpatrick and Ephraim McLean were directed
to prepare discourses as part of their trials for the ministry. Before the presbytery adjourned, Robert Guthrie, Robert Houston, Matthew Hall, and Samuel
Hodge were licensed as exhorters; and Alexander Anderson was approved for
ordination in May.[14]

When Cumberland Presbytery met in its regular session on October 4,
1803, at the Salem meetinghouse, James Porter was received as a candidate
for the ministry, after he had been examined on the languages,[15] experi-
mental religion, and motives for entering the ministry.[16] The revival party
gained additional strength by appointing six more exhorters: James Crawford,
Reuben Dooley, Robert Wilson, James Druggan, Michael Findley, and
David Foster.[17] The antirevival party lost one of their number when John
Hodge asked to be dismissed from presbytery because of change of address.[18]
Two days later, Cumberland Presbytery set a date for the ordination of
Ewing in November. This was the second ordination by the new presbytery.
As with the ordination of Anderson, only the preachers who promoted the
revival attended the ceremony. William McGee preached the sermon and
James McGready gave the charge. Later, at the ordination of William
Dickey, who had the favor of the antirevival group, the service was conducted by those who opposed the revival movement.[19] This situation clearly
indicates the existence of two distinct groups in the presbytery. The presbytery had been organized with the revival and antirevival factions equally
divided; however, at the end of its first year's proceedings, the revivalists
were in command of a decided majority:

| Revival Party | Antirevival Party |
|---|---|
| *Ordained Ministers:* | *Ordained Ministers:* |
| Samuel McAdow | Thomas Craighead |
| William Hodge | Terah Templin |
| William McGee | James Balch |
| John Rankin | Samuel Donnell |
| James McGready | John Bowman |
| James Haw | |
| Alexander Anderson | |
| Finis Ewing | |
| | |
| *Licentiates:* | *Licentiate:* |
| Samuel King | William Dickey |
| Ephraim McLean | |
| Hugh Kirkpatrick | |

*Candidate:*
James Porter

*Exhorters:*
Lawrence Rolleson
Robert Bell
James Farr
Robert Guthrie
Robert Houston
Matthew Hall
Samuel Hodge
James Crawford
Reuben Dooley
Robert Wilson
James Druggan
Michael Findley
David Foster

As Cumberland Presbytery began its second year, the revival party continued to increase. The antirevival ministers began to display a definite opposition to those who championed the revival. At the spring meeting of the presbytery at the Shiloh church, the antirevival party endeavored to prevent Ewing from being seated, but they were overruled by the revivalist majority. Before the meeting adjourned, James Porter was licensed as a probationer, James Farr and Thomas Nelson[20] were received as candidates, Thomas Calhoun and John Hodge were licensed as exhorters, and Samuel King was approved for ordination the following June. The revival group now gave the antirevival faction cause to feel that the whole synod would soon be controlled by the revivalists.[21]

The situation was growing critical. David Rice, who had suggested the licensing of laymen as exhorters, wrote to the General Assembly requesting advice concerning the "propriety of giving to persons permission to exhort publicly, without a view to the gospel ministry."[22] In reply to Rice, the Assembly of 1804 acknowledged his letter, spoke of "having perfect confidence in you [Rice]," and then gave its opinion:

The inquiry which you propose . . . concerning the propriety . . . of licensing and ordaining men . . . without a liberal education, is certainly of great magnitude. . . .

We do not say that a liberal education is absolutely essential to a man's usefulness in the ministry of the gospel; but reason and experience both demonstrate its high importance and utility. . . .

. . . It is the opinion of this Assembly, that where the field of labor is too extensive for the ordinary and regular ministry, certain assistants . . . may, under proper restrictions and limitations, be usefully employed in instructing the young in the principles of our holy religion. . . . It must be left solely to the regular and established judicatories of the church, according to the circumstances which may exist within their respective limits, to judge upon the subject. . . . They are not to be considered as standing officers in the church; but may be appointed, or removed, at the discretion of the Presbytery . . . but, *if possessed of uncommon talents, diligent in study, and promising usefulness, they might in time purchase to themselves a good degree, and be admitted in regular course to the holy ministry* [Italics not in the original].[23]

The time was auspicious for the minority group to take action against the "un-Presbyterian" activities of the Cumberland party. The revival faction had a majority in Cumberland Presbytery, but the antirevival faction had a majority in Transylvania Presbytery and in the Synod of Kentucky. The opponents of the revival took their case to the synod. The lines of battle thus were clearly drawn for an ecclesiastical conflict, with the Presbyterian Standards to be used as the weapon of the antirevival party.

The meeting of the Synod of Kentucky in October 1804 marked the beginning of the conflict between the synod and Cumberland Presbytery. It resulted in the unconstitutional censure of the presbytery by the synod, the dissolution of Cumberland Presbytery, the constitution of an independent Cumberland Presbytery, and the establishment of the Cumberland Presbyterian Church.

The mood of the 1804 meeting of the synod was affected by a number of occurrences during the preceding year. The previous meeting of the synod in 1803 witnessed the withdrawal of Robert Marshall, John Dunlavey, Richard McNemar, John Thompson, and Barton Stone, to form the Independent Presbytery of Springfield. The Synod of Kentucky immediately suspended them from the "exercise of the gospel ministry." [24]

One of the factors contributing to the *attitude* of the Presbyterian Church toward the Cumberland Presbyterians was the erroneous identification of the revival party in Cumberland Presbytery with this same "New Light" group. Referring to the New Lights, the Synod of Kentucky warned its people not to open "the door by which men of corrupt principles may enter and disseminate their poisonous sentiments." [25] The General Assembly received a request in 1804 from the Synod of Kentucky to send a committee to investigate the troubles within the synod. While the committee of the General Assembly was meeting with the Synod of Kentucky, the common fame letter of Thomas Craighead was presented to the synod in protest against the activities of the revival preachers in Cumberland Presbytery.[26]

It is very probable that the committee viewed the Cumberland ministers and the New Lights as belonging to one movement. When the committee reported to the General Assembly of 1805, the Assembly received at the same time a letter from James McGready asking the Assembly to issue a statement that the committee was not investigating the Cumberland ministers, but the New Light group consisting of Marshall, Dunlavey, McNemar, Thompson, and Stone.[27] The New Light preachers were active in northern Kentucky, about 200 miles from the Cumberland country. Thomas Craighead and others attempted "by private correspondence, to prejudice the minds of the distant members of the synod, by making them believe that the two works were the same."[28] Their efforts were partially effective. In 1824, Robert H. Bishop, professor of history at Transylvania University, wrote that the Cumberland Presbyterians had their origin in the "religious excitement" of the camp meetings.[29]

Nine years later, Samuel Miller, professor of ecclesiastical history in the Theological Seminary at Princeton, referred to the Cumberland Presbyterians as holding to an unscriptural creed, practicing "fanatical, revolting irregularities," and forming one "heterogeneous mass" with two other groups, the New Lights or "Stoneites" and the Shakers. Finis Ewing replied to Miller and listed seven errors made by Miller. Responding to Ewing, Miller said: "Dr. Bishop led me to assume with entire assurance the truth of all his statements." Miller agreed to investigate the matter in more detail. One year later, in June 1834, Miller made a retraction:

I am now convinced, that in representing the "New Lights," or "Stoneites," the "Shakers," and the Cumberland Presbyterians as exfoliations from the same disorderly body . . . I wrote from a misapprehension of facts. . . . I am sensible that in my statement, justice was not, in this respect, done to the Cumberland Presbyterians.[30]

Miller misrepresented the origins of the Cumberland Presbyterian Church, but he was willing to admit his errors; other writers, however—some of recent date—have made the same error of not inquiring into the evidences relative to the origin of the Cumberland Presbyterians.[31]

Two weeks before the 1804 synod met, Cumberland Presbytery convened at the Mount Pisgah meetinghouse on October 2. James McGready was elected moderator, and Ewing assumed the office of stated clerk. The evening session of the presbytery met in the home of Ewing. The first order of business was to license five exhorters, William McClure, Stephen Clinton, Samuel Blythe, William Moore, and Samuel Donnell. The activities of Cumberland Presbytery, the suspension of the Springfield group, the compromising letter of advice from the General Assembly to David Rice and Transylvania Presbytery, and a growing animosity between Craighead and Ewing, provided the background as the Synod of Kentucky opened its first session.

Craighead and members of the antirevival party in Cumberland Presbytery presented a written protest to the Synod of Kentucky concerning the procedures of the revival party.[32] The synod deferred action. It cited both parties to appear before the next synod to defend or refute Craighead's charges. In the meantime, the synod appointed a committee of five to inquire into the matter and report at the next session of the synod.[33] The synod also considered Craighead's protest against Transylvania Presbytery for licensing Finis Ewing and Samuel King.[34] The synod "enjoined" each presbytery to be governed in its business by the "rules laid down in the Constitution of our church and the Letter[35] of the General Assembly on that Subject." [36]

The revival party believed that the synod had overstepped its authority in citing them to appear before its judicatory for examination. The "appointment of a committee to act as spies upon the conduct of an inferior judicatory" has been condemned by one historian as an "assumption of power no Synod possesses." [37] The revival party felt that the presbytery had the sole power to judge and ordain ministers and that the synod had no authority to examine ordained ministers except through the process of appeal. This opinion was based upon the declarations set forth in the Constitution of the Presbyterian Church which states that "the presbytery has the power to examine and license candidates for the holy ministry: to ordain, install, remove, and judge ministers." The authority of the synod is different from that of the presbytery:

The synod has the power to receive and issue all appeals regularly brought up from the presbyteries; to decide on all references made to them; to review the records of presbyteries, and approve or censure them; to redress whatever has been done by presbyteries contrary to order; to take effectual care that presbyteries observe the constitution of the church.[38]

The Constitution further declares: "Process against a Gospel minister shall always be entered before the presbytery of which he is a member." [39]

Only one member of the committee, Archibald Cameron, attended the meeting of Cumberland Presbytery in April 1805, and he made no report to the synod. The citations would have been in order if the issue had come up before the synod by regular appeal or complaint. (The synod can exercise only appellate jurisdiction over ministers.) Apparently the committee realized that the citations directed to the two factions in the presbytery were "unwarranted and without law or precedent." The other members of the committee—David Rice, James Blythe, Samuel Rannels, and John Lyle—were not men who would neglect to carry out an instruction from a church court unless they thought the synod had exceeded its jurisdictional prerogative.[40]

Cameron, the committeeman attending the meeting of Cumberland Presbytery in April 1805, opened the session with a sermon on Ephesians 6:23, "Peace be to the brethren and love with faith." After the sermon, he refused an invitation to be seated as a corresponding member. The revival members of the presbytery viewed his presence with suspicion. Four of the exhorters refused to deliver discourses assigned to them as part of their trials. On the other hand, the presbytery boldly declared that William Dickey, Thomas Nelson, and Samuel Hodge would be ordained in June.[41] It is a curious fact that although Nelson and Hodge did not possess the necessary literary qualifications, these two men who performed in the presence of Cameron were received into the parent church four years later without being required to do further study.[42]

At the October meeting of the Synod of Kentucky in 1805, the presbyterial record book of Cumberland Presbytery was examined by a committee which reported the records to be "extremely defective." Among the irregularities noted were the admission of James Haw as a regular member of presbytery from the Republican Methodist Church;[43] permitting exhorters to minister "wherever God in his providence called them"; licensing persons as exhorters who lived within the bounds of Transylvania Presbytery; the use of the phrase "Finis Ewing's circuit";[44] a presbyterial letter recommending that people contribute to the support of the exhorters; and the licensure of James Farr, an "illiterate man."

The result of the report was the appointment of a Commission composed of ten ministers and six elders, who were invested with full synodical powers to confer with the members of Cumberland Presbytery and to adjudicate upon their presbyterial proceedings. The Commission was directed to convene at the Gasper River meetinghouse on the first Tuesday in the following December.[45]

When the Commission met in December, the following men had come under the care of Cumberland Presbytery since its organization in April 1803:

| Name | Status |
|------|--------|
| James Haw | Ordination ratified—April 1803 |
| Finis Ewing | Ordained—November 1803 |
| Samuel King | Ordained—June 1804 |
| William Dickey | Ordained—June 1805 |
| Samuel Hodge | Ordained—June 1805 |
| Thomas Nelson | Ordained—June 1805 |
| Hugh Kirkpatrick | Probationer—November 1803 |
| Ephraim McLean | Probationer—November 1803 |
| James Porter | Probationer—April 1804 |
| James Farr | Probationer—October 1804 |
| David Foster | Probationer—October 1805 |
| Robert Wilson | Probationer—October 1805 |
| Lawrence Rolleson | Exhorter—October 1802 |
| Robert Bell | Exhorter—October 1802 |

| | |
|---|---|
| Robert Guthrie | Exhorter—April 1803 |
| Robert Houston | Exhorter—April 1803 |
| Matthew Hall | Exhorter—April 1803 |
| James Crawford | Exhorter—October 1803 |
| Reuben Dooley | Exhorter—October 1803 |
| James Druggan | Exhorter—October 1803 |
| Michael Findley | Exhorter—October 1803 |
| John Hodge | Exhorter—April 1804 |
| Thomas Calhoun | Exhorter—April 1804 |
| William McClure | Exhorter—October 1804 |
| Stephen Clinton | Exhorter—October 1804 |
| William Moore | Exhorter—October 1804 |
| Samuel Donnell | Exhorter—October 1804 |
| Alexander Chapman | Exhorter—October 1804 |
| Samuel Blythe | Exhorter—October 1804 |

With the exception of Dickey, Hall, and Dooley, the above named men were investigated by the Commission of the Synod of Kentucky.[46] The older revival ministers were five in number—James McGready, John Rankin, Samuel McAdow, William McGee, and William Hodge. With the addition of William Dickey, the antirevival faction would have six members—Thomas Craighead, James Balch, John Bowman, Samuel Donnell, Terah Templin, and Dickey. If the revival ministers received by Cumberland Presbytery could be silenced or removed, the conservative, antirevival ministers would enjoy a majority control of presbytery.

The appointment of a synodical committee or commission to visit churches in order to establish the existing state of order or doctrine was not a procedure without precedent in the Presbyterian Church.[47] But the use of a "commission" vested with full synodical powers was without precedent and Presbyterian ministers pronounced such a commission unconstitutional.[48] The Commission of the Synod of Kentucky met on December 3, 1805, at the Gasper River meetinghouse. John Lyle, the moderator, opened the session with a three-hour sermon on the educational qualifications necessary for a Presbyterian minister, taking his text from Hebrews 5:4, "And no man taketh this honor unto himself but he that is called of God as was Aaron."[49] The attitude and policy of the Commission was presaged by the sermon.

The attitude of the constituency of Gasper River contributed to the antagonism existing between the Commission and the Cumberland ministers. The Commission "was stigmatized with the unhallowed name of an 'Inquisition,' sent down by the synod to destroy the revival of religion, and to cast off all the young preachers, because they had not learned Latin and Greek." Most of the people closed their doors to Lyle and the other Commission members. Only one man extended hospitality to the Commission, and he lived several miles from the meetinghouse. Both parties were guilty of using bitter words, and the strong prejudices of both groups nearly resulted in physical violence.[50]

All of the revival party had been cited to appear, including the licentiates and exhorters. Ten ordained ministers—James McGready, Samuel McAdow, John Rankin, William McGee, William Hodge, James Haw, Finis Ewing, Samuel King, Thomas Nelson, and Samuel Hodge—were present. Of these, the first five named had been ordained before coming to Kentucky and Tennessee; their ordinations were not in question.

On December 4, the Commission considered the case of James Haw, who had entered the Presbyterian Church from the Republican Methodist Church. Although Haw had been received by Transylvania Presbytery and had transferred to Cumberland Presbytery when it was formed from it, the Commission declared unanimously that Cumberland Presbytery had "acted illegally in receiving Mr. James Haw . . . without examining him on divinity, or requiring him to adopt the Confession of Faith of the Presbyterian Church." [51]

The Commission then proceeded to consider the charges against Cumberland Presbytery for "licensing and ordaining men to preach the Gospel contrary to the rules and discipline of the Presbyterian Church" and for requiring "only a partial adoption of the Confession of Faith by persons licensed to preach." When the defendants were asked to give their reasons for requiring the persons ordained or licensed to adopt the Confession of Faith only so far as they believed it to correspond with the Scriptures, Mc-Gready offered a defense on behalf of the revival party. He argued that since the Confession of Faith was of human composition and subject to human error, the revival ministers could accept it only insofar as it corresponded with Scripture.[52]

McGready's argument was very similar to that used by Jonathan Dickinson during the subscription controversy in the eighteenth century. Dickinson argued against an overture presented to the Synod of Philadelphia by John Thomson in 1727 which would require all ministers and ministerial candidates to subscribe to the Westminster Confession of Faith. Dickinson declared, "I think subscription to any human Composure as the Test of our Orthodoxy, is to make it the standard of our Faith; and thereby to give it the Honour only due to the Word of God." His argument was conducive to the wording of the Adopting Act of 1729 which made a distinction between the essential and necessary articles of the Confession and those not essential and necessary. The Adopting Act granted that the "essential and necessary articles" might be interpreted and stated differently by various presbyteries.[53] The Commission replied to McGready that if the men were required to adopt the Confession of Faith and Discipline "no farther than they believed to be the Word of God . . . no man can know what they believe in matters of Doctrine." [54]

When the Commission voted to proceed with the examination of those persons irregularly licensed and ordained, McGready, McAdow, William Hodge, Rankin, and McGee interposed for the "young men" [55] and refused to submit them to examination by a synodical commission on the basis that "they [Cumberland Presbytery] had the exclusive privilidge [sic] of examining and licensing their own candidates, and that Synod had no right to take the business out of their hands." [56] The synod had the power to deal with the presbytery for the alleged abuse of its authority, but it had no constitutional right to nullify what the presbytery had done in exercising its constitutional rights. The Constitution of the Presbyterian Church grants to the presbytery the power "to examine and license candidates for the holy ministry; to ordain, install, and judge ministers." [57]

On the following day, Saturday, the Commission called upon the young men "to submit to the authority which God has established in his church, and with which this Commission is clothed." The Minutes of the Synod of Kentucky state that the majority of Cumberland Presbytery requested leave in order to discuss the matter. In the meantime, the Commission and the antirevival members of the presbytery united in prayer to God for blessing and protection. [58]

Another account declares that when the young men were called upon to submit, Ewing arose and said, "It is said, 'If any man lack wisdom, let him ask God.'" Ewing then requested permission for the young men to retire for special prayer before giving an answer to the Commission. The moderator ridiculed the practice of going to the woods for secret prayer. Several other members sided with the moderator and the request was about to be denied when a member named Allen arose and said that he had seen men at the bar of justice and criminals about to be hanged but he had never known of a time when men were denied the privilege of prayer under any circumstances. The request of the young men was granted. [59]

When the young men returned to the meeting, the interrogation began. The question was put to them individually: "Do you submit or not submit?" (Submission meant to accept unconditionally the Standards of the Presbyterian Church, i.e., the Constitution of the Presbyterian Church, especially the Confession of Faith.) Each of them, except two, [60] refused to submit, stating that Cumberland Presbytery was a regular church judicature and competent to judge the faith and abilities of its own candidates. Furthermore, they pointed out that they had not been charged with heresy or immorality, and, if they had, the presbytery would have been the proper judicature to originate process against them. The Commission countered with a resolution "to prohibit the said persons from exhorting, preaching and administering ordinances in consequence of any authority which they have obtained from the Cumberland Presbytery, until they submit to our jurisdiction."

It was at this point that the Commission referred to the young men as being "illiterate." This is the first explicit reference to uneducated preachers, and it was brought out only in connection with the "common fame" charge made by Thomas Craighead, Samuel Donnell, and John Bowman. (A charge of this kind did not obligate the persons bringing the charges to assume the responsibility of the charges made.) Prior to this, the majority of Cumberland Presbytery were cited for irregular procedure in licensing men to exhort and preach, especially in not requiring unequivocal subscription to the Westminster Confession of Faith. The common fame charge was included in the decision rendered by the Commission:

WHEREAS the Commission of Synod have in a friendly manner, conferred with the Cumberland Presbytery and have examined into the proceedings of said Presbytery in licensing men to exhort and to preach . . . and have found that those proceedings were very irregular and *whereas*, when those men irregularly licensed were called upon to come forward to be examined by the Commission, Messrs. Wm Hodge, James McGready, Wm McGee, John Rankin, and Samuel McAdow interposed to prevent the examination, —and also that the moderator called upon the following persons (viz) Robert Guthrie, Saml Hodge, James Porter, David Foster, Finis Ewing, Hugh Kirkpatrick, Thomas Nelson, Thomas Calhoun, Samuel Donald [Donnell] Junior, Samuel King, Saml Blythe, and Robert Bell to come forward . . . they refused to comply, thereby virtually renouncing the jurisdiction of the Presbyterian Church, *and it being proclaimed by common fame that the majority of these men are not only illiterate but erroneous in Sentiment* [Italics not in the original]. *Resolved* that as the above named persons never had regular Authority from the Presbytery of Cumberland to preach the Gospel &c the Commission of Synod prohibit and they are [do] hereby solemnly prohibit the said persons from exhorting, preaching and administering ordinances in consequence of any authority which they have obtained from the Cumberland Presbytery, until they submit to our jurisdiction, and undergo the requisite examination.

The Commission further resolved "that the following persons (viz) James Fan [Farr], Lawrence Rollison [Rolleson], Robert Houston, James Crawford, Robert Wilson, James Duggins [or Druggan], Michael Findley, Ephraim McCain [McLean], John Hodge, Alexander Chapman, Wm McClure, Stephen Clinton and Wm Moore, who are now absent together with James Haw be laid under the same prohibition." [61] Altogether, the prohibition affected five ordained ministers, six probationers, and fifteen exhorters.

The Commission's suspension of the ordained ministers, probationers, and exhorters yields an interesting analysis. Ewing and King had been licensed by Transylvania Presbytery, but they were ordained by Cumberland Presbytery.[62] Transylvania also ratified the ordination of Haw from the Republican Methodist Church.[63] The other two ordained ministers, Samuel Hodge and Nelson, were both licensed and ordained by Cumberland Presbytery;[64] however, it is worth noting that Hodge and Nelson were the only two to be received back into the parent church—and they were received without a reexamination on educational qualifications.[65]

Of the six probationers (licensed preachers), McLean and Farr were licensed as exhorters, and Kirkpatrick was received as a regular candidate for the ministry by Transylvania Presbytery.[66] Porter was taken under the care of Cumberland Presbytery as a regular candidate for the ministry, and, like Kirkpatrick, he went through examinations in the languages.[67] Only Foster and Wilson were licensed both as exhorters and probationers by Cumberland Presbytery.[68] Two of the fifteen exhorters, Rolleson and Bell, were licensed by Transylvania Presbytery.[69]

Twenty-six men were suspended by the Commission. Three of the five ordained ministers, three of the six probationers, and two of the fifteen exhorters began their trials under Transylvania Presbytery; nevertheless, the activities of Transylvania Presbytery were never brought into the discussion by the Commission. Furthermore, the common fame letter of Craighead, Donnell, and Bowman was presented to the Synod of Kentucky almost a year prior to the ordination of Hodge and Nelson by Cumberland Presbytery; consequently, it seems that the authors of the common fame letter were directing their accusations—relative to *ordained* ministers—against Ewing, King, and Haw. The same three accusers—Craighead, Donnell, and Bowman—were the authors of the protest against the licensing of Ewing, King, and Alexander Anderson three years previously.[70]

After the business of the young men had been concluded, the Commission directed its attention to the older revival ministers. It informed McGready, William Hodge, McGee, Rankin, and McAdow that even though the Commission itself had synodical power to adjudicate upon their conduct for not submitting the young men to examination, it was citing the older ministers to appear before the next regular meeting of the Synod of Kentucky to account for their conduct. Before the ministers were dismissed, the Commission made direct accusations against three of them:

WHEREAS, *common fame* [italics not in the original] loudly proclaims that Rev. Messrs. Wm Hodge, Wm M'Gee, and John Rankin, hold and propagate doctrines contrary to those contained in the Confession of Faith of the Presbyterian Church, *Resolved* that they be and are hereby cited to appear before the Synod of Kentucky at their next session there to answer the above charge.[71]

The three men replied with a written refusal to obey the citation, alleging that the Commission had acted in an unconstitutional manner. The Commission reconsidered their action and countered with a more explicit accusation. Still basing their conclusion on common fame, they accused Hodge, McGee, and Rankin of denying election and believing that every person has a sufficiency of grace and the power within himself of obtaining more grace until he arrives at true conversion.[72]

The uncompromising attitude of the Commission may be explained to some degree by their next action, directed against Craighead. Craighead had initiated the controversy by making a common fame accusation against the revival party for denying election and for advocating a Pelagian concept of grace. The Commission probably realized that they had been led by Craighead to take unconstitutional action against individual ministers which was beyond their original purpose, which was to adjudicate upon *presbyterial* procedure.[73] When the Commission had disposed of the revival ministers, it directed its attention to Craighead:

> WHEREAS Common Fame loudly proclaims that the Rev. Thomas B. Craighead propagates doctrines contrary to the System of doctrines contained in our Confession of Faith, (viz) that he in effect denies the doctrine of election and that the special or supernatural operations of the Holy Spirit are necessary in order to believing conversion and sanctification; *Resolved* that at the request of Mr. Craighead, the Commission of Synod examine him in these doctrines.

After the Commission examined Craighead, he was remanded to the next regular meeting of synod to give an account of his doctrinal position.[74] Craighead was accused of the same doctrinal errors which be sought to attribute to the revival ministers. Since Craighead used a common fame letter to bring charges against the revival party, it may well be that he realized that in order to halt Ewing and the revival party, the most potent instrument in the Presbyterian Church would be doctrinal heresy. He used errors most familiar to himself—his own doctrinal views. He knew that the revival members of Cumberland Presbytery objected to the wording of the Westminster Confession on election because the revival preachers interpreted the confessional statement as teaching fatalism.

It is interesting that the concluding business of the Commission appears to be an attempt to mitigate some of the strong measures taken against the members of Cumberland Presbytery. The Commission approved the manner in which the presbytery had conducted the trial of James Balch, a member of the antirevival party.[75] In addition, the Commission admitted the irregular manner by which charges were preferred against Cumberland Presbytery:

> *Resolved,* also that the Rev Thos B Craighead, and Samuel Donald

[Donnell] and John Bowman, have acted irregularly in taking up the case upon *fama clamosa* [common fame] and not by dissent.[76]

The charges against the revival ministers were brought up in the same order as outlined in the common fame letter. This indicts the Commission by revealing that its decisions were based on testimony that came before it in an irregular manner. Davidson, a critic of the revival, has referred to the proceedings of the Commission as being "without precedent, and, thus far, without imitation." [77]

Several factors involved in the proceedings of the Commission may have elicited this comment from the noted Presbyterian historian: (1) The Commission based its decisions on evidence from a common fame letter, rather than from the evidence of the presbyterial record book. This was contrary to the original order of the synod that the Commission should "confer with the Members of Cumberland Presbytery and . . . adjudicate upon their Presbyterial proceedings which appear upon the Minutes of said Presbytery." [78] (2) The Commission acted contrary to the judicial process set forth in the Discipline of the Presbyterian Church by exercising original jurisdiction over individual ministers, a prerogative reserved solely for the presbytery—except in cases of appeal. (3) The Commission passed judgment upon the acts of one presbytery (Cumberland) for the actions taken by another presbytery (Transylvania). (4) The Commission acted contrary to the judicial principle that no minister can be reexamined or suspended except for heresy or immorality.[79]

After being in session for eight days, the Commission dissolved itself on December 11, 1805. Its members returned to their presbyteries and churches. The revival ministers determined to preach and administer the ordinances to their people while they explored the possibilities of resuming their ecclesiastical status in the parent church.

Efforts for reconciliation would continue for over four years, until several of the intransigent members would consider themselves forced to organize an independent presbytery on February 4, 1810. The revival party continued their functions in organized form by constituting themselves into a Council; they refrained, however, from any official presbyterial action from December 1805 until February 1810.

# 5

## UNRESOLVED DIFFERENCES:

## A NEW CHURCH

*Having waited in vain more than four years, in the meantime
petitioning the general assembly for redress of grievances, and a
restoration of our violated rights, [we] have, and do hereby agree,
and determine to constitute into a presbytery, known by the name
Cumberland presbytery.*

Samuel McAdow, Finis Ewing, and Samuel King, 1810

The Council of revival ministers suffered a series of reverses while they
were seeking a reconciliation with the Presbyterian Church during the years
1806-1810. Shortly after the organization of the Council, James McGready
withdrew, believing that the result could only be a complete separation of
the Council members from the parent church. McGready attempted to
remain uncommitted in his attitude toward the revival ministers and the
Presbyterian Church.[1] He failed to attend further meetings of the Council,
and he was not enrolled again in Transylvania Presbytery until 1809.[2]

Eight months after the Commission suspended the Cumberland ministers,
James Blythe, a prominent minister in the Synod of Kentucky, wrote to
William Hodge, the spokesman for the Council:

The differences which exist between the Presbytery of Cumberland and
the Synod of Kentucky I flatter myself will all be amicably adjusted. I think

66

this ought to be the inclination of every sincere Christian and lover of peace.

My principal object in writing you at this time was to instruct you, and thro[ugh] you our other dear brethren in Cumberland Presbytery to attend the approaching Synod, or as many as possible of you. You may rely upon the kindest reception from your brethren, and every endeavor to accommodate matters which is consistent with the word of God, and the government of our Church. Let us no longer suspect one another, but try and place confidence in each other, as being honest men, and sincere disciples of Christ. Could we meet in this temper, every thing would be rendered easier, and if favored with the divine blessing, every thing would be done right. We hope to meet with you, we hope to join our prayers with yours for your peace and prosperity.[3]

The Council directed Hodge and John Rankin to attend the Synod of Kentucky in October 1806, to attempt a reconciliation. Both Hodge and Rankin had been charged by the Commission, the previous December, with holding heretical doctrines. They told the synod that they were not attending in obedience to the synod's charge of heresy, but in response to the directive of the Council to effect a reconciliation. The synod appointed a committee to confer with the Council representatives. After a brief conference, the two men had convinced the committee of their doctrinal orthodoxy. They denied the idea that man is born with a spark of divinity or grace. They affirmed their belief in the doctrine of election, but they qualified their assertion by saying that they could not understand the mystery of election.[4] The committee were convinced of the falsity of the heresy charge against Hodge, Rankin, and William McGee, but they requested Hodge and Rankin to deliver to the Synod of Kentucky for examination the men ordained and licensed by Cumberland Presbytery. Hodge and Rankin refused. When the committee reported the decision, the synod immediately suspended the two ministers from the ministry until they would "manifest repentance and submission."[5] (William McGee refused to take sides with either party until October 1810, when he joined Cumberland Presbytery.) The suspension was another action by which the Synod of Kentucky executed original jurisdiction over individual ministers.[6]

The final act of the synod before adjournment was to dissolve Cumberland Presbytery and annex its members to Transylvania Presbytery, with the reason "that difficulties of a particular nature exist in Cumberland Presbytery so as in a great measure to incapacitate them for doing business."[7]

Blythe wrote to Hodge again in January 1807, three months after the meeting of the Synod of Kentucky:

The very unhappy situation of the Churches in your quarter has very much occupied my thoughts since I saw you. I am told that I have been suspected of impure motives in writing to you last summer, and desiring your attendance at Synod. Conscious that my motives then were pure, and relying upon your friendship, good sense and piety, I again write to you to propose another plan, by which I do hope this most unhappy difference may be accommodated, and the prosperity and peace of the church promoted. My plan is this, let both parties, you and the Synod, petition the next General Assembly to send a committee, which shall meet in Lexington next fall, and let all our differences be submitted to that committee—should said committee allow all your young men to preach, the Synod I know will acquiesce; should they think it proper that the young men should undergo any further trial they will appoint the persons before whom these trials shall be had. My dear sir, reflect well upon this matter, I do think the leading members of Synod would be willing to give you the whole of your young men rather than have a breach; but they cannot give up their right of judging of their qualifications to you; though I suppose they would willingly resign that judgment into the hands of a committee of the General Assembly. Should you think proper to meet a committee of the General Assembly at this place (which I most sincerely hope you may judge proper) a few of us here will write to Philadelphia, and I make no doubt we can procure such an appointment. I have the matter much at heart. I hope you will speedily consult with your brethren and adopt this or some other plan to prevent a breach. It will be necessary for you to recollect that it is not long before the meeting of the Assembly.[8]

The Council followed Blythe's advice and brought the dissension to the attention of the 1807 General Assembly through the "Letter of the Council of Revival Ministers to the General Assembly of 1807." [9] The document was written and signed by Samuel McAdow, William Hodge, John Rankin, and William McGee, on behalf of the Council. The letter reviewed the events from the Revival of 1800 until the organization of the Council in 1806. It explained that with the spread of the revival, the regular ministers could not supply the churches calling for preaching. Cumberland Presbytery licensed exhorters to fill the need of the vacant churches. The presbytery did not intend for the exhorters to be licensed for the regular ministry; however, if any of the exhorters should "purchase to themselves a good degree, they might be set apart for the holy ministry." [10] Some were licensed to preach after a long trial and after the presbytery had received signed petitions requesting their licensure.[11] The letter then gave its support for taking such measures:

From our personal knowledge of those men's good talents . . . from the numerous warm petitions of the people at large—from the example of many Presbyteries—from the silence of Scripture on literary accomplishments—from our own declaration in answer to Mr. Rice's letter, viz: "That human learning is not essential to the ministry"—from the exceptions made in the Book of Discipline, in extraordinary cases,—we humbly conceived that it would not be a transgression either of the law of God, or of the rules of our Church, to license men of such a description.

The Council said they had no desire to form a new party, unless it should become absolutely necessary. They denied the charge of doctrinal heresy and asserted their belief in election as a doctrine of the Bible, but said it was so mysterious that they could not understand it. To the charge of holding a Pelagian view of grace, the Council replied: "We utterly deny that man is born with a seed of grace." The basis for suspension of the revival ministers, the letter asserted, was for not submitting to the authority of the synodical commission.[12]

Since the case of the revival ministers had not come before the General Assembly by appeal from the Synod of Kentucky, the Assembly declined to render an official decision. The Assembly sent two letters, one to the Council and the other to the Synod of Kentucky. The letter to the Council criticized Cumberland Presbytery for ordaining men who did not possess the qualifications required by the Book of Discipline. The Assembly advised the members of the Council to conduct their affairs according to the Standards. The letter written by the Assembly to the Synod of Kentucky commended the synod for its zeal, but it questioned the insistence of the synod that the young men submit themselves to reexamination.[13] In addition, the Assembly questioned both the suspension of the irregularly ordained ministers without due process and the suspension of Hodge and Rankin for not agreeing to the reexaminations. The Assembly advised the synod to review its proceedings and "consider whether some of them ought not to be rescinded, and steps speedily taken to mitigate the sufferings, which your censure appears to have produced, and to remove at least a part of the complaints which it has excited." [14]

The attitude of the 1807 General Assembly is represented by a letter from a trustee of the General Assembly. The writer explained to the Council that no synod had the right to proceed against a minister, except by appellate jurisdiction; that only the presbytery could call its members to account for error in doctrine and practice. It agreed that even though a presbytery may have acted improperly in not requiring the necessary qualifications, once a person is ordained by a presbytery, not even a presbytery can depose him, except for cause or causes arising or made public subsequent to ordination. The writer believed that the synod's action in dissolving the presbytery and in annexing its members to Transylvania Presbytery had been proper, but had been "wholly improper in suspending ordained ministers, and still more improper was it for a Commission of Synod to do it." [15]

At its regular meeting in October 1807, the Synod of Kentucky considered the admonitions and criticisms of the General Assembly. The synod sustained its previous deliberations concerning Cumberland Presbytery by a majority vote. The synod then transferred the whole issue involving Cumberland Presbytery to Transylvania Presbytery for settlement. The Council would now have to deal with a lower judicatory than that which had passed judgment upon them. The members of the Council found themselves in an awkward situation. Before the Council members could get their case before the General Assembly, they would have to treat with Transylvania Presbytery, a lower judicatory than that which had delivered the suspension; they would then have to appeal to the Synod of Kentucky—the same body which had condemned them—and stand trial again before they could make a regular appeal to the General Assembly. It is very probable that the synod referred the Council to Transylvania Presbytery for the purpose of forcing the revival ministers to submit to a reexamination. The Council was in an impasse. The General Assembly would not render a decision on their behalf until the Council could make a regular appeal.

The Council petitioned the General Assembly again in 1808 to offer some relief in their peculiar situation. Again, the Assembly replied that as the matter had not been brought up by appeal from the Synod of Kentucky, it could give no relief, but it must refer the petitioners to the Synod of Kentucky as the only constitutional body competent to reverse the suspensions.[16] After the adjournment of the Assembly, James P. Wilson, pastor of the First Presbyterian Church in Philadelphia, wrote a letter to William Hodge:

*Reverend and Dear Brother in the Lord*: It was chiefly with a view to your case that I was in the Assembly this year. Many of us are anxious that you and your brethren should be relieved from your embarrassing situation. The great majority of the General Assembly were entirely disposed to do every thing in your favor that would be just and proper, or that you could reasonably have wished. If the records of the Synod of Kentucky had been before us, we should without difficulty have reversed your suspension; but we had no communication from that Synod, and could not concern with them absent. Yet this cannot essentially affect you; for if the work of their Commission was without constitutional authority and wholly void, and this is the better opinion; and also, if the ordinations made by you before the dissolution of your Presbytery, were by lawful authority, you are as truly in the ministerial office (though not a presbytery) as you can be. I beseech you to . . . continue as you are a little longer, and we have every reason to believe that your troubles will be ended at the next General Assembly. . . .

We are glad to hear of the prudence, diligence and success of the brethren you admitted. If they hold the form of sound words, and are steadfast in the faith, they will be as much beloved by the most of us, as though they had studied long and graduated. Yet our standards on the point of qualifications in the future had better be adhered to, as the church will be more stable . . . and the candidates will . . . be better qualified to cope with the more subtle enemies of the Gospel.[17]

It is rather ironic that the General Assembly was prevented from rendering a decision favorable to the Council because the Minutes of the Synod of Kentucky were not forwarded to the Assembly. The same synod had charged the ministers of Cumberland Presbytery with irregular procedure for not forwarding their record book to the synod.[18] This lack of action—whether deliberate or not—prevented the controversy from being settled for at least another year. Had the records of the Synod of Kentucky been sent to the 1808 General Assembly, the controversy might have been settled and the Cumberland Presbyterian Church would never have come into existence. What may have been a simple oversight profoundly altered the course of Presbyterianism in America.

Transylvania Presbytery, which now had the responsibility of dealing with the recalcitrant members of the former Cumberland Presbytery, met in October 1808 and drafted the following letter to the Council members:

Dear Brethren. We are anxious to see you & have a friendly interview with you respecting the difficulties which exist in your case. The Synod of Kentucky have directed us to endeavor to settle the business which lay before them respecting you. We hope you will meet with us . . . on Wednesday the 22d day of March next, & bring with you as many of those men who are declared by the Commission of Synod to be destitute of authority to preach the gospel as may to you seem proper that they may be sharers in the friendly interview.[19]

Hodge attended the meeting on behalf of the Council. The presbytery informed Hodge that it was invested with *full synodical powers* to decide on the charges against him and the other members of the Council. This assumption of powers was contrary to all Presbyterian belief and practice. A lower judicatory could not possibly be invested with the full powers of a higher judicatory.

The presbytery rendered its decision to Hodge in a written communication to be delivered to the Council:

Dear Sir. Agreeably to your request pby. have thought proper to address you by letter, & through all those likewise who are interested in you. . . . we with the same friendly spirit that was manifested in our late conference . . . do proceed to state those terms [for reconciliation]. . . . We think the ground of your suspension by synod just, and consequently the reasons for that procedure right & proper. With this impression we conceive your restoration can only be effected by a proper acknowledgement of the faith & submission to the authority of our church as contained in our book of discipline to which you are referred. The same will be required of those brethren who are yet under citation for not submitting to the authority of Synod as exercised by their commission. . . . From hence it may be easily inferred that an unequivocal adoption of our Confession of Faith is also indispensable.[20]

The Council rejected the terms: they virtually had been assured that the issue would be settled in their favor at the next General Assembly. The presbytery deposed Rankin because of his association with the Shakers, and cited McGready, McAdow, and McGee to appear at the next meeting.

The 1809 General Assembly was scheduled to meet just three months after the meeting of Transylvania Presbytery. Because the regular procedure would require the decision of Transylvania Presbytery to be placed before the next meeting of synod, which would be in October, the Council's appeal could not be heard by the General Assembly until 1810. The Council considered themselves assured by Wilson's letter that their case would be settled in 1809. With this in mind the Council directed Hodge to write a letter to the 1809 General Assembly. The Synod of Kentucky sent up two letters to the General Assembly describing the difficulties with the revival ministers. One of the letters was supposed to have been delivered to the General Assembly the previous year, but for some unexplained reason it failed to reach its destination. The Assembly reviewed the Minutes of the Synod of Kentucky with the accompanying two explanatory letters. John Lyle, from Kentucky, was present to defend the Synod of Kentucky. At the meeting of the Commission in 1805, Lyle had preached for three hours on the qualifications of the ministry. His sermon had influenced the Commission; he was equally effective before the General Assembly. He wept as he upheld the decisions of the Commission and the Synod. Even Robert Davidson admits that the Assembly was greatly influenced to support the synod when Lyle "wept freely as he portrayed in vivid colors the probable effects of the discomfiture and disgrace of the friends of truth and order." [21]

The General Assembly rendered a decision in favor of the synod:

> The Assembly took into consideration a letter from the Synod of Kentucky, and having also read another letter from their records, which by accident was detained from the last Assembly, were of opinion, that the Synod have in their letters exercised their unquestionable right of explaining their proceedings, which they have done, in a respectful and able manner, and to the full satisfaction of this Assembly: and the Assembly think it due to that Synod to say, that they deserve the thanks of the church for the firmness and zeal with which they have acted, in the trying circumstances in which they have been placed. [22]

The General Assembly had twice refused to take official action when the Cumberland party had sent up letters to the Assembly; yet the Assembly based its decision on two letters of explanation from the Synod of Kentucky.

In September 1809, John Connelly, an elder in the First Presbyterian Church in Philadelphia, wrote to Hodge, the correspondent for the Council:

Revd sirs,

Having attended the General Assembly this year as a lay Delegate from the first Presbyterian Church in this city, and having some knowledge of the business relating to your Presbytery, and the order taken thereon by the General Assembly at the request of the Synod of Kentucky—The gentleman to whom your letter of the 9th ult. was addressed not being a member of the General Assembly this year was pleased to favour me with a perusal thereof, and having considered its contents, I have thought it my duty to make you the following communication which I hope will be received in the spirit that dictates it—a love for the peace of Zion—

The last General Assembly had no tidings from the members of the late Cumberland Presbytery, but the Synod of Kentucky being represented, brought the business before the General Assembly for their approbation, which was obtained, as will appear from the printed extracts—First—on the representation that you had not complied with the request of the former Assembly, and that there was no probability that you ever would. 2dly—That the interests of religion were suffering by weakening the hands of the Synod of Kentucky; and lastly—from the powerful eloquence of one of the commissioners [John Lyle], that tears flowed down his cheeks—raised the sympathetic tear in the hearer's eye, affected his passions and silenced all opposition (yet the judgment of all were not convinced)—but had the Assembly possessed the information contained in your letter of the 9th ult. I am persuaded they would have arrested the business and that had you complied with their direction the year before, justice would have been done you. . . .

The question now is, what course are you to pursue? Hence you say "if the Assembly have not decided on our case—if you think we may yet forward an appeal with hopes of redress, etc."—to this I answer that you have had no trial, and though your case appears to have been decided in your absence and without your knowledge, upon the full and patient hearing of the representations of the Synod; yet if you seriously intended from the first reception of the letter to you from the General Assembly of 1808 to conform to its direction, and have a reasonable excuse for the delay—as far as I can see, the present aspect of your affairs would be wholly changed— of this you can judge; as to your pursuing the direction of the former Assembly—were I in your condition with my present views I should apply to the Synod as formerly directed, provided I had all along such intentions of conforming to their instructions, but if I had refused it hitherto I should now think it too late.

With respect to your constituting, I would abstain from that—it is doubtful, if not impossible as far as I can see, for you in a Presbyterian capacity, distinct from all other churches to maintain soundness of doctrine and strictness of order and discipline. I would much rather return into the bosom of the church one by one upon almost any terms, than injure the cause of Christ by multiplying division.

From your friend and the friend of peace
and order in the Church of Christ.

John Connelly[23]

The members of the Council had now waited for three and one-half years for redress of their grievances. When the General Assembly decided against them in favor of the synod, the Council met in August 1809, and appointed two commissioners to negotiate with the synod. The Council agreed to be examined by the synod, Transylvania Presbytery, or a committee appointed for that case decided as a body and not as individuals. In addition, they agreed to adopt the Confession of Faith, with the exception of fatalism. William Hodge and Thomas Nelson were commissioned to present these terms to the Synod of Kentucky. One week before the Synod of Kentucky convened in Lexington, Hodge appeared before Transylvania Presbytery and requested that his case be referred to the Synod of Kentucky. Hodge then presented the terms of reconciliation to the synod. The synod rejected the terms and offered a counterproposal that each member be examined individually by synod and that all of the Council members accept the Confession of Faith without reservation. Hodge agreed to report this to the Council; he also petitioned the synod to restore him into the Presbyterian Church. Petitions were also received from Samuel Hodge and Thomas Nelson. Synod referred the petitions to Transylvania Presbytery and ordered the presbytery to meet in December to rule on the petitions.

William Hodge reported to the Council on October 24 that the synod had complied with the terms of the Council. No mention was made of his own desire to come to terms with the parent church, nor is there any record of Connelly's letter being known by any person other than Hodge. The Council read the letter of the synod and promptly voted to reject the terms of reconciliation, because, in the opinion of the Council, the synod had not complied with the terms of the Council.

The vote was then taken, whether or not the council would put the resolution of last council into execution (which went solemnly to declare that unless the synod acceded to their propositions they would on this day constitute into a Presbytery) which was carried in the affirmative by a large majority. After which messrs. Wm. & Samuel Hodge, ministers, and Thomas Donald, Elder, withdrew from the Council, virtually declaring their intention to join the Transylvania Presbytery.[24]

William and Samuel Hodge, along with Thomas Nelson, met with Transylvania Presbytery in December. The presbytery received them back into the Presbyterian Church when they submitted themselves to the authority of the synod and accepted the Confession of Faith unconditionally.

The withdrawal of the Hodges and Nelson left the Council with William McGee, Finis Ewing, and Samuel King as the only ordained ministers. Samuel McAdow had moved to Dickson County, Tennessee. James McGready, just three weeks previous to this meeting of the Council, had come to terms with Transylvania Presbytery. The three remaining ordained ministers were prevented from constituting into an independent presbytery because McGee was in a state of indecision as to whether he should aid in constituting an independent presbytery or return to the parent body. This left the Council without the three ordained ministers necessary to constitute a presbytery. Ewing and King were alone. The members of the Council wanted to remain Presbyterian. Ewing rejected a suggestion to unite with the Methodist Church.[25]

The Council members formed themselves into a Committee and entered upon a discussion of the policy to be pursued. They agreed that each ordained minister, licentiate, elder, and representative should continue in union until the third Tuesday of the following March, at which time they were to meet at the Ridge meetinghouse. If three ordained ministers had not constituted into a presbytery by that time, they were to be released from the bond of union; otherwise, the Committee would consider the bond of union perpetual.

Ewing returned to his home, troubled over the churches' lack of enough ordained ministers to preach and administer the sacraments. He gave serious thought of constituting into a presbytery with only two ministers—Samuel King and himself. Ewing delayed, hoping that McGee or McAdow would take the initiative. Finally, on December 6, he took the initiative and wrote for advice to James Porter, a licentiate and member of the Committee:

Dear Brother:—My head aches; but I am not willing longer to defer dropping you a line. . . . I am anxious to hear how the brethren stand affected, on your side of the country [Tennessee], with respect to our situation in church affairs. . . . I will inform you that I have just visited Livingston county; and the brethren there seem bound to our Committee, by a stronger cord, if possible, than ever before. It is so with Casey's creek, Blooming grove, Spring creek, Lebanon, McAdow, &c. And what is strange to tell, Gasper river congregation have unanimously dissented from their preacher's act; and all declare for the "Committee." One of Mr. Nelson's congregations will discontinue him, and a portion of the other, if he joins the Synod. Therefore, on the whole, I do not know more than nine or ten families, in all this side of the country [Kentucky], who will be induced to leave their brethren, "the Committee." For my own part, the more I contemplate the thing, the more clear I see my way, and the more determined I am "not again to be entangled with a yoke of bondage." Therefore, I feel determined, for one, to go into a constituted state, if I can get no more than one ordained preacher to join me. You may perhaps be startled at this. So was I, when I first looked at the subject. But on a closer and more impartial examination of my aversion to such a measure, I was induced to believe that pride and tradition were the most formidable arguments against it. . . . I think the Presbyterian rule on this subject a good one; and I would not consent to depart from it only in a case of extreme necessity. Whether we will be necessitated to do so, I cannot tell, for I have not heard from Mr. McGee nor Mr. McAdow.

Brother Porter, if you will not think it discourteous, I will ask you a question on which I wish you seriously to think: whether it would wound your pride or your conscience to receive ordination from only two ministers? [26]

The response to Ewing from Porter is not known. It must be assumed that he persuaded Ewing to wait. After two months of waiting, Ewing could desist no longer. Before he would resort to the drastic measure of constituting a presbytery without the required three ordained ministers, he and King consulted Ephraim McLean, a licentiate and brother-in-law to Ewing, and persuaded him to go with them to Dickson County, Tennessee, and ask McAdow to assist in the constitution of an independent presbytery. McLean was carried along as insurance. If McAdow refused to constitute, Ewing and King would do so with McLean. The next morning, February 3, they departed for McAdow's, arriving there before nightfall. After spending considerable time in prayer, McAdow agreed to the organization of a new presbytery. On February 4, 1810, the presbytery was constituted and given the name of Cumberland:

In Dixon county Tennessee State, at the Rev. Samuel M'Adow's this 4th day of February, 1810.
We Samuel M'Adow, Finis Ewing, and Samuel King, regularly ordained ministers, in the presbyterian church against whom, no charge, either of immorality, or Heresy has ever been exhibited, before any of the church Judicatures. Having waited in vain more than four years, in the mean time, petitioning the general assembly for a redress of grievances, and a restoration of our violated rights, have, and do hereby agree, and determine, to constitute into a presbytery, known by the name of the Cumberland presbytery. On the following conditions (to wit) all candidates for the ministry, who may hereafter be licensed by this presbytery; and all the licentiates, or probationers who may hereafter be ordained by this presbytery; shall be required before such licensure, and ordination, to receive, and adopt the confession and discipline of the presbyterian church, except the idea of fatality, that seems to be taught under the mysterious doctrine of predestination. It is to be understood, however, that such as can clearly receive the confession, without an exception, shall not be required to make any. Moreover, all licentiates, before they are set apart to the whole work of the ministry (or ordained) shall be required to undergo an examination, on English Grammar, Geography, Astronomy, natural & moral philosophy, and church history. The presbytery may also require an examination on all, or any part, of the above branches of literature, before licensure if they deem it expedient.[27]

According to the agreement of the Council, when they had formed into a committee the previous October, a meeting was held at the Ridge meeting-house in March 1810. This was the first regular meeting of the new Cumberland Presbytery. Its ordained ministers were Samuel McAdow,[28] Finis

HOME OF SAMUEL MCADOW, BIRTHPLACE OF THE CUMBERLAND PRESBYTERIAN CHURCH, FEBRUARY 4, 1810

This is one of several pictures widely published in the Church. Each is an artist's conception, based on descriptions. The exact appearance of the original "Old Log House," in Dickson County, Tennessee, is not known.

Ewing, Samuel King, and Ephraim McLean. Licentiates included James Porter, Hugh Kirkpatrick, Robert Bell, David Foster, and James Farr. Its candidates included Thomas Calhoun, Alexander Chapman, William Harris, Robert Donnell, William Barnett, and David McLin. William McGee joined the presbytery in October 1810. These sixteen men are referred to as the founders of the Cumberland Presbyterian Church.[29]

The purpose in organizing an independent presbytery was not rebellion or schism; it was simply to meet the pressing demands which had been created largely by the revival which was still going on and to give proper authority to the ministers to preach and administer the sacraments. The purpose was not to project a new denomination.

At the March meeting the members of the new presbytery still expressed hope for reconciliation with the parent church; they agreed, however, that unless the reunion could be effected by October, no further efforts would be made. Before it adjourned its first meeting, the new presbytery adopted the Westminster Confession of Faith as its Standards, with the exception of the idea of fatalism. All who were able to adopt these Standards without reservations were permitted to do so, but provision was made for those who wished to make exceptions to the idea of fatalism in the doctrine of pre-destination. Formal college or seminary training was enjoined, but not re-quired; nevertheless, all candidates were to be examined on English grammar, geography, astronomy, natural and moral philosophy, church history, the-ology, and experimental religion. The presbytery ordered a circular letter to be drafted and sent "to the Societies and Brethren of the Presbyterian Church, Recently under the Care of the Council by the Late Cumberland Presbytery; in Which There Is a Correct Statement of the Origin, Progress and Termination of the Difference between the Synod of Kentucky, and the Former Presbytery of Cumberland, 1810." [30]

Efforts were made for reconciliation with the parent church until 1813. In the spring of 1811, West Tennessee Presbytery ordered James W. Ste-phenson to request advice from the General Assembly "respecting what line of conduct would be prudent for this presbytery to pursue towards those who style themselves members of the late Cumberland Presbytery." It also ordered Gideon Blackburn and Duncan Brown to be a committee to correspond with the members of "the late Cumberland Presbytery" in an endeavor to establish terms for reconciliation.[31]

The General Assembly sent an answer to Stephenson, stating that the ministers in question must adhere to the Standards, for "to relinquish prin-ciples set forth for the sake of peace is too dear a sacrifice." The Assembly then gave Stephenson a charge:

Take your stand, therefore, on the ground of the Confession of Faith and the Book of Discipline. Keep that ground. If these men wish to join our Church, they know the terms.[32]

The committee appointed to communicate with the Cumberland ministers reported in September 1811 that they had fulfilled their task, but no answer had been received from Cumberland Presbytery. Perhaps the Cumberland ministers were somewhat hesitant because of the tenor of the letter sent to them. The authors of the letter accused the members of Cumberland Presbytery of constituting into a separate body for the purpose of proselyting and using the name "presbyterian" to "mislead the unwary." They went on to say:

If the doctrines and discipline of our church were really so obnoxious to you as to produce a separation, why would you still desire to retain the name of Presbyterian—and hold communion with our body? . . . Can you suppose the work of the ministry ought to be committed to weak and insufficient men? . . . Those who would deny the utility of Academic study to qualify men for business, either in Church or state, must take leave of their senses; shut their eyes on the common occurrences of life, and add a momentum to the demoralizing principles of Illuminism. . . . Cautions which have been used . . . have been scarcely sufficient to prevent the Clergy and Laity from falling together into the vortex of ignorance and enthusiasm.

The letter concluded with a detailed discussion of the Cumberland ministers' error in believing that fatalism was taught in the Confession of Faith.[33]

One month later, Cumberland Presbytery did agree to meet with the presbyteries of West Tennessee and Muhlenberg. Ewing and McGee wrote to West Tennessee Presbytery requesting that the members of Cumberland Presbytery "be arranged as a body rather than as individuals." The request to be examined as a body rather than as individuals was an important issue with the Cumberland ministers who had a New Side heritage. To be examined as individuals would support the claim of the majority of the Synod of Kentucky that the synod had original jurisdiction over individual ministers; to be examined as a body denied the synod's right to examine candidates and ministers who had been licensed and ordained by the presbytery. James McGready argued this point for the Cumberland ministers before the synodical Commission which suspended the Cumberland group in 1805, but the Commission refused to grant the request. The Synod of Kentucky refused the same petition in 1809 during a discussion of terms for reconciliation.

Both the presbyteries held their meetings on April 7, 1812. Cumberland Presbytery appointed Ewing and McGee to confer with West Tennessee Presbytery, and Robert Bell and James Porter to confer with Muhlenberg Presbytery. West Tennessee Presbytery refused to entertain the request for the Cumberland ministers to be examined as a body. At the same session, West Tennessee Presbytery framed a lengthy and virulent "Pastoral Letter" against the Cumberland ministers and ordered that 500 copies be printed and distributed.[34] Ewing replied to the caustic letter in a series of five letters.[35] West Tennessee Presbytery retorted by passing a resolution that it would no longer recognize the Cumberland ministers and their congregations as being in any way connected with the Presbyterian Church:

Resolved that communion with that body of people called the Cumberland presbyterians in their present standing is considered irregular & unpresbyterial.[36]

Cumberland Presbytery met in November to consider their next move. The "Reply" of Finis Ewing was accepted as containing "a just exposition of our exception to the Confession of Faith upon the term fatality, and also a just view of the system of doctrine held by this Presbytery as fairly deduced from the Confession of Faith, so far as doctrines are treated of in that reply." [37] The presbytery then passed the following resolutions:

WHEREAS, Our brethren of the Muhlenburg and West Tennessee Presbyteries, instead of manifesting a spirit of reconciliation, have officially shut the door against the two bodies communing together.
Resolved, That this presbytery has, in substance, complied with our declaration in the circular letter relating to a re-union.
Resolved, It is our opinion that Muhlenburg and West Tennessee Presbyteries have, for the present, cut off all prospect of a union between the two churches.
Resolved, That we have always been, and expect to continue to be, willing and ready to have a union, on proper principles, with the general Presbyterian Church.[38]

When Cumberland Presbytery convened at the Beech meetinghouse in April 1813, it declared that no hope seemed to remain for reconciliation with the parent church. Since the presbytery had been making rapid gains in growth, plans were developed for a synod consisting of the presbyteries of Logan, Cumberland, and Elk with the following members:[39]

| Logan | Cumberland | Elk |
|---|---|---|
| Finis Ewing | Hugh Kirkpatrick | William McGee |
| William Harris | Thomas Calhoun | Samuel King |
| William Barnett | David Foster | James Porter |
| Alexander Chapman | David McLin | Robert Bell |
| | | Robert Donnell |

Cumberland Synod held its first meeting in October at the Beech meetinghouse, in Sumner County, Tennessee. The name of Cumberland Presbytery

### Mount Moriah Church

This church in Giles County, Tennessee, was organized in March 1810 by James B. Porter. It was the first to be organized as a Cumberland Presbyterian church. The pictured building was erected in 1855.

### Beech Church

"Old Beech," in Sumner County, Tennessee, is considered the oldest church in the denomination. It was organized in 1798 by Thomas Craighead and became a Cumberland Presbyterian church in 1810 under William McGee, its first pastor. A stone building with walls two feet thick was erected in 1828. The church was rebuilt after fires in 1940 and 1951; the pictured structure incorporates part of the walls from the early sanctuary. It serves a growing area near Hendersonville.

was changed to Nashville Presbytery. The synod elected McGee moderator and Ewing stated clerk. Two significant acts were passed: In one, a statement describing the "rise, doctrine, and progress of the Cumberland Presbyterians . . . was approved and ordered to be printed in the third edition of Buck's Theological Dictionary." This is notable as the first explicit reference to the "Cumberland Presbyterians" as a distinct ecclesiastical body. The other act was the appointment of a committee to "draw up and prepare for the press a Confession, Catechism, and Discipline in conformity to the avowed principles of this body." [40] The statement registered a dissent from the Westminster Confession in four particulars:

*First.* That there are no eternal reprobates.
*Second.* That Christ died not for a *part* only, but for all mankind.
*Third.* That *all* infants dying in infancy are saved through Christ and sanctification of the Spirit.
*Fourth.* That the Spirit of God operates on the world, or as co-extensively as Christ has made the atonement, in such manner as to leave *all men* inexcusable. [41]

With the organization of Cumberland Synod, the separation from the parent church was complete. The complicated events involved in the efforts for reconciliation from December 1805 until October 1813 indicate that the issues causing separation were not clearly delineated. The Cumberland ministers contended with presbyteries, a synod, and the General Assembly. If forbearance and tolerance had been shown by the various judicatories, it is very likely that reconciliation would have been a reality. As late as 1823, the Synod of Kentucky issued a *Brief History* to warn new people on the frontier about "those people who style themselves 'Cumberland Presbyterians' —a people who have no ecclesiastical connection with us whatsoever; and moreover, are not recognized by us as being in correct Presbyterian standing." [42] Two years later, however, the General Assembly gave full recognition to the Cumberland Presbyterians by declaring that they "are to be viewed in the same light with those of other denominations, not connected with our body." [43]

# 6

## OLD ISSUES REVISITED:

## AN INTERPRETATION

*We are conscious of the fact that our fathers were responsible
by their insensitivity to the needs of the frontier and by their
provincialism for a great share of the causes of the original schisms
and we, their descendants, wish to express to you, the loyal descendants of the founders of the Cumberland Presbyterian Church, our
sorrow for the part our Church played in the tragic division.*

General Assembly of the United Presbyterian Church
in the U.S.A., 1962

A fraternal delegate of the United Presbyterian Church in the United
States of America appeared before the General Assembly of the Cumberland
Presbyterian Church in Little Rock, Arkansas, at its 132nd meeting in 1962.
His presence was not unusual; the two churches exchanged delegates every
year. But his remarks to the Assembly constituted the most significant official
communication between the two groups since their separation in 1810. As
the Rev. W. Glen Harris began to speak, the Assembly suddenly realized
that something very meaningful was about to occur. A reverential silence
engulfed the Assembly as the assembled delegates became aware of the
speaker's words:

. . . that the 174th General Assembly approve the following message, and ask that it be delivered in person and read to the General Assembly of the Cumberland Presbyterian Church by the Rev. W. Glen Harris who is to be our fraternal delegate to that General Assembly.

Fathers and Brethren:

We are thankful that in these past several years we have begun to bridge the gulf that has existed between our churches. In the fellowship of the World Presbyterian Alliance and in less formal contacts and conversations we believe that the Holy Spirit has been healing the wounds and pain caused by the division of the Cumberland Presbytery in 1810, and by the only partially successful union of 1907.

We are conscious of the fact that our fathers were responsible by their insensitivity to the needs of the frontier and by their provincialism for a great share of the causes of the original schisms and we, their descendants, wish to express to you, the loyal descendants of the founders of the Cumberland Presbyterian Church, our sorrow for the part our Church played in the tragic division. We ask your forgiveness. . . . We would like to work with you as Christian brothers. We hope you will come to feel the same way towards us.

Yours in the name of our Lord Jesus Christ.

Marshall L. Scott, Moderator
Eugene Carson Blake, Stated Clerk.

The Cumberland Presbyterian General Assembly responded with a unanimous vote to send a similar letter to the General Assembly of the United Presbyterian Church, U. S. A., confessing their own faults and expressing a desire to work more closely together in the future.[1]

Over the past century and a half many reasons have been set forth for the separation of the Cumberland Presbyterian Church from the parent body during the early frontier days of Kentucky and Tennessee. Cumberland Presbyterian writers have attributed the origins of their church to controversies over the doctrine of election, the unconstitutional proceedings of the Synod of Kentucky in suspending members of the revival party in the original Cumberland Presbytery, opposition of antirevivalists to the revivalistic method of evangelism, controversy over the educational requirements of the Presbyterian Church, failure to adapt to the frontier, and the sociogeographic isolation of the frontier churches.

Previous investigators of the origins of the Cumberland Presbyterian Church have neglected to study the minutes of the judicatories involved in the disputes which occasioned the formulation of this Church. Most Cumberland Presbyterian writers have depended largely upon the interpretation published in 1835 by James Smith, who stressed the differences existing between the revival and antirevival parties; specifically, the concept of fatalism as expressed in the definition of election in the Westminster Confession of Faith.[2] After Robert Davidson wrote a critical account in 1847 of the frontier revival, referring to the ministers licensed and ordained by Cumberland Presbytery as "illiterate exhorters with Arminian sentiments," [3] Cumberland Presbyterian writers began to rationalize the issue of education by stressing other causative factors such as doctrinal differences and the unconstitutional proceedings of the synodical Commission which suspended the revival ministers of Cumberland Presbytery.

Franceway R. Cossitt, who wrote a rebuttal to Davidson's history and stressed the unconstitutional proceedings of the Presbyterian Synod of Kentucky as the cause of the separation, believed that the synod was aware that it had used illegal and unprecedented measures in dealing with Cumberland Presbytery. The synod knew that the proceedings of its Commission, which had suspended the Cumberland ministers in 1805, would have to be justified if the Commission was to escape the scrutiny of the General Assembly. The only way the synod could seek justification for its actions was to force the revival party to yield to the synod's unorthodox measures; therefore, unconditional submission was demanded in all cases. When the submission was made, lack of the literary qualification was no longer a factor in the admission of a person into the Presbyterian Church.[4] Three years after Cossitt's book appeared, E. B. Crisman wrote his *Origin and Doctrines of the Cumberland Presbyterian Church*.[5] He followed Cossitt in stressing the irregularity of the proceedings of the Synod of Kentucky.

A generation passed before other writers investigated the origins of the Cumberland Presbyterian Church. In 1888, Benjamin W. McDonnold listed several causes for the separation of the Cumberland preachers from the Presbyterian Church: opposition by the antirevivalists to the revival and to the methods of the revivalists, controversy over educational requirements, doctrinal differences, and the unconstitutional proceedings of the Synod of Kentucky.[6] Robert V. Foster added a new element to the study of the origin of the Cumberland Presbyterian Church by regarding the founding of the new church as a result of the failure of the Presbyterian Church to adapt itself to the frontier conditions.[7] Before the nineteenth century came to a close, two additional accounts of the origins of the Cumberland Presbyterian Church appeared. Thaddeus Blake published a "Defence" of the church in 1897, stressing the doctrinal issue as the primary cause for the origin of the new church.[8] The following year, John Vant Stephens attempted to explain the organization of the church and revealed his dependence on the past when he declared that although several factors were involved, "the final and principal cause . . . was one of Doctrine." [9]

Several theses have been written on various aspects of the origins of the

Cumberland Presbyterian Church. One student attributes the difficulties to the uncompromising attitude of the Scotch-Irish people,[10] but this is simply Cossitt's argument in different garb. Another student ascribes the causative factor to sociogeographic isolation,[11] but this is really another way of saying that the Presbyterian Church failed to adapt itself to frontier conditions—an argument used by nineteenth century writers. The writer of a more recent study of Cumberland Presbyterianism reiterates the thesis of sociogeographic isolation in providing a frame of reference for his survey of the social views of the Cumberland Presbyterian Church during the last quarter of the nineteenth century.[12]

Cumberland Presbyterian writers either have attempted to justify the use of ministers who failed to meet the usual educational requirements of the Presbyterian Church, or have ignored the question altogether. By placing less emphasis on the educational issue, stress has been given to the doctrinal and constitutional arguments. The question of education cannot be discounted. It was a factor. The issues of presbyterial and synodical authority, doctrinal differences, subscription to a creed, and the attitude towards the revival are all valid factors; they represent the same issues that ruptured the Presbyterian Church in 1741.[13]

Non-Cumberland Presbyterian writers have stressed the failure of the Cumberland ministers to meet the educational standards of the Presbyterian Church, often referring to the men as uneducated or illiterate. As noted above, Robert Davidson was the first historian of the Presbyterian Church to allude to the revival members of the first Cumberland Presbytery as "illiterate exhorters with Arminian sentiments."[14] Ten years later, in 1856, the Stated Clerk of the Presbyterian Church described Alexander Anderson, Finis Ewing, and Samuel King—the first three revival ministers to be ordained by Cumberland Presbytery—as "uneducated men of advanced age."[15] The noted historian of Calvinism, John T. McNeill, states that "the Cumberland Presbyterian church took its rise (1810) through the pleas of revivalists for the admission of untrained ministers to evangelize the new settlements, and the rejection of this by the Assembly."[16] A modern collection of source material in American church history allows over thirty pages for documents relating to the frontier activities of the "Stoneites," Methodists, and Shakers, but the Cumberland Presbyterians are dismissed with one sentence: "In 1810, revivalists of the Cumberland (Kentucky) Presbytery organized themselves into an independent body, which six [properly three] years later adopted the name Cumberland Presbyterian Church."[17]

The influence of Davidson is evident in other publications. William W. Sweet quotes Davidson's statement that the Cumberland ministers were "illiterate exhorters with Arminian sentiments."[18] Ernest T. Thompson, the historian of the Presbyterian Church in the United States, devotes a chapter in his history of Presbyterianism in the South to the "Frontier Schisms." Thompson is not only preoccupied with the lack of educational qualifications of the revival members of Cumberland Presbytery, but his account is based entirely upon Davidson's history and Sweet's collection of source materials,[19] without a single reference in his footnotes and bibliography to a Cumberland Presbyterian document.[20] The author of one of the volumes of the Studies in Presbyterian History, produced by the United Presbyterian Church in the U. S. A., declares that "the newly ordained ministers of the Cumberland Church were scantily educated."[21]

The uncritical assumption that the founders of the Cumberland Presbyterian Church were uneducated or illiterate and that the issue of education was the reason for the origin of the Cumberland Presbyterian Church is certainly belied by the veritable facts.[22] The suspension of the ministers of Cumberland Presbytery resulted from a written charge which Thomas Craighead, the senior member of presbytery, presented to the Synod of Kentucky in 1804, although the synod did not act upon it until 1805. The charge stated that the presbytery had licensed and ordained men who "were not only illiterate but erroneous in Sentiment."[23] This was a common fame charge. It was equivalent to "rumor"; it did not have to be substantiated by factual evidence. A common fame charge is no longer allowed in the Presbyterian Church. Craighead, who made the accusation, had also issued a written dissent to the licensing of Finis Ewing, Alexander Anderson, and Samuel King by Transylvania Presbytery in 1801. In his earlier charge, he referred to the men as "being destitute of classical learning."[24] A *classical* education meant the acquisition of a college diploma from an eastern or European university. The classical pretheological curriculum in Yale and the College of New Jersey, for example, included logic, grammar, rhetoric, geometry, arithmetic, physics, natural philosophy, and readings in the Greek and Latin classics. A candidate for the ministry studied divinity in the household of an eminent pastor-theologian. William Tennent included divinity studies in the regular curriculum of his Log College.[25]

Historians who depend uncritically upon Davidson for their information fail to recognize that many of the suspended ministers and candidates were educated. Finis Ewing studied under Thomas Craighead at the Springhill Academy, located about three miles east of Nashville. Ewing had a knowledge of Greek and he made an intensive study of Latin.[26] His knowledge of the languages and theology is evident in a series of letters which he wrote in reply to a pastoral letter from West Tennessee Presbytery in 1812.[27] Samuel McAdow, one of the three who founded the Cumberland Presbyterian Church, was ordained by the Presbyterian Church before he came to Tennessee in 1800. In North Carolina he had completed a three-year course at Mecklenburg Academy and had studied theology at David Caldwell's Log College.[28] James Porter, a licentiate at the time of his suspension, had completed his studies for the medical profession. He chose the ministry as his vocation and passed examinations in the classical languages administered by his presbytery.[29] Another licentiate, Hugh Kirkpatrick, was received into Transylvania Presbytery as a regular candidate for the ministry; he passed examinations in the languages before he was transferred to Cumberland Presbytery when it was organized in 1803.[30] Sweet, in his collection of Presbyterian documents, fails to reproduce the paragraph which refers to Kirkpatrick's examination in the languages, and he makes the glaring error of pointing out on one page that the case of James Porter is an example of "the absence of an examination on educational qualifications" even though two pages later he reproduces the minutes which state that "Mr. Porter's examination on the languages was sustained."[31] Ernest T. Thompson makes the same error about Porter by relying on Sweet's statement.[32]

The Cumberland Presbyterians refused to assume the responsibility of founding a new church until the doors of the Presbyterian Church were closed to them. They felt themselves compelled to take the step after eight years of effort (1805-1813) failed to effect a reconciliation. Were there reasons of sufficient moment to take such an extreme step? The justification for their decision rests on the historical interpretation of the events leading up to the constitution of an independent Cumberland Presbytery in 1810 and the actual organization of the Cumberland Presbyterian Church when the first Cumberland Synod convened in 1813.

It has been said that "it is impossible to interpret American Presbyterianism apart from the Great Awakening,"[33] and it is equally impossible to explain the origin of the Cumberland Presbyterian Church apart from the Great Awakening of 1740 and the Great Revival in the West, which began at the beginning of the nineteenth century. The issues which led to the division of the Presbyterian Church into the Old Side and New Side factions in the eighteenth century were the same as those involved in the division of the church in the early 1800s which resulted in the founding of the Cumberland Presbyterian: in the context of a religious revival, two theories, views, or philosophies of Presbyterianism came into conflict. The prorevival preachers had a New Side heritage; most of the antirevival preachers were of Old Side background. The basic differences between these two views of Presbyterianism were a major factor in preventing reconciliation. The following illustration sets forth the essential differences between New Side and Old Side Presbyterianism as they emerged from the eighteenth century:

| NEW SIDE (Liberal or Progressive) | | | OLD SIDE (Conservative) |
|---|---|---|---|
| Favored | — | REVIVAL | — Opposed |
| Exceptions in extraordinary cases | — | EDUCATION | — No exceptions |
| Modified Calvinism | — | DOCTRINE | — Strict Calvinism |
| Reservations allowed in nonessentials | — | SUBSCRIPTION | — Unequivocal; no exceptions |
| Only Presbytery has the jurisdiction over minister | — | ECCLESIASTICAL AUTHORITY | — Synod also has jurisdiction |
| Subjective; inner experience | — | DIVINE CALL TO PREACH | — Objective; act of ecclesiastical judicatory |
| Directed toward the conscience and conversion experience | — | HOMILETIC TECHNIQUE | — Directed toward the intellect and edification |
| Watts's Hymns | — | SUNG PRAISE | — Metrical Psalter |

On the western frontier, with its increasing consciousness of freedom from restraint, its optimistic view of the future, its emphasis on individualism, and its romantic faith in the "common man," the revival found a warm reception. The revival, however, brought division within the Presbyterian Church. As the number of converts began to be counted by the thousands and new churches multiplied, the Presbyterian Church failed to adapt itself to the frontier to meet the need of providing preachers to vacant churches. One small group with a New Side background favored liberality in licensing and ordaining men to preach who had failed to acquire a classical education. Like the Old Side group who opposed the New Side use of Log College graduates during the Great Awakening of 1740, the Old Side Presbyterians on the western frontier opposed any exceptions to the standard educational qualifications for the ministry.

Later Presbyterian historians have indicted the Presbyterian Church for its failure to adapt to the critical situation on the frontier. Robert E. Thompson believed the Church was wrong in insisting on "the rigidity of her polity in the manner of ministerial education."

She was right in setting up a high ideal. . . . She was wrong in refusing to recognize that there are times when a higher expediency demands a temporary relaxation of the rule. . . . On the frontier . . . the rigid exaction of a collegiate education for every candidate for the ministry was a fatal embarrassment.

Because the General Assembly insisted upon judging the needs of the frontier by the standards of Philadelphia, and insisted upon "making men gentlemen before it made them ministers," says Thompson, it lost its potential membership to the more resilient Baptists and Methodists.[34] Ezra H. Gillett believed that the "recluse scholar" with his "polished discourse read from the manuscript" could not meet the needs of the frontier. "Education and refinement were not in demand"; the West did not need preachers manufactured to order in colleges, but men who were trained on the field.[35] Referring to the failure of the Presbyterian Church to adapt to the needs of the frontier, another historian said: "The Presbyterians were heavily cumbered for advanced work by traditions and rules which they were rigidly reluctant to yield or bend, even when the reason for the rule was superseded by higher reasons." [36]

Education has received more attention than any other issue in statements concerning the separation of the Cumberland group from the Presbyterian Church.

It must be admitted that several men were licensed and ordained who had failed to acquire the classical education as expected by the Presbyterian Church, but this was neither unusual nor without precedent. This same factor was one of the wedges that forced the separation in the Presbyterian Church in the Great Awakening of 1740. After the Great Awakening, a ruling on educational requirements was set forth by the General Synod of New York and Philadelphia in 1777. Answering an inquiry from the Presbytery of New Castle, the synod declared:

The reference from the Presbytery of New Castle, respecting the propriety of admitting young men upon trials for the ministry without their having obtained a college diploma, was taken into consideration, in answer to which the Synod observe, that the superior advantages attending an education in public seminaries render it highly expedient to encourage the young men to finish their academical studies in such institutions as means of securing a learned ministry. . . . Yet as Presbyteries are the proper judges to determine concerning the literary and other requisite qualifications for the ministerial office, it is not intended to preclude from admission to trial, those who have not had the opportunity of obtaining public testimonials or degrees from public seminaries.[37]

Five years later, the synod reversed its position and stated the necessity of a liberal education.[38] The synod, in 1785, deferred a motion to extend the liberal college education to include two years of theological study.[39]

Although a standard was established in 1761 to recommend at least one year of theological study under the care of an approved minister in addition to a college degree,[40] many exceptions were made before and after the explicit adoption of a standard. At the first meeting of the Synod of New York and Philadelphia in 1758,[41] a request was received to ordain John Griffith to preach to a group of Welsh people. The synod considered the fact that he lacked a "liberal education," but because the circumstances were singular, the synod reasoned that "though he has not the measure of school learning usually required, and which they judge to be ordinarily requisite," he was ordained and attached to Philadelphia Presbytery.[42] The Presbytery of New Castle ordained John Rankin in 1778, although he had not received a college diploma.[43] In the case of Samuel Porter, who had studied under John McMillan, "the Presbytery [Redstone] allowed the usual course of study in his case to be curtailed" and ordained him in 1790.[44] Although William Paxton "had not the advantages of a college education," he was ordained by the Presbytery of New Castle in 1792.[45] James Turner received ordination by Hanover Presbytery in 1792, but "the full literary course required by the Presbyterian Book of Discipline was not exacted in his case, as it was judged to be one of those extraordinary cases which would justify a departure from the rule."[46] The General Assembly told David Rice, in 1804, that exceptions could be made in "extraordinary cases."[47] The Cumberland ministers, in their *Circular Letter* of 1810, listed additional exceptions to the educational standard, including "Mr. Beck, who was received by the Presbytery of North Carolina; Mr. Bloodworth, by Orange; Mr. Moore, by Hanover; Mr. Marquis, by Redstone; and Mr. Kemper and Mr. Abell by Transylvania Presbytery."[48] Even while the Cumberland Presbyterians were organizing into a General Assembly in 1829, the Presbyterian Church was still making exceptions to the rules. Two missionaries, who failed to meet the educational standard of the Presbyterian Church and who served for a year under the care of South Alabama Presbytery, were ordained "in consideration of the desolate condition of our country."[49]

Even with the numerous exceptions made to educational qualifications, the factor cannot be entirely discounted. The question of education did not become an issue until it was set forth in the common fame letter which caused the Synod of Kentucky to appoint a Commission to reexamine the men ordained and licensed by Cumberland Presbytery. It was an issue, but a minor one. In fact, it is difficult to find explicit charges against the Cumberland ministers for failing to maintain the educational standards of the Presbyterian Church. Davidson, the Presbyterian historian, coined the phrase "illiterate exhorters,"[50] but he also pointed out that "it was not the want of classical learning, but unsoundness in doctrine, the adoption of the Confession with reservations, that created the grand difficulty." [51]

From the time of the suspension of the Cumberland ministers in 1805 until the publication of Davidson's *History of the Presbyterian Church in Kentucky* in 1847, the question of education was never the predominant reason given as the cause of separation, nor the factor preventing reconciliation to the parent church. In 1805 the synodical Commission demanded that all persons licensed or ordained by Cumberland Presbytery submit to a re-examination by the Commission. When they refused, the Commission declared:

. . . it being proclaimed by common fame that the majority of these men are not only illiterate but erroneous in Sentiment.[52]

The charge of illiteracy was a common fame accusation; consequently, it was a common fame statement, and not a valid accusation, that caused the suspension of the Cumberland group. The action by the Commission was irregular and without warrant. Even the Commission admitted this in citing the authors of the common fame letter:

*Resolved,* also that the Rev Thos B Craighead, and Samuel Donald [Donnell] and John Bowman, have acted irregularly in taking up the case upon *fama clamosa*. . . .[53]

The decision of the Commission to suspend ministers by basing its proceedings upon testimony received in an irregular manner has been called an action "without precedent, and, thus far, without imitation." [54] The General Assembly of 1807 referred to the decision of the Commission as being of "at least questionable regularity." [55] A trustee of the same Assembly said it was "the decided opinion of the majority, in the General Assembly, that no Synod has the right to proceed against ministers or individuals except . . . by an appeal from the Presbytery," and the synod was "wholly improper in suspending ordained preachers, and still more improper was it for a commission of Synod to do it." [56] A commissioner to the General Assembly of 1808 assured the Cumberland ministers that the work of the Commission "was without constitutional authority and wholly void." [57] The same Assembly expressed its implicit disapproval of the censure inflicted by the Commission when the Assembly appointed James McGready a missionary in 1808, while he was under the censure.[58]

In March 1809, Transylvania Presbytery informed the suspended ministers of the terms for reconciliation:

We do humbly conceive that a formal examination . . . respecting doctrine and discipline is indispensable. . . . That an unequivocal adoption of our Confession of Faith is also indispensable.[59]

That Transylvania Presbytery was not concerned with educational qualifications is revealed by the decision to receive Samuel Hodge and Thomas Nelson—two of the men ordained by Cumberland Presbytery—without an examination on literary attainments:

Messrs Thos. Nelson & Saml. Hodge, two of the young men formerly licensed & ordained by the late Cumberland pby. & prohibited by the commission of Synod, came forward & expressed their desire to submit themselves to the wisdom & determination of this pby. whereupon pby . . . examined them so far as was thought expedient . . . & being satisfied with Messrs Nelson & Hodge in reference to their doctrinal qualifications for the gospel ministry, their aptness to teach, & after their accepting the Confession of Faith & discipline of our church & promising in a solemn manner conformity to the rules & regulations of the church & submission to the brethren in the Lord, their licensure & ordination were recognized & confirmed unanimously. . . . They were consequently recognized as members of this pby. & invited to take their seats which they did accordingly.[60]

In a letter to James W. Stephenson in 1811, the General Assembly warned Stephenson about his proposed plans to effect the reconciliation of the independent Cumberland Presbytery:

We do not object to your appointment of a committee to confer with these men, but we wish you to be careful not to yield any principle either in doctrine or government.[61]

The General Assembly issued an official statement, in 1814, relative to the Cumberland Presbyterians:

The grounds of their separation from us were, that we would not relax our discipline, and surrender some important doctrines of our Confession of Faith.[62]

The following extract from the *Brief History of the Synod of Kentucky* (1823) reveals the emphatic denial by the synod that the question of educational qualifications was a cause involved in the origin of the Cumberland Presbyterian Church:

It is moreover due to the cause of truth and candor, as well as to our Church at large, and the public generally, to correct a statement, or solemnly disavow the truth of a statement, widely circulated in the account given of the Cumberland Presbyterians in "Buck's Theological Dictionary," (fifth edition, by W. W. Woodward, p. 419.) It is there stated, that the "Commission exhibited many charges, &c. all of which were chiefly comprised in the two following, viz:—1st. Licensing men to preach the gospel who had not been examined on the languages. 2d. That those men who were licensed, both learned and less learned, had been only required to adopt the Confession partially, that is, as far as they believed it to agree with the word of God." *This latter charge is true, but the former is not.* And for the truth of this disavowal, we appeal to the testimony of those members of the Commission of Synod who are yet living. We appeal to the records of that Commission, where no such charge can be found specified or tabled against the Presbytery on that occasion. We appeal to the fact of the Transylvania Presbytery's having subsequently, under the connivance and approbation of the Synod, received two of those young men alluded to in the statement in question. And we appeal to the expressions of the Synod, in their explanation and defense to the General Assembly already given, which says: "Further, Synod thought that among so many young men there might be found at least a few, who would shortly be qualified for the office of the gospel ministry, could they be induced to use the proper means." *It is therefore denied that the charge under consideration is true.*[63]

The above statements from historians and several judicatories of the Presbyterian Church reveal that the central issue involved in the origin of the Cumberland Presbyterian Church was not educational qualifications.

The contributing factors to separation include the frontier and the revival which provided the sociological context, the question of education, the false identification of the suspended members of Cumberland Presbytery with the New Light group, and Craighead's letter to the Synod of Kentucky. When the Old Side majority of the Synod of Kentucky saw a real threat from the New Side or revival party, the synod used Craighead's common fame letter and the question of education to stop the growth of the revival party. During the Great Awakening in the eighteenth century, the same tactic was used by the Old Side party to halt the Log College men who promoted the revival.

According to New Side Presbyterianism, the suspension of the Cumberland ministers by a synodical commission was contrary to Presbyterian discipline; but according to the Old Side group, the synod had a valid right to examine or judge individual candidates and ordained ministers. The synod thought they were acting legally; the revival party thought the synod had acted unconstitutionally. Two different views or concepts of American Presbyterianism were in conflict. Failure to agree on doctrine and subscription prevented reconciliation. The revival group wished to make an exception to the doctrine of election. The synod would not yield; it insisted on the adoption of the Confession of Faith without any exception. The revival party wanted to be examined as a body rather than as individuals. The synod also would not yield this point, for to admit that they could be examined as a group and not as individual ministers would mean that the synod had no authority over them except by treating them as a presbytery. If the revival and the frontier provided the context for the conflict between Cumberland Presbytery and the Synod of Kentucky, if educational qualifications provided the pretext for reexamination by the synod, and if Craighead's letter of protest provided the instrument or the means for cutting off the revival party—then the issues of the doctrine of election, subscription, and ecclesiastical authority over licensed and ordained preachers maintained the wall of separation which the synod imposed in order to prevent reconciliation.

The issues of education, doctrine, subscription, and ecclesiastical authority, if dealt with separately, fail to explain the origin of the Cumberland Presbyterian Church. The individual issues must be considered as a group of concepts defining a distinct view of Presbyterianism. The members of the revival party were all products of a New Side liberal Presbyterian heritage. When the Scotch-Irish came to America in such large numbers during the first half of the eighteenth century, most of them settled on the frontiers in Pennsylvania, Virginia, and the Carolinas. They carried the Old Side influence into Kentucky and Tennessee.[64] The New Side influence was carried from Pennsylvania and New Jersey to Virginia and North Carolina, and thence into Kentucky and Tennessee. The men suspended by the Synod of Kentucky in 1805 shared this New Side heritage. Their opponents were Old Side men who had moved from the frontiers into the bounds of the Synod of Kentucky.

A definite lineage of New Side Presbyterianism can be traced from William Tennent's Log College to the members of Cumberland Presbytery who favored the revival movement. Among the graduates of Tennent's school were Gilbert Tennent, William Robinson, and two brothers, Samuel Blair, Sr., and John Blair. The Blair brothers established a Log College at Fagg's Manor in Chester County, Pennsylvania. Three of the graduates from Fagg's Manor were Robert Smith, Samuel Davies, and John Rodgers. Davies organized Hanover Presbytery in Virginia after William Robinson had planted the seeds of New Side Presbyterianism during a missionary tour. Davies was succeeded by John Rodgers, who had also studied under Gilbert Tennent.

Robert Smith, a Fagg's Manor alumnus, opened a Log College at Pequea in Lancaster County, Pennsylvania. Smith married the sister of Samuel Blair, Sr., and their two sons became eminent educators in Virginia. Samuel Stanhope Smith served as president of Hampden-Sydney College, and when he resigned to assume the presidency of Princeton, his brother, John Blair Smith, succeeded him. Other graduates of Fagg's Manor who established Log Colleges were Joseph Smith, John McMillan, and Thaddeus Dod, three of the "four horsemen of Redstone" who were constituted into Redstone Presbytery in 1781.[65]

Samuel Davies, another graduate of Fagg's Manor, propagated the New
Side heritage throughout the Presbytery of Hanover in Virginia and the Presbytery of Orange in North Carolina. David Rice, the first Presbyterian minister to settle permanently in Kentucky, received his theological training
under Davies and was married to the daughter of Samuel Blair, Sr.[66] David
Caldwell came under the tutelage of Davies at Princeton, studied theology
under Robert Smith at Pequea, and perpetuated the Log College influence
by opening an academy in Orange County, North Carolina.[67]

The ordained members of Cumberland Presbytery who came into conflict
with the Synod of Kentucky in 1805 were James McGready, William Hodge,
William McGee, John Rankin, Samuel McAdow, Samuel King, and Finis
Ewing. McGready was tutored by Joseph Smith and John McMillan in
Pennsylvania, and by David Caldwell in North Carolina. Caldwell also
taught William McGee, Samuel McAdow, and William Hodge.[68] The
father of Finis Ewing was an elder in David Rice's church at Peaks of Otter,
in Virginia. For the first ten years of Ewing's life—until Rice moved to
Kentucky in 1783—Ewing was under the pastoral care of Rice. It was Rice
who suggested that Transylvania Presbytery license Ewing and others as
exhorters.

McGready, Hodge, McGee, and McAdow were sent as missionaries to
Kentucky and Tennessee by Orange Presbytery during the years 1796-1800,
and they were incorporated into Cumberland Presbytery when it was organized in 1803. The other ordained members who were suspended by the
Synod of Kentucky in 1805 were Ewing, King, and James Haw. Ewing and
King were licensed by Transylvania Presbytery in 1802 and ordained by
Cumberland Presbytery in 1803. Haw was received as an ordained minister
from the Republican Methodist Church by Transylvania Presbytery in 1802
and was transferred into Cumberland Presbytery at its first meeting.

The Synod of Kentucky was predominantly Old Side in its attitudes and
heritage. When the New Side ministers arrived within the bounds of the
synod, the stage was set for an ecclesiastical war. Someone simply had to
light the fuse.

Thomas Craighead ignited the fuse when he sent his common fame letter
to the Synod of Kentucky in 1804. He accused the majority of the Cumberland Presbytery ministers—the revival members—of licensing and ordaining
men contrary to the Confession of Faith. Craighead's action has been interpreted by most writers as an attack by the antirevival party against those who
favored the revival.[69] Craighead's associates may have opposed the revival,
but the available evidence indicates that Craighead neither supported the
revival nor openly opposed the movement. Thomas Craighead's father was
a New Side minister,[70] and Thomas was pastor of his father's church fol-

lowing his father's death. Thomas's sister married David Caldwell, the teacher of most of the New Side preachers who were the actual leaders of the revival in Kentucky and Tennessee.[71] His accusations against the revival party reveal no antagonism toward the revival movement. In 1805 Craighead was charged with doctrinal errors similar to those with which he had charged the revival party of Cumberland Presbytery.

In referring to the men ordained by Cumberland Presbytery, the synod declared:

It being proclaimed by common fame that the majority . . . are not only illiterate but erroneous in Sentiment . . . the Commission of Synod prohibit . . . the said persons from exhorting, preaching, and administering ordinances in consequence of any authority which they have obtained from the Cumberland Presbytery, until they submit to our jurisdiction, and undergo the required examination.

Referring to three of the older ministers, the synod continued the accusations:

As Common Fame loudly proclaims the Rev Wm Hodge, William McGee, and John Rankin hold doctrines contrary to those contained in our Confession of Faith, (viz) that they in effect deny Election; and hold that there is a certain sufficiency of Grace given to every man which if he will improve he shall obtain more, and continue till he arrive at true conversion.

The charge against Craighead in 1805 was that

Common Fame loudly proclaims that the Revd Thomas Craighead propagates doctrines contrary to the system of doctrines contained in our Confession of Faith, (viz) that he in effect denies the doctrine of election and that the special or supernatural operations of the Holy Spirit are necessary in order to believing conversion and sanctification.[72]

Craighead had been charged with disseminating Hopkinsianism on the western frontier.[73] Barton Stone's biographer, Charles C. Ware, asserts that Craighead's influence upon Stone was the means by which a modification of Calvinism which developed in New England and was called the New Divinity, or Hopkinsianism, bore fruit in the New Light movement in northern Kentucky.[74] Richard McNemar and Matthew Houston, who entered the Shaker movement from the New Lights, were also infected with Craighead's views. Craighead's influence was so great that one of his accusers described him as "the grand heresiarch of the West, the prime mover of schisms in this section of our church."[75] Craighead was charged officially with "denying . . . the real agency of the Spirit in regeneration," and "denying the doctrines of divine foreordination, sovereignty, & election."[76]

If Craighead did not wish to halt the spread of the revival, why did he attack the revival members? Craighead was really trying to hinder the leadership and influence of one person—Finis Ewing. This leads to a very important factor relative to the suspension of the revival ministers of Cumberland Presbytery in 1805. This factor, which has never been explored, is the personal animosity between Craighead and Ewing. In order to understand the attack against Ewing, it is necessary to review Craighead's activities from his arrival in Tennessee in 1785 until his first attempt to block the licensure of Ewing in 1801. Directly involved with Craighead's personal feeling toward Ewing were family relationships which involved the two men. Craighead was the second senior member (next to Rice) when Transylvania Presbytery was constituted in 1786. Other members included Adam Rankin, Andrew McClure, and James Crawford. Craighead was absent from the first meeting, and he failed to attend a meeting of presbytery for a period of eleven years. In 1794, presbytery directed James Blythe to confer with Craighead concerning his absences. Blythe reported that Craighead could not attend because of the "distance and the danger of the roads." Another summons given to Craighead in 1796 prompted him to attend in March 1797.[77]

One reason that may have kept Craighead away from the presbyterial meetings seems to have been his dissatisfaction with Rice's having the preeminent position in presbytery, a position he probably desired for himself. This inference is supported by his request, at his first attendance in 1797, to have the presbytery seek a division into two presbyteries. Rice could head one; he could lead the other. Transylvania Presbytery refused to approve his proposal.[78]

From 1797 to 1802, Craighead attended two meetings of presbytery: those of April 1800 and October 1801. Both meetings were held at McGready's Muddy River Church, the scene of the Revival of 1800. During this same period, a series of important events happened which help to explain Craighead's opposition to the work of Ewing.

Finis Ewing came to Tennessee after both of his parents had died in Virginia. His father had been an elder in the Peaks of Otter Church and clerk of the Bedford County Court.[79] David Rice was pastor of Peaks of Otter until he moved to Kentucky in 1783.[80] In Tennessee, Ewing attended Craighead's church. Craighead was the rival of his former pastor, Rice. Ewing married Peggy Davidson, the daughter of General William Lee Davidson, in 1793, and two years later moved to Logan County, Kentucky. General Davidson's name was given to Davidson County, Tennessee, in which Nashville is situated; Davidson Academy in Nashville; and Davidson College in North Carolina.

Trouble was developing at that time in Davidson Academy. Ewing's uncle,

Ephraim McLean, Sr., served with Craighead, its teacher and president, on the Board of Trustees. The Ewings, McLeans, Davidsons, and Brevards were related through a series of intermarriages. The trouble involved the disposition of the Academy's funds. A suit was filed by Samuel Barton on September 4, 1797, against two members of the Board of Trustees, James Robertson and Lardner Clarke. Samuel Barton and James Shaw had agreed to give bond to John Buchanon to pay £640 in two installments for 640 acres of land to be given to Thomas Craighead as part of the price required by Craighead before he would accept the position in Tennessee as preacher and teacher of Davidson Academy. This transaction occurred in 1785. In addition to the land, Craighead would receive £50 annually in salary. Twenty subscribers had agreed to pay £236 over a period of three years. In the meantime, Shaw became "insolvent"; Barton was left holding the surety of paying Buchanon. Barton received very little of the £900 raised over the three-year period 1785-1788. Buchanon sued Barton for the cost of Craighead's property. Barton, in turn, sued Robertson and Clarke, claiming he had not received the money from the trustees as set forth by the original agreement. Barton also claimed that Craighead had received more "cash and property" than agreed upon. Barton felt he should not be responsible for the debt, and he called for a personal accounting "of Craighead and others." [81] The important thing to note is not simply the legal process, but that Craighead was the center of the controversy, and his daughter was married to Robertson's son. Ephraim McLean, Sr., was the *treasurer* of the Academy; Finis Ewing's uncle, Andrew Ewing, was clerk of the court which handled the case; and Davidson Academy was named for William Lee Davidson, the father of Ewing's wife.[82] This incident would have certainly caused a strong feeling between Craighead and the Ewings and McLeans, and it is not merely a coincidence that three years later Craighead opposed the licensing by Transylvania Presbytery of four men who included a McLean and a Ewing.[83] The diagram of the intermarriages of the Ewings, McLeans, Davidsons, and Brevards exhibits several important facts:

(1) Ephraim McLean, Sr., trustee and treasurer of Davidson Academy, married Elizabeth Davidson.
(2) Ephraim McLean, Sr.'s son, George, married Pamela Davidson, daughter of General William Lee Davidson.
(3) Ephraim McLean, Sr.'s daughter, Jane, married General Robert Ewing, brother of Finis Ewing.
(4) Finis Ewing married the daughter of General William Lee Davidson, first cousin to Ephraim McLean, Sr.'s wife.

Ephraim McLean, Sr.'s nephew, Ephraim McLean, and Finis Ewing were suspended because of Craighead's common fame letter.

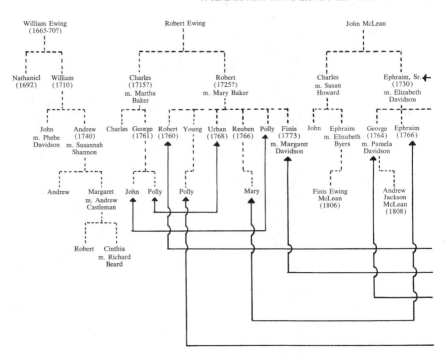

Craighead, who began his ministry in North Carolina, was acquainted with all these families. His father, Alexander Craighead, was a close friend of Ephraim Brevard, a leading patriot of the Mecklenburg Convention.[84] Andrew Jackson was a friend of Thomas Craighead; he was also a close friend of the Ewings and the McLeans. Jackson stood by Thomas Craighead during the latter's trial during the years 1808-1811, which resulted in his deposition from the ministry in 1811. George McLean, the son of Ephraim McLean, Sr., named one of his sons Andrew Jackson McLean, for Jackson. This was in 1808, during Craighead's trial, and during the time when the suspended ministers of Cumberland Presbytery were attempting to effect a reconciliation with the parent church. As President of the United States, Andrew Jackson appointed Finis Ewing as Registrar of the Land Office in Missouri in 1830.[85] Yet, Thomas Craighead struck across these mutual friendships to make his personal attack against Ewing. Ewing had been a member of the Polemic Society which met at Craighead's church; and since Ewing and his wife were members of Craighead's church, Craighead probably

THE EWING, McLEAN, DAVIDSON, AND BREVARD FAMILIES

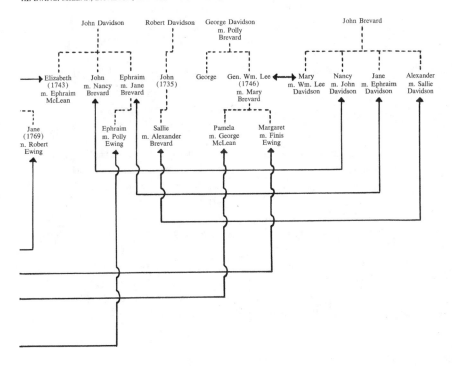

performed the marriage ceremony. It should be noted that the intermarriages of the Ewings, McLeans, Davidsons, and Brevards reveal that the Ewings and McLeans shared the same social stratum as the Davidsons and Brevards; consequently, the charge may be correct that Ewing and McLean lacked a classical education, but it would be difficult to refer to them as "illiterate" or "uneducated."

Before 1800, the lives of Ewing and Craighead were involved in the relation of parishioner to pastor. In 1795 Ewing and his wife moved to Logan County, Kentucky, and became members of James McGready's Muddy River Church. They joined on profession of faith, acknowledging that they had never known true conversion. On one occasion Ewing said to Craighead, "Your views of faith, sir, once came near destroying my soul." [86]

As noted above, Craighead attended presbytery twice between 1797 and 1801, both times at Muddy River, where Ewing was an elder. Craighead attended in April 1800, just as the Revival of 1800 was getting under way, and was appointed moderator. In October 1801, he journeyed again to Muddy

River, despite the "distance and the danger of the roads." He preached the opening sermon on a very appropriate text: "And this commandment have we from him, That he who loveth God love his brother also" (I John 4:21). Love was put to the test as Alexander Anderson, Samuel King, Ephraim McLean, and Finis Ewing presented themselves to presbytery to be licensed as exhorters. When this licensure was passed by presbytery, Craighead began his campaign to stop the ministerial activities of King, McLean, and Ewing.[87]

Craighead appeared at presbytery in 1802 and protested the licensure of King, McLean, and Ewing. But his opposition was not an expression of antirevivalism; it was an attempt to keep Ewing from being a part of Cumberland Presbytery. In a written protest, Craighead dissented from the "judgment of pby. in licensing Messrs Ewing & King . . . because their trials . . . consisted only in one short sermon & an examination on experimental religion & divinity, being destitute of classical learning, & they [Craighead and four other signers] discovered . . . no such extraordinary talents as to justify such measures."[88] Craighead did not refer to Ewing and King as "illiterate," but only lacking in *classical learning*.

Craighead's opposition to Ewing continued into Cumberland Presbytery when it was constituted in 1803. Craighead was recognized as the senior member. He preached the opening sermon and presided until a moderator was elected. Craighead was finally in a position of leadership, but he realized he had a rival in Ewing, who was transferred as a licentiate into Cumberland Presbytery.

Craighead was absent on the first day of the next meeting of Cumberland Presbytery in October. The presbytery chose this day to approve the ordination of Ewing for November. Craighead arrived the next day, but too late to oppose Ewing's ordination.

When the presbytery met the following April, with Craighead present, a move was made to prevent Ewing from being seated as an ordained minister. Craighead and his followers were overruled. Ewing was elected stated clerk at the October 1804 meeting of the presbytery.[89] Two weeks later, Craighead presented his common fame letter against the irregular proceedings of Cumberland Presbytery to the Synod of Kentucky.[90]

The April meeting of Cumberland Presbytery in 1805 convened with Craighead and the antirevival party enrolled. They wanted to be present when the synodical committee arrived, but only one of the appointed members attended—Archibald Cameron.[91]

In the fall meeting of the presbytery in 1805, Craighead, John Bowman, Terah Templin, and Samuel Donnell were absent on the first day. On the first evening, Ewing obtained a leave of absence—his first absence since becoming a member of presbytery. After Craighead's rival excused himself,

Craighead and Donnell appeared in presbytery the next morning. They were helpless to prevent the removal of charges against Ephraim McLean and the licensing of Robert Wilson and David Foster; they did, however, succeed in having the presbyterial record book "delivered to Mr. Donnell" to be presented to the next meeting of the Synod of Kentucky.[92] This was the last meeting that Ewing and the revival members would attend. The Synod of Kentucky examined the record book, condemned the proceedings of Cumberland Presbytery, and appointed a Commission to delve thoroughly into the matter. The Commission met in December and prohibited the revival members of Cumberland Presbytery from preaching or administering the sacraments.[93]

Cumberland Presbytery held two more meetings—April and October 1806—before it was dissolved and its members annexed to Transylvania Presbytery. Only the antirevival members were present. The rivalry between Craighead and Ewing in Cumberland Presbytery was ended, but this personal conflict had a strange and ironic sequel. In February 1810, Finis Ewing arranged a meeting with Samuel King at the home of Samuel McAdow in Dickson County, Tennessee, and organized the independent Cumberland Presbytery, an action which proved later to be in effect the constitution of the Cumberland Presbyterian Church. In April of the same year, Bowman was suspended by Transylvania Presbytery; six months later, Craighead was deposed from the ministry for preaching "Pelagian" doctrines.[94]

What were the factors involved in the origin of the Cumberland Presbyterian Church? Out of the years of revival and controversy—the period from 1800 to 1813—a number of decisive issues evolved, no one of which can be defined as the basic cause for the origin of a new denomination; but a series of elements, a number of causes, must be studied to understand their cumulative effect in forcing the organization of a separate body of Presbyterians. The revival in the West and the efforts of Cumberland Presbytery to adapt the standards of the Presbyterian Church to the frontier set the stage for the ecclesiastical drama to be enacted by Cumberland Presbytery and the Synod of Kentucky. Thomas Craighead's common fame letter, motivated by personal feelings against Finis Ewing, brought the internal strife of Cumberland Presbytery before the Synod of Kentucky. Added to the conflicting and confusing issues was the false identification of the Cumberland group with the New Light schism of 1803 in western Kentucky, which rejected all creeds.

The foregoing factors led to the *suspension*. But what prevented *reconciliation*? Reconciliation was prevented because of two divergent views of Presbyterianism. The synod was predominantly Old Side Presbyterian in its heritage, which caused a number of issues to enter into the conflict. The Old Side influence revealed itself when the synodical Commission acted with authority against individuals, a procedure which was contrary to the New Side concept that only the presbytery had original jurisdiction over its individual members. The revival party insisted, therefore, that they be examined as a body by Transylvania Presbytery or the Synod of Kentucky. In addition, the Cumberland ministers wanted to make an exception to the Westminster Confession of Faith on the doctrine of election, but the Old Side majority of the Synod of Kentucky insisted on unequivocal adoption. The suspended ministers of Cumberland Presbytery were claiming a right which was connected historically with the Adopting Act of 1729; the synod was claiming a position established by the Old Side Presbyterians in 1736 when the Adopting Act of 1729 was abrogated and replaced with a strict subscription policy which allowed for no exceptions.

The question of education was involved, but it was a question of relaxing of the requirements for a *classical* education rather than of licensing and ordaining men who were illiterate. The exception made by the Cumberland ministers to the Confession of Faith concerning the doctrine of election was not as important as the issue of strict subscription itself which the Old Side ministers wanted to enforce.

Underlying the entire controversy was the question as to the seat of ecclesiastical authority. Did authority over individual ministers reside in the presbytery or in the synod? The Old Side majority in the Synod of Kentucky held to the same view as the Old Side party in the eighteenth century: that the synod had a right to examine or reexamine candidates for the ministry. This was opposed by the New Side group in the eighteenth century as well as by the New Side Cumberland group within the Synod of Kentucky who believed the power to examine candidates for the ministry was vested solely in the presbytery. The leaders of the revival in the West, especially within Cumberland Presbytery, were in the stream of New Side Presbyterianism which flowed from the headwaters of William Tennent and the Log College alumni.

The entire controversy, with the various issues involved, reduces to one basic conflict: New Side Presbyterianism versus Old Side Presbyterianism. The issues which caused the schism in 1741 and the dissolution of New Brunswick Presbytery were the same that caused the separation of the Cumberland party and the dissolution of Cumberland Presbytery in 1806. The schism of the eighteenth century became final with the erection of New York Synod in 1745; the separation during the revival in the West became final when the New Side Cumberland ministers established Cumberland Synod in 1813.

# 7

## VAST FIELDS TO CULTIVATE

*Who would have anticipated, but a few years since, that our little, untaught, scoffed at and despised body would, in the course of ten years have grown into such consistency, respectability, and usefulness? Who would have thought that its congregations of respectable standing would by this time be scattered through or in six States and one or two Territories, whose preachers claim their full share of attention from the learned as well as the unlearned, from the noble as well as the ignoble?*

Finis Ewing in a letter to Robert Donnell, November 19, 1820

The issues involved in the formation of the Church continued to shape its development, but these were soon overshadowed by the missionary activities of Cumberland Presbyterians on the ever expanding American frontier. From October 1813, until the formation of a General Assembly in 1829 the Cumberland Presbyterian Church was governed by the "Cumberland Synod," otherwise called "The Synod of the Cumberland Presbyterian Church." [1] Every ordained minister was a member and was expected to attend and to bring along with him an elder. Absentees were called to account and occasionally admonished.

In the first meeting of the Synod, although twelve ordained ministers were present, only one ruling elder was enrolled. When the Synod named a committee to draw up a Confession of Faith and arrange for its publication each organized congregation was urged to send one of its most experienced elders to the next meeting of Synod to assist in deliberating upon the new

105

Confession.[2] At the second meeting of Synod, held at Suggs Creek, Wilson County, Tennessee, in April 1814, there was an attendance of ten ministers and seventeen ruling elders.

The principal item of business at the second meeting was the consideration of the new Confession of Faith. The greater part of four days was spent in deliberations upon the document, more than three days being given to the consideration of the Confession proper. It was considered section by section, along with amendments offered, and finally was adopted by unanimous vote on the morning of the fourth day of the deliberations. The Catechism, Discipline, Form of Process, and Directory for Worship were adopted in the course of the last day's sessions.[3] The Confession followed the chapter headings of the Westminster Confession but with significant changes in substance, especially in Chapter III (The Decrees of God), Chapter VIII (Christ the Mediator), Chapter X (Effectual Calling), and Chapter XVII (The Perseverance of the Saints).[4] The Larger Catechism was dispensed with, but an amended version of the Shorter Catechism was retained.

Finis Ewing and Hugh Kirkpatrick agreed to print the Confession of Faith "at eighty-seven and one-half cents per volume, upon good writing paper, neatly bound and lettered." [5]

The three presbyteries went about the task of carrying the gospel to the settlements on the frontier with unflagging zeal. B. W. McDonnold writes concerning the situation,

All three of the presbyteries had vast fields to cultivate, and those fields were continually expanding. The Nashville Presbytery, a few years after it began its separate presbyterial existence, found the whole western end of Tennessee opened by the purchase of the country from the Indians. But this expansion of this presbytery was a little thing compared with the vast fields thrown open on the frontiers of Logan and Elk presbyteries. In the case of the latter, soon after its organization, South Alabama was opened to American settlers, then Arkansas, then North-western Alabama, then Missouri. At one session of this presbytery petitions for preachers were received from five hundred pioneers in the new settlements of Alabama alone, and also from vast numbers in Arkansas and Missouri. Both Logan and Elk presbyteries tried to evangelize Missouri. In the wide bounds of Logan Presbytery Illinois, Indiana, and Ohio were opened to white settlements, and the earnest petitions of emigrants begging for the gospel were part of the stirring business coming up at every session.[6]

During the period of the Council, missionaries had been sent to the area of Huntsville, Alabama, and Robert Donnell was traveling and preaching in Alabama when news reached him of the organization of Cumberland Presbytery in February 1810.[7] During the period of the first presbytery John Carnahan, a candidate for the ministry, was ordered to form a circuit "on the Arkansaw, in the bounds of those settlements in which he lives, and report to Presbytery his success when he returns." [8]

It was not long after the organization of Cumberland Presbytery until some of the members of its churches emigrated to Indiana and Illinois. As early as 1811 a Mrs. Linzey, who had moved to a place near Petersburg, Indiana, wrote William Harris and Alexander Chapman urging them to come and preach to her and her neighbors. It is believed that Harris preached in Indiana as early as 1811.[9] In April 1817, Logan Presbytery ordered "that the Rev. Chapman ride three months. One month in the state of Indiana and the other two in the bounds of this presbytery as a missionary." The Rev. John Barnett likewise was to "ride" one month in Indiana.[10] Thereafter itinerants were sent regularly to Indiana. In August 1817, the first Cumberland Presbyterian church in Indiana was organized by the Rev. William Barnett in Gibson County. At first it was called Hopewell, but the name was later changed to Mount Zion.[11]

A Cumberland Presbyterian family named Tagert moved to southern Illinois in 1813. The first Cumberland Presbyterian sermon in Illinois is believed to have been preached near Golconda by John Barnett in 1815.[12] In 1817, the Rev. Green P. Rice settled in western Illinois. He preached occasionally at the French village of Saint Louis as well as in Illinois.[13] In 1818, the Rev. David W. McLin settled in southern Illinois.[14] It was he who organized the first Cumberland Presbyterian congregation in the state on June 8, 1819. It was at or near the present site of Enfield, in White County, and was called Hopewell.[15] Another congregation was organized later the same year by Rice in Bond County, in western Illinois, "at the home of William Robinson, some three miles north of Greenville." This church came to be known as Bear Creek.[16] A third center of Cumberland Presbyterian influence was in the "Sangamon country" to which the Rev. John M. Berry moved. The first church in this area was the Sugar Tree Church, which was located about ten miles south of Springfield.[17]

The first Cumberland Presbyterian minister to settle in Missouri was the Rev. Daniel Buie.[18] He settled near where the town of Glasgow was later built. He was already preaching in that area when, in 1819, the Missionary Board for Western Missions of the Cumberland Presbyterian Church, a woman's missionary society which had been formed with the encouragement of Finis Ewing, resolved to send a missionary to Missouri. The Rev. Robert D. Morrow, a young man then twenty-two years of age, was the one chosen.[19] Entering Missouri from Alton, Illinois, he proceeded to Pike County, where he found three Cumberland Presbyterian families, then to Calloway County and Howard County. He returned to Kentucky that fall to attend presbytery and synod, but he was back in Missouri to spend the winter preaching and was there the following spring for the organization of McGee Presbytery. After presbytery he laid out his first circuit in Missouri, which extended from Cape Girardeau to Clay County, a distance of at least 300 miles from east to west.[20] For the remainder of his life he made Missouri his home.

In the summer of 1815 Thomas Calhoun and Robert Donnell went on a preaching tour through East Tennessee, preaching first in the Sequatchie Valley, then at Washington, Morganton, and Maryville. The next year Calhoun returned to that area. In 1818, David Foster was sent to a regular circuit in East Tennessee, and in 1821 J. S. Guthrie was sent to the Hiwassee circuit. In 1823, Robert Baker and Abner W. Lansden were sent to that area, and in 1824, George Donnell and Samuel M. Aston.[21]

Cumberland Presbyterian itinerant preachers were sent to West Tennessee within less than a year after the area was bought from the Indians in 1819. In 1820, John L. Dillard and James McDonald began their work there. In 1821, Richard Beard was sent to the Forked Deer circuit. Soon thereafter campgrounds were established at Shiloh and McLemoresville, in Carroll County, and at Yorkville, in Gibson County.[22]

The first statistical report reflecting the status of the Cumberland Presbyterian Church came as a result of a resolution adopted in 1816:

> In order that we obtain a correct knowledge of the State of the churches under our care, Resolved, therefore, that each Presbytery produce, on the second day of each session of Synod, a correct statement of the number of societies and members in their respective bounds, and also the State of religion.[23]

In 1817 it was reported that

> The number of societies and members at present and number of conversions the last year were as follows: In Logan Presbytery, twenty-five societies, seven hundred and nineteen members, and two hundred conversions. In Elk Presbytery, thirty-five societies, seven hundred and two members, and one hundred and fifty conversions. In Nashville Presbytery, twenty-seven societies, six hundred members, and sixty-three conversions. In all eighty-seven societies, two thousand and twenty-one members, and four hundred and thirteen conversions.[24]

In 1818, however, the order regarding statistical reports was rescinded.[25] Instead, a committee on the "state of religion" was appointed each year. The reports on the "state of religion" usually included the number of conversions and the number of adult baptisms, the latter being adults "who had not received that ordinance in infancy." Reports for succeeding years yield the following figures: 1819, 1,130 conversions, 150 adult baptisms; 1820, 2,838 conversions, 415 adult baptisms; 1822, 2,718 conversions, 575 adult baptisms;

1823, 2,372 conversions, 500 adult baptisms; 1824, 3,021 conversions, 683 adult baptisms; and 1827, 4,006 conversions, 996 adult baptisms.

The reports on the "state of religion" reflect far more than mere statistical information, however. They abound in expressions of overflowing gratitude for the work that was being accomplished. The committee in 1817 observed that "in the course of the last year religion was in a more flourishing state than formerly; the different societies are more charitable, and the work of God abounding." [26] In 1818 various remarkable "displays of God's grace" are reported in particular areas. The report concludes, "There has no doubt been joy in heaven and joy on earth the last year, yet not unto us, not unto us, Oh Lord, but unto thy name be the glory." [27] The report for 1820 mentions the attention being given to the catechizing of children, the "impressive exhortations of many pious and gifted lay members," the attention to family prayers, and the "more than two-fold increase" of candidates for the ministry the past year. The report goes on to point out that

. . . Men and women of all classes are flocking to the standard of Jesus and fighting the battles of the Lord. We are prepared to answer a question once proposed by the Pharisees, "Have any of the Rulers believed on him?" Yes, glory to God, rulers and ruled, rich and poor, have forsaken all and are following Jesus. . . .[28]

After receiving a report of the 1820 meeting of Synod, Finis Ewing, who had moved to Missouri earlier that year, wrote in a letter to Robert Donnell:

. . . Who would have anticipated, but a few years since, that our little, untaught, scoffed at and despised body would, in the course of ten years have grown into such consistency, respectability, and usefulness? Who would have thought that its congregations of respectable standing would by this time be scattered through or in six States and one or two Territories, whose preachers claim their full share of attention from the learned as well as the unlearned, from the noble as well as the ignoble? [29]

In 1825, however, the committee on "the state of Religion" reported that

. . . Whether from pride, in consequence of your growing numbers, the cares of the world, the many devices of Satan, or all combined, the Lord seemed to hide his face. There appeared a want of spirituality in the ministry, and of humble dependence on God, a lack of public spirit and zeal in the cause, both amongst preachers and people, which in a few instances among the people have generated discord and a disposition in case of personal difference not to comply with the directions of Jesus, as enjoined by your discipline in such cases—"If thy brother trespass against thee, go and tell him his fault" & c.

Yet this state of affairs was but temporary, for "Even in those days of so much general deadness in the cause of God, some of the churches have been well watered." The report went on to state that

The Heaven directed and highly approved method of promoting the word of God, by encamping on the ground four days and four nights in succession which was introduced in the glorious revival of 1800 has been continued and owned of heaven.[30]

The territorial expansion of the Cumberland Presbyterian Church during this period is reflected in the organization of new presbyteries. A new presbytery would be formed in any particular area in which the Church was at work as soon as there were enough preachers residing in the area to constitute it. The usual number of preachers designated to form a new presbytery was four, which was one more than the number needed for a quorum, although in some instances there was a larger number.

The formation of McGee Presbytery, the first to be added to the three which constituted the Synod, was ordered by the Synod in its 1819 meeting. It was assigned all territory west of the Oakaw [the Kaskaskia] and the Mississippi; that is to say, western Illinois and the expanse of territory included in the Louisiana Purchase. Its original ministerial members were to be Green P. Rice, Daniel Buie, and Robert D. Morrow, of Logan Presbytery, and John Carnahan, of Elk Presbytery, "and any other members that may move into said bounds before said Presbytery be constituted, or any three of them." Its first meeting was designated to be held "at (or near) the place where Robert D. Morrow held a Camp meeting, on the Waters of Salt river, Missouri Territory," on the fourth Tuesday in May 1820.[31] Carnahan lived in Arkansas, Rice in Illinois, and Morrow and Buie in Missouri. Finis Ewing became a member of McGee Presbytery at its second meeting.[32] A number of candidates for the ministry came under the care of the presbytery during its first eighteen months of existence, and in 1821-1822 Ewing taught them theology in his home at New Lebanon, Cooper County, Missouri, and Morrow taught them literature and the sciences.[33] It was for this class of young preachers that Ewing prepared his *Lectures on the Most Important Subjects of Divinity*.[34]

The minutes of the Synod for 1822 reveal the existence of four additional presbyteries. Anderson, which seems to have comprised a portion of western Kentucky, eastern Illinois, and the state of Indiana, had as ministers William Barnett, David W. McLin, John Barnett, Aaron Shelby, William Henry, Woods M. Hamilton, and James Johnston. Lebanon, which had been created out of the eastern portion of Nashville Presbytery, had as its ministerial members Thomas Calhoun, William Bumpass, John Provine, John L. Dillard, James McDonald, Samuel McSpadden, and Daniel Gossedge. Tennessee Presbytery, which included the Tennessee Valley region of northern Alabama and some territory across the state line in Tennessee, had Aaron

Alexander, Albert Gibson, Robert Donnell, James S. Stewart, James Moore, and John Molloy as ministers. Alabama Presbytery, which lay still farther south, consisted of the following ministerial members: Robert Bell, William Moore, and Benjamin Lockhart.[35]

In 1822, Illinois Presbytery, comprising the state of Illinois, was created out of portions of McGee and Anderson presbyteries. The first meeting was held at John Kirkpatrick's home, in Montgomery County, Illinois, beginning the first Tuesday in May 1823.[36] Its original members were designated as Green P. Rice, David W. McLin, John M. Berry, and Woods M. Hamilton; however, Rice moved to the South before the presbytery met, thus leaving it to be consituted by the other three. Among the elders who were enrolled was John M. Cameron, who at the same meeting presented himself and was received as a candidate for the ministry.[37] Both Cameron and Berry were to play important roles in the life of Abraham Lincoln at New Salem in the early 1830s.[38]

By the time of the meeting of the Synod in 1823 it had become apparent that Alabama Presbytery as then constituted could function only with extreme difficulty because of the watercourses which separated the brethren from one another. Consequently, Alabama Presbytery was dissolved, and a new presbytery, known as Bigby Presbytery, was created with Robert Bell, John Forbes, John Molloy, and John C. Smith as members. Its territory was defined as

. . . Beginning at the mouth of the Mobile river, thence up s'd river to the mouth of the Black Warrior, thence up the Black-warrior to the road

FINIS EWING
(1773-1841)

From a portrait in McDonnold's *History of the Cumberland Presbyterian Church*. No likeness of either of the other founding members of the independent Cumberland Presbytery, Samuel McAdow and Samuel King, is known to exist.

leading from Florence to Tuscyloocy, thence with s'd road to Tennessee Presbytery line; thence with s'd line to the Tennessee state line; thence with s'd line to the Mississippy river, thence south to undefined boundaries; . . .

The first meeting was directed to be held at Abner Roan's home, in Monroe County, Mississippi, January 24, 1824. The remainder of the territory of Alabama Presbytery was attached to Tennessee Presbytery.[39]

In October 1822, a letter from John Carnahan asking for assistance in the work in the Arkansas country came before synod. The Synod recommended that an "intermediate presbytery" be arranged to be held by McGee Presbytery in Arkansas for the purpose of receiving candidates for the ministry. The Rev. William C. Long offered his services as a missionary for the ensuing winter and was directed to spend his time in Arkansas.[40] In the spring of 1823, McGee Presbytery ordained Robert D. King as an evangelist for the express purpose of sending him to Arkansas to participate in the intermediate session of presbytery. King, Long, and Carnahan were designated to meet at the house of John Craig, in Independence County, Arkansas Territory, on May 9, 1823, "for the purpose of hearing and receiving candidates for the holy ministry." [41] Reuben Burrow, then a licentiate, accompanied King to Arkansas, where they remained for several months, King working with Carnahan in the settlements along the Arkansas River and Burrow laying out a circuit in the area around Batesville.[42]

Thus preparation was made for the organization of Arkansas Presbytery, which was created by order of the Synod in its 1823 meeting. Its ministerial members were John Carnahan, William C. Long, Robert Sloan, and William Henry. Its first meeting was held at the house of John Craig, the place where the intermediate session of McGee Presbytery had been held the previous year. The date was the fourth Tuesday in May 1824.[43] After its first meeting Arkansas Presbytery experienced difficulty in maintaining a quorum. For the next three appointed meetings there was no quorum of ministers present.[44] The Synod, in its 1825 meeting, rectified the situation by attaching to Arkansas Presbytery "all that part of the McGee Presbytery lying south of the Missouri and east of the Gasconade Rivers, with all the ordained preachers within these bounds." [45]

In 1824 Alabama Presbytery was reactivated. Elk Presbytery had arranged for an intermediate session to be held in Alabama to ordain two licentiates who had moved thither.[46] Consequently, Alabama Presbytery was again ordered to be constituted at Alexander George's house in Perry County, Alabama, the first Friday in April 1825. This presbytery was bounded on the west by the Mobile, Bigby, and Black Warrior to Tuscaloosa, "thence by Bolivar's Road to the top of the mountain South of the Tennessee river, thence with the top of the mountain East to the Indian boundary line; thence south with s'd line to the Ocean." [47] Its ministerial members were William Moore, John Williams, James W. Dickey, and Benjamin Lockhart.

The boundaries of Bigby Presbytery, which apparently had failed to meet, were extended eastward in northern Alabama to the east boundary of Morgan County, and James S. Stewart, Green P. Rice, James Moore, and Carson P. Reed were attached to it. This presbytery, with its enlarged membership, was directed to meet at Concord meetinghouse, Lawrence County, Alabama, the second Tuesday in March 1825.[48]

Hopewell Presbytery, consisting of "the part of Nashville Presbytery which lies west of the Tennessee River," was directed to meet at Bethel meetinghouse, Carroll County, Tennessee, the third Tuesday in April 1825. Its ministerial members were William Barnett, Samuel Harris, John C. Smith, and Richard Beard.[49]

Indiana Presbytery, comprising the states of Indiana and Ohio, was created out of portions of Logan and Anderson presbyteries, by order of the Synod at its 1825 meeting. Aaron Shelby, Hiram A. Hunter, Alexander Downey, "and whatever ordained preachers may be living within the bounds of said Presbytery at the time of constitution" were to be members, and its first meeting was to be held at Portersville, Dubois County, Indiana, beginning the third Tuesday in April 1826.[50]

The Synod in its 1827 meeting created Barnett and Knoxville presbyteries. Barnett Presbytery included western and northwestern Missouri. Its members were Samuel King, Robert D. Morrow, Daniel Patton, and Henry

ROBERT DONNELL
(1784-1855)

THOMAS CALHOUN
(1782-1855)

Renick. Its first meeting was directed to be held at Lexington, Missouri, the third Tuesday in April 1828.[51]

Knoxville Presbytery, bounded on the north by Logan Presbytery, on the west by "the line dividing East and West Tennessee," on the south by the state line of Tennessee, and on the east by "undefined boundaries" was directed to meet at Concord meetinghouse, Knox County, Tennessee, on the third Thursday in April 1828. Its ministers were George Donnell, Samuel M. Aston, Abner W. Lansden, and William Smith.[52]

In 1828, at the last meeting of the General Synod, Saint Louis, Sangamon, and Princeton presbyteries were ordered constituted. Saint Louis Presbytery was to be "stricken off from the Arkansas Presbytery." It was bounded on the east by the Mississippi River, on the south by the Missouri-Arkansas state line to the Current River, up that river to a line to strike the head of the Gasconade River, thence down said river to the Missouri River, and down the Missouri to the Mississippi. Its ministerial members were Frank M. Braly, John R. Brown, John W. McCord, and John H. Garvin. It was directed to meet at Big River meetinghouse, Washington County, Missouri, April 20, 1829.[53]

Sangamon Presbytery, in Illinois, was composed of David Foster, John M. Berry, Thomas Campbell, Gilbert Dodds, and John Porter. Its first meeting was at the home of William Drennan, Sangamon County, Illinois, beginning April 20, 1829. Its boundaries were described as

. . . beginning at the mouth of the Illinois River, thence up s'd river to the north line of town ten; thence with s'd line to the Little Wabash, thence down s'd stream to south line of town seven, thence East with s'd line to the state line, thence north so as to include all bounds [?] north of the aforesaid lines.[54]

Princeton Presbytery's territory was not so large. It was to include "all that portion of Caldwell county, in Kentucky, lying between the Cumberland and Tradewater rivers, and the congregation of Piney Fork." Its members were Franceway R. Cossitt, David Lowry, John W. Ogden, and James Johnston. Its first meeting was set to be held at Cumberland College November 29, 1828. It was further directed that all candidates and licentiates coming to the college "shall be under the care and jurisdiction of the s'd Princeton Presbytery." They should produce a letter from the presbytery to which they last belonged, as in other cases of removal, and on leaving college should take like recommendations to their respective presbyteries.[55] This meant that the ministerial students in Cumberland College would be under the care of a presbytery consisting largely of the faculty of the college.

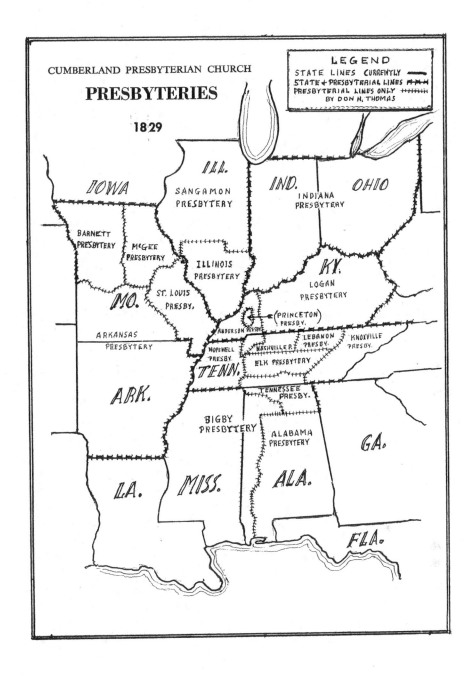

As early as 1824 consideration began to be given to forming a General Assembly. The following resolution was adopted:

*Resolved,* that it is hereby recommended to our several presbyteries to report to the next synod whether they wish a division of the synod or not, and if a division whether a General Assembly or a revision of the Confession of Faith so as to provide for forming a Delegated Synod.[56]

A constitutional majority of the presbyteries voted in favor of forming a General Assembly, but there was opposition, and the result was the postponement of the proposal.[57] One of the men opposed was Finis Ewing, who favored a delegated Synod. Concerning Ewing's stand on this question his biographer has written,

. . . He dreaded the imitation of other churches, lest the time might come when this Church would imitate others in things not profitable and praiseworthy. He had various other reasons which seemed mainly to grow out of his great aversion to pride and vain glory, and his heart-felt solicitude to preserve the minds of ministers and people in a state of deep humility, always sensible of their dependence on divine aid, for any degree of usefulness.[58]

In 1827 the question of forming a General Assembly was again taken up and again postponed.[59] In 1828 (Ewing being absent)

The subject of a General Assembly was again taken up, and after mature deliberation and fervent and solemn prayer, the great head of the Church in an unusual manner seemed graciously to afford his light, and a decision was made in favor of a General Assembly. The vote stood thus: for a delegated Synod, 20; for a General Assembly, 67.[60]

A resolution was then passed that four synods be constituted: Missouri Synod, to be composed of McGee, Barnett, Sangamon, Illinois, Saint Louis, and Arkansas presbyteries; Green River Synod, composed of Anderson, Princeton, Logan, and Indiana presbyteries; Franklin Synod, composed of Nashville, Lebanon, Knoxville, and Hopewell presbyteries; and Columbia Synod, composed of Alabama, Bigby, Elk, and Tennessee presbyteries.[61] These synods were constituted in the fall of 1829.

It will be observed that these four synods occupied about the same territory that the first four presbyteries had occupied in 1820; that is to say, Missouri Synod occupied substantially the same territory as had been assigned to McGee Presbytery nine years earlier (except that the entire state of Illinois was incorporated into Missouri Synod); Green River Synod was practically coextensive with Logan Presbytery as it had existed in 1820; Franklin Synod occupied about the same territory as Nashville Presbytery had occupied; and Columbia Synod occupied the general area which had been assigned to Elk Presbytery.

The Synod meanwhile had grown from a constituency of thirteen ordained ministers in 1813 to one of 120 in 1828.

The first General Assembly convened in Princeton, Kentucky, May 19, 1829. Thomas Calhoun was elected Moderator, and Richard Beard was chosen clerk.[62] Later in the proceedings of the Assembly F. R. Cossitt was elected "stated clerk" of the General Assembly.[63]

# PART II

*Growth and Development*

*of the*

*Cumberland Presbyterian Church*

*1830-1900*

At the beginning of the period 1830-1900, the Cumberland Presbyterian Church was still struggling to establish its identity in the family of American churches. The organization of a General Assembly in 1829 had been a major step in its growth as a denomination, but with fewer than 25,000 members, mostly in Tennessee, Kentucky, Missouri, and Illinois, it still was rather small and somewhat localized. The following chapters represent an attempt to tell how the Church matured in size and organization from 1830 to 1900.

The topical approach has been used so that the major areas of church activity could be presented systematically; however, chronological treatment of each topic has been used wherever feasible. An effort has been made to show how the Church's history related to or was affected by general developments and problems in American life. In order to get an idea of the overall coverage, the reader should scan these chapters before proceeding with his intensive reading.

# 8

## ANSWERING THE MACEDONIAN CRY:
## MISSIONS AND EXPANSION TO 1860

*The Board advises that you preach as often as your constitution and health will admit . . . administer baptism . . . form and organize congregations and ordain elders . . . attend to the simplicity of the gospel. . . . The Board entreats you to drink deep into the Spirit of your Lord and Master; to endure hardness as a good soldier; to watch and pray a great deal, and to believe much.*

William Harris in a letter to Alexander Chapman, October 24, 1820

The early Cumberland Presbyterian Church was almost entirely missionary in purpose and activity. The revivalistic fervor of its origin continued through the first few decades of its history. Practically every preacher was a missionary bent on carrying the good word to the spiritually "destitute," ever-moving frontier. Many ministers traveled, preached, and frequently organized churches on their own initiative. Some went on preaching tours from their homes in areas already settled; others moved westward with the frontier. The rapid growth and spread of the Church was due in part to such independent efforts. Most missionary effort, however, was at the behest of and under the direction of church courts, especially the presbyteries. The courts were composed almost exclusively of evangelists rather than pastors, since practically all Cumberland Presbyterian ministers were of that type. What was more natural than that they should set missionary tasks for themselves and for their young licensed preachers?

The presbyterial records and church histories give almost countless instances of presbyteries sending their candidates, licentiates, and sometimes ordained ministers on "itinerating" tours, frequently to areas hundreds of miles from their homes. Although there was some variation from time to time and place to place, the usual procedure was somewhat as follows: When a presbytery had young men (candidates or licentiates) available, it would request or order them to itinerate to a designated area for a specified period of time. Sometimes ordained ministers were sent on such missions. Most of the itinerants were truly missionaries, for they went into newly settled areas where there were few if any churches or preachers of any denomination. In some cases missionaries were sent into older sections of the country from which had come special requests for Cumberland Presbyterian preachers. Upon arriving in the assigned area, the itinerant traveled from place to place preaching wherever there was an opportunity—in private homes, in church houses (if there were any and they were permitted to use them), in offices, in places of business (even saloons), or out under the trees. On his first excursion through the region each preacher "laid out a circuit," arranging to preach at specified points on a regular schedule. If the proximity of preaching places permitted, he preached once or twice each day. The sparsity of settlers in some areas required more time for travel, and some of the circuits totaled three or four hundred miles. The term "circuit rider," usually associated with the frontier Methodists, was used by some Cumberland Presbyterians.

The itinerant missionary reported back to his presbytery the number of Cumberland Presbyterians already located on his circuit and the number of converts wishing to join. Then, when the numbers warranted it, the presbytery sent an ordained minister to organize churches. He baptized new members, ordained elders, and helped set up church sessions. Some of the congregations had as few as eight or ten members. Of course, if the missionary was an ordained minister, he could do these things without new instructions from presbytery. Missionaries were not supposed to organize a church in a locality unless there was a reasonable chance that the congregation could be supplied with at least occasional preaching by a licentiate or minister and with the "means of grace" as often as once or twice a year. (The term "means of grace" refers to the sacraments which required the presence of an ordained minister. A sacramental meeting usually was held on Sunday during a camp meeting.) As soon as a newly opened area had three resident ordained ministers (or presbytery could get some to go for the purpose), a new presbytery could be organized upon authorization from synod. The new presbytery then assumed responsibility for "missionating" within its bounds, which ordinarily extended indefinitely to include the contiguous frontier. Beginning about 1820 it was common for a new presbytery to constitute itself as a missionary society at its organizational meeting. It was largely through this process that the Church was extended south, west, and north from its birthplace. With only a few exceptions, efforts to move eastward met with much more limited success.

As older presbyteries were cut off from the frontier, their use of the itinerant system declined. However, itinerants still were used to "supply" vacant churches and to "missionate" within the now limited presbyterial bounds. Many of the older presbyteries remained interested in evangelizing the frontier. Missionary societies and boards at the local, presbyterial, and synodical levels were organized to raise money and send missionaries to "destitute" regions on tours or to settle. This procedure differed from the sending out of itinerants by presbyteries in that the societies and boards could and did send missionaries beyond as well as within presbyterial bounds.

Cumberland Presbyterians were committed wholly to the camp meeting and used it whenever and wherever possible in their missionary work. In the frontier areas they frequently cooperated with ministers and members of other denominations. The camp meeting was particularly well adapted to the needs of the frontier. Aside from its social benefits, it enabled a few preachers to reach many people.

By 1830 Cumberland Presbyterians had made the camp meeting a standard part of their regular religious life. They continued to participate in some interdenominational camp meetings (usually in cooperation with Baptists and Methodists). Most of the meetings, however, were organized and run exclusively by Cumberland Presbyterians. In the settled areas of the Church some congregations, but by no means all, held annual or semiannual camp meetings. Normally, the presbytery set the schedule for meetings at various places and assigned preachers to help at each. The favored period was from July to October. Some ministers became favorite camp meeting preachers and worked at many within their presbyteries and sometimes elsewhere on invitation. Robert Donnell attended an average of not less than twelve camp meetings a year for fifty years, having started at the height of the Great Revival in the early 1800s. He preached usually once or twice but sometimes three or four times daily at each and, in addition, prayed with and instructed mourners, exhorted sinners, and assisted in other ways.[1] From his intimate knowledge of the practices in Tennessee and northern Alabama, Donnell described the evolution of the housing used, saying that

the first shelters . . . were covered wagons and cloth tents. Next, rail pens were built, and covered with boards. Then log and frame huts were provided, and even brick cabins were, in some instances, erected for convenience.[2]

Although length and procedures varied, the schedule for camp meetings described by Donnell was quite common:

1st Day (Friday): Prayer and fasting. Preaching addressed to Christians usually on prayer and other duties connected with the meeting.
2nd Day (Saturday): Preaching, usually on human depravity.
3rd Day (Sunday): Preaching, usually on the plan of salvation.
4th Day (Monday): Appeals made to sinners and instructions given to lead the penitent to believe in Christ.
5th Day (Tuesday): Meeting closed with an exhortation to the new converts and to young Christians generally.[3]

As camp meetings became standardized, there were fewer exceptional "revivals" in connection with them. Yet they still had the purpose of reaching and converting "sinners," as well as of stimulating greater spirituality and piety among church members. There is evidence in the church papers and other literature that much was accomplished toward these ends, but there is evidence also that camp meetings became less effective and less popular. Except in sparsely settled areas, there was no practical need for camping. Many congregations changed to the "protracted meeting" as a substitute. The protracted meeting was similar in length, purpose, and procedures to the camp meeting; however, there was no camping overnight at the meeting site, which was a church building, a tent, or a brush arbor.[4] The one-week and two-week "revival" conducted by many congregations in the twentieth century appears to be a continuation of the protracted meeting tradition. In some areas camp meetings were continued for many decades, but in the pre-Civil War period "camp-meetings in all the older portions of the Church died a lingering death." [5]

In 1819 Cumberland Synod formed itself into a missionary board, primarily to support and oversee Charity Hall School in Choctaw Nation (Mississippi). As a board it operated with great difficulty and ceased to exist when the General Assembly was organized in 1829. Although the first six General Assemblies did not establish a general missionary board, some of them were active in that field. The third Assembly, in 1831, called upon each presbytery to form a Home Missionary Society, which in turn should try to establish an auxiliary society in each congregation. This Assembly also named five missionaries to go to western Pennsylvania in response to an appeal for Cumberland Presbyterian preaching. Two years later the Rev. George Donnell was assigned to the Carolinas for four months or more.

Members of the General Assembly became concerned with another problem which called for a type of missionary work. For several reasons many of the congregations previously formed were in need of help. The very rapid growth of the denomination, largely through evangelizing rather than proselytizing, had brought into the Church many who had little or no religious training. There always was a scarcity of ministers, never enough for the care of congregations and also for "missionating." Many ordained ministers were "secularized" (employed in nonministerial work), sometimes through choice but more often through necessity. By the 1830s the ranks of first-generation ministers, who shared a fierce revival spirit and held a set of doctrines in common, were becoming thinned by death, illness, and age. Fewer of the younger men burned with missionary zeal, and those who did tended to go to the front lines on the frontier. These several factors contributed to the lack of religious education and discipline among members and ministers and to increasing diversity in doctrine.

It was characteristic of the General Assembly that it adopted a missionary approach to a problem which had been created largely through missionary success. In this attempt to revive the earlier enthusiasm it called upon the founders and other "Fathers of the Church." The 1834 Assembly asked the founders to visit congregations throughout its bounds and "see how they do." [6] So far as can be learned, Finis Ewing and Samuel McAdow did not respond. But Samuel King and his son, the Rev. Robert D. King, visited Arkansas Synod and all of its presbyteries, traveled through Louisiana and helped with the organization of Louisiana Presbytery, and returned through West Tennessee. Samuel King reported that the Church "languished" through those regions and "though the forms of religion are maintained, there is but little of its power and vitality to be seen or felt among them." So many of the ministers had to labor with their hands for a living that not half of them were as devoted to church interests as they should be. The Kings were asked to tour through Kentucky, East Tennessee, Alabama, and Mississippi until the meeting of the next General Assembly. The Assembly also asked the Rev. Reuben Burrow and the Rev. William Bigham to travel through Missouri and Arkansas Territory.[7] All of this was done (except for travel in Arkansas), and the 1836 Assembly renewed the request that all the founders "missionate" among the churches.

A great hindrance to Assembly-sponsored missionary work was a lack of funds. In most cases it was expected that those sent out would be supported by the congregations they visited. The Kings, however, understood that they were to be compensated for expenses above the amount they collected. When they reported unavoidable expenses of $150 more than their compensation, a later Assembly refused to pay them, apparently taking the view that it was not the same body which had pledged compensation and was "not bound either morally or legally." As a consequence of this default, Robert D. King lost his property through inability to repay borrowed money. Happily for the Church, his resultant determination not to preach any more for the Cumberland Presbyterians did not last long.[8]

By the mid-1830s, church leaders were realizing the need for more formal organization for missionary work. In response to a memorial from Indiana Presbytery, the 1834 Assembly appointed a committee to draft a plan for establishing a Home Missionary Society. The committee's report was not acted upon. The next Assembly constituted itself into a board for both foreign and domestic missions and requested the presbyteries to become auxiliaries to it. This plan was modified in 1836 when a constitution for a Foreign Missionary Society was adopted unanimously. At the same time steps were taken toward making it auxiliary to the American Board for Foreign Missions, and for several years Cumberland Presbyterian aid to foreign missions was channeled through that organization. The society never was very active, perhaps because its president and corresponding secretary, the Rev. James Smith, became a very controversial figure in the Church. It never had a chartered board, partly because there was some opposition to chartered boards "as savoring of Church and State." [9]

It is uncertain whether or not the General Assembly continued as a board for domestic missions. The Assembly of 1837 considered and rejected a proposal that there be organized a Home Missionary Society distinct from the Foreign Missionary Society, saying that it was desirable but not expedient until other church institutions were settled on a permanent basis. One hundred dollars each was appropriated to the Rev. Samuel W. Frazier and the Rev. Amos Roark in 1838 for missionary work in the Republic of Texas (not a foreign field since it was within the bounds of the Church). The 1841 Assembly accepted a proposal that two missionaries be appointed to travel throughout the Church "to awaken your people to a sense of the duty and propriety of a rigid adherence to the doctrine and rule of the Confession of Faith," provided that such persons could be procured and that they be compensated by the churches they visited.[10]

When the 1843 Assembly met, concern for missions was stirring again. The Committee on Foreign and Domestic Missions declared: "It is time for us to awake from our past inattention and earnestly apply ourselves to the work, to which God in his Providence is calling us." A board to direct missionary efforts should be organized, it said, but this "may be more advisedly and efficiently done at a future meeting of the Assembly." [11] There being no General Assembly in 1844, the new Board of Foreign and Domestic Missions was not set up until 1845. The Rev. Franceway Ranna Cossitt, president of Cumberland University, was named president and twelve other prominent ministers and elders of the Middle Tennessee area were named to the board.

The earlier attempt to provide central leadership in mission work had failed, and it was quite difficult for the new board to get cooperation from synods and presbyteries. Several of those courts had missionaries working in distant places. Some were reluctant to turn over such work to the central board or even to send in regular reports on their own activities. The Assembly's board never was able to get full cooperation from throughout the Church, but significant progress was made before the Civil War.[12] During the sixteen years from 1845 to 1861 there were many evidences of growing interest in missions and of real accomplishment by the central board and its auxiliaries. Several articles on missions appeared in the church papers and in the *Theological Medium.* At first special sermons and then regular meetings on missions became features of General Assemblies. Receipts remained discouragingly low for several years. Even after the Rev. Isaac Shook was employed as secretary to the board in 1851, there was not significant improvement until he started devoting his full time to the work. It was Shook who, with Assembly approval, began the publication of a missionary magazine.[13]

Shook was succeeded as secretary in 1854 by the Rev. T. P. Calhoun. To raise funds both of these men relied on traveling agents, but with only indifferent success. The Rev. T. C. Blake, who became secretary in 1857, started abandoning the agency system and determined to depend entirely upon the preachers throughout the Church to collect for missions. Collections immediately began to climb, reaching a total of $22,471 during the last prewar year.[14] An attempt to correct some recognized deficiencies in organization and procedure can be seen in the adoption of a new constitution for the board in 1858. Leaders in the Church were making real progress in formal organization for mission work and toward awakening the membership to the needs and possibilities. Then the war came!

The Cumberland Presbyterian Church, especially in its first half-century, was predominantly rural. It had its origin and developed its distinctive characteristics in frontier conditions. As population increased, its members and ministers tended to shun the growing towns and cities, and there developed some prejudice against cities. This might have been due in part to the presence of congregations of Presbyterians and other older churches in the towns. In 1829 the only town in Middle Tennessee with an organized Cumberland Presbyterian congregation was Winchester, where a church had been organized in 1825. When George Donnell determined to work more in towns, there was some jeering and "an occasional intimation of personal vanity." [15] Some cities of considerable size had Cumberland Presbyterian churches by 1840, but they were exceptional. In the 1840s there arose a more general interest in promoting the establishment of churches in cities. Appeals for aid came to the General Assembly from struggling ministers and scattered members in towns and cities without congregations of Cumberland Presbyterians. Some of the most highly respected and influential leaders of the Church became interested in the opportunity for service which urban growth seemed to offer. It was largely in response to these appeals and this opportunity that the new Board of Foreign and Domestic Missions was set up in 1845.

Much of the money and effort of the Assembly's missionary board in the period 1845-1860 was devoted to missions in towns and cities. This was a definite departure from earlier efforts. Presbyteries, synods, and even the General Assembly had used missionaries previously for two purposes: (1) to carry the Word to those who were without it, especially to convert the unsaved, and (2) to rekindle the spirit in older portions of the Church where early enthusiasm seemed to be dying. In both cases the revivalistic approach was used: exhortation and enthusiasm, it was believed, would accomplish the desired ends. Of course, these aims and this approach remained important, but cities did not lend themselves to the "missionating" techniques with which Cumberland Presbyterians were familiar. Itinerancy and the camp meeting could not be applied. In most instances other denominations already were entrenched and there was not a considerable number of churchgoing people without a church to attend, as often was the case on the frontier. Ministering to a city congregation required more pastoral work, and that cost money. A church building was necessary, and city property came relatively high. The Cumberland Presbyterians overcame these difficulties only in a few places, but some progress, often slow and painful, was made by 1860.

Before the Civil War the central board, either independently or in cooperation with presbyterial or synodical auxiliaries, is known to have given some aid to nineteen town and city missions: Nashville, Jackson, Shelbyville, Murfreesboro, Chattanooga, and Clarksville, Tennessee; Philadelphia, Pennsylvania; Cincinnati, Ohio; Alton and Peoria, Illinois; Louisville and Paducah, Kentucky; Burlington and Colesburg, Iowa; Corinth, Mississippi; Evansville, Indiana; Leavenworth City, Kansas Territory; and two missions (one German) in Saint Louis, Missouri. The board also might have aided some other missions started by presbyteries or by individuals. Some of these mission points became self-sustaining after only brief periods of aid. Others were a burden and trial to the Church for many years; this was especially true of the main Saint Louis mission. A few, such as those at Peoria and Cincinnati, eventually failed.[16]

Through the efforts of energetic migratory members and ministers and of presbyteries, synods, and the General Assembly, the Cumberland Presbyterian Church continued its rapid numerical and geographical expansion in the period 1830-1860. There is little statistical information available, and it must be judged unreliable. During the period of the General Synod there was a decided prejudice against "counting." Once the Synod ordered statistical reports to be sent up, but the order was repealed at the next meeting.[17] This opposition continued in some quarters for decades. As late as 1859 someone at the General Assembly stated that "statistical intelligence begets a spirit of pride."[18] This opposition to statistics plus apathy, negligence, and lack of adequate procedures made it impossible for the Assembly or even synods to get requested information from presbyteries and congregations.

Beginning in the early 1830s, the Assembly received some reports and continually attempted to get the presbyteries to cooperate in gathering and submitting statistical data. In 1835, reports received from eighteen of the thirty-five presbyteries provided these totals: 167 ministers, 82 licentiates, 92 candidates, 243 congregations, and 17,719 communicants.[19] The totals for the entire Church surely would have been considerably less than twice these, since most of the seventeen presbyteries not reporting were in the most sparsely populated areas. There might have been as many as 250 ministers and 25,000 communicants. In 1859, after several different plans for collecting information had been tried, the Stated Clerk reported that 95 of the 101 presbyteries had sent reports, although many gave scanty data. He gave as incomplete totals the following: 890 ministers, 293 licentiates, 196 candidates, 1,189 congregations, and 82,008 communicants.[20] An examination of additional data scattered through the Assembly minutes of the period suggests that on the eve of the Civil War the Church had at least 1,100 ordained ministers and more than 100,000 communicants. One thing is certain: the rate of growth was steady and rapid, with nearly a fivefold increase in number of ministers, congregations, and members between 1835 and 1860.

Geographical expansion also continued apace. At the opening of the period 1830-1860 there were Cumberland Presbyterian churches in six states (Alabama, Illinois, Indiana, Kentucky, Missouri, and Tennessee) and in Arkansas Territory. In Mississippi there was a presbytery but no organized churches. In all there were nineteen presbyteries in four synods. At the period's close, twenty-five synods contained ninety-six presbyteries with churches in at least sixteen states, three territories, and two Indian nations. There also was a mission in Liberia. Much of the growth was in states where the Church already had a start; portions of all of them still were sparsely settled. But the greater accomplishment was the pushing into new frontiers.

Growth in East Tennessee was steady, if not spectacular, and in 1843 East Tennessee Synod was formed of Knoxville, Hiwassee, and Ocoee presbyteries. A year earlier work along the Georgia-Tennessee line had been started when the Rev. Hiram Douglas organized a church in what later became Whitfield County, Georgia. Although several more churches were formed and later Georgia Presbytery was established by East Tennessee Synod, expansion leveled off and there was little penetration into Georgia.[21]

Nashville Presbytery sent itinerants into the Western District of Tennessee within a year after it was bought from the Indians.[22] Progress was rapid. In 1824 Hopewell Presbytery was constituted, followed soon by Forked Deer and Hatchie. These were organized into Western District Synod in 1832. The name was later changed to West Tennessee Synod. Growth continued unabated until the Civil War, and West Tennessee Synod produced many able and energetic leaders for the Church.

By 1830 the Church was already strong in the Tennessee Valley portion of Alabama. In the central and southern areas of the state the beginning had been difficult and the future was uncertain. Although the Church had grown enough in that region for the formation of Union Synod (composed of Elyton, Alabama, and Talladega presbyteries) in 1836, for several reasons it languished. Its few preachers were nearly all missionaries rather than pastors. The presbyteries were unable to produce enough ministers; for example, of eleven candidates in Alabama Presbytery during a five-year period only one was ordained. There seems to have been an especially strong prejudice against the Cumberland Presbyterians. Finally, the social environment was not favorable. The tendency of most whites to move into towns, leaving rural areas to plantations worked by slaves, caused many rural churches to die. As the historian B. W. McDonnold put it, "A people relying on camp-meetings and circuit riders found their occupations gone when there was no place to preach in except towns." [23]

When Tombigbee Presbytery was formed in 1823, the only organized Cumberland Presbyterian activity in Mississippi was at Charity Hall, the Indian mission school. No congregation was organized in the state until after 1830. Only after Indian removal began in the early 1830s did the Church start to grow in northern Mississippi. In the spring of 1832 Mississippi Presbytery, bounded on the south by the Gulf of Mexico and with indefinite boundaries on the west, was formed by order of Columbia Synod. That fall the presbytery was joined with Alabama and Elyton presbyteries to form Mississippi Synod. Under great difficulties the Church in Mississippi made uneven progress. In 1836 there still were only five congregations in the state, and the largest had twenty-eight members. The presbyteries in Alabama were detached from Mississippi Synod in 1836. Until the formation of Texas Synod in 1842 Mississippi Synod was responsible for that area as well as Louisiana. Although membership remained rather small in Mississippi and Alabama synods, members and ministers in both states were among the most liberal in supporting church enterprises with energy and money.[24]

The first Cumberland Presbyterian church in Louisiana was organized near Springfield, Saint Helena Parish, in October 1831, at a camp meeting held by the Rev. Rainey Mercer and the Rev. Robert Molloy. By March 1832, the Rev. John W. Ogden had organized a church at Opelousas and one at Alexandria. Although Louisiana Presbytery was formed in 1835, the denomination made very little progress in that state. Other churches had a head start on the Cumberland Presbyterians. In 1849 most of Louisiana was placed within the bounds of Texas Synod, and the eyes of the Texans were turned toward the more promising fields to the west.[25]

Historians of the Church are high in their praise of the tremendous missionary accomplishments of Logan Presbytery. Its energy led not only to continued growth of the Church in Kentucky, but also to effective missionary work in Indiana, Illinois, and Missouri. Development in the Green River area and central Kentucky generally was rather rapid. Extreme western Kentucky was cut off from the central area by the Cumberland and Tennessee rivers. Missionaries from Tennessee (from Elk and Nashville presbyteries) worked in that region more often than did those from the presbyteries in Kentucky. The growth rate in Kentucky as a whole did not keep pace with that in Tennessee, Illinois, and Missouri. McDonnold attributed this to two factors: the strong opposition of antirevival Presbyterians, and the movement of large numbers of Kentuckians to new territories.[26] By 1830 foundations had been laid in both Illinois and Indiana. The Church grew so rapidly in Illinois that it soon rivaled and eventually passed that of Kentucky in membership. In 1860 the state had nine presbyteries in three synods.

Of particular interest to Cumberland Presbyterians is the fact that several of the men who had considerable influence on Abraham Lincoln during his formative years were members of their Church. These included James Rutledge, organizer of the New Salem Literary Society, in which Lincoln participated; John M. Cameron, in whose home in New Salem Lincoln boarded; Dr. John Allen; and the Rev. John M. Berry. The latter two have been credited with convincing Lincoln of the evils of "trafficking in" and using "ardent spirits." At the time Lincoln boarded in Cameron's home, Cameron was a licensed preacher, and later he was ordained into the ministry of the Cumberland Presbyterian Church.

In Indiana hopes aroused by the promising start were not realized. By 1860 Indiana Synod (the only one in the state) contained only three presbyteries, although the total number of communicants had more than doubled since 1830.

Missouri, although more distant from central Tennessee and Kentucky than were southern Illinois and Indiana, also was in the line of migration. The first Missouri Synod, organized in 1829, included Arkansas, Missouri, and part of Illinois. During the next three decades, as the Church grew rapidly and the number of presbyteries multiplied, there was much shifting of synodical lines. Eventually, however, the lines were stabilized somewhat along state lines. In 1860 there were three synods in the area: Missouri, McAdow, and Ozark. Missouri Synod, in addition to four presbyteries within the state, had jurisdiction over Kansas Presbytery and the presbyteries of California, Oregon, Pacific, and Sacramento until those in the far West were organized into Sacramento Synod in 1860.[27]

Settlements and church members remained widely scattered in much of Arkansas, so much so that in some cases circuits were formed entirely within the limits of a single congregation. Arkansas Presbytery was included in the original Missouri Synod formed in 1829. After considerable shifting of boundaries and names as new synods were formed, in 1852 there was a separate Arkansas Synod. By 1860 there were three synods—Arkansas, White River, and Ouachita—with a total of ten presbyteries entirely or mostly within the state.[28]

Cumberland Presbyterian expansion was mostly westward rather than eastward. Moderately successful efforts to plant the Church in East Tennessee and a slight penetration of Georgia have been noted. A few "missionating" tours into the Carolinas and Virginia created some interest. Some churches were organized in North Carolina, but they eventually died out.[29] The work in western Pennsylvania was notably different. The number of able preachers who shared in the work, the widespread interest it created throughout the bounds of the Church, and the rapidity of early growth there made it one of the most remarkable missionary episodes in the history of the Church. It also was one of the most thoroughly recorded developments.

As in so many cases the missionary opportunity in western Pennsylvania arose in the manner the Cumberland Presbyterians called "providential." In 1829 two ministers, Matthew H. Bone and John W. Ogden, traveled through portions of Ohio and Pennsylvania to raise money for the fledgling Cumberland College. As seems to have been a common practice of Cumberland College agents, they did more pleading for souls than for money. It is likely that news of their preaching and their denomination spread through the general region. In 1831 members of a Presbyterian church in Washington County, Pennsylvania, corresponded with F. R. Cossitt, president of Cumberland College, petitioning for a Cumberland Presbyterian missionary. In response to this appeal and similar ones from western New York, the 1831

General Assembly named five highly regarded preachers as missionaries to that field. Those named were Robert Donnell, Alexander Chapman, Reuben Burrow, John Morgan, and Alfred McGready Bryan.[30]

Morgan and Bryan, traveling together and preaching along the way, reached Washington, Pennsylvania, on July 14, 1831. At that time there was not a member of their denomination in the entire state. They were well received by the Methodists and by some Presbyterians. After Chapman joined them on July 22, the three preached at Washington and in its vicinity almost daily. Efforts of some Presbyterian ministers and members to persuade the people not to hear the "heretics" apparently only made them more eager to do so. The first Presbyterian church opened to them was "the Brick church." Then the Rev. Jacob Lindley and his congregation invited them to preach in Ten Mile Church. (Later, efforts of Lindley's presbytery to force the Ten Mile session "to close the doors against Cumberland preachers" was the last straw which led minister and congregation to join the Cumberland Presbyterians.)[31]

There was much interest but little "enthusiasm" during the first two weeks, but then evidence of "the mighty power of the Holy Ghost" appeared. As the missionaries "continued preaching from house to house and grove to grove . . . convictions multiplied in every direction." In mid-August the first Cumberland Presbyterian congregation was organized in a grove at William Stockdale's in Washington County. The first camp meeting began in early September with about 250 families tenting on the ground. Attendance on Sunday was estimated at from 5,000 to 6,000. Donnell and Burrow arrived just after the camp meeting started. A "remarkable" revival spirit was manifest, and Morgan reported that on several occasions as many as 250 of the "anxious" came forward at the same time. Reports on the number of conversions at the close of the camp meeting ranged from 220 to 300. In order that the new converts would not stampede into the Cumberland Presbyterian Church, there was a four-week delay in taking in members. Then, at a special meeting held for the purpose, Ten Mile congregation received 100 new members, 80 joined the Brick church, and about 80 united with the new Cumberland Presbyterian congregation.[32]

Following the camp meeting of early September the revival spread as the ministers extended their preaching to the surrounding area. Burrow, Donnell, and Chapman returned west in the fall, but Morgan and Bryan decided to stay permanently in Pennsylvania. By December five congregations, ranging in membership from 40 to 200, had been organized in the state. Early in 1832 Pennsylvania Presbytery was organized by order of Green River Synod. The Rev. Milton Bird and the Rev. Samuel M. Aston had moved to Pennsylvania, and soon several former Presbyterian and Methodist ministers joined the presbytery. By October 1833, it had twelve ordained ministers, three licentiates, and seven candidates. There were seventeen congregations and 2,800 members.[33]

After this almost spectacular beginning in Pennsylvania, the Church settled down to steady but not unusual progress. As in other areas most congregations were rural, but there was considerable success in towns and cities. Thriving churches were organized in Carmichaels, Uniontown, Waynesburg, and Pittsburgh. Union Presbytery was formed in 1837. Pennsylvania Synod (composed of Union, Pennsylvania, and Athens presbyteries) was constituted in October 1838. Although membership in Pennsylvania remained relatively small, that portion of the Church made important contributions to educational, publishing, and missionary activities.

The early history of Cumberland Presbyterianism in Ohio is intimately associated with that in western Pennsylvania. Bone and Ogden's 1829 tour had included portions of Ohio. Several of the ministers who worked in Pennsylvania in 1831 and 1832 preached at various Ohio points on their way to and fro. In late 1831 and early 1832 John Morgan preached several times in and around Athens but refused to organize a congregation because he saw no chance for it to be supplied with preaching. Morgan returned in the fall of 1832 to hold a camp meeting. He was accompanied by Jacob Lindley, who previously had been president of Ohio University and had organized the first congregation of Presbyterians in Athens. At this camp meeting in Alexander township, six miles from Athens, the first Cumberland Presbyterian church in Ohio was organized. A nearby Presbyterian congregation, at the time without a pastor, united with the new church. Lindley remained in the area several months. Under his influence the Presbyterian congregations at Beverly and Senecaville switched to the Cumberland Presbyterians. Isaac Shook, Matthew H. Bone, and Felix G. Black were other ministers who worked in the Ohio field. For several years some of the churches in Ohio were "supplied" by itinerants sent by Pennsylvania Presbytery. Growth was slow. As late as 1858 Ohio Synod (formed in 1833 of Athens, Miami, and Muskingum presbyteries) had only about twenty ministers and about 2,000 communicants.[34]

Cumberland Presbyterian entry into Texas occurred when it was still a part of Mexico. During the 1820s and early 1830s thousands of colonists from the United States settled there under the Austin grant. Under ordinary frontier circumstances churches and ministers would have been rare. In addition, all the colonists legally were required to join the Catholic Church, and until 1834 preaching by Protestants was forbidden.[35] Many colonists gave only lip service to the requirement of Catholic membership or ignored

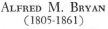

ALFRED M. BRYAN
(1805-1861)

F. R. COSSITT
(1790-1863)

it altogether. In fact, there was very little religious activity of any kind. Some Protestant preachers managed to violate the interdict on preaching. Methodist and Baptist preachers were there as early as 1824.[36] Not long afterward the first Cumberland Presbyterian preacher entered Texas.

When Sumner Bacon entered Texas in 1829, he was not really a Cumberland Presbyterian preacher; that is, he was not licensed to preach by any church authority. A native of Massachusetts and former soldier, he had professed Christianity at Fayetteville, Arkansas, in 1826. Feeling a strong call to go to Texas and preach, he requested ordination from Arkansas Presbytery but was not even accepted as a candidate because of his lack of preparation. Finally, after receiving some encouragement from Cumberland Presbyterians in Memphis, he decided to answer the call without formal church sanction. McDonnold summed up the later Cumberland Presbyterian view of this episode with these comments:

How blind we all are! God had specially trained up a man of his own choosing for a special work which no ordinary man could do. As a soldier in camp, then as a surveyor on a dangerous frontier, with Yankee energy and Cumberland Presbyterian zeal, this rough man was furnished for his wild, hard, dangerous, but exceedingly important mission. Because he was rough, wore buckskin, and had a special call, the dear brethren of Arkansas rejected him; but God will not be thwarted if men are blind.[37]

Working at least part of the time as an agent of the Natchez Tract Society, Bacon distributed Bibles in Texas during the next several years. Although not licensed to preach, he "exhorted" and conducted prayer meetings in defiance of Mexican law and of the policy of Stephen F. Austin, American colonizer. Most of the services reportedly were held out-of-doors so as to avoid having householders break the law. It was a hard life with more danger from the natural elements, rowdy and desperate whites, and Indians than from the authorities. On a trip back to Arkansas in 1832, Bacon again was turned down in his request for licensure. In 1833 he and a Methodist preacher held what was probably the first "unrestricted public camp meeting" ever held in Texas. From 1833 or 1834 to 1836 he was an agent of the American Bible Society in Texas.[38]

A change in official policy in Texas in 1834 was interpreted as legalizing Protestant preaching. Soon thereafter an opportunity finally opened for Bacon's ordination. The agent of the American Bible Society in Louisiana (a Presbyterian minister named Benjamin Chase) persuaded him to attend the organizational meeting of Louisiana Presbytery of the Cumberland Presbyterian Church in March 1835. On the plea of Chase the presbytery received Bacon as a candidate, licensed him, and ordained him all in the same day. The presbytery recorded that his was a special case and would not be regarded as a precedent. Bacon returned to Texas to devote even more time to preaching and to the interests of his Church.

With the outbreak of revolution late in 1835 all aspects of Texas life were disrupted. The war stimulated great interest back in the States. With Texas independence, in 1836, came much more Protestant activity, despite the unsettled state of affairs. On November 27, 1837, Texas Presbytery was organized by Bacon, Mitchell Smith, and Amos Roark. This was the first Protestant judicature or association in the state. It was not until 1840 that the first Methodist conference, the first Baptist association, and the first Presbyterian (Old School) presbytery were established.

Undaunted by political and social uncertainty, the founders of Texas Presbytery optimistically set up ambitious goals. By its very organization the presbytery assumed the task of "missionating" throughout the vast ranges of the new country. It resolved to establish a school and a religious paper. For several years progress was slow. One of the uncertainties facing the Cumberland Presbyterian Church in Texas was the question of its relationship to the Church in the United States, a foreign country. For a while there was a movement toward the formation of an independent church, and the presbytery even asked Mississippi Synod to rescind the order for the establishment of Texas Presbytery. The synod complied, but its action was reversed by the 1841 General Assembly. Meanwhile, Texas Presbytery had rescinded its earlier action, and the separation movement died.

When Texas Presbytery petitioned the 1842 General Assembly to form a synod in Texas, the Assembly refused because there were not three presbyteries in the state. This difficulty was removed by the formation of Red River Presbytery in December 1842 and Colorado Presbytery in March 1843. The 1843 Assembly then authorized formation of a synod. In October 1843, Texas Synod held its organizational meeting even though a quorum was not present. Recognizing "the peculiar circumstances of the country," the 1845 Assembly approved Texas Synod as being legally constituted.

After Texas was annexed to the United States—on December 29, 1845— the Church grew faster. In 1849 Brazos Synod was organized by withdrawing Trinity, Frazier, and Colorado presbyteries from Texas Synod. Five years later the General Assembly ordered the formation of Colorado Synod, to include Little River, Guadalupe, and Colorado presbyteries. By 1860 there were eleven presbyteries in Texas. Membership was still only about five or six thousand, but Texas was to become a stronghold of Cumberland Presbyterianism.

There was little penetration of the northern frontier beyond Illinois and Missouri by Cumberland Presbyterians. At Prairie du Chien, in a portion of Michigan Territory that became Wisconsin, an elder of the Church, General Joseph M. Street, became Indian Agent in 1827. His was the first Protestant family at that location. Street held prayer meetings and read sermons to agency employees and officers from Fort Crawford. In 1833 he was joined by David Lowry, a Cumberland Presbyterian minister from Tennessee, who, as subagent, was to open a school for the Winnebago

SUMNER BACON
(1790-1844)
"The Apostle of Texas"

Indians. A Protestant minister had preached at Prairie du Chien as early as 1818, but Lowry was the first to conduct regular church services there and he organized the first Protestant church. (Other Protestant missionaries began arriving in 1835.) Zachary Taylor, then a colonel stationed at the fort, reportedly attended services at Lowry's church. After the school was moved fifty miles farther west, in 1840, the congregation dwindled away. It had not been connected with any presbytery.[39] Later a few Cumberland Presbyterians moved into Wisconsin, but the Church never became strong there.

The Rev. Joseph Howard was among the early immigrants into Iowa, settling there in 1835, three years before the organization of the territorial government. The first Cumberland Presbyterian church in Iowa was formed at Howard's home in 1836 by the Rev. Cyrus Haynes. Growth was slow. Not until 1844 was Iowa Presbytery constituted. Few ministers settled there. In 1847 a church member wrote that he had been in Iowa seven years without hearing a Cumberland Presbyterian preacher. Some expansion occurred in the central and southern portions, but the northern area remained "destitute" for several years. Finally, in 1856, the Board of Missions sent the Rev. J. C. Armstrong and then the Rev. P. H. Crider to northern Iowa, and they organized several congregations. Iowa Synod (originally called Mississippi 2nd) was organized in 1857 and by 1860 included five presbyteries. Its ministers and congregations were scattered widely, however, and the total membership was probably not over 1,500.[40]

Immediately after Kansas Territory was organized in 1854 thousands of settlers rushed thither. We have no evidence that Cumberland Presbyterian ministers or members were active on either side in the struggle between slave state and free state forces there. In the midst of that strife a few ministers set about spreading the Gospel and setting up the Church. In early 1855 Round Prairie Church, probably the first Cumberland Presbyterian church in Kansas, was organized by the Rev. C. B. Hodges. Before the end of the year Kansas Presbytery was formed. In 1857 the general Board of Missions began to support some missionary activity in the territory. The work in Kansas, undertaken under extremely trying conditions, was just getting under way when the Civil War began. Kansas Presbytery, with the entire territory as its field, remained part of Missouri Synod until several years later.[41]

Several years before Cumberland Presbyterians are known to have been active in Kansas, some of them had made the long trek across plains, mountains, and desert to Oregon and California. It is possible that some members of the Church had gone to Oregon earlier, but the first minister to go was Josephus A. Cornwall. Cornwall was a self-starter who went without being sent. A real product of the frontier—born on the frontier of Georgia and reared on the frontier of Kentucky and Tennessee—he had been ordained in 1826 and had preached for many years in frontier Arkansas. With the exodus to Oregon under way, he determined in 1845 to form a company and go to the new frontier. He did not leave, however, until April 8, 1846. He left Batesville, Arkansas, with only his family, but they joined others at Independence, Missouri. Because of their late start and some delay on the trail, the company was caught by winter and had to stay in the Umpqua Mountains until spring.[42] Cornwall later wrote of the experience:

I lost most of my property, and lived seven months on wild meat, without either bread or salt. I finally succeeded in reaching the settlement by the 10th of May, . . . with my family all in good health, having been one year and one month on the road.[43]

The Rev. John E. Braly arrived later that year. In late 1847 or early 1848 he and Cornwall organized the first Cumberland Presbyterian church in Oregon. Although Missouri Synod in 1847 had authorized the formation of a presbytery, this was not done until November 3, 1851. Upon the discovery of gold Braly had gone to California in 1849. Two other ministers, Neill Johnson and Joseph Robertson, arrived in 1851 and joined Cornwall in forming Oregon Presbytery, which then took under its care four licentiates and accepted one candidate. There were only five congregations within presbyterial bounds, which embraced all of what became the states of Oregon and Washington. Total membership was given as 100, with perhaps seventy of these having come into the Church through profession of faith. Four years later the presbytery had ten ministers, eight licentiates, sixteen churches, and 423 members.[44] Though the growth was rather slow, compared to that in some other places, this was not really bad progress considering the newness of the territory, the great distance from the rest of Missouri Synod, the lack of assistance from the Church back in the States, and the necessity of ministers to earn their livings through "secular work." The Church in Oregon was off to a fair start, but controversy over slavery and secession divided the presbytery and so disrupted its work that it never really recovered.

Of the Cumberland Presbyterian ministers who went to California during the Gold Rush, it is not clear whether more went primarily to save souls or to gain wealth. Several of them were lured, only temporarily in some cases, away from their calling into the frantic scramble for gold. Of much more importance, many of them from the beginning or soon after arriving gave all or part of their time to the ministry.

Either John E. Braly or James M. Small was the first Cumberland Presbyterian minister to reach California. By July 4, 1849, Braly was preaching at Fremont after having moved from Oregon and opened a "boarding house" in a canvas structure. Later he moved to the Santa Clara Valley. Small came directly from the States, but the exact date of his arrival is not known. On September 12, the Rev. T. A. Ish arrived and settled in Sacramento. He later wrote that he "had something of the gold fever" for a while but "could not content myself to sit down an idler in the Lord's vineyard." By March 1850, John M. Cameron, a licentiate, had joined Ish in Sacramento and they had erected a small building where both preached each Sunday. Ish reported several church members in the area and hoped to organize a congregation soon. He regretfully noted that the gold fever had got some Cumberland Presbyterian ministers and named two who were "in the mines." [45]

The 1851 General Assembly ordered Brazos Synod (Texas) to establish a presbytery in California, but the California ministers already had acted. Among the new arrivals in 1850 had been some ministers who were active in preaching. On April 4, 1851, Cornelius Yager, Wesley Gallimore, and Braly constituted California Presbytery. This extraordinary action of forming a presbytery without authority from a higher court was taken as an emergency measure. Organization was needed to hold ministers and members to the faith in the face of the temptations around them of "getting rich quick." The presbytery received Small as a member and Cameron as a licentiate. The only two organized congregations in the presbytery were at Napa City and Martinez. At this organizational meeting the presbytery assigned members to various preaching tasks and set up a schedule for sacramental and camp meetings. The first camp meeting in California was held at Napa Valley in June 1851, with Small, Gallimore, Cameron, Braly, Ish, and J. J. May participating. Only two conversions were reported. Another, held in July in the Santa Clara Valley, created much more "excitement" and resulted in twenty-one conversions and twelve additions to the Church.[46]

Upon the appeal of California Presbytery the 1852 General Assembly approved the unusual formation of the presbytery and attached it to Missouri Synod. A request for missionary aid could not be met for several years, although the Assembly of 1855 instructed the Board of Missions to send a missionary to California before any other field was opened. The Board, lacking sufficient funds, was unable to find anyone to go until 1859. Then it sent the Rev. W. N. Cunningham to Stockton but paid only the cost of his travel with no provision for salary. Handicapped by distance, scarcity of ministers, and lack of missionary aid, the Church grew slowly on the west coast. The entire Pacific coast area remained under Missouri Synod until October 11, 1860, when Sacramento Synod was organized at Sonoma, California. It included California, Oregon, Pacific, and Sacramento presbyteries. At that time it was reported that the four presbyteries had a total of thirty-one ordained ministers but that "a large majority . . . are comparatively idle." The 1,049 members were described as "very imperfectly organized, if organized at all, and untrained." Here, too, the Church was almost entirely rural, with the list of church locations including only one town and not a single city.[47]

As a frontier people, early Cumberland Presbyterians had numerous contacts with Indians. Some of the "revival party" had preached to Indians before the new Church was founded. Occasional contacts were made along the edges of white settlements during the first decade of the Church's history. The first organized missionary work among the Indians, however, did not begin until 1820 with the establishment of Charity Hall School in Mississippi.

Organized missionary work among the Choctaws and Chickasaws in northern Mississippi by any church did not begin until 1818. In August of that year the Congregationalists started a mission among the Choctaws and eight months later opened a school.[48] At about the same time the newly organized missionary society of Elk Presbytery sent Samuel King and William Moore on a tour to the Tombigbee River area.

This led to interest in establishing a school for the Indians. In 1819, the Synod adopted the following resolution:

WHEREAS, Several letters were directed to the Moderator informing the Synod that several societies have been formed, the object of which was to raise funds to establish schools for literary and religious instruction of the Chickasaw and Choctaw nations of Indians, appointing the ordained ministers of this synod their board of trustees, which appointment was accepted.[49]

Also in 1819, Congress began appropriating money to support education for the Indians. Those funds, made available to churches in connection with their missionary efforts, stimulated the founding of schools. The number of such schools among all the tribes increased from three in 1819 to thirty-eight in 1835.[50] At first Elk Presbytery was unable to get government funds for starting a school within either the Choctaw or Chickasaw lands, but Robert Bell was appointed to open a school in the white settlements on the east side of the Tombigbee River.

Bell's school had been open only a few weeks when agents of Elk Presbytery and the chiefs of Chickasaw Nation reached agreement for a school on Indian land. The treaty was signed by the chiefs and Bell, Samuel King, and James Stewart on September 11, 1820, at the home of Chief Levi Colbert at Cotton Gin Port. On November 4, 1820, Bell moved to the site for the school, three miles below Cotton Gin Port and one mile west of the river.

Bell's younger son, also named Robert, immediately started erecting temporary buildings while the school got under way in the home of Colbert. Within three or four weeks the buildings were ready. Here, about halfway between Columbus and the present town of Aberdeen, Charity Hall School and mission maintained a precarious existence for about a dozen years.

Although the General Synod had assumed responsibility for supporting Charity Hall, its contributions averaged only $350 to $400 per year. About $300 was appropriated annually by the United States government. Contributions from both sources were uncertain, irregular, and insufficient. Frequently, Bell had to go into Tennessee and even Kentucky to beg for supplies and money. Much of the expense was paid from Bell's own property. Under intolerable financial and physical burdens, the Bells continued year after year. Bell did much of the farm labor himself, often with only the help of "an awkward set of Indian boys." He taught, preached regularly, conducted and assisted at camp meetings, traveled to raise money and supplies, and served as Indian Agent. Although some dozen different assistants were at the school during its existence, there probably never were more than two at the same time. With little help except the Indian girls, Mrs. Bell had the tasks of cooking, washing, and managing a household that included usually thirty or thirty-five students. She also taught the girls spinning and weaving. The many hardships, Bell later wrote, "would have induced me to have resigned . . . , had I not considered the credit and respectability of the C. P. Church, to be identified with the continuance and success of our Missionary School."

Despite these difficulties the school plant was expanded to include not only buildings for housing and for the school but also a tanyard, a farm cleared and fenced, a blacksmith shop, and a saddler's shop. Educational and spiritual accomplishments were less tangible and certain. Bell was encouraged by the pupils' progress in reading, writing, and arithmetic. He thought some learned the principal essential Christian doctrines and "often seemed serious," but he feared that none became truly converted. Nevertheless, he noted that most of the students remained sober and industrious after leaving the school, and he heard that some later filled high positions in their Nation after removal to the west.

In the early 1830s a fatal blow fell upon Charity Hall School. This was the government's decision to move the Indians west. All government and church aid to the school ended months before the removal treaty with the Chickasaws was ratified. Bell's effort to keep the school open without aid failed. The exact date of the school's closing is not known, but it apparently was between 1830 and 1832. Bell remained in Mississippi and was successful in organizing several churches after the whites settled the area.[51]

Not until about twenty-five years after the close of Charity Hall School did the general Church become active in work among the Southern Indians in their new location in what later became Oklahoma. There was some missionary work among Choctaws and Chickasaws by ministers on their own or with the support of lower courts. During the 1840s and early 1850s occasional pleas were made in church papers and in the General Assembly for the Board of Missions to send missionaries among the Indians. In 1854, after an appeal by David Lowry, who had spent years with the Winnebago Indians in the Northwest, the Board acted. It sent Lowry into Indian territory on an inspection tour with authority to appoint missionaries if he found suitable men.[52]

Lowry's report on his tour of several hundred miles through the Choctaw Nation revealed that earlier Cumberland Presbyterian preachers had been active there. He appointed two native preachers as missionaries—Israel Folsom, the first Choctaw ordained as a Cumberland Presbyterian minister, and Payson Williston, a licentiate. A white minister named Samuel Corley was appointed to ride and preach half-time among the Choctaws. Corley lived in Texas, only thirty miles from the Nation, and already was known and respected by the Indians. The Board added another white minister, R. W. Baker, and another native, George Folsom, as itinerant preachers. Under the combined efforts of white and Indian preachers Choctaw membership reached an estimated 600 to 700 by 1858.

When the Cumberland Presbyterian Board of Missions resumed Indian work, other denominations already had several schools in the Nations. The Board entered the educational field in 1855 by appointing Baker as superintendent of Armstrong Academy in Choctaw Nation. In 1859 this school had about 100 pupils. Arrangements were made also to open Burney Academy, a school for girls in Chickasaw Nation, with the Nation providing the buildings and the Board supplying the teachers. The first superintendent, F. D. Piner, supervised construction of the buildings but resigned before the school opened in 1859. The Board sent the Rev. R. S. Bell as superintendent in 1859. During the late 1850s several Choctaw and Chickasaw youths went to the church schools in Tennessee. Some of them were preparing for the ministry. This promising beginning among the Indians was disrupted by the Civil War. Bell and his wife remained in the field through those troubled times—to be joined by others after that storm was over.

Because of the location and lines of migration of the main body of Cumberland Presbyterians, they had little contact with Indians of the Northern tribes. The only minister known to have worked with them was David Lowry, who went to the area which is now Wisconsin in 1833, and he never was supported by any court or board. Lowry was employed as subagent with the Indian Agent at Prairie du Chien to set up a government school for the Winnebago Indians just across the Mississippi River.

At first the Indians opposed Lowry's school, and the "first session was without a single pupil." In 1837, however, enrollment reached forty-two. In order to get the Indians "farther away from whiskey and the contaminating vices of the frontier," the school was moved fifty miles west in 1840. With the departure of Lowry the congregation at Prairie du Chien dwindled away. In 1844 Lowry lost his appointment; he and some other Protestants believed this was due to the efforts of Catholics and "unscrupulous" whites. Regaining his position, he returned on May 1, 1846. Although the school continued to grow, achieving an enrollment of 125 by 1847, other problems arose. The pressure of white settlers had led to a new treaty, in 1846, by which the Winnebagos agreed to move farther north to lands to be furnished by the government. Disagreement between the Indians and the government delayed departure. This continuing uncertainty was a great hindrance not only to progress for the school but also to other aspects of the effort to get the Indians to settle down to the white man's ways. When finally force was used to move the reluctant Winnebagos, Lowry and his son helped in limiting or preventing actual conflict. During July 1848, the Lowrys accompanied the main body to their new lands in central Minnesota Territory. The following year Lowry reported that he had reopened the school with 125 pupils, with as many more willing to come if there had been room for them. After a few years Lowry again lost his appointment. By 1854 he was back in the South helping to get the Church to revive its work among the southern Indians.[53]

Cumberland Presbyterians were slow in beginning foreign mission work. (Missions to American Indians were considered foreign at first, but the Church later classified them as domestic.) The first mission to a foreign land was opened "providentially"—that is, with no special planning by the Church and, therefore, apparently through Divine Providence. J. Edmund Weir was a slave who had received "a good education." Having been ordained by Anderson Presbytery, he was manumitted so he could go to Liberia, Africa, as a missionary. In 1851 he visited churches in portions of the South raising money for the proposed mission. For five years after his arrival in Liberia in 1852 Weir preached without any official connection with or support from the Church in America.

In 1857 Weir visited the United States to try to get help from the Church. After being commissioned by the Board of Missions, he visited churches and raised money to erect a church building. In response to his pleas for more missionaries, the Board appealed to church members owning slaves who were ministers to free them so the Board could send them to Africa. The appeal went unanswered, and Weir returned alone with instructions to open a mission and build a church at Cape Mount, Liberia. With inadequate and uncertain support from the Church in America, Weir established and ran the mission. Repeated appeals of the Board for additional missionaries were fruitless. The Civil War cut off practically all aid to the mission. Some aid was sent after the war. In 1867 and 1868 Weir came to the United States asking for help. The 1868 General Assembly recommended suspension of the mission because of apparently unsurmountable difficulties. Being abandoned by the Cumberland Presbyterians, Weir returned to Liberia and joined the Congregationalists.[54]

Even more ill-fated than the Liberia mission was the attempt to start a mission in the Near East. J. C. Armstrong, a young man who had "missionated" on the Iowa frontier, felt a special call to preach the gospel to Moslems and persuaded the Board of Missions to send him to Turkey (the Ottoman Empire). Almost from the beginning the mission was beset with great difficulties. Leaving Nashville, Tennessee, on July 1, 1860, Armstrong, his wife, and their three-month-old baby went to New York and boarded the *Golden Rule,* a sailing vessel. On the Atlantic crossing the officers and passengers barely survived a mutiny in the midst of a violent storm. The trip from England to France and thence to Constantinople was pleasant. A period of several months of getting acquainted and of language study also went well. Then, before Armstrong could begin actual missionary work, disaster struck. The start of the Civil War in America cut him off from support and even communication from the Board of Missions in Lebanon, Tennessee. Also, his Southern sympathies led to his social ostracism by other American missionaries in Constantinople. For months he and his family survived on a little income from translation work and aid from his Turkish "servant" and from the chaplain of the British Embassy. An extended illness from typhoid fever shattered whatever hope he might still have held for beginning missionary work.

Armstrong's illness broke down all politically inspired animosity between him and the other American missionaries. They supplied all his wants and nursed him until he was well enough to undertake the voyage home. Then the American Board of Commissioners for Foreign Missions loaned him money for the passage. The family left Constantinople on July 11, 1862, and arrived at Quebec on August 19. Since Mrs. Armstrong was Canadian, they remained in Canada until the war ended before returning to Tennessee. After the war the Church paid Armstrong's debts and probably also paid him the arrears in salary. So ended the only Cumberland Presbyterian attempt to start a mission on the continent of Europe.[55]

# 9

## WEATHERING THE STORM

## OVER SLAVERY AND SECTIONALISM

*If a sectional religion divides us here, and destroys brotherly love, it will exclude us from heaven. There is no Northern or Southern religion there. . . . As we have loved each other heretofore, so let brotherly love continue. . . .*

Milton Bird to the 1861 General Assembly

The most shattering blow to fall upon the American churches during the nineteenth century was the secession of eleven Southern states and the Civil War of 1861-1865. Long before the war, Christians, North and South, had begun to take sides on the slavery question. Church membership did not shield very many from the moral and patriotic fervor aroused by slavery and war, and some churchmen were among the most fervent partisans on both sides. In the mid-1840s the two largest Protestant denominations split into Northern and Southern branches over the slavery issue, the Methodist Episcopal Church in 1844 and the Baptist churches in 1845. The third largest, the Presbyterian Church in the United States of America, had divided into Old School and New School branches over other matters in 1837.

When six Southern synods withdrew from the New School Church over the slavery question after the General Assembly of 1856, the New School Church became almost exclusively Northern in membership. The Old School

Church had a much larger Southern element, over one-third of its members living in slave states. Old School unity was broken in 1861, following the secession of eleven states and the General Assembly's adoption of the Spring Resolutions (resolutions introduced by the Rev. Gardiner Spring, of New York, in support of the Federal union). The seceding element organized as the Presbyterian Church in the Confederate States of America and later was joined by some of those who had left the New School Church a few years before. (After the war the name was changed to Presbyterian Church in the United States, and the denomination was popularly known as the Southern Presbyterian Church.) The Old School Church retained most of its members in the border slave states; however, the strong antislavery and unionist position it took late in the war caused a large defection to the Southern church immediately after the war.

Although not all Presbyterians in the North believed their church courts should become involved in secular issues, by 1861 most of them were anti-slavery. With the advent of the war they also were strongly unionist. During the war the New School Church and four of the five smaller Presbyterian bodies in the North consistently condemned slavery and supported the government's efforts to suppress the rebellion. The exception was the small Associate Reformed Church, which was not proslavery but which refused to make ecclesiastical pronouncements on the secular controversy. Among Presbyterian bodies, the Cumberland Presbyterian Church was in a unique position. By the end of 1861, it was the only one to have considerable membership in both the seceding and the nonseceding states.[1] To the strain of differing moral views on slavery had been added the political conflict of secession versus union. How the Church managed to avert ecclesiastical division under this great stress makes one of the most interesting chapters in its history.

In a "reflection" dated October 18, 1828, the Rev. Robert Donnell wrote:

O Lord, in Thy providence Thou has placed under my care a number of black people. For them I feel a deep interest. Help me, O my Master in heaven, to do for them what is right and to give them what is right.[2]

Donnell had a medium-sized farm near Athens, Alabama, which was worked by about fifteen slaves. When not on one of his many preaching tours he held morning and evening services with his family and slaves. Upon the complaint of the overseer that he could not get the farm work done, Donnell said he preferred less work to less worship.[3] In 1844 Donnell turned down an invitation to become pastor to the Memphis congregation partly because his removal would force the separation of some of his Negroes from their families. "This I could not think of doing; nor can I bear the idea of leaving

my black people here under an overseer, and removing without them." [4]
There is no evidence available that Donnell questioned the morality of the
institution of slavery.

The Rev. Finis Ewing also owned slaves, but slavery came to be distasteful to him. Soon after moving to New Lebanon, Missouri, in 1820 he
preached what was probably his first sermon against slavery. Extremely
critical of his fellow Cumberland Presbyterians who *"sell for life* their fellow
beings, some of whom are their brothers in the Lord," he especially condemned the separation of families. As for himself, he wrote that "after a
*long, painful,* and prayerful investigation of this subject, I have determined
*not to hold,* nor to *give,* nor to *buy* any *slave* for life. Mainly from the
influence of that passage in God's word which says, 'Masters give unto your
servants that which is *just* and *equal.'* " After deciding to free all his slaves,
Ewing tried to prepare them for freedom. He had some of the younger
ones taught to read and he made provision for the support of older ones. At
his death all were freed.[5]

There was no typical Cumberland Presbyterian attitude toward slavery.
These two examples, however, illustrate a common characteristic of those
whose views are known to us. This was a strong tendency toward soul-
searching in an effort to know and do what was right. As other examples,
both the Rev. David Foster and the Rev. Samuel McAdow moved from
Tennessee to Illinois reportedly because of opposition to slavery.[6] The *Revivalist* (Princeton, Kentucky), the first Cumberland Presbyterian paper,
came out in 1833 in favor of gradual emancipation. Believing that immediate
emancipation would create greater problems than slavery itself, the editor
contended that *"justice,* humanity, and religion, call for emancipation, and
*reason* dictates *gradual* emancipation. . . . By remaining inactive, we will
pull down upon our heads heaven's red-hot vengeance. Let us be up and
doing." [7] This position was maintained after the paper was moved to Nashville, Tennessee, and the name changed to the *Cumberland Presbyterian.*

Like the members of other denominations, Cumberland Presbyterians regarded the Negroes as responsible moral agents. Consequently, they not only
felt obligated to preach and teach Christianity to them but also accepted
them into the communion of the church. In most if not all cases, Negroes
were members of the same congregations as whites and sometimes attended
the same meetings. Frequently, however, when it was possible to do so,
separate meetings were held. An estimated 20,000 Negroes were members
of Cumberland Presbyterian churches in 1860. Some slaves who showed the
inclination and ability were authorized to preach to slave members. In a few
instances slaves and free Negroes were ordained as ministers. Through the
1840s and 1850s presbyteries in slave-holding areas frequently directed their

ministers and congregations to make special efforts and arrangements to see that the Negroes were supplied with preaching and the sacraments.[8]

Apparently, the attitudes of Cumberland Presbyterians toward the Negro and slavery differed little from those of the people among whom they lived. In the 1830s gradual emancipation was being suggested by many concerned persons in the upper South. The colonization in Africa of emancipated former slaves gained wide support as a means of removing what was regarded as an undesirable element from society. Beginning in 1833, the Cumberland Presbyterian General Assembly affirmed support for the American Colonization Society and urged ministers and members to aid it. The work of the Society, the Assembly said, would "ameliorate the condition of the free colored population" and "promote the cause of the Redeemer."[9]

As the sectional controversy over slavery became ever more bitter in the 1840s and 1850s, even moderate antislavery views became unpopular in the South. Both the secular and the religious press attacked abolitionism. Southern critics of slavery found it expedient to remain quiet or move to the North or West. Although radical proslavery opinion was not universal in the upper South, rational discussion on the subject was virtually impossible by the 1850s in the lower South and the Southwest. Cumberland Presbyterians were not immune from the passions of the moment. For example, a historian of the denomination in Texas cites instances of arguments given in defense of slavery and of condemnation of abolitionism, concluding that "the only way a Cumberland Presbyterian minister with abolitionist views could survive in Texas was to remain silent." Even in Texas there were a few who refused to keep quiet, though public pressure forced them to leave the state.[10] And while proslavery opinions were hardening in the South, Cumberland Presbyterians were becoming involved in the Northern abolition movement. Despite the extreme views of some members and ministers on both sides of the issue, the General Assembly refused to be drawn into the slavery controversy during the ante-bellum period. What were the reasons for this lack of official attention to the preeminent question of the day?

The apparent equanimity with which the Church faced the twin problems of slavery and sectionalism before 1861 was due to three main factors. First, the geographical distribution of the membership helps explain the scarcity of extreme partisanship. With no churches in the Northeast beyond Pennsylvania and relatively few in the states of the lower South, the membership was not afflicted with the most radical political leadership of the time. Slavery *was* an issue in the great midcontinent area where Cumberland Presbyterians were concentrated, but there were fewer extremists.

The second factor was the youthfulness of the Church. It was in a large measure a product of revivalistic fervor and was still in the stage of growth through revivalism. The first- and second-generation ministers who led the Church in the ante-bellum period were interested primarily in the salvation of souls through personal spiritual redemption. Few were theologians and even fewer were social reformers with concern for the possible relationship between condition of soul and condition of body.

Finally, the most direct factor was the deliberate decision and determination of Cumberland Presbyterian leaders to prevent the disruption of the Church. To most of them the unity of the Church was of much greater value than was any social or political reform. An illustration of this is the attitude expressed by Robert Donnell in 1844: "I have always endeavored to maintain a conservative position, both in church and State—believing that extremes are generally dangerous. Those questions which are now rending other churches, I hope will not get into ours; but that we will continue to maintain the unity of the spirit in the bonds of peace." [11] This determination was important in keeping down debate on the slavery question before the war. It also helped prevent a formal sectional division during the war and made reconciliation relatively easy after the war. A survey of developments within the Church relating to the sectional crisis makes this point clear.

During the ante-bellum period there was remarkably little attention to slavery and other sectional issues in the Cumberland Presbyterian press and in the deliberations of the General Assembly. In 1834 the editor of the *Revivalist,* after restating his support of gradual emancipation, declined to open his columns to a general discussion of the topic.[12] Other papers evidently followed a similar policy. The subject of abolition is not even mentioned in the General Assembly minutes until 1848. The Assembly of that year, in approving the report of the Committee on the Minutes of Pennsylvania Synod, expressed disapproval of any attempt by church courts "to agitate the exciting subject of slavery." Pennsylvania Synod, reversing a position taken a year earlier, had adopted this resolution: "That the system of Slavery, in the United States, is contrary to the principles of the Gospel, hinders the progress thereof, and ought to be abolished." The Committee believed that such resolutions would "gender strife, produce distraction in the Church, and thereby hinder the progress of the Gospel." [13]

The General Assembly of 1850 met in the midst of the controversies preceding the enactment of the Compromise of 1850 while some radicals in each section were suggesting division or secession. Without referring to the slavery question, the Assembly adopted unanimously the following resolution offered by Judge Robert L. Caruthers of Tennessee:

*Resolved,* That this General Assembly look with concern and disapprobation upon attempts from any quarter to dissolve the Union, and would regard the success of any such movement as exceedingly hazardous to the cause of religion as well as civil liberty. And this General Assembly would strongly recommend . . . prayer to Almighty God to avert from our beloved country a catastrophe so direful and disastrous.[14]

Later, after war had started, radical unionists were to refer to this deliverance as they appealed for a condemnation of "rebellion."

During the following year antislavery agitation was stepped up in the Pennsylvania and Ohio churches. The 1851 General Assembly received six memorials on the subject, signed by a total of about 150 members. The memorials were referred to the Committee on Overtures, whose report presumably was adopted by the Assembly. The report affirmed that the Church was "a spiritual body, whose jurisdiction extends only to matters of faith and morals" and included these resolutions:

*Resolved,* That, inasmuch as the Cumberland Presbyterian Church was originally organized, and has ever since existed and prospered, under the conceded principle that Slavery was not, and should not, be regarded as a bar to communion, we, therefore, believe that it should not now be so regarded.

*Resolved,* That, having entire confidence in the honesty and sincerity of the memorialists, and cherishing the tenderest regards for their feelings and opinions, it is the conviction of this General Assembly that the agitation of this question, which has already torn in sunder other branches of the Church, can be productive of no real benefit to master or slave; we would, therefore, in the fear of God, and with the most earnest solicitude for the peace and welfare of all the Churches under our care, advise a spirit of mutual forbearance and brotherly love; and instead of censure and proscription, that we endeavor to cultivate a fraternal feeling one towards another.[15]

Although some lower church courts continued to give attention to the slavery issue and the danger of disunity, the General Assembly took no further action until after secession had occurred. The Committee on the State of Religion reported with satisfaction in the General Assembly of 1858 that "our communion . . . is thus far free from the sectional elements which are distracting and rending other religious bodies. . . ." This condition, the Committee hoped, would continue "by the blessings of God, and a strict adherence to the spirit, teachings, and practice of our Lord and his apostles." [16] No further comment on the sectional crisis appears in the General Assembly minutes until after the dread threat of secession and war had become reality.

Only thirty-four days after the Civil War began with the firing on Fort Sumter, the 1861 General Assembly met in Saint Louis, Missouri, on May 16. The city was in an uproar. Union forces held a precarious military authority, but the preceding week had been marked by riotous skirmishes between the somewhat irregular Federal troops and mobs or gangs of Southern supporters. That the Assembly was able to hold even a three-day session under such conditions is remarkable. That its deliberations apparently were calm and restrained is a testament to the delegates' determination to protect the Church from the rising storm over disunion. This was the last Assembly to be really intersectional until after the war, and in this one only eight delegates attended from presbyteries located in seceded states. An additional twenty-two were from the border states of Kentucky and Missouri, and twenty-one came from free states. Only fifty-one of a possible 320 commissioners attended. They represented thirty-seven of the ninety-seven presbyteries in the Church. (In 1860 eighty of the ninety-seven presbyteries had been represented by 166 commissioners.) At this critical moment the Assembly turned to its principal voice of moderation, the Rev. Milton Bird.

Perhaps no other man was more widely known or more highly regarded by Cumberland Presbyterians than Bird. Four times (in 1842, 1848, 1851, and 1856) he had served as Moderator of the General Assembly, and he had been its Stated Clerk since 1850. Although respected as a preacher, he was better known for his editorial work and his writings. Perhaps by temperament but certainly by reasoned choice, his was the middle course. It was he who had popularized the term "medium theology" for Cumberland Presbyterian doctrines. His was not a complacent or an inactive conservatism; time and again he had interposed force of personality and persuasive argument to calm passions and reconcile controversies which threatened the peace of the Church.

Shortly before the 1861 General Assembly met, Bird had moved from Saint Louis to Jeffersonville, Indiana, possibly in the hope of avoiding the ·storms accompanying disunion. Through the pages of the *Cumberland Presbyterian Quarterly* he had made it clear that he was against secession, and he had assailed extremists on both sides:

Politico-religious fanatics are the worst of all classes to govern. How can the State hopefully attempt to curb that licentious liberty of conscience which they assume for themselves? . . . There is not and there cannot be freedom of conscience unregulated by reason and right. . . .
. . . . What crimson folly, to tear down the best government God ever made! As we conceive, false to the Constitution and faithless to the Union, northern extremists have provoked irritable southern extremists to co-operate with them in bringing upon us the existing calamities, and, in the delirium of the hour, they seem determined to involve us in a common ruin, and whelm us in fraternal blood. But shall they do it? O! God forbid! [17]

The outgoing Moderator not being present, Bird was asked to deliver the opening sermon. Using the text "Let brotherly love continue" (Heb. 8:1), Bird delivered a powerful and effective appeal for peace within the Church.

Its impact cannot be realized fully even by reading the complete sermon; here we can present only a few passages:

Brothers in Christ, though our country is divided and engaged in fratricidal war, we are brethren still, we can not afford to separate. Pure religion changes not. Its life is love, its atmosphere peace. . . . Love can not become hatred. . . .

. . . Christ is not divided, why should we divide? There is no sufficient cause. That which can not divide Christ should not be permitted to divide his people. . . .

Beloved brethren, we must not allow ourselves to be drawn into disputes about the things which belong to Caesar, and so become divided in things which belong to God. Each must allow others to follow their convictions of right in regard to the unfortunate condition produced by the Northern and Southern extremists who have dismembered our once happy and prosperous Union. Before this rupture our religion was not geographical or sectional, nor is it so since the rupture. If a sectional religion divides us here, and destroys brotherly love, it will exclude us from heaven. There is no Northern or Southern religion there, but God's redeemed in heaven come from the north and the south, from the east and the west. . . . As we have loved each other heretofore, so let brotherly love continue until all men shall be constrained to cry aloud, "Behold, how good and pleasant it is for brethren to dwell together in unity." [18]

"Through all those bitter years," B. W. McDonnold wrote, "the voice of Milton Bird rang out on the same key, nor did it ring in vain." [19]

This Assembly obviously was dominated by those committed to the spirit of Bird's message. The reports of the Board of Missions (written before the General Assembly convened), of the Committee on the State of Religion, and of the Committee on Missions all alluded to the coming of war and the necessity of preventing it from disrupting the Church. Also, the Assembly adopted unanimously a set of resolutions offered by Bird. Although the crisis in the Church and the "fratricidal war, the most terrible of all calamities," were regarded as evidence of God's "sore rebukes and heavy judgements," the members gave thanks that the Assembly could meet "in the unity of the Spirit and the bonds of peace" with representation from all sections. Resolving to try always "to cherish the true principles and pure spirit of Christianity" and to "walk in love and live in peace," they asked that the Church engage in unceasing prayer for God's blessing through the troublous times.[20]

Bird and other opponents of extremism continued to work for church unity, although there was increasing agitation in favor of involving the Church in the sectional controversy. The conservatives, however, still had full control of the 1862 General Assembly. Owensboro, Kentucky, had been chosen as a compromise site of the meeting. There were no delegates from the states of the Confederacy. Eighteen of the fifty-eight commissioners were from the border states of Kentucky and Missouri and forty were from the North. It should be noted that the developing controversy was not between Unionists and Confederates or specifically between antislavery and proslavery forces; rather, it was between those who wanted to commit the Church to a prounionist and antislavery position (radicals) and those who wanted to prevent involvement of the Church in those "secular" questions (conservatives).

The question of the Church's relation to the war was treated by the Committee on the State of the Church, of which Bird was chairman. As chairman he probably actually wrote the report. The Committee's report reflected only slight compromise with the more partisan (Unionist) views. Quotations from the Confession of Faith on duties to civil government were followed by resolutions which were adopted *unanimously* by both the Committee and the Assembly. The resolutions emphasized the separation of church and state as required by the Confession of Faith and by the civil constitution. Deploring the "carnage and demoralizing tendency of a war of brothers," they called for humility before God and prayer for "a speedy conclusion in a righteous peace." The determination of the Assembly to preserve unity can be seen in the following:

*Resolved,* That in this time of confused passion, we will, so far as in us lies, endeavor to allay and not exasperate the feelings of those who differ from us, and we most earnestly and affectionately advise our ministers and members to cultivate forebearance [*sic*] and conciliation; to avoid partisanship and sectionalism in Church and State, and to evidence their loyalty to Caesar by their loyalty to Christ in following his example and teaching; and thus continue in *brotherly love,* walking in the comfort of love and in the friendship of the Spirit.[21]

When the motion to adopt the report was before the Assembly, Moderator P. G. Rea, of New Lebanon Presbytery (Missouri), proposed that they kneel and ask the blessing and guidance of God "in this critical juncture." After the prayer, the report was adopted, whereupon the Assembly again knelt and gave thanks that the vote had been unanimous.

Having preserved unity in the 1862 General Assembly, the conservatives feared that the Church might become divided by action of the Southerners, who had not been represented. Therefore, Milton Bird went south on a mission of conciliation and reassurance. Richard Beard stated that Bird visited Nashville and Lebanon, Tennessee, but probably went no farther. "The passions of the people were very much inflamed," wrote Beard, "and he could have done but little." [22]

At the 1863 General Assembly at Alton, Illinois, the conservatives were on the defensive and barely averted actions which they feared would have split the Church. Although actual representation by area was little different from the year before, it was evident early that the "radical party" was much stronger. The first contest was over the selection of a Moderator. The radicals intended to elect the Rev. S. T. Stewart, of Pennsylvania Presbytery, if possible, while the conservatives supported Milton Bird. The Rev. J. L. Riley of Ewing Presbytery (Illinois) later claimed credit for seeing that a particular delegate (the Rev. G. W. Jordan, McLin Presbytery) was persuaded to vote for Bird rather than for Stewart. He noted also that some radical commissioners from Iowa and Illinois "providentially" were delayed from arriving until after the vote had been taken. If Jordan had voted for Stewart, Riley said, there would have been a tie vote which would have been broken in favor of Stewart by the late arrivals.[23]

In the fall of 1862 Ohio Synod had passed a "radical" memorial on rebellion and slavery. Upon its being presented to the General Assembly, it was referred to a special committee composed of one member from each of the eleven synods represented. According to Riley, this committee spent almost four days trying to agree on a report. Some members denounced the South "for the sins of rebellion and slavery" and favored separating from the Southern part of the Church. Riley told them he could see no consistency "in fighting secession in the state and advocating it in the church." Finally, they decided to let a radical write a statement on rebellion and a conservative prepare one on slavery. These were presented to the committee on the morning of the fourth day, and, after some grumbling, a compromise report was ready. Fearing interminable floor debate, the committee decided to ask the General Assembly to vote on the report without discussion.[24]

The statement on secession clearly was the work of the radicals and represented a definite change from the previous policy of noncommitment. It referred to the danger to church and nation from "a gigantic rebellion against the rightful authority of the general government of the United States. . . ." The Church, it stated, "cannot withhold her testimony upon great moral and religious questions . . . without becoming justly chargeable with the sin of hiding her light under a bushel." It was resolved that "treason and rebellion" were "heinous sins against God and his authority"; that they should hope and pray that the rebellion be put down; that they sympathize with those who had suffered because of loyalty to God and country and those who had been forced into the ranks of rebellion; and that they reindorse the statement adopted by the 1850 General Assembly which had affirmed the necessity or importance of political union.

On the other hand, the deliverance on slavery was consistent with the noninvolvement position formerly taken. It stated that the introduction of slavery was "an enormous crime" and that great evils would continue to be connected with it while it existed. But great minds had differed and been perplexed over the remedy. It called upon "those who, in the providence of God," had become connected with slavery to continue prayerfully to study God's word to determine their duty. Those not connected with it were urged to "exercise forbearance toward their brethren." As to the memorial before them, the committee stated that they were "not prepared to make the simple holding of slaves a test of membership." They proposed that the General Assembly "disavow any connection with, or sympathy for the extreme measures of ultra abolitionists, whose efforts, as we believe, have been and are now, aimed at the destruction of our civil government, in order to abolish slavery." [25]

Again recognizing the critical nature of its action, on motion of the Rev. Frederick Lack of Saint Louis, the Assembly called for the vote to be preceded by prayer to be led by the Rev. Woods H. Hamilton, the oldest minister present. After the report was adopted with only two dissenting votes, there was another "season" of prayer and thanksgiving led by the Rev. Joel Knight.[26]

The high tide of radical Unionist influence was reached in the 1864 General Assembly, which convened on May 19 in the Cumberland Presbyterian Church at Lebanon, Ohio. Tension apparently ran high. Milton Bird, as outgoing Moderator, delivered the opening sermon. True to his conservative position, he chose as texts John 18:36, "My kingdom is not of this world," and I Corinthians 13:13, "And now abideth faith, hope, charity, these three; but the greatest of these is charity." But his message did not have the magic of former years. Richard Beard later stated that the sermon "produced some dissatisfaction, and was afterwards published by Dr. Bird himself as a matter of self-vindication." [27]

The first clash arose over a proposal that the Assembly request that the national flag be raised over the church house "in token of our loyalty to the Federal government." After vigorous debate the resolution was adopted forty-five to eighteen on a roll call vote. Those voting "no" argued that the proposal had been introduced as a political matter and that they would not support it unless requested to do so by the state. Seven of those voting "yes" stated that they would not have voted for it if the question had not been presented as a test of loyalty. Most of those opposing it were from Kentucky and Missouri.

In order to handle the questions of slavery and "rebellion" the Assembly set up a special committee of one delegate from each of the twelve synods represented. Pertinent memorials were referred to this committee. Indiana Presbytery had requested the Assembly to adopt a clearer statement on the evils of slavery and to urge the Southern members to abandon "a system which is a reproach to our holy religion, and which has so imperiled our beloved Church, our free government, and our National Union." In response the committee majority declared slavery to be "contrary to the precepts of our holy religion . . . and the fruitful source of many evils and vices in the social system" and recommended that all Cumberland Presbyterians in both sections "give countenance and support to all constitutional efforts of our government to rid the country of that enormous evil." Although this was a more definite statement favoring abolition, it stopped far short of "excommunicating" slaveowners, which some radicals advocated.[28]

Richland Presbytery (Tennessee) had sent up resolutions appealing for continued church unity regardless of political unity or disunity. That the majority of the special committee well knew the import of their response is seen clearly in their statement that:

In this conflict we must stand by our Master, though it require us to sever the dearest ties of time, and as this Assembly has twice declared that obedience to the civil magistrate is a Christian duty . . . we must regard those who are or have been voluntarily in rebellion against the Government of the United States, as not only guilty of a crime against the Government but also guilty of great sin against God, and with such, without repentance and humiliation before God and the Church, we cannot desire fellowship.[29]

Conservatives attempted to block action on the majority report by moving that it be referred to the next General Assembly, with the presbyteries being asked to give their views. On a roll call vote eight Northerners joined twenty-three delegates from Kentucky and Missouri in voting for the referral motion. All but one of the twenty-six "Nay" votes were by Northerners. The conservative victory was short-lived. Immediately after the tally one delegate was allowed to change his vote from "Yea" to "Nay." The next morning, following who knows what pleas and pressures, three others changed from "Yea" to "Nay," bringing the vote to thirty against and twenty-seven for referral. Then, after more debate, the motion to adopt the majority report was passed by a vote of thirty-eight to twelve.

Had the General Assembly's action been accepted as the law of the Church, it would have had the effect of dividing the Church. The resolutions on slavery, mild as they were, likely would have antagonized many Southerners. But the statement on rebellion was, in effect, an attempt to read out of the Church (excommunicate) all those who voluntarily had aided the Confederacy. Apparently led by Bird, who had moved back to Kentucky, nine Kentuckians were joined by one delegate each from Missouri, Illinois, and Ohio in entering a protest against the Assembly's action. In this rather lengthy protest, they condemned "fanatical sectional agitation" and argued that: (1) the action did not accord with the fundamental law or doctrine of the Church; (2) the fundamental law of the Church could not be changed by the Assembly; (3) "agitation and violence" and their result were not consistent with "intelligence, order, piety, justice, and benevolency" because fanaticism feeds upon indulgence until it destroys; (4) the agitation was not demanded by a higher piety and benevolence but, rather, accorded with the passions of the multitude and the moment; (5) as the presbyteries had not acted, the report settled nothing, it being no more than agitation for the sake of agitation and an expression of the personal opinion of those voting for it; (6) the adoption of the report would contribute to secession in both the Church and the nation; and (7) it contributed to "alienation and disorganization in the Church" while doing no good.[30]

If the war had continued for two or three years longer or if the South had made good on the attempt to secede, it is probable that the rift in the Church would have been permanent. But when the 1865 General Assembly convened at Evansville, Indiana, on May 18 the war had ended. Although the Assembly made no concessions to the Southern element, it appears to have been hopeful that unity could be restored without great difficulty. Perhaps as a gesture of good will, the Assembly elected the Rev. Hiram Douglas of Georgia Presbytery (East Tennessee Synod) as Moderator. Douglas was from a predominantly Unionist area of Tennessee; the gesture was not a compromise with rebellion. In adopting the report of the Committee on the State of Religion, the Assembly reaffirmed the action of the 1864 Assembly as a basis for reconstructing churches whose members and ministers had been "involved in rebellion." This meant that "repentance and humiliation before God and the Church" were required of such rebels. Despite this requirement and the fear that missionary effort would be necessary in some areas, the Assembly rejoiced "that the root of bitterness will no longer be a disturbing element in the Church, to alienate feelings or to divide or distract the harmony of God's children."[31] The seating of twelve delegates from Tennessee indicated that the Assembly was willing to accept Southerners who had remained loyal or who accepted the conditions of 1864. The Assembly's optimism was shown in a prayer of special thanksgiving "for the evident presence of His Spirit, controlling and uniting the hearts of brethren from all parts of the Church," followed by singing and "fraternal congratulations, on account of the bright prospects of returning unity and good will throughout the whole Church."[32]

The war ended, then, with the radicals in firm control of the General Assembly and confident that their terms of reconciliation would prevail. Apparently they, as did Northern members of other denominations, assumed that military victory meant also ecclesiastical victory. However, they failed to reckon on the compromising spirit of some Northern and many border-state conservatives and the fact that the numerical strength of the Church lay in the South. Before turning to postwar developments it is appropriate to note some developments concerning the Church in the Confederacy.

As indicated earlier, secession and war cut off from the General Assembly that portion of the Church lying in the Confederate States. In the Confederacy normal church activities at all levels were disrupted, although many presbyterial and some synodical meetings were held. There was some sentiment favoring the organizing of a General Assembly; however, a series of conventions was held instead.

The first such convention met in August 1863, in Chattanooga, Tennessee. Over sixty persons were recognized as delegates, some appearing as individuals without credentials from their presbyteries. Some of them had strong feelings about the political situation, and a member moved that steps be taken toward separation from the Northern part of the Church. The Rev. Wiley M. Reed, a Confederate colonel, made a moving speech against the suggestion. As recorded by McDonnold, he said, among other things:

Those who are not satisfied with the form of our deliverances, but ask in addition that we put Caesar above Christ, and rend Christ's body, in order to show our patriotism, are not entitled to our respect. We want to please God, not politicians. Mr. Chairman, let us wait, and pray, and hope. I believe our church will remain undivided, no matter what comes of this bitter civil struggle.

The vote was unanimous against the motion: even the member who presented it voted "no." Later conventions also refused to heed the voices of separation. The next convention met at Selma, Alabama, in May 1864. With about 150 delegates, it was the largest of those held. The convention received a "most touching letter" from Milton Bird, whose appeal for the unity of the Church moved many to tears. The last convention met in Memphis, Tennessee, in 1865. Attendance was small. Apparently the expectation that all sections could be represented in the next General Assembly made further conventions unnecessary.[33]

As the war progressed, there was increasing pressure for the formation of a General Assembly in the Confederacy. Rumors of Unionist and antislavery statements by the General Assembly meeting in the North created much dissatisfaction. In the lower South some members left the Church for political reasons. Oxford Presbytery, in Mississippi, reportedly seceded from the denomination; however, it later sent delegates to the 1866 General Assembly. In Texas a "General Council" of presbyteries west of the Mississippi River was held at Corsicana in May 1865. Although its announced purpose was not clear, several presbyteries refused to send delegates because they believed the aim was separation. There apparently was some agitation in that direction, but no action was taken by the council.[34]

Understandably, there was much confusion at the end of the war. This was due in large measure to lack of information: members in each section did not know much about what had happened in the other, and there was a general uncertainty as to what the General Assembly had done. Rumors were rampant. The minutes of the wartime General Assemblies were not published until September 1865, at which time all those for 1861-1865 were issued in one publication. In the preface the Rev. J. B. Logan, of Alton, Illinois, expressed the hope that publication of the minutes would "dispel many erroneous notions, and groundless fears" and "tend . . . to prepare the way for a better understanding between different sections. . . ." [35]

Some members in the North and in the border states believed that the action of the 1864 General Assembly excluded "rebels" from the Church pending their "repentance and humiliation before God and the Church." As an example, Springfield Presbytery (Missouri) in an 1865 meeting concurred with the General Assembly "in extending pardons to returned rebel ministers who make the required confession." It also admonished and advised its "erring brethren to comply with the requirements of the General Assembly and the Constitution of the State of Missouri at their earliest convenience." [36] As the date for the 1866 General Assembly neared, it remained to be seen if this view was to prevail.

As delegates gathered at Owensboro, Kentucky, in May 1866, there was enough uncertainty to cause concern for the future of the Church. Richard Beard, in his restrained manner, later referred to the situation as "a delicate one." "There was," he wrote, "a great deal of inflammable material." [37] Over 150 commissioners from sixty-six presbyteries attended. Sixty-seven came representing presbyteries in the former Confederate states. Many of these and some of the forty delegates from Kentucky and Missouri surely had supported the "rebel" cause. Would they be admitted? Again the presence and personality of Milton Bird were decisive. As Stated Clerk he enrolled the Southern delegates, ignoring the question of their status in relation to the Church; to him they were members in good standing. This gave the conservatives an overwhelming majority in the Assembly. He then used his persuasive powers to get Beard's cooperation in organizing the Assembly on a plan for a peaceful settlement, a plan supported by "other wise and good men," as Beard called them.[38]

Again, as in crises of the past, Bird's prestige and talent for conciliation were called upon. He delivered the opening sermon from the text Romans 12:19, "Dearly beloved, avenge not yourselves, but rather give place unto

wrath: for it is written, Vengeance is mine; I will repay, saith the Lord."
Some extremists were not satisfied with the sermon, but it was appreciated
by most of the delegates. The Assembly was organized according to the "plan
for peace." Beard was elected Moderator and John Frizzell, an elder from
Winchester, Tennessee, became Recording Clerk, with A. E. Love of Columbus, Mississippi, as his assistant. From these selections and from the line-up
in voting on critical issues later, the nature of the "plan for peace" becomes
apparent: concessions to the Southerners were to be made in order to form
a Southern and border-state coalition against the Northern minority.

Early in the proceedings J. M. Howry, an elder from Oxford, Mississippi,
presented a resolution which was adopted on the motion of the Rev. James
A. Bowman, of Brownington, Pennsylvania. The resolution provided for
setting up a special committee of one member from each synod. Members
were to be selected by the commissioners from the several synods. This
committee was to consider the deliverances of former General Assemblies on
war and slavery and "to make such report thereon as the harmony of the
Church and the exigency of the times require." Communications on the same
subject from various presbyteries were referred to this special committee.
The membership of the committee was announced on Tuesday morning,
May 22. In view of the gravity of its task, the committee was given discre-
tionary leave of absence from Assembly sessions until its report was submitted.
It seems clear, however, that minds already were made up, since the com-
mittee was ready to report on the same afternoon.

The majority report was signed by all the Southern and border-state members (except the one from East Tennessee Synod) and by the member from
Pacific Synod—twelve in all. The arguments presented were essentially
those used by conservatives during the war—that the General Assembly
should not and could not legislate legally on nonecclesiastical concerns. The
fact that the majority of the members of Cumberland Presbyterian churches
were not represented in the wartime meetings of the Assembly was noted also.
The resolution stated: (1) that church and state were separate and distinct
and that "political differences were not incompatible with ecclesiastical allegiance, fellowship and unity"; (2) that the 1864 and 1865 deliverances
were disclaimed and had no binding force except on members who agreed;
(3) that as individuals they all "accept in good faith the results of the late
war, and acknowledge our allegiance to the Constitution and Government of
the United States"; (4) that, as slavery had been "abolished by the power of
the sword," all legislating and preaching on the subject should cease, "except
for the moral welfare of the African race"; (5) that they were grateful to
God for preserving the unity of the Church; and (6) that the Church should
avoid "legislation calculated to engender strife and discord" and that they

would do all they could "to heal any unpleasant feelings" that existed.

The seven Northern committee members, joined by Samuel B. West, of Knoxville, Tennessee, presented a short minority report. They found "nothing in the deliverances of former Assemblies, touching these questions, requiring modification or repeal" and believed that further action would "tend only to disturb the peace and harmony of the Church."

All other business of the Assembly was suspended while debate on this issue continued, beginning in the afternoon of May 22 on the motion to adopt the majority report. After almost a full day of discussion, apparently without progress toward agreement, Milton Bird presented a substitute report written by the Rev. J. C. Provine, of Nashville, Tennessee. As a compromise measure, the virtue of the substitute report was in its *general* nature: there were no references to specific actions or deliverances of former Assemblies and no statements regarding allegiance to secular constitutions and governments. Beginning with the "great truth" that Christ's "kingdom is not of this world" and with affirmation of the Cumberland Presbyterian teachings on—and the civil Constitution's requirement of—separation of church and state, it presented these resolutions:

*Resolved*, 1. That this General Assembly is opposed to every movement, coming from any quarter, that looks to a union of Church and State.

*Resolved*, 2. That we are opposed to the prostitution of the pulpit, the religious press, and our Ecclesiastical Courts, to the accomplishment of political and sectional purposes.

*Resolved*, 3. That any expression of political sentiment, made by any Judicatory of our Church, North, South, East, or West, is unnecessary, and no part of the legitimate business of an Ecclesiastical Court.

Members of the Northern faction were not satisfied with this attempt to skirt the issue, but they were unable to sway the majority. Among their attempts was a proposal by the Rev. S. R. Shull, of Atlanta, Illinois, that the substitute report be amended by adding "That these resolutions are not to be considered as nullifying any previous action of the Assembly touching the subjects of Rebellion and Slavery." Consideration of this proposal was postponed indefinitely by a vote of 104 to 51. A large majority of Southern and border-state delegates were joined by one delegate each from Kansas and California and two from Illinois to form the majority. Five of the seven from East Tennessee Synod and four of the twenty-two from Missouri voted with the Northerners.

After some additional efforts to amend the substitute report had been repelled, the Assembly permitted the Rev. A. B. Miller, of Waynesburg, Pennsylvania, to present a revised minority report. In it the Northerners made an important concession, adding to their report the provision that the expression of former Assemblies "which seems to require repentance and humiliation before God and the Church . . . is hereby disclaimed and rescinded." The motion to adopt the revised minority report lost by a vote of 42 to 110. Unwilling to accept merely a practical concession, the majority clearly were determined to reject the ruling of former Assemblies that slave-holding and rebellion were sinful. Northerners were just as opposed to any suggestion of approval of slavery and rebellion. Finally, on motion of the Rev. James Mitchell, of Houston, Texas, the substitute report offered by Bird was amended by adding this resolution: "That nothing in the foregoing shall be construed as an expression of opinion upon Slavery or Rebellion." In the late afternoon of May 24, the Assembly adopted the substitute report by a roll call vote of 112 to 40. This time only two delegates from East Tennessee and one from Missouri stayed with the Northern minority, while six from Illinois and one each from Ohio, Kansas, and California voted with the majority.

Two additional general resolutions relating to the unity of the Church were adopted. One was that Cumberland Presbyterian editors and publishers "be earnestly recommended to exclude from their columns such articles as may manifestly engender unholy strifes and divisions among brethren, and mar the peace and unity of our beloved Zion." The other, submitted by J. B. Logan and adopted on the motion of the Rev. G. T. Stainback, of Columbus, Mississippi, pledged the members to give full support to all the Church's enterprises and institutions.[39]

The sectional controversy did not again reach crisis proportions, but there continued to be some rumblings of discontent from the North. Pennsylvania Synod asked the 1867 General Assembly to say whether or not the decision of the 1866 General Assembly "repealed, nullified or set aside" the rulings of former Assemblies on the subjects of war and slavery. In response, the Assembly adopted (with but two dissenting votes) the following resolution introduced by B. W. McDonnold:

*Resolved,* That while the decisions of the General Assembly are of high authority, they cannot become a law binding on all the Churches, so as to set up a test of Church membership, without they are referred to the Presbyteries and there approved: Hence such decisions are not subjects of repeal, and the decisions of the last General Assembly did not repeal the decisions of former Assemblies on the subjects above named, nor did they acknowledge their authority, but simply disclaimed all jurisdiction over such questions.[40]

The 1867 Assembly closed on a hopeful and optimistic note with adoption of the following resolution:

*Resolved,* That we will, in the strength of the Divine Master, "forget the things that are behind, and push on to those that are before," rising in our might above all local prejudices and jealousies, and, with our hands united from the lakes to the gulf, we will labor in the same as brothers.[41]

Some Northerners, however, were not ready to regard the issue as settled. In its next meeting Pennsylvania Synod expressed dissatisfaction with the General Assembly's postwar rulings on the rebellion and slavery questions by resolving "That for the time being we will withdraw our cooperation from the General Assembly, in the way of declining to support the Boards of the Church, synodically or individually, or in any other way that would express our sympathy with said Assembly in her teachings on these questions." [42] Similar resolutions were introduced in other Northern church courts. In November 1868, the Board of Missions withdrew its promise of support for a missionary at Oskaloosa, Iowa, because he had voted for such a resolution. In the 1868 General Assembly the Committee on the Minutes of Pennsylvania Synod called attention to the resolution quoted above. Such action, the Committee reported, was "subversive of the best interests of the Church, and contrary to the genius of our ecclesiastical government." The Assembly, however, was determined not to reopen the controversy and laid the Committee's report on the table indefinitely.[43]

A much more moderate position than that of Pennsylvania Synod was taken by other Northerners. These apparently were willing to accept the 1866 Assembly's ruling that the wartime declarations on slavery and rebellion were not binding on the Church, but they wanted to reaffirm the Church's responsibility to speak out on moral questions. A memorial, signed by fifty-three ministers and eighty-seven elders, requested the 1868 Assembly to affirm as taught in the Confession of Faith and the Bible these propositions:

1. That things secular and civil belong to the State.
2. That things moral and ecclesiastical belong to the Church.
3. That in regard to things which are mixed . . . the secular and civil aspects belong to the State, and the moral and ecclesiastical aspects belong to the Church.
4. That it is the prerogative of the Church of Christ to sanction correct morals, to express its views through the pulpit, the press, and the various judicatories, on all moral questions, regardless of civil codes or political creeds.

The Committee on Overtures, to whom the above memorial was referred, presented a rather lengthy report. While appreciating the "sincerity and earnest desire" of the memorialists, it could not support the exact language of their statement. It was, the Committee wrote, "so liable to misconstruction that it would be unsafe as a form of a rule of practice." Chapter XXIII, section 3 of the Confession of Faith was quoted as much clearer than the first point of the memorial. It stated not only that civil magistrates must neither interfere in matters of faith nor assume any church functions but also that they must *protect* all Christians in the exercise of religion. The second point, the Committee said, failed to recognize that the state also has jurisdiction over moral questions. On the third point, the Committee quoted extensively from the Confession of Faith, the burden of the argument being that the church-state relationship is much more complex than the memorialists recognized. The Committee agreed fully with the fourth proposition, except for the phrase which implied that the church could defy or disregard the civil laws of the land. This reasoned report was adopted by unanimous vote. The relief of the delegates at again having averted dispute was expressed in special prayer of thanksgiving led by the oldest minister present, David Lowry of Iowa.[44]

Sectionalism did not disappear entirely from the Church, but the issues of secession and slavery were not again agitated in the General Assembly. In 1869 the Assembly's Committee on the State of Religion reported with satisfaction that "sectional animosities . . . have been buried with the past, and the bonds of Christian fellowship . . . have been re-established, we trust, never to be weakened." [45] Many times in following years Cumberland Presbyterians expressed pride in their Church's having preserved its unity. Certainly, a statement by A. B. Miller, Moderator of the 1877 General Assembly, showed that bitterness was dying, if not dead. Miller had been one of the "radical" element which had wanted the Cumberland Presbyterian Church to take and maintain a strong stand against secession and slavery. The corresponding delegate from the General Assembly of the Presbyterian Church, U. S. (Southern), in addressing the Assembly, alluded to the end of Reconstruction and the return to power of men who gave the people a fair chance, "a white man's chance." Miller, in his responding remarks, emphasized the *national* nature of the Cumberland Presbyterian Church, saying to the applause of his fellow commissioners, "It is a matter of history, sir, that when our country passed through a great revolution that sundered commercial, political, and social ties, we, as a Church, were able through the darkest of the storm to hold together, and we are here represented as one people today, for which we thank God." [46]

With the emancipation of the slaves and the close of the Civil War, the churches were faced with the problem of redefining the status of their Negro members. Previously, when slaves had received religious instruction and preaching, it usually had been on the initiative and under the control of masters who felt the responsibility. Negroes were members of the same churches or denominations as whites. For several reasons this pattern did not continue. Missionaries sent by Northern churches to work among the freedmen, upon finding most Southern churches closed to them, often encouraged Negroes to set up their own churches. Most of the Southern churchmen readily accepted the idea that the Negroes would be happier in their own churches where, with white aid, they could develop leadership ability. Negroes also accepted this idea; possibly it originated among them as they saw no hope of religious independence within the white-dominated churches. Consequently, in almost all instances separate Negro churches were organized during the Reconstruction period.

With the commissioners from former slave states gaining control of the 1866 General Assembly, Southern attitudes toward the freedmen dominated the policy of the Cumberland Presbyterian Church in the postwar period. The 1866 Assembly adopted a special committee's report on the moral and religious training of "colored people." A Northern delegate moved to strike out a statement that those most able and willing to aid the freedmen were the Southern people, but the motion was rejected. The report called upon presbyteries to aid Negro members of the Church by organizing Sunday schools for them, helping provide them with ministers, and assisting them to obtain church buildings. The next Assembly declined to establish a standing committee on the moral and religious training of "colored people" and made the subject a responsibility of the Committee on Education and the Committee on Missions. Both of those committees repeated essentially the same recommendations adopted the preceding year. Thus, in the immediate postwar period the General Assembly encouraged separation of the races in worship services and other church activities. The Assembly in May 1868 did recommend that Negro members be encouraged to attend services with the whites when they were not numerous enough to have congregations and worship of their own. Presbyteries were asked to take "measures to provide for them pious, able, and well-qualified ministers." However, "the leadings of Providence may hereafter show *more plainly* whether they should be constituted a separate ecclesiastical body." [47] This wording suggests that there already was talk of separation, but it is possible that the Negro leaders acted in response to the Assembly's statement.

At a convention of Negro Cumberland Presbyterians at Henderson, Kentucky, in October 1868, there was considerable sentiment favoring formation of a separate church. Action was deferred by this convention and by another at Huntsville, Alabama, in January 1869. A major step toward separation occurred in May 1869, at Murfreesboro, Tennessee, where the regular General Assembly and a called convention of Negro leaders both met. The Negro convention submitted a memorial to the Assembly which was taken (and since has been interpreted) as a request for aid in setting up a separate church. According to McDonnold, the Rev. Moses T. Weir (a brother of J.

Edmund Weir, the missionary to Liberia), in private conversation with a member of the Assembly, stated that this was the intention. As paraphrased by the Assembly's Committee on Overtures, the convention expressed "the opinion that it would not be for the advancement of the interest *of the Church,* among either the white or the colored race, for the ministers of the two races to meet together in the same judicatories." [48] The convention's request that synods be instructed to create presbyteries of Negro ministers was referred to the synods, which were authorized to form such presbyteries when considered in the best interests of the Negro members of the Church. The convention's proposal that the Assembly instruct that a synod be formed when enough presbyteries had been established was referred to the next Assembly. In none of the requests of the convention or actions of the Assembly is there clear evidence that either desired division into completely separate churches. In fact, the Assembly cautioned all the church courts "to confine themselves to such steps as are obviously necessary and proper for the present, and await the further developments of Divine Providence before determining upon an ultimate policy." [49]

When the 1870 General Assembly convened at Warrensburg, Missouri, Weir presented an informal commission from Greenville Presbytery, which had been formed of Negro ministers by authority of Green River Synod. Southern delegates feared that Weir was being used to foment political controversy, and there was considerable concern and debate for several days. Finally, the commission was laid on the table (rejected, but with no permanent ruling) on the grounds that the Assembly did not have official information about the establishment of Greenville Presbytery. The 1871 Assembly still assumed jurisdiction over the Negro element within the Church. At their request, it authorized the forming of Greenville Presbytery in Green River Synod and Huntsville and Elk presbyteries in Columbia Synod into a new synod. At this time there was clearly an intent of complete organizational separation, as the order was for the organization of the "First Synod of the Colored Cumberland Presbyterian Church" at Fayetteville, Tennessee, "on Friday before the first Sabbath of November, 1871. . . ." [50] The Assembly's records do not indicate whether the Negroes wanted complete separation or assumed that their synod and presbyteries would remain under the General Assembly.

Any remaining uncertainty about the relationship of Negroes to the Cumberland Presbyterian Church (white) was removed by the 1873 Assembly. On order of the Synod of Ozark, Missouri Presbytery had been constituted by Negro ministers. Members of Missouri Presbytery asked the Assembly to decide if they were members of one of the Negro synods in Kentucky and Tennessee or of Ozark Synod and therefore entitled to representation in the

General Assembly. Despite minority opposition, the Assembly ruled that they were not members of Ozark Synod and therefore could not be represented in the Assembly. In making this decision, the majority assumed that the Negro convention at Murfreesboro in 1869 had spoken for all Negro members and that the intent then had been to form a completely separate organization. The Negro Cumberland Presbyterians accepted this interpretation and on May 1, 1874, at Nashville, Tennessee, formed their own General Assembly. Thenceforward the two churches apparently remained on friendly terms and annually exchanged fraternal delegates or correspondence. However, spokesmen for the Negro church sometimes expressed disappointment at not getting more assistance from the white church.

Some Northern members of the Cumberland Presbyterian Church remained dissatisfied with the separation and at least once before the end of the century proposed union with the Cumberland Presbyterian Church, Colored. Acting at the request of Foster Presbytery, in 1883 the Synod of Central Illinois memorialized the General Assembly to initiate steps looking toward union to the extent of having only one Assembly in which the presbyteries of both groups would be represented. Repeating the view that separation had occurred at the request of the convention of Negro ministers in 1869 and alluding to the success of independently organized Negro churches, the Assembly did not grant the memorial.

It is probable that the prewar estimate of 20,000 Negro members of the Cumberland Presbyterian Church was an exaggeration. Even so, it is apparent that relatively few of those members went into the Cumberland Presbyterian Church, Colored. When the new General Assembly was organized in 1874, this church had an estimated forty-six ministers and only 3,000 communicants. The dislocations during and after the war surely caused many former slaves to lose their connection with the Church. In areas of Negro membership, congregations and presbyteries were disorganized or barely able to maintain the essentials of worship, so they could do little to help or hold Negro members even when inclined to do so. After the war the Northern branches of several denominations sent missionaries and money to aid the freedmen and help then organize churches. Beginning in 1866, the Cumberland Presbyterian Church was controlled by its Southern majority. Many congregations and presbyteries assisted their Negro brethren, but the Church as a whole failed to provide sufficient leadership or material aid to hold more than a small number of freedmen. Despite frequent and fervent statements recognizing obligations and affirming good intentions, the real aid the General Assembly gave the other church before 1900 was a modest contribution in the field of education. Lack of adequate resources was only a part of the explanation. As late as 1888, McDonnold decried the prejudice which caused anyone who tried to work with the Negroes to "be thrust out and lose caste." [51]

Despite its difficulties and small beginnings, the new church progressed. Statistical information was scarce and unreliable, but the white denomination's Stated Clerk estimated in 1886 that the Negro denomination had 200 ministers and 13,000 members in four synods and twenty presbyteries.[52] The rate of growth then slowed considerably, if the statistical reports were close to being accurate, because as late as 1895 the numbers were 215 ministers and 15,000 members in five synods and twenty-two presbyteries.[53]

# 10

## EXTENDING THE MISSIONARY FRONTIER,

### 1861-1900

*If we would accomplish our God-given purpose toward all men, we must give increasing attention to the changed social condition of the world and adopt such methods of evangelization as will meet the necessities of the times.*

Board of Missions, 1898

The Civil War, which very nearly split the General Assembly of the Cumberland Presbyterian Church, disrupted normal church activities at synodical, presbyterial, and local levels. In the North the absence of ministers and the general concern with matters related to the war prevented some synodical and presbyterial meetings and left many churches without leadership. But the impact was particularly heavy in the Southern and border states where about 75 per cent of the Cumberland Presbyterians lived.

For the Church, the loss of actual and potential church leadership was perhaps the worst feature of the war years. Many ministers and elders, North and South, entered the armies as soldiers or as chaplains. Among the latter were numerous men too old for regular military service.[1] In some cases wide areas were left without ministers. The lament of the Rev. R. O. Watkins of Texas might well have echoed through the land:

And now commenced the sad work of disastrous war, churches left without pastors, deprived of their rulers. . . . Calls everywhere by the destitute, sad, bereaved and suffering for someone to come to them in their sorrow and destitution to break to them the bread of life and give the consolations of the Gospel.[2]

Much of the loss was permanent as death or disability came to many who served in or with the armies. Merely as examples, cited because of the prominence of the fathers, Richard Beard lost two sons in the war and Reuben Burrow lost three, one being the Rev. Aaron Burrow, already highly regarded as a "very promising young man."[3]

At the end of the war there was much to be done. Watkins's description of conditions in Texas could have been applied to the Church throughout the South:

> In the fall after the war closed Texas Synod convened . . . , attendance small, and most of the members present were men enfeebled by age, pressed down with increased cares, mourning the loss of loved ones, and sad in view of the ruined conditions of the church. . . . the report from the committee on state of religion . . . came up, and sad indeed was the report made. Presbyteries nearly annihilated, churches left without preaching, many in disorganized condition, members sad, discouraged, not knowing what to do or where to go for aid, preachers pecuniarily ruined, pressed down with hard labours to secure even the bread necessary to feed their families.[4]

The synod's approach to the problem was in accord with Cumberland Presbyterian tradition: it called for a missionary to travel through the Synod to visit discouraged churches and to try to bring preachers and churches together. Watkins responded and devoted over a year to that particular work.

Variations of the missionary approach to the problems of reorganization were used widely. For instance, in March 1866, Indiana Presbytery organized a Presbyterial Board of Missions which was to employ missionaries, raise funds to support them, and aid vacant churches to secure pastors. "Religion was at a low ebb in most of the churches. . . . Fully one-half of the congregations were destitute of the ministrations of the gospel, and were being gradually absorbed by other denominations. [The Presbyterial Board] was designed to protect and save the life of these."[5]

Although most of the work of rebuilding was done at the synodical and presbyterial levels, the General Assembly continued its efforts to encourage and guide the missionary enterprises of the Church. The Board of Missions at Lebanon, Tennessee, was inactive during the war. Not only was it cut off from the General Assembly, which always met north of the Union lines, but also conditions in the South prevented it from carrying on its assigned activities. On this account the Assembly of 1862 set up a committee to handle mission work. The next Assembly, while disavowing any intent to dissolve the Lebanon Board, reorganized the committee and instructed it to take control of all missionary work of the Church.[6]

Under the leadership of the Rev. Frederick Lack as president and the Rev.
J. B. Logan as corresponding secretary, the new committee made progress
despite the unsettled conditions of the country. In its first two years it collected over $7,000 and aided missionary efforts in at least six states and in
Liberia. With approval of the General Assembly it also secured a charter
in Illinois and was organized in 1865 as "The Board of Foreign and Domestic
Missions of the Cumberland Presbyterian Church." Tentative plans were
being laid for special aid to churches in the areas overrun by the war. The
new Board (hereinafter referred to as the Alton Board), however, had begun
very limited work in the South when the primary responsibility for that area
was turned over to the Lebanon Board.

The first General Assembly (1866) after the war in which the entire
Church was well represented was confronted with reports from both the
Lebanon and Alton boards. In a spirit of reconciliation, the Assembly unanimously agreed to continue both boards under a plan designed to avoid
conflict between them and their respective supporters. The Assembly also
recognized the Pacific Synod Board of Missions as having a special position
and responsibility on the West Coast. The Alton and Lebanon boards both
suffered from lack of funds and lack of cooperation from the synods and
presbyteries within their areas. The Lebanon Board was able to give a little
aid to the mission in Indian Territory and to a few mission churches, but in
the South unsettled political, social, and economic conditions drastically
limited the work. The main problem of rebuilding absorbed the resources of
the Church. In 1869 the Lebanon Board reported that more churches had
been built and more pastors employed in the last three years than in the
previous twenty years. These accomplishments came almost entirely from
local efforts, with presbyterial and synodical encouragement, rather than from
efforts of the Board.

The multiple board system proved unsatisfactory. The 1869 Assembly decided to discontinue the Alton and Lebanon boards and establish a new
board at Saint Louis to be chartered by the state of Missouri. With the view
to future foreign mission work, it was to be called "The Board of Foreign
and Domestic Missions of the Cumberland Presbyterian Church." The
Pacific Synod Board (later the Permanent Committee on Missions) was
allowed to continue its special relationship to the Church. It collected and
disbursed mission funds in Pacific Synod and reported annually to the General Assembly.

The Assembly and its Board of Missions encouraged all synods and presbyteries to form missionary societies auxiliary to the general Board, and much
work was done at those levels. But progress was slow in getting synods and
presbyteries to coordinate their efforts through the general Board. Not only

was there lack of cooperation in fund raising and in selecting mission stations; the Board had great difficulty in getting reports on their mission work from the lower courts. Some improvement in coordination had been made by 1900, especially through the appointment of synod missionaries, but the problem persisted. The related problem of inadequate finances stubbornly defied the many approaches at fund raising used by the Board. In 1885 it reported that in the preceding year only one-fourth of the ministers and one-fourth of the congregations had aided the Board's work; contributions for both foreign and domestic missions averaged less than six cents per member of the entire Church. As late as 1899, out of a total of approximately 3,000 Cumberland Presbyterian congregations only about 1,100 contributed to missions.[7]

The low level of financial support for missions and other church enterprises was not due just to inadequate coordination and the lack of a tradition of systematic giving. A basic difficulty was the relatively low economic position of many Cumberland Presbyterians. The following illustration reflects a situation that was not typical but certainly was not uncommon. In response to an appeal for aid to missions published in the *Missionary Record* in 1891, a member wrote to the editor:

Dear Brother:—As we are a weak church at Popular Springs, we deem it unnecessary for us to give to "Missions," for we only have four members that are able to pay the pastor, and we are not able to pay him what he ought to have. We can only get men that are licensed and some of them are not willing to work for the sum we pay.

And the scripture says, "He that wont [*sic*] provide for his own house is worse than an infidel." So we are not able to provide for our own church, 'till we get stronger members. . . .[8]

Minor adjustments were made in the Board of Missions before the end of the century. In 1878 Board membership was reduced from twelve to five for the sake of efficiency. In 1856 a Board of Church Erection had been established to raise and administer a fund for making loans to congregations for the building of church houses. That board had been dissolved in 1867 and its work assigned to the Alton Board. The 1890 Assembly provided for the creation of a new Board of Church Erection, but the next Assembly authorized its consolidation with the Board of Missions. This resulted in the formation of the Cumberland Presbyterian Board of Missions and Church Erection.

A development of particular importance to mission work was the formation in 1880 of the Woman's Board of Missions. This was one indication of an increasingly active role of women in the Cumberland Presbyterian Church. From the early history of the Church, women had been involved in its activities in significant ways, though usually somewhat in the background in accord with custom. Ladies' missionary societies were being organized as early as 1818.[9] In those early years some women actually spoke out during church services. Richard Beard wrote of his aunt, Mrs. David Foster:

She sometimes, as long as I knew her, under the influence of high religious excitement, would break silence, and not merely shout aloud, but exhort her friends and bystanders. Her exhortations, too, were not the mere incoherent ravings of an unbridled imagination, but they were conceived and expressed with an astonishing degree of correctness. . . . The people sometimes said that when she threw aside her respect for the rules of order she was a better preacher than her husband. . . . Her case, however, was not an isolated one. We had other mothers in Israel who threw themselves as earnestly and decidely [sic] into the great work of the times. We witnessed without offense these outpourings of earnest hearts, which, we were satisfied from other sources, were right in the sight of God.[10]

Although this kind of "preaching" by women remained rare, Cumberland Presbyterian women spoke out in prayer meetings, taught and served as officers in Sunday schools, taught in church-sponsored schools and colleges, and wrote and edited some church literature (especially that designed for children). Despite this background, there was some opposition to the formation of the Woman's Board of Missions and to its early work. This opposition seems to have melted before the Board's considerable success.

The formation of the Woman's Board of Missions grew out of interest in foreign missions, and that remained its principal concern. The Rev. A. D. Hail, one of the Cumberland Presbyterian missionaries in Japan, and his wife wrote to the Rev. W. J. Darby of Evansville, Indiana, suggesting that efforts be made in the 1880 General Assembly to involve women more actively in foreign missions. Darby presented the idea to the women of the Evansville church. After getting approval of the Board of Missions, the Evansville women used the denomination's papers to call for a convention of women to meet at Evansville on May 25, 1880, at the time of the General Assembly. A three-day meeting, May 25-27, resulted in the drafting and adoption of a constitution and the selection of members of a Woman's Board of Missions.[11] Upon its being presented to the General Assembly then in session, the plan was approved by unanimous rising vote with a pledge of "most prayerful" sympathy and cooperation. The Board's headquarters was to be located at Evansville, and five of the seven original members lived in that city.

There might have been a few ladies' missionary societies already in existence, but most of the auxiliary societies were formed under the Board's prompting. At the end of one year the Board reported a total of ninety-nine auxiliaries, of which two were young ladies' societies and eight were children's bands. Many more would have been formed, the Board believed, "if [more] pastors had given their consent and assistance." The report included an explanation of the special concern with foreign missions:

The principal objection we meet is a claim for the paramount importance of the home work. This home work, we acknowledge, is essential, and should be accomplished; but it does not follow that the other should be neglected. Woman is indebted to Christianity for all the privileges she enjoys, and wherever the light of the gospel is shed, she is transformed from a state of existence worse than death, to the rank of man's counselor and friend.

Thus we see woman is called specially to organized effort in behalf of her sex; for as long as any portion of the earth is without the knowledge of Christ, we are in a manner responsible.[12]

Growth of organized women's aid to missions was steady and substantial if not spectacular. Annual contributions grew from $2,013.68 in 1880-1881 to $18,541.10 in 1898-1899.[13] In 1899-1900 the Board received contributions from 661 women's and young ladies' societies and 233 children's bands.[14] Many other societies had been organized, but some of them were inactive. Although most of the work of the Woman's Board was in the foreign field, it gave some aid to home missions.

In addition to evangelists and missionaries sent out by presbyteries, synods, and the general boards, there also were several independent Cumberland Presbyterian evangelists who "reported only to God." This type of evangelism was new in the post-Civil War period. The first Cumberland Presbyterian evangelist at large began that work in 1873; by 1880 the Church had twelve. There was some criticism of them for operating outside the regular organization and authority; however, they apparently kept on rather friendly terms with the Church. Some Cumberland Presbyterian preachers were independent evangelists only occasionally or for relatively short periods. Others devoted their lives to the work. Among the latter perhaps the best known were the Rev. R. G. Pearson and Dixon C. Williams, a lay evangelist.[15]

The Civil War and emancipation of slaves had resulted in a decline in total membership. The Stated Clerk in 1870 estimated the membership at 80,000 with about 1,100 ministers, 195 licentiates, and 222 candidates.[16] McDonnold estimated that there had been about 20,000 Negro Cumberland Presbyterians in 1860.[17] Although only a few of them went into the Cumberland Presbyterian Church, Colored, when it was organized a few years after the war, the 80,000 membership figure for 1870 apparently did not include Negro members. In 1870, then, the white membership was about what it had been in 1860. Some improvements were made in statistical reporting before the end of the century, but the Stated Clerk still had difficulty in getting complete and accurate data. According to his estimates, membership reached 100,000 in 1876, 151,929 in 1888, and 193,393 in 1895. Thereafter, the total given each year was the number actually reported by the congregations and presbyteries. In 1896 the total was only 165,847, but 420 of the 2,867 congregations did not report.[18] The report for 1898 was as nearly complete as any during the period. Information was received on all but 201 of the congregations besides those in Cherokee and Ouachita presbyteries, which did not report at all, and included the following:[19]

| | |
|---|---:|
| Synods | 15 |
| Presbyteries | 126 |
| Congregations (not including Cherokee and Ouachita presbyteries) | 3,021 |
| With installed pastors | 160 |
| With Sunday schools | 1,561 |
| Without houses of worship | 626 |
| With preaching every Sunday | 311 |
| Total number of members reported | 180,635 |
| Resident | 151,165 |
| Nonresident | 29,470 |
| Total number of ordained ministers | 1,694 |
| Connected with presbyteries | 1,599 |
| In transition | 95 |
| Licentiates | 287 |
| Candidates | 306 |
| Ordained ministers without a charge | 327 |
| Retired ministers | 120 |

Most Cumberland Presbyterian expansion from the Civil War to 1900 occurred within the geographical areas previously occupied. The Church retained much of its frontier orientation, but the last frontiers of the West were not so hospitable to church development. On the plains and in the mountains, populations were widely scattered or migratory or both. Nevertheless, the Church penetrated into some new areas. West Texas was the most fruitful new field as church members and ministers moved west. Despite noble effort by several self-sacrificing missionaries in Colorado and Nebraska and on the West Coast, little progress was made. Eastern movement was even more limited. Georgia and Florida presbyteries were formed but remained small. There were a few churches scattered in other eastern states. At one time the establishment of a New Jersey Presbytery was authorized, but the organization was not accomplished.

Although Tennessee kept its lead among the states in Cumberland Presbyterian membership with 41,512 reported in 1899, Texas had the greatest rate of growth in the period 1860-1900. By the end of the century membership in Texas had grown about fivefold to 29,905. Texas Synod (all of Texas and two presbyteries in Louisiana) had 320 ordained ministers, and Tennessee Synod (all of Tennessee plus Georgia Presbytery) was second with 300. Missouri was third in membership and ordained ministers with 26,443 and

271 respectively. Other states having over 10,000 members each were Kentucky—16,197; Illinois—14,892; and Arkansas—11,139. The remaining membership was distributed among the synods as follows: Pennsylvania—7,093; Alabama (including Florida Presbytery)—6,477; Indiana—5,902; Mississippi —5,485; Ohio—2,936; Kansas (including Nebraska Presbytery and some churches in Colorado)—2,826; Pacific (California)—2,106; Indianola (Oklahoma Territory and Indian Territory)—1,714; Iowa—1,572; and Oregon (including Washington)—1,379.[20] A few churches and members were scattered in other states. They either were unattached or were included in the bounds of presbyteries mostly in adjacent states. Members in foreign missions, of course, had a special relationship to the Church. The statistics given above are from incomplete data and in each case the actual membership probably was slightly larger.

In continuing to give primary attention to home missions, Cumberland Presbyterians, like American Protestants generally, were influenced by the late nineteenth century spirit of Manifest Destiny. Many Americans believed it was the destiny of the United States to lead the world to a better way. And for the Protestants among them, this better way was the path of Protestant Christianity. It was in this spirit that the Board of Missions used the slogan, "Save America to save the world." [21]

The Board gave some assistance to frontier missionaries in the West, but its attention increasingly was turned to the cities. Being primarily rural in background, Cumberland Presbyterians shared the view that cities were dens of iniquity and referred to them as "the seat of Satan's power." It was the Church's responsibility, they believed, to combat the spirit of worldliness and skepticism in urban life. In its 1898 report, the Board not only referred to the moral and spiritual aspects of the urban problem but also suggested a recognition of social responsibility for the Church. "Home missions," it said, "today have become largely a matter of city evangelization. To save our Godless cities, and thus save the moral life of our country should inspire to noblest effort all who can be moved by feelings of patriotism or love for humanity." After noting the tenfold increase in urban population since 1800, much of it in the past two decades, it continued:

This sudden increase in the city marks a profound change in civilization and demands the most careful consideration on the part of the church. It is an old and trite saying which modern experience is daily proving to be true that "as go the cities so goes the country." This mixed population, home born and foreign, this juxtaposition of great wealth and extreme poverty, affects the country in such a way as to compel consideration on the part of the church, and presents an opportunity which the Church has been slow to appreciate. That the Church cannot go on in the old-time way is becoming more and more manifest. If we would accomplish our God-given purpose toward all men, we must give increasing attention to the changed social condition of the world and adopt such methods of evangelization as will meet the necessities of the times.[22]

As was true of expansion earlier, much of the planting of churches in towns and cities from 1860 to 1900 resulted from initiative of presbyteries or synods and of individual ministers or groups of members. In some instances the Board of Missions appointed missionaries and sent them to selected locations. In other cases, it responded to appeals for aid from ministers or lay groups who already had begun trying to organize congregations. Aid usually was in the form of paying all or part of the salary of the missionary or pastor. Grants to help pay for church buildings were made infrequently. Loans from the church erection fund were made to some mission stations as well as to other congregations. Duration of aid varied from only a year or two to several decades. Between 1860 and 1900 the general Boards listed a total of 102 town and city missions, though the number given each year rarely was more than twenty. Their locations ranged from Pennsylvania and Georgia to the Pacific, and there was at least one in each of eighteen states and Oklahoma Territory. States with ten or more stations were Kansas, Illinois, Missouri, and Texas. A few of the town and city missions were abandoned. During the period, forty-seven were listed as becoming self-sustaining. No doubt many became self-sustaining without formal announcement to or by the Board, while the support of others was assumed by presbyteries or synods. Most of the missions were in towns or small cities; however, a few were in large industrial or commercial centers such as Chicago, Pittsburgh, Atlanta, Saint Louis, Memphis, and San Francisco.

Before the Civil War the Cumberland Presbyterian Board of Missions had begun work among the Chickasaws and Choctaws in Indian Territory (Oklahoma). The war cut off communication between the Indian missions and the Lebanon Board as well as the General Assembly. To general amazement, it was learned in 1866 that the Rev. Robert S. Bell and his wife had kept up their work among the Chickasaws at great hardship to themselves. One of the first actions of the revitalized Lebanon Board was to send financial aid to Bell. Cumberland Presbyterianism remained alive among the Choctaws, kept alive apparently by native ministers and members. In 1867 the Choctaw Nation was having eleven boys educated at Cumberland University and seven girls at Cumberland Female College, both at Lebanon, Tennessee. With the Board unable to find a missionary to send to the Choctaws, Bell began preaching to them as well as to the Chickasaws. A presbytery (Bethel) was organized under Texas Synod, and by 1871 it had four ordained ministers, two licentiates, three candidates, fifteen congregations, and 470 members. All the ministers, licentiates, and candidates, except for Bell, were native Indians. However, many of the members were whites or only part Indian.[23]

Gradually, the work in Indian Territory was expanded as white missionaries were sent or went of their own accord and as the number of native preachers increased. When death ended Bell's long service in 1880 or 1881, Bethel Presbytery had thirteen ordained and licensed native preachers, seven candidates, forty ruling elders, twenty-nine deacons, twenty-four congregations, and 527 communicants.[24] In 1877 the Rev. N. J. Crawford, who had been sent by the Board the previous year, organized the first Cumberland Presbyterian church among the Cherokees. Two years later he was joined by R. C. Parks, a Cherokee who recently had graduated from Cumberland University. At about the same time the bounds of Arkansas Synod were extended to include all of the Cherokee Nation and part of the Choctaw Nation. Then in 1884 Cherokee Presbytery was organized by Crawford, Parks, and David Hogan, an elderly minister who was devoting his declining years to missionary work.[25]

The opening of portions of Oklahoma to white settlers in 1889 and 1893 created problems for mission work among the Indians. There was a tendency for white ministers to work exclusively with the whites. Nevertheless, the number of Indian preachers increased and the Board managed to keep one or two white missionaries in the field. By 1897 there were two primarily Indian presbyteries: Cherokee in Arkansas Synod and Choctaw (formerly Bethel) in Texas Synod. In 1898 these two presbyteries plus South McAlester (Arkansas Synod) and Greer County and Chickasaw (Texas Synod) were organized into Indianola Synod. Choctaw and South McAlester were combined under the name of Choctaw Presbytery. The 1899 statistical report for Indianola Synod gave forty ordained ministers and 1,714 members; possibly fewer than 500 were "full-blood" Indians.[26] The Board had become quite discouraged over the situation, especially after the resignation in early 1898 of the Rev. A. B. Johnson, who for several years had been the Board's only white missionary working among the "full-bloods." However, its hopes were renewed after the appointment of the Rev. R. L. Phelps as synodical superintendent for Indianola Synod in 1899.

Cumberland Presbyterians contributed to the education of Indians in Oklahoma. Burney Academy in Chickasaw Nation was kept going by the Robert S. Bells through the Civil War and the Board of Missions resumed aid to it for a while. An attempt in the early 1880s to start a manual labor school for training preachers in Choctaw Nation failed. From 1887 to 1894 the Woman's Board paid the salary of Mrs. S. S. Phelps as a teacher in Hogan Institute, in a "half-breed" neighborhood adjacent to Cherokee Nation. The Woman's Board gave assistance to a few other schools, such as one run by Mrs. R. C. Parks at Muskogee, one run by the Rev. J. H. Dickerson at Durant, and another at Chelsea.[27]

The Liberia Mission had been the only foreign mission actually established by Cumberland Presbyterians before the Civil War, and it was abandoned by the Board of Missions in 1868. The attempt of the Rev. J. C. Armstrong to begin a mission in the Ottoman Empire (Turkey) had been aborted by the war and Armstrong's illness. In the early 1870s there was a revived and growing interest in foreign missions. The 1871 General Assembly instructed the Board of Missions to devise plans for raising money and carrying out foreign missionary activity. In 1873 it appeared that Venezuela was being opened providentially to Cumberland Presbyterians. Reportedly, some 800 square miles of land was to be made available to the Church to support mission work there. A church member, Dr. N. H. McGhirk, then living on Trinidad, evidently was responsible for arranging the grant of land through a company he was associated with.

In November 1873 the Board appointed the Rev. S. T. Anderson as missionary and McGhirk as lay helper. Anderson went immediately to Trinidad where he accepted an invitation to supply temporarily a mission church of the Free Church of Scotland at San Fernando. This and the agency of the American Bible Society provided a livelihood for Anderson and his family. Of course, it prevented him from starting a Cumberland Presbyterian mission and delayed the necessity of his support by his own denomination. The plan to establish a mission and organize a presbytery in Venezuela was never fulfilled. The Board soon realized that it could not expect any benefits from the land grant in the foreseeable future; also, it was unable to raise the money to send two additional missionaries as originally intended. Then Anderson resigned in May 1876 and returned to the United States.[28]

As early as the 1850s, the decade in which Japan was opened to contacts with the Western world, the Rev. F. R. Cossitt had urged the Church to turn its attention to Japan as a mission field. Again in the early 1870s its interest in Japan was stimulated when Pennsylvania Presbytery offered to support one of its young ministers as a foreign missionary. The Board of Missions failed to respond, partly because of its involvement in the Venezuela project. The young Pennsylvanian was the Rev. M. L. Gordon, a graduate of Waynesburg College and of Andover Theological Seminary. While retaining his Cumberland Presbyterian connection, he was sent to Japan by the American Board of Foreign Missions. Although the Cumberland Presbyterian Board chose not to unite with the American Board in foreign work, Pennsylvania Synod supported Gordon's work for several years.[29]

At about the time of the collapse of the Venezuela project, two brothers, the Revs. J. B. and A. D. Hail of Pennsylvania, volunteered for foreign service and were accepted by the Board. When Pennsylvania Synod pledged $1,000 to outfit him and $300 a year on his salary, the Board sent J. B. Hail and his family to Japan. They reached Osaka on January 30, 1877, settled in the Foreign Concession, and began the study of Japanese. Meanwhile, A. D. Hail had been studying medicine and awaiting a chance to join his brother. The chance came, and the A. D. Hails reached Osaka on November 1, 1878. After about two years of language study and other preparations, J. B. Hail preached his first Japanese sermon in a rented building. With increasing support from the Church, especially through the Woman's Board of Missions, the mission in Japan steadily grew under the admirable leadership of the Hails.

The work of the Hail families and the men and women who joined them in Japan was really remarkable. Just a listing of their activities would be too extensive for this general church history. By 1881 the two couples alone were conducting at least seventeen meetings a week: Bible reading and discussion, prayer meetings, classes in English and science, sermons, Sunday school, and others. In addition, the men continued their own language study, began translating some Cumberland Presbyterian literature into Japanese, and began making preaching tours in the country south of Osaka. By this time they were being assisted in some of the work by native converts, the first two of whom had been baptized on September 26, 1880. The arrival in November 1881 of Miss Alice M. Orr and Miss Julia L. Leavitt, the first two missionaries sent by the Woman's Board, enabled them to expand their work even more. The contributions of all new arrivals was quite limited during their first two or three years since they had to spend much of their time on language study.

Responding to the missionaries' repeated request for aid in establishing a girls' school and orphanage, the Woman's Board in 1883 sent Mrs. America McCutchen Drennan and contributed $3,000 for that purpose. The remarkable Mrs. Drennan, a widow in her fifties at that time, spent almost twenty years of dedicated service in Japan. A recital of her first nine months' work gives some indication of her energy and ability: she organized classes in English for young men, formed a Chautauqua Circle, organized a Christian Endeavor Society, conducted meetings in various parts of Osaka, adopted two children, and opened the Girls' School (later named Wilmina Girls' School).[30] She continued these activities at Osaka for several years and repeated many of them later at Nagoya, Ueno, and Tsu.

Before 1899, two additional men missionaries joined the Japan Mission, the Revs. George G. Hudson and G. W. Van Horn. Both were accompanied by their wives, who helped with mission work. Counting the four male missionaries' wives, a total of sixteen women served in Japan before 1900, some of them only briefly but others for several years.

In a letter to the Woman's Board in 1895, A. D. Hail recited the accomplishments of the several women missionaries:

The establishment of a girls' school, out stations opened, church houses built, men and women led to Christ by scores, ragged schools, reading-rooms, kindergartens and other forms of benevolence maintained, Women's Missionary Societies organized. . . . Sabbath school, singing, and English classes, woman's meetings, visitation work, general counsellors for any and all who may chance to come. It is not possible to tabulate the statistics of this kind of missionary effort. It is largely through their influence and cooperation that the churches at Yokkai-icha, Shingu, Tanabe, Wakayama, and . . . Tsu, have come into possession of churches of their own. By their influence not only have women been led to Christ, but of those some have been earnest workers among their own people, men also have been led to the Savior by their work, and some of these latter into the gospel ministry. Temperance and social purity work has been a prominent feature of their labor. There are Japanese women who but for them would have been doomed to wretched, wicked lives.[31]

From the beginning, the missionaries were cautious in bringing converts into the Church. They tried to make sure that the prospect or applicant understood what he was doing and was firmly committed to the Christian life. This was especially important because the convert usually was subjected to

A. D. Hail
(1844-1923)

J. B. Hail
(1846-1928)

strong direct and indirect pressures to pull him away from Christianity. They also adopted the principle that the Japanese Christians should be encouraged to assume control of their own church affairs as soon as possible. Because of the first principle, membership grew slowly at first. The first two members were accepted in 1880 and there still were only forty-two in 1883, several of them having come into the Cumberland Presbyterian Church by letter. Then in the next few years, with additional missionaries and some of the Japanese members beginning to be of real help, expansion was more rapid. The first church in Osaka was organized in February 1884; by the end of the year churches had been organized at Shingu and at two villages near Wakayama, Hikata and Mitani Mura. Two more were formed in 1885, at Wakayama and Tanabe. The locations of these churches reflect the rapid extension of the area in which the missionaries operated. There were several other mission stations and preaching places; some of the converts at these were able to have membership in the organized churches. By the end of 1888 there were seven congregations and 513 members.[32]

In accord with the policy of encouraging self-determination, the Japanese Cumberland Presbyterian churches were permitted to adopt their own rules and procedures. With the missionaries acting as advisors, delegates from the various churches and unorganized groups formed a temporary body which served the presbyterial function, pending the establishment of a regular presbytery when there would be three Japanese ordained ministers. It was in this spirit, too, that the missionaries approved the union of the Japanese Cumberland Presbyterian Church with the United Church of Christ in Japan in 1889. The United Church already had been formed by a union of the Presbyterian Church, U.S.A. (Northern), Presbyterian Church, U.S. (Southern), German Reformed Church, Dutch Reformed Church, and United Presbyterian Church of Scotland. The Declaratory Act of the United Presbyterian Church of Scotland was the basis of union, but later the Church of Christ in Japan drew up and adopted a simplified Confession of Faith. Although there was some criticism of this union among Cumberland Presbyterians back in the United States, it was supported by the Board of Missions and approved by the General Assembly.

The missionaries were not members of the Church of Christ in Japan ("United" was dropped from the name); they retained their home church and presbyterial connections. They did retain a close working relation with those churches and members who had been Cumberland Presbyterians, except for two congregations which asked to be transferred to another presbytery. Once established, the Japanese church formed its own missionary organization which worked with the foreign missionaries. By 1894 there were associated with the Cumberland Presbyterian mission about ten congregations with over 600 members. Some were supplied with preaching by the missionaries. Also working in them were several Japanese, including three ordained ministers, five licentiates, three lay evangelists, and five Bible women.[33] Many outstations (preaching places in outlying villages) also were served by the Japanese evangelists and foreign missionaries. In 1898 the annual report from the Japan Mission included a summary of its accomplishments of twenty years: twenty missionaries (fourteen still there), 1,086 persons baptized, 668 church members (many of those baptized had joined other churches or had transferred), six ordained Japanese ministers, a girls' school, a school for the training of Bible women, and several English schools, schools for the poor, and kindergartens established.[34]

The fortunes of Christian missions in Japan varied somewhat with shifts in public opinion and government policy toward foreigners. The first few years of Cumberland Presbyterian activity in the early and middle 1880s coincided with generally favorable policy and much curiosity about Western ideas and ways. One reason for the slower rate of mission growth in the late 1880s and early 1890s was the reaction against foreigners at that time. The Japanese were offended particularly by the refusal of Western countries to give up their extraterritorial treaty rights in Japan. In referring to the problem this situation created, the Cumberland Presbyterian Board of Missions expressed plainly the Christian aspect of America's "Manifest Destiny." Of course, the primary motive of missionary work was the salvation of souls, but the Board presented the social and cultural as well as the individual rationale. "If it were not indubitably true that Christianity is the sure pacificator of humanity," it said, the most ardent friends of Japan would be pessimistic over the future. However, it continued:

The peculiar emergency of the times rather bids Christians hasten with the sweet spirit of Heaven's love and Heaven's wisdom to direct their wandering hearts. On Christian America rests a very large share of this responsibility, for when with open Bible . . . Commodore Perry and crew sailed into port in front of Yokohama in 1853, the entrance was not only peaceable, but significant of a high-born purpose to deal with the nation in righteousness and the spirit of brotherly kindness. From that day forward the United States and its Christian subjects have been the foremost friends and benefactors of Japan. . . .

It is well that this should be. The eternal fitness of things requires it. The strength of our own national life, the providential environments, the Heaven-bestowed blessings through which we are the inheritors and the favored possessors of personal liberty and the beneficiaries of the purest spiritual Christianity, through which we are to-day the most powerful and wealthy of nations, make us pre-eminently debtors to all the less favored portions of humanity, and bid us be the leaders in race elevation. Of Christian civilization we are the Western exponents—Japan is our nearest Oriental neighbor

MRS. A. M. DRENNAN
(1830-1903)

Homemaker and teacher who, in middle age and twice widowed, was accepted as a missionary to Japan and served there with distinction over a period of two decades.

—itself in advance of all Asia in rapid changes from political despotism to constitutional government, and from superstitious enslavement to religious toleration.[35]

Not long after the Japan Mission was established, the Church turned its attention again to the Latin American field. American Protestants tended to view Latin America as a proper field for missionary activity. They regarded it as only nominally Catholic and actually pagan, or they thought of the people groaning under the burden of a corrupt priesthood. Responding to the growing interest, the 1881 General Assembly instructed the Board of Missions and the Woman's Board to cooperate in sending missionaries to Mexico as soon as possible. After considerable difficulty in raising funds and locating a volunteer, in 1886 the Board sent the Rev. A. H. Whatley, a recent graduate of the Theological School at Cumberland University. After over a year of language study and familiarization with the people and culture, Whatley located at Aguascalientes, a city of 35,000 which had no Protestant church. In 1887 he returned to the United States, married, and went on a tour publicizing the Mexico misson and raising funds to build a chapel and school. He returned to Mexico in August. In November the Whatleys were joined by the Rev. F. P. Lawyer, a graduate of Lincoln University and of McCormick Theological Seminary.[36]

The missionaries to Mexico found the people indifferent when not actually hostile. They concentrated on the establishment of schools to reach the children and young people and, through them, the parents. Whatley began preaching services twice weekly in January 1888. Though few attended, he was able to organize a church with five Mexican members within a year. A school was opened with twelve pupils in the first session. After several months of preparation, Lawyer and his wife opened a new mission at Guanajuato in April 1889. Whatley also started preaching at Asientos, a village near Aguascalientes. His report on an incident at Asientos illustrates one of the problems faced:

My helper, Donaciano Cortez, spent Sunday, April 28th at [Asientos], and in attempting to hold a service, an individual, the tool of the priest, assaulted the house, attempting to ride in on horse-back, with pistol in hand. This was repeated three times, the authorities finally arousing themselves sufficiently to arrest the disturber.[37]

The reports on the Mexico Mission during the 1890s reveal progress and reversals, hopes and disillusionments, and, overall, sound accomplishments achieved despite numerous obstacles. Three additional ordained ministers and their wives were sent, but in 1899 only two of the five couples remained. Five young women were sent by the Woman's Board and four were still there at the end of the century. Mission stations were set up at seven points, four in Aguascalientes and vicinity and three in Guanajuato and vicinity. Schools were established at six of the stations. In 1898, upon recommendation of the General Assembly and because of the resignation of one of the male missionaries, the work was consolidated in the area of Aguascalientes. The church in the city then had about 100 members. (This might have included some members living at the three outstation mission points.) There also was the newly organized Griffin Industrial School for Boys. Schools were being operated at Colegio Morales and Cosio, while Asientos had only preaching.[38]

In the face of growing difficulties of the Mexico Mission, the Board of Missions in 1897 asked the Church for patience and renewed effort:

But let us not anticipate a speedy overthrow of Roman Catholicism in Mexico. It is firmly entrenched in the hearts of the people; it is maintained by the tenacity of reverence, and is hoary with age. The people have been schooled in a religion of deception, they have been taught to believe an impure Gospel, they are slaves to a corrupt and powerful priesthood, which has utterly divorced morality from worship. Only by persistent effort, in the use of the most skillful means and by the highest Christian forbearance and patience, can they under the blessing of God be brought to comprehend properly the uplifting power of Protestant Christianity.[39]

During the period 1860-1900 the numerical and territorial expansion of the Cumberland Presbyterian Church was not nearly so rapid as in earlier decades. The Civil War hindered development dramatically. Though it made greater efforts than previously to enter the cities, the Church was unable to make significant gains in urban areas. Meanwhile, frontier conditions in which the Church had flourished were disappearing. Despite these hindrances, there was considerable growth. The number of members and of ordained ministers approximately doubled and there was almost a threefold increase in number of congregations. Geographically, further expansion within the United States was rather limited. Except in West Texas, the Church did not become strong in the Great Plains and Rocky Mountain area. There was some further penetration of Georgia and Florida, but the Church made little progress east of the Appalachians. Success in foreign missionary work was much more notable. The Japan Mission was especially well established, and, despite many difficulties, the Mexico Mission was maintaining a precarious existence.

Organizational progress was even more pronounced. By the end of the century the Assembly's reorganized Board of Missions was functioning more smoothly than ever. A Woman's Board of Missions had been organized and was making significant contributions, especially to foreign missions. Financial support had increased greatly, though it was still far too little to meet recognized needs. At the synodical level improvements in organization had been made. Synods had been consolidated to coincide in most instances with state lines. Synodical agencies had been established to help promote the work of the general boards of the Church as well as to carry out particular enterprises. In the following chapters some attention is given to progress in organization and accomplishment in such areas as education, publication, and Sunday schools.

# 11

## PREACHERS OF THE GOSPEL

*A man can feel that he fills the very avenue through which the grace of God might be communicated to save sinners, and therefore he feels the truth, "Woe is me if I preach not the gospel."*

Joel Knight, 1875

By the time the General Assembly was formed in 1829 many of the early practices in the Church had become rather standardized. The Church being almost exclusively missionary, the most important activities were those connected with preaching. That first generation of preachers, the "fathers" of the Church, came to be viewed almost with reverence by their successors. Their zeal and success in "bringing souls to Christ" and their endurance of countless hardships in answering their Master's call made some of them legends in their own time. In a real sense they created a church in their own image. Their strengths became its strengths; their limitations became its weaknesses. We can see much of their character in the legacy which they bequeathed to the Church. And the most important element of that legacy was the ideal of the "preacher."

The basic requirement for the ministry was a "call" from God, a belief shared with other evangelical denominations. Although it was assumed that there were outward signs or evidences of a true call, it was an entirely personal experience, similar to the experience of conversion. Just as the sinner under "conviction" had no peace until he received the grace to be saved, the person "called" to the ministry could not rest until or unless he became busy "in the Lord's vineyard." One of the clearest statements of that feeling was

189

made by a minister, Joel Knight, who had known many of the fathers and
who, of course, had experienced the call as they had:

With an appreciation of the true character of the sinner, and the fearful
prospects before him, and of the ample, full, and free salvation provided for
him, and offered to him, their feelings became so wrought up that they felt
like they could not live without trying to warn sinners, and persuade them to
be saved. Under such circumstances a man feels that he must try to open the
way for the grace of God to save sinners. A man can feel that he fills the
very avenue through which the grace of God might be communicated to
save sinners, and therefore he feels the truth, "Woe is me if I preach not the
gospel." [1]

The preaching prompted by this call and commitment was revivalistic and
"experimental." All the early ministers had some concern with doctrine, and
some became argumentative and combative in promoting and defending the
particular beliefs of their denomination. The emphasis, though, was on
preaching inspired by the Holy Ghost, which in turn descended upon the
hearers to "convict them of sin" and "lead them to Christ." After Alexander
Chapman, Alfred McGready Bryan, and John Morgan had begun preaching
in western Pennsylvania in 1831, a Presbyterian observer wrote of them:
"Having declared their peculiar [doctrinal] views, *they dropped non-essen-
tials, and commenced preaching Christ and him crucified.* This they did with
such power and demonstration of the Spirit, that many were cut to the
heart." [2]

The church literature is full of advice and anecdotes illustrating the
importance of "Holy Ghost preaching" and the overriding concern for the
souls of the unconverted. A second generation minister wrote in 1850 that
one of the fathers told him: "Never preach a sermon, nor deliver an exhortation, without telling the sinner how to come to Christ. . . . You know not
what may be the state of mind of some that may hear. The great question
with them may be, 'What shall I do to be saved?' You may never have another opportunity of answering it." [3] Late in his life Robert Donnell, one of
the greatest of the fathers, wrote:

. . . the most successful preaching is experimental preaching. Men who
preach experimentally, preach to the heart, and commend themselves to
every man's conscience in the sight of God. To tell what we have felt, will
have more influence on others than to tell what we know. . . . Our most
successful ministers and people are those who tell what the Lord has done
for them. Many preachers, who have but little doctrinal skill, have been most
successful in bringing souls to Christ. [4]

In many sources are found stories about the apparently ill-prepared, poorly
dressed, unprepossessing young preacher and the doubtful older minister

who expected little from the youngster and even seemed mortified at the prospect of having his pulpit disgraced—then the amazement over the eloquence and fire which shook the audience and touched off a burning revival. Although belief in the "calling" was practically universal among Cumberland Presbyterians and therefore not debatable, articles in support of it appeared in the church papers throughout the century. In 1875, for example, an elderly preacher, fearing that "our talented and educated ministers" might fail to preach "the simple truth of the gospel," raised the cry: "We want Holy Ghost preachers, whether learned or unlearned." [5]

The view of the ministry as a calling and therefore of the preacher as a vessel for the Holy Spirit had a profound influence on attitudes and activities in the Church. It contributed to the opinion, widely held, that formal learning was not necessary for and might even be a hindrance to successful preaching. Connected with the belief that God provides for those whom he calls, it helped support the tradition of inadequate pay for ministers. It obviously was a driving force in the tremendous exertions of generations of men truly committed to the missionary task. The success and contributions of the early ministers in the techniques of evangelism and revivalism (such as "missionating," itinerancy, and camp meetings) helped fix upon the Church an attachment to those techniques. In many instances much good resulted, but there was a tendency to rely primarily on revivalistic methods in meeting new problems. For decades the church courts sent out missionaries and evangelists to "awaken the churches" to any new or old recognized need. As much as was accomplished in this manner, it delayed the development of organized, systematic approaches to the promotion of and support for church enterprises.

Though they believed that God selected and called men for the ministry, Cumberland Presbyterians believed the church should not wait passively for him to act. "It is the duty of the church," said a minister in 1850, "to seek these men at the hand of God. 'Pray ye, therefore, the Lord of the harvest that he will send forth laborers into his harvest.' Matthew ix. 38." [6] In accordance with this admonition, the church courts frequently set aside special days of "humiliation and prayer" for God to call more men to the ministry and directed all ministers to preach on that subject. The continuing shortage of preachers in some areas usually was ascribed to the failure of the church in such areas to pray enough with the proper spirit.

The belief in a "personal call" to the ministry presented a practical problem to the presbyteries. Since the call was personal and internal, how could the presbyteries (charged with the responsibility of accepting or rejecting candidates) decide who really was called? The solution was not too difficult for the presbyteries willing to apply it. Those whom the Lord called, it was believed, He also qualified for the ministry, and these qualifications could be observed. Presbyteries were supposed to judge the candidates for the ministry and license only those who demonstrated through examination and a sermon that they did have the basic qualifications.

Actual practices in licensing preachers and ordaining ministers varied so much that no single statement can be accurate. It is quite clear, however, that presbyteries tended to accept as a candidate almost anyone who presented himself. The need for ministers remained desperate throughout the century; and who could tell what rough, unlettered lad (or middle-aged man, for that matter) might become another Harris or Donnell or Bryan? This tendency to accept candidates without adequate screening probably contributed to the widespread impression that Cumberland Presbyterians enforced no standards for the ministry.

Much evidence indicates that relatively few of the candidates ever were licensed to preach, and even fewer were ordained. Although presbyteries generally were lenient on educational standards, they did expect evidences of a "call" and demonstration of ability to preach effectively. There are numerous instances of candidates being denied licensure. Arkansas Presbytery in 1826, upon hearing a discourse read by James Miller, concluded "that his call was not to preach the gospel" and dismissed him "from under the care of this Presbytery in brotherly love and in good standing as a private christian. . . ." [7] During the same year Illinois Presbytery examined the case of Josiah Kirkpatrick, decided that "his gift and call were not to preach, and in the spirit of brotherly love" discontinued him as a candidate.[8] Of eleven candidates under the care of Alabama Presbytery in a five-year period, only one became an ordained minister.[9] Judge R. C. Ewing, a prominent elder in Missouri, estimated that hardly one in six candidates ever was ordained.[10] It is clear that many candidates were discontinued because presbytery was not convinced they truly were "called."

The influence of the church fathers can be seen in other ideal qualities of the minister. In the church literature "piety and devotion" and "learning" are listed almost as often as the "call" as desirable or necessary characteristics. The stories about the early successful ministers reveal an unabashed and manly piety which later generations admired even as they feared that it was disappearing. The list of other ideal qualities given by church writers includes several that reflect the influence of the pioneer preachers: natural endowments (the capacity to learn, even under adverse conditions), common sense and a knowledge of human nature, love for the Cumberland Presbyterian Church and a knowledge of its history and doctrines, willingness to sacrifice self to the calling, strong faith, a love for souls, humility, and the manners of a true gentleman (by which apparently was meant that natural grace which springs from sincerity and purity of heart and requires no special training).

Certainly few ministers of the first or succeeding generations possessed all of these characteristics. Those that were strong on some points were weak on others. For instance, T. C. Anderson wrote of Thomas Calhoun that he "was a man of strong passions and prejudices, and, when excited, his judgement was sometimes unconsciously biased." [11] Y. H. Hamilton, who had to contend with the rowdiness of life in Texas after the Civil War, once horse-whipped and ordered from town a bully who had abused an elderly minister by leading him through the village by his beard. On another occasion Hamilton reportedly "drew his gun" and held it on some ruffians throughout his sermon to prevent their carrying out a threat to break up the meeting.[12] Other examples could be given illustrating lack of humility or of other ideal characteristics. Some ministers in many denominations in the nineteenth century were argumentative, even belligerent, in presenting and defending their particular views. Some Cumberland Presbyterian preachers got involved in bitter disputes, sometimes with ministers in their own denomination, over secular as well as religious matters. In a few cases ministers were reprimanded or even deposed by their presbyteries for wrongdoing. Such limitations illustrate the frailty of human nature. They are remarkable *because* they were short of the ideal, and their recounting has been used by church writers to stress the importance of the ideal.

On the question of an educated ministry the Church was divided throughout the nineteenth century. Most of those ministers and members who wrote on the subject favored literary and theological education. The General Assembly, as the decades went by, became ever more insistent that the presbyteries enforce the educational requirements for ordination. Occasionally, however, opposition to or distrust of education appeared in the press. Most evidence of laxity came from the proponents of learning, as they described the practices which they decried. Both positions, as paradoxical as it may seem, were handed down by the church fathers in differing interpretations of their experiences. In his history of the Church (1888), B. W. McDonnold, a vehement defender of education, pointed to these conflicting interpretations in listing three errors he believed had prevailed in the Church:

One, [is] in overlooking "aptness to teach" and spirituality, which neither education nor the lack of it can ever supply. Another is in attributing the wonderful spiritual power of Calhoun and his associates to their lack of education. If lack of collegiate education gives this wonderful spiritual power, why is it that all the army of uneducated ministers in our church, and in other churches, to-day do not have it? The third error is in calling Ewing and

Donnell and their comrades uneducated men, and holding up their example as an excuse for laziness and stupidity, as, alas! so many of our presbyteries have done. True, these men were not graduates of any college, and what scholarship they had was not obtained according to regulation methods, but for all that they were educated men and profound thinkers. . . . They availed themselves of all the facilities in their reach. They carried text-books in their saddle-bags and studied at night. They studied men, and profoundly studied their English Bibles. Most that colleges do for men is to teach them how to think; these men had that lesson, no matter how they obtained it. Between these men and the lazy boy of to-day who has it in his power to secure a college education and will not do it, there is no similarity at all, and their example is a rebuke rather than an apology to all such.[13]

The founders of the Church, relaxing the Westminster Confession's standard of education, opened the door for the opponents of education. It is quite clear, however, that they were not opposed to education. In the organizational meeting in 1813, members of Cumberland Synod adopted a statement explaining their position. They were persuaded, they stated, "that God has and does call many to preach the Gospel who have no knowledge of the original languages [Hebrew and Greek], and who have been and are eminently useful in their profession." Therefore, they regarded a *classical* education "as not being *absolutely* essential," although they recommended it. There would be, then, "some learned and some *less* learned preachers. . . ." [14]

The Church was slow to provide opportunity for its ministerial candidates to acquire formal literary and scientific or theological education. Some presbyteries established, with varying degrees of success, presbyterial libraries for use by candidates. In 1826 Cumberland College was founded; however, few candidates attended and it had no theological department, although President F. R. Cossitt and others gave some lectures on theology. Even after several schools and colleges were in operation and some institutions had theological departments, most candidates got their education informally. In the early days some of them no doubt acquired very little learning, but, as McDonnold said of that first generation, they acquired the kind of education they needed for their missionary tasks.

Some of the early ministers were almost entirely self-educated. Robert Donnell's biographer wrote of him that:

He was not educated, in the popular acceptation of that term, but by self-directed mental labor, he became a respectable English scholar, and his Biblical knowledge was very profound, . . . his mother taught him the shorter Catechism of the Presbyterian church, before he was seven years old, and caused him to read the Bible through four times before he reached his twelfth year. When a boy, plowing in the field, he carried his book in his pocket, and when his horse required rest, he employed the time in reading. His leisure moments, by day and night, were devoted to mental culture; and when he set out upon his circuit as a preacher, he carried his books in his saddle-bags, and read and studied in the morning and evening, as well as while riding from one appointment to another. He also had the head of his cane so constructed as to furnish an inkstand, and when a thought occurred, while riding, worthy of preservation, it was reduced to writing.[15]

In another form of the "saddlebags" school the young man aspiring to become a preacher accompanied a minister on the circuit and to camp meetings—observing, assisting, and studying. At about the age of seventeen, in the mid-1820s, Silas Newton Davis was converted under the preaching of B. H. Pierson. Davis soon became "impressed to preach," but he was almost entirely without education and there were no schools in the region where he lived, the recently settled Kentucky portion of Jackson's Purchase. Pierson decided to "take him with me on the circuit, and teach him, as I might have opportunity, English Grammar and other things that I deemed important, and that, on becoming a candidate for the ministry, I knew the Presbytery would require him to know." Pierson found him to be an apt pupil with a remarkable memory. Despite Pierson's persuasion, the presbytery rejected Davis when he presented himself as a candidate in the spring of 1827, because of "his awkward appearance, his illiterateness, and . . . his homely costume." Davis then studied with Richard Beard in the fall of that year and was accepted as a candidate in November. With only one summer term of formal schooling, he went on to become a highly respected "doctrinal" preacher.[16] Many young men prepared for candidacy in this manner and continued to study "on the circuit" for licensure and ordination.

Sometimes the "saddlebags" school was combined with the "log cabin" school, or "Log College." In 1821-1822 Finis Ewing and Robert D. Morrow held their "school of the prophets" at New Lebanon, Missouri. Eight or ten candidates studied with them during the winter and accompanied them on preaching tours and at camp meetings during the summer. In 1836 Morrow opened a school at his home in Johnson County, Missouri.[17] David W. McLin, one of the church fathers in Illinois, conducted such a school for candidates, this being the only school available to them. The candidates attended McLin's school in winter and studied "theology from the Bible while on the circuit, with the Holy Spirit as teacher, or with some of the older ministers, while active operations in preaching and camp-meetings were kept up." [18]

Numerous examples could be given of the accomplishments of these "saddlebags" and "log cabin" schools. These practices were continued in some portions of the church up to the Civil War and possibly afterward. Many "graduates" of those schools became outstanding preachers, and some aspired to scholarship. An example of the latter is W. M. Allen, who grew up as an orphan and had probably no more than eleven months of formal schooling.

At the age of about twenty-three he became a candidate for the ministry in Mississippi. He prepared himself by traveling with other preachers, assisting them, and studying the course prescribed for ordination. He went far beyond the basic requirements and "studied Greek, mathematics, philosophy, Hebrew, and literature, carrying textbooks in his saddlebags as he went from appointment to appointment." In 1870 Allen became president of Chapel Hill College in Texas.[19]

The so-called "saddlebags" or "circuit riding" school and the Log College were already widely used methods of ministerial education before the Cumberland Presbyterians adapted them to their particular needs. Since these methods came to be accepted as normal and as especially well-suited to the needs of a pioneer ministry, some suspicions and fears were aroused when the Church started turning to formal education. Critics of college training in liberal arts and theology usually said that the Church needed *some* highly educated ministers—*"but."* The editor of the *Revivalist* wrote in 1833:

We know that learning, in the fullest sense of the word, is far from disqualifying a man to preach the gospel to an ignorant people. But are the preachers who are capable of measuring by an elevated standard in literary attainments, most ready to repair to those neighborhoods, where the people assemble to worship God in an *old* school-house, or in an *old* shell of a meeting-house, in which they sit on rough slab benches, and where there is little prospect of pecuniary reward for ministerial services? [20]

The 1835 General Assembly's Committee on the State of Religion revealed the mixed feelings prompted by the education question:

The sentiments of your people . . . on . . . improving your ministry in literature and theology, raise . . . mingled emotions of hope and fear. There is ground to hope that the facilities of your Church will soon present a host of intelligent and learned ministers, with the Lord at their right-hand, who will, unmoved, withstand the combined forces of infidelity; and, yet, there is ground to fear that high intellectual improvement, not directed in the proper channel, will be the occasion for many forgetting the bold arm of Israel's strength, vainly to trust in the arm of the flesh.[21]

During the 1840s and 1850s the General Assembly increasingly favored the education of ministers and urged presbyteries to enforce the standards of the Confession. Discussion of the question continued in the church papers. Writing for the *Banner of Peace* in 1846, Robert Donnell stated that a "suitable portion" of the ministers should:

. . . compare with any others in solid learning; but it is not necessary that all her ministers have the same portion of education to be useful members of the same ministerial body. —This was the opinion of the fathers and founders of the Cumberland Presbyterian church; and this is the standard they have left us; and from this standard the church should never be driven; not alone because it was the sentiment of our fathers; but because it is the language of common sense and of the Bible.

Donnell believed that a schism could be avoided if each group (the less educated and the more educated) recognized the importance of the other.[22] In responding to Donnell's comments, F. R. Cossitt, the *Banner of Peace* editor, agreed that the standards should not be too high or too low, and that those who favored more ministerial education did not advocate raising the standards in the Confession of Faith. He insisted, however, that presbyteries should know that God does not call a man who "is contented with ignorance or can indulge in indolence." [23] In the following year Donnell showed he was not opposed to more ministerial education by supporting the establishment of a theological department at Cumberland University and urging presbyteries, congregations, and individuals to aid candidates by sending them there or to some other good college.[24]

The Rev. David Lowry, noting that some men associated pride with an educated ministry, wrote in 1849: "For my part I am afraid of ignorance producing pride. At least I have not a very high opinion of that humility which is based on ignorance." [25] The Rev. Felix G. Black wrote a year later: "God has never sanctified ignorance, or consecrated it to his service. . . ." [26] The most frequently used argument of the advocates of an educated ministry was the necessity of "keeping up with the times": ministers could not defend the gospel unless they were as well-educated as the "purveyors of infidelity."

Throughout the century there were presbyteries where no more than lip service was given to even the minimum educational standards of the Confession of Faith. Such implied opposition to an educated ministry was largely silent and submerged, surfacing only in writings of its critics and in the reports of General Assembly committees. The published argument was really between two groups which favored more education but differed on urgency and emphasis. They apparently did not quite trust each other. Those less eager to promote advanced learning regarded education as secondary to spirituality and therefore not essential, though helpful under certain conditions. With some exceptions, they were not college trained. They identified with the church fathers and feared that the ministry was losing the zeal and piety of earlier years. Viewing the role of the Cumberland Presbyterian Church as still missionary and its method as revivalistic, they judged the ministry by the effectiveness of its "Holy Ghost" preaching as evidenced by the salvation of lost souls. One of them, writing in 1855, claimed to advocate a golden mean between the extremes of requiring a classical education for all preachers and of having little regard for learning. In actuality, he gave much more attention to the dangers of learning than to the dangers of ignorance. New moral truths, he said, cannot be discovered through worldly wisdom. "Religion is not dependent upon learning, but learning principally dependent upon religion; and should ever be subservient." Errors spring from a corruption of the simplicity of the gospel and "Learning serves as well to establish error as truth." That class of ministers who depended on learning, he believed, were much less effective than those who depended on Christ. Sanctified learning was good, but:

Are there not signs in our own church that, with some, learning is being substituted for religion, form for power? The aggregate of learning in the Cumberland Presbyterian church is, probably, double what it was fifteen years ago. But can she boast of a similar increase in pure heart-felt religion, burning zeal and all-melting, moving, prevailing prayer and preaching? Alas! it is believed by many that much of her zeal and life have departed. These, in many instances have surrendered the pulpit, the press and the congregation, to polite learning, logic and rhetoric. What a contrast between the ministry of twenty-five years ago and the ministry now! [27]

Members of the other group did not deny the primary importance of spirituality, but they believed that education was *essential* to the work of the ministry. Generally college trained, they stressed both liberal arts and theological education as necessary for the ministry of a settled church. Revivalistic preaching was still important, but the Church needed more and more professionally trained ministers who could serve as full-time pastors and help manage church enterprises. Milton Bird said that a man could not preach with inspiration *without study;* that is, God inspires only those who are prepared. "Ignorance," Bird insisted, "is the mother of superstition, not devotion. It is not the nourishment, but the poison of piety." [28] Those suspicious of learning tended to equate the decline of "Holy Ghost" preaching and revivalism with a decline in the Church as they saw "form" replacing "spiritual power." The aggressive proponents of education believed the Church was endangered *because of* the lack of men prepared to "refute error" and to lead and train the Church in such necessary forms as Sunday schools and systematic benevolence.

After the Civil War the group favoring more education became increasingly influential in the Church's higher councils. A survey of General Assembly deliverances reveals their progress. The 1865 Assembly recommended that:

No Presbytery should set apart any man to the work of the ministry, whatever may be his piety, or however churches may petition for his ordination, if he has not fully attained both in the spirit and the letter, to that degree of mental culture which is required by the Form of Government and Discipline of the . . . Church; and which is so necessary to place him abreast of the present age, and make him a workman that needeth not to be ashamed.[29]

Assembly statements continued to hedge, but pressure for an unequivocal commitment mounted. The revised Constitution, approved overwhelmingly by the presbyteries, was declared adopted in 1883. It declared as *indispensable* for ordination satisfactory examination on geography, English grammar, philosophy, astronomy, ecclesiastical history, the Holy Scriptures, natural and revealed theology, and the Government of the Cumberland Presbyterian Church. In addition, it "earnestly recommended that the Presbyteries . . . promote and encourage . . . the acquiring of a complete knowledge of the original languages, especially the Greek and the Hebrew, the utility of which, to a minister of the Word, is hereby unequivocally declared." [30] The wording is not much different from that of the first Constitution adopted by the Church; however, the emphasis here is upon attainment and conformity to the standards, whereas under the earlier statement it had been possible to emphasize the exceptions permitted.

Some presbyteries continued to license and ordain men who had little learning. According to one critic, older ministers even persuaded young men to leave their studies. He cited the case of a college student who was "stoutly urged by a friend to drop his studies and begin preaching, and was told that he was as ripe for the work as a shock of wheat, and that more study would fry the grease out of him and leave him as dry as a gristle." [31] The General Assembly recognized that some presbyteries violated the rule and in 1892 attempted to enforce conformity by adopting this preamble and resolution presented by the Committee on Education:

WHEREAS, The Constitution of our Church (page 101, section 56) prescribes the standard of literary attainment to be reached by licentiates preparatory to ordination, and emphatically states that a knowledge of the branches of literature therein enumerated is indispensable to ordination; and whereas, it is the habit of many of our Presbyteries to disregard often this requirement . . . and, by laying hands on men who have not reached the standard required, thrust into the ranks of the ministry incompetent men; therefore

*Resolved*, That we recommend to this General Assembly that it instruct the Synods under its jurisdiction to make more careful observations of the work of Presbyteries touching this matter, and where Presbyteries are found acting in violation of this law of the Church to administer to them a severe reprimand, and, if this fails to correct the evil, to proceed to dissolve said Presbyteries and distribute their ministers and Churches among other presbyteries according to the wisdom of the Synod so acting.[32]

This position was reaffirmed several times before 1900. In 1896 the Assembly's Committee on Education began calling attention to presbyteries which it said were lax in enforcing the constitutional requirements for ordination. It listed seven such presbyteries in 1896, eight in 1897, five in 1898, and five in 1899. The Assembly kept calling on synods to see that presbyteries followed the standards; however, it failed to support Arkansas Synod's censure of Porter Presbytery for ordaining a candidate although not fully satisfied with his educational qualifications.[33]

While the continuing debate over the desirability of an educated ministry went on, there was real progress in providing the means of formal theological training. One of the earliest ambitions of the trustees and other supporters of Cumberland University was to provide adequate theological as well as liberal arts education for prospective ministers. For about twenty years there had been sporadic consideration of establishing a theological school or department for the Church. In providing for Cumberland College the 1825 Synod resolved to annex a theological department. Foreseeing lack of funds at first, it suggested that the trustees appoint ministers to prepare lectures on theology to be read to the students.[34] The second General Assembly (1830) decided that the establishment of a theological department was inexpedient at that time. In this matter, as in many others, there was a widespread fear of centralization. The 1834 Assembly asked the synods and presbyteries to consider the expediency of establishing a theological school and to say whether they preferred several presbyterial and synodical schools or one institution under the Assembly. To this request, Indiana Presbytery responded by resolving that "one school would be safer than many, and at this time *none* would be better than any." [35] Actually, a majority of the presbyteries reporting their action to the next Assembly favored a central school, but about half sent in no report at all. That Assembly at first determined to go ahead with plans to set up a school or department but decided not to do so.[36]

During the 1830s and early 1840s a few young Cumberland Presbyterians attended the theological school at Princeton University (New Jersey). Some of their elders feared that they would be led astray by their Presbyterian teachers, and one of them, W. A. Scott, did leave the Cumberland Presbyterian Church—but this reportedly was for financial rather than theological reasons.[37] The desire of increasing numbers of young men for theological training and the prospect that they would go east to Andover, Lane, or Princeton seminaries stimulated a new general discussion of the question in the late 1840s. Beginning in 1846, President T. C. Anderson of Cumberland University and successive pastors of the Lebanon church (Robert Donnell and David Lowry) delivered theological lectures to candidates,[38] but this was no satisfactory substitute for a regular department. Richard Beard, F. R. Cossitt, Robert Donnell, and Thomas Calhoun were leaders among those supporting the establishment of a theological school. Calhoun probably was the author of a series of articles promoting the idea published in the *Banner of Peace* in March 1848.[39] The 1848 Assembly appointed a committee, with

Donnell as chairman, to poll the presbyteries on the proposal to establish such a school, to invite propositions as to its location, and to prepare a plan and suggest ways and means.

The replies of the presbyteries went to Donnell, who did not attend the 1849 Assembly and did not send a report on responses. Upon information from other sources, however, the committee concluded that a large majority of the presbyteries desired a theological school. Therefore, it recommended the establishment of a school or schools under the jurisdiction of the General Assembly. It suggested that schools be set up at both Cumberland College and Cumberland University to prevent antagonisms between the friends of each. By a close vote (thirty-nine to thirty-seven) the Assembly turned down the proposal to establish two schools. After extended debate, substitute resolutions, presented in a "spirit of conciliation," were adopted with only a few dissenting votes. These left the question open somewhat, stating that the Assembly was in favor of a school or schools and inviting the trustees of both institutions to create endowments for theological departments under the patronage of the Assembly.[40]

At the 1850 Assembly the Board of Trustees of Cumberland University reported its approval of the plan for theological schools. A revision in the charter had been secured to give the General Assembly power to approve appointments to the Board of Trustees. The endowment agent had been authorized to accept donations for a theological professorship as soon as the Assembly and the university trustees completed the plans. Cumberland College gave no official report, but President Beard said that its trustees favored the plan. The Assembly thereupon appointed a committee of seven, including the presidents of both the institutions, to perfect plans for the theological departments.[41]

The committee was unable to meet during the ensuing year because of an outbreak of cholera and for other reasons, so it was continued by the 1851 Assembly. But before the 1852 meeting an unexpected development spread dismay among the forces which had been working so hard for the theological school. West Tennessee Synod, under whose control Bethel College only recently had been organized, announced intention to add a theological department there and to appeal to the whole Church for support. Not only did this appear designed to undermine the other prospects, but there also was controversy over the soundness of the theological position of Reuben Burrow, the first professor of theology at Bethel. The effect of West Tennessee Synod's action seems to have been to stimulate the General Assembly's project as sentiment grew in favor of only one theological school, under Assembly control.[42]

The plan finally presented to the 1852 Assembly was quite comprehensive.

As amended and adopted by the Assembly, it provided for the possibility of establishing two departments, with carefully worded safeguards to ensure General Assembly control over selection of professors and curricula. However, the committee recommended setting up only one department for the time being, and the Assembly selected Lebanon as the location. Since President Richard Beard of Cumberland College acted as chairman of the committee and there was recorded no opposition, it appears that the Cumberland College forces agreed with this plan. As for the West Tennessee Synod project, "severe resolutions of condemnation" were presented "and after hot discussion were in a fair way to pass" until the Assembly was warned that their passage "would be the signal for the secession of West Tennessee Synod." The Assembly contented itself with asking all lower church courts to cooperate with the department at Cumberland University.[43]

On June 15, 1852, the university trustees adopted a resolution establishing a Theological Department, but there was considerable delay in getting it actually in operation. The professorship was offered first to F. R. Cossitt, but he declined. The trustees then selected Richard Beard, who accepted after much deliberation. The 1853 General Assembly approved Beard's appointment, but it was not until March 13, 1854, that he was inaugurated as professor of systematic theology. Although the trustees had appointed agents to raise an endowment, progress was slow and citizens of Lebanon paid Beard's salary at first.[44]

The Theological Department became firmly established, but it grew slowly. Beard was the only professor until 1860, when Benjamin W. McDonnold was added to the faculty. Enrollment reached nine regular and eleven "irregular" students that year. ("Irregular" students evidently were those registered in another department but taking some theological courses.) In addition, several other ministerial candidates attended theological lectures. Beard wrote volumes on systematic theology for basic texts for his course. Besides systematic theology, he taught classes in Greek and Hebrew. Before McDonnold joined the faculty, Beard was assisted by President Anderson, members of the Literary Department, and successive pastors of the church in Lebanon.[45] By 1860 the Theological Department endowment (on paper) was $45,000, but it was not very productive.[46]

The General Assembly and the trustees of the university were committed to providing candidates for the ministry with free literary and theological education. Several families of Lebanon provided free board for some of them,[47] but there were others who could not attend because of the expense of living away from home. In response to this need, Beard proposed to the 1854 Assembly the formation of an organization to aid them. Beard, Isaac Shook, David Lowry, H. A. Hill, and R. L. Caruthers were appointed a committee to prepare plans for such an organization. On the basis of the committee's report, the 1855 Assembly organized an Educational Society to raise money to aid needy ministerial candidates while they were in school. At the suggestion of R. C. Ewing, the Society also was asked to get from the heads of the Church's schools and colleges the names of qualified students who wished to teach school. This would help people find teachers for common schools and academies. The teacher placement plan did not work out, but some progress was made toward raising endowment for the Society to use in supporting the "young men."

The struggling Theological Department was struck down by war along with the rest of Cumberland University. In the reconstruction of the university economic necessity required that attention be given first to the College of Arts and the Law School, since those departments had the better chance of attracting students and would be largely self-supporting. Beard worked with President Anderson in reopening the College of Arts immediately after the war. Soon the Theological Department was reopened with Beard and others devoting part of their time to it. A gradual increase in endowment and other support soon made it possible for Beard to resume full attention to the department and for other professorships to be added. The General Assembly of 1885 encouraged wide support for the Theological Department by directing its own Board of Education to appoint an endowment agent. Previously the Cumberland University Board had had that responsibility. The new approach called attention to the fact that the school operated under the authority of and therefore was the responsibility of the entire Church. By 1898 substantial progress had been made; the Theological Seminary (as it came to be called) had a faculty of seven with sixty students enrolled. Many ministerial students in the College of Arts attended some of the lectures. At the century's close the endowment was over $80,000.[48]

Although the Theological Seminary at Cumberland University was the only one sanctioned and supported by the entire denomination, other institutions provided some theological instruction. Trinity University maintained a regular Theological Department, while others arranged for lectures in theology to be given to their ministerial students. Presbyteries and synods frequently provided special means for the education of their candidates who could not attend regular institutions. An example was the "Synodical Training School" set up by Pacific Synod in the late 1870s. Students lived in dormitories at San Jose, California, where they studied under a Committee of Instruction created by the synod.[49] There was some dissatisfaction with the location of the Theological Seminary at Cumberland University and also with the teachings of some of its professors, but the General Assembly turned down every proposal to move the school or to create a Bible institute entirely separate from any other educational institution. It first supported and then decided against a plan for starting another theological school to be in Chicago; however, it gave moral support to the efforts of Illinois Synod to do so.[50]

In several ways church members and institutions gave material aid to ministerial students. Customarily, church colleges required them to pay only nominal fees or no fees at all. In addition, they received assistance in meeting living costs. The basic responsibility for such aid lay with the presbytery, and many presbyteries met this responsibility in whole or in part. There were many candidates who could get an education only if support came from elsewhere.

Before the war the citizens of Lebanon had given free boarding to candidates for the ministry attending Cumberland University. After the war they were unable to continue this practice. Also, the war had brought to an end the Educational Society which had aided some students. At the suggestion of T. C. Blake, in 1868 an old boarding house with adjoining buildings was bought to house ministerial students attending Cumberland University. Congregations in the surrounding area contributed foodstuffs for meals. This "Camp Blake" provided living accommodations of from fifty to seventy young men for several years. In 1873 or 1874 three of the students died of typhoid. The remaining young men were moved out to board temporarily in private homes. Soon thereafter the Camp Blake project was abandoned and other means of housing and boarding ministerial students were adopted.[51]

Realizing the need for central encouragement and coordination of aid to the education of ministerial candidates, the General Assembly in 1881 resolved to establish a Board of Education to be located at Nashville, Tennessee. Though chartered soon thereafter, for several years the Board made little progress. By May 1886, it had received only $219.63 and aided only three students. By 1889 significant progress had been achieved, and during the 1890s it assisted by grants and/or loans between 100 and 150 students annually. Most of those aided were in preparatory schools and liberal arts colleges. Some were in the Theological Seminary. The Board was reorganized as the Educational Society in 1895. In addition to aiding ministerial students directly, the Board or Society raised endowment for the Theological Seminary for a while and paid the salary of one of the professors. It constantly urged presbyteries to encourage and help their probationers to get an education. In the 1890s it recommended a rather comprehensive six-year course of study for those who could not attend college or seminary. Many presbyteries adopted the course for their candidates and licentiates.[52]

The commitment of the General Assembly and a growing number of presbyteries and of members to the ideal of an educated ministry was bringing about real progress. Yet in the last decade of the century the overall picture and prospects were not very bright. In 1895 the Board of Education reported on the results of questionnaires sent to presbyteries asking for information on all of the 525 candidates and licentiates in the Church. Based on replies from eighty-four presbyteries, which were responsible for about two-thirds of the probationers, the Board estimated that only about 225 of the total were in school. Some were in the primary grades, some were in preparatory schools, and others were in college. The presbyterial clerks reporting indicated that thirty of the probationers did not want an education and that several of the others probably could not benefit from further schooling. About 85 per cent of those wanting education needed assistance to get it. Nearly half of the probationers reported on were married and many were doing "secular" work, mostly farming.[53]

First-generation Cumberland Presbyterian ministers and members established a tradition of inadequate support for the Church. This was manifest especially in the failure to pay the preachers. Some of the factors bringing this about can be identified: (1) On the frontier where the early preachers worked, money was very scarce; few church members had cash to contribute. (2) Even after the frontier stage Cumberland Presbyterian ministers worked mostly in rural areas among farmers with small incomes. (3) Many nineteenth century Americans had inherited a distrust of "ecclesiasticism"; they feared that a paid and professionalized clergy not only would assume too much authority over doctrine and worship but also would be parasites on the people. (4) The early preachers set an example of saying nothing to anybody about pay of any kind; consequently, the membership tended to be suspicious of anyone who appeared to be "out for the money." (5) The early pattern of "missionating," itinerancy or circuit riding, and camp meetings—in short, the lack of a settled ministry with a permanent relationship with congregations—made support of the preachers everybody's responsibility and, therefore, nobody's responsibility.[54]

McDonnold, with hundreds of records before him, concluded that of the early itinerants or circuit riders about one-third received no pay at all and one-third received "some socks" and up to twenty dollars a year. Of the remaining one-third, none received more than eighty dollars a year.[55] A few specific examples will illustrate the situation. In 1824 Robert Sloan formed a new circuit in Saint Charles and Montgomery counties, Missouri. For six months' preaching he received *"one three-cornered, white, cotton cravat."* [56] James McDowell, as a licentiate in Logan Presbytery, recorded in his journal that from April 20 to November 12, 1826, "I rode one thousand and thirty-eight miles; preached one hundred and sixty-one times. . . . I received by way of remuneration $27.25; my expenses, $3.62." [57] Apparently, McDowell was housed and fed free by church members or others on his circuit, as was the almost universal custom. William Calhoun Love, as a licentiate assigned to a circuit in West Tennessee in the early 1830s, during a six-month period traveled 1,620 miles, preached 150 sermons, and received $1.50 compensation.[58] In sending out intinerants, presbyteries rarely provided them with an income. Occasionally a presbyterial missionary society had some funds, but these were used to help finance "missionating" tours rather than regular circuit riding. Presbyteries did call upon congregations and the people to pay preachers on the circuit and at camp meetings. Sangamon Presbytery, for instance, in 1829 recommended that each neighborhood or congregation raise funds to pay preachers sent by presbytery to preach to them—"say $1.00 per day." [59]

In the early days ministers who preached regularly for settled congregations usually received little or no pay. "It was not expected that men who did not travel would be paid anything for preaching." This was true in the longer-settled areas as well as on the frontier. Robert D. King preached two years in Middle Tennessee in the 1830s and received no compensation at all from the people to whom he ministered.[60]

The itinerancy system had worked so well during the Church's first two decades that many ministers and members became committed to it, even coming "to think that pastorates were invented by self-seeking men who dreaded the hardships of an itinerant life and wanted big salaries." [61] The opposition to pastorates probably reached its height in 1830 when the General Assembly considered the advisability of removing from the Form of Government the chapter which provided for a pastoral relationship between minister and congregation and which referred to the pastoral office as the most important in the church. Such action, it was proposed, "would be for the honor of religion and the mutual affection of preachers and people." The Assembly, however, had second thoughts, recognizing that if that provision were removed, there would be no security for any minister who became pastor of a congregation. So, instead, it proposed replacing the chapter with a statement which would *permit* the pastoral relationship when it did not interfere with arrangements of presbyteries in assigning "supplies." The proposal was voted down by the presbyteries thirteen to two, with three not reporting.[62] Several years passed, however, before the Assembly came out with a strong statement favoring pastorates, and for decades the Church was divided on the question.

In the 1820s and 1830s some contracts were made between "pastors" and congregations. In most instances these did not establish a true pastoral relationship, since they normally provided for preaching only and usually just part-time. The practice developed of one preacher becoming the "pastor" for two, three, or even four different congregations. Full-time equivalent salaries were about $200 to $400 per year. Quite often congregations defaulted on even such low commitments.

With more and more congregations being without adequate preaching and teaching and even without regular sacramental services, increasing emphasis was placed on the importance of the pastoral system and paying ministers. Thomas Calhoun and other fathers publicly regretted not having taught the importance of "supporting the gospel." [63] In a sermon published in 1836 Finis Ewing said the lack of support of the ministry was a sin of omission and presented the scriptural basis and the necessity of giving.[64] The growing concern was reflected in the 1836 Assembly's recommendation to presbyteries and congregations to encourage pastoral relations when practicable, "as the Scriptural and best mode to water and build up the Church—to render her existence permanent." [65]

Until the Civil War there remained some tension between the commitment to itinerancy and the need for pastors. Each General Assembly call for more attention to settled pastorates was accompanied by a disclaimer of any intent to undermine the itinerant system. Several arguments supporting itinerancy were presented in the General Assembly and in the church press: (1) It was sanctioned by the example of Christ and the Apostles. (2) It was well adapted to plant new and supply feeble congregations over extensive areas, especially in new states and territories. (3) A term of itinerancy was excellent training for young ministers, adding practical experience to their academic education. (4) It was the best means for promoting the revival spirit among the churches. (5) It was a method of employing the services of all the preachers in ministerial work.

Despite these arguments, itinerancy declined except on the frontier. As in the case of "Holy Ghost" preaching, many Cumberland Presbyterians began to idealize itinerancy as an important element in an earlier "Golden Age" of the Church. This attitude is reflected in the 1848 Assembly's resolution urging presbyteries to resume the plan of "itinerant ministrations, as we deem it a most effective instrumentality in restoring the former energy, zeal, and life that so much characterized the earlier years of our beloved Church." [66]

As circuit riding was used less and less as a means of training licentiates and "supplying" churches, presbyteries began appointing special "evangelists" or "missionaries" to preach within presbyterial bounds. Sometimes the purpose was to promote some special cause; however, it usually was to encourage spiritual revival. A few ministers became professional revivalists, operating usually under the auspices of a presbytery or synod. A minister assigned to such a missionary task would lay out and publish a schedule, including appearances at as many congregations within presbyterial bounds as possible. Several such published schedules in the Middle Tennessee area during the late 1840s show average tours lasting twenty-five days with twenty-six sermons delivered at twenty-five different locations. This pattern of preaching was continued in many presbyteries through the latter half of the century. In some cases ministers were assigned to longer missionary tours. For example, J. M. Philips, a missionary for Saint Louis Presbytery, reported in 1877 that he had traveled 1,239 miles, preached 105 sermons, visited 10 counties, and preached to all but one of the congregations in the presbytery. He did not give the time covered, but it was probably the six months since the previous meeting of presbytery.[67]

After the 1836 Assembly statement positively favoring the pastoral system, later Assemblies and writers presented numerous arguments: (1) Since many ministers, because of poverty or family obligations, could not become itinerant preachers, they were almost useless as ministers. Congregations should support them and put them to work as pastors. (2) The system would enable the minister to read and study and to prepare better sermons. (3) A pastor could devote much of his time to promoting piety and education of young people and to home visiting, personal conversations, and prayer with individuals and families. (4) A pastor, as a presbyter, would help in the governing of the local church. (5) Pastors were necessary to build up and maintain churches organized by missionaries. (6) The ministry was a profession and ministers should be able to work at their profession and get paid; the ministry should not be regarded as a public charity.

In response to the increasingly favorable sentiment, the General Assemblies placed greater emphasis on the pastoral system. The 1843 Assembly prescribed procedures for electing and installing pastors and approved an installation ceremony. A committee report adopted in 1868 noted that the Form of Government stated that the "pastoral office is first in the Church, both for dignity and usefulness." By 1882 the pastoral system was coming to be regarded with much the same hope inspired by itinerancy thirty or forty years earlier. That year the Assembly adopted this statement, prepared by a committee: "It will infuse new life into your ministry, and inspire many of your weak, dispirited churches with confidence; it will bring the churches into closer sympathy with each other, bind them more strongly together, and its good results will no doubt be felt in every department of your work."[68]

Despite the denominational leaders' encouragement of pastorates and better pay, progress was slow. Pennsylvania Presbytery was exceptional; in 1833 all twelve of its ordained ministers were "living of the gospel." McDonnold, writing in the late 1880s, said no other presbyterial records showed such an instance; in fact, in some presbyteries none of the preachers had ever been fully supported. He attributed the strong support of pastors and missions by Cumberland Presbyterians in Pennsylvania to their Presbyterian training and background.[69] The same influence was exerted in Indiana and Illinois, but to a much lesser extent. Indiana Presbytery did not have its first installed pastor until 1844. In 1859 it had only two or three, and there was no increase during the next twenty years.[70] When the Rev. James B. Logan entered Illinois in 1853, there was not a congregation in the state wholly sustaining a pastor. All ten of the ministers present at an 1854 session of Vandalia Presbytery were receiving a combined total of less than $500 per year for their ministerial services. In 1876 at least eight ordained ministers in that presbytery were devoting full time to the ministry; the presbytery then had sixteen ordained ministers and one licentiate who were paid a total of $4,542 as pastors and supplies. An example of the progress of one of the more successful ministers in Illinois is the career of J. R. Lowrance. In 1845-1846 he supplied two congregations at a salary of $160 per year. In 1847 he was installed as pastor of Stouts Grove congregation, with a salary of $200 and board. Twenty years later, in April 1867, he became full-time pastor of the Union congregation, Lincoln, Illinois, at $600 and in December the same year moved to Danvers where he received $1,000 per year.[71]

REUBEN BURROW
(1798-1868)

J. B. LOGAN
(1820-1878)

The situation was worse in other areas. It was reported to the April 1850 session of Oxford Presbytery (Mississippi) that four of the eleven congregations within presbyterial bounds had lost organization "for the want of suitable attention" and that the members were without regular preaching and sacraments. Three other congregations were supplied with preaching only once a month and the remaining four twice a month. Of the nine ministers in the presbytery, one no longer preached because of illness and four others had no regular charges and preached rarely. In characteristic fashion, the presbytery appointed the Rev. S. G. Burney as a "missionary" to preach to the "destitute" portions of the presbytery.[72] Similar situations existed in many areas for decades. In the 1880s McDonnold gave statistics for one of the largest and most central presbyteries as an "average sample" of conditions throughout the Church. He said it had a total of forty ministers: three entirely supported by their congregations; two devoting full time to the ministry, whether supported or not; six engaged in church work under church boards; and twenty-eight secularized (earning their living in nonchurch work) although preaching on the Sabbath and getting a little pay.[73]

The "secularization" of the ministry, closely connected with inadequate pay, was another practice begun by the fathers of the Church. Most of them were farmers; some were teachers; others engaged in trades or business pursuits. A few had property enough to sustain them, so they were able to devote more time to the ministry. They labored with their hands "after the manner of the apostle," so that they "might not be chargeable to the churches." [74] Later generations of ministers followed in the footsteps of the "old men," but not always by choice. A sketch of the life of Hiram A. Hunter, published in 1883 shortly after his death, illustrates the versatility of some ministers. As a pioneer preacher in the Midwest during the 1820s and 1830s, Hunter had engaged in many secular activities.

His education had fitted him for both teacher and preacher, and his knowledge of medicine gave him calls to serve as a physician, which he did with a good degree of success. As a carpenter he built several houses for his own residences; as shoemaker he made shoes for his family; as a saddler he made his own saddles, saddle bags, and harness, and for three years he managed, though he did but little of the work upon a farm. All this was done without seriously interfering with his preaching.[75]

The last sentence says as much about the writer's view of the ministry as it does about Hunter's work.

The 1878 General Assembly's Committee on the State of Religion noted that hundreds of ministers were employed in secular work while hundreds of congregations were without pastors or were poorly supplied with preaching. In 1885 and 1886 proposals to set up an agency to bring unemployed ministers and vacant congregations together were presented but were not carried out. The 1891 Assembly appointed the Rev. M. Lowe as pastoral supply agent for one year to handle applications from ministers and congregations. His report in 1892 indicated that there was not enough interest or encouragement to warrant continuing the service. The century ended with the General Assembly still encouraging the establishment of pastorates and more pay for ministers, but with discouraging results.

In its growing concern with the economic welfare of ministers, the Church also became concerned with the plight of disabled or aged ministers and their dependents. In 1833 the General Assembly learned that one of the founders, Samuel McAdow, was "old and afflicted, and in circumstances quite necessitous." [76] For several years the Assembly raised money to help support him. It also provided the means of buying a small farm for the support of the widow and children of David McLin.

Various Assemblies called upon synods and presbyteries to see that afflicted or aged ministers and the families of deceased ministers did not suffer want, and some lower courts did establish organizations and procedures for their relief. In 1881, on authorization of the Assembly, a Board of Ministerial Relief was formed and chartered in the state of Indiana. Although it had

THORNTON HOME, EVANSVILLE, INDIANA

difficulty in getting general support and cooperation from the Church, the Board gradually built up its work. During the 1890s it gave aid annually to an average of about ninety individuals and families.[77]

In 1890 the Church realized a long-lasting dream of many of its members with the establishment of a home for aged ministers and the widows and orphans of deceased ministers. With money given by Mrs. E. Thornton of Petersburg, Indiana, a fifteen-room, three-story house with ten acres of land was bought at Evansville, Indiana. The Board of Ministerial Relief assumed control of it and immediately prepared it for occupancy.[78] It was named the Thornton Home in honor of Mrs. Thornton and soon became the residence of ten to fifteen persons ranging from orphaned children to elderly retired ministers.

# 12

## THE HANDMAID OF RELIGION

*Education is pre-eminently the handmaid of religion. No church can accomplish the ends of its creation without the correlative influence of education.*

1855 General Assembly

Between the Revolutionary War and the Civil War all the vast Mississippi Basin region passed through the frontier stage. At the end of that period the western fringe of the midcontinent area still was being peopled by pioneers. Crudity of frontier life was reflected in manners and morals as well as in physical conditions. Practically every portion of the trans-Appalachian West went through a churchless, schoolless, almost lawless stage which left the marks of ignorance, superstition, and intemperance upon communities and many of the people. In fact, the deterioration of manners and morals merely accentuated characteristics already quite prevalent among those in the vanguard of the westward movement. In every community, however, there were a few, mostly church members and ministers, who determined to improve conditions. They were largely responsible for bringing to the frontier the basic elements of "culture," defined by William Warren Sweet as "the enlightenment and discipline acquired as a result of mental and moral training."[1]

The most important religious influences in "civilizing" the frontier were exerted directly through church organizations such as congregations or societies, associations, presbyteries, and conferences. The churches, as organizations and through the independent efforts of members and ministers, also

213

were responsible for the establishment of most of the early schools and colleges. Churches continued to dominate education, especially at the college level, until after the Civil War.[2] As an illustration of this domination, 155 of the 182 "permanent" colleges established in the United States before the Civil War were founded by religious denominations.[3] Many more colleges were founded but lasted only a few years or a few decades, and hundreds of academies, institutes, seminaries, and other types of schools were set up under religious auspices.

Among the major denominations active in the Mississippi Basin, Presbyterians, Congregationalists, and Catholics were most committed to an educated ministry and membership and therefore were leaders in education in areas where they were strong. Baptists, Methodists, and Disciples of Christ, for socioeconomic as well as theological reasons, lagged somewhat but by the late ante-bellum period had entered the field with considerable energy and determination.

Because of the lateness and the circumstances of its origin, the Cumberland Presbyterian Church was among the relatively late entrants into the field of education. It had developed enough organization and self-consciousness, however, to participate fully during the period of greatest church educational activity, that being between 1825 and 1860. In proportion to membership, the Cumberland Presbyterian Church stood between the two groups of denominations mentioned above in educational interest and activity. It was perhaps less active and certainly less successful in founding schools and colleges than were the other Presbyterian, the Congregational, and the Catholic churches, but it was considerably more active, relative to membership, than were the Baptist, the Methodist, and the Disciples of Christ churches. The Cumberland Presbyterian purposes in promoting education were quite similar to those of other Protestant denominations; however, emphasis varied somewhat among the several groups.

The most immediate and the paramount purpose of Cumberland Presbyterians in their educational work was to provide literary and theological training for prospective ministers. Denominational interest was broader than the need for an educated ministry; an educated laity was needed as well. The following excerpt from a report adopted by the 1851 General Assembly not only illustrates the recognition of that need but also reveals a note of denominational pride. The report congratulated the Assembly and the Church

. . . upon its having fallen our lot to develop the character of our youthful denomination at an era whose spirit and genius frowns with a just indignation upon every intimation of opposition to popular education, and an educated ministry; and deprecates, earnestly, the very appearance of indifference to the great enterprise of training, intellectually, the masses of both sexes, and of affording every facility to young men of all the learned professions . . . every facility necessary to the attainment of high literary qualifications of their several stations.

We rejoice to be able to attest, that while the onward spirit of the times demands that the march of mind *in the Church,* keep pace with the intellectual progress of the world, in order that God's people may combat the evils of unsanctified literature and perverted science, and leaven the great masses with a spirit of consecration to the cause of Christ, the Cumberland Presbyterian Church is not—their means being considered—behind the foremost of the Christian Churches in the country, in the liberality and promptness with which they have responded to the demand.[4]

The use of education to promote denominational interests merged with broader religious aims. Education, the 1855 Assembly said, "is pre-eminently the handmaid of religion. No church can accomplish the ends of its creation without the correlative influence of education. . . . The God of Nature is the author of Revelation. Education is the talisman which unfolds the treasures, the mysteries, and the beauties of one, and of the other; of Revelation no less than of . . . Nature."[5] Education which would prepare the individual for life and for eternity would have to be Christian education. As the 1859 Assembly stated:

The education of females as well as males, must be such . . . as advances society in virtue as well as knowledge, and refines the character by purifying the heart and elevating its conceptions and aims.

Self-sufficient education is the parent of skepticism. It is to be deprecated as well as ignorance. . . . Education and religion mutually act and react upon each other. They are so inlocked that they cannot be separated. . . .

. . . . In our view, sanctified education is the most potent auxiliary in the hands of the church for the accomplishment of good and the advancement of man's welfare for time and eternity.[6]

Like many other Protestants of the nineteenth century, Cumberland Presbyterians regarded American institutions as peculiarly Protestant. Republican government, they believed, depended upon a people who had been educated in liberty of conscience and action. Finis Ewing expressed this view in a patriotic sermon delivered in Kentucky in 1814 during the War of 1812. Among the safeguards of liberty, he said, was the diffusion of useful knowledge:

It is necessary that the people, who are sovereign, should well understand their own rights. . . . Ignorance is the support, and main pillar, of either a despotic state or church; but it is *vice versa* as it respects a republic. . . .

. . . It is the interest of Popes and Kings to keep the multitude in ignorance; but it is the glory and strength of a Republic to have her citizens enlightened.[7]

Around midcentury the General Assembly and some individual writers echoed and elaborated on this theme. They not only encouraged the establishment of church schools and colleges but also believed the state should make education available for everyone. The 1849 Assembly, for example, stated that family, pulpit, school, seminary and college, the press, and all governmental branches and agencies "should cooperate to make education and its blessings as diffusive as the light of the sun, as universal as light or water. Away with a monopoly of knowledge." After pointing to the necessity of education for the free individual in a free society, it continued:

The christian and the patriot, the church and the state should cooperate in the cause of education. Each should second the endeavors of the other. . . .
In our view, the only safe palladium of our civil and religious institutions is secured by opening the door of the meeting house, school house, academy and college to every child of the Church and of the State—the child of the poor as well as of the rich—of the mechanic and farmer as well as the merchant and professional man. A people intelligent and virtuous can no more be oppressed than the light of the sun can be turned into darkness.[8]

In supporting "common schools" run by the state, Cumberland Presbyterians assumed that such education would be Christian education. Writing in 1860, the Rev. Milton Bird insisted that "Atheism does not plant the school; Pantheism does not endow the college. No form of infidelity blesses the people with a general school system. The true system of education has its foundation in true religion, and rests upon the Bible as its corner-stone." Therefore, he said, "The relation of religion to the school or college is such as to make it a *religious institution*. There cannot be a right system of education separate from the Bible." [9]

As the public school movement picked up momentum in the post-Civil War period, Cumberland Presbyterian writers gave it wholehearted support. In the period 1875-1900 editors of the *Cumberland Presbyterian* not only advocated more state support for schools but also came out for federal aid to the states for education. Editors and contributors continued to regard education for citizenship and patriotism as the basic purpose of the public schools, but they insisted that moral training was the most important part of preparation for citizenship. They therefore favored required Bible reading as the basis of moral training. These writers also advocated compulsory school attendance. While continuing to regard literary education as essential, they believed the public schools should provide industrial and physical training as well.

During the period 1830-1860 many American Protestants became alarmed at what they believed was a "Romanist" threat to American institutions. Apparently only a few Cumberland Presbyterians were radical anti-Catholics.

But as increasing numbers of Catholics came into the Mississippi Basin in the 1840s and 1850s and expanded their parochial school system, a general fear spread through the Church. A strong anti-Catholic statement was adopted by the 1855 General Assembly on the motion of J. G. White. (White then was a "missionary" in Saint Louis, which had a large Catholic German population. Probably because of his experiences there, he became the most vociferous anti-Catholic in the Cumberland Presbyterian Church.) The statement included a preamble noting the importance of education which includes *"freedom of thought"* and claiming that "Romanist" and Jesuit schools, though ostensibly for education, were actually established to "allure" American Protestant youth and "suppress the freedom of thought and instill into their pure and susceptible minds principles subversive to our civil and religious institutions. . . ." This was followed by resolutions condemning "Romanism," appealing to the church courts and churches to spread education and to circulate the Bible, and requesting that all members refrain from patronizing "Romish" schools—"as they value the institutions of their country and the precious souls of their children." [10]

One other reason for Cumberland Presbyterian activity in education, though personal rather than denominational, deserves mention because it resulted partly from the failure of the churches to pay their preachers. Many ministers turned to teaching, sometimes opening schools themselves, to earn a living. Most of such schools were short-lived, but some of them prospered in accomplishment if not in material benefits to their founders.

The first formal school established by the Cumberland Presbyterian Church was Charity Hall, a mission school opened in 1820 in the Choctaw Nation, Mississippi. During the early 1820s all the presbyteries discussed the possibility of a school for ministerial candidates. These discussions led to the decision of the General Synod to found a college for the entire Church. On October 22, 1825, while in session at Princeton, Kentucky, the Synod resolved to establish Cumberland Presbyterian College for liberal arts training. When funds permitted, a theological department was to be added. The Rev. Franceway Ranna Cossitt, a principal proponent of the college proposal, was familiar with the Fallenberg manual labor plan, which the Synod prescribed. To avoid class distinction, all students (not just those who could not afford to pay cash for board) would be required to work in the college farm two hours daily. The labor plan suited the equalitarian ideas of the church fathers, who also wanted to train a ministry for the rigors of frontier life. Accordingly, the Synod prescribed simplicity and economy in all phases of college life. [11]

The history of the Synod's and the General Assembly's relations with

Cumberland College is a tangled web of misunderstanding, recrimination, frustration, and failure. For nearly twenty years the Church was disturbed by the college question, which became one of the two major crises in the Church before the Civil War. (The other crisis was the dispute over the Rev. James Smith and the church paper.) The delegation named to procure a charter for the college dropped "Presbyterian" from the name, apparently to make it easier to get the charter and also in the hope of securing a broad patronage. This, the Rev. Richard Beard later wrote, "was perhaps the first error which was committed in the management of that ill-fated institution." [12] The charter for "Cumberland College" was issued by the legislature of Kentucky in January 1826. Princeton, Kentucky, pledged $28,000 for the college and was selected as the location. A farm of 400 to 500 acres near Princeton was purchased with borrowed money. On March 1, 1826, the college opened with six students in a large log house on the farm. Cossitt was the first president and apparently for a while the only professor. As enrollment increased other professors were added.

The greatest difficulties over the college were financial—the lack of money and the inability to develop a satisfactory system of fiscal control. The Board of Trustees started with a debt for the farm and buildings. This debt grew inexorably as plan after plan for raising money and managing business affairs failed. A basic handicap was the failure of the people of Princeton to fulfill their pledge. No more than a fourth of the $28,000 ever was paid. Beginning in 1826 the Synod and later the General Assembly sent agents on tours east, south, and west to solicit contributions. Results in cash were almost nil. Pledges and notes were easier to collect, but few of those were paid on schedule, if ever. The agents, usually young ministers, tended to turn to revivalistic preaching as collections for the college lagged. The first such tour was by Albert G. Gibson and Reuben Burrow. From the fall of 1826 through the summer of 1827 they traveled and preached through East Tennessee, through portions of South and North Carolina, and into Virginia. Upon returning and paying over the small sum collected for the college, they were reprimanded for failing to stick to the purpose of their tour and were released from the agency without compensation, although each had had expenses of about seventy-five dollars.[13] Others sent out as agents included Laban Jones, John W. Ogden, Matthew H. Bone, James Smith, and President Cossitt. All had indifferent success. In 1827 a plan to sell "scholarships" at $1,000 each brought in very little, and a request to the Kentucky legislature for a donation of land or loan of money went unheeded. Beard recalled later that the members of the first General Assembly (1829) at one point became so discouraged over the college's financial embarrassment that a recess was called so that all could retire and pray "for light and guidance in their darkness and trouble." This worked, he said, to provide temporary relief.[14]

During the 1830s the financial crisis continued as debts mounted. Two ministers, John Barnett and Aaron Shelby, attempted unsuccessfully to manage the business affairs of the college under a leasing arrangement. Similar efforts by the Cumberland College Association, a joint-stock company, also failed. Meanwhile, intermittent appeals for donations were made to the Church. The 1842 Assembly heard the depressing news from the Cumberland College Association that foreclosure was imminent unless $2,400 in new funds was provided almost immediately. This was the proverbial "last straw." Many of those who had given notes and pledges in the latest endowment drive were at the Assembly. Since the property had not been turned over to a new Board of Trustees free of debt, as they had expected, they considered themselves absolved from payment of their subscriptions. The consequence was a decision to consider moving the college to a new location, a decision prompted partly by an offer from citizens of Lebanon, Tennessee. A commission was set up to receive propositions from any other places (not excepting Princeton), to accept the most desirable offer, to secure incorporation of a board of trustees (if necessary), but not to obligate the Assembly financially "or in any way compromise the good faith and reputation of our Church." [15]

The commission, meeting at Nashville, Tennessee, in July, received bids and accepted that of Lebanon. A remonstrance from Cumberland College Association against the decision was ineffective, and another Cumberland College was chartered and in operation at Lebanon under the presidency of Cossitt before the next General Assembly met. That Assembly was a stormy one. The commission defended its action as being in accordance with instructions. Members of Cumberland College Association opposed the move, claiming the Assembly was legally and morally bound to continue supporting the college at Princeton. By a fairly close vote of thirty-six to twenty-eight the Assembly approved the commission's action and denied any legal connection with the Cumberland College Association.

Despite the high feelings aroused over this question and the controversy over publishing activities, practically all Assembly commissioners were agreed that such difficulties should be avoided in the future. With only six dissenting votes, the following was adopted:

Resolved by this General Assembly, that it would be unwise, impolitic, inexpedient, and contrary to the genius of presbyterian government to enter into any connections of a pecuniary nature giving it the supervision of any literary institution, newspaper, or otherwise become embarrassed by the control of pecuniary matters, so as to give occasion for its moral principle and good faith to be called in question.[16]

Also, Richard Beard, Milton Bird, and other leaders succeeded in an "effort to keep off the meeting of the next Assembly two years, to give time for the passions of men to cool." [17]

One of the ironies of the Cumberland College case was that the college became clear of debt almost immediately after the 1842 Assembly's decision to seek a new location. Only three weeks after the commission had chosen Lebanon, it was announced in the papers that the college at Princeton would continue in operation and that it was free from debt. This "miracle" had been accomplished through sale of the farm and all other property except the college buildings and ten acres of land. Thus ended the manual labor aspect of the college program, a feature which has been regarded by some as a principal source of difficulty.

Cossitt having left to become president of the new college at Lebanon, Richard Beard was called to head the older institution. He was a graduate of Cumberland College and a former teacher there. For several years the college maintained a stable existence with the support of Green River Synod, which in 1845 on invitation assumed the responsibility of appointing members of the Board of Trustees. The 1850 General Assembly offered to assume the same power over appointment of its trustees as it had over Cumberland University, provided the trustees desired it and the charter were amended. There was, quite naturally, no response from the Princeton people. When Beard resigned to become the first professor of theology at Cumberland University in 1853, the Rev. A. J. Baird became president. Within two years enrollment grew from fifty-five to eighty, and prospects were so good that plans were made to move the college to a new campus closer to town. However, a new crisis led to the sudden resignation of Baird in January 1855, and the plan was abandoned. The Rev. Azel Freeman then served as president *pro tempore* until May 1855, when Milton Bird took office. Bird's chief interests were in pastoral and publication work. Apparently he gave inadequate attention to the college, which declined under his administration. In a "last desperate effort" to keep the college going, in 1858 the Board appointed the Rev. H. W. Pierson of the Presbyterian Church as president. The entire school with all assets and liabilities was turned over to Pierson and the two other faculty members for a ten-year period with no strings whatever. This action was approved by Green River Synod. Thus ended Cumberland Presbyterian connection with Cumberland College. The college operated with some success until Pierson left at the end of the 1859-1860 term without even notifying the Board. The final Board meeting was held on January 8, 1861, and the end of Cumberland College was officially recorded.

The direct involvement of the General Synod and the General Assembly in the financial affairs of Cumberland College no doubt contributed to its difficulties. Those bodies also interfered directly in the internal affairs of the school. They prescribed standards for hiring faculty and set up rather strict regulations of behavior of faculty members. The Assembly even required reports from department heads. Student behavior also was closely regulated. All luxuries, such as feather beds, were prohibited and economy was demanded of all. For a while uniform clothing of plain material and style was required of both students and faculty. All students had to work on the farm and, until about 1840, eat in the college dining hall. The Assembly also made specific recommendations or regulations concerning the location and construction of buildings, crops to be planted, vacation periods, and courses to be offered. The Board of Trustees enacted these regulations and supplemented them with other rules such as those forbidding dueling and quarreling, sedentary games and gambling, and the keeping of musical instruments or dogs in dormitory rooms. It is little wonder that there were disciplinary problems. President Cossitt reported that he sometimes received letters threatening his life and that he had to expel some "vicious young men."[18] With the end of the General Assembly's connection with the college and the beginning of Beard's administration, there was a decided change in the atmosphere. "It was," said McDonnold, "like passing out of Mosaic rigor into Christian freedom."[19]

From its beginning Cumberland College had to offer preparatory courses, as there were few opportunities for students to attend school in their home communities. In 1842 the preparatory courses required for entrance into college work were English grammar, Latin grammar, Greek grammar, Mair's *Introduction,* six books of Vergil's *Aeneid,* and common arithmetic. The classics weighed heavy also in the college work, but course requirements in Latin and Greek did drop from 42 per cent of the entire program in 1826 to 28 per cent in 1842. There was progressively more emphasis on mathematics, natural science, and the social sciences. The emphasis on classical learning was in accord with the prevailing practices and aspirations of the time, but it probably contributed to limiting the number of students and graduates.

Enrollment in the college was affected by general economic conditions, incidence of disease (especially cholera), student reactions to internal college practices, and variations in the outside controversy discussed earlier. On March 1, 1826, the school opened with only six students but by the end of the year there were sixty. (Enrollment figures include prep students.) In 1827-1828 there were eighty students from ten states. Until the college closed in 1860 enrollment varied from a high of 125 in 1830 to a low of twenty-five in 1843.

Only a few were graduated with baccalaureate degrees—a total of ninety-six or ninety-seven during the thirty-four years of the college's history. Seventy-seven of these entered the professions of law, the ministry, teaching, and medicine. The largest number, thirty-eight, went into law. Twenty-eight graduates were or became ministers, but almost half of these devoted most of their careers to teaching. Three or four others became teachers, and eight became physicians. Cumberland College graduates played leading roles in the Church's history from the 1830s to the end of the century, especially in education and theology. Its sons who entered law were prominent as lawyers and judges from Maryland to Texas, and one, John Selden Roane, became governor of Arkansas. Despite the gloom and storm which surrounded the struggling institution, it made significant contributions to the development of the Church and to the culture of the region.

The relations of the Cumberland Presbyterian Church with Cumberland University were much happier than those with Cumberland College. There were difficulties and some controversies, but the General Assembly avoided direct involvement in the financial affairs of the institution. It did approve the appointment of members of the Board of Trustees under an 1850 revision in the charter and for a while even ratified appointments to the faculty. Actually, it had legal authority over only the theological department. Nevertheless, the university was a Cumberland Presbyterian institution. In the nineteenth century, practically all its trustees and most of its professors were members of the denomination. Although it purposely attracted students from as wide a field as possible, it enjoyed the special patronage of the Cumberland Presbyterian Church.[20]

In the midst of the 1842 crisis over Cumberland College, citizens of Lebanon, Tennessee, influenced by the Rev. George Donnell and his church session, sent a petition to the General Assembly recommending Lebanon as a location "in case that body should deem it wise to locate a new institution. . . ."[21] Donnell's biographer, the Rev. T. C. Anderson (who was an observer of the events of 1842), said that Donnell was "the moving spirit" in getting the college located at Lebanon.[22] Initially, the intent was to move Cumberland College, as evidenced by the use of the same name and the appointment of the same president. In 1844, however, the name was changed to Cumberland University partly because the college at Princeton, Kentucky, continued in operation. Also, the trustees had decided to organize the institution on the university plan of a number of professional schools grouped around a liberal arts college. From the beginning the trustees determined to build up an institution of the first rank. McDonnold gives Robert L. Caruthers much of the credit for the university's initial and continuing success. A highly respected lawyer and a Cumberland Presbyterian elder, Caruthers was president of the Board of Trustees during the university's first forty years. But he was only the first among many citizens of Lebanon and Middle Tennessee who were its moral and financial mainstay for many years. The Rev. Robert Donnell, a well-known and beloved "father" of the Church, also lent his considerable influence to the support of the university.

The Literary (that is, liberal arts) Department of the new institution opened on September 20, 1842, in temporary quarters with the Rev. C. G. McPherson as the only professor. There also was a preparatory department under one of the college students. (Throughout its early history the university maintained a preparatory department mainly because of the inadequate schooling of candidates for admission to the Literary Department.) Cossitt arrived in February 1843 to assume duties as president and teacher. By September 1844, in addition to the president, there were three professors (of Latin and Greek, mathematics, and modern languages) and a tutor. Enrollment increased rapidly, reaching 138 by 1847. Thirty of these were candidates for the ministry.[23] From the beginning the university charged no tuition to ministerial candidates, whether Cumberland Presbyterian or of other denominations. In 1844 Cossitt resigned to devote full time to his work as editor of the *Banner of Peace and Cumberland Presbyterian Advocate.* T. C. Anderson became president, a position which he filled with distinction until the Civil War interrupted the life of the university.

Determined to broaden the offerings of the university, in 1845 the trustees appointed Nathan Green, Sr., professor of constitutional and international law and political economy. After he declined the appointment, Judge Abram Caruthers was selected. (Abram and R. L. Caruthers were brothers.) Apparently Caruthers failed to take the appointment, although possibly he delivered some lectures. Two years later the trustees resolved to establish a Law Department. After R. L. Caruthers agreed to meet any deficits in the $1,500 annual salary, Abram Caruthers resigned from the bench to become the university's first professor of law. The Law Department opened in October 1848, with classes being taught in the offices of Judge R. L. Caruthers. Only seven students were present at the opening, but enrollment rose to thirteen by the end of the first five-month session.

When the proposal to add law to the curriculum was presented, there was an outcry of protest from those who thought a theological department should be added first. In the face of increasing opposition, the trustees publicly pledged in July 1848 that the Church never would be asked to help support the Law Department. This quietened the protest and the new department grew rapidly. Abram Caruthers, as a pioneer in the teaching of law in the South, not only developed teaching methods which set standards for the teaching of law in Tennessee but also wrote two textbooks for use in his classes. He used a modified case method and moot court and had systematic, day-by-day assignments and examinations. By the end of the third year there were forty students in the department and the 1858-1859 enrollment of 188 was the largest of any law school in the nation. Nathan Green, Sr., a judge on the Tennessee Supreme Court, began giving lectures in 1848, and four years later he resigned from the bench to devote full time to teaching. Among other additions to the law faculty was Nathan Green, Jr., a member of the first graduating class. He was appointed in 1856; in 1873 he became the university's first chancellor. According to the 1859 Cumberland University catalogue, students came from all parts of the country to study with Caruthers and the elder Green and "flocked around them as the youth of Athens used to gather about their philosophers." [24]

While the Law Department was prospering, the Literary Department (preparatory and college) continued to grow. By 1851 it had three professors, two tutors, and 125 students. The endowment was given as $60,000, but that figure is misleading. The endowment was mostly in the form of notes on which the donors paid annual interest while retaining the principal. Interest payments were erratic and little principal ever was paid. Incidentally, this $60,000 figure was given for the Literary Department endowment nearly every year through 1860. The largest pre-Civil War enrollment for the entire university was in 1858 with 490 students and eleven professors distributed as follows: Literary (college and prep)—292 students and six professors; Law—188 students and four professors; Theology—five students and one professor (about forty-five ministerial students in the Literary Department also took lessons or attended theological lectures); Engineering— five students. [25] Engineering courses were offered by Alexander P. Stewart, professor of mathematics and later a general in the Confederate States Army.

The Civil War, McDonnold wrote, "wiped out the endowment, burned down the buildings, destroyed the library, and filled all the friends of the university with despair." [26] All departments were closed. Despite the desolation, almost immediately after the war efforts were made to revive the university. The Rev. T. C. Blake set out as agent to raise money. Richard Beard and T. C. Anderson opened the Literary Department while Nathan Green, Sr., and Nathan Green, Jr., opened the Law School. From 1866 to 1873 B. W. McDonnold was president, and from 1873 to 1902 Nathan Green, Jr., filled the new office of chancellor. Under their administrations Cumberland University not only was rebuilt; it was expanded in size and service with the Literary and Law faculties being especially notable. The Theology Department also was revitalized and its faculty included several

BENJAMIN W. McDONNOLD
(1827-1889)

ROBERT L. CARUTHERS
(1802-1882)

of the most capable and well-known ministers in the Church.

Most Cumberland Presbyterian institutions of higher education were early to adopt coeducation. Cumberland University was a long-time holdout against pressure from the Church on this point, but its trustees finally gave in and opened most of the departments to women in the late 1890s.

At the end of its first fifty years the university had awarded 478 degrees in liberal arts (B.A.—394; B.S.—56; M.A.—18; Ph.D.—10), 1,425 in law, 204 in theology, and 25 in commerce. Although total enrollment seldom reached 500, the university's alumni continued to bring it much glory. A list of positions achieved by its graduates, prepared in 1938, is really remarkable:[27]

| | |
|---|---|
| College Presidents | 47 |
| College Professors | 107 |
| United States Senators | 9 |
| United States Representatives | 66 |
| U. S. Supreme Court Justices | 2 |
| Federal District Court Judges | 10 |
| Federal Circuit Court Judges | 4 |
| United States Secretary of State | 1 |
| Ambassadors to Foreign Countries | 4 |
| State Supreme Court Justices | 42 |
| State District Court Judges | 65 |
| Judges of Chancery Courts | 20 |

Judges of State Courts of Appeal ............................. 12
State Governors ........... ............. . ...... 11
Members of State Legislatures ........................... 862
Ministers  . . . . . . . . . . . . . . . . . . . . . . . . . . . . . . . . . . . . . . . . . . . . . . . . . . 1,205
(Twenty-one of the ministers had been moderators of national church as-
semblies.)

Control of Cumberland University passed from the Cumberland Presbyterian Church to the Presbyterian Church, U. S. A., as a result of the
union movement in 1906, but Cumberland Presbyterians justly could be
proud of having created such a productive institution.


While General Assembly interest in education was absorbed in Cumberland College, Cumberland University, and the question of a theological
school, Cumberland Presbyterians throughout the bounds of the Church
had their particular educational interests and activities. Being among the
few literate members of their pioneer communities, ministers frequently
taught in whatever schools were provided. Many lower schools were established interdenominationally by congregations or even by the members of a
single church. Sometimes an individual would open a school and look to
the entire community for patronage. Preachers frequently taught in the
public "common schools." There is no record of the extent of involvement
of Cumberland Presbyterians in those lower schools, although there are
many references to such participation.

Fragmentation of Cumberland Presbyterian effort and enterprise is demonstrated in no area more fully than in education. While the General Assembly
was pleading for support for its projects, secondary schools and colleges pro-
liferated under the auspices of synods and presbyteries. Only a few had been
founded before 1840, but in the next two decades dozens of them cropped
up from Pennsylvania to California.[28] The General Assembly at first encouraged the formation of new schools. In a report adopted in 1845, ministers
and members were recommended to work toward a comprehensive educational system to consist of: lower schools within the bounds of every
congregation (preferably in cooperation with others in the community,
but alone if necessary); preparatory schools in every presbytery; and Cumberland University and the colleges at Princeton, Kentucky; Beverly, Ohio;
and Uniontown, Pennsylvania, providing higher education. But as academies, institutes, and colleges multiplied, the Assembly and several contributors to church publications expressed alarm over the generally low quality
of education provided and the absorption of the Church's resources in so
many enterprises, many of which they believed were bound to fail.

During the nineteenth century, synods, presbyteries, congregations, and individual church members founded or assumed control over about fifty-five schools at the secondary level. Every state with a significant Cumberland Presbyterian membership had at least one academy, institute, seminary, or comparable school under church control or operated "in the interest of the church." The eighteen schools in Tennessee, the eight in Illinois, the six in Missouri, and the six in Kentucky accounted for more than half of them. About 70 per cent of these schools were established before the Civil War. The mortality rate was high. A few became "colleges" or were transferred from Cumberland Presbyterian control, but most closed because of lack of patronage, mismanagement, the effects of the Civil War, or the growth in public education.

There was widespread criticism of the lower and the "secondary" or preparatory schools for failure to establish and maintain standards. Much of this criticism came from persons connected with the better colleges, professors and officials who claimed the schools were not preparing students adequately for college entrance. As applied to most of the schools, this charge no doubt was well founded. It was true despite the fact that most secondary education, at least that for boys, was pointed toward college entrance requirements, but it surely was a case of poor education being better than no education at all, and a few of the schools gained well-deserved reputations for excellence.

In addition to Cumberland College and Cumberland University, which were established by the General Synod and the General Assembly, about thirty-seven institutions called "colleges" or "universities" were founded by and/or controlled by Cumberland Presbyterian courts during the nineteenth century. They were scattered from Pennsylvania to California and were distributed as follows (counting Cumberland College and Cumberland University): Texas—ten; Tennessee and Missouri—six each; Illinois—three; Arkansas, California, Mississippi, Oregon, and Pennsylvania—two each; and Ohio and Kentucky—one each. A common criticism by those who opposed proliferation and supported higher educational standards was that many of the institutions were not real colleges. All but two or three of the twenty-two founded before the Civil War had failed by 1861 or closed during the war. Some were reopened after the war and fifteen new ones were established by 1900. Epidemics, fire, financial troubles, and factionalism took their toll and only a few endured into the twentieth century. Although others certainly merit attention because of their temporary or lasting importance, attention will be given here to the early histories of only Bethel College, Waynesburg College, Lincoln University, Trinity University, and Missouri Valley College. These, together with Cumberland University, were the members of the Cumberland Presbyterian Inter-College Association which was active during the 1890s.

Because the Cumberland Presbyterians of western Pennsylvania and Ohio were rather distant from the institutions at Princeton, Kentucky, and Lebanon, Tennessee, they determined to have a college of their own. After Madison College of Uniontown, Pennsylvania, suspended operation in the mid-1830s, its Board of Trustees (forty-five Presbyterians, Methodists, and Episcopalians scattered through several states) arranged for Cumberland Presbyterian patronage and appointed as president J. P. Weethe, a young Cumberland Presbyterian candidate for the ministry and recent graduate of Ohio University. Despite "sectarian" opposition, the college prospered under Weethe's leadership. Among the teachers were John Morgan, Milton Bird, Azel Freeman, and A. J. Baird. One of the innovations introduced by Weethe with approval of the trustees was the admission of women as students. This made Madison one of the earliest coeducational colleges in the nation. (Cumberland Presbyterians generally favored "female education" and several of the secondary schools and colleges established before the Civil War were coeducational.)

With Madison College's growth came increasing rivalry for control. In 1842, the majority of the Board having decided to sever the connection with the Cumberland Presbyterians, Weethe and the Cumberland Presbyterian members of the faculty resigned. Within two years the college was floundering again and the trustees turned full control of it over to Pennsylvania Synod. This time, however, no cure could be effected, and in 1846 the college again ceased operation.

Meanwhile, Pennsylvania Synod had resolved in 1840 to endow its own college rather than cooperate with the General Assembly in supporting Cumberland College. In 1842 the synod accepted an invitation from Beverly, Ohio, to cooperate in founding a college there, and a charter was obtained in 1843. J. P. Weethe was Beverly College's first president and for a while its only teacher. During the first session (1842-1843) there were no building and no funds; Weethe taught the few students in his hotel room. The project did not succeed; Beverly College never did graduate a student. By 1848 it apparently was inoperative, as the property was offered to the General Assembly for use as a theological seminary. The offer was not accepted, and when Ohio Synod was formed in 1853 the property was turned over to it.

Still determined to have a college, in April 1849, Pennsylvania Presbytery appointed a committee to seek a location. That autumn the presbytery accepted the offer of Waynesburg, Pennsylvania. Almost immediately thereafter the Rev. Joshua Loughran went there to begin a high school which later was merged into the college. With the completion of a new building, Waynesburg College went into operation in November 1851. In 1853 control of the college was turned over to Pennsylvania Synod.

Among those first appointed to the faculty were Joshua Loughran as president and A. B. Miller as tutor. Miller was in the first graduating class in 1853 and immediately became professor of mathematics. After Loughran resigned in 1855, Weethe became president. Although Weethe had left the Cumberland Presbyterian Church, he apparently had the confidence of the synod upon beginning this work. Dissatisfaction developed over his theological views and his management of the college, however, and he resigned in 1858. Miller was named to the presidency in 1859 and filled that position with distinction for about four decades. Although the college had a $3,000 debt in 1859, its prospects were good. There were six professors and 150 students.[29]

In these early years Waynesburg College did not accept women as students working toward the baccalaureate degree, but from the beginning there was a Female Department which granted a diploma. From 1850 until her death in 1874, Mrs. A. B. Miller (the former Margaret K. Bell) was principal of that department. The Millers were primarily responsible for the survival of the college during the difficult war years and for its revival afterward. President Miller later summed up the trials of the war years and postwar decade:

For the sake of my fellow-educators, I wish to say to my Church, from my heartfelt sorrows in this respect, that *an incompetent support is a great hindrance to the usefulness of a college president or professor.* I have been compelled to preach in order to live, sometimes supplying points twenty miles distant; I have been compelled to deny myself books greatly needed; to stay at home when I should have traveled; to walk many miles, because I could not afford to pay hack-fare; to be harassed with debts that have eaten up the mind as cancers eat up the flesh. . . . I once turned superintendent of schools, and walked all over Greene county, in order to save a little money, and still the college went on—while the nation was fighting battles. At another time I edited the *Cumberland Presbyterian,* did all the necessary correspondence of the office and kept the books, at the same time teaching six hours a day in the college, exercising general oversight of its financial affairs, and often preaching twice on the Sabbath. How imperfectly all these things were done, no one is more painfully sensible than the writer, and he sincerely prays that a like apparent necessity of trying to do so many things at the same time may never come again, though he is scarcely less busy today.[30]

Upon becoming president, Miller had felt the job to be more "to make a college than the honor of presiding over one." His work was done well. By 1898 the enrollment had reached 355 with a faculty of fourteen. The property was valued at $100,000, and there was a productive endowment of $40,000 and a nonproductive endowment of $20,000. More importantly, the college had produced many church leaders, among whom were the Hail brothers the Cumberland Presbyterian Church's first missionaries to Japan, and the Rev. William Henry Black, first president of Missouri Valley College.

In the ante-bellum period West Tennessee Synod was one of the Church's largest synods in membership. Much of the time it was rent with factionalism and controversy. There apparently was considerable rivalry between some leading West Tennessee ministers, such as Reuben Burrow and C. J. Bradley, and the "Lebanon men" after Lebanon became a center of educational and publishing activity. It is not clear that Bethel College grew out of that rivalry, but the majority in West Tennessee Synod certainly was not deterred by any desire to join in a consolidated church effort in education.

Bethel College developed out of Bethel Seminary, which was established under West Tennessee Synod in 1842 at McLemoresville, Tennessee. In 1847 Bethel Seminary was chartered with the provision that it could become a college when $50,000 in productive endowment had been raised. Unable to raise the endowment, the trustees got that provision repealed in 1850 and received the right to organize a college at its discretion. In 1850 the first session as a college began with the Rev. J. N. Roach as president. B. W. McDonnold was one of the two professors. Since it grew out of the already successful Bethel Seminary, there was a considerable enrollment (about 150) the first year. The high school apparently was continued as a preparatory department of the college. In 1852 a theological department was added. Enrollment increased gradually during the next several years, reaching 165 in 1858. This included fifteen in the Theological Department, whose professor, Burrow, had attracted quite a following.

From the beginning, the Bethel College faculty determined to emphasize scholarship. The four-year college curriculum was heavy on Latin, Greek, mathematics, and science, but students could substitute modern language study for part of the Greek requirement. Some history, political science, and economics courses were included, as were the more traditional philosophy, rhetoric, and composition. President Roach was known as a strict disciplinarian, and student life was sternly regulated.

The Civil War forced the closing of the college in 1861, and during the war the buildings were occupied by Union forces. Although it was reopened in 1866, it later was closed for the last time at the McLemoresville site. With a measure of recovery from the effects of the war, West Tennessee Synod was able to reestablish Bethel in 1872 at a new location, in McKenzie, Tennessee, about ten miles from McLemoresville. The reopened college was made coeducational. In 1891-1892, the enrollment reached 275. Six years later enrollment had declined to 185, probably because the growth in public secondary education was reducing the need for a preparatory department.[31]

OLD MAIN BUILDING, BETHEL COLLEGE
This was the first building erected on the McKenzie, Tennessee, campus after the college was moved from McLemoresville in 1872. It was later
enlarged and remodeled, and it stood until 1931.

The decision to establish Lincoln University grew out of the desperate
need for ministers and education in the Midwest during the Civil War.[32]
The proposition originated in the Synod of Indiana with the Revs. James
Ritchey, Elam McCord, and Azel Freeman its principal proponents. In
Illinois it was supported by the Revs. J. R. Brown, A. J. McGlumphy, J. B.
Logan, J. H. Hughey, and J. G. White, among others, while the Revs. J. R.
Lowrance and W. F. Baird were among the leaders in Iowa. Many laymen
also lent their support. All five synods located in Indiana, Illinois, and Iowa
cooperated in the enterprise. In the fall of 1864 a commission of one member
for each synod was appointed to receive bids for a location and to select a

place. Among several bids submitted, that of Lincoln, Illinois, was judged best. The Illinois legislature approved the charter on February 6, 1865, and work on a building was begun before the end of the year. With the completion of the $60,000 building, the first session started on November 16, 1866, with Freeman as president. From the beginning women were admitted on equal terms with men. Both preparatory and college work were offered.

President Freeman's contribution to the founding and early growth of Lincoln University has been regarded as of "incalculable value." However, he resigned in 1869, partly because there was some criticism of his strict discipline and of his theological views. Under his successor, the Rev. J. C. Bowden, there was less emphasis on discipline and scholarship and more on general culture. At Bowden's death in 1873 the school had a faculty of seven with 150 in the preparatory department and forty-eight doing college work.

The next president, A. J. McGlumphy, tried to establish professional schools within the university; however, a law school and a theology department each lasted only one year. Due partly to the original policy of selling scholarships as a means of raising an endowment, the institution soon was beset with financial problems and went through several years of bare existence. In 1882 enrollment in all college departments had dropped to twenty-five. It was not until the early 1890s under the administration of Archelaus E. Turner that significant improvement occurred. By 1898 college enrollment had increased to 150; productive endowment was over $53,000 and nonproductive endowment was $22,000.[33] Lincoln University was in a reasonably healthy condition when it became a part of James Millikin University in 1903.

At the close of the Civil War Cumberland Presbyterians in Texas had three small colleges, none of which was strong enough to provide an adequate program. In 1866 the synods of Texas, Colorado, and Brazos began exploring the possibilities of combining efforts in one institution. Joint commissions were appointed, and work was begun which resulted in the formation of Trinity University.[34]

Although it was not really a town, having only one trading house, and was situated six miles from the railroad, Tehuacana was selected as the site of the school. It did have the advantages of being centrally located and having an environment conducive to good health. Also, its smallness presumably made it free from vice and extravagance.

Trinity University opened on September 23, 1869, in the former home of John Boyd, a local supporter of the institution. A charter was received on August 13, 1870. The Rev. William E. Beeson was the first president and for a while the only teacher. He had only seven students when the first session began, but enrollment increased to 100 by the end of the year. By the fifth year there were 420 students in the primary, preparatory, and college departments. The school was fully coeducational from the beginning. Stringent rules governing social contact between the sexes were established and reportedly strictly enforced.

After a few years of rapid growth, there was a decline in enrollment due to the development of public schools and the establishment of several more colleges, a few of which were Cumberland Presbyterian. In 1877 a theology department was started, and it was continued for the rest of the century. A law department was maintained for a time. Beeson stepped down from the presidency in 1877. Tenure of presidents tended to be short; those serving as acting or permanent president to 1900 included the Rev. S. T. Anderson, the Rev. B. G. McLeskey, L. A. Johnson, J. L. Dickens, and B. D. Cockrill. In 1894 the enrollment was slightly over 300; there were six professors and six assistant professors. Productive endowment was given at $31,000 and nonproductive at $45,000.[35] By the end of the century enrollment had declined to about 250, and shortly thereafter the school was moved to Waxahachie.

In one respect the history of the founding of Missouri Valley College contrasts sharply with that of most other Cumberland Presbyterian institutions established during the nineteenth century. Much greater care was taken to ensure adequate financial support than was true in other cases.[36] In the late 1860s Ozark, McAdow, Missouri, and Missouri Valley synods began to consider establishing a centrally located college. Interest increased after the closing of McGee College in 1874. On October 27, 1874, representatives of the synods in Missouri met at Sarcoxie to plan for a new college. This resulted in the selection of a joint commission to raise an endowment of $100,000. This commission, with only a few changes in personnel, worked for over a decade toward raising the endowment and securing a building fund.

By 1887 about $25,000 in cash had been raised. Sedalia, Missouri, proposed to donate $40,000 to the endowment, fifteen acres of land for a campus, and $25,000 to the building fund, provided an additional $25,000 could be raised. This having been accomplished and Sedalia's offer formally presented, the commission advertised for other bids. It accepted the best offer, that of Marshall, Missouri: endowment—$46,000; building fund—$38,000; seventy-four city lots—valued at $22,000; and forty acres for a campus—valued at $32,000, for a total of $138,000. The charter for Missouri Valley College was issued on June 30, 1888. On September 11 the commission held its final meeting and turned over to the Board of Trustees $104,381.08 endowment in cash, notes, and securities, $38,000 for the building fund, and deeds for land valued at $56,000. The Board set general policies for the college, including full coeducation. A year later the college opened with A. J. McGlumphy as chairman of the faculty. Initial enrollment was ninety-two, but it increased to 153 by the end of the year. In 1892 enrollment reached 270 and remained close to that level for the rest of the decade. These figures include students in the preparatory department.

In the summer of 1889, shortly before the college opened, George L. Osborne, president of the State Normal School at Warrensburg, was elected president of Missouri Valley College, but he declined. Then William Henry Black, pastor of the Lucas Avenue Cumberland Presbyterian Church in Saint Louis, was offered the presidency. He also declined at first, but in February 1890, the offer was repeated and he accepted. Black was an outstanding educator and an effective administrator. While emphasizing high academic and moral standards, he was liberal-minded and well-versed in up-to-date educational theory. The college curriculum was a mixture of the classics and "modern" subjects and included Greek, Latin, German, French, physics, chemistry, biology, history, elocution, music, and fine arts. In addition, Bible instruction was required. During the 1890s usually about three dozen students were studying for the ministry.

The mortality rate was high among schools and colleges founded by all denominations in the pre-Civil War period. Most of the lower and secondary schools which did not expire for other reasons eventually fell before the expansion of the public school system. Many of those schools were converted into public schools; some others evolved into colleges. The mortality rate of church colleges founded before the Civil War was extremely high in the West, as shown by the records for Arkansas—almost 100 per cent, Texas and Kansas—95 per cent, and Missouri—90 per cent. In older states the rate was not so high but still averaged around 50 per cent.[37] This includes those that closed permanently during and after the Civil War as well as those that failed before the war. The Cumberland Presbyterian college mortality rate of slightly over 80 per cent was about the same as the overall rate in the West. It should be noted that some of those early colleges were sacrificed in the movement to provide stronger institutions, as when three presbyteries in Texas surrendered their colleges to the formation of Trinity University by Texas Synod in 1869. Considering its relatively small membership and its youth, the Cumberland Presbyterian Church bore its share of the burden of bringing education to the midcontinent.

# 13

## PROBLEMS WITH PUBLICATIONS

*There is nothing . . . that so truly represents the mind and spirit of a church to the outside world as its publications. These go where preachers and teachers cannot be heard.*

Editorial, *Cumberland Presbyterian*, May 3, 1883

The religious press rivaled church schools and colleges as an influence in bringing "culture" to the trans-Appalachian West. Religious journalism in America began in the 1740s, but only twelve religious journals had appeared before the Revolutionary War. Several of those were short-lived, and although others were started soon after the war, in 1800 only ten were being published. In the early decades of the new century there was a phenomenal increase in the number of periodicals, but there also was a high rate of attrition. Of the 532 that appeared between 1743 and 1830, only 174 were still being published in the latter year. There were over 300 new starts in the next decade, but most of them had only a brief existence. Two hundred fifty of those begun before 1840 were frontier publications.[1] About half of the religious periodicals were official publications of specific denominations or were published privately "in the interest of" particular denominations. The others either had broader religious purposes or represented more narrow sectarian or special interests.

All the major denominations were quite active in the publishing field in the pre-Civil War period. Presbyterians sponsored the largest number of periodicals, but some Methodist papers had more subscribers. The religious press also was quite active in printing and distributing Bibles, books, tracts, and Sunday school literature. The American Bible Society, the American Tract Society, and the American Sunday School Union were, of course, leaders in the distribution of religious literature.[2] Several of the churches founded boards of publication or "book concerns," not only to promote their denominational interests but also to further the cause of religion generally.

Before 1830 Cumberland Presbyterian publication had been limited to two editions of the *Confession of Faith and Shorter Catechism*,[3] an edition of Finis Ewing's *Lectures*, a hymn book (in addition to one published by the Rev. William Harris), and a small number of articles and pamphlets. Upon providing for the founding of Cumberland College, the 1825 Synod had proposed eventually connecting with it a printing office to publish a paper, books, and other religious material. The Synod and the trustees of the college did not find it expedient to establish a press. In early 1830 the initiative was taken by President F. R. Cossitt and the faculty of Cumberland College acting as private individuals. They began publishing at Princeton, Kentucky, the *Religious and Literary Intelligencer* as a weekly with Cossitt as editor and the Rev. David Lowry, who owned the press, as his chief assistant.[4]

When the 1830 Assembly met in Princeton, Cossitt and his associates offered to give the Assembly authority to appoint the editor if the *Religious and Literary Intelligencer* were made the recognized organ of the Church. The offer was accepted, and Lowry was appointed editor. Thus began the chapter which McDonnold called "the darkest one in all the history of the Cumberland Presbyterian Church."[5] Lowry served satisfactorily for over two years; however, without prior approval of the Assembly he moved the paper to Nashville, Tennessee, in 1832. The name was changed to the *Revivalist* and the Rev. James Smith became a partner and assistant editor. A few months later Lowry sold out to Smith, leaving him in full control as publisher and editor. At that time Smith seems to have been highly respected with many friends throughout the Church. Although the Assembly tended to accept any *fait accompli* and hope for the best, there is no specific evidence of any opposition to the approval of Smith as editor. The 1833 Assembly even made him general agent for its "Book Establishment." It was certainly with hindsight that McDonnold described him as a risk to the Church because of his tendency to plunge in business ventures and to overtax his energies and credit in a wide range of activities.[6] In justice to Smith, it should be noted that the mid-1830s was a period of unrestrained business optimism and even wild speculation, especially in what was then the West.

By 1834 Smith was in financial trouble, for which he blamed the Church in part for failing to give adequate patronage to the paper. The Assembly recognized an obligation to him, and the commissioners, as representatives of their respective presbyteries, agreed to lend him $1,200. The Assembly resolved to increase to 4,000 the subscription list of the paper, which now was called the *Cumberland Presbyterian*. The first commitment was met, but the subscription list never reached 4,000, being only 3,400 in 1835 and falling to 3,060 in 1836. Each year the Assembly expressed its confidence in Smith as editor and renewed its pledge to help increase circulation of the paper. In 1836 it did not mention specifically the 4,000-subscription goal in its renewed pledge. By this time quite a bit of criticism of Smith had developed in the Church, and the Assembly resolved that it "discountenance all attacks upon the *Cumberland Presbyterian,* and view them as attacks upon the acknowledged organ of the Church."[7]

As Smith's financial situation worsened, so did his relations with the Church. Although the Assembly continued to appeal for better patronage for the paper and continued to sanction it, there was increasing criticism of Smith's business practices and editorial policies. A principal difficulty was that the Assembly "appointed" the editor and regarded the paper as its official organ but did not exercise any control over either its editorial policies or its financial management.

Early in 1839 Smith, who already had been quite outspoken in criticism of some Cumberland Presbyterian practices, started calling more insistently for reform in the Church. He proposed adequate pay for ministers, the establishment of pastorates, and more education of ministers. His editorials stimulated a general discussion, although there was much resentment over his tone. McDonnold wrote:

While justice requires it to be said that the evils which he denounced were beyond the possibility of exaggeration, and the excoriations which he gave the church were all richly deserved; yet the terrible denunciations were not always of a nature to be endured, even by those who believed about those matters as he did.[8]

No General Assembly was scheduled for 1839. Smith was joined by others in calling for a meeting to consider means of bringing practices in the Church up to the standards of the Book of Discipline. Smith also was deep in financial trouble and announced his intention of stopping publication of the paper, so there was pressing need for arrangements to keep the *Cumberland Presbyterian* going. Instead of calling an unscheduled Assembly meeting, the Rev. Hiram A. Hunter, as incumbent Moderator, asked the presbyteries to send delegates to a convention to consider these matters.[9]

This convention met in Nashville, Tennessee, in May and was attended by thirty-seven of the leading ministers and elders in the Church. Eight men (including Smith), who had not been sent by presbyteries as delegates, were present and were allowed to participate. Smith, however, did not take part in the discussions and decisions concerning the church paper. The convention members resolved to work toward reform in the Church by trying to get their presbyteries to enforce ordination standards and make it possible for ministers to devote their full time to the ministry. It also proposed a plan to renew publication of the *Cumberland Presbyterian* by an association of presbyteries. The convention adopted a statement commending Smith for his service to the Church, admitting that the Church was partly responsible for his financial difficulties, and pledging to do all they could to help relieve him "from his pecuniary embarrassments." [10] This determination, however, did not extend to buying the subscription list of the *Cumberland Presbyterian,* reportedly because the asking price was too high.

The committee on publication appointed by the convention decided to have the paper published at Lebanon with the Rev. George Donnell as editor. It decided to delay publication until after the fall meeting of the presbyteries. Then in September Smith started issuing the *Cumberland Presbyterian* again, this time from Springfield, Tennessee, claiming that it still was the official organ of the Church. McDonnold described what ensued:

Parties rapidly formed. Angry feelings were stirred up. The presbyteries nearly all took action in favor of one party or the other. Finis Ewing and John L. Dillard both threw their great influence on the side of Smith's paper. Logan Presbytery passed resolutions condemning the convention, and declaring Smith's paper the true organ of the church. Alabama Presbytery did likewise. Richland Presbytery and all of Columbia Synod, with Robert Donnell at their head, took the side of the convention and requested the members of their congregations not to take Smith's paper.

Secession, division, disruption were the words floating in the air.[11]

During the winter and spring of 1840, controversy continued, though it abated somewhat after appeals were made to halt the dispute until the next General Assembly could consider the question. To avoid a showdown, the publication committee decided to postpone publication of the new paper at Lebanon until the General Assembly made some decision. Smith continued to press charges against the convention and claims against the General Assembly in his paper and in visits to churches and presbyteries. In the midst of this turmoil a well-named monthly paper, the *Banner of Peace,* appeared. It was published and sent free throughout the Church by F. R. Cossitt, president of Cumberland College. Without taking sides, he called for peace in the Church. In this plea he was joined by many others, although he also published an article in which Smith "declared the church to be in its death agonies." "To F. R. Cossitt, more than to any other human agency," McDonnold wrote, "does the church owe its escape from wreck in the General Assembly of 1840." [12]

The commissioners who assembled in May 1840 were divided on the question of Smith's claims against the Assembly. After much discussion an acceptable compromise was reached. Without specifically accepting responsibility for Smith's losses on the paper, the Assembly admitted that the Church had failed to increase circulation to 4,000 as resolved in 1834 and 1835. It agreed to pay Smith $1,925 to compensate him for that particular failure and called upon Assembly members to assist in raising the amount. Over two-thirds of the amount was provided by commissioners to the Assembly canceling debts owed to them by Smith. The remainder was paid in cash, less the amount Smith owed the Church Fund. (Formerly he had held the Fund but had been unable to pay all of it over to his successor.) The Assembly graciously blamed nothing but the generally bad business conditions for the suspension of publication of the *Cumberland Presbyterian.*

Smith again had stopped issuing his paper, and the Lebanon group never started one. The Assembly failed to designate any paper as the organ of the Church. In response to widespread appeals, Cossitt decided to continue publishing the *Banner of Peace* and made it a weekly. Smith remained a dissatisfied and controversial figure in the denomination for a few more years. He managed to antagonize more and more of his associates. In June 1844, the Rev. Robert Donnell wrote to a friend: "I did not see Smith. He left Memphis two days before I got there. It is generally understood, however, that he intends joining the Presbyterian church, and our brethren say they hope he will." [13] Soon thereafter he did so. His efforts to persuade others to go with him resulted in his carrying only the Rev. John W. Ogden. His predictions that others, including Richard Beard, would be "driven out" of the Church as he had been also were not fulfilled. He believed that the Church would neither support nor tolerate an educated ministry. He was only partly right, and Beard, Cossitt, and others chose to work toward proving him entirely wrong. Years later, recalling the Smith episode, Beard said, "He was an extraordinary man, and we ought not to have lost him." For a while, Beard wrote, Smith was idolized by Cumberland Presbyterians, but then came the quarrel and separation, and with his departure "his sun went down." [14]

The Cumberland Presbyterian Church did not have an official paper again until 1874. But in the 1840s and 1850s several were published as private enterprises in the interest of the Church. Most of them lasted only a short time and some changed locations, names, and editors frequently. A listing of those started by 1860 presents a profile of those publication efforts: [15]

1. *Cumberland Presbyterian Pulpit.* Published by James Smith at Nashville, Tennessee, in 1833. Lasted about two years.

2. The *Banner of Peace*. Established by F. R. Cossitt at Princeton, Kentucky, in 1840. Moved to Lebanon, Tennessee, in 1843 and to Nashville in 1853. Lasted under succession of owners and editors until its subscription list was sold to the denomination's Board of Publication in 1874.

3. *Union and Evangelist*. Established by John Morgan at Uniontown, Pennsylvania, in 1840. Taken over by Milton Bird after Morgan's death in 1841. Name changed to *Evangelist and Observer* and shifted to Pittsburgh. Moved back to Uniontown with name *Cumberland Presbyterian* in 1846. Under succession of owners and editors published at Uniontown, Brownsville, and then Waynesburg until 1868 when its subscription list was sold to J. B. Logan, who published a paper under the same name at Alton, Illinois.

4. The *Ark*. Established by Robert Frazier at Athens, Tennessee, in 1841. Moved to Memphis by 1846. Sold to W. D. Chadick in 1850 and combined with the *Banner of Peace*.

5. The *Texas Presbyterian*. Established by A. J. McGown at Victoria, Texas, in 1846. Moved to Houston and then to Huntsville. Publication ceased about 1856.

6. *Watchman and Evangelist*. Established by Milton Bird at Louisville, Kentucky, in 1850. After several changes in editors was consolidated with *Missouri Cumberland Presbyterian* in 1858 to form *St. Louis Observer*.

7. The *Ladies' Pearl*. Established by W. S. Langdon and J. C. Provine at Nashville, Tennessee, in 1852. Bought by J. B. Logan and W. W. Brown and moved to Alton, Illinois, in 1857. Was published, with various editors, until 1884.

8. *Missouri Cumberland Presbyterian*. Established by J. B. Logan at Lexington, Missouri, in 1852. Moved to Saint Louis in 1853. Moved to Alton, Illinois, in 1856. United with *Watchman and Evangelist* to form *St. Louis Observer* in 1858.

9. *St. Louis Observer*. Formed in 1858 by union of *Watchman and Evangelist* and *Missouri Cumberland Presbyterian*. Milton Bird was its first editor. List sold in the early 1860s to the *Cumberland Presbyterian* of Waynesburg, Pennsylvania.

10. The *Theological Medium*. Established by Milton Bird at Uniontown, Pennsylvania, in 1845. Published successively as a monthly, a quarterly, a monthly, and again as a quarterly at different places and under different names. Became *Theological Medium and Mississippi Valley Review* and then *Theological Medium and Quarterly Review*. Suspended publication because of low circulation in late 1850s.

11. The *Presbyter*. Established by T. M. Johnston at Alamo, California, in 1860. Name changed to *Pacific Cumberland Presbyterian* and then to the *Pacific Observer*. Sold to D. E. Bushnell in 1871 and published for short time in San Francisco.

12. The *American Presbyterian and East Tennessee Cumberland*. Begun in 1851 with J. B. Dobson as editor. No record of longevity.

13. *Texas Medium*. Published in 1852. No other information.

14. *Texas Pulpit*. Edited by James Sampson, James Guthrie, and M. Priest in 1851. No other information.

Each of these periodicals played its part in helping develop denominational self-consciousness of Cumberland Presbyterians. None had a large circulation, but they reached a considerable number of ministers and laymen. There sometimes was rivalry and even disputes among them. They brought to church members not only news and views of Cumberland Presbyterians but also more general religious and secular news. Among their readers were members of other denominations, who gained some knowledge of Cumberland Presbyterians. The *Banner of Peace* was the most important of the weeklies. Published from the heartland of the Church, it generally maintained a broad view and tried to appeal to all of the Church. Occasionally the Assembly was asked to try to consolidate the several weekly papers and issue an official periodical for the entire Church, but no definite steps were taken in that direction until after the Civil War. The *Theological Medium* deserves special mention. Through the pages of the *Medium* important contributions were made to the development of a Cumberland Presbyterian theology. The General Assembly recognized its importance and several times praised Bird's efforts and resolved to work toward increasing circulation of the journal.

Cumberland Presbyterians were quite interested in the distribution of religious literature, but they were rather slow in developing a denominational literature. Before 1829 the Synod had sanctioned the publication of two editions of the *Confession of Faith,* a hymn book, and Finis Ewing's *Lectures.* Many ministers and members had worked with and for Bible societies and tract societies. As early as 1817, only a year or so after the formation of the American Bible Society, the Green River (Kentucky) Bible Society was organized with William Harris as president. Such societies usually were interdenominational, but Cumberland Presbyterians were active in many of them. Harris probably was the first to distribute religious tracts in his area.[16] Many ministers served as agents for Bible and tract societies; others distributed Bibles and tracts without pay. Such literature quite often was added to the already bulging saddlebags of pioneer preachers. During the period 1830-1860 the General Assembly frequently urged presbyteries, congregations, ministers, and members to support the work of the American Bible Society and the American Tract Society and their local affiliates. Like other Protestant groups, Cumberland Presbyterians regarded as essential the free distribution of the Bible among all classes of mankind "in their own vernacular."[17]

During the early 1830s the General Assembly maintained a "Book Concern" through which church literature was distributed by a general book agent and various local agents. There was continuing difficulty with this system. In 1835 the Assembly was in debt to its general book agent, Joseph B. Hill, for the printing of Ewing's *Lectures* and the *Confession of Faith*. In return for release from the debt the Assembly turned over the remaining books to Hill as his property and urged its members to aid in selling them. This probably ended the Assembly's "Book Concern" for several years. Various synods made their own arrangements for publishing and distributing the *Confession of Faith*. In 1840 a special publications committee was set up, but three years later it was discharged after having accomplished nothing.

Despite the recent unfortunate development in financial matters relating to the college and to the newspaper, and the previous inability to operate a "Book Concern," some church leaders still worked to revive publishing activity. By a vote of forty-nine to twenty-three the 1845 Assembly decided to establish a "Publishing Association" as a joint-stock company with presbyteries as investors. It was to begin operations only after $3,000 had been raised. Still acutely aware of past misfortunes, the Assembly disavowed any relation with the Publishing Association "that would imply pecuniary responsibility." [18]

The Church responded to the project with varied reactions, and the Publishing Association never functioned. The 1846 Assembly was faced with so many conflicting views that it suspended the project until the next meeting. The 1847 Assembly abandoned that plan and approved an alternate proposal. A constitution for an incorporated Board of Publication of the Cumberland Presbyterian Church was approved. The five members of the Board were to be appointed by the Assembly and could be removed at its pleasure. An Examining Committee, also appointed by the Assembly, would approve authorized works to be published. Business must be done on a cash basis and there were to be no debts greater than the assets. The Assembly was to bear no liability, but any profits were to go to it. Money would be raised by voluntary contributions. Milton Bird, Laban Jones, F. E. McLean, A. M. Phelps, and James L. Stratton were appointed members of the Board. Robert Donnell, T. C. Anderson, and Richard Beard made up the first Examining Committee. [19]

The Board of Publication was chartered by the legislature of Kentucky and located its work in Louisville. For a while Milton Bird was both president of the Board and its publishing agent. He resigned as publishing agent in 1850 and was replaced by the Rev. Lee Roy Woods. When Bird moved from Louisville to Princeton, Kentucky, in 1854, he resigned from the Board. Two years later he was appointed to the Examining Committee. Woods was succeeded as publishing agent in 1854 by the Rev. Jesse Anderson.

From the beginning the new Board was in financial difficulty. Initial costs of publication were not offset by sales, so a debt soon was acquired, first to the publishing agent in unpaid salary and then to the printers. During the mid-1850s donations declined almost to the vanishing point and debts mounted, partly because in 1852 the Board adopted a credit plan for distributing books to presbyteries. Although there was a considerable debt, the liabilities of the Board never were greater than its assets.

In 1855 there were complaints in the Assembly about inadequate reporting and accounting from the Board and its agent. The Assembly appointed a committee to audit the Board's books and report to the Church. Such a measure, so common in more recent times, probably was unprecedented in Cumberland Presbyterian history. Despite an improving financial situation, due mainly to the work of the new general soliciting agent, H. M. Ford, dissatisfaction with the Board increased. Personnel of the Board changed rapidly because of frequent resignations. Finally, the 1857 Assembly ordered the Board "to wind up its business during the coming year, incurring no further liabilities, and settling all debts of the concern. . . ."[20] The next Assembly approved a new plan for carrying on publishing activities. It was prefaced by a brief statement which summed up the general view on the necessity to continue the publishing work:

. . . The necessity of a supply of cheap denominational works seems to be acknowledged by all. It is a want, too, which must be deeply felt. Thought is the food of the mind, and reading furnishes material for thought. It is difficult to find sufficient material without reading. In order to reading [sic] we must have books. The masses of the people do not read many nor large books. A cheap practical literature is better suited to their circumstances. If we believe the doctrine of our own Church to be true, we ought to furnish our people with such works as will contain plain and scriptural expositions of those doctrines.[21]

The new plan was designed to avoid the pitfalls which had endangered all previous efforts of the Church to conduct affairs involving finances. As adopted by the Assembly, it set up a Committee of Publication whose members were to live close together and were to be practical businessmen who were devoted to the interests of the Church. Specific regulations were laid down concerning financial management and annual reporting to the Assembly. The old Board was directed to wind up its business and hand over all proceeds and property to the new Committee on Publication as soon as possible. Finally, provision was made for a group of seven commissioners to accept bids from various cities on the location of a book depository and store, which, if prospects became good enough, might become a publishing house. Andrew Allison, the Rev. W. E. Ward, and the Rev. Wiley M. Reed, all of Nashville, Tennessee, were appointed as the Committee on Publication.

The Committee went immediately to work. It transferred the old Board's property to Nashville but was unable to locate the stereotype plates for some of the books in print. Although there was a long discussion in the 1859 Assembly over the publication question, the Committee was instructed and encouraged to continue with its work. The committee on a book depository and store reported that it had received only one proposition, that being from A. F. Cox of Saint Louis. No action was taken on Cox's offer.

On the eve of the disaster of secession and war, it appeared that the publishing work of the Church finally was on an even keel. Although unable to locate the plates of the *Confession of Faith, Infant Philosophy,* Ewing's *Lectures,* Donnell's *Thoughts,* and Porter's *Foreknowledge and Decrees,* the Committee had published a total of over 13,000 copies of four titles by May 1, 1860. Almost 10,000 copies of the hymn book had been sold. It was operating on a cash basis and reported a sound financial condition. Since the charter from the Tennessee Legislature had been issued to the "Board of Publication of the Cumberland Presbyterian Church," the Assembly approved the change of name. It also directed the old Board to surrender its charter to the state of Kentucky. The Assembly was pleased especially with the report of the Committee (Board) of Publication and praised it as clear, concise and full, specific, and definite. A Board that could elicit that kind of praise from the Assembly had a good chance of getting the wide support so much needed for the success of its work.

The bright hopes inspired by this promising new start in publication activity were shattered by secession and the Civil War. While the war raged, the Board at Nashville was unable to function. Since the wartime General Assemblies met north of the lines, the Board was cut off from the parent body. The 1862 Assembly appointed a special Committee on Publication to try to confer with the Board and, if unable to do so, to act as a Publishing Committee. Since that committee failed to act and there was still no report from the Board, the 1863 Assembly appointed a new committee to be located at Pittsburgh, Pennsylvania, and authorized it to raise money and publish denominational books. After considerable difficulty, including the necessity of putting up some of their own money to pay claims against the Nashville Board, the new committee transferred the plates and book stock to Pittsburgh. Despite the moderate success of the committee, the Assembly was dissatisfied with some vagueness and inexactness in its report. In 1865 a new permanent committee consisting of J. N. Cary, S. T. Stewart, and Alexander Postly was appointed to continue the work at Pittsburgh. These men organized as a Board of Publication on June 19, 1865, and secured a charter March 16, 1866.[22]

A. J. BAIRD
(1820-1884)

MILTON BIRD
(1807-1871)

With the return of Southern delegates to the General Assembly in 1866, there was an unsuccessful effort by the Southerners to have the publishing work returned to Nashville. Then in 1867 there was a struggle among proponents of Pittsburgh, Nashville, and Saint Louis. The Nashville group won and the Rev. A. J. Baird, the Rev. L. C. Ransom, and D. C. Love were appointed as the new Board. While the Assembly expressed gratitude to the Pittsburgh Board, it believed that the work had not been as successful as desired because it was not centrally located and the plan of operation (as established by the General Assembly) had been "radically deficient." This action of the Assembly, together with dissatisfaction over the post-Civil War deliverances on slavery and rebellion, led Pennsylvania Synod temporarily to recommend that its churches not cooperate with the general boards of the Church.

During the rest of the century the Board of Publication made steady if unspectacular progress. It became one of the most successful general enterprises of the denomination. Although its headquarters remained in Nashville, beginning in 1880 the enlarged membership included prominent ministers and laymen from other portions of the Church. A succession of able men served as president: A. J. Baird, W. E. Ward, John Frizzell, John M. Gaut, and J. C. Provine. The Board was also fortunate in getting as publishing agents and general managers several well-qualified persons, including the following: J. C. Provine, William E. Dunaway, the Rev. T. C. Blake, John D. Wilson, the Rev. W. J. Darby, T. M. Hurst, and John M. Gaut. Aside from the building up of a denominational literature (including Sunday school literature), the most important accomplishments of the Board were the purchase and publishing of a weekly paper, the *Cumberland Presbyterian*, and the establishment of a publishing house.

For about forty years before the Board acquired the *Cumberland Presbyterian*, individuals had published papers in the interest of the Church. The Church had no official connection with any of them after James Smith suspended publication of his *Cumberland Presbyterian* in 1839. The Assembly of 1858 had expressed its desire to see two or more of those papers consolidated, but no action had been taken. In the late sixties and early seventies, with the publishing work showing greater promise, the Assembly proposed that the Board purchase and consolidate two or more of the weeklies then being issued by private interests. This goal finally was accomplished in 1874 with purchase of the good will (including subscription lists) of the *Banner of Peace* (Nashville) from the Rev. S. P. Chesnut, the *Cumberland Presbyterian* (Alton, Illinois) from the Rev. John R. Brown and T. H. Perrin, and the *Texas Cumberland Presbyterian* (Tehuacana) from the Rev. J. H. Wofford. Also, a printing press and some other machinery were bought from Brown and Perrin. The total cost was $25,000, of which $5,650 was paid in cash.

With the consolidated paper being published at Nashville under the title the *Cumberland Presbyterian* (after the name *Banner-Presbyterian* was tried and dropped), the Board selected John R. Brown as editor. Brown had been coeditor and part owner of the Alton, Illinois, paper and it was hoped that having a northern editor would placate the fears and disappointments of some of those who objected to the consolidation; however, there was no unanimity over this matter. In the Assembly of 1875 one presbytery protested the concentration of denominational papers at Nashville. It urged the establishment of additional papers and the removal of the *Cumberland Presbyterian* to Saint Louis. Another presbytery memorialized for the location of the paper at Memphis. Dissatisfied elements charged that the Board had overstepped its authority, but its actions were upheld by the Assembly.

Despite grumbling from several quarters, the *Cumberland Presbyterian* under Board management got off to a good start. In 1876 the subscribers numbered a respectable 7,680. Largely from profits from the paper and from Sunday school literature, by 1878 the debt had been reduced to less than $5,000. A modest amount was realized from bequests and payments on donation notes. But already trouble, financial and otherwise, was brewing. The Board had assumed that private publishing interests would be subordinated and the consolidated paper would receive patronage from throughout the denomination. Soon, however, new privately published papers were being issued. By 1877 the Rev. Philip Axtell was publishing the *Religious*

*Pantagraph* at Pittsburgh and a new *St. Louis Observer* was being edited by the Rev. W. B. Farr. Possibly other enterprises had been started. Here was another example of divided interest and fear of centralized power in the Church. The controversial question of the right or propriety of such private papers was debated in several Assemblies in the late 1870s. The 1876 Assembly insisted that members were obligated not to compete with the *Cumberland Presbyterian*. Two years later the Assembly, though still strongly urging support of the central paper, stated that it did not presume to prohibit the publication of papers by individuals nor require them to get the Assembly's permission.

The Board viewed these developments with dismay. As the controversy deepened, it watched in frustration as payments on donation pledges and the circulation of the *Cumberland Presbyterian* declined. The 1878 declaration of the Assembly opened the field of publishing to even those who had been deterred by the previous ruling. For example, J. H. Wofford, who had sold out to the Board in 1874, in 1879 began publishing the *Texas Observer* (later the *Texas Cumberland Presbyterian*). Disillusioned and discouraged, all members of the Board resigned in 1879. In his letter of resignation, W. E. Ward, the Board president, reviewed the developments of the past few years —the high hopes and aspirations and early progress followed by growing opposition and finally the Assembly's surrender to that opposition. "And can the Church," he asked, "expect her men to roll the stone forever to the top of the hill, when, like Sisyphus, they must see it elude their grasp and roll back to the bottom?" Fearing that the Church no longer was willing to support that particular Board, he concluded his letter with these poignant words:

It is, therefore, in my opinion, useless, if I had the time and strength, to work longer in this cause. I have loved the cause of publication; have believed, and now believe, consolidation to be the great power for elevating and unifying our Church; for it I have suffered some reproach and ridicule; have been held up as "Caesar" and "Bishop," and I feel that I am no longer called upon to work in a cause that invites so much criticism.

With malice to none, I beg now to retire to the wide and peaceful fields of education.[23]

Ward and W. C. Smith leaving no alternative, the Assembly accepted their resignations, but it did not accept those of John Frizzell, John M. Gaut, and P. H. Manlove. It complimented the Board on its accomplishments under difficult conditions and again called upon the entire Church to support the central publishing interests. With this crisis over, the Board's work again showed progress. *Cumberland Presbyterian* circulation rose to over 10,000 in 1881 and fluctuated between about 8,000 and about 13,000 during the rest of the century. Publication of Sunday school literature, tracts, religious books, the *Confession of Faith*, and a "hymn and tune book" brought respectable profits except in times of general economic depression. At such times donations also fell off and the Board had difficulty in paying operating costs and debts.

John R. Brown was sole editor of the *Cumberland Presbyterian* until 1883 when the Rev. David Madison Harris of Lincoln, Illinois, joined him as associate editor. About eighteen months later, desiring a more aggressive personality in the editorial chair, the Board asked Brown to resign. Harris became principal editor and the Rev. John M. Howard of Carmichaels, Pennsylvania, was named assistant editor. The ousting of Brown stirred up considerable criticism, but the Assembly accepted the action. In 1885 it assumed the duty of selecting editors; however, that authority was returned to the Board a year later. With the resignation of Harris in 1890, Howard probably assumed the chief editorial duties, although a policy of "impersonal" editorship recommended by the Assembly was started. The Rev. Ira Landrith, a native of Texas, replaced Howard in 1895 and was managing editor for the rest of the century. From 1896 to 1898 he was assisted by Laban Lacy Rice.

For several decades a dream of many church members was the establishment of a publishing house. In the 1830s the Assembly had sponsored a generally unsuccessful "Book Concern." The successive Boards of Publication from the late 1840s to 1871 employed book agents to handle sales of works and tracts which were printed under contract with various printers. Then in 1871 the Church's first bookstore was opened in rented space at 41 Union Street in Nashville.[24] This was the location also of the general publishing and editorial offices and of the printing machinery owned by the Board after it began issuing the *Cumberland Presbyterian*. As the work expanded, this rented space and the equipment became increasingly inadequate. In 1888 the Board requested and received permission to start soliciting donations for the construction of a publishing house. Proposals or bids were received in 1889 from Evansville, Indiana; Lincoln, Illinois; and Nashville, Tennessee. Nashville's bid of $10,000 was accepted and a lot on Cherry Street was purchased. The building was constructed in 1891-1892. Total cost of the property was $81,603.57 but it included an older building which was rented out at $600 per year and an adjacent lot valued at $10,000. The new indebtedness was acquired at an unfortunate time as the financial panic of 1893 and the following depression cut deeply into the business of the Publishing House. Nevertheless, by 1900 considerable progress toward paying off the debt had been made and the house had been able to add more and improved equipment and expand the variety and amount of publications.

After the Civil War there was renewed interest in and encouragement of the publishing of a review journal like the prewar *Theological Medium*. In 1870 T. C. Blake responded and began publishing a new series with the name *Theological Medium and Cumberland Presbyterian Quarterly*. This quarterly was purchased by the Board of Publication in 1872, and the Rev. M. B. DeWitt became editor soon thereafter, holding that position until 1879. Despite repeated General Assembly appeals for patronage, the subscription list declined from over 500 in 1873 to about 300 in 1879. Nearly every year it was published at a loss. Then the theology faculty of Cumberland University assumed control and financial responsibility and published it as the *Cumberland Presbyterian Quarterly Review* until they sold it to W. C. Logan of Saint Louis in 1883. Logan was able to maintain it only about two years. Again responding to appeals from members and church courts, in 1889 the Board of Publication reestablished a quarterly with the title *Cumberland Presbyterian Review*. J. M. Howard, the Rev. R. V. Foster, and M. B. DeWitt successively were editors. Again there was insufficient patronage and the review was a financial burden. With circulation dropping toward 300, the Board stopped publication in 1892. Seven years later it was revived but for only a short period.

# 14

## THE CHURCH AND THE "WORLD"

*The cause of Christ demands that the children of God should live
soberly, as well as righteously and godly, in this world—cleansing
themselves from all ungodliness and worldly lusts, and taking up
their cross and following their Master in meek and holy living—
thus, by their walk and conversation, letting their light shine, and
truly commending the religion of Christ to the confidence and acceptance of all men.*

1870 General Assembly

Nineteenth century American Protestants had an ambivalent attitude
toward the state. On the one hand, most Protestants, lay and clerical, favored
separation of church and state. The religious dissenting tradition, supported
by late eighteenth century rationalism, had brought about a successful dis-
establishment movement during the Revolutionary period, although the
movement was not completed in New England until the 1830s. Once
accomplished, however, the separation of church and state seems to have
been accepted as good also by most members of the churches formerly favored
by state policy. On the other hand, there remained a strong theocratic strain
in the Protestant churches. Very many ministers and members believed the
state had the duty of protecting the Christian (Protestant) elements in
American culture and enforcing Protestant (Puritan) standards of behavior.
The real "theocrats" were those who viewed the United States not merely as
a Christian nation but also as the new "Israel." Americans were a "chosen
people" who were bound by God's law as a nation. Though agreeable to

250

the separation of the state from any particular church, the "theocrats" worked for what amounted to the establishment of Protestant Christianity. They believed that all aspects of American life, including politics and government, must be Christian.

Other Protestants rejected the notion that America was an Old Testament-type, though Christian, "Israel." Stressing the relation of God to the *individual*, they not only opposed state control of religion but also feared that denominational and nondenominational boards, associations, and societies would limit religious liberty. Nevertheless they, too, worked toward creating a Christian environment and regarded American institutions as essentially Protestant. This attitude was quite common on the frontier, especially in the denominations that originated in the West.

Another factor affecting Protestantism's relation to the state and society was the widely held idea that the church is *in* this world but not *of* it. This posed problems. Should preachers get involved in politics? How should the Christian's religion relate to his business, his politics, and other aspects of his secular life? This view can be seen also in the insistence of many churches that their members shun all "worldly" pleasures.

In meeting the questions of church and state and of the proper role of the Christian in the "world," Protestants relied primarily upon denominational efforts. They also tried to extend the Christian influence through voluntary interdenominational and nondenominational associations, including the American Bible Society, the American Tract Society, the American Sabbath Union, the American Temperance Union, and a host of others. Missionary effort, education, moral suasion, the press, and church discipline were their principal weapons, but on some matters there was a demand for the use of governmental power. On the liquor question, most of the churches went beyond advocacy of temperance to support for legal prohibition. Also, the state was expected to protect the "American" Sabbath, to keep the Bible in the public schools, and in general to safeguard republican (Protestant) institutions.[1]

In meeting problems of the "world," Cumberland Presbyterians shared the dilemma and joined the efforts of other Protestants. Within the Church there always were some who opposed efforts to organize to promote activities such as missions, education, and publication. There was opposition also to involvement, direct or indirect, in politics or other secular means of abolishing social evils. This position was held by those who believed that centralized power, church or secular, was a threat to individual liberty and by those who insisted that improvement of man and society could come *only* through the redemption and moral regeneration of *individuals*. Others gave strong support to organized denominational, interdenominational, and nondenominational enterprises and even of state action to promote Protestant Christianity and protect Americanism.

Articulate Cumberland Presbyterians had a profound concern for the worth and good order of society. Many of them believed that the spiritual and moral development of the free individual depended in large measure upon the institutions which nurtured him. They shared the belief that American institutions were Protestant institutions. Accordingly, they looked with suspicion or outright hostility upon anything which seemed to threaten the American family, the American Sabbath, American education, or American republicanism.

Cumberland Presbyterians were among the first in the West to become active in the temperance movement. Before 1820 each of the first three presbyteries "declared it to be an offense worthy of discipline to make, sell, give away, or drink intoxicating liquors." [2] Many new presbyteries adopted temperance resolutions at their organizational meetings or soon thereafter. It became customary for the pioneers to form a temperance society when they organized a church.[3] Finis Ewing's biographer called him the "father of the temperance reformation in central and western Missouri." Soon after he moved to Missouri in 1820, Ewing organized what may have been the first temperance society in the state.[4] In 1828 Cumberland Presbyterians joined Presbyterians in organizing at Trenton the first temperance society in West Tennessee. This was shortly after Richard Beard preached the second temperance sermon ever delivered in that part of the state.[5]

The highest church court was somewhat slower to take a definite position. At the Synod of 1827, one year after formation of the American Society for the Promotion of Temperance, the subject of temperance was first brought "prominently" before the Church. Although presented with a powerful appeal by the Rev. Henry F. Delany, the temperance resolutions were rejected. "The good old men were taken by surprise," Beard later wrote. "None of them were in favor of drunkenness; but they thought the resolutions aimed a blow at their freedom. It was the old objection. They claimed the right of using what they pleased themselves, and in their families." [6] A year later the Synod did adopt a mild resolution calling on ministers and members "to discountenance the unnecessary use of ardent spirits in the several congregations, settlements, and families, and wherever else their influence may extend." [7]

While the General Assembly was slow to reach an extreme position on temperance, some lower courts were less reluctant. For example, Washington Synod in 1834 (one year before becoming Missouri Synod) recommended that its presbyteries require that all church members who made or sold "ardent spirits" be suspended from the church.[8] The Assembly, on the other hand, limited itself in 1836 to recommending that no minister, elder, or member "shall engage in retailing ardent spirits or disposing of them in any other way."[9] Assemblies continued to adopt moderate statements declaring the liquor traffic to be an evil and encouraging the temperance movement. Finally, in 1851, the Assembly declared "that to make, buy, sell, or use as a beverage" any intoxicating liquors was an immorality; "that it is not only unauthorized, but forbidden by the Word of God."[10] Two years later the Assembly stated that it was the duty of a Christian to work for legal prohibition.

This temperance and prohibition position was maintained through the 1850s, but the Assembly was reluctant to make total abstinence from drinking intoxicants a test of membership. In 1855 it left that question to the presbyteries, after suggesting that members who persisted in drinking after being informed of its evils should "be dealt with as disorderly."[11]

The Civil War interrupted many of the "normal" interests and activities of the Church, but by 1870 the Assembly was reaffirming its temperance position. It renewed its practice of appointing a committee on temperance each year, and it adopted increasingly stronger statements. The 1873 Assembly declared "that it is a sin to make, buy, sell, or give, or in any way use as a beverage, intoxicating drinks of any description." This was the first Assembly statement specifically branding participation in the liquor traffic as a personal sin. It was followed by an urgent request that church sessions "deal with such offenders and free the Church from the guilt and scandal of such unchristian conduct."[12]

During the last quarter of the century the Cumberland Presbyterian Church stood in the front ranks on the temperance question. The Assembly recognized that in many places the Church was far below the standards it had set. It continued to urge total abstinence and in 1877 recommended to all its churches the use of the pure "fruit of the vine" in the observance of the Lord's Supper.[13] The Assembly of 1878 recognized the right of the state to make and enforce laws to regulate, modify, restrict, or abolish the whiskey traffic and stated that there was no moral right enabling a man to engage in it or a state to license it.[14] Licensing and taxing came to be regarded as forms of approval, and in 1886 the Assembly advocated absolute constitutional prohibition. The following year the obligation "to pray for, labor for, and vote for" such constitutional amendments was declared a Christian obligation.[15]

Opposition to political means surfaced in 1889 when the majority report of the Committee on Temperance urged ministers and members "to rely not so much upon the success of secular movements as upon the power of the gospel" to remedy the liquor "evil." The minority insisted that nothing short of state and national constitutional amendment would be satisfactory and declared the Church "squarely for prohibition." After much debate and an amendment denying the intent to endorse any political party, the minority report was adopted by an overwhelming vote.[16]

There was no withdrawal from this stand during the remainder of the century. The Assembly continued to favor prohibition by the state and total abstinence for the individual. It urged the use of moral suasion and offered encouragement to all temperance societies. Though unwilling to commit the Church to any party platform, the 1899 Assembly stated it to be the duty of Christians to separate from every organization which compromised with the liquor traffic, to unite with some organization which opposed it, and to vote against it.

The *Cumberland Presbyterian*, published weekly after 1874 as the official organ of the denomination, devoted much attention to the liquor question. Editorially, the paper favored local option over the license system and absolute prohibition over local option. The editors reported contests in various states and urged their readers to vote for and work for prohibition; however, they refused to support the Prohibition Party movement. Editors and contributors presented a wide range of arguments against the use of intoxicants and in favor of prohibition. The paper no doubt helped maintain and solidify the Church's position of total abstinence and absolute prohibition.

Temperance sentiment among Cumberland Presbyterians also was applied to the use of tobacco. The General Assembly first acted on this question in 1855 by declaring "that the use of tobacco, by chewing and smoking, is unnecessary—is a useless expenditure of money . . . ; is extremely nauseous and offensive in our churches, especially to the ladies—and is injurious to the health of those who use it." [17] In 1870 and 1871 the Assembly refused to adopt proposed statements on the subject. In 1880 the Committee on Temperance reported that it regarded the "excessive" use of tobacco as a great evil and would "disapprove and discourage" its use by the young. The Committee believed, however, that the evil must be referred to the individual conscience, to church sessions, and to presbyteries. Even this mild censure of the use of tobacco was not adopted. Some thought it too weak, but after a delegate argued that it looked to the "arraignment of venerable members and ministers," the entire item was postponed indefinitely by a vote of eighty-five to sixty-eight.[18]

The question would not die. Although its editors cautioned enthusiasts to "hasten slowly," antitobacco articles began to appear frequently in the *Cumberland Presbyterian*. The 1881 Assembly refused to act on an antitobacco resolution. In 1883, after rejecting a resolution that would "discountenance the use of tobacco in all its forms," the Assembly adopted by a vote of ninety-one to sixty-six this statement: "The use of tobacco is an evil which should be discouraged, especially in the rising ministry."[19] The Board of Education was instructed in 1889 to give "no aid to any candidate for the ministry in securing an education who uses tobacco."[20] Despite continuing opposition, the majority in several later Assemblies before 1900 supported mild resolutions critical of the use of tobacco; however, such use was not declared to be sinful.

Antitobacco writers for the church paper used many arguments. They dwelt upon the discomfort it caused others and the way it degraded the "sensibilities" of the users. They cited professional reports and hearsay as evidence of tobacco's harmful mental and physical effects. Great stress was put on the cost—the waste of money by tobacco-using ministers and church members. One writer forcefully summed up several of the arguments by listing reasons why he was pained to see a minister using tobacco:

1. Because he stinketh.
2. Because he maketh himself filthy with his spittle.
3. Because he sinfully wasteth his Lord's money.
4. Because he injureth his health and shorteneth his life.
5. Because he wickedly setteth a bad example before the small boy.[21]

In common with other evangelical churchmen in the nineteenth century, Cumberland Presbyterians were outspoken in denouncing "worldliness" as being out of harmony with the Christian spirit. The General Assembly of 1852 expressed the opinion held by the Church throughout the century:

WHEREAS, there is no specific law in the Discipline of this Church, forbidding the members thereof attending fashionable balls and parties, theatres, circuses, and such places of worldly amusement for carnal indulgence of mere human merriment, gotten up and mainly sanctioned by those who are not connected with the evangelical church.
*Resolved,* therefore, by this General Assembly, that in all such instances where members of our Church are known to attend such places for purposes of participating in them, be held responsibile in each case to the church session of the congregation where such member holds his or her membership, and that church sessions be and they are hereby instructed to adopt such rules in their respective congregations as may forbid such conduct.[22]

A later Assembly (1870) stated that Christians "should live soberly, as well as righteously and godly, in this world—cleansing themselves from all ungodliness and worldly lusts, and taking up their cross and following their Master in meek and holy living. . . ."[23] Soon thereafter a minister stated that *"Christians are to seek their pleasure in the Lord—in the discharge of religious duty and nowhere else."*[24]

To Cumberland Presbyterian critics of manners and morals the trend toward "popular amusements" was quite disturbing. The true Christian, they insisted, found joy and pleasure in his religion above any offered by the world. Since man's lot was to work, his highest joy should be in work. Amusements were necessary for recreation—to enable a person to return to his work with renewed vigor—but the Christian should not engage in amusements which could have any moral ill effects. Pleasure, they maintained, was wrong when engaged in for its own sake. Although dancing and the theater were the favorite targets, a wide range of activities were condemned in the church press. These included church entertainments to raise funds, sports (especially boxing), card playing, gambling, "high art," and popular literature.

From their beginning as a denomination, Cumberland Presbyterians believed in strict Sabbath observance. It was an attitude and practice of rural America which the church fathers had inherited and which they passed on. As new ways of earning a living, of transportation, and of recreation accompanied city growth and the beginnings of industrial development, new Sabbath activities emerged. Not until 1845, however, did the General Assembly adopt a statement on the subject. It then encouraged ministers and members to promote the sanctification of the Sabbath and expressed disapproval of these activities on the Sabbath: unnecessary travel, visiting, "indulging in idle sports and vain amusements," and the operation of railroad, canal, or steamboat lines.[25] The 1852 Assembly stated that anyone traveling to or from the General Assembly on the Sabbath should be dealt with for an immorality.

After the Civil War the Assembly began to express real concern over threats to strict Sabbath observance. In 1874 it pointed to the danger in the efforts of "Rationalism, Infidelity and Romanism" to turn the Sabbath into a day of recreation and amusement. With increasing urbanization and greater immigration of non-Protestants there was a definite tendency toward the "Continental" Sabbath. Americans increasingly came to look upon Sunday as a day of rest and relaxation after the week's toil. By 1900 some of the Protestant churches had retreated and no longer expressed great alarm over Sabbath desecration. Others, especially minor denominations, continued to demand strict observance. The Cumberland Presbyterian Church was among the latter group. In 1879 the Assembly set up a Committee on the Prevention of Sabbath Desecration. A year later this became a Permanent Committee on Observance of the Sabbath with instructions to correspond with other such committees and with the International Sabbath Association.

During the remaining years of the century the General Assembly con-

tinued to support strict Sabbath observance. It opposed efforts to repeal existing Sunday laws and even called for more stringent ones. In 1891 it adopted
a comprehensive list of unacceptable activities: social visiting and feasting,
idleness or frivolous pastime, nonattendance at church by children, Sunday
newspapers, Sunday trains and excursions, baseball, picnics and similar
amusements, and Sunday mail service.[26] A later report added reading and
bicycle riding to the list. These official pronouncements together with many
articles in the church publications show that Cumberland Presbyterians did
not relax in any way their stand for the "American" Sabbath.

During the period 1835-1860 many Protestants were caught up by the
Native American movement, which found its main expression in anti-
Catholicism. The tone of Protestant anti-Catholic literature was set with the
publication in 1836 of Samuel F. B. Morse's *Foreign Conspiracy Against
the Liberties of the United States.* The *Awful Disclosures* of Maria Monk
was the prototype of a more scurrilous and sensational literature, but the
more respectable preachers and editors shied away from it. Morse's "revelation" of a supposed Austria-backed popish plot to take over the United
States made a profound impression on the minds of men already conditioned
to see the Pope as "the man of sin" or "Anti-Christ." The immigration of
large numbers of Irish and German Catholics in the period lent plausibility
to Morse's "conspiracy" idea.

Cumberland Presbyterian concern with Catholic influence has been noted
in reference to the Sabbath question in this chapter. The General Assembly
did not pronounce on the Catholic question until 1845, but then it took
the typical Protestant position of the time. It was time, the Assembly declared, to raise a warning against "the dark designs and mischievous policy
of the man of sin." The Papacy was seen as "a well-organized political
power, and opposed to liberty of all kinds, and especially to that of the soul,
and the right to worship God according to the dictates of conscience." [27]

At about the same time the leading Cumberland Presbyterian paper, F. R.
Cossitt's *Banner of Peace,* increased its attention to the Catholic question.
During a three-month period in 1846 that weekly paper carried ten anti-
Catholic articles written by Cumberland Presbyterians plus eighteen reprint
articles, letters, and news items about Catholics. The quarterly journal,
published and edited by the Rev. Milton Bird, also devoted considerable
space to such literature. This interest was reflected in additional strong
anti-Catholic resolutions adopted by the General Assembly in the 1850s.
Beginning in 1853, the Assembly also frequently offered encouragement
for and urged support of the American and Foreign Christian Union, which
had as its main purpose the "conversion" of Roman Catholics.

After a return to somewhat normal activities following the Civil War, Cumberland Presbyterians in General Assembly and in the church press renewed their verbal attack on "Romanism." In the 1870s and early 1880s there were several anti-Catholic statements by the Assembly. While the Rev. John R. Brown was editor of the *Cumberland Presbyterian* (1874-1885), many editorials and articles of the extremist type were published. With the change in editorship, in 1885, there was a marked change in the *Cumberland Presbyterian's* treatment of the Catholic question. The Rev. David Madison Harris and his assistant and successor as editor, the Rev. John M. Howard, also believed that Catholicism was opposed to American institutions, but they saw no real danger and were inclined to deprecate the activities of the alarmists. Denunciation of "Romanism" and angry debates with priests, they believed, would do little good. To be successful in the competition, Protestants would have to evangelize the urban population. Harris and Howard even commented favorably on evidences of a liberal trend in Catholicism, such as the Pope's support for the working man and the permitting of Catholic parents to send their children to public schools. Inconsistently, however, they occasionally warned that such actions were merely ruses by which the Catholic power wished to lull loyal Americans into a false feeling of security. During this period there also was less concern expressed by the General Assembly. Oddly, anti-Catholicism among Cumberland Presbyterians was declining even while there was another upsurge of nativism, as evidenced by the short though energetic life of the American Protective Association. By the end of the century, however, there was growing rapport throughout the country between American Protestants and Catholics except for the more fanatical in each group.[28]

One of the greatest challenges to American Protestantism in the late · nineteenth century was that presented by the problems growing out of industrial expansion and the growth of cities. Could Protestantism, nurtured in a predominantly middle-class rural society, adjust to the conditions of an industrialized urban society? The religious consensus in the pre-Civil War period was that the existing socioeconomic system was divinely ordained. Free enterprise and individualism were sanctioned, while governmental regulation and collective action to control or improve the economic system were considered unnatural and ungodly.

In the post-Civil War period prosperity seemed to be vindicating the laissez-faire doctrines once and for all. Protestantism honored the newly rich industrialists and showed little awareness of the fundamental social and economic changes which were occurring. The moralistic attitude toward poverty and other social ills remained dominant, as individual failings were blamed for poverty and suffering. There was much charity among church people. It was, however, a charity ill adapted to the problems of slum tenements, large foreign-born populations, new labor relations, urban crime, and many others created by rapid industrialization.

By the end of the century numerous Protestant spokesmen had challenged the traditional views of the majority. They had offered numerous proposals for applying Christian principles to the problems of industrial society— proposals collectively called Social Christianity or the Social Gospel. Although the holders of the new ideas remained a minority before 1900, their influence on the Christian conscience and church programs in the twentieth century was to be profound.[29]

The Cumberland Presbyterian Church as a whole, according to negative evidence in the General Assembly records, took little note of new social questions. But some members were aware and interested. Their opinions, drawn from the pages of the *Cumberland Presbyterian* and other church periodicals, ranged from the traditional or conservative support of the status quo to a rather severe criticism of existing laws and practices.

John R. Brown, editor of the consolidated *Cumberland Presbyterian* from 1874 to 1885, showed only mild interest in new social questions. He was able to lift the curtain of tradition enough to see that capital was partly to blame for unrest among workers. Orthodoxy descended again, however, as he placed the blame for suffering, disorder, and depression upon such evils as intemperance, extravagance, speculation, and the operation of railroads on Sunday. No new remedies for social ills were offered by Brown or contributors.

David Madison Harris and John M. Howard brought a freshness and vigor which permeated all departments of the paper during the decade, 1885-1895, when one or both were chiefly responsible for its editorial content. They and several others writing for their paper and for the quarterly journal were in that stream of social awareness and criticism called the Social Gospel. They were motivated by a fear of socialism, by a deep sympathy for the oppressed classes, by a high regard for human dignity, and by a realization that the churches were losing contact with the masses. Extremely critical of capitalistic abuses, especially those of monopoly, they defended labor's right to organize but feared that unions would become as tyrannical as capital had been. They approved strikes in principle but believed strikes too often led to violence. Boycotts and other devices which seemed to interfere with individual rights were condemned. As practical solutions to labor strife they suggested such measures as compulsory arbitration, profit-sharing, cooperatives, and laws to abolish trusts and to insure free competition. Holding society largely responsible for poverty and crime, they believed that the only cure for social problems was the application of Christian ethics—the spirit of the Golden Rule—to all secular affairs. They urged their readers to take their Christianity into their daily lives, to participate in reform movements, to minister to the bodies as well as to the souls of the poor and oppressed, and to abolish those artificial class distinctions which were driving the masses away from the churches.

After the Rev. Ira Landrith succeeded Howard as chief editor of the *Cumberland Presbyterian* in 1895, there was a definite falling off of editorial interest in new social problems. Fewer contributed articles on the subject were published. Landrith did condemn trusts and monopolies, sympathize with workers, predict social revolution, suggest arbitration in labor disputes, and favor old age insurance, but such topics were treated rarely and with much less fire than by his predecessors.

The participation of some editors and a few contributors in the Social Gospel movement does not reveal the social views of the rank and file Cumberland Presbyterian membership. The supporters of economic reform probably were in the minority. Although some orthodox conservatism continued to appear, relatively few ministers and members left written expressions of their views. Nevertheless, the dissemination of progressive views through the church publications must have had some influence on the thinking of the readers.

Cumberland Presbyterians, like members of other religious groups, were faced with problems created by science and scholarship.[30] The controversy centering around Darwin's theory of evolution was the most spectacular development in this area, although the questions of higher criticism, Bible revision, and other evidences of intellectual revolution contributed to the unsettled state of theological thought. Darwinism was the severest challenge to orthodox theism in the nineteenth century. It not only cast doubt on the Genesis story of creation; it also seemed to endanger many other elements of the orthodox evangelical Christian faith. If the Genesis account were discredited, could the Bible be accepted as the actual word of God? If man never had been in a state of perfection, how could the doctrine of the fall and redemption be explained? If the universe and organic life were subject to natural laws and nothing else, how could a person continue to believe in a personal God who was interested in his welfare? Underlying the whole conflict was the question of the influence of evolutionary thought on the concepts of absolute truth and of purposeful creative design in nature.

These points seemed irreconcilable to many Christians who rejected Darwinism and charged "modern" science with atheistic tendencies, but by 1900 liberal Protestant thinkers had adjusted to the implications of Darwinism. Some resolved the difficulty by saying that science and religion were mutually exclusive, seeing the Bible as a guide to faith and not concerned with scientific knowledge. Others preferred to consider the account in Genesis as allegorical and claimed that it anticipated and supported the evolution hypothesis. More progressive theologians substituted the concept of immanence for the theory of literal creative design, theism having its rational basis in the idea of an indwelling power which worked through the trial and error method of evolution. Thus Christianity was seen as a progressive unfolding of higher ethical and spiritual values. Protestantism was not united, however, in the acceptance of Darwinian science. Perhaps most ministers and laymen continued to reject it or remained unaware of the whole question.

Throughout the late nineteenth century there was wide diversity of opinion among Cumberland Presbyterians on evolution and related questions. Of those who presented their views in the church press, the conservatives made up the largest group. The conservatives saw a threat to Christianity in "modern" science and philosophy. They either rejected all scientific discoveries or believed that there was no conflict between religion and "true science," a term which they usually failed to define. Holding fast to the orthodox faith, they retained a literal interpretation of the Bible and resisted new interpretations. To many of them modern thought represented a vague but dread threat to the "faith of the fathers." To protect the faith they used a variety of approaches, ranging from flat rejection with no attempt at rational argument to closely reasoned attempts to refute and discredit scientific theories, especially Darwinism.

The second largest group of Cumberland Presbyterians who reacted to Darwinian thought might be called moderate compromisers. Although they were cautious about accepting new discoveries or theories, they were not "dead set" against scientific developments. They were suspicious of "science so-called" and its speculations, including the more "disagreeable" aspects of Darwinism. They saw the conflict as being between science and theology rather than between science and religion and believed that theology must adjust its interpretation of revelation as "definite" scientific laws threw additional light on basic religious truths. Moderate compromisers respected science, but they insisted that scientists could neither discover nor destroy spiritual truth. They were willing to accept the "facts" of science but would draw a line beyond which science could not go. Many of this group believed that science discovered how the hand of God worked through nature. They accepted the findings of geology and thought of the "six days" of creation as geologic ages. Darwinism was regarded as a possible explanation of how living things were "created." There was more hesitation in accepting the theory as applied to man, but even that was accepted as a possibility. The essential point was that after man's body was created, in whatever manner, God breathed into it something which made man a "living soul."

The smallest group of those who commented on modern science were the liberal compromisers. Readily accepting new scientific discoveries and theories, they seemed as a group to have a better understanding of contemporary intellectual currents. They insisted that theology must accept the revelations of science, and they pleaded for more liberality toward new ideas and for freedom of thought and discussion within the broad framework of Christianity. The contention that science and religion could not be reconciled was rejected completely. Positive arguments were presented to show that modern science supported theism and contributed to a grander conception of God and a clearer understanding of Christianity. The more liberal thinkers were in agreement tht the evolution theory was well established and that it could have no adverse effect on Christianity. After all, they said, the great question was not about how man was created but about what he is and what he is destined to be. Since religion and science were complementary, both being means of revelation, Christianity and the Bible had nothing to fear from scientific investigation.

On the questions of Bible revision and Biblical criticism, Cumberland Presbyterians also were divided. Most of them opposed both revision and criticism and defended the Authorized (King James) Version. Any tampering with it, they feared, would undermine faith in the Bible as the "word of God." Others, a few, believed that the higher criticism was necessary to a better understanding of the Bible.

In all likelihood the main body of Cumberland Presbyterians were conservative in their reactions to new intellectual trends, if they were concerned at all. There is evidence, however, that the Church as a whole was willing to make some concession or adjustment to new scientific knowledge. In 1882 the General Assembly unanimously approved a revision of the Confession of Faith and submitted it to the presbyteries. One hundred of the 116 presbyteries approved the revised Confession.[31] One change is significant to the present discussion. The phrases "of nothing" and "in the space of six days" were omitted from the section on creation. While the proposed revision was before the Church, there was much discussion of it in the *Cumberland Presbyterian,* but there was only one article objecting to the specific change noted here. The article revealed the opposing attitude quite clearly. The author claimed there was an attempt to revise "Moses rather than Ewing." Particularly, he was opposed to the reason given for the change (presumably by the revision committee), which he quoted as follows:

Again, the words, "in the space of six days," are . . . very properly omitted. The developments of the physical history of the earth have clearly established the fact, if human science ever positively established any truth, that the progress of the earth from its original or formless state to its present condition, occupied a very long period of time. It is utterly useless to deny it.

"These words are omitted," the critic declared, "not because they are not scriptural, but because science has settled the question against Moses. Poor, old, deluded Moses! I guess he would have been a very clever historian if he had only lived in this scientific age." [32]

There were several additional moral and social problems to which Cumberland Presbyterians gave their attention. Many of them were concerned particularly with the evils in partisan politics and corrupt government. The basic remedy, they believed, was the participation of "good men" in politics and government. The *Cumberland Presbyterian* editors and some other writers supported several specific reforms, such as the secret ballot, a merit system for the civil service, and the popular election of United States Senators. There was considerable concern over lynchings, "mob rule," and general disrespect for the law. These evils were blamed generally on inefficient legal processes and abuse of the court system. Reform in the legal system was deemed imperative by those writers.[33]

It appears that Cumberland Presbyterians did not differ significantly from the main body of American Protestants in the diversity and tendencies of their opinions on nineteenth century moral, social, and intellectual questions. They had a strong moralistic attitude toward those questions and tended to regard themselves as guardians of public and private morals and of American institutions. They differed among themselves as to the proper approach in meeting the problems. None denied the importance of moral suasion and evangelism, but an increasing number urged the government to help abolish or prevent social and moral evils.

# 15

## "A POSITION OF USEFULNESS
## AND RESPECTABILITY"

*. . . We are assuming a position of usefulness and respectability,
side by side with sister denominations, who have the prestige of an
older and more extensive history.*

Board of Publication, 1868

One of the keys to understanding any organization is to study how its
members view it; an association is to a large extent what its members think it
is. Self-consciousness among Cumberland Presbyterians was displayed in
positive self-analysis and in reaction to how others treated them. Their developing attachment to the "Cumberland" part of the denominational name
revealed increasing confidence and maturity.

During the first three or four decades of the Church's history members
appear have taken the name for granted. Though more or less accidentally
acquired, it was for several years descriptive of the local nature of the Church.
Then, too, the early leaders were so busy with missionary and organizational
work of prime importance to them that the question of the appropriateness
of the name probably just was not raised. Sometimes they were upset when
derisively called "Cumberlands," but they were much more resentful when
their critics failed to distinguish between them and the "Stoneites," or New
Lights, and the Shakers, groups which they regarded as heretical.

By midcentury, however, there was some sentiment favoring choosing a
name more descriptive of the expanding Church. Union and Allegheny
presbyteries of Pennsylvania requested a change to "American Presbyterian

264

Church"; this not only would emphasize the increasingly national nature of the Church but also would recognize its birth in America. In denying the request the General Assembly showed no particular enthusiasm for the existing name but saw no reason for changing.[1] Union Presbytery renewed this request in 1865 and was turned down again.

In the early 1880s there was more general agitation over changing the name. A memorial from Rushville Presbytery (Illinois) to the 1880 Assembly requesting a change was rejected as impracticable and undesirable. This was followed by much debate of the question in the church press. Then the 1881 Assembly was presented with several memorials. Nashville and Athens presbyteries suggested "American Presbyterian," California Presbytery preferred "Presbyterian Church of America," and Indiana Presbytery proposed "Evangelical Presbyterian." The Assembly adopted a report proposed unanimously by the Committee on Overtures denying these memorials. After citing practical objections (examples being the impossibility of agreeing on another name and the necessity of changing names of schools, boards, and papers), the Committee noted that "Cumberland" had become "sacred in the hearts of our people" and that the denomination's particular doctrines had become associated with the name. Confusion and dissatisfaction would result from any change, as they still would be called Cumberland Presbyterians by others.[2] After a while interest in the issue died down but was revived in the 1890s. Finally, the 1895 Assembly, acting on memorials from Arkansas Synod and Yazoo Presbytery (Mississippi), asked that all agitation on the subject cease.

Looking back across sixty years of service to the Church, the Rev. Richard Beard wrote in 1880, "The first generation of Cumberland Presbyterians were the most intensely spiritual people that I have ever known." He insisted on this, although he recognized that old men tend to magnify the past.[3] This emphasis on spirituality runs through church literature—sermons, the press, and reports of boards and committees to church courts. Warning voices continually were being raised against trends away from that spiritual purity. As early as 1836 the General Assembly's Committee on the State of Religion saw "the spirit of this world prevailing to an alarming extent." "Enthusiasm" had not disappeared, for "still the tented grove resounds with songs of praise, the prayers of saints, the groaning of penitents, and the hallelujahs of new-born souls." Yet there was a "fearful and almost universal" decline in "personal piety, holiness of life, self-denial, devotion to the cause of Christ, interest for souls, zeal for the prosperity of the church and the glory of God." [4]

Again and again church spokesmen held up the example of that first generation. Even allowing for extravagance of nineteenth century style, a sincerity of commitment to the ideal of spirituality can be seen in this 1870 statement about the early period:

All the churches felt the pulsation of a divine and mighty life. That life was all the more powerful for the heavenly unction, and for the simplicity with which it was clothed, and the energetic self-reliance which gave tone, power and efficiency to our early operations. . . . A fire was there, which did burn.[5]

Cumberland Presbyterians saw the growth of "formalism" as the greatest threat to the vitality of the Church. A committee of the 1859 Assembly detected some indication of formalism "which, it is to be hoped, will never be allowed to cast its blight over the vital elements of [the Church], and thus mar its beauty, and break the arm of its strength." It urged all members

to avoid formalism, and all effort at conformity to the caprice of a fashionable world, and a fashionable religion, which can only offer to the world a lifeless, sapless trunk, without capacity to bear fruit to the honor and glory of God, and impart vital energy to the souls of men, and give to them the hope of life, and a glorious immortality beyond the grave.[6]

Among the many voices raised in warning, that of the Rev. John R. Brown, editor of the *Cumberland Presbyterian*, may be taken as an example. Writing in 1875, Brown thought it evident that Cumberland Presbyterians in many instances were yielding their traditional spirituality and "giving place to the formalities of the world." The Cumberland Presbyterian Church, he said, could not become "fashionable" without yielding both its doctrine and its spiritual life. He feared that "as a Church, we are not maintaining our original standard of piety, and in the proportion that this is not done, [we are] losing our power over the world as a Christian people."[7]

The history of the Church in the nineteenth century was affected greatly by this emphasis on spirituality. Its effect can be seen in the tendency toward exhortation rather than organization to promote support for church enterprises. The insistence of the Rev. Milton Bird and like-minded men that the Church was "not of this world" helped account for the ability of the Church to survive the crisis over slavery and secession without a definite rift. Though never denying (and even emphasizing) the political and social responsibilities of individual Christians, the Church was reluctant to get involved in social issues except those (such as temperance and prohibition) which were considered to be basically moral according to traditional concepts of morality. Except for the stronger opposing positions on slavery and secession or "rebellion" taken by Northern and Southern branches of some of the other denominations, this was normal for religious bodies in the nineteenth century.

Cumberland Presbyterians saw much evidence of the working of special providence in their history. A quotation selected from among many similar expressions will illustrate this conception. One of the Church's historians wrote in the 1870s:

A true history of the Church is but a record of God's providences and dealings with men. . . . Not an unimportant portion of these special dealings and providences has God communicated to the world through the medium of the Cumberland Presbyterian Church. I know of no branch of the Church, for the time it has existed, which has been attended with greater marks of approbation from the great Head and King of Zion, than has been vouchsafed to us as a people.[8]

The first half of the nineteenth century was a period of vigorous religious controversy. Sometimes particular debates degenerated into name-calling contests as disputants were carried away by passion. In other cases learned and dispassionate men carried on profound and lengthy published arguments on questions of fundamental importance in the development of American religious thought and practice. Being to a considerable extent a product of conflict, personal as well as institutional, Cumberland Presbyterians retained a measure of aggressiveness. Most of this spirit and fire was directed toward missionary effort and attacks upon infidelity, atheism, and "worldliness" in general. But in some cases it involved them in disputes with members of other churches—and even among themselves—and these disputes frequently led to hard feelings. Despite some unfortunate effects, argumentation helped Cumberland Presbyterians establish their particular position on the American religious scene, in their own eyes as well as in the eyes of others.

During their early history while the emphasis was on missionary revivalism, Cumberland Presbyterians cooperated (especially in camp meetings) with ministers and members of several other denominations. About the only revivalistic group they shunned was the "Stoneites" or New Lights. In fact, position on revivalism became the general criterion for practical cooperation. In his history (1888), B. W. McDonnold wrote, "Men of any [denomination] who oppose revivals can not work well with us, nor we with them." However, he noted, "As to communing at the sacrament of the Lord's Supper, we put no barrier in the way, but refer the question to men's own consciences. I have seen Unitarians communing with our people. It is not our custom to require any test. . . . This has always been our custom, and is the obvious meaning of our standards." A few dissented from this interpretation and insisted that membership in some orthodox church (through baptism) be a prerequisite to communion.[9]

In their relations with the mother Presbyterian Church, Cumberland Presbyterians had considerable difficulty on several matters. They struggled long and hard to get Presbyterian writers to stop identifying them with "heretical" and "disorderly" groups such as the Shakers and the New Lights. Somewhat related was the problem of explaining and defending their "medium theology," the Presbyterians insisting that the Cumberland Presbyterian position must be Arminian if it were not Calvinist. Then there was the charge of an "illiterate" ministry, a charge which bothered some Cumberland Presbyterians not at all but which was of deep concern to others, partly because it could not be refuted easily.

In its official relations with other Protestant bodies the Church followed a policy of cautious friendliness. This caution was particularly noticeable in relations with Presbyterians. The mother church had not recognized the Cumberland Presbyterians as a denomination until 1825. Soon thereafter the Presbyterian Synod of Tennessee appointed a committee to confer with the Cumberland Presbyterians on a plan for friendly correspondence. (It might be noted that, of all the Presbyterians, those in Tennessee had the best opportunity to know the "Cumberlands.") Cumberland Synod responded in 1827 by appointing a similar committee. The Presbyterian General Assembly intervened, stating that the initiation of such correspondence was its prerogative. Accordingly, the Synod of Tennessee withdrew its proposal and the 1828 Cumberland Synod dissolved its committee.

The 1835 General Assembly turned its attention to the possibility of "friendly correspondence" with the adoption of a preamble and resolution presented by Robert L. Caruthers. Noting that some editors and writers had been agitating the subject of "friendly intercourse" with other churches, it resolved that the Cumberland Presbyterian Church

entertains sentiments of friendship and brotherly love, for all worthy members of all other churches, and will, with great pleasure, at all times embrace, evry [sic] opportunity of manifesting to other denominations, collectively and individually, the sincerity of their professions, and will unite with them, on all suitable occasions, to advance the grand cause of the Christian Religion.[10]

The very next year the Assembly responded to an invitation of the Evangelical Lutheran Church by instructing the Stated Clerk to propose that a plan for an interchange of delegates be devised.

Nothing came of that proposal, but in the 1840s there was a widespread general interest in closer relations—even union—among the evangelical churches. By 1845 several churches were exchanging delegates among their church courts. In 1845 the Synod of Pennsylvania suggested to the General Assembly that it investigate the possibility of union with the Evangelical Lutheran Church. This led to arrangements for an exchange of corresponding delegates, but that is as far as the Assembly was interested in going. When the Synod of Ohio suggested union with the same church in 1859, the Assembly declined to act in the absence of any communication from the Evangelical Lutherans.

A flurry of excitement ran through the church in the late 1840s with consideration of a limited degree of union with the Constitutional (New School) Presbyterians. (The New School—Old School schism in the Presbyterian Church in the United States of America had occurred in 1837.) The New School General Assembly, responding to considerable interest from the membership, in 1846 appointed a committee to correspond with the permanent committee on correspondence of the Cumberland Presbyterian Church. Neither committee .was authorized to go beyond the gathering of information; however, they not only proposed exchanges of delegates between General Assemblies and lower courts but also recommended that vacant churches of either denomination be permitted to employ ministers of the other as temporary supplies. The Cumberland Presbyterian Assembly of 1847 accepted only the proposals for exchange of delegates between General Assemblies, synods, and presbyteries. The New School Assembly of 1847 postponed action, partly because of uncertainty as to the Cumberland Presbyterian doctrines and position on slavery. The New School body, being mostly Northeastern, was antislavery. Richard Beard, who had appeared as corresponding delegate, was embarrassed and chagrined at the failure to recognize him and at the questions raised about his Church.[11]

With the New School decision on exchange of delegates pending, there continued much discussion of the subject by Cumberland Presbyterians. For example, the Synod of Missouri noted that such discussion "has, and still is producing excitement, and in many instances unpleasant discussion, and disunion of feelings to some considerable extent, among the ministers and members of the Cumberland Presbyterian Church."[12] Meanwhile, the New School Assembly of 1848 was approving the exchange of delegates.[13] In declining to move toward actual union, both churches expressed feelings of fraternal love and unity of Christian spirit, but each believed it could serve the cause best while preserving its separate identity. It is apparent that both were deterred also by opposition within the ranks and the desire to avoid internal controversy.

Another milestone in relations with the Presbyterians came when the first Old School corresponding delegate attended and was seated in the 1860 General Assembly. McDonnold later wrote, "While Cumberland Presbyterians naturally waited for Presbyterians to move first in this matter, yet they hailed this movement with great joy."[14] Despite McDonnold's recollection, there actually was some hesitation as the 1860 Assembly failed to approve a resolution proposing negotiations over terms of correspondence between the two bodies. The next year it named a delegate, however, and in

1862 the Rev. S. T. Stewart became the first Cumberland Presbyterian delegate to the Old School Assembly. Correspondence with both the New School and Old School Assemblies continued until their reunion in 1869 and thereafter with the reunited church.

After 1861 both the Old School and New School churches were Northern. The six Southern New School synods had withdrawn in 1857. In December 1861, following the adoption of the nationalistic "Spring Resolutions" by the Old School Assembly the previous May, Presbyterians in the seceding states organized the Presbyterian Church in the Confederate States of America (later named the Presbyterian Church in the United States). Since Cumberland Presbyterian Assemblies during the war met north of the military lines and Southern members remained in the Church, there was no chance for correspondence with the newly formed Southern Presbyterian body. With the war over, in 1866 official contact began with an unexpected suggestion of possible organic union between the two churches.

Claiborne A. Davis, pastor of the Memphis congregation, was appointed as corresponding delegate to the Assembly of the Southern Presbyterian Church to meet in Memphis in December 1866. Entirely on his own initiative, Davis suggested that the time was right for a movement looking toward organic union of the two churches. The Southern Assembly then appointed a special committee to find out "how far the way is prepared for an organic union between the two bodies *upon the basis of the Westminster standards.*" [15] This qualification should have been enough to discourage the Cumberland Presbyterians; however, the 1867 Assembly appointed a similar committee. The two committees met at Memphis and exchanged proposals and counterproposals. In their final presentation the Cumberland Presbyterians failed to agree to an unqualified acceptance of the Westminster standards on the doctrine of "fatality or necessity"; therefore, the Southern committee and Assembly rejected the proposal. There clearly had been no real chance of union. As soon as news of the suggested union spread, there was much discussion and disagreement within each of the denominations. However, the movement did lead to a period of friendly correspondence through the exchange of delegates or letters between the two Assemblies. Relations cooled somewhat in the late 1870s and early 1880s, in part because of a failure in communications regarding a change in policy on correspondence. The opposition of some Southern Presbyterians to the admission of the Cumberland Presbyterian Church to the Pan-Presbyterian Alliance also placed a considerable strain on their relations.[16]

With the reunion of the Old School and New School Presbyterians in 1869 and the general surge of ecumenical spirit in the 1870s, some Cumberland Presbyterians again were caught up in the movement. This time it was the Rev. A. J. Baird who, as corresponding delegate to the 1873 General Assembly of the Presbyterian Church, U. S. A. (Northern), took it upon himself to suggest organic union. Consequently, the Assemblies of both churches appointed committees to study the question and consult together. The committees met at Nashville, Tennessee, in February 1874. As in the case of the early exchanges with the Southern Presbyterians, the basic differences concerned the Westminster Confession. The Cumberland Presbyterian group proposed what amounted to a merging of their church into the Presbyterian, provided that the Confession of Faith of either church could be accepted by members and ministers and that all literature and records of both churches be retained as the teachings and history of the united church. The Presbyterian committee saw the Cumberland Presbyterian interpretation of the Westminster Confession as standing in the way, but they insisted that their view of God provided "as thorough conviction of human freedom and accountability" as was found in the other church. Further contact and understanding, they believed, would make this evident, whether or not there was organic union. The Cumberland Presbyterian group countered with the suggestion that it might be a providential time for slight changes "in the language of these time-honored Standards as will fully adapt them to the faith of both churches." Both committees agreed to submit a progress report to their Assemblies and recommend the appointment of a joint committee to continue consideration of the question.[17]

An unfortunate failure in communications permitted a widespread impression among Cumberland Presbyterians that the two committees had agreed to the suggested plan of union. This probably helped account for the heated debate on the question in the 1874 Assembly, which ended with the decision to discontinue the committee and take no further action. The Presbyterian Assembly of 1874 continued its committee, but the next year it also was discharged on account of the Cumberland Presbyterian decision. As in earlier cases of suggested organic union, it is quite clear that favorable sentiment was not really widespread enough to give such proposals a chance of adoption. However, these exchanges and continuing fraternal correspondence did help members of the different churches to get to know each other better. Later, in the controversy over the admission of the Cumberland Presbyterian Church into the Pan-Presbyterian Alliance, the Church found it had many advocates among the Northern Presbyterians.

A development of great and gratifying interest to Cumberland Presbyterians occurred in the 1870s and 1880s. This was a cordial correspondence with the Evangelical Union of Scotland. Hearing that there might be an organization in Scotland holding doctrines similar to theirs, the 1870 Assembly instructed the Stated Clerk, Milton Bird, to try to open correspondence with it. Bird made initial contact with members of the Evangelical Union. In the 1870s and 1880s the two groups exchanged letters, church literature, and even delegates on a few occasions. Each appears to have been overjoyed to learn of the other's existence and that they had so much in common in history and doctrine. Both had experienced what they thought of as persecution from other Presbyterians for their liberal doctrines. Both also believed their influence was contributing to a movement away from strict Calvinism or "fatalism" in the other churches. Mutual interest seems to have waned in the late 1880s, and no record of further correspondence appeared in the General Assembly minutes after 1890.[18]

No doubt many Cumberland Presbyterians cared little about how their Church was regarded by other members of the Presbyterian family. Some made it quite clear that they wanted nothing to do with the "Calvinists." There were others, however, who did care. Though loyal to the doctrines of their own Church, they seem to have wanted the "respectability" which clothed more orthodox Presbyterianism. In addition to a sincere commitment to ecumenism, this was a reason for the pleasure over fraternal correspondence and attempts at organic union. It also helps account for the great interest in the question of whether or not the Church would be admitted into the Pan-Presbyterian Alliance. Since the Cumberland Presbyterians' deviation from the Westminster Confession was presented as an argument for their exclusion, the issue was of international Presbyterian interest.

The 1873 General Assembly of the Presbyterian Church, U. S. A., adopted a resolution looking toward closer union among Presbyterians. It appointed a committee to correspond with other churches holding the Westminster standards about the desirability of holding an ecumenical council. That committee invited the Cumberland Presbyterian Assembly to appoint a committee to meet with others in a planning conference. The letter of invitation was signed by Howard Crosby, Moderator; Edwin F. Hatfield, Stated Clerk; and James McCosh, president of the College of New Jersey (Princeton). Evidently, these men did not consider the Cumberland Presbyterian "exceptions" to the Westminster standards important enough to exclude them from the conference. The Assembly appointed a committee of five to attend the planning session, but the committee did not report back, apparently not having participated. When "The Alliance of the Reformed Churches Throughout the World Holding the Presbyterian System" was formed in London in 1875, the Cumberland Presbyterian Church was not represented and therefore was not a member. The Rev. W. E. Ward had been appointed as delegate but had not attended.[19] In all probability, had the committee participated in the planning or had Ward attended the London meeting, the Church would have entered the Alliance as a matter of course.

At first there must have been little interest among church members in the Pan-Presbyterian Alliance (as the new organization popularly was called), for no delegates were appointed to its 1877 meeting at Glasgow, Scotland. The next meeting was scheduled for Philadelphia in September 1880. Although his denomination was not a member of the Alliance, William Henry Black, pastor of a congregation at Pittsburgh, became chairman of a local committee to arrange for a visit of the Alliance to Pittsburgh. He participated only after he was assured that the Cumberland Presbyterians had not been "counted out." In explaining his action, he wrote in the denominational paper:

If Cumberland Presbyterians want to command respect, they must respect themselves. Self-respect comes first. If we want to have a place among the denominations of the world worthy of us, we must assume it ourselves and not "wait to be invited." Shall we, as a denomination, have a place in that Alliance at Philadelphia next autumn? Have we enough self-hood to claim a position which is rightly ours? [20]

Whether or not because of Black's prompting, the 1880 Assembly appointed nine delegates to the Philadelphia meeting. Black and John R. Rush, an elder, were the only ones to attend, and the burden of seeing that the Cumberland Presbyterian case was considered fell upon Black. In the credentials committee the Southern Presbyterian delegate and two delegates from Scotland opposed the seating of Black and Rush, the Scots being sure the Cumberland Presbyterians were heretical since they were on intimate terms with the Evangelical Union of Scotland. The committee's report recommended that Black and Rush not be seated on the grounds of lack of evidence that the Cumberland Presbyterian creed was in harmony with the Consensus of the Reformed Confessions. Although the report was adopted, it soon became clear that most of the delegates had not understood the significance of the issue—or even that the vote excluded the Cumberland Presbyterian Church from the Alliance. In fact, apparently most of the European members had never heard of the Cumberland Presbyterians. As soon as understanding dawned, general dissatisfaction spread and the question was reopened. After much debate a substitute report was adopted:

*Resolved,* That the Council are unable, *hoc statu,* to admit as members brethren representing churches whose relations to the Constitution have not been explained and can not now be considered.[21]

This was a diplomatic measure to avoid a showdown vote on the question of doctrinal requirements for admission to the Alliance. It stated that the Council could not consider the Cumberland Presbyterian Church for membership because it had not adopted the Constitution of the Alliance. The ruling also excluded the small Reformed Presbytery of Philadelphia; however, it called a meeting, adopted the Constitution, and was accepted.

The issue of Cumberland Presbyterian membership in the Alliance stimulated much debate on both sides of the Atlantic. Generally, on this side, Presbyterians in the Southern and Midwestern parts of the United States opposed admission while those in the Northeastern United States and Canada favored. Across the Atlantic Scots opposed and those on the continent favored admission. The religious press also took sides. Among the papers and journals taking editorial positions, the following have been noted:

| For Admission | Against Admission |
|---|---|
| *Independent* | *Presbyterian Banner* |
| *Evangelist* | *Central Presbyterian* |
| *Christian at Work* | *Herald and Presbyter* |
| *Missionary Review* | *Presbyterian Journal* |
| *Presbyterian Review* | |
| New York *Observer* | |

Among the Cumberland Presbyterians there was much gratification at the attention their Church and its doctrines were receiving, but there was disagreement over whether or not application for membership should be renewed at the next Council meeting at Belfast, Ireland, in 1884. Among the advocates of the continued effort to enter the Alliance, W. H. Black appeared the most aggressive. It should be done, he argued, because (1) their "own dignity and denominational independence" demanded it, (2) they owed it to their friends in other denominations who supported them, and (3) they owed it to the world which was looking to see if Cumberland Presbyterians had enough denominational manhood to demand their rights.[22] Opposition to renewing the application was based in part upon a fear that, under the circumstances, it would represent a doctrinal concession. The majority in the General Assembly, however, took the view that no such concession would be involved. A "Consensus of the Reformed Confessions" did not exist in fact, as no attempt had been made to define such a consensus. The Council at Philadelphia in 1880 appointed a committee to consider the advisability of defining the consensus and report at the next meeting. The Cumberland Presbyterians took the position that, if a decision on their conformity to the "Consensus" was to be made, it was up to the Council of the Alliance to make it. Accordingly, the 1881 Assembly formally approved the Constitution of the Alliance and the 1882 Assembly appointed delegates to the Belfast meeting.

In its official letter to the Alliance, the 1883 Assembly listed the main

Cumberland Presbyterian doctrines and stated the issue plainly:

It is well known to the religious world that our Confession of Faith and Catechism are revisions of the Westminster Confession of Faith and Shorter Catechism, expressing our understanding of the teachings of God's word. Now, dear brethren, if the difference between our statements of doctrine and those of the Westminster Confession of Faith is inconsistent with our being represented in your body, you will so decide.[23]

Many members of other churches shared the desire to make the issue a doctrinal one. Some wished admission of the Cumberland Presbyterian Church, which could be interpreted as a general liberal shift further away from strict Calvinism by the Presbyterian churches. Others wanted its exclusion, which could be seen as a victory for orthodoxy.

When the Council of the Pan-Presbyterian Alliance convened at Belfast in June 1884, twelve delegates from the Cumberland Presbyterian Church presented their credentials. These delegates, who were paying their own expenses, came armed also with copies of various documents, including a summary of the Church's history and the recently adopted Revised Confession of Faith. Interest in the issue was so intense that a Belfast firm printed 3,000 copies of the Confession. The Committee on Consensus appointed by the previous Council unanimously reported against trying to define or clarify the consensus at that time. The acceptance of that report in effect made it impossible for the Council to use a doctrinal criterion in ruling on the Cumberland application. Nevertheless, interest remained high and the Credentials Committee was enlarged to seventeen members to insure that all shades of opinion were represented. The committee meeting was attended by sixteen of the members. The member representing the Presbyterian Church, U. S. (Southern), missed the committee meeting, later explaining that he had been unable to learn where it was being held. In a unanimous report the committee noted that the first Council had placed the responsibility for deciding whether or not they ought to join the Alliance on the churches themselves. It recommended:

. . . without pronouncing any judgement on the church's revision of the Westminster Confession and Shorter Catechism, to admit the Cumberland Presbyterian church into the Alliance, and to invite the delegates now present to take their seats.[24]

Heated and extended debate ensued. Southern Presbyterians, supported by several delegates from the Scottish and the Irish churches and a smattering of others, vehemently opposed adoption of the report. Clearly they regarded the Cumberland Presbyterians as outside the pale of the Westminster standards and believed that their admission would open the doors to a "watering down" of those standards. There were warnings that adoption of the report might well break up the Alliance, an implied threat of secession.

Those favoring the report did so for various reasons. Some were of the opinion that exclusion of the Cumberland Presbyterians would be a slap at all the Reformed churches which did not hold strictly to the Westminster Confession. Also, some of the European churches never had adopted it and actually differed from it more than the Cumberland Presbyterians did. There were even threats of withdrawal if the latter were excluded. Moderates pointed out that the as yet undefined consensus certainly was not identical with the Westminster Confession and that, after all, it was not necessary for the Council to judge the applicant's doctrines.

Finally, in a move apparently intended to mollify the Southern Presbyterian delegates, the last part of the report was amended to read:

> The Council, without approving of the church's revision of the Westminster Confession and of the Shorter Catechism, admit the Cumberland Presbyterian church into the Alliance and invite the delegates now present to take their seats.[25]

As amended, the report was adopted by a vote of 112 to 78.[26] Unfortunately, the vote cannot be interpreted along doctrinal lines. Many, if not most, of those voting "Nay" favored admission without qualification. Some of those voting "Aye" did so because they interpreted the qualification as a rebuke to the Cumberland Presbyterians for deviating from the Westminster standards. Others supporting the amended report regarded the qualifying statement as an unimportant concession to the conservatives for the sake of continued unity in the Alliance. These conflicting interpretations were carried over into opinions expressed by editors and correspondents in the religious press. Regardless of differing views, there was general satisfaction with the way the problem had been handled. And at least one Southern Presbyterian paper, the Saint Louis *Presbyterian,* approved admission of the Cumberland Presbyterian Church on the basis of its presbyterianism.

Never before had the Church and its doctrines received such attention. So much of it was favorable, too! Satisfaction among Cumberland Presbyterians was general but not universal. The 1885 Assembly unanimously adopted a preamble and resolutions approving or accepting membership in the Alliance. It was careful to note that the Council's action placed "the Alliance upon a basis not inconsistent with our creed. . . ."[27] When it was learned that the Church was being assessed about $500 per year to help meet Alliance expenses, several presbyteries proposed withdrawal, but without success. The first notable practical effect of Alliance membership on the Church was in the area of foreign missions. Under an Alliance plan for greater cooperation in foreign fields the Cumberland Presbyterian Church in Japan was merged with other Presbyterian and Reformed churches there to form the Church of Christ in Japan. The missionaries, of course, retained their denominational connections.

During the surge of ecumenical spirit in the 1870s, the Cumberland Presbyterians renewed fraternal correspondence with the Evangelical Lutheran Church. By the early 1880s enough interest in possible organic union had developed in both churches that committees were appointed to consult on the matter. Consultation was entirely by letter and both committees reported that the time did not appear ripe for organic union.[28]

An abortive movement toward union with still another church occurred in the 1880s. W. H. Black, who obviously strongly favored ecumenism, was the first Cumberland Presbyterian delegate to the General Conference of the Methodist Protestant Church at Pittsburgh in 1880. He suggested the possibility of union of the two bodies. In 1885 committees were appointed by both churches to consider that possibility. Their joint report suggested that only minor points of doctrine and easily adjusted differences in government separated the two churches, but as in the several previous cases the movement collapsed because of lack of general support.

All the recent proposals for organic union originating with Cumberland Presbyterians had been on the initiative of individuals rather than the General Assembly. The Assembly tried to stop the practice in 1886 by requiring that no further overtures be made without its prior instruction. The lack of cooperation with this directive brought on another more explicit order in 1898. The Assembly had established fraternal correspondence with some other evangelical churches, but in none of those cases had it become involved in a movement toward organic union.

Cumberland Presbyterians lent their support to nondenominational and interdenominational organizations whose purpose was to Christianize America. Individual ministers and members were among the earliest supporters in the West of the work of the American Bible Society, the American Tract Society, and the American Sunday School Union. Numerous ministers served as agents for those groups. The second Assembly (1830) noted the work of these and similar organizations and resolved to "cooperate with them so long as they are conducted on liberal and prudent principles and free from sectarian influence."[29] Although the General Assembly never was able to give much financial assistance, it and the lower church courts consistently lent encouragement and moral support.

The Sunday School Union was influential in getting the Church interested in the "Sabbath school" idea. Initially, the usual practice was to participate in Union schools, but there was a gradual turn toward the forming of denominational programs. As early as May 1832, the Beech congregation established one.[30] The original purpose of the Sunday school had been to reach children whose religious and moral training was being neglected, that is, orphans and children of nonmembers. The trend was toward denominational schools to supplement the home religious education of the children of church members.

The record of the Sunday school movement in the Cumberland Presbyterian Church is a good example of the development of churchwide organization. Before the Civil War the General Assembly took an interest in Sunday schools and frequently encouraged the churches to establish them. It saw them as a means not only "to lead the youthful mind to Christ" but also to give adults an opportunity for service as teachers. The Assembly started appointing a Committee on Sabbath Schools in 1852 but was unable to report actual practices in the churches for lack of statistical information.

Shortly after the war, interest and activity picked up. The Rev. T. C. Blake began publishing the *Sunday School Gem*, the first such literature published especially for Cumberland Presbyterians. The 1867 Assembly established a standing committee to work at establishing a denominational Sunday school literature in addition to Blake's *Gem*, which was commended to the churches. Two years later, the committee not having made significant progress, the task was assigned to the Board of Publication. Beginning with some children's books and then turning to periodicals, over the next twenty-five years the Board built up a considerable Sunday school literature. It purchased the *Gem* from Blake and later started *Sunday Morning* with comments on the International Sunday School Lessons; *Our Lambs* for the youngest "scholars"; *Comments, Rays of Light*, and *Lesson Leaf* as aids to older children; *Bible Study* for teachers; a Home Department *Quarterly*; and a Junior *Quarterly*. Progress was made both in "grading" the literature and in "upgrading" its quality. In 1898 the Rev. John A. McKamy was appointed as full-time editor of the Sunday school literature. Until then that had been part-time work of other editors or of the Sunday School Superintendent.

During the last quarter of the century there also was much improvement in churchwide organization of the work. In 1883 the Rev. M. B. DeWitt was chosen to fill the newly created office of General Sunday School Superintendent. As no salary was provided, he never actually assumed the duties and resigned in 1886. The Rev. J. H. Warren then was appointed. After he had devoted several months part-time to the job without salary, the position was made permanent and a modest salary provided. Following Warren, successive superintendents were DeWitt in 1889 and the Rev. George O. Bachman in 1894. The economic depression of the mid-1890s forced a cutback in expenses, so Bachman resigned in 1895. For a while H. H. Buquo served as acting superintendent without pay, and he was followed by the Rev. Taylor Bernard, who served with a nominal salary of fifty dollars per year.

Even before the office of General Sunday School Superintendent was set up, there was much progress through synodical and presbyterial organizations. Cumberland Presbyterians had begun cooperating in Sunday school conventions and teachers' institutes, both denominational and Union. By the end of the century, with the aid and encouragement of the General Superintendent, most of the synods and presbyteries had appointed Sunday school superintendents and were conducting the work in an energetic and systematic fashion. An annual "Children's Day" offering provided funds for the general and synodical activities.

As in other areas of church work, statistical information on Sunday schools long was either nonexistent or unreliable. The first estimate of total enrollment was given in 1876 at 150,000, not including those in Union schools.[31] In 1887 the Superintendent estimated that Cumberland Presbyterian churches had 1,306 denominational and 918 Union schools.[32] That these estimates were much exaggerated is shown by 1895 estimates based on much more reliable data: 1,285 denominational schools and 420 Union schools for a total of 1,705, with membership of 6,436 officers, 9,818 teachers, and 103,909 pupils.[33] Despite lack of cooperation in some areas of the Church, at century's end Sunday school work was flourishing and preparations were being made for a special drive to increase membership and to raise more funds to finance expanded activity.

The increasing importance of women in organized church work in the last quarter of the century was quite notable. They served as teachers and sometimes as officers in Sunday schools. Their contributions in the missionary field and in church schools and colleges have been discussed in an earlier chapter. Late in the century they began efforts to acquire the right to participate in church government. Actual practices probably developed before being noted in the church courts or the press. As early as 1877, Pennsylvania Presbytery approved the appointment of "female members" as trustees and deacons in congregations.[34] Apparently, there was little opposition to their being given such duties, but the question of their ordination as elders or ministers was quite controversial.

The General Assembly first touched upon that question in 1887. Oregon Synod had invited congregations to send women to its meetings to speak and advise. The Assembly declared the synod's action illegal, but on the grounds that there was no provision for calling lay members into a church court as advisers rather than on the grounds of sex. When confronted directly with the question of the ordination of women as ruling elders, the Assembly acted indecisively and inconsistently. The 1892 Assembly, by a vote of 105 to 90, ruled that such ordination was not prohibited by church law and left the question to be decided by lower courts on the basis of local needs. Mrs. P. L. Clagett of Nolin Presbytery (Kentucky) appeared as a delegate and was seated in the 1893 Assembly. In an attempt to get a definite policy adopted, this Assembly presented two constitutional amendments: one specifically would have excluded women from the offices of ruling elder and deacon; the other specifically would have made them eligible for those offices.

Despite widespread interest and much published debate, the presbyteries voted against any change, so the policy remained uncertain. The 1896 Assembly ruled that Indiana Synod violated the constitution by seating Mrs. S. K. Hart as a representative, but the next Assembly accepted as legal Kansas Synod's seating of a Mrs. Squires as a ruling elder. The 1898 Assembly refused to attempt clarification of the policy and so the situation remained at the end of the century.

Controversy over the ordination of women as ministers centered around the case of Mrs. Louisa M. Woosley. In 1889 Nolin Presbytery ordained Mrs. Woosley to the full work of the gospel ministry. Kentucky Synod in 1890 declared that the presbytery had no authority to ordain her, but it failed to revoke the ordination. In August 1893, Nolin Presbytery elected Mrs. Woosley as an alternate delegate to the General Assembly. The synod then reaffirmed its earlier ruling, declared her election null and void, and directed the presbytery to retire her name from its list of ministers. Mrs. Woosley appeared at the 1894 Assembly with her credentials and appealed the action of Kentucky Synod. Nolin Presbytery, which had failed to obey the synod's order, asked Assembly to reverse the action. By a close vote of eighty-five to seventy-eight the Assembly denied Mrs. Woosley's appeal and refused to seat her, ruling that she was not a regularly ordained minister. Nolin Presbytery refused to abide by the decision and asked the 1895 Assembly to reconsider. The Assembly turned down the request, asserting that it could not reopen a case after "final judgment" had been rendered. Here the matter rested so far as church law was concerned. But the issue was not resolved, as Mrs. Woosley's presbytery continued to support her. Other presbyteries were accepting women as probationers for the ministry. The Assembly's Stated Clerk, on its instructions, continued to omit their names from the official presbyterial rolls.[35]

MRS. L. M. WOOSLEY
(1862-1952)

A portrait of the first woman minister in the Cumberland Presbyterian Church, from her book, *Shall Woman Preach? or, The Question Answered*, published in 1891.

In its early history the government of the Church, except at the local level, clearly was dominated by the clergy. In the General Assembly there usually were about twice as many ministers as elders before the Civil War. In addition, moderators and stated clerks always were ministers and most committees had ministers as chairmen. Some laymen were appointed to boards, especially in the 1840s and 1850s as attempts were made to bring business efficiency into the management of church enterprises.

After the Civil War there was a decided increase in the role of laymen. The Assembly of 1865, recognizing what probably was already a widespread practice, ruled that ruling elders could transact session business without the presence of the minister. When Milton Bird died in 1872, John Frizzell of Tennessee, a ruling elder, was elected Stated Clerk, a position he held until 1883. In the 1870s presbyteries began electing elders as moderators, the earliest reported in the church press being the election of James Cunningham by Union Presbytery (Pennsylvania) in 1871.[36] When the question of the constitutionality of this practice came before the Assembly in 1881 and 1882, the delegates were almost evenly divided but voted against stating a definite policy.[37] Despite protests, this inaction was taken generally to mean that the election of elders as moderators did not violate church law.

The struggle clearly was over when the 1884 Assembly elected Frizzell as Moderator. Other elders serving as Moderator of the General Assembly before 1900 were Nathan Green (the younger), of Lebanon, Tennessee, in 1887; E. E. Beard, also of Lebanon, in 1891; and H. H. Norman, of Murfreesboro, Tennessee, in 1898. This recognition of the growing importance of laymen in church government was reflected in an increase in the proportion of elders in the Assembly. By the late 1890s the ratio of ministers to elders was usually about six to five. More laymen also were active on the several general church boards and in other church enterprises.

When Cumberland Presbyterians looked at how their church government actually worked, they were at a loss to describe it in traditional terms. While presbyterian in theory, in practice at the local level it probably was closer to being congregational. The dearth of settled pastors, especially in the early decades, limited clerical influence and guidance in church sessions. The frequent failure of congregations without pastors to send representatives to presbytery and synod further isolated them from the higher courts. Consequently, laymen (elders and deacons) played a more important role in local church government than strict conformity to presbyterian polity would have required. Some members believed it necessary to adopt a middle-ground governmental system along with a medium theology to avoid the extremes of Calvinism and Arminianism. Certainly practices varied greatly from place to place and time to time. When appeals and memorials relating to government came up to the General Assembly, they frequently reflected either a lack of knowledge of or a disregard for church law, especially the deliverances of the Assembly.

There was lack of contact or communication in both directions. Except in the very early years, until the late 1890s about 20 per cent to 50 per cent of the synods annually failed to send their records for inspection by the Assembly. After the Stated Clerk began distributing statistical report forms to presbyterial secretaries, it was decades before he could rely on general compliance. And the difficulty was almost as great in the other direction. As a minister wrote in 1879:

When we meet in General Assembly (our war council), we plan with ability great unanimity, and issue tremendous orders; but, when we get home our notions are as far apart as our homes. If this were to occur once or twice it would not be strange, but it has become a rule, a settled habit, and unless we can change it, of course we can never mass our forces on any one thing.[38]

This lack of cooperative effort was due in part to the failure of General Assembly rulings, requests, and orders to reach the masses of ministers and members. Relatively few members received church papers. Time after time the Assembly urged the presbyteries to force their ministers to transmit orders and information to congregations. Apparently the main difficulty was that the negligent ministers also controlled the presbyteries—or even failed to attend presbyterial meetings.

Another reason for the lack of unity was the distrust and even fear of central authority in religious matters which many members shared. We have noted this as a factor in opposition to various general enterprises. Obviously, there were many members, ministers, and presbyteries that did cooperate and conduct affairs of the Church in an orderly and businesslike manner. Yet the general problem persisted and yielded only slowly to efforts at reform. McDonnold summarized his view of the situation in 1888 in commenting on the earlier establishing of a board of missions:

There were fears by some that the general board would become a pope. But the danger in the Cumberland Presbyterian church has never been in the direction of the pope, but in the other direction. Independence, which regards neither session, presbytery, assembly, nor the general welfare, has more frequently paralyzed our enterprises. There is a medium between the centralization which makes a pope and the private independence which makes anarchy. God in his providence is slowly leading the church to this medium ground.[39]

The movement which McDonnold noted was being evidenced in several areas of activity: publication, education, Sunday schools, missions, systematic benevolence, and others. Then in the 1890s the General Assembly stepped up its efforts to improve church government. It directed the presbyteries to order "idle" ministers to serve "vacant" churches, suggesting that a minister's failure to obey would be grounds for expulsion.[40] This directive was renewed annually for several years. It set up a uniform and comprehensive schedule of reports for use by all lower courts. A long-standing ambition was realized in 1899 with the publication of the *Cumberland Presbyterian Digest*, prepared by the Rev. John Vant Stephens. Its descriptive subtitle was "A Compend of the Organic Law of the Cumberland Presbyterian Church, Together with the Organic Law of its General Agencies, and the Judicial Deliverances of its Supreme Judicatory." With this excellent guide in hand, with well-organized and relatively smoothly functioning general enterprises in operation, and with a growing spirit of cooperation, the Church entered the new century with rising confidence and optimism.

# *16*

## A PROGRESSIVE THEOLOGY

*Let it be understood, in short, that ours is not a fixed and change-less, but a progressive creed; and through all the decades we are to seek a more and more nearly exact statement of the truth revealed in Scripture, and believed by our own people.*

J. M. Howard, 1883

The schism in American Presbyterianism in 1810 which produced the Cumberland Presbyterian Church was in part a theological movement. As such, its immediate roots were in the New Side wing of American Presbyterianism which formed in the first half of the eighteenth century under the leadership of a group of ministers called the Log College preachers. These men, who were active in the Great Awakening of 1740, exerted a strong influence on the ministers who went into Virginia and North Carolina with the tide of Scottish Presbyterian migration into these states during the middle of the eighteenth century. The first Cumberland Presbyterians came largely from the congregations of these Virginia and North Carolina preachers who represented the Log College-New Side theological tradition. The first Cumberland Presbyterians did not regard the theological views which they held as novel in American Presbyterianism, something produced by frontier revivalism. Rather, they believed they were propagating a theology already present in the Presbyterianism which they had known in North Carolina and Virginia. The characteristic mark of this theology was its tendency to modify the claims of the Westminster Confession concerning the unconditional sovereignty of God and to enlarge the scope of human freedom and activity.

Finis Ewing was aware of this theological tradition and identified himself with it. This is evidenced by his comparison of the revival spirit in Cumberland Presbytery with the spirit of the Great Awakening in Brunswick Presbytery in New Jersey, which had been the stronghold of the Log College-New Side preachers.[1] He argued that a tradition of modified Calvinism had existed not only in American Presbyterianism but in Presbyterian and Reformed theology from the time the Westminster Confession was written. As evidence, he called attention to the fact that Richard Baxter, a prominent seventeenth century English Puritan, had "rejected in the Confession what we call fatality." [2] Ewing's knowledge of this theological tradition of modified Calvinism made it possible for him to affirm without apparent hesitation, "The Calvinistic system of doctrine with the exceptions we have made is nearest Scriptural of any with which I am acquainted." [3]

What was called fatalism, the belief that some persons, before the foundation of the world, had been predestined to be lost, was avoided in Log College-New Side theology throughout the eighteenth century. The universal character of the atonement was implicit in the very approach of revival preaching. Emphasis in revival preaching on the experience of regeneration was more compatible with the idea of conditional election—an election based on the conditions of repentance, faith, and obedience. The theological modifications which this emphasis encouraged were matched by a further weakening of the doctrine of predestination under attacks which charged that it was an insult to the spirit of democratic justice.

Samuel Davies, a second-generation Log College preacher and perhaps the most influential leader in Presbyterianism in Virginia and North Carolina in the mid-eighteenth century, is a good example of an advocate of modified Calvinism. Davies was very sensitive to the difficulties created by the doctrine of predestination, particularly the charge that it cast a "stain of Cruelty and Injustice upon the Gospel." [4] In an attempt to soften the fatalism suggested by the Westminster Confession he said, "This you may be sure of, that if you have not made yourselves fit for destruction, . . . by your own wilful sin, you shall never be doomed to it by virtue of any decree of God." [5] He was impatient with all talk about the "high mystery of predestination" and the "secret counsel of God," and charged that it was just such unprofitable speculations that caused controversies. In a ringing declaration he anticipated the later Cumberland Presbyterian cry concerning a "whosoever-will gospel." Said he, "I venture to assert that Christ died for every man, in such a sense as to warrant all that hear the gospel to regard the offer of salvation by his death as made to them without distinction." [6]

This theological tradition represented by Davies was carried to Kentucky and Tennessee in the migrations of Presbyterians from Virginia and North Carolina at the end of the eighteenth century and the beginning of the nineteenth century. It was this theological tradition that informed the preaching during the Great Revival of 1800, in which the first Cumberland Presbyterians were involved. James McGready, a central figure in the revival, urged caution in the manner in which the doctrine of Divine Decrees was interpreted. He wrote, "Someone in his great zeal for the truth contends warmly for predestination, election, and final perseverance, and unless he is very cautious, he will do it in the wrong manner." [7] As Davies had done, he argued that a man's eternal destiny is not fixed until the final judgment; hence one could in complete sincerity invite all unbelievers to repent and be born again.

Before the schism of 1810, the revival ministers of Cumberland Presbytery, who had been suspended and charged with serious doctrinal deviations, insisted that the views they held were not unusual in American Presbyterianism. The only scruple any of them had ever raised concerning the Westminster Confession was in regard to "the concise manner in which the highly mysterious doctrine of divine decrees is expressed, which is thought led to fatality." [8] In 1812, in the first formal statement of the theological position of the reconstituted Cumberland Presbytery, Finis Ewing again stated that "fatality is the only objection." [9] The positive counterpart to this objection was a conditional election and an unlimited atonement. As Ewing put it, "We do not believe in the doctrine of *eternal* reprobation. We do not believe that Christ died for a part of mankind only. We do not believe that a part of the infants who die in infancy are lost." [10]

In the first authorized theological statement of the newly formed Cumberland Presbyterian denomination, prepared by Finis Ewing and Robert Donnell and published in the 1814 edition of Charles Buck's *Theological Dictionary,* a position is taken in opposition not only to the "rigid Calvinists" but also to the "extreme Arminians." This was the first formulation of what came to be the identifying mark of Cumberland Presbyterian theology—a medium position "between the opposite extremes" of Calvinism and Arminianism.[11] Ewing and Donnell may have found this description in the writings of Ewing's former pastor and sponsor, David Rice, a New Side minister, who in his book, *A Lecture on the Divine Decrees,* published in 1791, had said that both Calvinists and Arminians "in the warmth of debate on the subject . . . have run into wide extremes." [12] Rice had urged that a mediating position be found between the extremes.

In the view of Ewing and Donnell, "extreme Calvinism" meant the doctrine of double predestination as set forth in the Westminster Confession, or the removal of human agency altogether from the determination of a man's salvation or reprobation. "Extreme Arminianism" was identified as the view that man can, without special assistance, turn to God and be saved. The "intermediate position" of Cumberland Presbyterian theology was said to be the view that redemption is offered conditionally to all men, but that no man can lay hold of this redemption without the special grace of God. Such grace is available to all, however, in the form of illumination and influence of the Holy Spirit.

It soon became clear to Ewing and Donnell and other Cumberland Presbyterians that their theological position required not simply scruples about certain interpretations of the Westminster Confession, but the more drastic action of a deletion of some sections and a revision of the wording of other sections. This they proceeded to do. The newly formed Synod in 1813 appointed a revision committee consisting of four ministers—Ewing, Donnell, William McGee, and Thomas Calhoun. This committee, with Ewing doing the major part of the work,[13] drafted a revision of the Westminster Confession which was adopted by the Synod in 1814.

Though significant changes were made in several sections of the Confession, the most noticeable ones were in those on Divine Decrees, Providence, and Effectual Calling. Large portions of these sections were deleted, thereby eliminating some of the most objectionable features of "extreme Calvinism." In the "Preface" to the 1814 revision of the Confession, it was stated that the intention of the committee was "to erase from the old Confession the idea of fatality *only*."[14] This claim was far too modest, for in addition to doing this through the substitution of conditional election and reprobation for the unconditional and irresistible decrees of God, the revision both restricted the effects of the Fall on man and enlarged man's freedom and his natural abilities in preparing himself for conversion.

Statements in the Westminster Confession concerning the decrees of God had long been a problem for the New Side-Log College wing of Presbyterianism. It was in this section, in particular, that the idea of fatality seemed to be suggested. The Cumberland Presbyterian revision of 1814 virtually eliminated this section and inserted in its stead a long footnote explaining the deletion and setting forth the Cumberland Presbyterian position. In the portion of the section that was retained, the decrees of God were changed from absolute pretemporal determinations of people and events to a pretemporal determination of general conditions or laws to which man in his freedom might respond. The committee on revision correctly saw that this change from unconditional to conditional election required a corresponding change in those sections of the Confession dealing with man's ability and freedom. The Westminster Confession said bluntly that man's fall into sin left him without ability "to convert himself, or to prepare himself thereunto." [15] This was softened to read that man "is not able by his own strength to convert himself, or to prepare himself thereunto without Divine aid" (C. P. C., 1814, ix, 3). Conditional election creates a situation which calls for some action on man's part; thus it cannot be the case that he is wholly without ability for goodness. Whereas the Westminster Confession attributed salvation wholly to God, even including the faith by which man received the gift, the Cumberland Presbyterian revision made it a cooperative work in which man also does his part. This is clearly stated in the 1814 Revision in the footnote to the section on Divine Decrees: "The plan of the Bible is grace and duty. God calls (grace); sinner hearken diligently (duty); God reproves (grace); sinner turn (duty); God pours out his Spirit (grace); sinner resist not the light, but improve it (duty)" (C. P. C., 1814, footnote to iii, 2).

The 1814 revision of the Westminster Confession brought the creedal statement of Presbyterianism in line with the kind of theology that had been more or less explicit in the preaching of the New Side-Log College ministers for many decades. It gave the growing number of Cumberland Presbyterian preachers a solid theological footing for the preaching of a "whosoever-will gospel."

Two members of the revision committee, Ewing and Donnell, soon established themselves as articulate interpreters of the "medium theology," giving the new and expanding denomination its first formal theological works written from the point of view of the revised Confession. In 1827 Ewing published a book entitled *A Series of Lectures on the Most Important Subjects of Divinity,* which consisted of lectures he had given at a school for ministers that he had established in Missouri. In this book may be found the basic ideas that informed the 1814 revision of the Westminster Confession. The controlling concept in Ewing's theology was that of the moral law. He advised his students that if they wanted to be "well grounded in the fundamental truths of the gospel, to study well the law." [16] He defined the moral law as that "which is good, right, and fit in its own nature; consequently always right, and must eternally continue to be right." [17] It was in accordance with this law that God had determined to deal with men. Though this law was to be found in the Bible, it was also written "in less or more legible characters, on every man's heart, and impressed by the divine Spirit, in a less or greater degree on every man's conscience." [18] If it were the case that God dealt with men in terms of a clearly published law, it could not be true, as the Westminster Confession claimed, that God determined men's destinies by secret decrees. Moreover, if God dealt with men in terms of the moral law, they should be able to perform as well as understand its conditions. The first man, Adam, failed to perform the condition of obedience; therefore all men were placed under the penalty of death. The gospel is the good news that Jesus Christ *has* performed the conditions of the law for man, freed him from the penalty of death, and given him a new set of conditions which he is able to meet. Under the new covenant, man is required to believe in Jesus Christ as the proper act of obedience to the law.

Like Ewing, Donnell developed his theology around the concept of the moral law, the rational principle that was the underlying basis for harmony in all relations. As Donnell saw it, the moral law is not the same as the will of God, rather it is that to which even the Divine Will must be conformed. "There is a universal immutable law, generally called moral, which is not dependent on sovereign power for its existence, but grows out of the eternal reason of things. . . . This is the great platform on which heaven itself is built." [19] It is this law that defined Adam's relation to God, a state of trial. When Adam failed his probation and placed all his descendants under a penalty of death, it became necessary to create a new set of conditions for man. This Christ did by his death, satisfying the penalty imposed on mankind by Adam's sin. The new conditions are that men are commanded to believe in Jesus Christ. All who pass this new state of trial are confirmed to eternal life. It is clear that man determines his own destiny. His fate is not sealed by some secret decree of God before the foundation of the world.

It is necessary for the will of man to determine, while the condition of this covenant is before him, to be saved by the second Adam. Soon as this determination takes place, he is justified—entitled to heaven. . . . On the other hand, the sinner that determines to reject Christ, after having had a fair opportunity of embracing the benefits of his death, is also sealed to everlasting misery.[20]

Nothing sounded more reasonable, to men imbued with the sense of democratic justice that prevailed on the American frontier, than a gospel in which God gives man a "fair opportunity." It is not surprising that Donnell felt that the Cumberland Presbyterian Church exactly fit the American way. "She was born in this land of liberty, and is properly called an American church, if not the only one." [21]

The "medium theology" as interpreted by Ewing and Donnell was a system in which God exercised his sovereignty in determining that man's life should be within a system of moral law, and in dealing out the rewards and retributions appropriate to the system. God's grace is manifested in the second chance he gives man in the new covenant in Jesus Christ—in the alteration of the conditions so that man now has a fair trial, despite the sin of Adam. Man exercises his freedom, with a full knowledge of the consequences, in obeying or disobeying the new command. The mystery of God's election had thus been transformed into the rational conditions of the moral law.

The first generation of Cumberland Presbyterians did not set out to construct a new theology. They intended only to revise the creedal statement of the Church to bring it into line with the theology which was already in fact being preached. They regarded their theology as a modified Calvinism, even as their Confession remained the Westminster Confession, appropriately modified. The second generation of Cumberland Presbyterians had fewer ties with the old theological tradition. The existence of the new denomination was now securely established and out of the growing denominational self-consciousness there began to come demands for a theology with a specifically Cumberland Presbyterian label. In 1840 the General Assembly appointed a committee to prepare for publication a standard work on Cumberland Presbyterian theology.[22] Though this project failed to materialize, in 1845, the Rev. Milton Bird, who had been a member of the committee, began publication of a quarterly theological journal to which he gave the significant title *The Theological Medium.* This quarterly continued with almost unbroken publication throughout the remainder of the nineteenth century under various titles and editors, and it became an important stimulus to and repository of Cumberland Presbyterian theological writings.

The beginning of the publication of the *Theological Medium* coincided with a growing interest in a more precise definition of Cumberland Presbyterian doctrine—the medium theology—in relation both to Calvinism and to Arminianism. It soon became clear, however, that it was easier to talk about a middle position than to define it. The result was that some writers began to charge each other with too much deviation from the middle toward one extreme or the other. "Conservative" and "liberal" positions began to emerge, the former being more inclined toward Calvinism and the latter toward Arminianism. Milton Bird was a leader of the "conservatives," and Reuben Burrow, a professor at Bethel Academy (afterward Bethel College), was a leader of the "liberals."

The point at which the divergence of views began to be apparent was in the doctrine of faith. Bird was disturbed that the doctrine was being interpreted in such a way as to make it an autonomous act of man, performed apart from special divine aid. It was the published views of Reuben Burrow that were the particular object of his concern. Although the Revision of 1814 had restricted the effects of original sin on the will, it still insisted that natural man was incapable of actions connected with his salvation, except with divine aid. Burrow removed even this restriction. From his point of view, man is now as capable of goodness as Adam ever was. "Man's soul is so perfectly free in its responsible actions as to be necessitated by no moral sensibilities or qualities apart from that self-moving volition given at first, and never taken away by the giver or lost by the receiver." [23] Therefore, Burrow rejected not only the view that faith is a gift of God, but also the claim that it is a joint act of God and man. "The assumption therefore, that faith is both the act of the creature and the gift of God, makes it no better, because it not only holds that God must give grace but also faith." [24]

Unwilling to permit such a veiw to go unchallenged, Bird replied, "I cannot adopt the hypothesis, that faith is neither more nor less than *a single act of the mind,* wholly at the pleasure of the human will performed whenever and wherever it pleases." [25] Though he did not charge Burrow with intentionally holding heretical views, he nevertheless felt they were heretical. "In the doctrine of faith the error of the Socinians is to be avoided, as well as that of the Calvinists." [26] Bird argued that the fact of man's bondage to sin means that he cannot of himself originate faith. God must perform a work in man first, "otherwise the principle of faith can neither exist, nor act, either in its first degree, higher, or highest, or most mature steps." [27] Bird acknowledged that he did not know how to define it, but he was certain that faith was the result, in some sense, of a cooperative work of God and man. At times, he spoke of it as a concurrence of Divine and human agencies, and again he described it as a process in which God performs the initial act, which is then followed by a response from man. In its inception faith is the gift of God; it does not "originate in the human will." [28] Bird was willing to acknowledge that natural man possesses a certain freedom, but he is not autonomous—"man is free but not independent." [29] Though the initial act (usually called illumination) which God performs in man is something short of salvation, it is nevertheless performed prior to any action on man's part. "The choice and action of the sovereign will of God opens the way for, and gives to man the power of concurrence or conformity to that choice and will." [30]

It seemed to Burrow that Bird was saying exactly what the Westminster Confession said, except in different language. He saw little difference in the claim that God, at his own initiative, regenerated a man and gave him the faith to accept the salvation in Jesus Christ, and the claim that God, at his own initiative, illuminated a man and gave him "the power of concurrence or conformity to that choice and will." Apart from the question of whether Bird's views were at this point significantly different from the Westminster Confession, it should be noted that Bird denied that God's election was irresistible. He held that man cannot act autonomously in faith, but that he may and does originate absolutely the act whereby he rejects God's initial gift.

The divergence of views expressed by Bird and Burrow continued to be felt in the Church as more and more efforts were expended to define a theology that was peculiarly Cumberland Presbyterian. It was this difference that produced on the one hand requests for a further revision of the Confession of Faith, and on the other hand warnings about moving too far toward Arminianism. Between 1849 and 1852 a number of overtures were sent to the General Assembly from presbyteries and synods "praying a revision of the Confession of Faith." [31] (The exchange of views between Bird and Burrow appeared in the *Theological Medium* in 1846.) In 1852 the Assembly issued something of a rebuke to those pressing for revisions by warning, "Should the walls once be thrown down, it would be difficult, if not impossible, ever to build them up so as to suit the peculiar taste of each." [32] Undaunted by this warning, in 1853 West Tennessee Synod again sent an overture to the Assembly asking for a committee to be appointed to prepare a revision of the Confession. This effort met with success and such a committee was named by the Assembly. It is significant that the membership of the committee included Burrow, but it did not include either Bird, Burrow's theological opponent, or Richard Beard, the newly appointed professor of theology at Cumberland University, who shared Bird's "conservative" views. In 1854 the committee presented a report calling for a limited revision of the Confession, but the report was not approved. The proposed changes were generally along the lines of those made in the Revision of 1814. Perhaps the most important recommendation was that which would have rearranged the order of the chapters in the Confession so that those on Repentance and Saving Faith would have preceded the chapter on Justification, all in accordance with the idea of a conditional election. Also, the title of the chapter on Effectual Calling would have been changed to Divine Influence.[33]

Though the effort at a revision of the Confession failed in 1854, there was a sizeable minority that had favored it (sixty-four against and forty-one for revision). One of the leading opponents of revision was Beard, who, like Bird, was disturbed by what seemed to him to be a "prevailing tendency to Arminianism," and expressed the hope that there was "conservatism enough to keep it [the Church] in its primitive doctrinal status." [34] He felt that Ewing and Donnell had "considered their theology as a modified Presbyterian or Calvinistic theology," [35] and he intended to remain true to the founding fathers—to prevent the "wall" from being "thrown down."

As late as 1880, only a few months before his death, in an address to the General Assembly, Beard said of the 1814 Confession, "I think that this is the sort of Confession of Faith any man needs. . . . Any conservative man can adopt it. Let it alone." [36]

Beard regarded his monumental three-volume work entitled *Lectures on Theology* as an exposition of the 1814 Confession, and he believed that his writings were in keeping with the views of Ewing and Donnell. Though not commissioned by the General Assembly as such, Beard's *Lectures* were in fact the standard work on Cumberland Presbyterian theology that had been sought earlier. Written at about the midpoint of his tenure of twenty-five years (1855-1880) as professor of theology at Cumberland University, the *Lectures* constitute a complete theological system according to the "medium principle"—a full-scale apologetic for the doctrines of the Cumberland Presbyterian Church.

As an apologist for Cumberland Presbyterian theology, Beard sought to show that this theology was at the same time "Scientific, Experimental, and Practical." [37] By scientific, he meant that its basic propositions could be demonstrated to the reason to be true. By experimental and practical, he meant a theology that fit human experience, that corresponded to human feelings, and that met human needs. Beard's concern for a practical theology led him to adopt as a theological method a procedure based on an analysis of human consciousness. In this analysis, he found two essential elements —an awareness of dependence and an awareness of freedom. It was clear to him that these elements of human consciousness corresponded to the fundamental doctrines of the medium theology—the theology of grace and duty.

An Ewing and Donnell had done, Beard interpreted grace primarily in terms of law. The gospel is a "supplement to the law." [38] Man's dependence on God is described as moral obligation—the moral law. It is the moral law that conditions God's sovereignty so that he determines to deal with man in terms of a conditional covenant. Atonement in Jesus Christ is a satisfaction of the penalties of the moral law, so that man may have a second chance. It is law that structures God's acts toward man, that determines the framework of man's dependence on God.

If the element of dependence in human consciousness, with its correlative of grace, is to be understood in terms of moral law, it could easily be shown that the other element derived from consciousness, human freedom, with its correlative of duty, is also to be understood in terms of law. It is law that poses the condition necessary to the exercise of freedom. God's government of the world is a government of law, and "such a government implies freedom of action." [39] Man is "free to observe or violate those laws of conduct which

God has prescribed for him." [40] Duty is the action of man when he, in freedom, obeys the demands of the moral law.

Beard was in complete agreement with the 1814 Confession that the plan of the Bible is grace and duty, and he believed that he had shown that this plan is practical—that it corresponds to human experience. While it is true that "salvation is of grace, . . . grace does not exclude the idea of duty." [41] Nothing is more plainly taught in the Scriptures than that "whatever God may do for man, unless man do something for himself, he will never be saved." [42]

Though Beard was determined to maintain a balanced emphasis on grace and duty, like other apologists for the medium theology, he had difficulties with the doctrine of faith. Taking a position similar to that of Bird, he wrote, "I shall insist, that grace, and grace alone, enables us to believe; but I shall insist as strenuously that the believing is our own act." [43] At the same time he acknowledged that he could not untangle this paradox. This matter, he said, lies "beyond the range of human investigation." [44]

Beard's successor in the chair of systematic theology at Cumberland University was Stanford G. Burney. Burney had been an advocate of further revision of the 1814 Confession of Faith and had been a member of the committee that had drafted the unsuccessful revision in 1854. Less than a year after Beard's death in 1880, the General Assembly appointed another Revision Committee with Burney as its chairman. This committee met with more success than the one on which Burney had first served, for in 1883 the radically revised Confession of Faith which the committee drafted was finally approved by the Church.

From 1850 to 1875 Burney was pastor of the First Cumberland Presbyterian Church in Oxford, Mississippi. In 1852 he founded Union Female College at Oxford and served as its president until 1860. In 1860 he was elected Moderator of the General Assembly. At various times during his pastorate at Oxford he taught philosophy at the University of Mississippi. In 1877 he became a professor of Biblical literature at Cumberland University, and, following Beard's death in 1880, he was appointed to the chair of systematic theology. In addition to his published works on anthropology, psychology, soteriology, and ethics, Burney frequently contributed articles to the *Theological Medium*. Through his teachings and writings, and as chairman of the committee which prepared the 1883 revision of the Confession of Faith, he left a permanent imprint of his ideas on the theology of the Cumberland Presbyterian Church.

In his writings Burney accomplished three objectives. First, with the use of a faculty psychology that was current in America in the nineteenth century, he defined human freedom as complete autonomy of the will, and, unlike Beard, he did not shrink from the consequences of this claim. Second, having established complete autonomy for man, he interpreted religion as man's autonomous ethical activity. These two developments were, in a sense, an extension of the two facts which Beard had derived from his analysis of human consciousness—human freedom and the moral law. The third objective of Burney was the removal from Cumberland Presbyterian theology of all the basic concepts and images of Federalism carried over from the Westminster Confession in the 1814 revision of the Confession.

In his analysis of the self, Burney distinguished three faculties: the intelligence, the sensibility, and the will. While he believed these three faculties worked in harmony, they were nevertheless absolutely distinct from each other. The function of the intelligence and the sensibility is to present alternatives of action to the will, whereas it is the function of the will to choose. In its choice the will is absolutely free. "All volitions, both divine and human, are primary or uncaused causes." [45] Burney insisted that "our acts are our acts, not because we consent to them, or commit ourselves to them, but because we actually originate them." [46] In line with this view, Burney described faith as the autonomous act of man in response to the Scriptures and to divine influence.

According to Burney, man in the Fall lost none of his freedom or ability, only his original condition of righteousness. With his will unimpaired, man is fully capable of initiating actions toward God. This must be the case, or there would be no ground for moral accountability. It is not surprising, therefore, that Burney should have openly advocated a religion of works. "Everyone is rewarded according to his works. This is the ethical law given in the Scriptures." [47]

The most ambitious and far-reaching part of Burney's theological activity was his effort to eliminate the basic concepts and images that had been carried over into Cumberland Presbyterian theology from the Westminster Confession. These were the foundation of a system of theology known as Federalism or Covenant Theology. The term "Federalism" was derived from the claim that Adam as the "federal head" or representatitve of mankind had entered into a covenant of works with God, but then broke this covenant, placing all mankind under the penalty of death. God, who was conceived as the moral governor of the universe, was obliged to uphold the law. The role of Jesus Christ, the second Adam, was that in his death he satisfied the penalty of the law, thereby making it possible for God to pardon man without appearing to have relaxed the law. This system of theology was completely repugnant to Burney. He rejected the "federal headship" idea as being inconsistent with individual moral responsibility; he said God is properly conceived as a father, not a governor; and he maintained that it was a blot on the character of God to claim that God had to punish someone for Adam's sin before he could forgive man.

Though Burney nowhere acknowledges a dependence on Horace Bushnell, a Congregationalist minister and the leading figure of late nineteenth century liberalism in American theology, there is a similarity of his ideas to those of Bushnell. Bushnell had rejected the Federalism of New England theology as being sterile and unrelated to life. He interpreted the covenant in terms of family relations rather than the contract relations of civil government. With just such a change in mind, Burney said, "Happily for Christianity the divine fatherhood is coming into greater prominence in the pulpit and religious literature than has been accorded for centuries." [48]

Like Bushnell, Burney claimed that the sin of Adam is transmitted by heredity. Bushnell had also argued that a parent could transmit a propensity toward good to his children; therefore, a child reared in a godly home should be able gradually to "grow up a Christian, and never know himself as being otherwise." [49] Burney seems to mean essentially the same thing when he says he thinks "children under highly advantageous circumstances may come to love Christ and actually pass from a state of death unto life before they are capable of any distinct sense of moral accountability." [50] This view is obviously quite different from the early Cumberland Presbyterian emphasis on a definite, conscious, time-and-place experience of the new birth.

The images dominant in the theology of Ewing, Donnell, and Beard were legal ones, the images of Federalist theology. Adam was the legal representative of man; God was the moral governor; the covenant was a legal agreement; the atonement was a legal satisfaction of the penalty of death which God as moral governor was obliged to uphold. All this theology Burney swept away, putting in its stead a theology which employed the images of the family relation. "Not until men recognize God as their Father who loves them, protects them, pities them as kind parents pity their children do they trust him, reverence him, love and obey him with a cheerful, happy delight." [51] A comparison of this view with that of Ewing will reveal how far removed was the theology of Burney from that of the founders of the Church, who, as good Presbyterians, believed a man was never converted until he had been "slain by the law." Ewing said, "The idea of man first seeking God from love, or being moved thereto by a principle of love in the heart of God, is extremely preposterous. What! an unconverted sinner moved by love to seek God?" [52] As he saw it, the only motive sufficient to produce repentance was a fear of the awful judgment of God. This had been the approach of the revival preaching out of which the Cumberland Presbyterian Church had

STANFORD G. BURNEY
(1814-1893)

RICHARD BEARD
(1799-1880)

grown. It is clear that Burney had accomplished his objective—a new theology. With Burney as chairman of the committee appointed in 1881 to revise the Confession of Faith, it was to be expected that ideas from his theology would be reflected in the new Confession.

The Committee on Revision appointed by the General Assembly in 1881 was actually two committees: one composed of Burney, the Rev. A. Templeton, and John Frizzell, an elder, and the other composed of C. H. Bell, J. W. Poindexter, A. B. Miller, W. J. Darby, ministers, and R. L. Caruthers, an elder. The instructions of the General Assembly were, "Let the work of the first, of three, be revised, and if need be, corrected by a second committee of five." [53] Accordingly, the first committee met for a week at Cumberland University, November 18-24, 1881, and prepared the revision. The second committee, with only three of the five members present—Bell, Darby, and Caruthers—met jointly with the first committee the following week to review the proposed revision. The report of this joint committee to the General Assembly in 1882 spoke of "a wonderful harmony of opinion" and seems to suggest that the review of the second committee produced no significant changes in what the first committee had written.[54] The 1882 Assembly made only minor, verbal changes in the proposed revision and submitted it to the presbyteries for approval. The 1883 Assembly reported that 100 out of 116 presbyteries had voted their approval, and the new Confession was declared the official creed of the Church.

When compared with the Confession of 1814, the Confession of 1883 reflects several important changes. These may be grouped under two headings. First, there are changes like those proposed in 1854. These include additional restrictions on the sovereignty of God, a further weakening of the effects on man of the Fall, and an increase in man's freedom and ability, and a rearrangement of the order of the chapters in the Confession so that those on Repentance and Saving Faith preceded the chapter on Justification. The other group consists of changes similar to those made by Burney in his theology, when he replaced the legal concepts and images of Federalism with the personal concepts and images of the family relation.

The new Confession affirms that God is "unchangeable in his being," but it avoids all suggestions that his actions are unchangeable, predetermined before the foundation of the world. God in his actions must have the flexibility which a conditional system demands. Accordingly, the new Confession deletes the statement which speaks of God "working all things according to the counsel of his own immutable and most righteous will," as well as the claim that "nothing is to him uncertain" (C. P. C., 1814, ii, 1,2). Likewise, while it affirms the general providence of God over all creatures and special providence over the church, it stops short of the statement in the 1814 Confession which said that the providence of God governs "all creatures and things, from the greatest even to the least" (C. P. C., 1814, v, 1).

One of the criticisms made of the 1814 Confession by the Committee on Revision was that many of its expressions could not "be construed in intelligible thought in light of our modern psychology." [55] This comment is a clue to some of the more important changes in the new Confession. According to the 1814 Confession the image of God in man was the "righteousness and true holiness" with which God had endowed him (C. P. C., 1814, iv, 2). The Fall resulted in the loss of this image. Man fell from his "original righteousness and communion with God," and was thus "indisposed, disabled, and made opposite to all good, and wholly inclined to all evil" (C. P. C., 1814, vi, 2,4). His will is in bondage to sin until "God converts . . . and translates him into the state of grace, . . . and by his grace alone enables him freely to will and to do that which is spiritually good" (C. P. C., 1814, ix, 4). The new Confession, reflecting the psychology of Burney, defines the image of God in man as the faculties of "intelligence, sensibility and will." [56] Though man is still said to have lost his original condition of righteousness in the Fall, he did not lose the image of God, in particular the faculty of will—"man is still free and responsible" (C. P. C., 1883, Sec. 36). This enlargement of the capacities of natural man makes it possible to redefine faith as an act of man rather than a gift of God. The 1814 Confession had spoken of it as "the grace of faith, . . . the work of the Spirit of Christ, . . . ordinarily wrought by the ministry of the word" (C. P. C., 1814, xiv, 2).

The new Confession describes it as man's act of assenting to the truth of the Scriptures and of "receiving and resting upon Christ alone for salvation" (C. P. C., 1883, Sec. 45).

The Confession of 1814, as a modification of the Westminster Confession, retained most of the essential features of the Federalist system of theology. As an example, God's covenant with man was said to have been one in which "life was promised to Adam, and in him to his posterity" (C. P. C., 1814, vii, 2). The 1883 Confession deletes the "Federalist clause"—the promise of life to all men in Adam—and says simply that the promise was to Adam. The Federalist idea was also eliminated from the doctrine of the Fall. The 1814 Confession said of the sin of Adam and Eve, "by their sin all were made sinners" (C. P. C., 1814, vi, 6). This is changed to the generalized statement that through them "sin entered into the world" (C. P. C., 1883, Sec. 18). Burney had argued that the claim that any man is made a sinner by another's act is inconsistent with the principle of individual freedom and responsibility.

One of the features of Federalist theology was the satisfaction theory of atonement. In this view Adam's sin required a punishment of death in order that the conditions of the law might be satisfied. Were God to forgive man without exacting this penalty, he would appear to be lax in upholding his law. This dilemma is solved when Jesus Christ offered himself as a substitute —as the second Adam—to make satisfaction through his death. In keeping with this view, the 1814 Confession stated that Jesus by his death "fully satisfied the justice of his Father" (C. P. C., 1814, vii, 5). Again, it is claimed that "Christ, by his obedience and death, did fully discharge the debt of all those that are justified, and did make a proper, real, and full satisfaction to his Father's justice on their behalf" (C. P. C., 1814, xi, 3). In the 1883 Confession the latter statement is eliminated altogether, and the concept of satisfaction in the former is changed to that of propitiation—Jesus "became the propitiation for the sins of the whole world" (C. P. C., 1883, Sec. 31). One instance of the use of the term "satisfaction" remained in the new Confession (Section 48), and the idea seems to be suggested in the reference in Section 49 which speaks of justification as "strictly a legal transaction."

It should be noted that in his major work on the atonement, in which he rejected the concept of satisfaction, Burney employed instead the concept of propitiation. He defined "propitiation" as that which effects reconciliation in a broken personal relation. He argued that this was something different from satisfaction, where the payment of a penalty is required. Introduction of the term "propitiation" in the new Confession (Sections 27 and 31) coupled with the deletion of the concept of satisfaction in certain key passages would seem to suggest the influence of Burney.

Apart from changes in the content, the 1883 Confession differed significantly from the 1814 Confession in the simple matter of length. For example, the chapter on Repentance was reduced from six to three sections, and the chapter on Good Works from seven to two sections. In its report to the General Assembly, the Revision Committee suggested at least one reason for this severe pruning and condensation. The old Confession, they said, was "too long, unnecessarily diffuse and tedious, especially for children." [57] It is also possible that the committee was influenced by the prevailing mood of liberal Protestantism toward the end of the nineteenth century, in which creeds tended to lose their status as repositories of the faith once-for-all delivered to the saints, and to become broad generalizations of the bare essentials of theology. In October of 1881, apparently with the forthcoming revision of the Confession in mind, William H. Black, a leading Cumberland Presbyterian clergyman and later president of Missouri Valley College, expressed the impatience of late nineteenth century liberalism with creeds and, for that matter, with theology itself. He wrote, "There is a growing feeling that theology has been too complicated in times past; that we need to throw aside much of the old cumbrous machinery and to concentrate on the vital facts." [58] A. B. Miller, another prominent clergyman, president of Waynesburg College, and a member of the Revision Committee of 1881, described a creed as "but a temporary halting place in the march of mind." [59] In view of its temporary nature, Miller went on to say, a creed should contain "brief summaries of only the essential doctrines." [60] He obviously felt that this had been achieved in the 1883 Confession. The immediate and widespread popularity of the new Confession is an indication of how accurately the revisers had gauged the mind of the Church.

The 1883 Confession and the background theological literature that surrounds it marked the era in which the Cumberland Presbyterian Church became a full and recognized partner in the family of Presbyterian and Reformed churches in America. Though it was denied membership in 1880 in the newly formed Alliance of Reformed Churches Throughout the World Holding the Presbyterian System because of the objections of some members of the Alliance to its Confession of Faith, the Cumberland Presbyterian Church did become a member in 1884. This was despite the fact that the Church had in the meantime adopted a new Confession that was even less like the Westminster Confession, the creedal statement of most of the members of the Alliance, than the previous Cumberland Presbyterian Confession had been.

In its meeting in 1885 the General Assembly took note of the admission of the Church to the Alliance and resolved to "continue to fraternize cordially with the liberal and progressive churches composing the Alliance." [61] The terms "liberal" and "progressive" used in the report adopted by the Assembly are perhaps descriptive of the self-image which the leaders of the Cumberland Presbyterian Church at the end of the nineteenth century had of their Church and its Confession, in comparison with other Presbyterian and Reformed churches. W. J. Darby, a member of the 1881 Revision Committee, confidently predicted that history would record "that the Church has nobly served in the forefront of those who have wrought out the triumphs of liberal Presbyterianism in this country." [62] He went on to describe the 1883 Confession as an admirable statement of "the views of liberal Presbyterianism." [63]

That the theology of the Church at the end of the nineteenth century was different from what it had been at the beginning of the century when the Church was formed was clearly evident, but this was felt to be a compliment to the Church. The view expressed by the Rev. J. M. Howard concerning the 1883 Confession appears to have been shared widely throughout the Church. He wrote, "Let it be understood, in short, that ours is not a fixed and changeless, but a progressive creed; and that through all the decades we are to seek a more and more nearly exact statement of the truth revealed in Scripture, and believed by our own people." [64] An article had appeared in the *Cumberland Presbyterian* in 1878 in which it was warned, "If a Church is so impolitic as to refuse to adopt [*sic*] her creed to the progress of the age, revolution will be the consequence." [65] The article went on to suggest that it was just such an impolitic attitude that had resulted in the "rebellion" of 1810 that produced the Cumberland Presbyterian Church. The Confession of 1883 was the response to such a warning. As the Church neared the end of the first hundred years of its existence, it appeared determined to remain faithful to one of the fundamental characteristics of its tradition, openness to theological change.

# PART III

*The Cumberland Presbyterian*

*Church in the Twentieth Century*

*1901-1970*

*On the occasion of the ninetieth birthday of the Cumberland Presbyterian Church, in February 1900, Dr. Ira Landrith, editor of the* Cumberland Presbyterian, *suggested that as it entered upon the last decade of the first century of its existence the motto of the Cumberland Presbyterian Church should be, "Four thousand churches and half a million members before the Centennial Anniversary" [1910]. This mood of optimism was negated, however, by the interjection in the year 1902 of a proposal for union with the Presbyterian Church in the United States of America, which proved to be a divisive issue. Although the "union" received the support of a majority of the presbyteries and was declared to be an accomplished fact, a substantial remnant was determined to perpetuate the Cumberland Presbyterian Church.*

*The struggle to rebuild, the attempt to broaden the Church's horizons during the 1920s, difficulties faced during the depression, the reassessment of its mission and potential following World War II, and the subsequent strengthening of the institutional life of the denomination are successively narrated in chronological order.*

# 17

## MOVING IN TO POSSESS THE LAND

*The Cumberland Presbyterian Church has passed through the wilderness, and by the guiding hand of its Lord has reached its Kadesh-barnea. Is there faith enough to go forward and possess the land? Shall we, in the strength of Jehovah, make an aggressive movement to capture and seize upon our inheritance? Do we realize that we are well able to overcome it, that in fact fully three-fourths of the people in this country are in sympathy with the doctrines and policies peculiar to our beloved church, assuming them, erroneously, to be the doctrines and policies of their own denomination? Shall we make our impress upon the people and the institutions of this country, claiming for our number all who are at heart with us? Shall we have our own?*

W. C. Morris, in sermon at the opening of Tehuacana Presbytery,
November 16, 1899

William Warren Sweet, recent American church historian, has written, "The most significant single influence in organized religion in the United States from about the year 1880 to the end of the century and beyond, was the tremendous increase in wealth in the nation." He goes on to point out that just as the log house gave way to more comfortable dwellings, church members were no longer willing to worship in crude and unsightly meetinghouses, and there was an era of church building. Denominational colleges flourished as never before. The emotional type of religion which had characterized the frontier "was gradually giving way to a more easygoing re-

305

ligion." The churches which had ministered to the poor were being transformed into churches of the upper middle class. The old camp-meeting
grounds were transformed first into Chautauqua assemblies and later into
middle-class summer resorts.[1]

Another factor which Sweet mentions is the tendency toward the consolidation of political and economic institutions. The power of the federal
government was growing at the expense of the states, and the great corporations had arisen.[2] The efficiency of such combined organizations in business
and industry was soon to be used by proponents of organic union as an
argument for the union of the Cumberland Presbyterian Church with the
Presbyterian Church in the U. S. A.[3]

Many heads of corporations were also churchmen who devoted large sums
of money to church-related educational institutions. Among these were John
D. Rockefeller, who contributed large sums to the endowment of the University of Chicago, and Daniel Drew, Cyrus H. McCormick, and the Vander-
bilts, whose names are perpetuated in institutions which benefited from
their gifts.[4]

This was also the period of the rise of the Social Gospel with its emphasis
upon the ethical teachings of Jesus and the Old Testament prophets. This
development tended to shift the theological emphasis from individual salvation to the problem of the sins of society. Consequently, there was a diminish-
ing interest in theological issues having to do with the "plan of salvation" and
an increasing interest in what were considered to be the more practical aims
of the church.[5]

This was also the age of American imperialism. As a result of the Spanish-
American War of 1898 the United States came into possession of Puerto
Rico and the Philippines. These immediately claimed the attention of the
American churches as fields for evangelization. At the same time, there was
resistance in the Orient to the increasing foreign influence.[6] In China, this
opposition came to a head in the Boxer Rebellion, which represented an
attempt on the part of a secret Chinese organization to kill off all foreigners
and Chinese Christians (the latter because they had accepted a foreign
religion).

At the dawn of the twentieth century the Cumberland Presbyterian
Church was continuing its characteristic evangelistic and missionary work
in the areas recently opened up for settlement. One such area was the territory of Oklahoma, comprising the western part of the present state of Oklahoma. One report indicates that at the fall meeting of Greer Presbytery in
1899 eleven new churches were received under the care of the presbytery.[7]
The report of the General Assembly's Board of Missions in 1901 states that

the Rev. R. L. Phelps, the synodical field man for Indianola Synod, had organized thirty-eight churches during the two preceding years.[8] During the period from July 1899 through December 1903, the *Cumberland Presbyterian* contains reports of the organization of some ninety new churches. Of these, twenty-one were in Oklahoma and the Indian Territory.

Another area which was being entered by the Cumberland Presbyterian Church was in West Texas, in the western portion of what was then Abilene Presbytery. Churches were organized during this period at Big Spring, Colorado City, Midland, Snyder, and Tahoka. These were in the area later occupied by Snyder. Presbytery, which was created by order of the Synod of Texas at its 1904 meeting.

Although new churches were reported in sixteen states and territories during the 4½-year period mentioned, fifteen of the new churches were in Tennessee, the cradle and stronghold of the Cumberland Presbyterian Church. These included two new churches in Memphis (Walker Heights and McLemore Avenue) and one in Nashville (Ninth Church). Included also were churches in smaller towns such as Algood and Mount Pleasant and rural churches such as Poplar Grove (Obion Presbytery); Ruth's Chapel, near Livingston; and Saint John (Clarksville Presbytery).

The Cumberland Presbyterian Church had been slow in moving into the cities. Establishing churches in the city cost money, and rural people on the whole could not easily see the necessity of contributing toward the building of expensive edifices in the city when they themselves were worshiping in quite ordinary buildings. The urgency of entering the cities was coming to be increasingly recognized, however, as part of the evangelistic task of the Church. In 1900, the General Assembly's Board of Missions and Church Erection listed nine ministers as home missionaries, all of whom were laboring in urban fields: R. H. Fry, who was at Carthage, Missouri; C. G. Watson, Columbus, Ohio; A. B. Welch, Drexel Park, Chicago, Illinois; A. W. Hawkins, Decatur, Illinois; E. H. Liles, Denison, Texas; J. J. Dalton, Henderson, Kentucky; H. F. Smith, Topeka, Kansas; Taylor Bernard, Raymond Place, Saint Louis, Missouri; E. E. Thompson, Seattle, Washington. Churches at Fort Smith, Arkansas; Sheffield, Alabama; and Portland, Oregon, which formerly had been mission churches, had become self-sustaining.[9]

The Board's report for 1901 showed the addition of Los Angeles, California; Denver, Colorado; and Washington, Pennsylvania, to the list of mission churches. A movement had been launched also for establishing a church in San Francisco, California. New buildings had been erected at Washington, Pennsylvania; Topeka, Kansas; and Oklahoma City.[10]

In 1903 twenty-one home mission churches were listed. Nine of these had been added during the preceding year: Columbus, Mississippi; Denison, Texas (which for a time had been taken over by the Board of Missions of Texas Synod); Durant, Lehigh, and Sulphur, Indian Territory; Ensley, Alabama; Hot Springs, Arkansas; Broad Street, Louisville, Kentucky; and Scott City, Kansas.[11] Missionary work was being conducted in other urban areas by some of the synods and presbyteries.

The Cumberland Presbyterian Church, like other churches, was experiencing an era of church building. In the Minutes of the General Assembly for 1901 are listed sixty-one new churches which had been dedicated the preceding year. Most of these were relatively inexpensive, although $22,500 had been spent in building a new church at Macon, Missouri, and $16,000 in erecting the building at Washington, Pennsylvania.[12] There were still, however, 543 congregations without houses of worship. Of these, 218 were in Texas Synod, 100 in Arkansas Synod, and sixty-three in Indianola Synod.[13] The last figure represented more than half the congregations in the synod.

A mountain mission project was launched in January 1897, under the sponsorship of the Woman's Board of Missions, when the Rev. R. F. Johnston and his wife opened a school at Barnard, North Carolina.[14] By 1899 more than two hundred pupils were enrolled at Jewell Hill Academy, as the school was called. In that year the name was changed to Bell Institute, and a new school building and chapel were completed. On December 23, 1899, a church was organized with forty-three members. This church was received under the care of East Tennessee Presbytery April 1, 1900.[15] By 1906 this church had a membership of 150. Meanwhile, schools had been founded at Red Hill and Hopewell, in the vicinity of Barnard. The Red Hill school later became known as Mount Neta School, in honor of Miss Neta Boyd, the first teacher.[16]

Work was being continued among the Choctaw Indians in the Indian Territory. The Rev. Martin Charleston, a Choctaw minister, was employed by the General Assembly's Board of Missions and Church Erection. Need was expressed for the help of a trusted white man, such as the Rev. A. B. Johnson had been, to advise the Choctaws in locating the forty or fifty acres of land to which each was entitled. It was claimed that persons of mixed racial descent were taking possession of the best land, leaving only the comparatively worthless land for the fullblood Choctaws. A strong appeal had been made by the people in that area to have Johnson reappointed by the Board, but this had been impossible because of a lack of funds.[17] By 1902, however, Johnson, Mrs. Johnson, and Charleston were all listed as missionaries whose support was coming from the Woman's Board of Missions.[18]

In January 1894, a school for the Chinese was opened in San Francisco with Mrs. Naomi Sitton as teacher. Mrs. Sitton's interest in the children helped her win the confidence of the parents. Some of the Chinese had a superstitious fear of having a child die in the home. Therefore Mrs. Sitton would take sick children into her home and nurse them back to health. From among these children she adopted five and reared them as her own. Her only daughter, Miss Guerdon Sitton, gave up getting a college education to care for these children. All finished high school, and one graduated from the University of California. In January 1898, a Sunday school was begun.[19]

In September 1901, Mrs. Sitton resigned as superintendent of the San Francisco mission, and the Rev. B. F. Whittemore was chosen as her successor.[20] Shortly thereafter the Rev. Gam Sing Quah and his wife were added to the staff. Early in 1904 a Chinese congregation was organized with Tom Jung and Wong Hong as elders. This church first was listed in the Minutes of the General Assembly for 1905, at which time it reported nineteen resident and thirteen nonresident members.

In November 1899, a night school for Chinese was opened in Hanford, California, by the Woman's Board.[21] The following year the work was expanded to include the Japanese, and by 1903 the work at Hanford had become entirely Japanese.[22] A mission school was also opened in April 1900, at Merced, but by 1904 it had been discontinued because the pupils had left the city. Gam had served at Hanford and Merced as a preacher and interpreter prior to his becoming connected with the mission at San Francisco.[23]

In addition to maintaining missions which had been planted earlier in Japan and Mexico, the Cumberland Presbyterian Church, at the turn of the century, had recently begun a mission in China. In 1895 the General Assembly had asked the Board to consider the advisability of starting mission work in Africa and China. By the time of the meeting of the General Assembly in 1897 the decision had been made to open a mission in China. G. W. Freeman, of Mansfield, Missouri, had proposed to contribute $1,000 to assist Dr. O. T. Logan through a postgraduate course in medicine and to pay his salary for one year in China.[24] The 1895 class of the Theological Seminary and the Synod of Alabama joined efforts in making provision to send the Rev. H. L. Walker to China. The Christian Endeavor Society of the denomination pledged the means to send an additional missionary. Logan, Walker, and the Rev. T. J. Preston were consecrated to mission work in China during the 1897 General Assembly.[25]

Logan, his wife, and Preston sailed for China in September 1897. After spending some time in the study of the Chinese language and in seeking out a suitable location, Dr. and Mrs. Logan arrived at Chang-teh, in the province of Hunan, on Christmas Day, 1898. Preston arrived a few days later.

At the 1899 General Assembly, Gam Sing Quah and the Rev. William Kelly, a doctor, were set apart as missionaries to China, and the Rev. J. C. Worley and his wife were commissioned as missionaries to Japan.[26] Kelly was soon afterward sent to China as a medical missionary, but after considerable correspondence with missionaries and with others whose position and experience made them competent to advise, it was decided that Gam could not work to advantage among the Hunanese and should be sent to Canton, in his native province.[27] As has already been noted, he was sent instead to California to work among the Chinese on the West Coast.

Meanwhile, Dr. and Mrs. Logan had to return to the United States because of the doctor's ill health. Kelly and Preston continued with the work at Chang-teh until after the outbreak of the Boxer Rebellion in 1900. In the latter part of July the missionaries left Chang-teh upon the advice of the Board. Kelly went to Shanghai, where on August 22 he was married to Miss Carrie Elizabeth Goodrich, of the Foreign Christian Missionary Society.[28] She died only a few months later.

In May 1901, Preston and Kelly returned to Chang-teh, where they were accorded a hospitable welcome and found that no loss of property had occurred during their absence. Dr. and Mrs. Logan returned to China in November of that year, their support being provided by Salt River Presbytery (Missouri). Meanwhile, the first appeal ever made by the Board of Missions to the Sunday schools to undertake a special work was made on the first Sunday in October 1901, when they were requested to make an offering for the purpose of building a hospital in Chang-teh. A total of 397 schools responded, and $2,706.10 was contributed.[29] At this time the Christian Endeavor societies in Texas were contributing to Preston's support, and the societies in other states to Kelly's support.

During the year 1902 a hospital was erected, and shortly after its completion a chapel and a residence for the missionaries were built. The latter was named the L. M. Rice Home in honor of L. M. Rice, of Louisville, Kentucky, who made the first and largest contribution for the residence.[30] In October 1903, the mission forces in China were augmented by the sending of the Rev. George F. Jenkins, Mrs. Jenkins, and the Rev. I. G. Boydstun; however, Kelly had resigned from the mission.[31] During 1905 two additional missionaries, Mrs. Mable Martin Boydstun and Miss May Beekley, arrived in China.[32]

Medical, evangelistic, and educational missions were carried on in Hunan province. During the year 1904 a total of 137 inpatients were treated in the hospital, and more than 6,000 outpatients were given treatment. By the spring of 1904 there was a church of eleven members at Chang-teh, and during the year another mission station was opened at Taoyuen, thirty miles west of Chang-teh, under the direction of Mr. and Mrs. Jenkins. A school for girls had been begun as early as 1903 with Mrs. Logan as the teacher, and during 1905 the John Miller School for boys was founded.

In 1900 the Cumberland Presbyterian Church had churches in twenty-five states and territories[33] and missions in three foreign countries. It comprised sixteen synods and 121 presbyteries. There were 2,937 churches with a total reported membership of 180,192, but there were only 1,642 Sunday schools with a total enrollment of 103,545. There were 1,596 ordained ministers, 245 licentiates, and 260 candidates for the ministry. Forty-nine ministers had been ordained during the church year ending April 30, 1900.[34]

The denomination was experiencing a gradual growth in membership, although the number of local churches was declining. From 1896 to 1905 there was an increase in reported membership from 165,847 to 185,756. The peak for this period was reached in 1905. The number of churches had reached its peak in 1898 when 3,021 churches were listed. In 1905 there were 2,922 churches listed.

The number of ordained ministers reached its peak in 1904 when 1,649 ministers were listed. The number of licentiates and candidates, however, had steadily declined since 1897, when there were 301 licentiates and 324 candidates. In 1905 there were 132 licentiates and 163 candidates. Concern over the inadequate number of persons being educated for the ministry was expressed in 1903 when it was reported that, although the enrollment in the Theological Seminary at Cumberland University had reached a new high, there were only ten probationers in the senior classes of all the colleges of the Church and only ten in the junior classes.[35]

Some new presbyteries were being created on the growing edge of the Church, while in other areas consolidations were taking place. Among the new presbyteries created during the period from 1899 to 1905 were Oklahoma and Washita, in Indianola Synod; Leitchfield, in Kentucky Synod; and Snyder and South Louisiana, in Texas Synod. On the other hand, the number of presbyteries in Kansas was reduced from five to three, and the number in Arkansas Synod from eleven to seven. Trinity Presbytery, in Texas Synod, had been consolidated with Texas Presbytery, and three presbyteries in the state of Louisiana had been combined to form Louisiana Presbytery. The presbyteries of Albion and McLin, in Illinois Synod, had been combined to form Mount Vernon Presbytery. Georgia Presbytery had been dissolved and its churches added to Chattanooga Presbytery. There had been some other realignments of presbyteries, and the names of several had been changed. Altogether, the number was reduced from 123 in 1899 to 118 in 1905.

An unfortunate aftermath of the consolidation of presbyteries in the Synod of Arkansas was the secession of most of the ministers and churches which formerly had constituted Porter Presbytery and the subsequent formation of the Reformed Cumberland Presbyterian Church. Porter Presbytery had been organized in 1891 out of the eastern portion of King Presbytery. It comprised the counties of Scott, Logan, Yell, and Perry, together with that part of Conway County lying south of the Arkansas River. By action of the Synod of Arkansas in the fall of 1901, Porter Presbytery was consolidated with Fort Smith Presbytery.

On February 20, 1902, Porter Presbytery met at the time and place appointed for the meeting of the consolidated (Fort Smith) presbytery, but no one came from the previously existing Fort Smith Presbytery except one ruling elder, who was invited to a seat as a member in council. Porter Presbytery proceeded to act as a presbytery in disregard of the action of synod, elected commissioners to the General Assembly, and sent a memorial to the Assembly "relative to Presbyterial Lines." [36]

When the General Assembly met in May 1902, the Stated Clerk reported having received credentials of commissioners from Fort Smith Presbytery, which had failed to meet at the time appointed by synod, and from Porter Presbytery as well. The Assembly's Committee on Credentials recommended that the commissioners from Fort Smith Presbytery be enrolled, but expressed the opinion that the commissioners from Porter Presbytery, who were elected subsequent to the synod's action dissolving the presbytery, were not entitled to seats. Since, however, Fort Smith Presbytery as enlarged by the consolidation with Porter Presbytery would be entitled to four commissioners, it was recommended that the Rev. A. B. Williamson, who was present with a commission from Porter Presbytery, be seated as a commissioner from Fort Smith Presbytery. He, however, respectfully declined to sit in that capacity.[37] The Assembly further decided that since Porter Presbytery had been dissolved by Arkansas Synod it could not take cognizance of the paper purporting to be a memorial from Porter Presbytery. There was also before the Assembly a notice of appeal by the stated clerk of the former Bartholomew Presbytery, which also had been dissolved by Arkansas Synod, protesting the action of synod, but since it was not accompanied by supporting evidence and no one appeared to prosecute the appeal, it was dismissed.[38]

In July 1902, the ministers and elders of Porter Presbytery formulated a communication to Arkansas Synod asking the synod to rescind its former action dissolving the presbytery.[39] The request was not granted, although a petition to reestablish Bartholomew Presbytery was granted.

The petition to synod having failed to accomplish its purpose, the members of Porter Presbytery held a council at Ellsworth, Arkansas, on November

17, 1902, in which the decision was made to reorganize as an independent presbytery. The Declaration adopted at that time was signed by nine ministers and six ruling elders. It was alleged that Arkansas Synod had acted in haste. The presbytery, so the Declaration stated, was being organized for the purpose of perpetuating the Cumberland Presbyterian Church in the rural districts.[40]

On July 17, 1903, the independent presbytery meeting at Pilot Prairie, in Scott County, resolved to form a new church. A "Declaration of Principles" was adopted and signed by ten ordained ministers, one licentiate, and thirteen ruling elders. The presbytery would be governed by the principles of the doctrine and government of the Cumberland Presbyterian Church until it could edit a Confession of its own. It expressed the determination "to hold up the Doctrines of the founders of the C. P. Church from which we feel the present C. P. Church to be drifting." A committee consisting of the Rev. T. J. Hampton, the Rev. S. M. McKinney, the Rev. J. L. Durham, and two ruling elders, T. J. Moore and G. S. Williamson, was appointed to compile a Confession of Faith and Form of Government. This committee was instructed to "conform as closely to God's word as possible, regardless of what men may have written."[41] The Confession of Faith and Form of Government was adopted November 21, 1903.[42] It was printed by Wagner Printery, Paris, Arkansas, in pamphlet form and consisted of twenty-four pages.

Although the Confession as a whole represents a rather free rewriting of the 1883 Confession of Faith of the Cumberland Presbyterian Church, there are significant differences. The "word of God" was declared to be "composed of all the books found in what is known as the Bible and as set forth in King James' translation."[43] (The American Standard Version had been published in 1901.) Discarding the doctrine of the two covenants derived from the "Federal" theology, the Confession mentioned the covenant of Sinai as having been "offered to the one-ninth family of Abraham's posterity; to which family it was not given for the purpose of their eternal salvation but for the purpose of bringing so much of mankind to a test of unaided personal conformity to God's demands as would show the utter inability of fallen humanity to meet divine demands on their own strength and merit."[44] This, it would seem, represented a true insight into the apostle Paul's understanding of the purpose of the Law. There was no reference to sanctification or to the baptism of infants, although belief in the latter doctrine is implied in this statement: "In the new dispensation baptism stands to the church as did circumcision in the old."[45]

Trials for licensure and ordination were to embrace, "when applicable, the highest order of human bearing known to the Presbytery," yet no man was to be rejected for lack of technical learning if he could gain men for Christ.[46] Provision was made for the licensure of exhorters and for the licensure and ordination of women as ministers.[47] The Form of Government provided for a synod, but its powers were to be limited. It was to be only a court of review, appeal, and complaint.[48] Actually, the Reformed Cumberland Presbyterian Church during the brief period of its existence consisted of only the one presbytery.

No reference to the "union" controversy which was going on in the Cumberland Presbyterian Church appears in the records of Porter Presbytery until May 1905, just after the meeting of the General Assembly at Fresno, California, at which the presbyterial vote on the proposed union with the Presbyterian Church in the U. S. A. was announced. In a meeting held at Old Union, in Logan County, on May 26-27, 1905, noting that "the attempted swallowing up of the C. P. Church . . . by the Presbyterian Church in the United States of America" was now "an accomplished fact," the presbytery voted to drop the word "Reformed" from its name and to be known simply as "this Cumberland Presbyterian Church." [49] Thereafter the members of Porter Presbytery did tend to identify with the antiunionists in the Cumberland Presbyterian Church. At a session held on July 29-30, 1905, copies of the *Cumberland Banner,* an antiunion periodical begun in 1904, were distributed and subscriptions solicited.[50] A year later the *Banner* was adopted as the official organ of the presbytery.[51]

At a meeting held October 12-13, 1906, a memorial to Arkansas Synod was adopted and a commission consisting of four ministers and four ruling elders appointed to attend the meeting of Arkansas Synod with instructions "to ask the Arkansas Synod to enroll the Porter Presbytery as a part of the Loyal Cumberland Presbyterians in Arkansas." [52] The request was granted by Arkansas Synod meeting at Russellville on October 26, and Porter Presbytery was enrolled and its ministers and elders present seated as members of the Synod.[53] At that time Porter Presbytery reportedly had twenty-three preachers, twenty-eight congregations, and about 1,200 communicants.

Why did Porter Presbytery withdraw from the Cumberland Presbyterian Church? Why did Arkansas Synod refuse to rescind its action consolidating Porter Presbytery with Fort Smith Presbytery while at the same time reestablishing Bartholomew Presbytery, which also had been dissolved in 1901? Why did Porter Presbytery decide in 1906 to return to the Cumberland Presbyterian Church?

The only reasons assigned by Porter Presbytery for attempting to perpetuate its existence in defiance of the action of Arkansas Synod have already been mentioned, namely, that Arkansas Synod had acted in haste, and that the presbytery felt that its own perpetuation was necessary if the rural churches were to be supplied with preaching. Fort Smith Presbytery, to which Arkansas Synod attempted to attach Porter, did have several town churches, and it was perhaps believed, even if mistakenly so, that the ministers of those churches would not be sympathetic to the problems of the rural churches. The rebellion against the synod was therefore a rural reaction against what was considered to be the high-handed measures of the town preachers. This rebellion was an isolated instance arising in what was at that time a rather isolated area of the Church.

Porter Presbytery continued to operate as a presbytery in disregard of the synod's action, whereas Bartholomew Presbytery accepted the synod's decision but petitioned for a restoration of the presbytery. Consequently, Porter Presbytery did not receive the consideration at the hands of the synod which Bartholomew Presbytery received.

In what respect was the situation changed to cause Porter Presbytery to seek readmission to Arkansas Synod in 1906? Arkansas Synod had been for some years a delegated body; that is, it was composed of equal delegations of ministers and ruling elders elected by the presbyteries (although the ministers usually constituted a majority of those actually attending). Most often the ministers chosen to attend synod were pastors of the town churches. These were the ministers by and large who went with the union in 1906. For example, of twenty-one ministers who attended Arkansas Synod in 1904, only three remained in the Cumberland Presbyterian Church after 1906, although 40 per cent of the total ministerial membership in the synod remained. Thus the members of Porter Presbytery probably believed that those who were responsible for the dissolution of their presbytery were now gone, and they would find themselves in more congenial company among those who remained.

In 1900 there were ten colleges, universities, and preparatory schools under the control of the Cumberland Presbyterian Church: Cumberland University, Lebanon, Tennessee, which consisted of a preparatory school, college department, law school, and theological seminary; Waynesburg College, Waynesburg, Pennsylvania; Missouri Valley College, Marshall, Missouri; Trinity University, Tehuacana, Texas; Lincoln University, Lincoln, Illinois; Bethel College, McKenzie, Tennessee; Auburn Seminary, Auburn, Kentucky; Arkansas Cumberland College, Clarksville, Arkansas; Southern Female College, West Point, Mississippi; and Texas Female Seminary, Weatherford, Texas. Auburn Seminary was a preparatory school. Records of that period mention, also, the College for Young Ladies, Lebanon, Tennessee, and Maddox Seminary, Little Rock, Arkansas. These were operated by Cumberland Presbyterians but were not under the control of the Church.

In the interest of its educational institutions the General Assembly in 1899 launched the most ambitious financial campaign which had ever been promoted within the Cumberland Presbyterian Church. The Centennial Endowment Movement was designed to raise $1,000,000 for educational purposes by the time of the centennial of the denomination, February 4, 1910.

Five schools were selected to be recipients of the proposed fund: Cumberland University and the Theological Seminary were to receive $300,000; Waynesburg College, $100,000; Lincoln University, $150,000; Trinity University, $150,000; and Missouri Valley College, $150,000. In addition, it was proposed that $100,000 be raised to establish a college on the Pacific Coast and $50,000 for a postgraduate divinity school to be established in connection with the University of Chicago.

The denomination was divided into six areas. Pennsylvania and Ohio were to be the special territory of Waynesburg College. Indiana, Illinois, and Iowa were the territory of Lincoln University. Missouri, Kansas, Nebraska, and Colorado were expected to contribute to the support of Missouri Valley College. Washington, Oregon, and California would be called on to raise money to establish a college on the Pacific Coast. Texas, Louisiana, and Indianola Synod were the territory of Trinity University. Kentucky, Tennessee, Georgia, Mississippi, Alabama, and Arkansas were to be the special territory of Cumberland University. The whole Church was to be the territory of the Theological Seminary. An Educational Commission was named to promote the campaign.[54]

In 1900 the schools which were to benefit from the campaign had endowments in approximately the following amounts: Theological Seminary, $81,014.65; Cumberland University (Literary Department), $25,000; Waynesburg College, $42,000; Lincoln University, $61,038.83; Trinity University, $40,000; and Missouri Valley College, $110,000.[55]

Both Bethel College and Arkansas Cumberland College sought to be included in the campaign. An agreement was worked out in April 1900, whereby Cumberland University agreed to refrain from canvassing for endowment funds in the five presbyteries of West Tennessee (Hopewell, Madison, Memphis, Obion, and Savannah) until June 1, 1901. After this date, if Bethel continued to canvass for funds, the agents of Cumberland University should enter only those churches which Bethel agents had previously visited. Meanwhile, Bethel College was advised, in view of its lack of endowment, to refrain from offering bachelor's degrees after the end of the current school term until such time as adequate equipment and endowment should have been secured.[56] The Synod of Tennessee recommended that unless Bethel College should succeed in raising a productive endowment of $50,000 by February 4, 1910, it should take its place as a training school in articulation with Cumberland University.

A request from the trustees of Arkansas Cumberland College that the state of Arkansas be assigned as the territory of this college was granted with the understanding that the action should not be interpreted as debarring the agent of Cumberland University from soliciting funds within Arkansas Synod. The right of Arkansas Synod to support its own school was recognized, but Arkansas Cumberland College was not recognized as one of the colleges of the educational system of the Church.[57]

Both in 1900 and in 1901 there were memorials asking the General Assembly to eliminate from the Centennial Endowment Movement the project of endowing a postgraduate divinity school in affiliation with the University of Chicago.[58] A memorial from Kirksville Presbytery (Missouri) in 1901 was based on objections raised to "certain doctrinal teachings of the theological professors" in the University of Chicago. A special committee appointed to consider this memorial recommended that the action taken in 1899 providing for this project be rescinded since there seemed to be no immediate prospect of raising the funds. This recommendation was adopted.[59]

This conduct of the "million-dollar campaign" was largely left in the hands of the financial agents of the institutions which were to benefit, with the Educational Commission supplying promotional materials. Consequently, the movement was carried forward with varying degrees of success in different areas. In 1901 it was reported that $235,000 had been raised in cash and pledges for four of the institutions. (This did not include the Millikin gift mentioned below.)[60]

The whole movement was profoundly affected by two events: the offer of James Millikin to make a substantial gift, under specified conditions, to establish an institution which would be under the control of the Cumberland Presbyterian Church, and the removal of Trinity University from Tehuacana to Waxahachie, Texas.

In May 1900, it became known that Millikin, a banker in Decatur, Illinois, had offered to contribute $200,000 and sixteen acres of land for an industrial school to be located at Decatur, provided the citizens of Decatur would contribute $100,000. He further proposed that if the Cumberland Presbyterian Church would move Lincoln University to Decatur, he would give the above amount to this institution, provided the denomination would raise a reasonable sum (later set at $100,000).[61] Although Millikin was a member of another denomination, his father was a ruling elder in a Cumberland Presbyterian church in Pennsylvania, and his wife was the daughter of a Cumberland Presbyterian minister, the Rev. S. M. Aston.

The General Assembly in 1900 expressed the hope that the synods of Illinois, Indiana, and Iowa would place themselves in a position to receive this gift.[62] Subsequently the three synods took favorable action and appointed a commission to work out the details. It was decided to amend the charter of Lincoln University so as to name the school James Millikin University. The school would have two branches. One, to be known as Lincoln College, would remain at Lincoln. The other, to be known as the Decatur College and Industrial School, was established at Decatur. Decatur was made the headquarters of the university.

The conditions having been met, the first four buildings of the school at Decatur were completed, and on June 4, 1903, Theodore Roosevelt, then President of the United States, delivered the dedicatory address.[63] The school opened in September of that year.

In the meantime, Millikin also made a gift of $50,000 to the college at Lincoln, and the citizens of Lincoln raised $25,000 for the erection of a new building.[64]

At the meeting of Texas Synod in the fall of 1900 memorials were received from five presbyteries asking that action be taken looking to the removal of Trinity University from Tehuacana (where it had been in operation since its foundation in 1869) to a larger town or city. By a vote of fifty-five to forty-four action was taken stating that "it is the sense of this Synod that the best interest of the Church and its educational work would be conserved by the removal of said institution from its present location to some good city within our bounds." A committee of seven was appointed to consider all questions involved in removal and to receive bids for the location of the school.[65]

In 1901 the committee, after having considered proposals made by Corsicana, Itasca, and Waxahachie, recommended Waxahachie as being the most suitable place for the location of the university.[66] The citizens of Waxahachie proposed to give $80,000 in cash, land, and notes. It was decided that immediate steps should be taken to remove Trinity University to Waxahachie, and the Board of Trustees was empowered to convey by quitclaim deed the campus and the building thereon together with vacant lots owned by the institution to such person or persons as might be designated by the people of Tehuacana, with the understanding that all endowment, apparatus and furniture, and all other property, except the campus and building, should be transferred to Waxahachie or disposed of in the interest of Trinity University.[67] The buildings planned at Waxahachie were completed in time for the opening of the fall session in 1902, and the school opened there on September 9.

NATHAN GREEN, JR.
(1827-1919)
Law Professor, 1856-1919,
at Cumberland University;
Chancellor, 1873-1902

MEMORIAL HALL, CUMBERLAND UNIVERSITY,
LEBANON, TENNESSEE

JAMES MILLIKIN UNIVERSITY, DECATUR, ILLINOIS

The main emphasis in the synods of Illinois, Indiana, and Iowa was necessarily given to meeting the conditions necessary to receiving the Millikin gift, and the attention of Texas Synod was temporarily diverted from the raising of endowment by the question of the relocation of Trinity University and the need for buildings in the new location. Nevertheless, the Educational Commission in its report to the General Assembly in 1904 noted that more money had been secured for college endowment during the four years of the Commission's existence than had been secured for that purpose during the previous ninety years of the denomination's history.[68] The greater part of the actual money raised was that contributed from various sources to the founding of James Millikin University. No apparent progress was made toward establishing a school on the Pacific Coast. There is no doubt, however, that the status of the five schools designated to be beneficiaries of the million-dollar campaign was much improved as a result of the increased emphasis on education.

The Thornton Home for aged ministers and their wives and widows was being operated at Evansville, Indiana, under the direction of the Board of Ministerial Relief. In 1899, Texas Synod, sensing the need for a similar home in its bounds, appointed a committee to formulate a plan for establishing such a home and to receive proposals for its location.[69] In 1903 it was reported that a stone residence and eleven and three-fourths acres of land in the town of Round Rock, together with other donations of money and property, had been secured for such a home. The home, which was designated as the Sheppard Home, was established at Round Rock with these Texans as trustees: the Rev. John Hudson and H. B. Sheppard, Round Rock; R. M. Castleman, Austin; Henry Adkinson, Rutledge; and F. M. Hedrick, Taylor. The gifts of money and property totaling an estimated $11,000 in value had been secured through the efforts of the Rev. W. D. Wear at an expense of $80.80.[70] The home was opened for occupants on December 1, 1904.

Books published by the Cumberland Presbyterian Publishing House during the years 1900-1903 included *Life in Japan,* by Miss Ella Gardner; *Elect Infants,* by the Rev. J. V. Stephens; a revised and improved edition of *Alice McDonald,* by the Rev. J. B. Logan; *Dancers and Dancing,* by the Rev. J. M. Hubbert; *The Organized Sunday School, The Teaching Problem,* and *The Superintendent's Handbook,* by J. W. Axtell; *How Missions Pay,* by the Rev. J. W. Laughlin; *We Are Ten* (a book in the Missionary Series), by Mrs. George W. Shelton; and *Be Ready,* by the Rev. Ira Landrith. These titles are indicative of interests claiming the attention of leaders within the Cumberland Presbyterian Church during this period: missions, doctrine, morals, and Sunday school work.

Objection was raised to the Rev. R. V. Foster's *Systematic Theology* (published in 1899) because, contrary to the order of subjects in the Confession of Faith, he treated faith and repentance as consequents of regeneration. Logan Presbytery sent an overture to the General Assembly in 1899 asking that the Assembly express its approval of Foster's purpose to revise the chapter on regeneration. The Assembly, however, declined to take action.[71] The following year the presbyteries of Colorado, Little River, and Obion asked for the removal of Foster from the chair of systematic theology in the Theological Seminary of Cumberland University on the ground that "his teachings, in some important points, are out of harmony with our system of Theology and the teachings of the Bible." San Antonio Presbytery petitioned the Assembly against taking such action.[72] It was pointed out in the General Assembly that Foster had not had sufficient time to revise his book, and, on the basis of his statement that he "approves of every statement of our Confession of Faith as containing the system of doctrines taught in the Holy Scriptures," the Assembly declined to grant the requests for his removal.[73]

During this period an amendment to Article 47 of the Constitution providing for the election of ruling elders and deacons for limited terms was passed.[74] On the other hand, the General Assembly declined to recommend to the presbyteries an amendment proposed by two presbyteries relating to Section 101 of the Confession of Faith regarding the mode of baptism. This amendment would have omitted the word "rightly" before the word "administered" and would have deleted the sentence which reads "Yet the validity of the Sacrament does not depend upon any particular mode of administration." [75]

The question of the ordination of women continued to come before the General Assembly in one way or another. In April 1899, Owensboro Presbytery received Mrs. L. M. Woosley as an ordained minister by letter from the defunct Nolin Presbytery. An appeal was filed against its action. The Synod of Kentucky ordered her name dropped, but Owensboro Presbytery refused to comply. The Stated Clerk of the General Assembly, however, omitted her name from the published list of ministers.[76]

In 1901 Miss Vianna Woosley, of Leitchfield Presbytery, appeared as a commissioner to the General Assembly on the part of the eldership. A resolution challenging her right to retain her seat as a member was presented but after lengthy discussion was laid on the table. A resolution was then adopted instructing the presbyteries not to send women to represent them in future Assemblies but stating that "this shall not unseat or lead to the unseating or expelling of any Commissioner in this General Assembly." [77]

In 1903, the General Assembly received a memorial from Walla Walla Presbytery, in the state of Washington, asking that a constitutional amendment be submitted which would provide for the ordination of qualified persons to the ministry regardless of sex. On the basis of previous deliverances of the General Assembly prohibiting the ordination of women the memorial was not granted.[78] The same year the ministerial directory forwarded by the stated clerk of Walla Walla Presbytery contained the name of a woman as a probationer for the ministry. The Stated Clerk of the General Assembly reported that he had erased her name in accordance with his understanding of the implied instructions of the General Assembly.[79]

# 18

## ENDURING THROUGH CRISIS

*The division in our church over the union question is a result of a difference of opinion as to the effect of the revision of 1903. Those opposed to union on the proposed basis are firmly of the opinion that the union brethren are wrong in their contention that the Presbyterian Church has come to our doctrinal position. . . . The majority of those favoring union are of the opinion that the recent revision brings the Westminster Confession to our historic position.*

W. P. Bone, professor of New Testament at Cumberland University, 1905

In 1902, the Cumberland Presbyterian Church was in many respects enjoying unprecedented prosperity. Although the number of candidates for the ministry had declined, new churches were still being established, and a renewed interest in education promised to put the five strongest of the colleges and universities on a sound financial basis. Yet during the next four years it was to be shaken to its very foundation by a movement to effect a union with the Presbyterian Church in the U. S. A. That denomination, since the secession of most of its Southern presbyteries during and shortly after the Civil War, had been confined principally to the North and West.

As a culmination of some fifteen years of discussion, the General Assembly of the Presbyterian Church, U. S. A., in its 1902 meeting, submitted to its presbyteries several amendments to its Confession of Faith. For convenience these amendments may be divided into three classes:

(1) Three amendments involved changes in the existing text. It was proposed to amend Chapter XVI, Section VII, so that instead of saying that works done by unregenerate men, even though they be works commanded by God, are "sinful, and cannot please God," it would state that such works "come short of what God requires." In Chapter XXII, Section III, this statement would be deleted: "Yet it is a sin to refuse an oath touching any thing that is good and just, being imposed by lawful authority." Chapter XXV, Section VI, which labeled the Pope as "that antichrist, that man of sin, and son of perdition," was to be so changed as to read that "the claim of any man to be the vicar of Christ and the head of the Church, is unscriptural, without warrant in fact, and is a usurpation dishonoring to the Lord Jesus Christ." [1]

(2) Two new chapters pertaining to "the Holy Spirit" and "the Love of God and Missions" were proposed to be added as Chapters XXXIV and XXXV. The latter chapter, especially, seems to contradict the basic tenets of the Westminster Confession to which Cumberland Presbyterians had objected. It declares that God has provided a way of salvation sufficient for and adapted to the whole lost race of men, that he offers this salvation to all men in the Gospel, that he desires that all men should be saved, promises eternal life to all who truly repent and believe in Christ, invites and commands all to embrace the offered mercy, and by his Spirit pleads with men to accept his gracious invitation. This chapter of itself would seem to have been quite satisfactory to Cumberland Presbyterians.

(3) A "Declaratory Statement" designed to interpret Chapter III, on the Decrees of God, and Chapter X, Section III, concerning the salvation of infants dying in infancy, was to be added. The text of the "Declaratory Statement" follows:

While the ordination vow of ministers, ruling elders, and deacons, as set forth in the Form of Government, requires the reception and adoption of the Confession of Faith only as containing the System of Doctrine taught in the Holy Scriptures, nevertheless, seeing that the desire has been formally expressed for a disavowal by the Church of certain inferences drawn from statements in the Confession of Faith, and also for a declaration of certain aspects of revealed truth which appear at the present time to call for more explicit statement, therefore the Presbyterian Church in the United States of America does authoritatively declare as follows:
*First,* With reference to Chapter III of the Confession of Faith: that concerning those who are saved in Christ, the doctrine of God's eternal decree is held in harmony with the doctrine of His love to all mankind, His gift of His Son to be the propitiation for the sins of the whole world, and His readiness to bestow His saving grace on all who seek it. That concerning those who perish, the doctrine of God's eternal decree is held in harmony with the doctrine that God desires not the death of any sinner,

but has provided in Christ a salvation sufficient for all, adapted to all, and freely offered in the Gospel to all; that men are fully responsible for their treatment of God's gracious offer; that His decree hinders no man from accepting that offer; and that no man is condemned except on the ground of his sin.

*Second,* With reference to Chapter X, Section 3, of the Confession of Faith, that it is not to be regarded as teaching that any who die in infancy are lost. We believe that all dying in infancy are included in the election of grace, and are regenerated and saved by Christ through the Spirit, who works when and where and how he pleases.

The General Assembly also adopted a "Brief Statement of the Reformed Faith" designed "to inform and enlighten the people in regard to the significance and religious meaning of the Reformed Faith and not with the view of becoming a test of Orthodoxy for ministers, elders and deacons." It was emphasized that this statement in no wise was intended to take the place of the Confession of Faith.[2]

Some talk of union among various churches was in the air. The General Synod of the Reformed Church had appointed a special committee of five clergymen to study the possibility of a federation of the twelve churches in this country holding the Presbyterian system. There had been before the General Assembly of the Presbyterian Church, U. S. (popularly known as the Southern Presbyterian Church), a petition from some ministers and laymen of the Nashville area requesting the opening of negotiations for union with the Reformed Church in America; however, since this petition did not come to the Assembly through regular channels, the Assembly declined to take action. During the summer of 1902 a sizable group of ministers and laymen of the United Brethren in Christ petitioned their bishops to open negotiations with churches similar in polity and doctrine to theirs. Specifically mentioned were the Methodist Protestant, Evangelical, United Evangelical, and Cumberland Presbyterian churches. Those five churches had at that time a combined membership of about 800,000. Publicity was given this petition through the columns of the *Cumberland Presbyterian.*[3]

That union would be an issue in the forthcoming General Assembly was made certain early in September 1902, by the almost simultaneous passage by Lincoln and Decatur presbyteries, in Illinois, of similar resolutions memorializing the General Assembly of the Cumberland Presbyterian Church, contingent upon approval of the proposed amendments to the Confession of Faith by the presbyteries of the Presbyterian Church, U. S. A., to take action looking to a union of these two denominations. The resolution adopted by Lincoln Presbytery was introduced by Dr. J. L. Goodknight, then dean of Lincoln College, at the suggestion of the Rev. W. J. Darby, corresponding secretary of the Educational Society of the General Assembly, who visited the meeting of that presbytery. Darby had taken a lively interest in the founding of the new James Millikin University. James Millikin, who had given considerable sums toward the establishment of this institution, had made a trip to the East, in the course of which he had visited some of the great eastern universities. The project he was fostering seemed inglorious by comparison. Although the Cumberland Presbyterians of Iowa, Illinois, and Indiana, who were the sponsors of James Millikin University, had raised the $100,000 originally stipulated, they had been slow in coming through with the matching funds stipulated by Millikin as a condition to his making additional gifts. Consequently, he had become dissatisfied with their performance. What better way could be devised to obtain the needed money than to take the whole project into the Presbyterian Church and let it provide the matching funds? Darby suggested to Goodknight that he believed Millikin would be pleased if the two presbyteries in which the twin colleges which made up James Millikin University were located would adopt memorials proposing union with the larger Presbyterian body.[4]

On September 10, at the meeting of Lebanon Presbytery at LaVergne, Tennessee, resolutions looking to union were introduced by John M. Gaut, a Nashville attorney and ruling elder, but a substitute resolution expressing the opinion that "the occasion is not now opportune" was adopted instead.[5] On September 11, Darby introduced in his own presbytery (Indiana) a resolution favoring union. This resolution, so the editor of the *Cumberland Presbyterian* stated, was "practically identical" with the one introduced the day before in Lebanon Presbytery.[6] A special committee to which this paper was referred mentioned the suggestion emanating from an "Arminian" group (the United Brethren) for union of certain Arminian bodies and Cumberland Presbyterians and made a point of saying, "We are Presbyterians, and not Arminians." This suggests that Indiana Presbytery was motivated, at least in part, by a desire to forestall the possibility that union with the "Arminian" groups would receive serious consideration.

Meanwhile, the editor of the *Cumberland Presbyterian,* the Rev. Ira Landrith, counseled that the move for union was premature, and that Cumberland Presbyterians should have waited for the Presbyterian Church to take the initiative. He recognized that "There are those in both the Presbyterian and the Cumberland Presbyterian churches who do not regard the proposed revision [of the Presbyterian Confession of Faith] as satisfactorily complete." At one point early in the discussion Landrith wrote, "They [Cumberland Presbyterians] ought to make haste to stop for the present this premature union movement." He suggested that the presbyteries which had taken favorable action would do well to call meetings and reconsider and indefinitely postpone the proposal.[7] Nevertheless, Darby, with the support of a few other ardent advocates of union, persisted in his course.

By the time of the meeting of the General Assembly, which convened in Nashville in May 1903, memorials favoring some kind of action looking to union of the Cumberland Presbyterian Church with the Presbyterian Church, U. S. A., had been received from the presbyteries of Colesburg, Decatur, Indiana, Kirksville, Lincoln, New Lebanon, Tehuacana, Vandalia, and Wabash, and the synods of Indianola and Missouri. There were memorials unfavorable to the proposal from the presbyteries of Chattanooga, Chickasaw, Clarksville, Cookeville, Louisville, Mound Prairie, Owensboro, Princeton, Robert Donnell, and South Louisiana.[8] Memorials favorable to union were introduced in several other presbyteries but were defeated. Texas Synod adopted a resolution urging that the Church pursue "the even tenor of her way" and discouraged precipitation of the union issue until the way should be opened for a full, open, and authoritative understanding of the doctrinal attitude of those with whom it was proposed to unite.[9] Thus the division within the Cumberland Presbyterian Church on this issue was apparent from the outset.

Meanwhile, two presbyteries of the Presbyterian Church, U. S. A., Mattoon and Dayton, expressed their pleasure that the Cumberlands were considering union with the larger Presbyterian body. The initiative had been taken, however, by persons and judicatures within the Cumberland Presbyterian Church.

The Cumberland Presbyterian General Assembly responded to the memorials by appointing a Committee of Nine, on Presbyterian Fraternity and Union,

to confer with such like Committees as may be appointed by other Presbyterian bodies, in regard to the desirability and practicability of closer affiliation and organic union among the members of the Presbyterian family in the United States, and if, in any particular case, after conference and investigation, union shall seem to be desirable and practicable, to suggest suitable means for its accomplishment, and to report such basis of union as may be mutually agreed upon to the next General Assembly.[10]

The General Assembly elected the Rev. W. H. Black, president of Missouri Valley College, to serve as chairman, and for the purpose of electing the other eight members the commissioners were divided according to synods into four groups, each of which was to meet and nominate two persons. Those chosen by the caucuses of commissioners from the various areas included Ira Landrith and E. E. Beard, of Tennessee; the Rev. S. M. Templeton and M. B. Templeton, of Texas; the Rev. B. P. Fullerton, of Missouri; Judge W. E. Settle, of Kentucky; the Rev. D. E. Bushnell, of Illinois; and

A. E. Turner, president of Waynesburg College, Pennsylvania. Meanwhile, by resolution, Dr. R. M. Tinnon, Moderator of the General Assembly, was added to the committee, and later, by motion, the committee was further enlarged to include the Rev. W. J. Darby and the Rev. B. G. Mitchell. Thus a committee of twelve was formed. The Stated Clerk of the General Assembly, the Rev. J. M. Hubbert, was named to act as secretary for the committee until it should meet and organize.

Before its final adjournment the General Assembly received a telegram from the General Assembly of the Presbyterian Church, U. S. A., meeting in Los Angeles, California, announcing that it had appointed a similar committee. No other Presbyterian bodies took favorable action.

Meanwhile, the proposed revisions of the Confession of Faith of the Presbyterian Church, U. S. A., had been approved by an overwhelming majority of the presbyteries, despite some opposition, and were put into effect by action of the General Assembly in 1903.

The first joint meeting of the committees of the two churches was held in Saint Louis, Missouri, beginning September 29, 1903, and continuing until October 2. Since the committees could not complete their work at that time, certain details were referred to subcommittees composed of equal numbers of committeemen from the two churches. These subcommittees met in Cincinnati December 29-31, 1903. A final meeting of the two committees was held February 17-20, 1904, in Saint Louis, at which time the Joint Report on Union was adopted and signed. The report received the unanimous approval of the Cumberland Presbyterian committee, but two members of the committee from the Presbyterian Church, U. S. A., presented a statement of dissent.[11]

Proceedings of the committees were not revealed until the Joint Report on Union was in final form; however, Landrith, who apparently had ceased his opposition to the union proposal following his appointment to the committee, assured readers of the *Cumberland Presbyterian* that the interests of the Cumberland Presbyterian Church were being well cared for. After the first joint meeting he wrote:

Lest unnecessary anxiety should be felt in any quarter, we desire to say very positively that the Cumberland Presbyterian Committee did not volunteer, nor was it asked to consent to, any compromise or surrender of its historic doctrinal position. If the Cumberland Presbyterian Church is ever united with the Presbyterian Church in the United States of America, the union will be a real one, faithful alike to our history and to our consistent creedal contentions. Upon this point there is no difference of opinion in our committee, and none, we believe, in the committee with which we are negotiating.[12]

In the fall of 1903 Landrith resigned as editor of the *Cumberland Presbyterian* to become general secretary of the Religious Education Association, with headquarters in Chicago. On January 1, 1904, he was succeeded as editor by the Rev. James E. Clarke, pastor of the Addison Avenue Cumberland Presbyterian Church in Nashville and former president of the Board of Publication. Clarke did not open the columns of the paper to discussion of the union question until after the committees of the two churches had formulated their report. The Joint Report on Union was published in the *Cumberland Presbyterian* of February 25, 1904. By that time many of the commissioners to the 1904 General Assembly had been elected.

The Joint Report on Union consisted of three sections: (1) the Plan of Reunion and Union of the Two Churches, (2) eight Concurrent Declarations, and (3) three Recommendations.[13]

The Plan of Reunion and Union provided that the Presbyterian Church in the United States of America and the Cumberland Presbyterian Church should be united under the name and style of "The Presbyterian Church in the United States of America"; that the union should be effected "on the doctrinal basis of the Confession of Faith of the Presbyterian Church in the United States of America, as revised in 1903, and of its other doctrinal and ecclesiastical standards"; and that the Scriptures of the Old and New Testament should be acknowledged as "the inspired word of God, the only infallible rule of faith and practice." The basis of union was to be submitted to the presbyteries of the two churches, which should meet on or before April 30, 1905, to express "their approval or disapproval" of the plan.

Of the Concurrent Declarations, the first is of special importance:

1. In adopting the Confession of Faith of the Presbyterian Church in the United States of America, as revised in 1903, as a Basis of Union, it is mutually recognized that such agreement now exists between the systems of doctrine contained in the Confessions of Faith of the two Churches as to warrant this union—a union honoring alike to both. Mutual acknowledgement also is made of the teaching and defense of essential evangelical doctrine held in common by these Churches, and of the divine favor and blessing that have made this common faith and service effectual.

It is also recognized that liberty of belief exists by virtue of the provision of the Declaratory Statement, which is part of the Confession of Faith of the Presbyterian Church in the United States of America, and which states that "the ordination vow of ministers, ruling elders and deacons, as set forth in the Form of Government, requires the reception and adoption of the Confession of Faith, only as containing the system of doctrine taught in the Holy Scriptures." This liberty is specifically secured by the Declaratory Statement, as to Chapter III and Chapter X, Section 3, of the Confession of Faith. It is recognized also that the doctrinal deliverance contained in the Brief Statement of the Reformed Faith, adopted in 1902 by the General

Assembly of the Presbyterian Church in the United States of America, "for a better understanding of our doctrinal beliefs," reveals a doctrinal agreement favorable to reunion.

It was further provided that all ministers and churches of the two denominations should be admitted to the same standing in the united church which they should hold in their respective connections at the consummation of the reunion; that the boundaries of the various presbyteries and synods should be adjusted by the General Assembly of the united church; and that the institutions of learning under the control of the Cumberland Presbyterian Church should remain in charge of their respective boards of trustees with no greater control to be exercised by the General Assembly or other ecclesiastical courts of the united church than was being exercised by the corresponding judicatory of the Cumberland Presbyterian Church.

The most controversial of the Recommendations was the following:

1. It is recommended that such a change be made in the Form of Government of the Presbyterian Church in the United States of America, as will allow additional or separate Presbyteries and Synods to be organized in exceptional cases, wholly or in part, within the territorial bounds of existing Presbyteries or Synods respectively, for a particular race or nationality, if desired by such race or nationality.

As soon as the proposed plan of union was publicized and the columns of the *Cumberland Presbyterian* again were opened to discussion of the question, division over the issue again became apparent. On the one hand, there were those, including the editor of the *Cumberland Presbyterian,* who believed that the objectionable features of the Presbyterian Confession of Faith had been satisfactorily explained away by the "Declaratory Statement." It was urged that Cumberland Presbyterians would be inconsistent, now that the difficulties which led to the formation of the Cumberland Presbyterian Church had been removed, if they remained a separate denomination.[14] Dr. R. V. Foster, professor of systematic theology in the Theological Seminary at Cumberland University, labored to prove that the Confession of Faith of the Cumberland Presbyterian Church was essentially Calvinistic.[15] It had only protested against an abuse of the caution contained within the Westminster Confession itself as to how the "high mysteries" of the doctrine of predestination should be handled.

That the union would make for greater efficiency was urged by John M. Gaut, of Nashville. The result would be a large national church with prestige and power. The union would heal a breach in the Christian Church which the fathers had deplored.[16] Some of the advocates of union suggested that the Cumberland Presbyterian Church had the fields, and the Presbyterian Church, U. S. A., the money to develop those fields. Noting that the statement had been made that the Cumberland Presbyterian Church could enter a hundred new towns in Oklahoma and the Indian Territory if it had the money, the Rev. J. R. Sharp, of Covington, Tennessee, wrote, "The gold mine is largely in our hands, the smelter in the hands of our neighbors." [17] It was predicted that several of the border synods in the North and Northwest would disintegrate unless the union became a reality.[18]

In the other hand, many Cumberland Presbyterians were disappointed to learn that apparently no concessions had been obtained by the Cumberland Presbyterian committee. The name of the reunited church was to be the Presbyterian Church in the United States of America. The union was to be on the basis of the Confession of Faith of the Presbyterian Church in the United States of America as revised in 1903. The result would be absorption rather than union. Cumberland Presbyterians would be giving up their name and their Confession of Faith. The Presbyterian Church, U. S. A., would be giving up nothing.

The Rev. J. L. Hudgins, pastor of the Cumberland Presbyterian Church at Washington, Indiana, felt that a new confession of faith should have been formulated.[19] The Rev. W. T. Dale inquired why, if the Presbyterian Church intended the "Declaratory Statement" to take the place of Chapter III, it did not strike out Chapter III and substitute the "Declaratory Statement" for it. Furthermore, the "Declaratory Statement" proposed to interpret only Chapter III and Chapter X, Section III. Other parts of Chapter X were left untouched. Chapter XVII, which based the doctrine of the perseverance of the saints on "the immutable decree of election," was unchanged. There were questions in the Larger and Shorter Catechisms which taught the doctrine of unconditional election and reprobation just as surely as did the Confession proper.[20]

The Rev. W. P. Bone, professor of New Testament literature in the Theological School at Cumberland University, likewise regarded the revision of the Presbyterian Confession as being far from satisfactory. He cited statements made by members of the revision committee in which they declared that the system of doctrine had not changed. He objected to Concurrent Declaration No. 1, which declared that there was "sufficient agreement" between the systems of doctrine of the two churches to warrant union, on the ground that he simply did not believe it to be true.[21]

Why, it was asked, did the Presbyterians need the "Brief Statement" to interpret the Reformed faith to the laity? Did not its promulgation suggest that the meaning of their official creed was doubtful and needed explaining? "Why should we return to dogmas and barnacles that must have a new interpretation with each succeeding age?" inquired a newspaper editor, T. A.

Havron, of Jasper, Tennessee.[22]

The education requirements of the Presbyterian Church for ordination had been accepted, apparently without question. It was estimated that not more than one-fourth of the approximately 1,600 ministers of the Cumberland Presbyterian Church were seminary graduates. Would not the others be, according to the language of the Form of Government of the Presbyterian Church, "a reproach to religion and dangerous to the Church"?[23] The Rev. J. P. McDonald, of Chestnut Mound, Tennessee, suggested the need not only for the writing of a new confession of faith but also for an educational standard sufficiently elastic to be applied to the rural districts as well as to the university city.[24]

There was also objection to the disposition of the race question. There was no attempt, as far as is known, to involve the Cumberland Presbyterian Church, Colored, in the union. The Presbyterian Church, U. S. A., however, had done a great deal of missionary work among the Negroes in the South following the Civil War and thirteen presbyteries composed of Negro churches had been organized in Virginia, North Carolina, South Carolina, Georgia, Alabama, Mississippi, Tennessee, Arkansas, and the Indian Territory. This area overlapped to a considerable extent the territory occupied by the Cumberland Presbyterian Church. The question at issue was, Would the proposed change in the Form of Government make it possible for the white constituency (in case the Cumberland Presbyterian Church should enter the proposed union) to request and obtain separate presbyteries for the whites? Or would the organization of separate presbyteries be contingent upon the request of the Negro constituency? E. E. Beard, son of the theologian Richard Beard, believed that under the proposed change the white constituency could ask for and obtain separate presbyteries. The Rev. M. M. Smith, of Kentucky, interpreted the proposed change to mean that the Negroes must request separate presbyteries if such were to be set up.[25] There appears to have been no substantial difference between those favoring union and those opposed as to the desirability of having separate presbyteries for the two races. It was rather a question as to whether or not the proposed change would effect the separation. The "separate but equal" doctrine with reference to public accommodations for the races had been sanctioned by the United States Supreme Court less than ten years previously and probably represented the prevailing point of view in most of the area occupied by the Cumberland Presbyterian Church.

Recognizing that the editor of the *Cumberland Presbyterian* was receiving far more articles on the union question than he could publish and that some advocates of union had expressed their intolerance of views expressed by those opposing, the Rev. A. M. Buchanan began publication in April 1904 of a paper at Moberly, Missouri, in opposition to the union. This paper, known as the *Cumberland Banner,* was begun as a twelve-page monthly publication.

Obion Presbytery petitioned the General Assembly to decline to submit the plan of union to the presbyteries "for the reason that the terms of same are not equitable to us as a Church." New Hope and Owensboro presbyteries adopted similar memorials.[26]

The General Assembly of the Cumberland Presbyterian Church met in May 1904, at Dallas, Texas. As was to be expected, the union question overshadowed all other issues.

In addition to submitting the Joint Report on Union, the Committee on Fraternity and Union submitted a Supplemental Report which was in reality a series of arguments in support of the proposed plan of union.[27] As to the history of the union movement, the committee stated that

It was spontaneous in both Churches, there being no previous agreement or agreements, but individuals, Presbyteries, and Synods acted independently, in both Churches, in favor of the movement, after the publication of the action of the General Assembly of the Presbyterian Church in the United States of America of its acts of revision, the Declaratory Statement and the Brief Statement.

It was pointed out that the founders of the Cumberland Presbyterian Church did not seek independence but liberty of belief, which, it was urged, was now secured by the Declaratory Statement. It was argued at length that "Revision has revised." The existence of "great combinations in trade, manufacture, commerce and labor" was cited as proof that men were sinking their individual interests for the sake of "the greater economy, efficiency, and resources of larger organization." The age was practical, not philosophical. Men were not asking for psychological distinctions but for results. Presbyterianism and Protestantism were on trial before the world. It was also noted that the Presbyterian Church, U. S. A.,

which is the greatest Presbyterian Church in the world, heartily desires a truly national field for its work and workers. It wishes its aggressive evangelizing operations carried on in the South as well as in the North, and seriously objects to being called the "Northern" Presbyterian Church. This being the ideal of the Presbyterians, naturally they would hail union with our Church as a providential means to its realization.

The Committee on Church Cooperation and Union of the Presbyterian Church, U. S. A., presented its interpretation of the union negotiations to its General Assembly which met in Buffalo, New York.[28] Concerning the revision of the Confession of Faith completed in 1903, this committee stated,

It was made clear to the brethren of the Committee on Fraternity and Union of the Cumberland Presbyterian Church, at the outset of our conferences, that the Revision of the Confession of Faith recently undertaken by our Church was not occasioned by any pressure from without, but was purely a movement within our own denomination. It was also stated that the purposes of the movement were two: to disavow inferences drawn from certain statements in the Confession of Faith, and also to set forth some aspects of revealed truth which appeared to call for more explicit statement. In addition it was declared that the effect of the adoption of the Declaratory Statement as a part of the Constitution, was simply to give legal standing to interpretations of Chapter iii and of Chapter x, Section 3, which previously had seemed to have merely the force of private opinion, and that the revision of the Confession of Faith had effected no material change in the doctrinal attitude of our Church.

It was recognized that "union would make our Church strong and potential in the Middle South and Southwest, and also give to it a national character commensurate with its name, its history and its responsibilities." It was pointed out, however, that a considerable increase in home mission contributions would be needed if the work of evangelization in this area was to be done effectively.

Concerning Concurrent Declaration No. 1 with regard to doctrinal agreement, the committee of the Presbyterian Church hastened to point out that this declaration was not a part of the basis of union. The language finally adopted, it stated, was primarily the language of the Cumberland Presbyterian committee and should be interpreted in light of the fact that preceding it the statement was made that the Cumberland Presbyterian Church was to adopt the Confession of Faith of the Presbyterian Church, U. S. A. Although, according to this committee, the language of Declaration No. 1 "was not satisfactory to them or to us," it was felt that the inclusion of some such statement was due a church which, according to the proposed plan of union, would yield its name and adopt the Presbyterian standards in their entirety.

With reference to the declaration as to liberty of belief contained in the second paragraph of Concurrent Declaration No. 1, the committee stated that "it was understood that no more liberty of belief was expected by the Cumberland brethren, than is now accorded under the Revised Confession to our own ministers and elders." With regard to the reference in this paragraph to the "Brief Statement of the Reformed Faith" it was noted that

the brethren of the Cumberland Presbyterian Church understood clearly that the Brief Statement was not a part of the Constitution but simply a doctrinal deliverance, that it had force as interpreting the Reformed Faith only so long as it should be acceptable to the Church, and that it could be altered or rescinded by any General Assembly.

Thus it is apparent that the interpretations of the effect of revision as submitted by the two committees to their respective General Assemblies differed radically.

Concerning the recommendation that provision be made for separate presbyteries for members of a particular race or nationality the Presbyterian committee reported that

no effort was made by the Cumberland Presbyterian Committee to secure any change as to the Church relations of the colored ministers and congregations now in connection with this General Assembly. It was understood that these relations were matters that belonged to our Church alone.

The question of permitting separate presbyteries for members of different races had been referred in 1903 to a Special Committee on Territorial Limits of Presbyteries. At the time of its appointment there was referred to it an overture from the Synod of Tennessee asking that the rule forbidding the organizing of two presbyteries in the same territory be rescinded. There were overtures from several presbyteries on the same subject. An overture from the Presbytery of Cimarron suggested the organization of an African Presbyterian Church. These overtures had been formalized before the question of union with the Cumberland Presbyterian Church came before the General Assembly. In its report to the 1904 Assembly, this committee, after paying respect to certain great and unalterable principles—principles regarding the brotherhood of man—to which the Presbyterian Church, U. S. A., had always borne consistent witness, mentioned a number of presbyteries situated in the South which were made up solely of Negro churches. The committee went on to say,

In all this vast region it is not possible to organize a white church in connection with our General Assembly for the reason that such church would be under the care and control of a colored Presbytery. White Presbyterians, seeking such an organization, must ask of the Colored Presbytery permission to do so, and come under their control. Say what we please about the evils of social prejudice and racial antipathies, the fact remains that white churches will not associate themselves with colored Presbyteries.

The Committee recommended that the General Assembly send down to the presbyteries for their action the following overture:

Shall Chapter x, Section 2, be amended by adding to it the following words, "but in exceptional cases a Presbytery may be organized within the boundaries of existing Presbyteries, in the interests of ministers and churches speaking other than the English language, or of those of a particular race; but in no case without their consent"; and the same rule shall apply to Synods.[29]

This was almost, but not quite, the same as the proposed change called for in Recommendation No. 1 of the Joint Report on Union. The words "but in no case without their consent" were added. This addition did not help eliminate the vagueness which existed in the version contained in the Joint Report on Union. Whose consent must be obtained? That of the whites, or that of the Negro constituency, or both?

The proposal for separate presbyteries for those of different races did not originate as a concession to the Cumberland Presbyterian Church but was designed to meet a practical problem within the Presbyterian Church, U. S. A. Its purpose was to make possible the organization of white churches within the areas occupied by existing presbyteries composed of Negroes.

The plan of union was put before the General Assembly of the Cumberland Presbyterian Church in the form of a resolution providing "that the included Joint-Report on Union be adopted; and that the Basis of Union be and is recommended to the Presbyteries of the Cumberland Presbyterian Church for their approval or disapproval." The resolution further provided that the Moderator and Stated Clerk "be instructed to submit the Basis of Union, contained in said report, to the Presbyteries of the Cumberland Presbyterian Church, in the usual constitutional manner" upon receipt of official notification of the adoption of the report by the General Assembly of the Presbyterian Church, U. S. A.[30]

Discussion on the resolution was begun at ten o'clock Tuesday morning, May 24, and continued through the sessions of Tuesday and Wednesday. When the Assembly resumed its meeting at eight o'clock Wednesday night the decision was reached that the Assembly would hear one more speaker on each side of the question and then proceed to vote. There were 251 commissioners enrolled in this Assembly. Of these, 236 were present when the vote was taken. The affirmative vote was 162; the negative vote, 74. Four more affirmative votes were secured than the two-thirds required to refer a constitutional change to the presbyteries.[31]

The General Assembly of the Presbyterian Church, U. S. A., also adopted the Joint Report on Union and submitted the Basis of Union to its presbyteries. If the General Assembly meeting in 1905 should find that the Basis of Union had been approved by two-thirds of the Presbyteries, then the necessary steps should be taken, "if the way be clear," to complete the union with the Cumberland Presbyterian Church. In this connection the General Assembly adopted the following:

*Resolved,* 4. That the Assembly, in connection with this whole subject of union with the Cumberland Presbyterian Church, places on record its judgment, that the revision of the Confession of Faith effected in 1903 has not impaired the integrity of the system of doctrine contained in the Confession and taught in Holy Scripture, but was designed to remove mis-apprehensions as to the proper interpretation thereof.[32]

This was the Presbyterian answer to the Cumberland Presbyterian committee's argument that "Revision has revised." [33]

Following the action of the two Assemblies the contest for the presbyterial vote, especially in the Cumberland Presbyterian Church, began in earnest. Both advocates and opponents of union organized their forces. Before the commissioners left Dallas, opponents of the proposed basis of union met and appointed a steering committee composed of three Tennessee laymen: Judge Joe H. Fussell, of Columbia; J. N. Parker, of Dyersburg; and T. A. Havron, of Jasper. Beginning on September 29, 1904, a general meeting of opponents of the proposed union was held at the Epworth Hotel in Saint Louis, the arrangements having been made by the Rev. A. N. Eshman, president of Southern Female College, which had a booth at the World's Fair then in progress. At this meeting, which was attended by about sixty persons, resolutions were adopted, one of which declared the intention

to adhere to the confession of faith and doctrines of the Cumberland Presbyterian church, without any deviation therefrom, or any compromise whatever with any other different religious faith or doctrine. . . .

It was further declared

that we will maintain with Christian fortitude and faith the organization of the Cumberland Presbyterian church intact, and zealously guard the possession of all rights and interests to which we are entitled by virtue of our membership in the Cumberland Presbyterian church.[34]

One result of the Saint Louis conference was the merging of the *Cumberland Banner,* above mentioned, and the *Cumberland Evangel,* which meanwhile had been launched by Havron, in Jasper, Tennessee. The *Cumberland Banner* was the name chosen for the new paper. It became an eight-page weekly and was published at Jasper, with Havron as editor.

The unionists also organized by forming a Voluntary Committee on Union Information. Ira Landrith, from his headquarters in Chicago, served as the committee's corresponding secretary.[35]

After the 1904 Assembly, the editor of the *Cumberland Presbyterian,* with the approval of the Board of Publication, threw the weight of the church paper unhesitatingly on the side of union. Although he continued to receive and publish contributions by persons opposed to union, his editorial policy was avowedly in favor of union. He defended his policy on the ground that the General Assembly had "adopted" the Joint Report on Union which included Concurrent Declaration No. 1 affirming the existence of such agreement between the systems of doctrine of the two churches as to warrant union. Since the Assembly had decided that the Westminster Confession had been revised, it was his duty as editor to enable the readers to see that the Confession had indeed been revised.[36]

Dissatisfaction arose early in the Assembly year because the Stated Clerk of the General Assembly assumed the prerogative of announcing through the columns of the *Cumberland Presbyterian* that the presbyteries would not be expected to vote on the union question until their spring meetings.[37] Having made this announcement, he departed for a tour of Europe without having sent out the official ballots. The reason given was that by spring it would be known whether or not the presbyteries of the Presbyterian Church, U. S. A., had voted favorably on the proposed change in their "Form of Government" providing for separate presbyteries for those of different races. This withholding of the ballot was considered by some to have been an unwarranted action on the part of the Stated Clerk. The fall meetings were usually better attended than the spring meetings, and it was believed desirable that as full a representation as possible should be present to vote on so important a question.[38] Because the question had not been submitted in the regular manner, a prounion minority in Marshall Presbytery, in Texas, which was one of the first to vote on the union question, filed a protest against the action of the majority on the ground that the question was not properly before the presbytery.[39]

The Voluntary Committee on Union Information, however, had its own method of dealing with the situation. Prior to the fall meetings a letter was sent out by the corresponding secretary to representatives in the various presbyteries. In it the suggestion was made that if the Stated Clerk had not communicated with the presbytery on the subject, the question of union could be brought up by asking for the appointment of a "Committee on the Minutes of the General Assembly." This further suggestion was made:

3. If your Presbytery, even after a full discussion, seems likely to be doubtful, or "anti-union," postponement should be urged, as that would be wiser than final adverse action. Six months of patient education on union will bring around enough votes to carry the Presbytery into the union column next spring, though if adverse action is taken now, reconsideration next spring may be impossible. Vote if you can win; postpone, rather than run the risk of being defeated.

It was stated that the Committee was ready "with literature and if necessary, with visiting debaters" to render any legitimate assistance in presbyteries where the issue was uncertain. Presbyterial representatives were requested to keep the Committee informed as to the prospect for carrying their respective presbyteries for union:

Who are the leaders against union, their names, addresses, arguments, influence, etc., etc.? What literature is being circulated against union? (Send me sample copies if you can.) Tell me anything you can about the methods, accusations, etc., of the anti-unionists. In a word let me have everything you know for or against the union movement in your Presbytery. The value of this information to our Committee and to the cause cannot be over-estimated.[40]

The circulation of this letter provoked the charge that the unionists' methods were "political." The unionists, on the other hand, claimed their methods were legitimate and were no more "political" than those of their opponents who had sent out their "Special Instructions" as to how those opposed to union should react under certain contingencies. These instructions urged that copies of the Confession of Faith of the Presbyterian Church, U. S. A., as revised in 1903 be circulated in order that the people might know exactly what they were being asked to accept as a doctrinal standard. Congregations were urged to instruct their delegates as to how to vote in presbytery. Presbyteries voting against union were urged, in addition, to protest the whole procedure as "unlawful, unauthorized and revolutionary." In case a presbytery was considered likely to vote for union, it was suggested that antiunion members get excused from voting and enter a protest on the grounds of the alleged illegality of the proposal. All who were opposed were urged to make a "continual protest" and to continue in the organization.

Meanwhile, the discussion through the papers and through the publication of leaflets became increasingly bitter. Wild accusations were hurled against the leaders of the union movement. It was alleged that the Cumberland Presbyterian Committee on Fraternity and Union had received a promise of $100,000 for the publishing house at Nashville, $100,000 for the theological seminary, and other considerations which "look like a round million dollars" if union were achieved. These allegations were denied by the unionist leaders. There is no doubt that the prospect of the availability of home mission funds from the Presbyterian Church, U. S. A., to supplement the salaries of ministers in areas occupied by the Cumberland Presbyterian Church was used as an argument for union. That any promise of financial benefits was made by the Presbyterian committee seems unlikely.[41]

The alleged spontaneity of the union movement, used by some advocates as proof that it was inspired by the Holy Spirit, was a more vulnerable point of attack. It was pointed out that some leaders of the movement, especially the secretary of education, W. J. Darby, had put forth widespread efforts to obtain the passage of memorials favoring union. Not only had Darby fostered the presentation of memorials in Lincoln and Decatur presbyteries, but he had been present at the meeting of Lebanon Presbytery at LaVergne, Tennessee, in September 1902, where he had argued that the Presbyterian revision would remove all the doctrinal differences between the two churches.[42] At a meeting of Memphis Presbytery a letter from Darby, suggesting the passage of a memorial favoring union, was read on the floor of presbytery by the Rev. H. S. Williams, pastor of the Court Avenue Cumberland Presbyterian Church in Memphis. The matter was referred to a committee which reported favorably, but the presbytery rejected the committee's report.[43] Robert Donnell Presbytery, in Alabama, in addition to asking the General Assembly to maintain "a dignified silence" on the union proposals, went on record as regretting the use, by the secretary of education, of his official position and influence to further this "scheme" and asking that the boards see to it that the men sent out by them to do definite work devote themselves to that work alone.[44] All this suggests that the movement was not quite as spontaneous as its warmest advocates claimed it to be.

There was much dissatisfaction because the people did not have a greater voice in determining the outcome of the presbyterial vote.[45] The voting was done, of course, by the ordained ministers and the ruling elders representing churches. While opponents of the proposed union were urging congregations to inform themselves and instruct their delegates to presbytery as to how they should vote, John M. Gaut asserted that "The congregation is not a church court. It has no power to vote on any such question as the union question." The vote of the majority, he stated, would not be binding on the delegate to presbytery. Elders were usually better informed than the average church member, and the elder elected to presbytery should listen, reflect on what he heard, and then vote his convictions.[46] An antiunionist countered with the query as to why, if a vote of a congregation was required to move a church building from one site to another within a local community, the members should have no voice as to whether or not they should be transferred to another denomination? [47]

Relatively early in the discussions Ira Landrith, as corresponding secretary of the Voluntary Committee on Union Information, noted that nearly all of the recognized leaders of the Church—living ex-Moderators, college presidents, board members, and others in official positions—were supporting the union. He did not claim this as an argument for union, but used it rather to refute charges made by antiunionists that "mercenary motives" and "political methods" characterized the unionists. It was unlikely, he argued, that so many well-informed and "probably devout" men would be influenced by such motives.[48] The fact that most of the opponents of union were relatively unknown was taken up and used by others as an argument for union. A. T. Cory, of Scott City, Kansas, urged the Church to trust its leaders: "Why should these unknown anti-union leaders have the brazenry to set themselves up to uncover our eyes and disillusion us as to the alleged deception practiced upon us by trusted men, is the question that has puzzled us." [49] In response to such attacks made on leaders of the opposition, the Rev. T. Ashburn, of Evansville, Indiana, came to their defense. "While they have no desire to assume leadership in our church," he wrote, "no ambition for official position, nevertheless, no better or safer leaders could be found if they should happen in any way to be forced to the front." [50]

As the voting progressed, it was pointed out by some unionists that the presbyteries opposed to union had had fewer additions to the church and had given less money to denominational enterprises than those favoring union. The Rev. F. H. Ford, of Milan, Tennessee, noted that thirty-six presbyteries voting for union gave $19,427 to five denominational enterprises, whereas thirty-two presbyteries voting against union gave only $8,377. The figures indicated, he concluded, "that the opposition is not only anti-union but anti-church erection, anti-missions, anti-education and anti-everything." [51]

As the pattern of the voting began to be apparent, some unionists began to interpret the opposition as being dictated by sectional and racial prejudice. In February 1905, the editor of the *Cumberland Presbyterian* wrote under the caption, "Union and the Relation of Races":

In connection with this subject there is one great responsibility which stares us fairly in the face: If union fails, the verdict of the world will be that it failed chiefly because of sectional suspicion and prejudice.

He went on to say,

Things have come to such a pass that now, if for no other reason, union should be consummated in order that we may avoid the awful stigma of having permitted mere sectional feeling to separate Christian men, when it can no longer separate soldiers and politicians. [52]

The Rev. W. L. Livingston, of Henderson, Kentucky, after noting that only two presbyteries east of the Mississippi and south of the Ohio had voted for union, while two presbyteries west of the Mississippi and north of the Ohio had voted negatively, asked,

Can it be that the people south of the Ohio and east of the Mississippi have different theological views from their brethren north and west? I do not believe it. Can it be that those of us south of the Ohio and east of the Mississippi are less informed than our brethren north and west? It certainly cannot be. What then? The "negro," that is all. We have said we are not a sectional church. Does not the vote prove to the contrary? [53]

That there was resistance among Southern Cumberland Presbyterians to the idea of becoming part of a "Northern" church is apparent. Although provision was being made for separate presbyteries for those of different races, some were convinced that social mingling of the races would be the inevitable result of union. In any case, there would be Negroes in the General Assembly.[54]

Probably most Cumberland Presbyterians believed that the setting apart of the Negro constituency in 1871 to form a separate denomination was a wise move. It was pointed out that while the Freedmen's Bureau of the Presbyterian Church, U S. A., had succeeded in enlisting 12,000 Negroes in the Southern states, the Cumberland Presbyterian Church, Colored, had gathered a membership of approximately 50,000.[55] W. B. Young, of Clarksville, Tennessee, while asserting that the principal argument used against union was doctrinal, not racial, could not see leaving a church which had settled the racial problem by having a separate church to go to one where the status of the Negro was uncertain.[56]

On the other hand, the Saint Louis resolutions had not mentioned race. The Rev. W. H. Berry, of Texas, writing in December 1904, thought it unfortunate that the question of race had been injected into the issue at all, for he regarded the doctrinal issue as far more important.[57] Individuals in two Southern presbyteries, reacting against Clarke's February editorial in the *Cumberland Presbyterian,* stated that in their presbyteries it was not the race problem but the doctrinal issue which caused their presbyteries to vote against union. Judge J. J. McClellan, of West Point, Mississippi, wrote concerning the vote in New Hope Presbytery:

The people of the South will not mix with the colored brother, either socially or religiously. The proposed solution of the race problem is not altogether acceptable to them, but that is not their chief reason for opposing union.[58]

Likewise, the Rev. T. G. Randle, of Louisiana, wrote:

In behalf of the Louisiana Presbytery let me say (and I can get the proof if requested) that it was not a "sectional feeling" as Mr. Clarke states that caused that Presbytery to vote against union, for the leading issue in that discussion on both sides was on the revision of the book of the Presbyterian Church, U. S. A., chapters 3 and 10.[59]

What appeared to be a vote along sectional lines may be accounted for by another factor. In the South the Cumberland Presbyterian Church was generally well entrenched and felt no need for union with a larger body. On the other hand, there is considerable evidence that in the outlying presbyteries, especially in such states as Iowa, Colorado, California, Oregon, and Washington, the generally small Cumberland Presbyterian churches were having a difficult time maintaining themselves alongside the usually stronger Presbyterian churches. The Rev. E. N. Allen, of Portland, Oregon, found the outlook for the Cumberland Presbyterian Church in the West "exceedingly discouraging." He quoted the Rev. E. E. Thompson, of Seattle, Washington, as urging, "Vote the union through and thus end the agony of our work in the West." [60] The Rev. R. L. Vannice, of Iowa, noted the decline of the Cumberland Presbyterian Church in that state because it did not early plant itself in the centers of population, and because the Presbyterians were preaching as free a gospel as Cumberland Presbyterians. Now that revision had come, he saw no reason for Cumberland Presbyterians to contend for a separate existence. [61] The Rev. P. A. Rice, of Colorado, believing that the Presbyterians "have come to our ground," declared that "we are left without a single argument" to justify the continuing existence of the Cumberland Presbyterian Church. He predicted that if the union should fail "it would be difficult, if not impossible, for us to hold the ground already occupied, to say nothing of extending our work." [62] It was largely in these outpost synods that the deciding vote for union was won.

Overshadowing all else was the doctrinal issue, whether or not the Presbyterian Confession of Faith had been so revised that Cumberland Presbyterians could accept it. Among the advocates of union within the Cumberland Presbyterian Church were a few avowed Calvinists. Referring to a statement made by Dr. W. H. Roberts, Stated Clerk of the General Assembly of the Presbyterian Church, U. S. A., that "Our church regards itself as having made no material change in its doctrinal standards," the Rev. W. P. Thurston, of Owensboro, Kentucky, commented:

Of course; and if they had made any "material change," we most surely could not go in with them. We do not want the Calvinistic theology materially changed. We have never "impaired the system of doctrine" taught in the Westminster symbols, and could not go in with any church which would do so. The utmost charge of the fathers was that fatality "seemed" and "appeared" to be contained in some parts of those symbols, and their extremest request was for such a modification of the language as would remove that "inference." Mankind knows that that has now been done, and we do not want the other church to go any further in that direction; that way lies Arminianism. [63]

"If the revision of 1903 impaired the integrity of the system of doctrine," wrote R. A. D. Dunlap, a layman of Gadsden, Alabama, "I myself should oppose union." [64] Most Cumberland Presbyterians who favored union, however, adopted the view taken by the Committee on Fraternity and Union that "Revision has revised."

From the point of view of those who opposed the union, the doctrinal issue was well summarized by W. P. Bone when he wrote:

The division in our Church over the union question is a result of a difference in opinion as to the effect of the revision of 1903. Those opposed to union on the proposed basis are firmly of the opinion that the union brethren are wrong in their contention that the Presbyterian Church has come to our doctrinal position. They are supported in their view by Presbyterian standard literature, and by most Presbyterians, North and South. Even the Editor of The Texas Christian Advocate very properly sees that we are about to abandon our Confession for one which contains the severe predestinarian doctrines which we formerly repudiated. Some of our union brethren have been telling us all along that we can get further revision when we get into the other church. Some of them say we will simply ignore the doctrines which we have always counted as objectionable, and yet the majority of those favoring union are of the opinion that the recent revision brings the Westminster Confession to our historic position, as interpreted by the Preface to our Confession. This opinion, however, is an erroneous one. . . .[65]

Meanwhile, the several periodicals of the Presbyterian Church, U. S. A., reflected a lively interest in the proposed union. None of these were official church papers in the sense that the *Cumberland Presbyterian* was the official organ of its sponsoring body. Consequently they reflected diverse points of view.

The *Presbyterian,* of Philadelphia, which had opposed the revision of the Confession, noted that the two churches were approaching the proposed union with different understandings of the effect of revision. Shortly after the 1904 Assemblies the *Presbyterian* expressed itself editorially thus:

The fact is not to be ignored, or minimized, that both our own and the Cumberland General Assembly have favored the plan of Union and Reunion by overwhelming majorities; but it is equally patent that they have done so in different ways and with different understandings. Our Assembly did so with the distinct avowal that our Confessional revision did not impair the integrity of our system of doctrine as taught in Holy Scripture. The Cumberland Assembly did so with the declared understanding that our doctrinal system had been radically changed. Which is right? How can there be harmony and agreement in a union brought about under such misapprehension? Will not a Confession received and interpreted in this way be more a matter of contention than of unification? [66]

There was a continuing controversy between the *Presbyterian* and the *Cumberland Presbyterian.* The editor of the latter was obviously embarrassed by expressions contained in the former which indicated that the welcome being extended to Cumberlands by the larger Presbyterian body was far from unanimous.

Some Presbyterians feared lest the Calvinism of the Presbyterian Church be diluted by the influx of Cumberland Presbyterians. Replying to an ardent advocate of the proposed union, one minister questioned the assumption that voting in "at one gulp" 2,102 ordained ministers, licentiates, and candidates for the ministry reared on "Arminian theology" would not add to varieties of doctrine already existing within the Presbyterian Church.[67]

The editor of the *Interior,* published at Chicago, while acknowledging that the Confession had been revised, asserted that

very few Presbyterians have at any time in the last century accepted the book, even unrevised, in a sense offensive to the average Cumberland Presbyterian. The revision wrote out a supplement that Presbyterians had previously been carrying around in their heads.[68]

The *Herald and Presbyter,* of Cincinnati, while giving cautious support to the union proposal, made clear its belief that the Presbyterian Church was still Calvinistic and that if Cumberland Presbyterians voted for the union it would be because they accepted the doctrinal standards of the Presbyterian Church in their historic sense.

Believing that the Cumberland brethren are honest and intelligent, we believe that if they vote for union, it will be because they accept our system of doctrine. If they are Arminians, as some claim, or anything else than Calvinistic Presbyterians, they will vote against union.[69]

Others were more enthusiastic in urging that the union be approved. The Rev. John Donnan Countermine, writing for the *Presbyterian Banner,* of Pittsburgh, saw the coming of the Cumberlands to the Presbyterian fold as the prodigal son returning home. Noting that the initiative had been taken by the smaller denomination, it was a case of "the boy coming to himself and returning of his own free will to the old home, seeking admission." Like the father, the Presbyterian Church ought to hasten to receive the returning prodigal.[70]

A contributor to *Christian Work and Evangelist,* of New York, interpreted the initiative taken by the Cumberland Presbyterians for union as a cry for help.

The Cumberlands need their Northern brethren, need them greatly and need them now. It is that need which speaks in their overture for union; that need which declares duty more significantly in the terms and spirit of the protest. For the people to be left to such leadership, when they cry out to be delivered, is a sin against duty by a failure to grasp opportunity. The people need the touch and power of a large and progressive church. The men who have the best knowledge of their needs are bringing them to the hands held out to uplift and strengthen them. To discourage or to postpone acceptance of the offer and the trust is too momentous and far reaching to be risked by factious opposition or fearful delay! [71]

As a result of several consolidations, the number of presbyteries in the Cumberland Presbyterian Church was reduced from 118 in 1903 to 114 in 1905. Sixty presbyteries voted for the union, while fifty-one disapproved. Florida Presbytery did not report any action; Ozark Presbytery, in Missouri, first voted against union, then reconsidered, and tabled the matter; and Cookeville Presbytery, in Tennessee, voted for union conditionally. At that time a constitutional change required only the approval of a majority of the presbyteries, each presbytery voting as a unit. Thus an affirmative vote of fifty-eight presbyteries was required. Two more than that number voted for union. In the presbyterial voting, however, more individuals had cast votes against the proposal than had voted for it. A total of 691 ministers and 649 ruling elders voted for union, making a total affirmative vote of 1,340, while 470 ministers and 1,007 ruling elders voted against union, making a total negative vote of 1,477. The presbyteries voting against union also represented a somewhat larger constituency than did those favoring union.

The strongest opposition came from the states of Tennessee, Kentucky, Alabama, and Mississippi. All except two of the thirteen presbyteries in Tennessee, one of the seven in Kentucky, and one of the five in Mississippi voted against union. All five of the presbyteries in Alabama were opposed. The synods of Texas, Arkansas, Indianola, Illinois, and Missouri were divided on the question. Eight of the twenty-one presbyteries in Texas Synod, four of the six presbyteries in Indianola Synod, and five of the eight presbyteries in Arkansas Synod voted against union, as did three of the ten presbyteries in Illinois Synod and four of the thirteen in Missouri Synod. One presbytery, Morgan, of the three in Indiana Synod also voted against the proposed union. The deciding factor was the vote of the "border" presbyteries in the East, North, and West. All of the twenty-two presbyteries which made up the synods of Iowa, Kansas, Ohio, Oregon, Pacific, and Pennsylvania voted for union. These had in 1905 a combined membership of 17,198, a total only slightly larger than the membership of Kentucky Synod, which cast seven presbyterial votes.

At the General Assembly which met in Fresno, California, in May 1905, a Special Committee on Organic Union was appointed to canvass the vote. Majority and minority reports were offered.[72] The majority report affirmed that the union had been constitutionally agreed to by the Cumberland Presbyterian Church. The minority report insisted that there was no authority in the Constitution of the Church for the action taken, and that the standards of the Church had not been changed as prescribed by its Constitution. It was pointed out that the amendment adopted by the Presbyterian Church,

JOSEPH H. FUSSELL
(1836-1915)
Opponent of the union movement.

"Go on, if you will, and join another
church, forsaking the home of your
childhood, but know now and ever
that somewhere in the sunlight of
God's love the Cumberland Presbyterian Church will live on."

U. S. A., regarding separate presbyteries for those of a particular race was not
the same as that embodied in the Joint Report on Union.

There followed eight hours of debate, beginning Monday afternoon and
ending late Tuesday afternoon. It was in the course of this debate that Judge
Joe H. Fussell, in closing the debate favoring the minority report, made the
statement which made him famous among Cumberland Presbyterians: "Go
on, if you will, and join another church, forsaking the home of your childhood, but know now and ever that somewhere in the sunlight of God's love
the Cumberland Presbyterian Church will live on." [73] The minority report
was rejected by a vote of 137 to 111, after which the majority report was
adopted by a vote of 137 to 110.

Against the adoption of the majority report a protest signed by ninety-
one commissioners was submitted by J. J. McClellan, of Mississippi. This
protest pointed out the impossibility of bringing the doctrinal positions of
the two churches into harmony with each other; expressed the opinion that
the "Declaratory Statement" was not revisional in either intent or effect,
but was rather a reaffirmation of the doctrine of decrees taught in the
Westminster Confession; affirmed that the union would not be a union in
reality but rather a merging of the membership and assets of the Cumberland
Presbyterian Church into the Presbyterian Church, U. S. A.; called atten-

tion to the bare majorities by which "union" had been carried; and contended that there was no constitutional authority for merging the Cumberland Presbyterian Church into another denomination. Although the adoption of the Confession of Faith of the Presbyterian Church, U. S. A., was contemplated in the plan of union, the question of its adoption was not referred to the presbyteries, but only the question of union. The protestants pleaded that the discussion the preceding year had revealed that the Cumberland Presbyterian Church as a whole was not yet ready for union; that the movement was "confessedly premature"; and that "coercive measures can only produce confusion." [74]

The answer to the protest insisted that the General Assembly, as the "supreme court" of the Church, had the sole right to pass upon the legality of the steps taken toward union, including the steps taken by the Assembly itself. Since the General Assembly had declared that every step taken had been legal, it must necessarily be so. The same argument was used with reference to the question of doctrinal agreement: "Two General Assemblies and a majority of our Presbyteries believe that doctrinal agreement does exist." [75]

Meanwhile, the General Assembly of the Presbyterian Church, U. S. A., meeting at Winona Lake, Indiana, found that the Overture on Territorial Limits providing for the organization of separate presbyteries and synods for members of a particular race had been approved by a vote of 188 presbyteries to 45. Only a majority of the presbyteries was required to amend the Administrative Standards. On the Joint Report on Union there was an affirmative vote of 194 presbyteries and a negative vote of 39. Eleven of the presbyteries voting against union were those composed of Negro churches. This was their way of protesting the provision for racial presbyteries. Otherwise the principal opposition came from presbyteries in New York, New Jersey, and Pennsylvania.[76]

Details for putting the union into effect were left to be worked out during the ensuing year. For this purpose the Cumberland Presbyterian Committee on Fraternity and Union was enlarged by the appointment of nine additional members—most, if not all, of whom had opposed the union. Three of those appointed declined to serve.

In 1906, the General Assembly of the Cumberland Presbyterian Church met at Decatur, Illinois. Prior to the Assembly the opponents of union filed a bill in the Circuit Court at Decatur enjoining the commissioners to the General Assembly individually and collectively from taking the final steps to merge the Cumberland Presbyterian Church with the Presbyterian Church, U. S. A. Judge W. C. Johns, of the Circuit Court, overruled the motion on the ground that "The decisions of the Supreme Judicatory [of the Church) as to matters of faith, procedure, and practices are final, and binding on secular courts." The decision was read to the General Assembly and spread upon its minutes.[77]

The report of the Committee on Fraternity and Union, embodying a Joint Report on Reunion and Union, submitted by the committees of the two churches was adopted by a vote of 165 to 91.[78] (Later twelve commissioners who were absent when the vote was taken, requested, and were granted, the privilege of putting on record the fact that they would have voted in the negative had they been present.) This report provided, among other things, that after each General Assembly should have received telegraphic notice from the other of adoption of the Joint Report, the Moderator should make public declaration of the fact and publicly announce "that the basis of reunion is now in full force and effect." After this declaration, no further business would be in order in the General Assembly of the Cumberland Presbyterian Church except a motion to adjourn *sine die* as a separate Assembly.

Against the action of the General Assembly in adopting this report and agreeing to adjourn *sine die,* Fussell, a commissioner from Columbia Presbytery, submitted a protest signed by one hundred commissioners. The reasons given for the protest were as follows:

1. This Assembly is without power to declare the Cumberland Presbyterian Church, as a separate organization, at an end.
2. This Assembly has no power or right to declare that the Confession of Faith of the Presbyterian Church in the United States of America, as revised in 1903, and its other doctrinal and ecclesiastical standards, have been adopted by the Cumberland Presbyterian Church, in accordance with its Constitution, and, in the opinion of these protestants, such statement is not correct.
3. Said Assembly had no power to transfer the allegiance of the ministers, elders, deacons, officers, particular churches, judicatories, boards and committees to another denomination of Christians, and make them amenable to another church creed and constitution.
4. Said Assembly had no power to direct the Presbyteries of the Cumberland Presbyterian Church to send representatives to the General Assembly of the Presbyterian Church in the United States of America.[79]

The second point in the protest questioned the constitutionality of the procedure. Obviously there was no express provision in the Constitution of the Cumberland Presbyterian Church for bringing about its merger into another church or otherwise terminating its existence. Nor was there any provision permitting the adjournment of the General Assembly *sine die.* Although a majority of the presbyteries voted for the proposed Basis of

IRA LANDRITH
(1865-1941)

J. L. HUDGINS
(1857-1939)

Union, there was a real question whether or not a constitutional amendment was submitted to the presbyteries. A supreme court judge in one state was later to note that no amendment to the Confession of Faith was submitted to the presbyteries, but only a basis of union.[80] It was implied in the plan of union that the doctrinal and ecclesiastical standards of the Presbyterian Church, U. S. A., were to be adopted, but these documents were not submitted. If the Confession of Faith of the Presbyterian Church, U. S. A., had been submitted in its entirety to the presbyteries as a substitute for the Confession of Faith of the Cumberland Presbyterian Church, would the vote have been the same?[81]

Involved also was the matter of religious liberty. Did the General Assembly have a right to transfer the allegiance of its constituents to another church and make them amenable to another creed? A substantial number of Cumberland Presbyterians did not think so.

Prior to its adjournment, the General Assembly, in addition to appointing a committee to formulate a reply to the Fussell protest, named a Committee on Pastoral Oversight to draft a "Pastoral Letter" to the Cumberland Presbyterian churches. The Committee was also continued "to act upon any matter coming under its jurisdiction in the interim until the meeting of the General Assembly of the reunited church in 1907." This committee consisted of the Moderator and Stated Clerk of the General Assembly and one representative from each of the seventeen synods. The "Pastoral Letter" ad-

(FORMER) FIRST CHURCH, DECATUR, ILLINOIS

The 1906 General Assembly, a majority of whose members voted to unite the Cumberland Presbyterian Church with the Presbyterian Church in the U. S. A., convened in this church. The inset portrait is of the Rev. J. W. McDonald, pastor host.

GRAND ARMY OF THE REPUBLIC HALL, DECATUR, ILLINOIS

The G. A. R. Hall served as the rallying place for 106 antiunionist commissioners to the 1906 General Assembly. They elected new Assembly officers and acted to continue the Cumberland Presbyterian Church.

dressed to Cumberland Presbyterians everywhere and "appointed to be read in the churches" sought to "caution" Cumberland Presbyterians against statements which probably would be made by those who were unwilling to go into the union. It also warned the members and officers of the churches against ignoring their vows to submit themselves to the various church courts and to "study the peace of the Church." It was urged that very little change would be felt locally as a result of the union.[82]

A telegram having been received from the General Assembly of the Presbyterian Church, U. S. A., that it had adopted the Joint Report on Reunion and Union and had made the declaration therein called for, the Moderator of the Cumberland Presbyterian General Assembly, Ira Landrith, publicly announced that the basis of reunion and union was in full force and effect and that the Cumberland Presbyterian Church was now reunited with the Presbyterian Church in the United States of America as one church. The motion to adjourn *sine die* was adopted *viva voce*.

Ever since the Saint Louis conference it had been apparent that even if the union proposal carried, the attempt would be made to perpetuate the Cumberland Presbyterian Church. It came as no surprise, therefore, when Fussell announced immediately following the *sine die* adjournment that the meetings of the General Assembly of the Cumberland Presbyterian Church would be continued in the Hall of the Grand Army of the Republic, inasmuch as use of the church building had been denied it for that purpose. In the continued session some one hundred commissioners were enrolled. J. L. Hudgins was elected Moderator, and the Rev. T. H. Padgett was named Stated Clerk. After filling vacancies on the various Assembly boards occasioned by the exodus of members to the Presbyterian Church, U. S. A., and transacting other routine business, the General Assembly adjourned to meet at the birthplace of the Cumberland Presbyterian Church in Dickson County, Tennessee, in May 1907. Thus was perpetuated the General Assembly of the Cumberland Presbyterian Church.[83]

# 19

## THE BROKEN BODY

*All who are willing to follow the General Assembly in uniting
with the Presbyterian Church, U. S. A., will stand on the left side.
. . . All who are not willing . . . will stand on the right. . . .*

Mound Prairie Presbytery, July 18, 1906

Following the adjournment of the General Assembly at Decatur, Illinois,
in May 1906, the unionists considered the union of the Cumberland Presbyterian Church with the Presbyterian Church, U. S. A., an accomplished
fact. According to their point of view, all churches, ministers, and church
members formerly in the Cumberland Presbyterian Church were now in the
Presbyterian Church, U. S. A. The Rev. James E. Clarke, editor of the
*Cumberland Presbyterian,* wrote:

> It is too late now for any former Cumberland Presbyterian to say "I do
> not intend to, and will not, become a member of the Presbyterian Church."
> Each and every former member of the Cumberland Presbyterian Church,
> unless since union was consummated he has taken a letter of dismission, is
> now a member of the Presbyterian Church. . . .

Taking notice of the fact that the commissioners opposed to union had
met together after the adjournment and had organized "what they called the
'Cumberland Presbyterian General Assembly,'" the editor contended that
this "Assembly" had no legal status. He recognized that some of these
brethren had been elected as commissioners for the avowed purpose of opposing the union. But as soon as Moderator Landrith's gavel fell, he insisted,

353

the commissions of these men were terminated, and they had no further powers as commissioners. "They say they have formed a 'General Assembly,'" continued Clarke, "but it is a body which has no synods, no presbyteries, no churches, no ministers, and no members." He went on to suggest that

if, after due deliberation and prayer, they wish to form a religious organization based on the Cumberland Presbyterian Confession of Faith and constitution, then the way to do it is for the ministers to secure regular letters and get together and form presbyteries. Then those presbyteries can regularly, in accordance with the form of government, select commissioners to make up a General Assembly.[1]

Numbers of Cumberland Presbyterians, even among those who had opposed the union, believed that since the General Assembly and presbyteries had voted for union, it was their duty to go along. Ministers and ruling elders had taken a vow at their ordination to be submissive to their brethren in the Lord assembled in the various church courts. Others, while recognizing that they had taken such a vow, insisted that they had done so within the context of the Cumberland Presbyterian Church. They had also, at their ordination, received and adopted the Confession of Faith of the Cumberland Presbyterian Church as containing the system of doctrine taught in the Holy Scriptures. They believed that the Assembly had no right or power to transfer their allegiance to another denomination and make them amenable to another church creed and constitution.

At the presbyterial level the lines were quickly drawn. As the various presbyteries met in their summer or fall meetings the question would arise, Is this a presbytery of the Cumberland Presbyterian Church, or is it a presbytery of the Presbyterian Church, U. S. A.? When this question was decided by majority vote, the minority would withdraw to form a presbytery according to its understanding of the matter. With the exception of possibly two dozen presbyteries which went solidly, or almost solidly, with the union, the various presbyteries passed through the ordeal of division.

The first presbytery to divide was Obion, in the Synod of West Tennessee. This presbytery had vigorously opposed the union movement from the beginning. In the vote on union, six ministers had voted for union and nineteen against, while forty ruling elders representing as many churches had voted solidly against union.

Obion Presbytery was called to meet in special session at Rives, Tennessee, Thursday, June 14, 1906, at one o'clock, to consider, among other specified items of business, "The instruction of the congregations within our bounds and under our jurisdiction as to their attitude to the question of union with the Presbyterian Church in the U. S. A." At this meeting the Rev. P. F. Johnson presented a paper recommending endorsement of the action taken by the commissioners who perpetuated the General Assembly of the Cumberland Presbyterian Church at Decatur and instructing the churches to report to the Rev. T. H. Padgett as Stated Clerk of the Assembly and to send their benevolent offerings to the boards created at Decatur. The Rev. D. T. Waynick then presented a substitute paper declaring Obion Presbytery to be a presbytery of the Presbyterian Church, U. S. A., and calling upon the churches to act in accordance with that view. The Rev. J. L. Hudgins inquired whether Waynick presented the paper as a Cumberland Presbyterian or as a Presbyterian. When he replied that he presented it as a Presbyterian, the moderator, the Rev. R. L. Keathley, ruled the paper out of order. After an attempt at postponement, Johnson's paper was adopted. A communication was also sent to the Moderator and Stated Clerk of the General Assembly of the Presbyterian Church, U. S. A., requesting that Obion Presbytery be omitted from the roll of presbyteries of that church, since this presbytery had never adopted the Confession of Faith of that church, was not organized in accordance with its Constitution, and was therefore under no obligation to submit to its government.

Waynick then withdrew and was followed by a few other persons who met in the Rives schoolhouse and were constituted as the Obion Presbytery of the Presbyterian Church, U. S. A. Six ministers joined in constituting this presbytery, and two others were received by letter. Three churches were represented. The ministers who had voted for the paper presented by Johnson were dropped from the roll for having renounced their allegiance to the Presbyterian Church in the U. S. A., but all churches were retained on the roll.[2]

On the evening of the same day Snyder Presbytery, in Texas Synod, met in the school building in the rural community of Dora, Nolan County, Texas. The retiring moderator was W. W. Beall, an attorney from Sweetwater, who had been one of the commissioners who helped perpetuate the Cumberland Presbyterian General Assembly at Decatur. Noting that Snyder Presbytery at its previous meeting had adjourned as a presbytery of the Cumberland Presbyterian Church, the moderator declared that in this capacity the body was now meeting. He suggested that as the roll should be called, each minister and delegate be enrolled as a minister or ruling elder of the Cumberland Presbyterian Church or of the Presbyterian Church, U. S. A., as he might designate. The stated clerk, however, refused to call the roll of Snyder Presbytery of the Cumberland Presbyterian Church, asserting that there was no such presbytery or church. He announced his readiness, however, to call the roll of Snyder Presbytery of the Presbyterian Church, U .S. A. As Beall refused to act as moderator of such presbytery, the stated clerk assumed the chair, declared a recess for fifteen minutes, and requested the ministers and delegates to assemble at a home some three or four hundred yards away. There the presbytery of the Presbyterian Church, U. S. A., convened, while the Cumberland Presbyterian presbytery continued its sessions in the schoolhouse.[3]

When Austin Presbytery met at Shady Grove, Burnet County, Texas, June 29, it was found that those who chose to remain Cumberland Presbyterian had only two ordained ministers present, the Rev. John Hudson and the Rev. J. L. Stevenson. Accordingly, those present adjourned to meet at the Sheppard Home in Round Rock on July 5. There these two ministers, together with the Rev. Jesse Marshall, who lived in the home, constituted the presbytery and ordained W. G. Griffith, a licentiate, to the full work of the ministry. Seven churches were represented in this meeting.[4]

Lebanon Presbytery met September 10 at Mount Tabor Church, near Murfreesboro, Tennessee. This presbytery, in the bounds of which were both the publishing house and Cumberland University, had voted for the union. Since the Mount Tabor Church session had voted to let the Cumberland Presbyterians use the church building, the unionists, consisting of twenty ministers and eighteen elders, adjourned to meet that night at Murfreesboro. Those remaining, with four ministers present and twenty-four churches represented, elected the Rev. Thomas Buchanan moderator and R. L. Baskette, a Nashville layman, stated clerk.[5]

Mount Vernon Presbytery met with the New Bethel Church in Marion County, Illinois, September 18. After the opening sermon had been preached and the constituting prayer offered, the Rev. W. M. Freeze inquired whether this was the Mount Vernon Presbytery of the Presbyterian Church, U. S. A. When answered in the affirmative, he stated that those who did not wish to recognize the union wished to withdraw and proceed with the work of Mount Vernon Presbytery of the Cumberland Presbyterian Church. The pastor of New Bethel Church then read a paper which had been passed by the local congregation stating that the congregation was loyal to the action of the higher courts of the Church, desired that no discord be created, and forbade the use of the church building, manse, or grounds for the purpose of carrying on the work of the antiunionists. When the spokesman for the antiunionists had bid the unionist brethren godspeed, five ministers—J. W. Borah, W. M. Freeze, G. W. Green, E. M. Johnson, and Joseph Wood—together with other persons in sympathy with them, met in the public road "under the shade of a friendly tree," and continued the organization of Mount Vernon Presbytery of the Cumberland Presbyterian Church. J. W. Borah was elected moderator, and E. M. Johnson, stated clerk.[6]

Usually the "unionist" presbytery would take no further action regarding the ministers who renounced the union other than to drop them from the roll for having renounced the jurisdiction of the Presbyterian Church, U. S. A. In some instances the stated clerk was directed to report to their respective church sessions ruling elders who did not go along with the union. Likewise the Cumberland Presbyterian presbyteries dropped the names of ministers who declared their allegiance to the Presbyterian Church, U. S. A. In a few instances, as in the presbyteries of Little Rock and Decatur, more severe measures were attempted.

Little Rock Presbytery, which then consisted of nine ordained ministers and eighteen churches, had voted for the union but in 1906 had elected one unionist and one antiunionist commissioner. This presbytery met at the Gum Springs Church, near Searcy, Arkansas, the evening of July 19. There were five ministers present. Two of these had declared their intention of going along with the union, while three were determined to perpetuate the Little Rock Presbytery of the Cumberland Presbyterian Church. Seeing that they did not have a quorum of ministers, the two unionist ministers, the Rev. J. N. Cunningham and the Rev. J. H. Barkwell, together with an elder who had accompanied them, adjourned to meet at Little Rock the next morning and caught a night train back to Little Rock. There they were joined by the Rev. A. S. Maddox in constituting Little Rock Presbytery of the Presbyterian Church, U. S. A. Three ministers—J. S. Hall, J. E. Martin, and J. G. Robinson—together with four ruling elders, continued the meeting of the Cumberland Presbyterian presbytery at Gum Springs. The Little Rock Presbytery of the Presbyterian Church, U. S. A., preferred charges against Hall, Martin, and Robinson and cited them to appear on August 23. They disclaimed the jurisdiction of that presbytery and did not appear.[7]

In Decatur Presbytery, in Illinois, charges were preferred against the Rev. J. H. Hughey, an aged minister, for insubordination and for disturbing the peace of the churches. Hughey had joined with the Rev. W. L. Bankson and the Rev. J. M. Wyckoff in perpetuating Decatur Presbytery of the Cumberland Presbyterian Church.[8]

In other cases the separation was carried out more amicably. McGee Presbytery met in a called session with the Bethany Church, near Keytesville, Missouri, July 23. After the object of the meeting had been stated and a few questions asked, a spokesman for the unionists, recognizing that the local congregation was opposed to the union, asked all the nonunionists to stand in front of the pulpit, and while a hymn was being sung the unionists would shake hands with the nonunionists and pass out of the building. The request was granted, and while the audience sang "How Firm a Foundation," the unionists shook hands with the nonunionists and retired from the house.

It was noted that sixteen representatives remained with the group opposed to union and that this faction had six ministers while the unionists had nine.[9]

Mound Prairie Presbytery, in southwestern Arkansas, met at Lockesburg on July 18 at 11 a.m. The opening sermon was preached by the Rev. James E. Baggarly from Psalm 26:9, "Gather not my soul with sinners, nor my life with bloody men." After the noon recess the following paper was read and adopted:

All who are willing to follow the General Assembly in uniting with the Presbyterian Church, U. S. A., will stand on the left side of the house as the roll is called. All who are not willing to follow the General Assembly in uniting with the Presbyterian Church, U. S. A., will stand on the right side of the house as the roll is called.

The minutes of Mound Prairie Presbytery of the Presbyterian Church, U. S. A., go on to state that

In deference to Rev. W. E. Dooley, pastor-host, the Presbytery yielded the Presbyterian church house for the present to the dissenters. And the Presbytery repaired to the Methodist Church and elected Rev. A. B. C. Dinwiddie, Moderator, and Rev. I. N. Clack, Stated Clerk and Treasurer.

Nine ministers went with the "dissenters," seven with the union.[10]

In White River Presbytery, in northern Arkansas, the unionists and anti-unionists apparently were reluctant to separate, for the presbytery, after meeting for a night session, continued in session until after noon the following day before it came to the parting of the ways. At 10:30 in the morning, A. M. Colson, a licentiate, preached a trial sermon preparatory to his ordination. A unionist minister moved that the ordination be conducted according to the Confession of Faith of the Presbyterian Church, U. S. A. After some discussion, the presbytery recessed for the noon meal. In the afternoon, after further discussion, the motion was lost. After another recess of ten minutes, four ministers and the representatives of three churches withdrew. The three ordained ministers who were left—J. S. Bone, E. W. L. Jennings, and G. W. Thompson—proceeded to ordain Colson, as their next presbyterial act.[11]

By the time of meeting of the 1907 General Assembly, the Stated Clerk of the Cumberland Presbyterian General Assembly had reports from eighty presbyteries. Included was Porter Presbytery, which had become independent in 1902 but had been received back into Arkansas Synod in 1906. Two of these presbyteries did not have a quorum of ministers, and several barely had a quorum. Meanwhile a consolidation of presbyteries had been begun. Texas Synod, in its 1906 meeting, consolidated Abilene and Snyder presbyteries to form Sweetwater Presbytery, and Fort Worth Presbytery was consolidated with Weatherford. Missouri Synod had combined Neosho Presbytery with Ozark. The Stated Clerk of the General Assembly, in 1907, listed thirty presbyteries as being in a disorganized condition. Two of these, Amarillo and Cherokee, were later reorganized.

While the lines were being drawn at the presbyterial level a contest for the allegiance of the people at the local church level was taking shape. This contest was complicated in turn by the struggle over property rights which soon found its way into the civil courts.

The Committee on Pastoral Oversight appointed by the General Assembly of the Cumberland Presbyterian Church just before it voted to adjourn *sine die* lost little time in getting around to instructing the unionists as to how they should deal with "seceders"—that is, ministers, church officers, or members who refused to go along with the union. If a pastor, by any specific act, should indicate that he renounced the union, this, it was said, would be equivalent to resigning his office as pastor, and the session would be justified in calling, through the presbytery, another pastor. Elders renouncing the union would in effect resign their offices. Church members renouncing the union would forfeit their rights as members, and those who were loyal to the union would be justified in ignoring them as members. Those ministers, officers, and members who were loyal to the union would alone constitute in law the true ministers, officers, and members of the Church, and in them would be vested all the rights of possession and control of the property.

Included in the instructions were the following:

TRUSTEES.—Should the trustees of your church undertake to prevent you from controlling and using the building, or should they offer to allow the seceders to use it for separate services, such trustees would be guilty of a breach of trust, and any loyal member or members of the united church, whether elders or not, would have the right to file a bill in equity to remove such trustees or restrain them from such breach of trust, and to enjoin the seceders from interfering with the control, possession or use of the property. This right is wholly independent of the fact whether a majority of the congregation are seceders or not.

The loyal members of a congregation constitute the congregation whether they be a majority or a minority; the loyal members of the session constitute the session whether they be in the majority or the minority; and the loyal members of the presbytery, be they a majority or a minority, constitute the presbytery. Whenever it becomes necessary, a loyal minority can separate itself from the majority and elect its own officers and conduct its business free from the annoyance or obstructions of the seceding majority. Whenever they do so it is the duty of the trustees to allow this loyal session to control the church property.

Arrangements had been made with John M. Gaut, of Nashville, Tennessee, a member of the committee and an attorney, to give legal advice and make suggestions to pastors, sessions, church members, boards and committees.[12]

On July 25 an injunction suit was filed at Fayetteville, Tennessee, by the unionists. This was the case known as *Ira Landrith* et al. v. *J. L. Hudgins* et al. It was filed in the name of the members of the executive committee of the Committee on Pastoral Oversight; the unionist elders of the churches at Fayetteville, McKenzie, and Kenton, Tennessee; and "all other members of the Presbyterian Church in the U. S. A." Named as defendants, with Hudgins, were T. H. Padgett, a few other leaders of the continuing Cumberland Presbyterian Church, and the antiunionist elders of the churches named. All ministers, officers, and members of the Cumberland Presbyterian Church who repudiated the union or renounced the united church were enjoined from the following acts:

1. From interfering with or molesting the pastors, elders, deacons, church members or other ecclesiastical agencies who adhere to and recognize said United Church, in the use, enjoyment, possession and exclusive control of all houses of worship, parsonages, endowment funds or other property or effects which belonged to the Cumberland Presbyterian Church or any of its boards, committees, judicatories, congregations or institutions or are held in trust for them.

2. From instituting or prosecuting any suit at law or in equity for the purpose of asserting any right which they, or any of them, may claim to have, possess, control or use any said property.

3. From using the name of the Cumberland Presbyterian Church as the name or any part of the name of any of their organizations, congregations, sessions, Presbyteries, Synods, general Assemblies, boards, committees or other ecclesiastical judicatories, institutions or agencies, in connection with the claim, on the part of said judicatory, organization or agency, or any one acting for it, that it is a judicatory, organization or agency of the original Cumberland Presbyterian Church as organized in 1810.

4. From manufacturing or selling the Confession of Faith of the Cumberland Presbyterian Church or any other of its copyrighted books, pamphlets, or publications.[13]

Shortly thereafter a similar injunction was obtained by the unionists in Warrensburg, Missouri, in the Circuit Court of Johnson County.[14]

The full force of the injunction in Tennessee was felt for a period of about two months. During that time any worshipers within the state who assembled as Cumberland Presbyterians laid themselves liable to being cited for contempt of court. On one occasion the entire official board of the church at Jackson, Tennessee, was placed under arrest.[15] On September 22, however, the injunction was dissolved as to the third and fourth prohibitions. The first prohibition was modified to permit alternate use by complainants and defendants of the property at Fayetteville, McKenzie, and Kenton, pending final hearing of the case. The second prohibition was interpreted as not inhibiting the institution of suits deemed necessary for the protection of property interests.[16]

At Atlanta, Georgia, a suit was filed by the remaining Cumberland Presbyterians enjoining certain officers of the church from transferring the property of the First Cumberland Presbyterian Church of Atlanta to the Presbyterian Church, U. S. A. Judge John T. Pendleton granted the injunction, declaring the union to be null and void.[17]

On the other hand, a decision favorable to the unionists was rendered in the District Court of Marion County, Texas, with reference to the church at Jefferson where the antiunionists had filed suit.[18] There had been similar decisions in the case of the churches at Washington and Vincennes, Indiana.[19] The Illinois case, in which the antiunionists had sought to enjoin the General Assembly from completing the union, had been carried to the Appellate Court of the Third District of Illinois. Such was the situation when the two General Assemblies met for their 1907 meetings.

In contrast with the acts of the Committee on Pastoral Oversight which seemed determined to crush all opposition to the union, voices were raised in behalf of a better way of settling the property dispute. The Rev. J. S. Groves, a former Cumberland Presbyterian minister living in Texas, wrote:

At this time, when the world is presented with the humiliating spectacle of brethren going to law about church property, we should not forget that there are things of greater value than a legal title to property. It is better to be just than to possess property. No church and no individual should seek to possess property to which they have no moral right. They may have a title that will hold good in any court, yet if that property rightfully belongs to another it will be a curse if it remains in their hands. . . .

He urged that a congregation refusing to go into the union should be allowed to hold its property unmolested if there was no division. In the case of a church which was divided, he contended, there ought to be an equitable division of the property.[20]

The Rev. William Laurie, who in the General Assembly of the Presbyterian Church, U. S. A., in 1905 had requested that his negative vote on the union question be recorded, protested through the columns of the *Presbyterian* against the obviously extreme provisions of the Tennessee injunction.[21] Another writer in the *Presbyterian,* who identified himself only as "Senex Presbyterianus," strongly urged that the schools and other property held by the boards of the Cumberland Presbyterian Church be returned to that portion of the Cumberland body which declined to come into the union. This, he urged, should be done, first of all, because it was right. Furthermore, the Presbyterian Church had no need for this property. "Another theological seminary, for example, would be as useless to us as a fifth wheel to a coach," he stated. Such a step, he insisted, would also avoid unseemly contention and strife.[22]

The Synod of New Jersey, meeting in October 1906, sent the following overture to the General Assembly:

> *Resolved,* That Synod would overture the General Assembly to appoint a committee of mediation and arbitration, to treat with our Cumberland brethren who refuse to come with us, and thus obviate all necessity for litigation.[23]

Similar overtures were addressed to the Assembly by the presbyteries of Erie and Vincennes.[24] Unfortunately for the remaining Cumberland Presbyterians, these voices did not prevail in the councils of the Presbyterian Church.

The General Assembly of the Cumberland Presbyterian Church met May 16, 1907, at the birthplace of this Church in Dickson County, Tennessee. For practical reasons the sessions, with the exception of the initial one, were held in the town of Dickson under a tent prepared for the purpose. During the first day's session the Assembly sent greetings to other religious bodies then in session, including the General Assembly of the Presbyterian Church in the U. S. A., then in session at Columbus, Ohio. That evening an additional paper was approved to be sent to the Assembly at Columbus. This paper deplored the "cruel and relentless effort" being made in the name of the Presbyterian Church, U. S. A., "to coerce unwilling Cumberland Presbyterians" to go into the larger Presbyterian body, or failing in that, to force them to give up their name, organization, Confession of Faith, and property. Passages from the "Pastoral Letter" sent out by order of the 1906 General Assembly were cited as evidence that many who were leaving the Cumberland Presbyterian Church had been "misled" by statements to the effect that the Presbyterian Church had abandoned the Westminster Confession and had accepted the doctrines of the Cumberland Presbyterian Church. A fervent appeal was made to the Presbyterian Assembly to leave the Cumberland Presbyterian Church in control of its property.[25]

The General Assembly of the Presbyterian Church in the U. S. A. met in Columbus, Ohio, the same day that the Cumberland Presbyterians met in Tennessee. The opening sermon was preached by the Rev. Ira Landrith who had been Moderator of the Cumberland Presbyterian General Assembly in 1906. He took as his text Deuteronomy 33:23, "Possess thou the west and the south." [26]

The paper from the Cumberland Presbyterian Assembly reached the Presbyterian Assembly on Monday. The minutes state that "A paper received from Rev. T. H. Padgett and others was referred to the Moderator and Rev. Ira Landrith, D. D."[27] Later three other persons, including one other former Cumberland Presbyterian, were added to the committee.[28] On the last day the Assembly authorized the Moderator to make any necessary verbal changes in the letter sent in reply.[29] The reply was directed "to the Rev. T. H. Padgett and Others Meeting at Dickson, Tenn., May 16, 1907."[30] This letter expressed regret that the persons addressed and their associates had "declined to concur in the constitutional action" of the General Assembly and presbyteries of the "former Cumberland Presbyterian Church." It administered a stern rebuke to them for suggesting that anyone had ever claimed that the Presbyterian Church, U. S. A., had abandoned the Westminster Confession and for the interpretation they had placed on passages quoted from the "Pastoral Letter." Regret was expressed that the unwillingness of some to accept the union had rendered it necessary to ask the courts of several states to determine the property interests involved. The hope was expressed that they (the persons addressed) would come to "recognize the wisdom of yielding to the legally expressed will of those who have long been your brethren in the Lord."

The refusal of the Presbyterian Assembly to recognize the continuing existence of the Cumberland Presbyterian Church was to affect fraternal relations between the two churches for several years. Not until 1919 did either Assembly again send fraternal greetings to the other.

The General Assembly of the Presbyterian Church, U. S. A., replaced the Committee on Pastoral Oversight with a committee of eleven to have charge of all legal matters arising out of the "Reunion."[31] Any expenses incurred were to be paid by contributions from persons or organizations interested, which meant that the ex-Cumberland Presbyterians would pay the bill. This policy was not uniformly adhered to, however, for in 1910 the General Assembly granted an appropriation of up to $10,000 to assist in carrying the Missouri property suit to the federal courts.[32]

On June 1, 1907, the Appellate Court of the Third District of Illinois rendered a decision favorable to the unionists. This was in the case of *J. H. Fussell* et al. v. *J. B. Hail* et al. in which the antiunionists sought to enjoin the General Assembly of the Cumberland Presbyterian Church meeting at Decatur in 1906 from putting into effect the pending union. The main points supporting the decision were: (1) the General Assembly of the Cumberland Presbyterian Church had ruled that sufficient doctrinal agreement existed between the two churches to warrant union, and its decision must be accepted as final; (2) the General Assembly's right to enter into a union, though only implied, was defended on two grounds: first, on the basis of the constitutional provision giving the General Assembly the power "to concert measures for promoting the prosperity and enlargement of the church," and, second, because other unions among Presbyterians had been formed on the basis of an inherent or implied right of churches to unite.[33] This case was appealed to the Supreme Court of Illinois, which on February 20, 1908, rendered a decision against the appellants. It was pointed out that no property was involved in this suit, and that "the civil courts deal only with civil or property rights. They have no jurisdiction of religious or ecclesiastical controversies." [34]

Meanwhile, in an opinion handed down August 9, 1907, the Supreme Court of Georgia reversed the decision of the lower court in the Atlanta case on the ground that "the General Assembly as the highest church court, has determined the question arising as to the alleged differences in doctrine." Since the Assembly had decided that it was best that the reunion take place, the court saw no reason for interference in the controversy.[35]

On the other hand, on February 27, 1908, the Court of Civil Appeals at Texarkana, Texas, reversed the judgment of the District Court of Marion County which had left the Jefferson church property in the hands of the unionists. This decision said in part,

Those who remained with the original organization were sufficient in number to maintain its existence and perpetuate the Cumberland Presbyterian denomination. Those who consented to the union proceedings and went into the Presbyterian organization thereby abandoned the former organization. As long as that original organization was kept alive it retained its identity, and as members of that society only can any of the parties have an interest in the property in question.[36]

Early in 1909 two important decisions were rendered in favor of the unionists. The Court of Appeals in the state of Kentucky rendered a majority decision in favor of the unionists in the Sturgis case. This decision was followed by the closing of a number of church buildings in Kentucky against the nonunionist Cumberland Presbyterians. Likewise, the Supreme Court of Texas reaffirmed the decision of the District Court of Marion County giving the Jefferson church property to the unionists. In Texas, the property generally was already occupied by the unionists, and the decision in the Jefferson case merely confirmed the existing situation. Following these decisions many Cumberland Presbyterian congregations in Kentucky and Texas set themselves to the task of erecting or purchasing new buildings.

A decision which gave hope to the remaining Cumberland Presbyterians and produced dismay in the ranks of the unionists was that delivered by Judge M. M. Neil of the Supreme Court of Tennessee on April 3, 1909, in the case of *Ira Landrith* et al. v. *J. L. Hudgins* et al. While recognizing that civil courts in this country have no power to intermeddle with religious matters as such, the judge noted that when church organizations take title to property they enter the domain where civil courts control. He set forth the principle that "when it clearly appears that the ecclesiastical tribunal is wrong it should not be followed." Two aspects of the case received major consideration. In the first place, it was pointed out that Concurrent Declaration No. 1 of the plan of union merely expressed the opinion of the two Assemblies that "such agreement" or "sufficient agreement" between the doctrinal systems of the two churches existed as to warrant union. The court therefore must determine whether the two systems of doctrine were substantially the same. If this were found not to be the case, the property could not be diverted. It was the opinion of the court that the two systems of doctrine were not substantially the same. It was pointed out, also, that no amendment to the Confession of Faith of the Cumberland Presbyterian Church was submitted to the presbyteries, but only a Basis of Union. The decision of the court stated,

Our conclusion of the whole case is, that the proceedings taken for union were not effective to merge the Cumberland Presbyterian Church into the Presbyterian Church in the United States of America; that the Cumberland Presbyterian Church still maintains a vital, and independent organization, with a General Assembly, Synods, and Presbyteries; that the defendants are truly identified therewith in doctrine, polity, and organic subordination; that the complainants are not so identified, but have united themselves with another and different ecclesiastical organization; and that the defendants are entitled to the Church property in controversy at Fayetteville, and the complainants have no interest therein; and that the complainants' bill should be dismissed with costs.[37]

In consequence of this decision most of the local church property in Tennessee which had been held by the unionists reverted to the remaining Cumberland Presbyterians. The latter moved back into church buildings from which in many cases they had been excluded for almost three years. The changed situation in Tennessee was noted by the General Assembly of the Presbyterian Church in the U. S. A. in its 1909 meeting. It was stated that as a result of the Tennessee court decision

many of the congregations connected with the General Assembly of the Reunited Church in that [Tennessee] Synod have voluntarily relinquished their church edifices, and some have been required to surrender their edifices to other parties by order of the Courts.

The denominational property at Nashville and the Theological Seminary at Lebanon, it was pointed out, were in jeopardy. To alleviate the situation the General Assembly authorized and directed the Board of Home Missions and Church Erection to take immediate steps to provide a special fund of not less than $100,000 to assist the Presbyterians of Tennessee in building new churches "in the place of these taken from them by reason of the legal decision in that State." [38]

On June 8, 1909, the Missouri Supreme Court, following the lead of the Tennessee decision, held in the Warrensburg case that the Cumberland Presbyterian Church had no authority to unite with the Presbyterian Church, U. S. A., without first amending its creed and constitution. [39] On the other hand, a decision of the District Court at Bloomington, Illinois, left the property of the church at Lincoln, Illinois, in the hands of the unionists. [40]

Following the Tennessee and Missouri decisions, the unionists sought to throw the matter into the federal courts. This was understandable in the case of the denominational property, such as the publishing house at Nashville, which was awarded to the Cumberland Presbyterian Board of Publication in 1910. It was the property of the whole denomination, and there were board members living in other states. The attempt was now made to have the federal courts take jurisdiction in several local church cases by having non-resident members domiciled in other states file claims of interest in the church property under the plea of "diversity of citizenship." On August 9, 1909, Judge E. T. Sanford, of the Federal District Court at Knoxville, Tennessee, held that the federal court had no jurisdiction in the case of the Oak Street property in Chattanooga. [41] Later, however, the federal courts, upon instruction from the United States Supreme Court, assumed jurisdiction in several Tennessee church cases, among them Grace Church, Nashville; Court Avenue, Memphis; Bethel, near Clarksville; and the churches in Greenfield, Columbia, Springfield, and Savannah. In this way several pieces of church property in Tennessee came to be awarded to the Presbyterian Church, U. S. A. [42]

In July 1913, the United States District Court in Memphis rendered a decision favorable to the unionists in the case of the Court Avenue Church, of Memphis. It was claimed that of a membership of about two hundred all had acquiesced in the union for some three years, but after the Tennessee decision some eight or ten members declared themselves Cumberland Presbyterians and sought possession of the property. The federal court refused to go behind the decision of the General Assembly, as is indicated by the following excerpt from the opinion rendered:

I think, upon principle as well as upon authority, that two churches should be left to determine for themselves whether there was a valid union between them. The highest authority of both churches having determined that there was such a union, that question should be left to so remain in so far as the civil courts are concerned.

The steps leading to the union were directed by [more] learned men of their respective organizations than it is possible for the judge of any civil court to be, and it would seem that these learned and pious men, whose life work is going about the world doing right themselves and exhorting others to like conduct, would have conducted this effort at union fairly and under a correct interpretation of the laws of the respective churches, and that the result of the union as announced by the two general assemblies followed the wishes of the two organizations as fairly, legally, and constitutionally expressed.[43]

In August of the same year Grace Church, of Nashville, was awarded to the unionists by the Federal District Court in Nashville. Here the membership was almost equally divided on the question of union. The property had been awarded to the Cumberland Presbyterians somewhat belatedly in January 1912. A claim to an interest in the property was filed by four nonresident members living in other states, one of whom was said to have been a resident of Mississippi who had united with Grace Church while a student in Nashville.[44] When the adverse decision came, the Cumberland Presbyterians who were ejected from the property numbered about 125.

The property in Missouri was likewise thrown into the federal courts. The Synod of Kansas had an interest in Missouri Valley College, and a suit was filed in the federal court covering not only the college property but all Cumberland Presbyterian property in the state of Missouri. On August 16, 1913, the United States District Court at Kansas City upheld the validity of the union and enjoined members of the Cumberland Presbyterian Church forever from interfering with the use by the Presbyterian Church, U. S. A., of church property in Missouri.[45] In April 1915, this decision was sustained by the Appellate Court at Saint Louis which declared the Presbyterian Church in the U. S. A. to be the owner of Missouri Valley College and all other church property of the "former Cumberland denomination." [46] The United States Supreme Court affirmed the decisions of the lower courts on May 6, 1918.

Numerous lawsuits had been filed in various places. On April 26, 1910, the Illinois Supreme Court decided in favor of the unionists.[47] Although the Appellate Court of the State of Indiana had twice ruled in favor of the remaining Cumberland Presbyterians, the Indiana Supreme Court rendered a decision in favor of the unionists.[48] A decision adverse to the Cumberland Presbyterians was rendered by the Mississippi Supreme Court in the West Point church case in June 1911.[49] In November 1911, a similar decision was rendered in the District Court in the Oklahoma City case.[50] A few months later the Wagoner, Oklahoma, case was decided in favor of the

Presbyterian Church, U. S. A. Little church property in Oklahoma remained in Cumberland Presbyterian hands to be affected by these decisions.[51] As late as the fall of 1914, however, a suit was filed by the Presbyterians for possession of a church building at Chickasha.[52]

The task of gathering the scattered remnants and rebuilding local Cumberland Presbyterian churches was a gigantic one. Many difficulties were faced by those who in good conscience could not see their way clear to go into the union.

In the first place, about two-thirds of the Cumberland Presbyterian ministers went into the union. The Minutes of the General Assembly for 1906 list 1,514 ordained ministers. The Minutes for 1907 list 570. The latter figure included fifty who were ordained during the year 1906-1907. Included, also, were sixteen ministers in Porter Presbytery, which was received back into Arkansas Synod in the fall of 1906.[53] Many of the 570 ministers were nearing the age for retirement from active service, as the growing mortuary rolls of the next few years testify.[54]

The majority of the church buildings were in the hands of unionists, and Cumberland Presbyterians who still occupied their church houses were threatened with the possibility of losing them. Those who chose to remain Cumberland Presbyterian often had to worship in courthouses, opera halls, lodge halls, store buildings, or wherever else a place of worship could be found.

The General Assembly's Board of Missions was unable to come to the relief of churches which needed help. In its report to the Assembly in 1907 the Board noted that many congregations which in the past had supported the work of the Board were now themselves in need of assistance.[55]

Finally, the pressure was upon all, ministers and congregations, to go along with the union. As has already been indicated, Cumberland Presbyterians were told that they were already in the Presbyterian Church, U. S. A.

In a number of instances pastors were able to lead their congregations to declare themselves Cumberland Presbyterian. In many instances, on the other hand, whole congregations followed their pastors into the union. Still other churches—and these were numerous—were divided.

An atmosphere of tension prevailed as unionists and antiunionists sought to win the allegiance of the people. Recognizing the key role of the pastor, the Rev. A. N. Eshman, chairman of the Advisory Board named by the continuing Cumberland Presbyterian General Assembly, sent out a letter of advice containing the following:

Cumberland Presbyterian Pastors Only. Our churches should be supplied with a Cumberland Presbyterian pastor or be unsupplied until our new boards come to their relief. No pastor at all is infinitely better than a union pastor for our churches. Better be supplied with a preacher of any other denomination than a unionist; but we emphasize the suggestion that your church have a Cumberland Presbyterian pastor or be vacant.

This advice was construed by the Committee on Pastoral Oversight to mean "better be lost than listen to a union preacher." [56]

On the other hand, in a letter dated June 28, 1906, signed by J. M. Patterson, who was corresponding secretary of the former Cumberland Presbyterian Board of Missions and Church Erection at Saint Louis, the following advice was sent to unionist leaders in the various presbyteries:

Another matter of great importance. Find out quickly where the anti-union agitators are at work and camp on their trail. Stay right with them. Leave none of their misrepresentations unanswered for twenty-four hours. Expose their methods in the city and town papers wherever you can get in. Drive them from the bounds of your presbytery as quickly as possible. . . . [57]

Such was the temper of the times.

Much of the work of gathering and reorganizing the scattered remnants was done by missionaries appointed by the new Board of Missions named at the continued session of the General Assembly at Decatur. This Board secured the services of the following men to act as its representatives: the Rev. J. D. Lewis, in West Tennessee Synod; the Rev. T. E. Hudson, in Tennessee Synod; the Rev. R. D. Shook, in Alabama; the Rev. J. T. Barbee, in Kentucky; the Rev. T. H. Padgett, in Arkansas (in addition to his duties as Stated Clerk of the General Assembly); the Rev. H. G. Nicholson, in Colorado; and the Rev. S. C. Lockett and the Rev. B. E. Bowmer, in Texas.[58] Several of these men were continued by their synods as synodical missionaries. A number of presbyteries appointed missionaries to do the same kind of work.

The Rev. F. A. Brown, who as early as 1911 was serving as secretary of missions for Indianola Synod, has left correspondence revealing his manifold activities during those trying times. Frequent drouths plagued the work in Oklahoma. The synodic board had to borrow money to meet its obligations. On one occasion when the treasury was emptied two board members paid the balance of the board's obligations out of their pockets. Brown sometimes went without his salary in order that others who could not get along as well might have the money. Besides serving a church called Rock Creek, near his home, he preached regularly once a month to a church about 250 miles away. His correspondence includes letters to missionary pastors urging them to hold on a little longer, to laymen seeking to impress upon them that the Lord had need of their service in a more definite way, and to a group of women in New Jersey who wished to know more about the Indians and their way of life. He seems to have attended nearly all the meetings of the five presbyteries which composed the synod and was present for the reorganization of Cherokee Presbytery in December 1911.[59]

Brown's activities took him to Tennessee in the fall of 1911. The denominational Board of Sunday School and Young People's Work had promised $500 to the work in Oklahoma, but the money had to be raised. Brown therefore attended meetings of the synods of Tennessee and West Tennessee to present the cause of missions in Indianola Synod.

Limitations of space forbid the telling of the whole story of the efforts of ministers and laymen who labored to rebuild the Cumberland Presbyterian Church during this period. Only a few examples can be cited.

A number of churches in Tennessee, such as those at Knoxville, Dyersburg, Union City, and Jackson, remained virtually intact, although, as has been noted, the pastor and official board of the last-named church felt the weight of the Tennessee injunction on one occasion.

The churches in Nashville, on the other hand, were divided over the union question, and in most of them, if not all, the remaining Cumberland Presbyterians were temporarily deprived of the church property. West Nashville Church, locked out of its building, organized a Sunday school in a building formerly used as a drugstore.[60] Arrington Street Church worshiped in a building formerly used as a carpenter shop and stable.[61] The Addison Avenue Church divided in September 1906, when following a morning worship service Frank Slemmons, an elder, requested all loyal Cumberland Presbyterians to repair to the primary room. Although threatened with an injunction, twenty-six members met and elected four elders to serve with the two who had remained Cumberland Presbyterian. The Rev. Thomas Buchanan, pastor of Beech Church, and one of the few nonunionist ministers remaining in Lebanon Presbytery, ordained and installed the elders.[62] After the Tennessee Supreme Court decision in 1909, these churches regained possession of their property.

Prior to 1906, Court Avenue Church was the leading Cumberland Presbyterian church in Memphis, although there were four other small congregations in the city and its environs. One of these was Central Church, which had a frame building located on Union Avenue. Late in 1906, the Rev. C. A. Davis, presbyterial missionary for Memphis Presbytery, reorganized Central Church with seven members. Shortly thereafter, the Rev. C. H. Walton, a member of Walker Heights Church and a carpenter, who recently had been ordained to the work of the gospel ministry, began preaching at Central. At first he was employed for two Sundays a month.[63] Eventually the property on Union Avenue was sold, and property was purchased at Linden and Dudley, where a new building was erected. This building was first occupied March 16, 1913. Remnants of other congregations in Memphis soon found their way to Central.

The First Cumberland Presbyterian Church at Evansville, Indiana, of which the Rev. T. A. Wigginton was pastor, went with the union, but Jefferson Avenue Church, which was being served by the Rev. T. Ashburn, remained Cumberland Presbyterian. In January 1907, Ashburn resigned to become pastor of the church at Knoxville, Tennessee. In the fall of that year, Indiana Presbytery of the Presbyterian Church, U. S. A., moved to take possession of the Jefferson Avenue Church. The five nonunionist elders —M. H. Vaught, H. J. Graf, A. C. DeForest, Peter Zapp, and William Reister—were ordered to appear before the above mentioned presbytery. This they refused to do on the ground that Indiana Presbytery of the Presbyterian Church had no jurisdiction over them or their church, whereupon the presbytery ordered them to cease acting as elders. The unionist elders secured a preacher for the following Sunday, and the Cumberland Presbyterians were barred from the church building by an injunction, the doors locked, the windows nailed down, and a guard posted. The Cumberland Presbyterians therefore met in the home of Albert Shultz, with sixty-one persons present.[64] They accepted the use of the Jewish Temple as a temporary meeting place. Soon a lot was purchased and a temporary building erected. This building was dedicated December 28, 1907, by Ashburn, the former pastor.[65] The Rev. R. L. Kirkland served as pastor for one year beginning early in 1908. He was succeeded by the Rev. C. M. Zwingle, under whose ministry the church and Sunday school grew rapidly. A new sanctuary was built in time for the meeting of the General Assembly in 1911. By that time the church had some three hundred members and an enrollment of five hundred in Sunday school.

In June 1907, the Rev. J. D. Lewis went to Birmingham, Alabama, at the request of the Board of Missions. Cumberland Presbyterians and Presbyterians, U. S. A., were having their Sunday schools at the same time in different areas of the building, and Lewis preached on Sunday afternoons.[66] Subsequently the Cumberland Presbyterians had to vacate the building and worshiped elsewhere until a building was erected in 1912. During this time Lewis rendered a ministry to other congregations in the area. Oak Grove, a rural church nearby, had been closed by the unionists, but a citizen of the community, not a member of the church, somehow managed to get the impression of the lock in a cake of soap and had a locksmith make a key. Thereafter Lewis preached at Oak Grove one Sunday afternoon each month. In the fall of 1908 he reported having visited Gadsden, where he preached to forty-three Cumberland Presbyterians.[67]

On July 15, 1906, a group of Cumberland Presbyterians in Dallas met at the Ross Avenue Baptist Church, and, after a sermon by the Rev. S. C. Lockett, elected four elders and two deacons.[68] Soon a lot was purchased on East Main Street and a building fund started to build a church. For a time during the summer of 1907 preaching services were suspended, but a "Whosoever Will Club" met each Sunday morning at the home of H. A. R. Horton, one of the newly elected deacons.[69] On September 1, 1907, the Rev. W. H. Berry preached to the Dallas flock in its own chapel on East Main Street and Hill Avenue. The Rev. John R. Morris, the Rev. J. W. Pearson, and the Rev. W. J. Lackey served successively as pastors. Meanwhile, the chapel was sold and property purchased on the corner of Washington Avenue and Simpson Street, where a more commodious building was erected. There was an indebtedness against this property, however, and it was about to be sold when on May 9, 1915, at the urgent request of the Rev. W. A. Boone, of Marshall, secretary of the synodic board of missions, the Rev. H. R. Allen became pastor. He and Horton signed the notes, and the church was run by faith, as no mission funds were available. In August of that year there were still only eighteen active members, but the Sunday school had increased from fifteen to fifty.[70] This church enjoyed a gradual growth, although it was still cumbered by debt when the General Assembly, which met in Dallas in 1918, gave assistance in paying off the indebtedness.[71]

On October 4, 1908, the Rev. N. C. Pyles, of Mansfield, Texas, reorganized the remaining Cumberland Presbyterians in Fort Worth with a membership of eighteen.[72]

On June 10, 1908, a minister, John Hudson, went to Austin, Texas, and ordained two elders, installed another, and received R. M. Castleman into the church by letter.[73] Here the former Cumberland Presbyterian property was sold to a Baptist congregation by the Presbyterians, who had no need for it since their own edifice was directly across the street. Regular services were not held, however, until early in 1914 when Castleman invited the Rev. W. A. Boone to visit the city. He spent some twelve days there, and on March 8, 1914, the church was reorganized with fifty-seven members.[74] On April 30 a committee from the Central Baptist Church sent a written proposal to sell its property (the former Cumberland Presbyterian property) to the reorganized congregation for $23,000. The proposal was accepted, Castleman subscribing $10,000 of the amount. Soon the Cumberland Presbyterian congregation was worshiping at its former location. The Rev. J. H. Zwingle was called as pastor.[75]

In June 1906, J. T. Barbee reported that he had found two women at

Sturgis, Kentucky, who were taking the names of those who wished to remain Cumberland Presbyterian. They had fifty-eight names on their list.[76] As has already been noted, the decision in the Sturgis property case was adverse to the remaining Cumberland Presbyterians, but they soon had $4,000 for a church building and the offer of a lot on which to build. This story was repeated many times over at various places in Kentucky as Cumberland Presbyterians built or purchased buildings to replace those which had been lost.

The Cumberland Presbyterians at Bowling Green did not wait for a court decision before proceeding with plans to build. In July 1906, a majority of the elders cast their lot with the Presbyterian Church. The minority met at the home of one of the elders, and, after canvassing the situation, decided that the possible loss of property would not put an end to Cumberland Presbyterianism in Bowling Green. The Rev. S. H. Eshman was called as pastor and began his work there in September 1906, serving both the Bowling Green church and Mount Olivet, which was nearby. The auditorium of a school was secured for services for a time. Later the congregation met in the circuit court room. A lot was purchased for $4,500 and within two years was paid for. In August 1909, the cornerstone of a new building was laid. A brick building was erected at a cost of about $20,000 and was dedicated May 29, 1910.[77]

Eshman had been pastor of the church in Paducah, Kentucky, which in 1906 had 150 members. Shortly after the Decatur Assembly, finding himself out of harmony with a majority of the congregation on the union question, he resigned as pastor. On March 5, 1907, J. T. Barbee, missionary of Kentucky Synod, met the Rev. D. W. Fooks in Paducah. Meetings were held for three nights in the First Christian Church. On the third night fifty members met and elected four elders. Fooks became pastor of the church, and the following year a house of worship was purchased.[78]

In 1909, the Rev. O. A. Barbee, pastor of the church at Greenville, Kentucky, organized a Sunday school in Owensboro and began preaching in the circuit court room of the Daviess County courthouse one Sunday night each month. On August 22, a temporary organization was effected with nine members, one of whom had been an elder in the original Owensboro Cumberland Presbyterian Church. After some lapse of time during which the group was without regular worship services, the organization was completed in October 1910, by the Rev. W. T. Galloway. Shortly thereafter a mission church was purchased from the Walnut Street Baptist Church for $400.[79] The Rev. J. L. Price and the Rev. G. B. McDonald served successively as pastors. In October 1914, O. A. Barbee became pastor and served until June 1932.

### STURGIS, KENTUCKY, CHURCH

The pictured building was erected in 1910 and is shown in a photograph taken that year, some thirty years after the organization of the church in Sturgis. It is representative of church houses built to replace property involved in litigation after 1906 and awarded to the Presbyterian Church in the U. S. A. It has subsequently been remodeled and enlarged.

### McKENZIE, TENNESSEE, CHURCH

This church was organized in 1867 and has been attended by generations of Bethel College students. Its building, erected in 1892 and remodeled and enlarged some years later, is representative of church property involved in litigation after 1906 but retained by Cumberland Presbyterians. The church was originally known as the Bethlehem Church, the name being changed in 1889.

Cumberland Presbyterians began anew, usually with very small remnants, in a number of other strategic places where formerly there had been substantial congregations. In April 1908, services were begun at Springfield, Missouri, under the leadership of the Rev. B. F. Logan, with an attendance of six in Sunday school and fifteen in the worship service. Soon a church building was purchased.[80] On the night of February 3, 1910, a group of Cumberland Presbyterians in Harrison, Arkansas, held a prayer meeting with twenty-four persons present, commemorating the one hundredth anniversary of the birth of the Cumberland Presbyterian Church. Out of this occasion grew a weekly prayer meeting, and from the prayer meeting came a church.[81] In May 1911, the Rev. J. M. Russell held a revival meeting in Sedalia, Missouri. A lot was purchased and a tent pitched on it. In July the cornerstone for a new church building was laid, and in October a building was completed.[82] In September 1913, the Rev. L. B. McCaslin went to Russellville, Arkansas, where there was a very small remnant of Cumberland Presbyterians. Serving at the same time as pastor of the Shiloh and Dover churches, he led in the purchase of a lot and the erection of a building in Russellville.[83] In 1914, a congregation of six members built a church at Fayetteville, Arkansas.[84]

There were numerous instances, also, in which sizable groups of Cumberland Presbyterians refused to go into the union, but because of a lack of adequate ministerial leadership or because of the failure to obtain a permanent place of worship, the attempts to continue as churches were frustrated. At Brownwood, Texas, for example, some seventy-five members declined to go into the union. For two years the Rev. J. D. Caldwell ministered to them. Services were held for a while in an opera house and later at the Carnegie Library.[85] When Caldwell left, no minister was secured. At Denton, Texas, a remnant continued for several years to meet in the courthouse. Among the elders of this congregation was John Bacon, son of Sumner Bacon, pioneer Cumberland Presbyterian minister in Texas.[86] This congregation, in consequence of being unable to secure ministerial leadership, dwindled in numbers but was never dropped from the presbyterial roll. When the church was reactivated in 1932, one elder, J. C. Parr, and a few other members, who had constituted the continuing congregation after 1906, participated in the reorganization.

Although most of the churches above mentioned were in towns or cities, the Cumberland Presbyterian Church after 1906 was more predominantly rural than before. A larger proportion of the town churches went with the union than was the case with the rural churches. In many presbyteries the country churches were the strongholds for the perpetuation of the Cumberland Presbyterian Church. In several instances—including those of Owensboro, Paducah, Fort Worth, Central Church in Memphis, and Addison Avenue Church in Nashville, all cited above—rural ministers helped plant churches again in the towns and cities.

As to the number of members who went with the union, the number who remained Cumberland Presbyterian, and the number who went into other communions, accurate information is not available. In 1906, there were 2,869 churches and a total reported membership of 185,212, of whom 145,411 were reported as "resident" members. The Presbyterian Church, U. S. A., had 8,118 churches and 1,158,682 members. For the next several years the statistics were complicated by the fact that both denominations continued to carry on their rolls nearly all of the churches that had been Cumberland Presbyterian before 1906. Indeed, in many instances, the membership figures for 1906 were carried forward. At one time the *Cumberland Presbyterian Banner* claimed that "not less than one hundred thousand members" still adhered to the Cumberland Presbyterian Church.[87] The letter addressed by the Cumberland Presbyterian General Assembly to the General Assembly of the Presbyterian Church, U. S. A., in 1907 suggested that one-fourth of the membership had gone into the union.[88] On the other hand, the *Cumberland Presbyterian,* which continued to be published as a unionist organ and tended to belittle both the number and quality of those who did not go along with the union, claimed that only about one-eighth of the former membership of the Cumberland Presbyterian Church stayed out of the union. Noting that there were 145,411 resident members in 1906, and that the General Assembly tax was paid in 1907 to the Presbyterian Church, U. S. A., on 126,876 members of former Cumberland Presbyterian churches, the editor of the *Cumberland Presbyterian* estimated that a number amounting only to about 12.5 per cent had stayed out of the union.[89]

Obviously the truth lay somewhere between the figures quoted by the spokesmen of the opposing groups. R. L. Baskette found through an analysis of the statistical tables of the Presbyterian Church, U. S. A., for 1907, that 1,216 former Cumberland Presbyterian churches actually reported to stated clerks of the Presbyterian Church, U. S. A. These churches reported a total of 80,522 members. There were 1,680 former Cumberland Presbyterian churches which made no report to the Presbyterian Church, U. S. A.[90] The total membership figure for 1906, rather than the number of "resident members," was used for those churches which did not report. Such churches were indicated by an asterisk. J. V. Stephens, professor of church history in the Theological School at Cumberland University, is reported to have estimated that 90,000 Cumberland Presbyterians went with the union and that 55,000 "stood pat" or became affiliated with Methodist or Baptist churches.[91] In 1916, after most of the lawsuits had been settled and the presbyterial rolls (with few exceptions) purged of churches which had gone into the union, the Cumberland Presbyterian Church reported having 1,446 churches and a total lay membership of 63,735.[92]

A study completed in 1970 by the Rev. W. Loran Waller calls attention to the number of churches which neither were retained long upon the rolls of the Presbyterian Church, U. S. A., nor continued as Cumberland Presbyterian churches. Of the 2,877 churches which were on the rolls of the Cumberland Presbyterian Church in 1906, it was found that 978, or approximately one-third of the 1906 total, were not to be found on the rolls of either denomination in 1921. Only 971 were still listed on the rolls of the Presbyterian Church, U. S. A., while 1,078 (including 170 which appeared on the rolls of both churches) were still listed as Cumberland Presbyterian churches.[93] Many former members of the Cumberland Presbyterian Church had gone into other churches, especially to the Methodist bodies and to the Presbyterian Church in the United States (often called the Southern Presbyterian Church), while many others were "as sheep without a shepherd."

Meanwhile, consolidations of presbyteries and synods had become necessary in many instances. Of three presbyteries in Iowa, only one small presbytery remained. It was attached to Missouri Synod, and in 1919 its constituency was added to McGee Presbytery. Three presbyteries which formerly made up Indiana Synod were consolidated in 1910 to form one presbytery, which was attached to Illinois Synod. By 1914, the twenty-one presbyteries in Texas Synod were reduced to twelve. In the State of Missouri, eight presbyteries remained where there had been thirteen. In Illinois, the number of presbyteries had been reduced from ten to five. Kentucky Synod retained all of its presbyteries except Louisville. The one remaining Cumberland Presbyterian church in this presbytery, Bethel, near Harrodsburg, was added to Cumberland Presbytery. Arkansas Presbytery was combined with Fort Smith in 1907, and a few years later the presbyteries of Little Rock and Burrow were combined. In Indianola Synod the presbyteries of Washita and Greer were combined, and for a while the territory of Cherokee Presbytery was added to Choctaw Presbytery; however, as has been noted, Cherokee Presbytery was later reorganized. Only in the synods of Alabama, Tennessee, and West Tennessee did all presbyteries continue to function.

Not all the energies of Cumberland Presbyterians were spent in reorganizing the remnants of previously existing churches, for new fields were entered. A survey made by Dr. J. L. Goodknight, then Stated Clerk of the General Assembly, and published in the spring of 1914 indicated that during a period of six and one-half years following the 1906 Assembly eighty-nine new churches had been organized. Of these, twenty-five were in Indianola Synod and forty-five in Texas Synod. Ninety-four churches had been built, and thirty-six purchased or improved. In Kentucky Synod, twenty-two new church buildings had been erected since 1906, and in Texas Synod, twenty-four.[94]

Waller's study shows that between 1906 and 1921 there were 212 new churches added to the rolls of the Cumberland Presbyterian Church. This number included seventeen which were received with the readmission of Porter Presbytery in the fall of 1906.[95]

A step was taken toward planting Cumberland Presbyterian churches on the south plains of Texas when in late July 1908, Sweetwater Presbytery met at Union, twenty miles north of Tahoka. This was near the line between Sweetwater Presbytery and Amarillo Presbytery, which had been reorganized in November 1907. Two ministers of the latter presbytery, B. H. Baker and C. W. C. Norwood, attended. Following presbytery, Baker and Norwood held meetings at Block 20 and Lubbock. The Rev. J. L. Elliott and D. B. Norman, a licentiate, remained for a series of services at the place where presbytery had met. The Rev. L. B. McCaslin, the Rev. W. M. Bennett, and the Rev. E. R. Skiles held a meeting at Tahoka.[96] Each of these meetings resulted in the organization (or, in the case of Tahoka, the reorganization) of a church. The Lubbock church was organized at the home of E. P. Earhart on August 8, 1908, with seven members. Elliott became the first pastor. He preached at Floydada, Emma, Block 20, and Union, also.

In 1912, the General Assembly received a communication from the Rev. M. L. Bullard, the Rev. O. W. Carter, and the Rev. E. D. Dysart, all of whom lived in New Mexico, appealing for aid to purchase a tent for use in evangelistic work.[97] The Board of Missions loaned them forty-five dollars, and the tent was purchased.[98] During a revival held in August 1912, a small congregation was organized at Elkins, New Mexico. Another had been organized about a month earlier by Bullard near the Capitan Mountains.[99] Another was organized at Roswell. On January 11, 1913, by order of Texas Synod, the Roswell Presbytery was organized at Roswell, New Mexico, by the above named ministers. A licentiate, Noah Webb, was ordained.[100] Soon afterward two other ministers were received. The Rev. Willie H. Stephens was named as presbyterial evangelist. Later a small congregation near Pecos, Texas, was received into this presbytery.

In 1915, the General Assembly ordered the formation of the Synod of West Texas and New Mexico to consist of the presbyteries of Amarillo, Brownwood, Roswell, and Sweetwater. Its first meeting was held at Lubbock in September 1915.[101] Only four meetings of this synod were held, however. The 1919 meeting failed for lack of a quorum, and in 1920 the territory of this synod was added to Texas Synod. The disruption caused by World War I and the severe drouth of 1917 and 1918 resulted in the scattering of many of the small congregations in this area. Roswell Presbytery ceased to exist, and in 1921 the territory of Sweetwater Presbytery was divided between the presbyteries of Amarillo and Weatherford.[102]

# 20

## GATHERING TOGETHER THE PIECES

*The publishing house in Nashville was in the hands of the unionists. Cumberland Presbyterians were without Sunday school literature of their own, and the* Cumberland Presbyterian *was a unionist organ. The property of all the colleges and universities of the Church was in the hands of the Presbyterian Church.*

Of the members of General Assembly boards as constituted prior to 1906 only one remained in the continuing Cumberland Presbyterian Church. This was Dr. W. G. Ralston, of Evansville, Indiana, president of the Board of Ministerial Relief since its organization in 1881. Two members of the Woman's Board of Missions, which was elected by the Woman's Missionary Convention, remained: Mrs. Mattie Ashburn and Mrs. Mary M. Graf, both of Evansville.

Only two missionaries remained: the Rev. Gam Sing Quah, of the Chinese mission in San Francisco, and Miss Sallie Herbert, a teacher in the mountain mission school at Barnard, North Carolina. The mission at Barnard passed into the control of the Presbyterian Church, U. S. A. The Chinese mission in San Francisco had been destroyed by the earthquake and fire of April 1906.

The publishing house in Nashville was in the hands of the unionists. Cumberland Presbyterians were without Sunday school literature of their own, and the *Cumberland Presbyterian* was a unionist organ.

The property of all the colleges and universities of the Church was in the hands of the Presbyterian Church. Although a majority of the Board of

Trustees of Bethel College, McKenzie, Tennessee, which was operated by the Synod of West Tennessee, remained Cumberland Presbyterian, the property was being held for the Presbyterian Church by the president of the school, W. E. Johnston.

The Thornton Home for aged ministers, at Evansville, was likewise in the hands of the Presbyterian Church, U. S. A. The Sheppard Home, which was under the control of Texas Synod, was jointly administered for a time by trustees appointed by the synods of the two churches, although a later court decision was to award the property to the Presbyterian Church, U. S. A. For a period of time, however, it afforded a home to one Cumberland Presbyterian minister, the Rev. Jesse Marshall, and his wife.

The continuing session of the General Assembly in 1906 named persons to the various boards in place of those who had indicated their intention to go with the union. The General Assembly in 1907 augmented their numbers so as, in most cases, to bring the boards up to their normal membership of nine.

The Board of Ministerial Relief had been created in 1881 to give aid to aged ministers and their wives and widows. This Board reported to the General Assembly in 1906 that it had ninety-four beneficiaries.[1]

In 1906 three men were named to constitute the Board of Ministerial Relief. During the year 1906-1907 this Board received offerings totaling $611.76, and eleven beneficiaries were aided.[2] In 1907, the Board was enlarged to nine members. Officers elected in addition to W. G. Ralston, who continued as president, were the Rev. R. D. Miller, vice-president; the Rev. J. H. Milholland, secretary; and the Rev. J. M. Wyckoff, treasurer.

The offerings gradually increased, and so did the number of beneficiaries. In 1910-1911 offerings totaled $2,564.37, and there were eighteen beneficiaries. In 1911 the Board employed its corresponding secretary and treasurer, Wyckoff, to devote his whole time to the work of the Board at a salary of $600 for the year and expenses.[3] In 1912-1913 the offerings totaled $4,929.65. There were twenty-nine beneficiaries at that time, and the Board had assumed responsibility for support of the orphans' home at Bowling Green, Kentucky.[4] In the years immediately following, the offerings ranged from $2,952.97 (1915-1916) to $4,650.84 (1913-1914), while the number of beneficiaries rose to thirty (not counting those in the home at Bowling Green) in 1917.

The home at Bowling Green was first mentioned in the Minutes of the General Assembly in 1905. It came into the possession of the Church through the bequest of Miss Victoria W. Jackson. The General Assembly endorsed the project and appointed a committee "to take visitorial control of said orphanage." [5] This home passed into the hands of the Presbyterian Church, U. S. A., in 1906, although, according to the terms of the bequest, it was to be under the supervision of a board of managers all of whom must be members of the Cumberland Presbyterian Church of Bowling Green. Preference was to be given (1) to needy orphan children of Cumberland Presbyterian parentage of Bowling Green and Warren County, Kentucky; (2) to needy orphans of Cumberland Presbyterian parentage who were residents of any of the United States or territories; and (3) to needy orphans of Bowling Green and Warren County of any religious persuasion. [6]

Early in 1912 the opportunity of obtaining the home arose rather unexpectedly. In March of that year J. M. Wyckoff, who was traveling for the Board of Ministerial Relief, was asked by Dr. J. L. Goodknight, Stated Clerk of the General Assembly, to go to Bowling Green to investigate the home. Upon his arrival he learned that it had been intimated that the Presbyterian Church might turn the home back to the Cumberland Presbyterians.

The local Cumberland Presbyterian church was at first reluctant to elect a board of managers if there were financial obligations involved, as it had just built a new house of worship and had all the financial obligations it could carry. The Board of Ministerial Relief, however, agreed to finance the home if the local church would agree that it should be a home for the retired ministers, their widows, and the missionaries of the Cumberland Presbyterian Church as well as for orphan children. On this basis the local congregation appointed a committee to confer with the Presbyterian board of managers to ascertain whether this board was willing to turn the home back to the Cumberland Presbyterian Church.

It was found that the Presbyterian board was willing to make the transfer. The Bowling Green congregation, therefore, on April 23, 1912, appointed a board of managers, and on April 29 a contract was entered into between the Board of Managers of the Cumberland Presbyterian Orphans' Home at Bowling Green, Kentucky, and the Board of Ministerial Relief. The Board of Managers would select the person or persons to superintend the home, but the Board of Ministerial Relief would have control of the financial phase of any agreement with such person or persons. [7]

Under this arrangement the Rev. S. H. Eshman and his wife were elected to have custody of the home, and Eshman, who also was serving as pastor of the Bowling Green church, became pastor of the home. Dr. T. W. Stone was named as the home's physician, and H. H. Denhardt was named attorney for the two boards.

The home was presented to the General Assembly meeting in Warrensburg, Missouri, in May 1912, with appropriate ceremonies and was accepted by the Assembly;[8] however, the actual transfer was not made until May 31. On June 23, 1912, after some repairs had been made, the home was dedicated in the presence of a large congregation of people, the Rev. J. L. Hudgins preaching the dedicatory sermon and J. H. Milholland offering the dedicatory prayer.[9]

The home was situated on a lot one hundred feet wide and four hundred feet long near the new Cumberland Presbyterian church. It was described as being a commodious brick structure with a frame building at the rear attached to the main building. It was appraised at $10,000 and the contents at $1,100.[10]

The one orphan boy, Brooks Scruggs, who was in the home at the time of the transfer was a member of the Presbyterian Church, U. S. A. He was taken from the home by a ruling elder in the local Presbyterian church, although it had been agreed that he might remain in the home. Mrs. S. V. M. Brown, widow of the late Rev. J. R. Brown, was brought to the home from Evansville, Indiana, and subsequently the Rev. J. M. Ashford and his wife were admitted. The first orphan child admitted under the new management was Irene Monroe, whose parents had been members of the Union Church, in Ewing-McLin Presbytery, Illinois. Thus, when the next General Assembly convened in Bowling Green in May 1913, there were three aged residents and one orphan child in the home.[11]

In the summer of 1913, following the resignation of Eshman as pastor of the Bowling Green church, Mrs. W. E. Phalan became matron of the home. She served in this capacity until 1918. In 1914 there were three orphan children and one aged inmate in the home; in 1915, five children and two aged inmates; and in 1916 and 1917, one minister and five children.[12]

In 1915 the Board of Ministerial Relief reported receipt of two bequests. J. L. Goodknight had bequeathed $500 to the Board, and Mrs. Brown, who died at the home on February 10, 1915, had left to the Board about $600 in cash together with her household goods and other personal property not otherwise disposed of in her will. The Board decided to use the proceeds of Mrs. Brown's will for the home. The Board also reported to the General Assembly the loss by death of both its president, W. G. Ralston, and its corresponding secretary-treasurer, J. M. Wyckoff.[13] Following the General Assembly the Board was reorganized by the election of the Rev. E. M. Johnson, president; the Rev. W. H. Hutchinson, vice-president; the Rev. Charles R. Matlock, recording secretary; and J. H. Milholland, corresponding secretary-treasurer. Milholland served in the latter capacity until June 1916, when he was succeeded by the Rev. John A. McLane, who had become a member of the Board in 1915.

The Board of Missions as named by the General Assembly in its continuing meeting in 1906 consisted of the Rev. J. L. Joyner, of Cordell, Oklahoma; William Clark, of Jefferson, Texas; and the Rev. W. M. Robison, F. Y. Hall, and F. H. Prendergast, all of Marshall, Texas. The office of the Board was established at Marshall, the only paid employee the first year being a part-time secretary who was paid fifteen dollars per month.[14] In 1907, Robison was made secretary of the Board at a salary of fifty dollars per month.[15]

At first the Board's attention was largely occupied with the attempt to secure representatives in various areas of the Church to head up the work of holding together or reorganizing the remaining Cumberland Presbyterians. Beginning in January 1907, fifty dollars per month was given toward the support of Gam Sing Quah, pastor of the Chinese Church in San Francisco.

With the assumption in 1907 of the expense of the San Francisco mission by the Woman's Board of Missions, the General Assembly's Board was left free to devote its attention to other fields. Beginning in 1907, payments of twenty-five dollars per month were given to aid Central Church, of Memphis. In 1909, the Board pointed out that Memphis was still receiving assistance, but that "under the plan suggested by us for the future, Memphis, being in one of the strong synods, would be expected to receive its aid locally, from the Presbytery or Synod and not from the Church at large." [16] The Board continued to aid the Memphis church, however, until the end of 1909.

Beginning in December 1907, aid in the amount of twenty-five dollars per month was given to a group which was carrying on a Sunday school at Colorado Springs, Colorado. Beginning in February 1908, a like amount was given to aid the struggling congregation at Pueblo, where the Rev. H. G. Nicholson was pastor. Subsequently, Nicholson ministered to both groups. Aid was given until early in 1912 when the pastor resigned. No replacement was secured, and Colorado was lost to the Cumberland Presbyterian Church.

Attention was also given to the needs in Oklahoma. The General Assembly in 1908 directed the Board of Missions to proceed with plans to place a missionary in Indianola Synod.[17] Already some aid had been given the Rev. J. S. Lish, of McCurtain, Oklahoma. Under the program begun in November 1908, aid in the amount of $66.66 per month was given through the Rev. F. A. Brown, superintendent of missions in Indianola Synod.[18] Meanwhile, the Board of Sunday School and Young People's Work took over the task of raising money, as a missions project, through the Sunday schools for the support of Lish, as a missionary in Choctaw Presbytery. Beginning about 1912 the Board of Missions aided at Wagoner and

Pryor, Oklahoma, where the Rev. J. S. Hall was pastor.[19] Beginning in 1913, the Rev. D. F. Blasingame, presbyterial missionary in Cherokee Presbytery, was aided by the Board.[20] Later the Rev. T. G. Reid served the church at Pryor, and Hall worked at McAlester and other points.[21]

Aid in the amount of twenty-five dollars per month was given the church in Dallas, Texas, from October 1908 until November 1913. The Rev. W. J. Lackey was the pastor during this period.[22]

In 1910 the Board of Missions resigned as a body in order that a new board might be constituted with headquarters in Missouri to act under the charter previously used in that state.[23] A board of seven members was created, five of whom were residents of Missouri. The Rev. A. M. Buchanan was elected president, and the Rev. J. W. Duvall, secretary-treasurer.

About 1911, attention began to be given to the work on the Pacific coast. During 1911-1912, the amount of $300 was given to help build a house of worship at Fresno, California, where the Rev. J. R. Walker was pastor. There a church building purchased from the United Presbyterian Church was moved onto a lot which the Cumberland Presbyterians had purchased, and a basement was put under it.[24] In April 1913, the Board began supplementing the salary of the Rev. W. D. Hawkins at Merced.[25] Hawkins resigned in February 1914 and was succeeded by the Rev. E. W. Johnson, who served until 1917, when he resigned to return to school. The Rev. J. D. Lewis succeeded him. In 1915 the Rev. C. H. Walton went to Los Angeles as pastor, and his salary was supplemented by fifteen dollars per month.[26]

Smaller amounts were given at some other places, and some gifts were made toward the erection of church buildings. Over a three-year period a little more than $1,000 was given on the building at Birmingham, Alabama, and during the year 1913-1914 the sum of $500 was given on the church building at Marshall, Missouri.[27]

During the period from 1906 to 1918 the annual receipts of the Board of Missions averaged no more than $2,500 annually. Some mission work was carried on by presbyteries and synods. In 1907-1908 a total of $11,456.15 was reported as having been given for synodic and presbyterial mission work; in 1910-1911, $4,880.02; 1911-1912, $7,906.40; 1912-1913, $2,413.87; and 1913-1914, $1,753.40.

Frequent appeals for aid in building churches appeared in the *Cumberland Presbyterian Banner,* and there was some response. In 1913-1914 the General Assembly's Board of Missions proposed to pay the last one hundred dollars of the indebtedness on the Memorial Church at Dickson, Tennessee. Publicity was given through the columns of the *Banner,* and the sum of $1,090.89 was received, leaving only the last $96.56 to be paid by the Board.[28]

Early in 1907 the Woman's Board of Missions was reorganized by enlisting Mrs. Thomas Jordan, Mrs. Tillie M. Stone, Mrs. Lydia E. Tupman, Mrs. Frances Varner, and Mrs. Anna M. Conn to fill the existing vacancies. Mrs. Jordan died just before the 1907 Convention. At this Convention Mrs. Gertrude Shulz, Mrs. Johnie Massey Clay, and Mrs. Ella L. Goodknight were added to the Board.

When the Convention met in 1907 the work of the women throughout the Church was in a very disorganized condition. Not a single synod or presbytery was fully organized. The structure had to be rebuilt from the bottom up, and with inexperienced workers. Some local missionary auxiliaries were functioning, but total receipts of the Board for the year had been only $509.62, of which $460.26 was still in the treasury. The Woman's Board found itself in the peculiar position of "being a Missionary Board without a missionary, and with no definite work in sight." [29]

During the General Assembly and Missionary Convention held at Dickson, Tennessee, in May 1907, the General Assembly's Board of Missions requested the Woman's Board to assume one-half the salary of Gam Sing Quah. Later the Woman's Board was asked to assume full charge of the San Francisco work. [30] When Gam returned to China in 1908, it was the Woman's Board which sent him. Thus it happened that the foreign mission work of the Cumberland Presbyterian Church was committed to the women of the Church.

During the 1907 Convention, Mrs. Clay suggested the annual observance of Woman's Board of Missions Day. [31] This observance afforded not only the

MRS. JOHNIE MASSEY CLAY
(1871-1963)

A leader in the Church's missionary enterprise for many years, being elected a member of the newly reorganized Woman's Board of Missions in 1907 and serving as its president from 1916 to 1936, as editor of the *Jubilee Journal,* and as the first editor of the *Missionary Messenger.*

opportunity for the people to make an offering to missions but also a means of bringing the work of the Woman's Board to the attention of the Church.

Through the cooperation of T. A. Havron, editor of the *Cumberland Presbyterian Banner,* space was given in the *Banner* for a regular Woman's Board of Missions department. Mrs. Clay edited this department from 1907 until 1917. Mrs. Walter Crawford, of Paris, Tennessee, succeeded her. After the *Cumberland Presbyterian* was returned to the Cumberland Presbyterian Church in 1910, Mrs. C. M. Zwingle edited a similar department in that periodical.

Miss Mary H. Stephenson, of Petersburg, Illinois, edited the *Monthly Topic Leaflet* providing program suggestions for the auxiliaries. Upon her resignation in 1911, Mrs. J. T. Slaton accepted this responsibility.

Until 1911 the Woman's Board maintained its office in the home of Henry J. Graf, in Evansville; Mrs. Graf had been named its secretary-treasurer in 1907. Subsequently, until the office was moved to Nashville in 1925, space was rented in commercial buildings in Evansville: in the Hartmetz Building, 1911-1917, and then in the American Trust Building.

Mrs. Mattie Ashburn became president of the Woman's Board in 1907 and served until December 1910. When she resigned, the first vice-president, Mrs. Conn, was elevated to the office of president and served until the Convention at Birmingham in 1916, when she was succeeded by Mrs. Clay.

Until 1916 organizers were employed for periods of time to work in the various synods. Among those who are known to have served in that capacity were Mrs. Joanna Alexander and Miss Kate Vaughn, Tennessee; Miss Julia McCaslin and Miss Ollie Glass, Texas; Miss Louvinia Wilson, Kentucky; and Mrs. Anna Knoch, Illinois. By 1916 the organizing and sustaining of new auxiliaries was left to the synods and presbyteries.

In August 1908, Gam Sing Quah announced his intention of returning to China as a missionary to the people of his native land. Shortly after he communicated to the Board his call to China, his wife died; nevertheless, he determined to go ahead with his plans to return to China. The missionary auxiliary of the church at Knoxville, Tennessee, where Mrs. Ashburn was then residing, assumed the greater part of his salary. On October 21, 1909, Gam and his young adopted son, Finis Ewing Gam, sailed for China. (He subsequently remarried.) The Knoxville auxiliary continued with the major support of Gam until 1918, when Kentucky Synod assumed that responsibility.

Following Gam's departure, the Rev. Wong Hong became acting superintendent of the San Francisco mission. He was succeeded by the Rev. W. D. Hawkins, who served from September 1910 until November 1911.

The Rev. J. S. Draper became superintendent in January 1912. A number of other persons worked in the mission during this time, among them the Rev. Tom Jung, who became pastor of the church in 1916; Miss Sallie Herbert, formerly of the mountain mission in North Carolina; and Miss Julia McCaslin.

Sometime during the year 1912-1913 a mission was opened among the Chinese in Oakland, California, with Hawkins as superintendent. A small congregation was organized there in 1917 or a little earlier.[32]

Meanwhile, after many difficulties in obtaining a place to hold public worship services, Gam opened a mission in Canton, China. He supplemented his regular preaching services by street preaching, visitation, and personal work. A reading room was set up at the mission, and, in February 1911, a girls' school was begun. Churches at Canton and Sha Kai were organized in 1912 and came under the care of California Presbytery. During 1914, missions were begun at Honam and Ti Won, and in 1915 at Tai Chung.[33]

During this period the Woman's Board aided considerably in the home field, sometimes by direct gifts and sometimes through the General Assembly's Board of Missions. In 1908, Miss Herbert was sent to assist in the work at Colorado Springs. In 1910-1911, $900 was given through the Assembly's Board for the work in Colorado, Arkansas, and Oklahoma. In 1911-1912, $750 was given for the work in Missouri, Iowa, Ohio, and Pennsylvania. That given Missouri was used to supplement the salary of the pastor at Sedalia. In 1911-1912 the Woman's Board gave a total of $3,250 to special home mission projects; in 1912-1913, $2,657.50; and in 1913-1914, $835.03.[34]

Named to constitute the Board of Sunday School and Young People's Work in 1906 were the Rev. T. Ashburn, the Rev. J. T. Barbee, William Reister, of Evansville, Indiana, and William Reiber, of Decatur, Illinois.[35] The General Assembly in 1907 directed that there be two departments: a Sunday school department and a Christian Endeavor department. The latter was urged to arrange as early as possible a Denominational Reading Course for the education of the young people in the history, doctrines, policy, and spirit of the Cumberland Presbyterian Church.[36] In 1908, Ashburn was nominated by the General Assembly to be a member of the Board of Trustees of the United Society of Christian Endeavor.[37]

In 1908, also, a recommendation was adopted that the money contributed by the Sunday schools and young people's societies be used for the support of one or more missionaries among the white congregations in Choctaw Presbytery, Indianola Synod. J. S. Lish was the missionary aided by this Board, and in 1908-1909 the amount of the support was $283.60.[38] Some support for the mission work in Oklahoma was continued through this Board until 1913.

Meanwhile, the Board promoted the organization of Sunday schools and young people's societies and the holding of institutes and conventions in different parts of the Church. Emphasis was placed upon the Teachers' Training Course, organized classes, the cradle roll and home departments, grading of schools, and a more general observance of special days. In 1915 it was recommended that a teacher-training textbook be edited and published by one or more persons to be designated by the General Assembly.[39] The Rev. O. A. Barbee, the Rev. C. M. Zwingle, and T. Ashburn were appointed to this task. The result was the publication in 1920 of a textbook known as *The Student's Lamp,* written by Barbee.

Dissatisfaction over the participation of the Church in the United Society of Christian Endeavor was expressed by some. The Committee on Sunday School and Young People's Work, in its report to the General Assembly in 1908, while expressing the belief that the Church should have a distinctive denominational organization for its young people "when the time is ripe," expressed the opinion that the time had not yet come for such an organization.[40] In 1909, mention was made of the feeling expressed by some that the young people should be taken out of the Christian Endeavor organization because in Christian Endeavor conventions they would be associated with members of the Presbyterian Church, U. S. A. The young people would be more loyal to the Cumberland Presbyterian Church, it was claimed, if they were kept out of the interdenominational Christian Endeavor conventions. The Board pointed out, however, that no form of young people's organization could be made more denominational than Christian Endeavor, and the belief was expressed that the young people would be benefited by the broadening influence of such conventions. It was pointed out, too, that Christian Endeavor leaders were the first outside the denomination to recognize the Cumberland Presbyterian Church as still in existence after 1906, and that it was worth much to be thus recognized.[41] The question of withdrawal from Christian Endeavor came before several Assemblies, but the Board of Sunday School and Young People's Work stood firm in its conviction that the Church should not withdraw, and this position was supported by the General Assembly. Permission was given local churches, however, to organize their young people under whichever form was desired, either as Christian Endeavor societies or as Cumberland Presbyterian Young People's Societies.

In 1906, the publishing house at Nashville, Tennessee, passed into the hands of the Presbyterian Church, U. S. A. The *Cumberland Presbyterian* was continued under the editorship of the Rev. James E. Clarke as a Presbyterian paper. Those who stayed out of the union, however, had a fearless advocate in the *Cumberland Banner,* which since 1904 had been published as a privately owned enterprise by T. A. Havron, at Jasper, Tennessee. As of May 3, 1907, the name was changed to the *Cumberland Presbyterian Banner.* In December 1907, the *Banner* was moved to Tullahoma, Tennessee.

To meet the need for Sunday school literature, Tennessee Synod, in its meeting in the fall of 1906, appointed a committee to arrange for the publication of such literature.[42] This committee entered into contract with the Rev. J. R. Goodpasture, of Nashville, to produce and circulate six pieces of Sunday school literature: a *Senior Quarterly,* a *Junior Quarterly,* a *Primary Quarterly,* the *Cumberland Visitor, Our Little Children,* and a *Lesson Leaf.* If the enterprise made a net profit, Goodpasture was to receive up to $125 a month. In December 1908, the General Assembly's Board of Publication assumed the responsibility of publishing the literature, retaining Goodpasture as editor and business manager.[43]

On February 13, 1910, the Supreme Court of Tennessee affirmed the decision of the Chancery Court which gave the publishing house to the Cumberland Presbyterian Church. Meanwhile legal respresentatives of the Presbyterian Church, U. S. A., applied to the Federal District Court at Nashville for a restraining order to prevent the Cumberland Presbyterian Board of Publication from taking possession of the publishing house, but in March the case was dismissed for want of jurisdiction. The unionists then appealed to the United States Supreme Court.

Meanwhile, at 5 p. m. on February 23, 1910, the publishing house and all its business affairs were surrendered to the Board of Publication of the Cumberland Presbyterian Church.[44] Already the Board had elected R. L. Baskette as general manager. The Rev. A. N. Eshman was named to serve temporarily as editor of the *Cumberland Presbyterian.* Both were members of the Board. Effective June 1, 1910, J. L. Hudgins was elected editor of the *Cumberland Presbyterian* at a salary of $1,800 per year. Goodpasture surrendered the business part of his contract to the Board as of March 1 but continued to serve as editor of the Sunday school literature. The week following the surrender of the publishing house, Clarke, who had been editor of the *Cumberland Presbyterian,* began publication of the *Presbyterian Advance* at another location in Nashville.

Although there was rejoicing among Cumberland Presbyterians over recovery of the publishing house, the acquisition of this prize proved not to be an unmixed blessing. In the first place, the operation prior to 1906 had been geared to supplying the needs of a denomination with 185,000 members, a considerably larger operation than could be maintained under the changed conditions in which the Church now found itself. Although the publishing house prior to 1906 had shown a net profit from $6,000 to $10,000 annually, such success could not be realized under conditions existing in 1910, when the volume of business was necessarily reduced.

Furthermore, the total indebtedness of the publishing house, as reported in 1910, was $50,648.09. This figure included a bonded indebtedness of $20,500. It included, also, some $15,000 in accounts payable to the Presbyterian Board, mostly for books and supplies which had been shipped to the book depository established at Nashville upon the taking over of the publishing house in 1906.[45]

Again, possession of the publishing house brought up the question as to who should be editor of the *Cumberland Presbyterian*. Many people assumed that T. A. Havron, who had published the *Banner* on his own since 1904, would be named editor, yet this did not happen. The Board considered purchasing independent papers and merging them with the *Cumberland Presbyterian* but decided that this should not be attempted until the pending litigation should be finally settled. Meanwhile the *Cumberland Presbyterian* was to be published "without prejudice to any other paper."[46] The failure of the Board to consider seriously the election of Havron as editor resulted in many expressions of dissatisfaction on the part of his friends. Leaders in the Church became divided over the policy of the Board, those who approved advocating a two-paper policy, and others contending that there should be one church paper with Havron as editor.

The Board of Publication also became involved in a lawsuit brought by W. B. Baird, manager of the publishing house under the Presbyterian Church, U. S. A. The occasion for this suit was the publication of the Board's report to the General Assembly in 1910 and an article in the *Cumberland Presbyterian* supposed to have been written by R. L. Baskette containing references which Baird interpreted as reflecting upon his integrity.

Although not directly due to the transfer of the publishing house, another vexing question arose concerning actions of the Board with relation to J. R. Goodpasture, editor of the Sunday school literature.

The financial affairs of the publishing house seem to have reached a crisis sometime prior to the meeting of the General Assembly at Warrensburg, Missouri, in 1912, for in that year, along with the report of the Board of Publication, a minority report was submitted by Baskette, who since the previous Assembly had resigned as general manager. The minority report alleged that the Board's report was not in reality a report of the Board of Publication, since the Board, due to lack of a quorum, had not met to consider it. He cited various instances of abnormal valuations which gave the impression of an increase in assets when in reality there had been no such increase. Actual control of the affairs of the publishing house, he alleged, was not in the hands of the Board, but of one member of the Board. Exception was also taken to the fact that all reference to the Sunday school literature was omitted from the Board's report. Baskette tendered his resignation as a member of the Board and urged that the Assembly appoint an entirely new Board of Publication or that the "Lackey Law" be enforced.[47] The latter reference was to a resolution introduced by W. J. Lackey and adopted by the General Assembly in 1909. This resolution provided that there should be no more than nine members on any board, that one-third of the members of each board should be elected of "new material" each year, and that no individual should be a member of more than one board.[48]

The matter of Goodpasture's employment came to the attention of the General Assembly's Committee on Publication even though there was no mention of the matter in the Board's report. In a meeting held on May 5, 1911, the Board, allegedly without previous notice, had voted to reduce Goodpasture's salary by the amount of twenty-five dollars per month effective July 1, 1911.[49] This action was taken in apparent disregard of the terms of a contract made on August 30, 1909, which provided that at least thirteen weeks' notice must be given in case of a termination of the contract, and that this must be done only at the beginning of a quarter. Whether or not the General Assembly in 1911 was aware of the action taken by the Board, it adopted a recommendation that Goodpasture be reelected as Sunday school editor, but with no mention of salary.[50] The Committee on Publication appointed at the General Assembly in 1912 made a report on the troublesome questions before it in which it asserted its belief that "that which is herein recommended has been divinely inspired and that it is for the glory of God and for the advancement of His cause through the agency of the Cumberland Presbyterian Church." Included was a recommendation "that our present editor, Rev. J. R. Goodpasture, be continued as editor of our Sunday School literature on a salary of $1,500.00 per annum."[51]

Apparently the Board of Publication did not accept the doctrine of the "plenary inspiration" of the Committee's recommendations. It construed the Assembly's action as a recommendation and not as an order. Since July 1911, Goodpasture had been accepting the one hundred dollars per month under protest as "on salary." Now when a check for this amount was tendered him he refused to accept it because it did not include the full amount which the Assembly had directed. Thereafter, and until the General Assembly met in 1913, the Board paid him nothing.

Among those who were critical of the policies of the Board of Publication were some of the leaders in Missouri Synod. The Board therefore sent J. L. Hudgins as its representative to the meeting of Missouri Synod. When a resolution was introduced calling on the Board of Publication to give reasons why it was not paying Goodpasture the salary recommended by the Assembly, Hudgins made a speech defending the Board's position. He alleged that Goodpasture had failed to look after orders for Sunday school literature as he (Hudgins) had looked after subscriptions to the *Cumberland Presbyterian;* that he spent time writing a novel which should have been devoted to the work for which he was hired; that he devoted much time to superintending his farm; that the action of the Assembly in fixing Goodpasture's salary at $1,500 was the result of a compromise and was "railroaded" through the Assembly; and that Goodpasture had not entered into the fight in defense of the policy of the publishing house.[52] Goodpasture requested Lebanon Presbytery, of which both he and Hudgins were members, to investigate these allegations. A committee of the presbytery, after investigating the matter, made a report completely exonerating Goodpasture.[53]

In the spring of 1913, A. N. Eshman, who was still a member of the Board, prepared a circular letter, a copy of which was procured and published by the editor of the *Cumberland Presbyterian Banner.* In it Eshman denounced Havron, Goodpasture, and, without calling his name, J. L. Goodknight, Stated Clerk of the General Assembly. He described the work of the editor of Sunday school literature as an "easy-chair—hammock—shade tree—work-when-you-feel-like-it-job" which he said Goodpasture would be glad to do for $600 a year if he could not get the Board to pay him more. Men could be found in almost any synod, he asserted, who could do the job as well as Goodpasture was doing it. Havron was accused of stirring up opposition to the boards of the Church, and Goodknight, it was implied, had not given a proper accounting of the funds he had handled.[54] A partial retraction of the latter charge, submitted by Eshman, was later published at Goodknight's behest.[55]

Thus the stage was set for an airing of the controversy at the 1913 General Assembly. The Board of Publication in its report cited three situations as barriers which had hindered the work of the publishing house: (1) the fact that the house was in litigation, (2) that the various receiverships which the unionists had attempted against the house had caused creditors to press for their claims, and (3) that editorials and contributions tending to destroy confidence in the Board of Publication had appeared in the columns of the *Cumberland Presbyterian Banner.*[56] The Board presented its interpretation of the Goodpasture matter. Goodpasture, as editor of Sunday school literature, also made a report to the General Assembly in which he reviewed the history of his relationship to the enterprise. This report, though excluded by Assembly action from being published in its Minutes, was printed in full by the *Banner.*[57] The Committee on Publication recommended that $300 be paid

Goodpasture out of the General Assembly's treasury and that "the Board of
Publication be urged to meet its acknowledged obligation to Brother Goodpasture out of the first available funds." The following recommendation
regarding the status of Goodpasture was adopted:

It is the sense of your committee that Rev. J. R. Goodpasture is an employee of this Assembly, under the direction of the Board of Publication,
and as such he is entitled to a salary of $1,200.00 per year and we recommend
that he be continued as Sunday School Editor at the salary stated.

Regarding the issue between the Board of Publication and the editor of
the *Banner,* the following recommendation was adopted:

We recommend that the *Banner* be requested to refrain from all adverse
criticisms of all the enterprises of the Church for the Assembly year and
that Brother A. N. Eshman be requested to send out no more letters concerning this unfortunate question and the membership of the denomination be
requested to withdraw their support from any one who may violate these
arrangements.[58]

Shortly after the 1913 General Assembly, Goodpasture resigned as editor
of the Sunday school literature. The Rev. T. H. Padgett was then chosen
editor of the *Senior Quarterly* and the *Advanced Quarterly;* Rev. A. C.
Biddle, editor of the *Junior Quarterly;* and Miss Allie May Taylor, editor
of the *Primary Quarterly* and the children's papers. Several other contributors
were chosen with a view to enriching the content of the literature. There was
no general editor of Sunday school literature after Goodpasture's resignation
until 1917, when T. Ashburn became editor.

The appeal of the unionists to the United States Supreme Court resulted
in a directive to the Federal District Court in Nashville to assume jurisdiction and try the publishing house case. The result was a decision, rendered
in July 1913, that although the Cumberland Presbyterian Board of Publication was legally in control, it must conduct the affairs of the publishing house
for the benefit of the Presbyterian Church, U. S. A. The recognition of the
Cumberland Presbyterian Board as being legally in control made it possible
for this Board to negotiate several matters. The Board of the Presbyterian
Church, U. S. A., agreed to turn over to the Cumberland Presbyterian
Board all plates of books which were distinctively Cumberland Presbyterian,
the subscription list and good will of the *Cumberland Presbyterian,* and all
manuscript material which was in hand. It also agreed to change the name of
the corporation within six months so as to eliminate the name "Cumberland
Presbyterian." [59]

At this juncture, A. N. Eshman, who owned a printing plant in the Radnor area of Nashville, offered to publish the *Cumberland Presbyterian,* the Sunday school literature, and a limited number of denominational books for one year from September 1, 1913, without loss to the Board. This was with the understanding that the Board would turn over to him certain books which had been received through the compromise settlement with the Presbyterian board. He was to be allowed one hundred dollars monthly salary provided the business should earn it.[60]

Following the loss of the publishing house, J. L. Hudgins, on his own initiative and through the columns of the *Cumberland Presbyterian,* appealed to the Church at large for gifts and subscriptions in the amount of $10,000 as a trust fund to equip a modest printing plant for the use and benefit of the Board of Publication. The response was encouraging. Subscriptions totaled $12,500. The Board of Publication voted to accept the cash and subscriptions thus raised, subject to approval of the General Assembly, and made Hudgins trustee of the fund.[61] The General Assembly in its 1914 meeting approved this action and urged that in purchasing and operating a printing plant the Board avoid incurring any indebtedness. The plant should be operated to publish the needed literature of the Church and not for commercial purposes; however, the Board was allowed the privilege of doing such printing as would not interfere with the object for which the plant was established.[62]

The same General Assembly directed the Board of Publication to procure a charter from the state of Tennessee and divided the membership of the Board into three classes with terms to expire at the end of one, two, and three years in accordance with the General Assembly's regulations. The charter was procured on May 11, 1915.

Meanwhile a compromise was reached in the libel suit brought by W. B. Baird whereby $750 was awarded to the plaintiff.[63] This sum, together with attorney's fee of $100 and costs of $215.36 in the publishing house suit in the federal court, was raised by Eshman through private subscription.

The 1915 General Assembly authorized the purchase of Eshman's printing equipment; however, the actual purchase was not effected until October 22, 1915. The amount authorized to be expended in the purchase was $10,000, and the inventory of machinery and equipment totaled $11,706.84. Eshman, who was elected general manager for the year ending October 1, 1916, guaranteed that the profit from the operation would be at least $1,706.84, and this amount was credited on the purchase price. The face of the notes for money which had been borrowed by Eshman from the publication fund, totaling $4,561, was also credited on the purchase price, and the Board executed notes for $1,869, for $1,800, and for $1,800 respectively, to be paid at the end of one, two, and three years after the date of purchase;

however, Hudgins had collected a sufficient amount for the publication fund that $1,469 was paid at the time of purchase, thus reducing the indebtedness to $4,000.[64]

The General Assembly in 1916 consolidated the Board of Publication and the Board of Sunday School and Young People's Work. T. Ashburn, who since 1906 had served on the latter board and was familiar with this phase of the work, was employed as field man to give all of his time to the development and expansion of Sunday school and young people's work. He began his work September 8, 1916. Eshman continued as manager of the printing plant until January 6, 1917, when he resigned. Hudgins was then made business manager, the duties of this position being added to his work as editor of the *Cumberland Presbyterian* without additional salary.[65] In his report as manager to the 1917 General Assembly the printing plant was referred to as the New Cumberland Press, a name which it bore for the next several years.[66]

Unfortunately, the controversy between the *Cumberland Presbyterian Banner* and the Board of Publication continued. In 1917 the Board complained of articles having appeared in the *Banner* which reflected on the honesty and integrity of members of the Board.[67] The *Banner* had lost support because of its controversial character. Many people grew tired of its continuing references to the union controversy. The battle was over, they held, and the Church ought to give itself to more constructive pursuits. Yet because the Presbyterian Church, U. S. A., had thus far refused to recognize the existence of the Cumberland Presbyterian Church, the editor of the *Banner* insisted that Cumberland Presbyterians ought not to have fraternal relations with ministers or other representatives of the Presbyterian Church, U. S. A. Cumberland Presbyterian ministers, it was contended, ought not to participate in ministerial associations to which ministers of the Presbyterian Church, U. S. A., belonged. Preceding the meeting of the General Assembly at Memphis in 1915, when the pastor host, C. H. Walton, addressed a letter to both papers asking that commissioners and visitors to the Assembly exercise restraint in their references to the Presbyterian Church, U. S. A., while attending the Assembly, the *Banner* refused to publish the letter.[68]

The Board of Education in its report to the General Assembly in 1907 was unable to report any school as being under the control of the Cumberland Presbyterian Church. The Assembly did recommend Radnor College, a school for young ladies which was owned and operated in Nashville by A. N. Eshman, as being a suitable place for Cumberland Presbyterians to send their daughters.[69]

In July 1907, however, announcement was made by the Board of Trustees of Bethel College that a building had been secured and that Bethel College would open in September.[70] The building obtained was a store building located on Stonewall Street in McKenzie, which was rented for twenty dollars per month. While President Johnston and his faculty continued to operate a school under the auspices of the Presbyterian Church, U. S. A., in the college building on Cherry Avenue, the Cumberland Presbyterian Board of Trustees opened a rival school in the rented building. J. W. Burney was president for the first three months of the 1907-1908 session, at the end of which time he retired. Charles H. McCord was then placed in charge, but at the end of the third quarter he was forced to give up the work on account of failing health, and the school closed. During the year the General Assembly's Board of Education contributed $800 toward the operation of Bethel College.[71]

Meanwhile the General Assembly's Board of Education made arrangement with the Board of Trustees of Bethel College for the opening of a theological school at the college and named the Rev. P. F. Johnson dean. The Board of Trustees of Bethel College named Johnson president of the college also, and during the school year 1908-1909 he served in a dual capacity. Associated with him on the college faculty were J. R. Garrett, Miss Iva Owen, Miss Gerda Pratt, Miss Nell Gains, Miss Grace Garrett, and Miss Edna Stevenson (some of whom were in charge of classes below the college level). The report of the Board of Trustees to West Tennessee Synod in October 1908 stated that Bethel had students from four states: Tennessee, Kentucky, Mississippi, and Texas. The treasurer's report for the preceding year showed receipts of $1,638.39, including the $800 contributed by the General Assembly's Board of Education, and disbursements of $1,640.64, part of which was spent in equipping the rented building.[72] At the end of the 1908-1909 school year Johnson resigned as president of Bethel College to devote his full time to the theological school.

Following the decision of the Tennessee Supreme Court in the Fayetteville case, the Board of Trustees filed an injunction to obtain possession of the college property. Possession was obtained in time for the Cumberland Presbyterian school to occupy the college building for its 1909 commencement exercises. By decree of the Chancery Court at Huntingdon in January 1910, the college property in McKenzie was awarded to the Cumberland Presbyterian Church. The Presbyterian Board of Trustees agreed not to appeal the case or allow the names of its members to be used in making an appeal, and the Cumberland Presbyterian Board agreed not to prosecute its suit for damages for the period the property had been in the possession of the unionists.[73]

Johnson was succeeded as president by N. J. Finney, a graduate of Cumberland University, who had served as president of Cumberland Female College at McMinnville, Tennessee. During the year 1909-1910, Finney taught languages and sciences; J. R. Garrett, English and mathematics; B. F. Hooker, language and mathematics; Miss Gerda Pratt, music; Miss Ollie Dinwiddie, expression; Mrs. T. H. Baker, art; and J. W. McDonald, telegraphy.[74] Receipts for tuition in 1909-1910 totaled $2,015.25; in 1910-1911, $1,260.25; and in 1912-1913, $2,339.25. In 1909-1910 the $2,015.25 received was divided equally among Finney, Garrett, and Hooker. The other teachers received only fees paid by students taking private lessons. In 1910 the Board of Education arranged to supplement the salaries of the president and two teachers in Bethel College so as to provide a salary of $,1,000 for the president and $750 for each of two teachers.[75] According to the report of the Board of Trustees of Bethel College to West Tennessee Synod in October 1911, the Board of Education contributed $1,014.75 to Bethel College during the preceding year.[76]

Despite lean years the school was continued in operation. In 1911-1912, Finney, in addition to his duties as president, was teaching Greek and natural sciences; Garrett, English and biology; and W. N. Calhoun, Latin and mathematics.[77] In 1913-1914 Finney was teaching Latin, Greek, and philosophy, while G. L. Meek was teaching mathematics and English, and Garrett, history, political science, and biology.[78] Among teachers of special subjects during this period were Miss Opal Pratt, voice; Mrs. Gladys Gwin Kelley, piano; Miss Grace A. Ross, oratory and physical culture; Mrs. Gertrude Green, expression and physical culture; Mrs. Ollie Dinwiddie Smith, expression and physical culture; and Miss Bess E. Dewitt Finney, violin.

In the fall of 1913 a committee of four was appointed by West Tennessee Synod to meet with the Board of Trustees to formulate plans for a "Greater Bethel." A goal of $20,000 was set: $5,000 for improvements and equipment and $16,000 for endowment. By the time of the meeting of synod in 1914, $1,289.60 in cash had been received, and $2,998.15 had been pledged by individuals and churches in the synod and $1,330 by the businessmen of McKenzie.[79] Apparently only a relatively small portion of these pledges was ever paid; however, two notes representing indebtedness which had been incurred in the operation of the college were paid, and some needed improvements made on the building.

During this period the enrollment varied, but during several sessions it exceeded one hundred. A considerable number of these were ministerial students who were charged only half tuition.

A new crisis was faced in the fall of 1917, because of the involvement of the United States in World War I. The Board had to borrow money to insure the operation of the college. The sum of $600 was borrowed to supplement tuition receipts. It was agreed that any tuition receipts over and above $825 would be used to repay the loan. If the tuition receipts should exceed $1,425, the three teachers in the literary school would reap the benefit of such receipts.[80]

Meanwhile, Cumberland Presbyterians in Texas became interested in establishing a college. In October 1910, Texas Synod appointed a committee to investigate the possibility of building a school in Texas.[81] This committee was offered college property at Leonard, Texas, consisting of an eight-acre campus on which were a three-story school building and a girls' dormitory. This property, formerly occupied by Manton College, was offered to Texas Synod on condition that it pay off a debt of $7,000 and establish a school.

At a called meeting of synod held at Leonard June 29, 1911, the property was accepted and arrangements made to open the school in September under the name of Cumberland College. A board of trustees was named, consisting of the Rev. J. W. Pearson, Joe F. Hall, John W. Groves, W. W. Witcher, and B. B. Braly.[82] Pearson was elected temporary president of the school. He, with four other teachers, opened the school September 12, 1911, with an enrollment of nineteen students in the literary department, eleven in music, and four in art.

At the regular meeting of synod in October, John W. Groves, of Olney, Texas, was appointed to superintend the raising of $10,000: $7,000 to pay the debt on the buildings and grounds, and $3,000 for repairs. Key men were appointed in the various presbyteries to assist with the campaign, and $850 was pledged before synod adjourned.[83]

Texas Synod meanwhile had become the beneficiary of the bequest of Mrs. Tennie C. Sheppard, of Round Rock, Texas, whose husband had given the Sheppard Home, which was still in litigation. Anticipating that the original Sheppard Home would be awarded to the Presbyterian Church, U. S. A., she left her home in Round Rock to be used as an old ministers' home. She also bequeathed $6,000 to Texas Synod, $1,000 being designated for each of the following causes: the Cumberland Presbyterian school in Texas (for endowment), the education of young ministers in Texas Synod, ministerial relief in the synod, church extension in the synod, home missions, and foreign missions. The bequest was an endowment fund. Only the interest was to be used. Before synod adjourned a motion was passed authorizing the lending of the $6,000 to Cumberland College.[84] With the loan and additional funds raised, the $7,000 debt was paid.

The lending of the proceeds of the Sheppard bequest to Cumberland College proved to be but the beginning of sorrows. The number of students continued small (usually about twenty-five). Funds came in very slowly, and there were deficits the first two years. By March 1914, W. J. Lackey, who meanwhile had become president, held unpaid claims of $709 for money he had advanced for the operation of the school, and there was other indebtedness totaling $2,553 besides the Sheppard bequest. Opposition to continuing the school had developed within the synod, based on a lack of faith in its ultimate success.[85] In the fall of 1915, the Rev. W. A. Boone, who was employed by the Board of Trustees of the Cumberland Presbyterian Theological Seminary to teach theology to the ministerial students in Cumberland College, was serving as president.[86]

For a time there was a glimmer of hope. When synod met in October 1916, the Rev. I. V. Stine had been in the field for five months raising money for the school. Working at a salary of eighty dollars per month and expenses, he had visited most of the churches in Denton, Dallas-Bonham, Marshall, and Texas-Greenville presbyteries. He had collected $958.95 ($241.21 above his salary and expenses) and had received $7,829.50 in notes payable one-tenth each year. Although the indebtedness was now $5,841.27, not counting the Sheppard bequest on which no interest was ever paid, there was hope that through a continuation of his work adequate support would be forthcoming.[87] This hope was frustrated, however, by his death in May 1917.

On December 28, 1917, a called meeting of synod was held, and the Board of Trustees recommended that the school be closed January 8, 1918, and the property sold.[88] On January 2, 1918, the two banks in Leonard

A. N. ESHMAN
(1865-1951)

J. L. GOODKNIGHT
(1846-1914)

filed suit and levied on the property, and it was sold to the banks for $1,000. Later this judgment was set aside, and the property was sold for a better price with the understanding that the proceeds would be prorated between the banks and the teachers and other persons at Leonard to whom money was owed.[89] The Board of Trustees of Texas Synod also brought suit to recover the Sheppard bequest. When the property was sold and other debts settled, Texas Synod received only $248.35 of the $6,000 loaned to the college.[90]

Thus the attempt to found a college in Texas ended disastrously. A number of ministerial students were educated there, and probably as many as two dozen pulpits in North and East Texas were supplied by students of Cumberland College during its brief existence. The division within the synod over the policies followed in maintaining the school, however, was difficult to heal, and a sense of failure hung over the Cumberland Presbyterian Church in Texas for years. Bethel College had escaped a similar fate by limiting teachers' salaries to tuition receipts.

As early as 1907 the need for a theological school was emphasized, and a committee was appointed to negotiate with the trustees and faculty of Bethel College in regard to establishing a theological school in connection with that institution.[91] As has already been indicated, the Board of Education established such a school at McKenzie in 1908 with P. F. Johnson as dean and sole professor. The school was opened September 1, 1908. Enrollment the first year reached twenty-two, of whom twenty-one were Cumberland

N. J. FINNEY
(1846-1931)

P. F. JOHNSON
(1852-1925)

Presbyterians. A salary of $800 was paid to Johnson.[92] In 1909-1910 there were thirty-seven students. These were also taking work in Bethel College. The following year there were forty-four students, and in 1911-1912, fifty-five.

Meanwhile, action was taken looking toward establishing a permanent theological school. On May 5, 1911, the Board of Trustees of the Cumberland Presbyterian Theological Seminary (appointed in 1910) applied to the state of Tennessee for a charter of incorporation.[93] Suit was filed for possession of Cumberland University. Early in 1913 a compromise settlement was proposed by the Board of Trustees of Cumberland University. The sum of $37,500 would be paid to the Cumberland Presbyterian Church if it would relinquish all claims against Cumberland University. The General Assembly voted to accept the compromise provided the attorneys would accept 10 per cent of the proceeds as their fee. Action was taken setting aside this fund to be held intact as a trust fund, the income alone to be used for educational pruposes.[94] The $33,750 thus received gave the Cumberland Presbyterian Church its first educational endowment since 1906. Meanwhile, the theological school had graduated its first class in 1913. A member of this class, the Rev. A. D. Rudolph, served on the General Assembly committee which recommended acceptance of the compromise and was influential in having the fund designated as endowment.

The Board of Trustees of the Theological Seminary took charge of the school as of October 17, 1913. Thereafter the work of the Board of Education consisted mainly of providing financial aid to ministerial students attending college and seminary. In the fall of 1914 the Rev. S. H. Braly was added to the faculty of the Seminary, and the election of both Johnson and Braly was confirmed by the General Assembly in 1915. The same Assembly directed the Board of Trustees to elect an additional faculty member and place him at Cumberland College, in Texas.[95] W. A. Boone was the person elected.

In 1914 an effort was launched to raise an additional $100,000 for the Theological Seminary: one-third for buildings and equipment and two-thirds for permanent endowment.[96] By 1916 the endowment had increased to $36,410, and $2,144.40 had been received as income from endowment. Johnson was receiving $1,000 a year, Braly, $750, and Boone, $600. Additional subscriptions for endowment in the amount of $21,000 were reported.[97]

The General Assembly of 1917 was asked to take steps to locate the Theological Seminary permanently and to discontinue the practice of dividing the funds with Cumberland College; however, the Assembly directed that a teacher be provided at Cumberland College another year.[98] Cumberland College was closed before another year passed.

A Committee on Tithing was first appointed at the General Assembly in 1913 following an address by Vint N. Bray, of Springfield, Missouri. The committee recommended that Bray, a ruling elder, be made the General Assembly's Tithing Secretary, that his address be published in pamphlet form, that pastors preach on tithing, and that "our people *be exhorted to adopt this plan,* secure in the belief that the blessings of *the Most High will surely follow."* [99]

In 1914 a Board of Tithing, consisting of nine members, was appointed.[100] By 1916, a total of about 2,500 tithers were enrolled, but it was reported that only about 300 of these were men.[101] In 1917 it was recommended that a field man be employed, and, at the platform meeting of the Board of Tithing, some $1,400 was received in cash and subscriptions for this purpose.[102] The employment of the man and the nature of the work accomplished belong to the next period of the denomination's history.

Such is the story of the development of the institutional life of the Cumberland Presbyterian Church from the state of chaos which existed in 1906 to about the year 1917. Of those who were thrust into places of leadership in this crisis, few were experienced in the kind of work they were called to do. What was done was accomplished through much sacrifice. Cumberland Presbyterians did not support the enterprises of the Church with their means as they might have done, although this failure may be partly explained by the fact that many of them, though not all, were having to rebuild churches in their home communities. The litigation growing out of the attempted union was also expensive. Nevertheless, the enterprises of the Church were reorganized and foundations were laid, without which the gains of subsequent years would have been impossible.

# 21

## BROADENING OF HORIZONS

*It should be done; it can be done; therefore, it must be done.*
Hannibal S. Seagle, in launching the campaign
for the educational movement, 1918

The United States of America officially entered World War I on April 6, 1917. The General Assembly of the Cumberland Presbyterian Church, which met in May at Lincoln, Illinois, apparently paid little attention to the fact that the nation was at war. The only action taken which recognized a state of war was the adoption of a resolution commending three men for appointment as chaplains in the armed forces.[1]

At the General Assembly held at Dallas, Texas, a year later, however, a patriotic service was held the first night.[2] On Friday afternoon a memorial service honoring the American soldier boys was held with addresses delivered by F. A. Seagle, T. A. Havron, and the Rev. I. K. Floyd, a chaplain in the United States Army who was then stationed at Camp Bowie, near Fort Worth. A large service flag was dedicated in honor of the Cumberland Presbyterian boys in the armed forces. A special War Work Committee was appointed, and a petition that the General Assembly set apart May 30, 1918, as a day of fasting and prayer, in accordance with President Woodrow Wilson's proclamation, was adopted.[3]

The War Work Committee recommended the creation of a special War Work Commission composed of five members. The duties of this body had mainly to do with forwarding to the War Department applications of Cumberland Presbyterian ministers who desired to be chaplains, assisting persons desiring to enter the army YMCA service, and supplying Cumberland Presbyterian chaplains with necessary equipment and with religious tracts and literature.[4]

A resolution was adopted endorsing the stand taken by President Wilson regarding the war, pledging him the support of the Church in his efforts to raise and equip a great army and navy, endorsing and encouraging the purchase of Liberty Bonds, Thrift Stamps, and War Savings Stamps, and pledging support to the Red Cross, the YMCA, and the YWCA in their war activities.[5]

Cumberland Presbyterians on the whole gave full support to the war effort and joined in the spirit of the times in regarding participation in the war as a campaign to make the world safe for democracy. The denomination's two papers supported the war effort. Lists of contributors to the War Work Fund being raised by the War Work Commission were published regularly in the *Cumberland Presbyterian Banner,* the editor of which served as the Commission's treasurer. Various articles, some written by others than Cumberland Presbyterians, appeared in the *Banner* supporting the righteousness of the American cause. When the Fourth Liberty Loan Drive was about to be launched, the editor of the *Cumberland Presbyterian* expressed the view that "We can conceive of no higher religious duty than that of aiding our government to back up the millions of young men now under the colors of the country in our interests." [6] The ministers of the Cumberland Presbyterian Church on the whole joined with those of other churches in selling Liberty Bonds and War Savings Stamps. Apparently these were sometimes offered for sale in the churches at the Sunday morning worship hour, for at least one minister protested against this practice.[7] The writer remembers, also, a pastor who raised some questions regarding the assumed righteousness of the American cause, to the dismay of some of the members of his flock. It is probable, however, that his attitude was the exception rather than the rule.

Some ministers had gone so far as to proclaim that American soldiers who died in this war would be assured of eternal life. Cumberland Presbyterian ministers, however, seem not to have espoused this point of view. Soldiers, like anyone else, would be saved only through repentance and faith.[8]

Altogether, eight Cumberland Presbyterian ministers received appointments as chaplains in the armed forces. These were I. K. Floyd, M. L. Clemens, A. C. Stribling, W. Y. Durrett, T. L. Wood, Thomas Dyer, J. G. Stewart, and John A. Deaver. The last-named chaplain was killed in battle in France on October 12, 1918. Clemens was severely wounded.

Beginning in 1919, relations with the Presbyterian Church, U. S. A., took a turn for the better. The General Assembly of that church, meeting at Saint Louis in May 1919, sent a communication of greetings to the Cumberland Presbyterian General Assembly for the first time since 1906. This communication did not reach the Stated Clerk of the General Assembly until November 9, 1919, and was presented at the 1920 Assembly. The Assembly accepted and reciprocated the greetings, joining in the desire "for the day when all barriers against a common fellowship shall have been removed."[9] Thereafter greetings between the two bodies were regularly exchanged.

With the decision of the United States Supreme Court in the Missouri case in May 1918, the era of the lawsuits resulting from the attempted union came to an end; however, the expense of the litigation had not been paid in full, and contributions to the Legal Fund had diminished to a mere trickle. To meet the remaining sum due W. C. Caldwell, an attorney of Trenton, Tennessee, who had been employed by the Cumberland Presbyterian Church in several cases, as well as amounts due individuals who had advanced money for court costs and legal fees, the General Assembly in 1916 resolved to ask each presbytery to contribute an amount equal to five cents per member annually over a four-year period for the Legal Fund.[10] This effort was only partially successful, for in 1924 it was reported that thirteen presbyteries had paid their quotas in full, seventeen had paid part, and thirty-seven had paid nothing.[11] Meager contributions continued until the year 1928-1929 when it was reported by the Legal Fund Committee that nothing had been received.[12] In 1929 the Committee was dismissed.

Meanwhile, claims had been filed by Lamb and Lamb, a law firm of Fayetteville, Tennessee, for services rendered in connection with the publishing house suit, for which $2,300 was yet due, and a claim of $2,750 for services rendered in carrying suits in Alabama and Mississippi to the supreme courts of those states. In 1927 the General Assembly directed the Board of Publication to pay Lamb and Lamb the $2,300 due in the publishing house case at the rate of $500 per year. It also voted to pay for the Alabama and Mississippi cases out of rents received from a wheat farm in Kansas which had become the property of the Church by bequest.[13] Final settlement with Lamb and Lamb was made in 1929. Thus was written the final chapter in the lengthy and expensive litigation growing out of the controversial "union" attempt of 1906.

During and shortly after World War I, two steps were taken by the Cumberland Presbyterian Church which were to have great effects on its subsequent development. One was the adoption of a plan to raise $500,000 as endowment for a literary and theological school. The other was the setting up of a denominational budget to finance the boards and agencies of the General Assembly.

On February 20, 1918, an Educational Convention met in Memphis, Tennessee, for the purpose of considering the educational needs of the Church. Thirty-four persons attended. Recognizing that the educational needs of the denomination were being met only in part, and believing that the time had come when some definite plan for concerted action should be adopted, the Convention proposed that the General Assembly establish and maintain one educational institution which should include both literary and theological departments. The Assembly was asked to provide for the raising of an endowment of $500,000 for the literary department. Provisions for the raising of this endowment were not to interfere with the existing plan to raise a theological endowment.[14]

This plan was brought before the General Assembly at Dallas in May 1918 and received the Assembly's enthusiastic support. An Endowment Fund Committee of nine persons was appointed to promote the campaign for the half million dollars. This committee was headed by Hannibal S. Seagle, of Chattanooga, Tennessee. The editors of both the *Cumberland Presbyterian* and the *Cumberland Presbyterian Banner* tendered the services of their papers in the promotion of the campaign. During the General Assembly word was received by telegram of a bequest made by Mrs. Cynthia Smith, of Decatur, Illinois, to the Cumberland Presbyterian Church. The Assembly resolved to place the proceeds of this bequest in the Educational Endowment Fund.[15]

Soon after the Assembly, by agreement of the committees involved, the campaigns for the two endowment funds were merged with the understanding that one-fifth of the amount raised would go into theological endowment until the amount of $100,000 was raised for that purpose. It was also agreed that subscriptions should become binding when $250,000 had been subscribed.

The actual beginning of the campaign was delayed on account of the war, but it was launched in February 1919, with full-page announcements in both church papers. Meanwhile, key men had been appointed in the various presbyteries, and 50,000 subscription notes had been printed. Using as a motto "It should be done; it can be done; therefore, it must be done," Seagle opened the campaign with an address at Chattanooga on the first Sunday in February. He then visited in Kentucky Synod and later spoke in Knoxville, Greeneville, and Nashville, Tennessee. At this point be contracted influenza and pneumonia and died on March 22, 1919. His brother, F. A. Seagle, took up the mantle thus laid down and as acting secretary reported to the General Assembly in May that subscriptions had passed the $100,000 mark.[16]

At the General Assembly in 1919 F. A. Seagle was appointed a member of the Endowment Committee in place of his deceased brother, and the committee was changed to a Commission on Educational Endowment and directed to be incorporated. Meanwhile, at the suggestion of the Rev. Hugh S. McCord, tithing evangelist, a movement had been launched to endow a Hannibal Seagle chair of English Bible in the college to be established. This movement received the approval of the General Assembly.[17]

In the meantime, West Tennessee Synod offered Bethel College to the General Assembly on condition that it be adopted and maintained by the Assembly as a school for the whole Church. The Assembly deemed it unwise to accept the offer with the conditions accompanying it, but expressed a willingness to accept the college if it were left free to dispose of the property as it should see fit.[18] Bethel College was temporarily taken under the care of the General Assembly, however, and the income from the Cynthia Smith legacy was designated to be used to aid Bethel College until needed by the greater school to be established.[19] In 1919, the General Assembly received an unconditional offer of Bethel College, which was accepted. In its offer the Board of Trustees of Bethel College described the property as follows:

One building on four acres of ground, well situated; building in front is three stories high, in back, two stories; front hall seating capacity 200, and two class rooms. Auditorium on second floor, 40 x 70 feet; dormitory with sixteen rooms on second and third floors, dining room and kitchen in basement. With an expenditure of five thousand dollars, the building used only for teaching purposes, could accommodate three hundred students. The value of building and grounds for school purposes is, perhaps, about twenty thousand dollars—that is, a building similar to the college would cost at the very least twenty-five thousand dollars. As real estate, it is worth eight thousand dollars.

It was also stated that the total indebtedness of Bethel College was $724.13.

Bethel College was kept open during the war, the Board of Trustees stated, "only because our three literary teachers, Prof. N. J. Finney, Prof. J. R. Garrett, and Miss Grigsby, have been true and loyal to our school's interest." They had taught regardless of meager salary. There were fifty-three students during the year 1918-1919, but a number of these were ministerial and missionary students or children of preachers, who were charged only half tuition.[20]

The Board of Trustees of the Theological Seminary anticipated in the spring of 1918 that the Seminary might have to be closed, and the General

Assembly authorized the Board to use its discretion in the matter.[21] Fortunately the school was kept open, and seventeen students were enrolled.[22]

When the Educational Endowment Commission made its report on April 17, 1920, more than $222,000 had been subscribed to the endowment fund. By the time of the meeting of the General Assembly the $250,000 mark had been reached, and subscriptions became due and payable.[23] The Assembly appointed a committee of seven men, with an alternate for each, to receive proposals and bids for the location of the proposed literary and theological school.[24]

When the General Assembly met at Greenfield, Missouri, in 1921, a total of $291,893.60 had been subscribed to the endowment fund, and $132,006.37 had been paid. The committee to receive bids for the location of the school reported receipt of seven proposals. These came from Memphis, Chattanooga, Jackson, and McKenzie, Tennessee; Bowling Green, Kentucky; Greenfield, Missouri; and J. E. Eberts, of Warrensburg, Missouri.[25] By a vote of fifty-five to forty-three, the Assembly delayed the selection of a location for the school.[26]

The next General Assembly met at Greeneville, Tennessee, in May 1922. At this meeting only four proposals for the location of the school were received. When the vote was taken, McKenzie was the choice of forty-nine of the ninety-six commissioners participating and so was chosen as the location for the school. Nashville received forty-one votes; Jackson, four; and Memphis, two. McKenzie proposed to deed to the proper board of the Church eleven acres of land adjoining the Bethel College campus and to contribute $75,000 in cash.[27]

At this same Assembly three boards which had to do with the educational interests of the Church were merged: the Board of Education, the Board of Trustees of Bethel College, and the Board of Trustees of the Theological Seminary. The new board was called the Cumberland Presbyterian Board of Education. At the same time the following recommendation was adopted:

We further recommend that Bethel College be merged into, and become a part of the new school, should it finally be located at McKenzie, Tennessee; that for the present, said school shall be known as Bethel College.[28]

Following the acceptance of Bethel College by the General Assembly, some efforts were made to give financial relief to the college. In July 1919, the Board of Trustees met in joint session with the General Assembly's Board of Education "to consider with them the grave problems that confronted our Church along educational lines." [29] It was agreed that a faculty was needed, and that teachers should be guaranteed a sufficient salary to maintain themselves. The Cynthia Smith bequest had not yet become productive. Nevertheless, definite salaries were promised, and one teacher was added to the faculty. During the year 1919-1920 Bethel College received $715.70 from the Smith estate. During the year 1920-1921 the Board of Education aided Bethel College to the amount of nearly $3,000.[30]

In 1921, N. J. Finney was made president emeritus but was continued as a teacher. During the next two years the Rev. R. L. Keathley served as president. The General Assembly in 1921 recommended that the Endowment Commission pay to the trustees of Bethel College 70 per cent of the income from the endowment fund.[31] Under this plan some $4,900 was provided for the college during the ensuing year.

In 1923, the arrangements for the permanent location of the school at McKenzie having been completed, the school was organized with five departments: training school, literary, home economics, music, and theological. A faculty of sixteen persons was secured. Among the new faculty members was Shelton L. Beatty, of Milan, Tennessee, a graduate of the University of Tennessee who was employed to teach English and education. He reached his twenty-second birthday shortly after the opening of the school year. The following year he was made acting dean, and in 1925 he became dean of the college. The Rev. John W. Dishman came from the pastorate of the church at Milan to serve as Hannibal Seagle Professor of Bible. Joseph Rutledge Whitmer, of Kentucky, was elected president in time to be introduced to the General Assembly during its meeting at Fairfield, Illinois, in May 1923.[32] He was, at the time, one of the youngest college presidents in the United States, being thirty-three years of age.

The new Administration Building, erected with the $75,000 given by the people of McKenzie and vicinity, was completed in time to be dedicated on February 4, 1924.[33] In the meantime, the Church was the recipient of $100,000 bequeathed by John T. Laughlin, of New London, Iowa. The General Assembly in 1923 set aside $50,000 of this amount to be used in the erection of a girls' dormitory. This dormitory was ready for occupancy at the opening of school in the fall of 1924 and was named Laughlin Home. The Assembly appropriated $10,000 of the proceeds of the Laughlin bequest to furnish and equip the Administration Building and designated the remainder as endowment. The old college building, or a portion of it, was used as a boys' dormitory. Thus the reorganized Bethel College began its work auspiciously.

The "honeymoon" proved to be of short duration, however, for the Committee on Education appointed at the General Assembly at Nashville in 1925 found itself confronted with several grave problems. A student in Bethel College, James Denney, the son of one of the members of the new Board of Education, had been fatally injured in a football game with Union

ADMINISTRATION BUILDING, BETHEL COLLEGE, McKENZIE, TENNESSEE

"THE OLD LOG HOUSE" AT BETHEL COLLEGE

This campus landmark was raised as an approximate replica of the Church's birthplace and as a reminder of its heritage, with funds from a campaign initiated by students in the 1920s. It has become popularly known as "the Log Cabin," although in pioneer days a distinction was made between a solidly built "log house," such as Samuel McAdow's, and the ruder type of dwelling called a "cabin."

University in the fall of 1924. This brought about a demand, which found embodiment in memorials from two presbyteries, that "match games" with other schools be discontinued. The family of young Denney did not share in this demand.

The Board of Education pointed out the need for completing the basement of the Administration Building and the construction of a gymnasium. The need for a more up-to-date and comprehensive library was also emphasized, and the Board asked that any surplus in the ministerial aid fund might be used for the benefit of the library.

There had also been a growing demand, arising out of the fundamentalist-modernist controversy which was going on in several of the larger denominations, that some sort of creedal statement be required of teachers employed by Bethel College.

The most serious problem, however, had to do with the theological department. Despite the increase in enrollment in Bethel College, the number of those taking work in the theological department had decreased. Only thirteen students took courses in this department during the year 1924-1925. Eight of these were taking the major part of their work in the college or in the preparatory school. For some time there had been a demand that some younger men be placed on the theological faculty. In 1921 the Board of Trustees had elected the Rev. W. H. Butler as a teacher in the Theological Seminary to succeed the Rev. S. H. Braly. Butler, however, declined the position. In 1925, the Rev. P. F. Johnson, dean, who was seventy-two years of age, and Braly, who was seventy-five, remained as the department faculty. Both were graduates of the Theological School at Cumberland University. When the General Assembly met in 1925 the Board of Education had not elected a theological faculty for the ensuing year.

A committee appointed by the Board of Education to study the needs of the theological department had recommended that the school cease granting the Bachelor of Divinity degree. It recommended that the course for ministerial and missionary students leading to the Bachelor of Arts degree include subjects in Christian education and courses dealing with the distinctive doctrines of the Cumberland Presbyterian Church. A year's work in religious education beyond the Bachelor of Arts degree was also recommended, the courses to be such as could be transferred to other schools of religious education.

The General Assembly's Committee, however, disapproved the proposed changes in curriculum. The memorials seeking the abolition of intercollegiate athletics were also denied. Seeing a greater need for better dormitory facilities than for completing the basement of the Administration Building or constructing a gymnasium, the $40,000 remaining in the Laughlin fund was designated to be used in building a boys' dormitory, which would be named Laughlin Hall. The Board was instructed to proceed to the election of a theological faculty "with all diligence."

A recommendation was adopted that all persons employed as teachers in the school be required to subscribe to the following "avowal of hearty acceptance of the fundamentals of the gospel":

I accept and believe the Bible account of creation as the direct act of God; the Bible record of miracles; the immediate and infallible inspiration of the holy Scriptures as the very word of God; that Jesus Christ was conceived of the Holy Ghost, born of the virgin Mary, was the only begotten Son of God, and that he came from heaven to die as an atonement for sin; that he was crucified and died, and the third day arose from the dead by a bodily resurrection; that he ascended to heaven, from whence he will in due time return again. I believe, further, that heart repentance toward God and faith toward the Lord Jesus Christ bring spiritual regeneration, without which the accountable soul cannot be saved. As a teacher I will, without compromise, steadfastly stand for these fundamental things, and actively resist every encroachment upon them within my sphere of service.[34]

This creed would be more accurately described as evangelical than as fundamentalist, although it was doubtless prompted by the fundamentalist-modernist controversy.

In a meeting held on June 10, 1925, the Board of Education elected the Rev. George W. Burroughs as dean of the Theological Department for a term of two years. Braly was continued as a teacher for the year 1925-1926, and the Rev. J. J. Cobb was elected to teach beginning with the school year 1926-1927. Johnson, who was named dean emeritus, died a few days later. Burroughs and Braly accepted the positions to which they were elected, but Cobb declined.[35]

When school opened in the fall of 1925 only three persons enrolled as graduate students in the Theological Department. The work of the graduate students was therefore correlated with the work of those in the junior and senior years in college, so as to serve a larger number of students through the Theological Department. For those who were unprepared for such work, two or three courses were provided in addition to the necessary literary work.

Burroughs soon came into collision with President Whitmer over their respective philosophies of education. Whitmer was interested in securing recognition of the college by the Tennessee State Department of Education to facilitate the certification of teachers, and the college curriculum had been organized with this aim in view. Burroughs felt that a college founded and supported by a church should embody in its program a stronger Christian element than state institutions were free to do. He also found himself at variance with the president over the classification of students enrolled in courses in his department. When he felt that his attitude and efforts were misunderstood, he decided to resign the office of dean and devote his efforts solely to teaching for the remainder of the year.[36] On January 29, 1926, he filed with the secretary of the Board of Education his resignation "as dean of the Theological Department of Bethel College." On the preceding day, Mrs. Hugh S. McCord, who was serving as matron of the boys' dormitory, submitted her resignation.

The Board met on February 9 to consider these resignations. Without having Burroughs appear before the Board, the Board proceeded to accept the resignations and to elect others to fill the vacancies. Braly was advanced to the office of dean, and the Rev. John W. Dishman, who was teaching Bible in the college, was elected to teach in the Theological Department. The Rev. Daniel W. Perry was elected to teach Bible in the college.

On February 11 a telegram signed by seventy-one students of Bethel College was sent to the president and the secretary-treasurer of the Board. The telegram read as follows:

We, the undersigned wish the board to meet at once and reconsider the action taken in regard to Brother Burroughs. Numbers are thinking of withdrawing from the institution their support, and we feel that under the present conditions we cannot recommend the school to anyone.

In response to this telegram, a meeting of the executive committee of the Board was called for February 12. Four other board members attended. President Whitmer, Dean Beatty, and Dean Braly were asked for a report on existing conditions. The committee instructed the secretary-treasurer of the Board to write letters to certain students and teachers (some of whom had become involved in the disturbance), and those out of harmony with the school were called upon to reaffirm their loyalty. This action was taken without calling in the students and faculty members allegedly involved. At a second meeting the replies were considered, and the faculty was instructed to investigate and deal with students found guilty by them of causing confusion. Seven students were subsequently placed on probation. They appealed to the Board of Education which, after consideration of statements made by both sides, dismissed the appeal without formal trial, removed the penalty, and exonerated the students.[37]

In the meantime, the views of the students and faculty members at variance with the administration were given wide circulation through publication of a paper called the *Cumberland Presbyterian Bulletin,* edited by

Charles H. McCord, who had served briefly as Bethel's president some years before and who was the brother of Hugh S. McCord. In the two issues of this paper the attempt was made to discredit the administrative officers of the college and the methods used by President Whitmer in promoting the school. Thus an unsavory situation developed.

How did it happen that matters reached such a state? In the first place, the letter of resignation submitted by Burroughs was subject to more than one interpretation. Some members of the Board who had never been enthusiastic about employing him in the first place pointed out that he had been elected "dean ·of the Theological Department" and that he had resigned from this position. Had he clarified the matter by stating his willingness to continue as a teacher to the end of the school term, much trouble might have been avoided. On the other hand, he expected to be called before the Board,[38] but this did not happen.

Furthermore, the disturbance in the school was badly handled because a proper distinction between the functions of administration and faculty, on the one hand, and those of the Board, on the other, was not observed. The Board, or rather its executive committee acting with the support of other members of the Board, assumed authority in dealing with individual students which rightly belonged to the administration and faculty.

The Committee on Education appointed at the General Assembly at Columbus, Mississippi, in May 1926, was unable to agree on a report. Majority and minority reports were submitted. Both reports were rejected, and a commission was set up to consist of the Moderator of the General Assembly and twenty other persons to be appointed by him "to investigate and correct conditions at the school at McKenzie and the Board of Education." [39]

The Commission met in McKenzie June 22 and continued in session until July 1. The Commission condemned the Board of Education for leaving the details of its work in the hands of the secretary-treasurer. It likewise condemned the executive committee of the Board for passing sentence on students and faculty members without giving them a hearing. It instructed the Board to employ G. L. Meek as headmaster of the Preparatory Department and to restore Mr. and Mrs. Meek as superintendents of the dining hall and purchasing agents for Laughlin Home for the next school year. (The Board of Education, prior to the General Assembly, had elected others to these positions.) It recommended that President Whitmer be retained for the next twelve months, but that he not be granted the year's vacation which had been agreed to by the Board and reported to the Assembly. It expressed the view that Whitmer's connection with Bethel College should cease at the end of the next school year.[40]

On the matter of carrying out the Commission's recommendations the Board of Education was divided. Three of the nine members contended that the recommendations ought to be carried out in detail. The majority, however, felt that to do so would involve the violation of contracts the Board had entered into in good faith and acting within its rights as a corporation. Involved were contracts with various persons for the posts for which the Commission ordered the employment of Mr. and Mrs. Meek. The school was already in difficulty with the State Department of Education over the accreditation of the Preparatory Department because Meek's qualifications did not meet state requirements. J. R. Garrett, whom the Board had elected headmaster of the Preparatory Department, possessed these qualifications. The Commission instructed the Board to employ Garrett as a teacher in the Preparatory Department, but the fact that the department was being reduced to two years (junior and senior years) seemed to make impractical the employment of an additional full-time teacher. Whitmer's vacation was also a matter of contract. The majority of the Board believed themselves to be under moral obligation to fulfill these contracts and to take such action as they deemed best for the school.

Just when it seemed possible that some adjustment might be worked out, I. K. Floyd, Moderator of the General Assembly, wrote Meek directing him to remain in the place in which the Commission had placed him and informed the Board that he expected no further interference or lack of co-operation. The Meeks remained in their living quarters in Laughlin Home until after school opened. Finally, on September 30, a compromise settlement was effected whereby upon payment of $1,500 to Meek (that being his annual salary as specified by the Commission), he and Mrs. Meek surrendered possession of the dining room and the living quarters occupied by them.[41]

The failure of the Board of Education to carry out in detail the recommendations of the General Assembly's Commission provoked a strong reaction. Fourteen memorials were directed to the General Assembly by presbyteries and synods, nearly all of them asking that the Commission's actions be sustained. Some asked for the removal of the six members of the Board of Education who had voted against carrying out the Commission's directives. Some asked for the removal of President Whitmer and Dean Beatty.[42] There was a decrease in the enrollment of the school, since a number of the students who had been involved in the disturbances did not return. Instead of the year's vacation which the Board had originally granted Whitmer, he was paid on the basis of twenty-two weeks of accumulated vacation to which the Board decided he was entitled, and he went on a world cruise according to previously arranged plans. Beatty was in charge of the school during his absence. The faculty of the Theological Department in 1926-1927 consisted of John W. Dishman, as dean; the Rev. Ewell K. Reagin; and S. H. Braly, who was employed to teach on a part-time basis.

The issue concerning the Board's failure to carry out the Commission's recommendations came before the next General Assembly, which met in Lakeland, Florida, in May 1927. Early in the session a special committee was chosen with a view to reaching a compromise agreement. Inasmuch as the previous Assembly had failed to elect members of the Board of Education to succeed those whose terms expired, the Board, acting in accordance with its by-laws, had reelected the same three persons to serve until the next General Assembly. This action had been approved by the Assembly's Commission. Consequently, the terms of six members expired in 1927. A solution was reached by electing six new members, three being nominated by those who had supported the Board's viewpoint and three by those who supported the Commission.[43] This had the effect of giving the antiadministration forces a majority of one within the Board. Meanwhile, Whitmer announced his resignation, and the Board was given a free hand in electing his successor. The compromise with Meek was approved, but other recommendations of the Commission were ordered placed in immediate effect.[44]

The Board as now constituted elected one of its number, Edgar Baker McEuen, of Owensboro, Kentucky, to serve as president of Bethel College. Thus peace was restored, although the effects of the controversy still remained. The progress of the school had received a severe setback. One of the most lamentable results was the loss to the school of a number of persons whom it sorely needed in its program. On the one hand, the failure of the Board to communicate with Burroughs when he submitted his resignation and the mishandling of the resulting disturbances led to the loss of Burroughs, the McCords, and John T. Younger, a teacher of mathematics and social science. When their supporters in turn demanded the removal of Whitmer and Beatty, the school lost the services of these capable educators. Beatty continued with the school one more year but left in 1928 to pursue further graduate study. For some years he served, until his retirement in 1966, as dean of men at Pomona College, Claremont, California. Whitmer spent the greater part of the remainder of his life as a highly respected member of the faculty of Western Kentucky State College, at Bowling Green.

Prior to 1919, each General Assembly board made its own financial appeal to the Church. Certain months were designated for collections to be taken by each of the various boards. The results of this procedure, even before 1906, had never been spectacular.

In December 1918, representatives of the various boards met at Clarksville, Tennessee. Growing out of this meeting, an informal conference of commissioners and visitors to the General Assembly in 1919 was held, and a special committee was appointed which made recommendations relative to a denominational budget. A goal of $90,000 was set for the year 1919-1920. Each congregation was asked to raise an amount equal to $1.50 per member. An apportionment was made on a percentage basis to the various General Assembly boards, including the Educational Endowment Commission, which was allotted 5 per cent for campaign expenses. An Executive Committee consisting of one member from each participating agency (seven in all) was named, with Frank McDonald, of Chattanooga, Tennessee, as its secretary-treasurer and general director.[45]

During the year 1919-1920, $30,000 was received. This was far short of the goal which had been set, but was more than twice the total collections of the various boards for any previous year since 1906. Every board except the Board of Ministerial Relief received more money than it had received the year before. The General Assembly in 1920 adopted a recommendation that the Budget Plan be continued "as the permanent method of financing the Boards of our beloved Church." [46]

On November 1, 1917, Hugh S. McCord began work as tithing evangelist under the direction of the Board of Tithing. He traveled extensively, not only preaching tithing as the Bible plan for financing the Church but also promoting the total work of the Church. Mrs. Vint N. Bray continued to serve as secretary-treasurer of the Board.

At the General Assembly in 1923 the Board of Tithing and the Budget Committee were consolidated to form the Board of Tithing and Budget.[47] McCord was continued as tithing evangelist, and Mrs. McCord was made general treasurer with an office at McKenzie. During the year 1923-1924 McCord delivered 240 messages, each relating to some vital question of the life of the denomination. He personally enrolled 250 new tithers and obtained subscriptions to the denominational budget totaling $8,500. Much of his work was done in the rural districts and among the smaller congregations.[48]

Early in 1926 both Mr. and Mrs. McCord resigned. The Board did not employ a field secretary until December, when the Rev. A. N. Eshman began his work in that capacity. He attempted literally to sow down the Church with literature, especially in the form of a budget booklet which he prepared. He recommended a goal of $107,000 for the year 1927-1928. The General Assembly was not as optimistic, however, and set a goal of $50,000.[49] In 1927-1928 a budget of $34,321.71, the largest until that time and for many years thereafter, was raised, but the expense of raising it went $2,500 beyond the 10 per cent allotted for that purpose. The General Assembly expressed its disapproval of this policy but increased the percentage to the Board for the following year.[50]

During the years 1928-1929 and 1929-1930 the Board carried on its work through synodic, presbyterial, and congregational key men. In 1930, it recommended the employment of ten synodical field men who should represent both the cause of missions and the budget. Again the Board had expended funds beyond its designated percentage, and a note of $1,500 for borrowed money remained unpaid.[51] In place of the Board's proposals, the General Assembly adopted a recommendation that a budget field man again be employed, and the Board's percentage was again increased.[52]

Following the initiation of the denominational budget plan, annual receipts of the Board of Missions and Church Erection more than doubled. Consequently, there was an increase both in the number of fields aided and in the amount of aid given. In 1918-1919 aid was given to eight fields. The largest amount given any one field (except for $1,293 paid on the Dallas church debt) was twenty-five dollars per month.[53] In 1920-1921 regular monthly aid was given to sixteen fields; lots had been purchased in Los Angeles and in Kansas City, Missouri; and a mortgage of $975 on the church at Sedalia, Missouri, had been taken over by the Board.[54]

Prior to this time the Board had been under the necessity of expending the greater portion of its income to save the Church organically; that is to say, the salary of a minister would be supplemented to help make it possible to perpetuate the life of a presbytery or a synod.[55] Even now much of the aid given went to supplement salaries of ministers who were serving some of the weaker churches. Altogether, during the period from 1918 to 1930, aid was given by the Board of Missions and Church Erection to some seventy fields. These included presbyterial and synodic mission programs, city churches, town and country churches, and groups of churches. Several new fields were entered, however, the development of some of which will be noted.

The church which was begun at Kansas City, Missouri, was in a very real sense a project of the Board of Missions and Church Erection. In 1921, the Board reported that it had purchased a lot in Kansas City for the sum of $1,025.[56] In 1922, the General Assembly directed that the columns of the *Cumberland Presbyterian* be opened for the solicitation of funds to build a church in Kansas City.[57] Some time elapsed, however, before a man could be found to take charge of the work, and the church was not organized until March 8, 1925. On that date a church of fifty-nine members was organized in the home of J. J. Miller, by Thomas Dyer, who had been employed as the missionary pastor, assisted by the Rev. Fred C. Hughes, the Rev. C. B. Parkhurst, and the Rev. J. A. Bozarth.[58] The first service was held in the basement of the new church on July 26, 1925. Substantial aid was given this project from the beginning. Aid in the amount of $113.33 per month was given until February 1, 1926, when it was decreased to $83.33 per month.[59] In 1928, under the ministry of the Rev. W. R. Reid, a sanctuary was built.

About the year 1920 three Cumberland Presbyterians living in San Antonio, Texas, met and became interested in establishing a church there. Two of these were P. D. Starr and Miss Dessie Gibbins, who subsequently were married. In December 1921, the group learned of five other Cumberland Presbyterian families in San Antonio. In February 1922, the Rev. J. S. Eustis, presbyterial missionary, was sent to San Antonio to survey the field. On the fourth Sunday in February he preached in the auditorium of the Woman's Club. On March 19, an organization was begun with eight persons expressing a desire to become members. On August 20, five others came into the organization, and Eustis, assisted by the Rev. J. W. Hornbeak, a retired minister living in the city, ordained Starr and J. W. Williams as ruling elders. By the end of the year there were seventeen members. Services were held once a month in the auditorium of the YMCA until July 1923. No services were held from then until March 1924, when the Rev. Hugh Watson came and preached in the YWCA building. He accepted the pastoral oversight of the group, and aid in the amount of fifty dollars per month was given by the Board of Missions and Church Erection. A lot was purchased, and in 1925 a small chapel was built. The first service in the chapel was conducted on June 14 by I. K. Floyd, Watson meanwhile having resigned. On August 1, 1925, the Rev. J. R. Haws became pastor, and the Board supplemented his salary in the amount of seventy-five dollars per month.[60] In 1929, when the Rev. T. J. Tanner became pastor, there was a membership of about sixty.

In February 1923, Mr. and Mrs. Henry J. Graf moved from Evansville, Indiana, to Tampa, Florida. About the same time the Rev. J. D. Lewis moved to Tampa and built a home and a small chapel. On July 1 a church was organized with twenty-three members. In 1925, the building hitherto occupied by the Cumberland Presbyterian Church at Lakeland, Florida, was moved to Tampa and placed on an adjoining lot.[61] By 1928 this congregation had a membership of one hundred. During its earlier stages the Tampa church was not aided by the Assembly's Board; however, the General Assembly in 1928 directed that a loan of $500 be granted it.[62] In 1930 the Board reported that it was aiding the Tampa church in the amount of twenty-five dollars per month.[63] Graf, who meanwhile had been ordained to the work of the ministry, was serving as pastor. (Lewis had died June 12, 1929.) The church subsequently was named the Lewis Memorial Church.

In September 1925, the Rev. T. E. Bright held a revival meeting in Alabama City, an industrial area adjacent to Gadsden, Alabama. A church of sixteen members was organized. The Rev. J. S. Hall served as pastor until the first of January 1926, when Bright returned to minister to the church. Within six months from the time of organization of the church there was a Sunday school with 115 persons enrolled and an average attendance of eighty-five or ninety. Two lots had been purchased and a tabernacle built.[64] In 1927, the Board of Missions and Church Erection was giving twenty-five dollars a month to aid the church in Alabama City.[65] The following year the church was reported to be self-sustaining. In 1929, the General Assembly directed that a loan of $3,000 previously granted the Alabama City church be made a gift.[66] A new building had been erected at a cost of about $16,000. This church became the Forrest Avenue Church, of Gadsden.

In the fall of 1928, the Rev. B. O. Wolfe, of Jackson, Tennessee, became interested in the establishing of a Cumberland Presbyterian church in Detroit, Michigan. He secured the names of persons in the Detroit area who were subscribers to the *Cumberland Presbyterian* and wrote to each of them enclosing the names of the others. Soon these persons became acquainted with one another, and in 1929 they sent a petition to the General Assembly requesting that steps be taken to establish a church in Detroit,[67] and the Board of Missions was instructed to do so immediately.[68] In September 1929, the Rev. S. T. Byars was sent to Detroit as missionary, and on October 12 a church was organized with fifty-four members.

Efforts of the Board to aid Negro Cumberland Presbyterian churches did not have the support of the General Assembly. The Board first called attention to the needs of the Negro denomination in 1922. It was supplementing the salary of the Rev. W. A. Covington, in Bowling Green Presbytery, in the amount of twenty-five dollars per month.[69] Aid was continued to this field until February 1, 1925. In 1925, the Board was aiding a mission in Kansas City, Kansas, where the Rev. S. A. Nelson was laboring, in the amount of $12.50 per month.[70] With regard to this item the Committee on Missions stated that "By reason of the fact that the colored church is not affiliated with, or a part of, our Church, we recommend that all funds contributed through the channels of the Church be used wholly for our own Church." [71]

The following year there was an appeal from the Cumberland Presbyterian Church, Colored, at Dyersburg, Tennessee, asking for assistance in the erection of a church building. While recognizing this as a worthy cause, the Committee on Missions again expressed the feeling "that it would be inadvisable to contribute to this cause at this time, when appeals from our own fields go unanswered for lack of funds." [72] Thus the General Assembly in two successive years denied its missionary obligation to its black brethren of like faith. The denial was the act of the Assembly and not that of the Board of Missions and Church Erection.

From 1910 until 1929 the Board of Missions and Church Erection was composed almost entirely of persons living in Missouri. In 1922, both the Rev. A. M. Buchanan and the Rev. J. W. Duvall, who long had served as president and secretary-treasurer, respectively, were retired from membership on the Board. At this time Dr. R. M. King was elected a member of the Board. Subsequently he was elected secretary-treasurer and served in this capacity until 1938. In 1929, in response to memorials from Lebanon and Memphis presbyteries, the General Assembly voted to make the membership of the Board denomination-wide. The number of members was increased from seven to nine, and five members were named from areas other than Missouri. [73]

Meanwhile the Woman's Board of Missions was expanding its work. During the General Assembly in 1918 more than $1,500 was obtained in cash and pledges for the purchase of a lot for the Chinese mission in San Francisco. [74] Soon thereafter a lot was purchased.

In 1920 the Rev. Gam Sing Quah returned to the United States for the first time since beginning his work in Canton, China. An awareness of the need led the Missionary Convention to determine to build two missions: one in Canton and one in San Francisco. At a joint meeting of the General Assembly and Convention more than $10,000 was subscribed. Gam subscribed one month's salary to the building fund. During the year the women sang to the tune of "Where He Leads Me I Will Follow,"

> Build two missions in 1920.
> We can do it if we will.

July 31 was set as "Build a Mission Day." [75] During the Assembly year 1920-1921 more than $36,000 was raised for this purpose. Twenty thousand dollars was borrowed so that the mission building in San Francisco could be built immediately, and the Rev. D. W. Fooks went to San Francisco to superintend the erection of the building. [76] The mission at Canton was not built until 1922, but with the money allotted for this building two missions were built, at Canton and Honam. [77]

In 1924, at the request of Gam and the Woman's Board of Missions, the General Assembly commissioned Fooks to represent the General Assembly and the Woman's Board of Missions in the organization of a pres-

FIRST CHINESE CHURCH, SAN FRANCISCO, CALIFORNIA

The building at 855 Jackson Street, in the heart of Chinatown, was completed in 1921, when this picture was taken. An earlier building had been destroyed in the San Francisco earthquake and fire of 1906.

bytery in China to be known as Canton Presbytery. It also requested Texas Synod to take the necessary steps to order the organization of the presbytery. Gam and Fooks were commissioned to organize the presbytery by receiving the Rev. Leung Wing Gan from the Alliance Mission and the Rev. Ug Shek-hing from the American Swedish Mission. The new presbytery was to be attached to Texas Synod.[78] Acting under these instructions, appropriate action having been taken by the synod, Canton Presbytery was organized in Canton on October 24, 1924. Five ministers were enrolled as members: Fooks, Gam, Leung, Ho Qui Dok, and Low Don Foo. Seven congregations were enrolled.[79]

As early as 1913, there were young people in the Cumberland Presbyterian Church who were interested in becoming missionaries to South America.[80] In 1920 the suggestion was made that the proposed mission be named in memory of the late Chaplain John A. Deaver.[81] In 1922 the Woman's Board agreed to assist the Rev. W. L. Swartz and his wife in a course of training in Moody Bible Institute, Chicago, with the understanding that they would become missionaries to South America.[82] They were commissioned during the General Assembly at Nashville in May 1925.[83] In November, Swartz sailed from New York to seek a location for the mission. Colombia, where there were only thirty evangelical missionaries among seven million people, was chosen. In the city of Cali, Swartz met the Rev. C. P. Chapman, of the Gospel Missionary Union, who encouraged him to begin work there. In March 1926, Mrs. Swartz joined her husband in Colombia.

The first Colombian worker enlisted was Martiniano Fajardo, who had accepted Christ in a service at Palmira. Soon afterward his younger brother, José, was converted and was the first person baptized by Swartz in Colombia.

On March 11, 1928, Miss Bernice Barnett, of Missouri, and Miss Ethel Brintle, of Oklahoma, were commissioned as missionaries to Colombia.[84] Soon after their arrival they visited the Fajardo family farm, in the Department of Tolima, and encouraged José to enter the Colegio Americano which was to open in Cali in September. There were twenty-eight students the first year.

On February 4, 1929, a church was organized in Cali with about fifteen members. During this year the work was expanded to include Dagua, Lomitas, and El Pinal as preaching points. During 1929, also, property was purchased from the Plymouth Brethren at Pereira, a city about one hundred miles north of Cali.

In 1930 Swartz resigned his appointment. In anticipation of his resignation the Woman's Board had sent the Rev. Elbert L. Conyers and his wife to the Colombian field.

JOHN A. DEAVER
(1885-1918)
Cumberland Presbyterian chaplain from Jackson, Tennessee, killed in action in World War I, for whom the mission in Colombia was named.

As early as the spring of 1924 Mrs. Adele Helsley, of the Knoxville church, was engaged in misson work in a community known as Cox's Cove, in Yancey County, North Carolina, where she taught school and did community work. This work was sponsored by the Ladies' Bible Class of the Knoxville church. Auxiliaries of some other churches in Knoxville Presbytery later helped.[85] In March 1924, the presbytery appointed a committee to visit the community and investigate the outlook for a mission school.[86] The decision was favorable, and the presbytery decided to attempt to build a school; however, an insurmountable obstacle was encountered when it was found that all land in Cox's Cove was owned by a corporation which refused to subdivide and sell the land.[87] Another location was then sought. By March 1926, the Tackett's Creek mining section, at Anthras, Tennessee, had been selected as the site, and a deed to the necessary land had been obtained.[88] That summer a building was completed at a cost of $7,343.15 and was dedicated on September 12.[89] During the first two years the Rev. L. B. Saxon, Mrs. Saxon, and Miss Annie McCroskey taught in the school, which was called the Finis Ewing School. Through Mrs. Helsley's house-to-house visitation as community worker, approximately one hundred pupils were enrolled the first year.

In March 1927, Knoxville Presbytery requested the Woman's Board of Missions to take over the mission. The Board agreed to assume this responsibility at the end of the Convention year, in May 1928.[90] From 1928 to 1930 the Rev. George E. Coleman served under the direction of the Woman's Board as superintendent of the mission. During his term of service a church of twenty-three members was organized.[91] Others connected with the mission during this period included Miss McCroskey, Miss Verna Briggs, and Miss Nora McCoy, teachers; Miss Artie Robey, community nurse; and Mrs. George E. Coleman, community worker. In the spring of 1930 Coleman resigned the work at Anthras to accept a pastorate in Kansas City, and the Rev. J. B. McCollum was chosen as his successor, with Mrs. McCollum as community worker. Other teachers during McCollum's administration were Miss Briggs and Miss Sophronia Simmons.[92]

In 1919 the Board of Ministerial Relief began supplementing its income through the promotion of an Easter offering. The Rev. John A. McLane, secretary-treasurer of the Board, proposed that each Sunday school pupil bring to Sunday school on Easter Sunday at least one egg. It was suggested that suitable containers be brought to each church to take care of the eggs and that they be sold on Monday morning and the proceeds sent to the Board of Ministerial Relief. It was estimated that if every Sunday school pupil in the Cumberland Presbyterian Church would respond, $1,200 would be added to the Board's treasury.[93] Nearly 300 Sunday schools responded, and more than $1,800 was received. The Board was able to increase its payments to each beneficiary by 25 per cent. This plan, which reflected the rural character of the Cumberland Presbyterian Church, proved to be popular, and in 1926 annual receipts from this source passed the $5,000 mark.

The number of children cared for in the Home at Bowling Green increased from five, in 1918, to twenty-one, in 1924. From 1918 until 1921 Mrs. C. G. Chick was in charge of the home, being assisted by her husband, a minister. Other directors served in the years that followed. The operating budget of the home rose to a figure of $4,647.75 for the year 1925-1926. When in 1928-1929 something like $4,000 was spent for maintenance of the Home, the General Assembly's Committee on Ministerial Relief considered that amount an excessive sum for the maintenance of fifteen children.[94]

As early as 1921 a question was raised as to the title of the property of the Home. The Board of Ministerial Relief pointed out to the General Assembly that this was not the property of the Cumberland Presbyterian Church or of the Board of Ministerial Relief.[95] By 1922, however, the decision apparently had been reached that the title was satisfactory, for the building had been enlarged to sixteen rooms and a heating plant installed. These improvements had cost $9,234.26, and there was an indebtedness of $4,500.[96]

In 1929 the matter of the relationship of the Home to the Church was again an issue. The General Assembly adopted a recommendation that the Board of Ministerial Relief assume full control of the Home, employing all help and establishing the rules and regulations by which it was to be operated. All monies advanced by the Board to the Home since 1912 were to be considered a loan to the local board and lien on the property. Should the Board of Control refuse to accept this agreement, demand for payment with 6 per cent interest should be made, and a suitable location secured for the Home.[97]

The local board felt that under the provisions of the Jackson bequest it could not turn over the Home to the Board of Ministerial Relief; however, its management was given over to the Board until the next General Assembly. The Board recommended that the General Assembly withdraw from the situation at Bowling Green and seek a new location.[98] A special committee appointed the previous year recommended solving the problem of the dual management of the Home by placing on the Board of Ministerial Relief some members from Bowling Green and vicinity.[99] Instead, the General Assembly appointed a commission composed of three persons to take under advisement the selection of a site for the location of an Orphans' and an Old People's Home for aged ministers, their wives or widows, to be the property of the Cumberland Presbyterian Church subject to the ratification of the General Assembly.[100]

The number of children in the Home had decreased until there were only seven in 1930. In September, the Board moved the children to the home of G. T. Johnson, at Auburn, Kentucky.[101] Thus was terminated the Board's connection with the home at Bowling Green.

Early in 1919 the *Cumberland Presbyterian Banner,* together with the machinery and equipment belonging to T. A. Havron, the editor, were purchased by the Board of Publication for the sum of $10,500. It was agreed that Havron and the Rev. J. L. Hudgins, who was serving as editor of the *Cumberland Presbyterian,* would serve jointly as editors of the combined publication which retained the name *Cumberland Presbyterian.* Hudgins was continued as manager with Havron in charge of the printing plant. The first issue under the joint editorship was that of February 7, 1919. The Board recommended to the General Assembly that a location be chosen for the publishing house, and that if it was to remain in the Nashville area it should be moved into the city.[102]

On November 9, 1919, the Rev. T. Ashburn died, and the Rev. W. H. McLeskey was elected to fill out his term as field secretary and as editor of the Sunday school literature.[103]

In June 1921, Hudgins resigned as editor-afield and business manager. The Board accepted his resignation and did not reelect Havron. Instead, the Rev. J. W. Stiles was made editor of the *Cumberland Presbyterian* and business manager effective July 1, 1921. After serving about three months in this capacity Stiles had a board meeting called and offered his resignation. He had found that "he did not care to give his life to the editorship of a paper or bury himself in a printing plant." His resignation was accepted effective November 1, and Hudgins was again elected business manager and editor.[104] In 1923 the Rev. S. L. Noel was named as his assistant.[105]

By the spring of 1923 the Board of Publication was out of debt. In 1924 the Board reported having purchased property in Nashville at Eighth and McGavock for the sum of $22,000, of which $12,000 had been paid. On the front was a two-story brick building which was rented and would later be used for offices. A machinery hall was being constructed at the rear.[106] In 1925 this property was occupied by the Board of Publication.[107] During this year, also, the office of the Woman's Board of Missions was moved to Nashville from Evansville, space being provided in the publishing house.[108]

By action of the General Assembly in 1926 Hudgins was retired from his position as editor-manager with one half salary for twelve months, and Noel was employed in his stead.[109] This stipend to Hudgins was continued for only the one year.[110]

Interest in the creation of a Board of Young People's Work was manifested as early as 1920 when a communication on that subject from the Rev. H. R. Allen, representing a delegation from Arkansas, Texas, and Oklahoma, was brought before the General Assembly.[111] The request was denied; however, a resolution was adopted instructing the Board of Publication to appoint a superintendent of young people's work who should be put in the field as soon as practical.[112]

In June 1922, the Rev. Charles R. Matlock was elected field secretary and supervisor of young people's work. He prepared and had published a *Cumberland Presbyterian Young People's Annual* and an *Efficiency Chart*.[113] In 1924, upon the recommendation of the incumbent, Allen, Matlock was chosen to serve as trustee for the denomination in the United Society of Christian Endeavor.[114]

Plans were made for a Young People's General Assembly to be held in connection with the meeting of the General Assembly at Austin, Texas, in May 1924. This Assembly was organized by the election of the Rev. H. C. Walton, of Birmingham, Alabama, as president, and Miss Mollie Walkup, of Nashville, secretary.[115]

In 1927 the General Assembly created a Board of Young People's Work.[116] Since only a little more than $400 was turned over to this board and only 3 per cent of the denominational budget allotted to it, an appeal was made to the young people themselves for pledges and contributions. Acting largely on faith, the Board employed the Rev. Clark Williamson as general secretary. He had just completed his theological education at Gordon College. During the summers of 1925 and 1926 he had worked in the field as Matlock's assistant.

The character of the Young People's General Assembly was now changed. No longer did it meet with the General Assembly, but in the summer of 1927 it was held on the campus of Bethel College. Beginning in 1928, courses in Christian education arranged by the Educational Council of the Board were offered. A service program was recommended to the young people's societies. Mountain missions was made the missionary objective of the young people.[117] Subsequently the various synodic camps, some of which were already in operation, were converted into standard leadership training schools. During 1928, two accredited schools and one accredited class were held. In 1929, six standard training schools and six classes were conducted, and 342 credits were issued.[118]

During the period from 1918 to 1930 three synods were dissolved. The dissolution of the Synod of West Texas and New Mexico has already been noted.[119] The other two, Pacific and Mississippi, were likewise in areas where Church membership was relatively small.

For some time conditions in Pacific Synod had left much to be desired. A minister who had been deposed by Los Angeles Presbytery was ordered by synod to be placed on the roll of California Presbytery. The General Assembly in 1924 found that in reality Pacific Synod was defunct, for, not counting the minister who had been placed on its roll by the synod, California Presbytery had only two ordained ministers, and there were only three presbyteries in the synod. The General Assembly therefore declared Pacific Synod defunct, directed that its constituency be formed into one presbytery, and added this presbytery to Texas Synod.[120] This presbytery, which was called Pacific Presbytery, held its first meeting at Fresno, California, in September 1924.

Mississippi Synod likewise was composed of only three presbyteries, one of which was very weak. Hugh S. McCord placed his membership in Yazoo Presbytery in order that it might have a quorum, but during the year 1927 the other two ministers died. Thus when the General Assembly met in 1928 it found that Mississippi Synod was unable to function. It therefore placed the presbyteries of Mississippi and New Hope in the Synod of Alabama, which became Alabama-Mississippi Synod.[121]

One new synod, however, was created during this period. In 1925, in response to a memorial from Knoxville Presbytery, the General Assembly made provision for the creation of East Tennessee Synod, subject to ratification by Tennessee Synod at its next meeting.[122] The concurrence of Tennessee Synod having been given, East Tennessee Synod held its first meeting at Knoxville, in November 1926. It was composed of the presbyteries of Chattanooga, East Tennessee, and Knoxville.

In 1921, the year following the achievement of woman suffrage on a national level, the ordination of women as ministers, elders, and deacons was legalized. The controversy over the ordination of Mrs. L. M. Woosley during the 1890s has been mentioned.[123] In 1911, Leitchfield Presbytery (the successor to Nolin Presbytery) restored Mrs. Woosley's name to its ministerial roll, and the action went unchallenged by Kentucky Synod. In 1907, Mrs. Bessie C. Morris was received as an ordained minister from the Methodist Protestant Church by Dallas-Bonham Presbytery. From 1916 through 1920 at least four other women were ordained as ministers within the Cumberland Presbyterian Church: Miss Mabelle Robison, by Ozark

Presbytery, September 1, 1917; Miss Birdie Lee Pallette, by Lexington Presbytery, 1916 or 1917; Mrs. Chloe Kratli, by Springfield Presbytery, April 2, 1919; and Mrs. Ada Slaton, by Louisiana Presbytery, November 5, 1920.

In 1920, in the attempt "to bring our Constitution into harmony with our present practices," a committee of three was appointed to prepare an amendment to the Constitution on the question of the ordination of women.[124] Instead of recommending the several constitutional changes that would have been involved, the General Assembly in 1921 adopted the following deliverance which was embodied in a minority report presented by E. B. McEuen, of Owensboro Presbytery, a ruling elder and a member of the Committee on Judiciary:

We most respectfully submit that the word "man" with reference to a human being is a generic term, and as used in the Holy Scriptures, and Constitution and the other confessional statements of our Church has no reference to sex, but should be construed to, and does, in fact, include the human being whether male or female.[125]

Thus the Cumberland Presbyterian Church gave legal sanction to a practice already begun, becoming one of the earlier Christian bodies officially to approve the ordination of women. Several years were to elapse before the larger Presbyterian bodies would take a similar step.[126]

In 1904-1905 a minority of votes carried a majority of presbyteries for the proposed union with the Presbyterian Church, U. S. A. The desirability of changing the amending process so as to require the affirmative vote of a larger percentage of the presbyteries was suggested editorially by J. L. Hudgins in December 1925.[127] In 1927, the General Assembly received memorials from the presbyteries of Madison, Memphis, Brownwood, and Hopewell regarding this matter. The memorials from Madison and Memphis presbyteries asked that the Constitution be so changed as to require the approval of three-fourths of the presbyteries to amend the Confession of Faith, Catechism, Constitution, or Rules of Discipline. Brownwood and Hopewell asked that the approval of two-thirds of the presbyteries be required.[128]

Some of these memorials were doubtless prompted by fears of a movement to carry the Cumberland Presbyterian Church into another denomination which had arisen as a result of rumors connected with the difficulties at Bethel College in 1926.[129] B. O. Wolfe, then a ruling elder in the Jackson, Tennessee, church, who introduced the earliest of these memorials in his presbytery (Madison), is reported to have expressed the opinion that if a union with another denomination were ever carried by a three-fourths vote of the presbyteries it would be because the Church as a whole desired it.[130]

In response to these memorials the General Assembly recommended to the presbyteries an amendment to require the approval of 75 per cent of the presbyteries for future constitutional changes.[131] During the ensuing year, thirty-four presbyteries voted for the change, four voted against, and twenty-three made no report.[132] Thus the amendment was approved by majority vote.

In 1929, the General Assembly recommended an amendment designed to require a larger majority for referring amendments to the presbyteries. A three-fourths majority of those voting, rather than two-thirds, would be required, and there must be present and voting not less than 75 per cent of the full membership of the General Assembly based upon the complete representation of every presbytery.[133] This amendment received the approval of forty-nine of the sixty-one presbyteries.[134]

# 22

## PULLING THROUGH A DEPRESSION

*The members of the present faculty [of Bethel College] have shown a spirit of extreme unselfishness in their attitude to our financial situation when we were unable to meet salary payments promptly. And every member of the faculty cheerfully consented to the salary reduction asked by the General Assembly last year. Salaries accepted for next year are less than salaries received by high school teachers in many of our small towns.*

Board of Education, 1933

The depression of the 1930s, which was precipitated by the stock market crash of October 24 ("Black Thursday"), 1929, began to be felt throughout the Cumberland Presbyterian Church by the summer and fall of 1930. In that same year there was a severe drouth throughout much of the South and Southwest.

One effect of the depression, of course, was a marked decrease in contributions both for the work of local churches and for denominational causes, for there was widespread unemployment and prices of farm products had taken a downward plunge. Bank failures were frequent. The General Assembly's treasury lost $400 in the Farmers Bank of Fulton, Kentucky, which closed on October 15, 1931.[1] Income from endowment funds decreased, as borrowers were unable to pay the interest on their loans. Local churches which had erected buildings on which there was an indebtedness found themselves in crisis situations. The First Church of Nashville lost its building. Such churches as Columbus, Mississippi; East Gadsden, Alabama;

432

West End, Birmingham, Alabama; and Central, Memphis, Tennessee, were saved from a similar disaster by the timely use of denominational funds.

The General Assembly which met at Evansville, Indiana, in 1931 had before it two memorials calling for financial retrenchment. Suggestions included a reduction in the number of board members, consolidation of some boards and agencies, and a limitation of the salaries of secretarial and administrative personnel. The majority of the commissioners to this General Assembly, however, were as yet in no mood to talk seriously about retrenchment, at least where Bethel College was concerned.

The Board of Education reported to this Assembly that it had elected the Rev. Edgar Hart Guynn as president of Bethel College for a five-year term at a salary of $5,000 a year. (The president had been receiving $3,000.) At the same time, the Rev. Ewell K. Reagin, who had left the Theological Department of Bethel College in 1928 to become pastor of the church at Knoxville, Tennessee, was recalled from the pastorate to serve as dean of the Theological Department at a salary of $3,000 per year. Salaries of classroom teachers ranged from $1,500 to $2,200. President-elect Guynn had great plans for the school. A larger campus was needed. A schedule was being arranged whereby faculty members might absent themselves for advanced study in leading universities. Courses of study were being revised. Guynn requested that "instead of the undignified term, 'Theological Department,' permission be given to designate this department as 'The Cumberland Presbyterian Theological Seminary of Bethel College.'"[2] The general expectation seemed to be that under his administration miracles would be performed.

Although there was a minority report signed by two members of the Board who favored the election of Reagin as president at a salary of $3,000 a year, the majority report was accepted.

During the year 1931-1932, Bethel College had an enrollment of 252 students, compared with 160 the preceding year; however, the operating deficit, which had gradually increased since the reorganization of the school in 1923, was increased another $11,000 for the current school year, and salaries of teachers, when the Board made its report in 1932, were three months in arrears. Guynn had resigned, giving as his reasons "that he felt his health breaking under the strain of his heavy work" and that he felt that he was "unable to realize his ambitions for Bethel College because of the retarding influence of the world-wide economic situation."[3] The Rev. Leonard L. Thomas, who had been added to the faculty in 1929 to teach in the Theological Department, was made acting president. The following year he was elected president.

During the year 1931-1932 the income from funds in the hands of the

Educational Endowment Commission totaled $9,000 as compared with $16,-000 the year before. Teachers had taken a voluntary reduction of 10 per cent in their salaries for the coming year. The General Assembly requested that they accept an additional 10 per cent reduction.[4]

In 1933, radical financial readjustments had to be made. Although a successful year's work was reported, with an enrollment of 270 students, receipts from the Educational Endowment Commission were only slightly more than $7,000. Bethel College now had a total indebtedness of $65,000. Under the leadership of President Thomas, a policy of operating under a strict budget was inaugurated. The budget of 1933-1934 was set at $21,000. Salaries of the president of Bethel College and the dean of the Theological Seminary were set at $1,600 each. H. B. Evans, dean of the college, was to receive $1,300, and salaries of classroom teachers ranged from $900 to $1,160.[5]

During the next few years there was a gradual improvement in the financial condition of Bethel College. During the year 1933-1934 some $6,000 was raised by the Church toward retirement of the deficit. Subsequently smaller amounts, usually ranging from $2,000 to $3,000 a year, were contributed to this cause. Receipts from endowment also increased. Although the Educational Endowment Commission had to foreclose on a number of pieces of real estate, the endowment fund on the whole weathered the storm well.

Although salaries continued to be low, with only small increases from year to year, it was possible under existing economic conditions to employ persons with the doctor of philosophy degree at salaries of less than $2,000. At least two members of the faculty who had served since the 1920s earned the doctoral degree during this period, also. In 1938-1939 there were five persons on the faculty who held the doctorate.[6] National Youth Administration funds were available for student jobs, and a Civilian Conservation Corps camp established near McKenzie brought a number of young men to Bethel College who otherwise would not have been in school. During the year 1936-1937 the enrollment reached a record high of 353 students.[7] Thereafter the enrollment decreased somewhat as government aid to students decreased. During the year 1940-1941 there were 227 students, of whom 92 per cent were receiving some kind of financial aid.[8]

In 1939 Thomas resigned as president and was succeeded by Ewell K. Reagin. Thomas was assigned to the Hannibal Seagle Bible Chair made vacant by the death of the Rev. John W. Dishman in April of that year. Under Reagin's administration a music department was developed. Beginning in 1940 an annual pastors' conference was held on the Bethel campus, the second session of which attracted an attendance of ninety-five visiting ministers besides local ministers and students in the college and seminary.[9]

Through the cooperation of the town of McKenzie and the use of government funds and some contributions from the Church, the John W. Dishman Gymnasium was built on a site adjoining the campus. This property was later deeded to the college.

Enrollment in the Theological Seminary also increased. During the early part of this period there were few graduate students enrolled in the Seminary. In 1938-1939 there were fourteen students in the Seminary as compared with four the preceding year. The following year there were fifteen.[10]

In 1941 the General Assembly approved plans covering a three-year period, 1942-1944, during which a "Forward Movement" was to be promoted to enlist the interest, patronage, and financial support of the Church in behalf of Bethel College and to liquidate the indebtedness which long had hampered its progress.[11] This program was inaugurated in recognition of the fact that the centennial of Bethel College would be observed in 1942. The indebtedness at that time was reported to be $48,597.65.

In the fall of 1930 the Board of Tithing and Budget employed as a field man Thomas C. Stockton, a young businessman living in Memphis. He traveled throughout the Church at a salary which netted him less than $100 per month, since he paid his own expenses; but despite the best efforts that could be put forth, the denominational budget for the year 1930-1931 was only $16,611.17.[12] During the meeting of the General Assembly in 1931, announcement was made that Bun E. Rodden and two of his sisters, Miss Sarah Rodden and Miss Iona Rodden, members of the Pine Tree Church, near Longview, Texas, had deeded to the Board of Tithing and Budget a one-fourth interest in the mineral royalty on a tract of land within the newly discovered East Texas oil field. During the ensuing year a budget slightly in excess of $20,000 was raised, and of this amount the sum of $7,392 was credited as "Texas Synod Personal." Besides making a handsome contribution to the denominational budget, Rodden made a special contribution which enabled the Board of Tithing and Budget to pay off an operating deficit which had been carried forward for several years. The amounts coming in from local churches were, for the most part, "widow's mites," as the Board noted in its report to the General Assembly in 1932.[13]

Stockton, who meanwhile had entered the ministry, resigned his position as field man early in 1933 to accept a pastorate. Thereafter for a period of some three years the promotion of the budget, other than what could be done by mail, was committed to presbyterial and synodic directors. During the year 1933-1934, with the partial recovery of the economy, contributions from the churches increased by some $4,000; however, the income from oil royalties was down, and the total budget was $18,874.93.[14]

In about 1935 the Board of Tithing and Budget began giving increasing attention to the importance of the installation of a systematic plan of finance in local churches. A booklet written by I. M. Vaughn, secretary-treasurer of the Board, entitled *Solving the Financial Problems of Cumberland Presbyterian Churches,* was used. In 1936 the Board reported that during the past year seventy-seven congregations had installed a systematic plan for local church finance for the first time.[15] Subsequently the "Cumberland Plan" was recommended, a "Cumberland Plan" church being one which contributed to the denominational budget at least 10 per cent of its income exclusive of building funds.[16]

In 1936, the Board employed Mrs. Euline C. McLeskey as assistant secretary. She had charge of routine matters in the Board's office, edited the *Budget News,* of which six issues were published in 1936-1937, and taught courses in "Christian Stewardship" and "Financing the Work of the Church" in a number of synodic youth camps.[17] Joe Forbis, president of the Board, produced at his own expense a motion picture entitled *The Cumberland Presbyterian Church at Work* which he presented to the Board in 1938.[18] Following the General Assembly that year, the Rev. Wayne Wiman began his work as field man for the Board. His principal task was to show the picture in every congregation and enroll churches in the "Cumberland Plan" of finance. During the first year the picture was shown to 20,250 people in 270 exhibitions.[19] Mrs. McLeskey, whose marriage to Thomas C. Stockton took place in 1939, resigned as assistant secretary in that year, and the work of the office, as well as the field work, devolved upon Wiman. His efforts in showing the picture, *The Cumberland Presbyterian Church at Work,* were augmented by those of the synodic field men employed about this time under the direction of the Board of Missions and Church Erection.

The immediate results were not phenomenal, as far as the increase in receipts for the denominational budget was concerned, but changes were being made in the financial practices of many Cumberland Presbyterian churches. Actually, the denominational budget reached a total of $26,890.28 in 1937-1938 and continued around $25,000 or $26,000 throughout the remainder of this period.

Statistics appearing in the report of the Board of Tithing and Budget for the year 1940-1941 reveal the continuing rural character of the Cumberland Presbyterian Church. At that time there were sixty churches in cities of 10,000 people or more. Of these, fifty-three contributed a total of $4,786.11 to the denominational budget. There were 147 churches in towns, of which 126 contributed a total of $4,915.95, while of 802 country churches, 505 contributed $11,021.27 to the denominational budget.[20]

The Commission appointed in 1930 to take under advisement the selection of a site for an orphans' home and a home for aged ministers and their wives or widows recommended locating the home at or near McKenzie, Tennessee. The Carson farm, lying just outside McKenzie, had come into the hands of the General Assembly's Board of Trustees by bequest. It offered one possibility. Another possible site was the property of the McTyeire School, a preparatory school for boys formerly operated by the Methodist Church but now closed. On this property where was a mortgage of $25,000. It was believed the property could be obtained for the amount of the mortgage.[21]

To the 1931 General Assembly four memorials were addressed relative to this matter: Hopewell Presbytery asked that the home be located on the Carson property, Obion Presbytery that it be located at or near McKenzie, Dallas Presbytery that it be located at Fort Worth, Texas, and Gregory Presbytery that it be located within the bounds of Texas Synod. The Assembly's Committee on Ministerial Relief felt that the memorials from Texas did not rest on a firm enough foundation to be acted upon favorably at this time, although it recognized the desirability of locating some one of the General Assembly's institutions west of the Mississippi River. The Carson property could not be developed without a considerable outlay of money, and the assumption of the obligation necessary to obtain the McTyeire property would have required immediate payment of at least $10,000. The General Assembly could not provide the outlay of funds that would be needed, and it continued the commission as a committee to make further investigation.[22]

In the meantime there were developments within Texas Synod which had a bearing on the location of the home. Early in 1929, G. T. Morrow, of Lubbock, Texas, died leaving a will in which substantial amounts were bequeathed to various charitable institutions. After various sums were appropriated for specific causes, one-third of the residue of the estate was bequeathed to "The Cumberland Presbyterian Orphans' Home of Fort Worth, Texas." There was no such institution. The fact that children of two former pastors of the Lubbock Cumberland Presbyterian Church had been reared in the Masonic home at Fort Worth probably led Morrow to assume that there was a Cumberland Presbyterian home there. It was clear that he wished for the Cumberland Presbyterian Church, along with others, to benefit from his estate. Texas Synod, therefore, in a called meeting held at Fort Worth June 11, 1929, took steps to establish such a home by appointing a board of trustees and entering into an agreement with A. H. Smith, who owned land adjacent to the Cumberland Presbyterian Church in Fort Worth, for the purchase of a lot for the sum of $1,000. Smith donated an additional lot.[23]

This clause in the Morrow will was contested by a brother of the deceased. In 1931, a compromise settlement was reached whereby 50 per cent of the item in question was awarded to the Church. Since the General Assembly was now seeking a site for its orphans' home, Texas Synod, in October 1931, voted to offer the assets of the proposed synodic home to the General Assembly if it would locate its orphans' home in Texas. A commission was appointed to visit possible sites and communicate its findings to the General Assembly. It was believed that altogether the synod would have assets of approximately $5,000 to offer.[24]

The synodic commission selected a six-acre tract of land in the southwest part of Denton, Texas, on which there was a nine-room house. This property could be obtained for $4,000. The Chamber of Commerce of Denton proposed to raise $1,000 of the amount.

Believing the Texas proposal to be something the General Assembly could handle, the Committee on Ministerial Relief appointed at the 1932 Assembly proposed that if Texas Synod would give to the General Assembly the proposed site in Denton unencumbered, it would recommend that the Home be located there. A meeting of commissioners present from Texas Synod was called, and it was their belief that the Committee's proposal could be met. The Committee therefore recommended to the General Assembly the following:

WHEREAS, Texas Synod offers to give absolutely free to the General Assembly of the Cumberland Presbyterian Church for a Ministerial and Orphans' Home a six-acre tract of land, well improved, at Denton, Tex. We recommend that the General Assembly accept said property and it shall become the Ministerial and Orphans' Home of the Cumberland Presbyterian Church.[25]

Subsequently, Texas Synod approved the agreement, and the property in Denton was purchased and deeded to the General Assembly's Board of Ministerial Relief, the vendor accepting instead of a lien on this property a lien on the Fort Worth lots for the balance owed him. The children, now six in number, were temporarily placed in the home of the Rev. J. L. Elliott and his wife, who cared for them while repairs were being made on the Home. Mrs. G. T. Johnson, the matron, together with her husband, arrived early in 1933 and served until 1936, Elliott meanwhile having been designated as superintendent. In 1938 Mr. and Mrs. L. J. Springer came to the Home as superintendent and matron, respectively. By this time there were fifteen children in the Home.[26]

In 1939 the Board of Ministerial Relief reported that it had purchased a tract of land of about ten acres a short distance from the existing Home at a cost of $3,850. There remained more than $13,000 in a building fund.[27] The greater part of the building fund had come from the estate of the late H. P.

CUMBERLAND PRESBYTERIAN CHILDREN'S HOME, DENTON, TEXAS

King, of Van Buren, Arkansas, who had bequeathed one-fourth of the greater portion of his estate to the Board of Ministerial Relief, one-fourth to the Board of Missions and Church Erection, and one-half to the Educational Endowment Commission. A building was erected on the new property at a cost of about $18,000. This building was dedicated on June 20, 1941, during the meeting of the General Assembly at Denton.[28]

In 1934, in response to a memorial from Lebanon Presbytery, an effort was approved to raise $100,000 endowment for ministerial relief.[29] At that time the Board of Ministerial Relief had an endowment fund of about $14,000. The Rev. J. L. Hudgins, who in his time had raised considerable sums of money for various enterprises of the Church, was appointed campaign manager on a commission basis. This was not a propitious time for raising large sums of money, however, and the Board's report for 1940, the first after the death of Hudgins, showed total endowment funds of slightly more than $22,000.[30]

When the General Assembly met in 1931 two crisis situations in local churches were brought before it. The church at Columbus, Mississippi, had applied to the Board of Missions and Church Erection for the sum of $5,000 to save its property from foreclosure. Columbus was considered to be an important field, as it was the only Cumberland Presbyterian church in Mississippi having the full-time service of a minister. The church in East Gadsden, Alabama, was also in financial trouble. The General Assembly directed the Board to use any funds available to save the property at Columbus and East Gadsden.[31] The Board gave the church at Columbus the sum of $1,095.64 and granted a loan of $1,500. East Gadsden was granted a gift of $550 and a loan of $1,700.[32] In 1932, Fifth Church, in Memphis, which had been organized in the summer of 1929, was in difficulty. The General Assembly directed that a loan of $800 be made to this church.[33] In 1933, the Board was directed to give assistance to Central Church, of Memphis. There was an immediate need for $1,000.[34] During this period aid of one kind or another was given to four of the five churches in Memphis.

As its income from the denominational budget decreased, the Board of Missions and Church Erection was forced to curtail its aid to a number of fields. The General Assembly in 1932 directed the Board to reduce its aid to the Detroit church from $100 to $50 per month.[35] In 1933 the General Assembly directed that the Board supplement no pastor's salary so that it would be more than $100 per month and manse, or $125 per month if there were no manse.[36] At the beginning of the year 1934 the Board asked the churches receiving aid to take a 25 per cent reduction in the amount of aid received.[37]

Aid was given to many fields during this period, although usually in small amounts. Although it was necessary for some aid to be given to rural churches, in general these probably fared better than did the urban churches. There was widespread unemployment in the cities, which seriously affected the financial structure of the churches. For example, the Rev. William T. Ingram, Jr., served the church in Fort Worth, Texas, in 1933 and 1934 at a salary of forty dollars per month while attending Texas Christian University and Southern Methodist University. He and his wife lived in the room which was designed as the pastor's study and used the church kitchen in the basement. Only three members of the church had a regular income. Some members could not attend services because they did not have carfare. During 1933 the Board of Missions and Church Erection aided the Fort Worth church on its building debt in the amount of $25.00 per month. In 1934 the aid was reduced to $18.75 monthly.[38]

The General Assembly in 1935 recommended that a missionary be placed in every presbytery in which there was not already an active program of missions. Where entire self-support was not possible, the General Assembly's Board was to supplement the missionary's salary in an amount agreed upon by the missionary and the Board. The Lord's Acre Plan was recommended, especially among rural churches, to aid in making the program self-supporting.[39] It was recommended by the Board that 20 per cent of the proceeds of the Lord's Acre Plan be dedicated to presbyterial missionary work and the remaining 80 per cent to the local church program. By 1936 it was reported that this program had been adopted by thirty-two of the sixty presbyteries.[40] The 1936 General Assembly, however, concurred in the opinion of its Committee on Missions that the suggestion of placing a missionary in each presbytery should have more elasticity. Some presbyteries could not use a missionary to advantage, and a small amount to supplement salaries of men in charge of groups of churches would be of greater benefit. It was also recommended that each presbytery receiving aid from the General Assembly's Board form a missionary committee or board to supervise the activity of the missionary or pastor receiving aid.[41]

In 1937, a comprehensive program was recommended by the Board of Missions and Church Erection and approved by the General Assembly. It embraced general policy, policy in making loans, policy in aiding churches, synodical missions, presbyterial missions, and missions in the local church.[42] It was designed to strengthen the local church program and to make each church a missionary unit. It was an effort to make the Board of Missions and Church Erection something more than an agency to receive and disburse mission funds.

The same General Assembly adopted a resolution introduced by Ewell K. Reagin asking the Board of Missions and Church Erection to create within the Board a committee to study the needs and conditions of the Cumberland Presbyterian Church, Colored, to offer assistance to its leaders, and to make recommendations to the General Assembly of the Cumberland Presbyterian Church regarding such action as was deemed advisable.[43] The following year this committee recommended that each presbytery study the needs of the Cumberland Presbyterian Church, Colored, within its bounds; that the Board of Christian Education consider the possibility of sponsoring youth camps and local training schools for the young people of that church; and that its young ministers be given the privilege of taking correspondence courses from Bethel College.[44] Although the General Assembly referred these recommendations to the appropriate agencies, several years were to elapse before the sort of cooperative program envisioned was to become a reality.

In 1938, the General Assembly's Committee on Missions and Church Erection recommended "that an effort be made to secure a field man in each of the respective synods, these men to be nominated by their synod and approved by the board." [45] By 1940 there were five synodic field men, all ministers: D. C. Murphree, Alabama-Mississippi Synod; D. J. Francis, Arkansas Synod; M. F. Allen, Texas Synod; J. Elmer Kelley, Indianola Synod; and R. W. Furkin, Missouri Synod. The Rev. Rayson Going was serving as missionary for Choctaw Presbytery.[46] These men were receiving a major portion of their salaries from the General Assembly's Board. Their activities included visiting the churches, attending presbyterial meetings, holding revivals, forming groups of churches and helping them secure pastors, soliciting subscriptions to church periodicals, organizing missionary societies, surveying communities with a view to planting new churches, and showing the motion picture, *The Cumberland Presbyterian Church at Work.*

Although the scarcity of funds hindered the Board of Missions and Church Erection from venturing far into new fields, some new churches were organized.

In 1931, Indiana Presbytery employed the Rev. J. B. Foster to do mission work in southwestern Ohio, the bounds of Illinois Synod and Indiana Presbytery having been extended to include Michigan and Ohio.[47] By the end of the decade at least four churches had been organized in Ohio, and one church, Mount Zion, which had chosen to remain Cumberland Presbyterian in 1906, was reactivated. Unfortunately, almost all of these churches were later lost to the Cumberland Presbyterian Church.

Following the decision to locate the Orphans' Home at Denton, Texas, J. L. Elliott, who was living in Denton, intensified his efforts to reestablish the church there. On September 6, 1932, the Denton church was reorganized with twenty-one members.[48] Some of these members came from the Sunnydale Church, a rural congregation nearby, and eventually the remaining active members of that church came into the Denton church. A loan of $3,000 was obtained from Elmira Chapel, a church near Longview, Texas, which had several oil wells on its property, and a brick-veneered church building was erected.

On November 30, 1934, under the leadership of the Rev. W. R. Reid, pastor at Searcy, Arkansas, and W. L. Oliver, an elder, a congregation of seven members was organized in the Rose City area of North Little Rock, Arkansas. This congregation, with the Rev. Alvin D. Gregory as its first pastor, worshiped in a store building until November 1935, when a temporary building was erected on a site which had been acquired nearby. In September 1937, under the leadership of the Rev. L. P. Turnbow, who became pastor in February of that year, a stone sanctuary was erected. In 1939 there were 106 members.[49]

While serving churches in Louisiana and in eastern Texas, the Rev. Thomas H. Campbell became aware that a number of Cumberland Presbyterians had moved from those areas to Shreveport, Louisiana. In the fall of 1938 he made two visits to that city. In January 1939, he returned with M. F. Allen, field man for Texas Synod, and a church organization was begun with five persons participating. Before the charter membership roll was closed, the number increased to fourteen: two men and twelve women. The congregation was supplied with preaching twice a month by various ministers until June, when Campbell moved on the field. Services were held at first in the home of one of the members, but later two rooms of the house where the pastor lived were equipped as a chapel. Growth was slow, and three years later when the pastor resigned there were still only about thirty members. In 1941, Bun E. Rodden, of the Pine Tree Church, near Longview, Texas, purchased a lot for $1,500 and donated it to the church. A building fund of some $1,200 had also been gathered by the end of 1941. In 1942 a small first unit was built, and about two years later, during the ministry of the Rev. N. A. Woychuk, a vacant church building at Jefferson, Texas, which had been donated to the Shreveport church by the Board of Missions of McAdow Presbytery, was torn down and the materials were used in erecting a sanctuary for the Shreveport church.

In its report to the General Assembly in 1941 the Board of Missions and Church Erection mentioned a new church at Lexington, Tennessee, which was being served by the Rev. J. T. Buck.[50] A church building which had been vacated as a result of the merger of two Methodist churches in Lexington was purchased.

One factor which had hindered the establishing of new churches was the lack of available building funds. The Board of Missions and Church Erection for some years designated a portion of its income as a loan fund for building purposes but had not been especially successful in collecting these loans as they became due. In 1932 the General Assembly made what proved to be a wise decision when it named the Rev. D. W. Fooks, Stated Clerk of the General Assembly, as a member of the General Assembly's Board of Trustees. It also suggested that he be made financial agent for the Board.[51] Under his management certain trust funds which had come into the hands of the Board of Trustees were loaned to churches. Loans were made for a ten-year period with 5 per cent of the principal, plus the accrued interest, being due and payable each six months. In addition to a first mortgage on the church property, a joint note signed by a number of responsible individuals was required. Under this program loans were made to such churches as Edgefield in Nashville and First Church in Dallas for the erection of educational buildings; to East Lake, Birmingham, Alabama; Rose City, North Little Rock, Arkansas; Margaret Hank Memorial, Paducah, Kentucky; Fellowship, Camden, Arkansas; Watkins Park, Nashville, Tennessee; and East Side, Memphis, Tennessee, for the erection of church buildings, and to Murfreesboro, Tennessee; Cloyds, Mount Juliet, Tennessee; and Gurley, Alabama, for the purchase or erection of manses.

The Board of Ministerial Relief, through use of its endowment funds, rendered a similar service on a smaller scale. A loan of $5,000 was made to the West End Church, Birmingham, in the summer of 1936 to save that church from foreclosure. The following year a loan of $3,000 was made to enable the First Cumberland Presbyterian Church of Detroit, Michigan, to build.[52]

The Jubilee Convention of Cumberland Presbyterian missionary women, originally planned to be held in observance of the fiftieth anniversary of the organization of the Woman's Board of Missions, was delayed one year in order that the observance might be held at the birthplace of that board, Evansville, Indiana. This Convention held in May 1931 was the largest held up until that time. More missionaries were present than at any previous Convention. Among them was the Rev. Gam Sing Quah. In January 1930, a monthly publication, the *Jubilee Journal*, was begun by the Board. After the Jubilee Convention it was continued under the name of the *Missionary Messenger*.

Before another year had passed, the Woman's Board, like other agencies of the Church, began to feel the effects of the depression. In 1932 the Finis Ewing Mountain Mission was turned back to Knoxville Presbytery. Expenditures had to be cut in other fields. Offerings to the Woman's Board reached their lowest figure in 1933-1934 when the total was only about $14,000. Thereafter there was a gradual increase, with contributions in 1939-1940 exceeding $30,000.

On February 18, 1937, Gam Sing Quah, Cumberland Presbyterian mis-

GAM SING QUAH
(1863-1937)

SAMUEL KING GAM
(1911-1955)

sionary to the Chinese for many years, died in his native country. Fortunately his son Samuel King Gam, who had been educated in the United States, had returned to China in the fall of 1935. At his father's death Samuel King Gam succeeded him as superintendent of the South China mission. At this time there were ten organized churches in Canton Presbytery, and a total church membership of 1,142. Reverses were soon to come, however, for in the fall of 1938 the Japanese overran the Canton area. Gam was forced to flee to Hong Kong, although he was later permitted to return. Mission work was begun in Hong Kong, but the work around Canton, although not entirely stopped, suffered greatly.

There were frequent changes of personnel on the mission field in Colombia. Late in 1931 the Rev. Elbert L. Conyers and his wife returned to the United States because of the illness of their son. The Rev. Davis O. Bryson and his wife were sent in their stead. Meanwhile, José Fajardo, the "first-fruits" of the Cumberland Presbyterian mission in Colombia, accompanied the Conyers family to the United States and entered the University of Oklahoma High School, living with Miss Ethel Brintle's family. In 1933, Miss Brintle was married to Plutarco Roa, member of a family who had moved to Colombia from Guatemala. Miss Betty Smith, of Fort Worth, Texas, was sent as a missionary in 1932. In December 1935, she was married to Leon Terrell, an instructor at the government aviation school in Cali. After a few months he was transferred, and she resigned from the missionary staff. Miss Ollie Mae Preston was commissioned as a missionary to Colombia on December 1, 1935, but remained on the field only a short time. Meanwhile, Miss Bernice Barnett was married to Moises Gonzalez, who shortly afterward entered the ministry. In 1936, Conyers and his family returned to Colombia. He superintended the erection of the new building for the Colegio Americano on a site which had been purchased overlooking the Cali River. In 1939 the Conyers family returned to the United States, and in January 1940 the Rev. Paul F. Brown and his wife were commissioned to serve in Colombia.

Despite the changes in personnel, there was growth. A rural church known as La Helvecia, situated a few miles from the city of Armenia, which since about 1925 had formed the principal nucleus of a movement known as the "National Evangelical Church," decided to become affiliated with the Cumberland Presbyterian mission. It called as its pastor Alfredo Cardona and had the distinction, according to the missionaries, of being the first Protestant church in Colombia to employ its own pastor and pay his salary. In 1934 Bryson and his wife were sent to Pereira, where a session was organized. Meanwhile a chapel was built at Restrepo, in the mountains northwest of Cali.

In 1934, the Woman's Board of Missions requested the General Assembly to extend the boundaries of Texas Synod to include the Cauca Valley area of Colombia.[53] This petition was granted. In the fall of that year, Texas Synod passed an order for the organization of Cauca Valley Presbytery.[54] On March 8, 1935, Cauca Valley Presbytery was organized with three ordained ministers participating: Mrs. Roa, Miss Barnett, and José Farjardo. The Rev. James W. Elder, a chaplain in the armed forces then stationed in Panama, was present as an advisory member. Bryson, who had been named by Texas Synod to preside at the organization, was prevented by illness from attending. Four churches were represented: La Helvecia, Pereira, Restrepo, Cali. José Fajardo was elected moderator. At this meeting four probationers were received under the care of the presbytery: Martiniano Fajardo, Alfredo Cardona, Antonio Sepulveda, and Robert Grazales. Cardona was ordained at this meeting.[55]

In 1937, work was begun in Alameda, a *barrio,* or district, of Cali. In this same year the new building for the Colegio Americano was completed.[56] In 1937 and 1938, the members began to move away from La Helvecia. Some of them moved to Armenia, where services were begun in 1938. In the summer of 1939 a church was organized there with nineteen charter members.[57] Services were also begun in El Paraguay in the home of Obdulio Barrios. Plutarco Roa, who meanwhile had dedicated himself to the work of the ministry, and his wife took charge of the work at Armenia. A lot was purchased with the help of the congregations at La Helvecia, El Paraguay, and Bethel. In 1941, Roa was ordained to the full work of the ministry. Meanwhile, several members of the Pereira church moved to Cartago, where a new congregation was organized with fifteen charter members on July 14, 1940.[58]

The Rev. Clark Williamson, who more than any other one person was responsible for the development of the Christian education program of the Cumberland Presbyterian Church, continued to serve as General Secretary of the Board of Young People's Work. Beginning about 1933, the Rev. Morris Pepper, a student in the Cumberland Presbyterian Theological Seminary, assisted him on a part-time basis. In 1935 a total of 600 local young people's societies were listed, and the following year fifty-two presbyterial young people's societies were functioning.[59] Notable progress was made in leadership education work, especially as it was promoted through summer camps. During the year 1930, 336 credit certificates were issued in YPGA, three synodic camps, and six classes conducted in presbyteries and local churches.[60] In 1934, 1,201 credit certificates were issued through YPGA, nine synodic and five presbyterial camps, and twenty-four classes.[61]

In 1930, the Board of Publication also inaugurated a program of leadership education. To a considerable extent it overlapped the work being done by the Board of Young People's Work.

Meanwhile, the Board of Publication encountered problems within the publishing house. Dissatisfaction arose because the manager, the Rev. S. L. Noel, permitted a political paper, which was being handled as job printing by the publishing house, to run up an account of several thousand dollars which there seemed little hope of collecting. In 1931, C. C. Brock, who already was serving as foreman of the shop, was made manager of the publishing house. Noel was continued as editor of the *Cumberland Presbyterian* one more year, but in 1932 the Board elected the Rev. O. A. Barbee, of Owensboro, Kentucky, as editor.

As early as 1931 a young people's paper published monthly but in weekly parts was being produced under the direction of the Board of Young People's Work in cooperation with the Board of Publication. The Rev. Ky Curry was serving as editor.[62] Afterward the *Cumberland Crusader,* as this paper was called, became a project of the Board of Publication and was edited by the Rev. T. A. DeVore. The General Assembly in 1935 directed that at the earliest practical date all the literature, including the *Cumberland Crusader* and the *Young People's Quarterly,* be edited by the publishing house staff.[63] Thomas H. Campbell, of Texas, who was added to the editorial staff shortly thereafter, became editor of the *Crusader* and it was made a monthly magazine. When he left the publishing house in August 1937, he was continued as editor of the *Crusader* on a nonresident basis.

The fact that there were two boards promoting leadership education curricula prompted Alabama-Mississippi Synod to direct a memorial to the 1936 General Assembly asking that the Assembly instruct the Board of Young People's Work, the Board of Publication and Sunday School Work, and the Woman's Board of Missions each to appoint two members to constitute a committee on Christian leadership training work, through which all leadership education should be done.[64] A memorial from Dallas Presbytery urged a greater emphasis within the leadership curriculum on courses of study for Sunday school teachers. It also called for representation of Sunday schools in the presbyterial youth rallies.[65]

These memorials were referred to a special committee which recommended the appointment of a Board of Christian Education, the functions of which should be to

(a) Take over all the work that is now being carried on by the Board of Young People's Work.

(b) Take over all that work which is now being carried on by the

Board of Publication and Sunday School Work which pertains to organization, promotion of Sunday schools and their work, setting up standards and forming curriculum for training Sunday school teachers and workers, and the supervision of the work of Sunday schools throughout the denomination.

(c) That it shall be the duty of this Board to promote all phases of Young People's and Sunday School Work, prepare and set up standards of training and curricula for the training of Sunday school teachers and workers and young people's leaders.

(d) That this Board shall be the only agency authorized to determine courses to be offered and issue credits therefor.

The Board of Publication and Sunday School Work was instructed to transfer to the newly created Board of Christian Education "all of its work pertaining to the setting up of standards and curricula for the training of Sunday school teachers and workers and the promotion of Sunday school work together with all the materials, charts and standards." [66]

The question which remained unanswered was, Who would produce the Sunday school literature? The Board of Publication was jealous of its interest at this point, for the Sunday school literature, especially the adult quarterly, was its principal source of income. Profits from the sales of Sunday school literature were enabling it to operate and make annual payments of $2,000 to $4,000 each year on the publishing house debt. This Board, in its summer meeting in 1936, sought to defend its right to produce the Sunday school literature by placing its own interpretation on the General Assembly's action. [67]

On the other hand, there were those who believed that more of the proceeds from the sales of Sunday school literature ought to be used in the improvement of the literature. Although instructions were given in 1931 to make funds available for the production of a young people's quarterly, this quarterly did not become a reality until 1936. The Board of Christian Education, although maintaining a noncommittal attitude on the matter, could hardly see how it could accomplish all that was expected of it without having some voice in the production of the Sunday school literature. Following its meeting in the fall of 1936 the secretary of the Board of Christian Education, the Rev. Daniel W. Perry, made a report to the *Cumberland Presbyterian* which included the following statement:

For the working out of its program committees were appointed on organization and curriculum but while this program is in process of development it was the mind of the Board that for the present we will continue with the literature for Sunday school and young people's organizations and the personnel producing it. [68]

This was interpreted by some persons connected with the Board of Publication to mean that the Board of Christian Education did plan to take over production of the Sunday school literature at a later date.

Beginning in January 1937, a campaign was launched through editorials in the *Cumberland Presbyterian* and letters to the editor designed to secure to the Board of Publication full control of the Sunday school literature.[69] These efforts were augmented by the activities of board members who visited presbyterial meetings. Twelve memorials were addressed to the General Assembly by various presbyteries, ten of them in the state of Tennessee, all asking that the production and publication of the Sunday school literature remain in the hands of the Board of Publication and Sunday School Work.[70]

The Board of Christian Education, in its report to the General Assembly, recognized the importance of the Sunday school literature to the financial structure of the Board of Publication and denied any intention of assuming such control over its production as would jeopardize the financial status of the Board of Publication. It proposed that editors and contributors to the Sunday school literature be nominated by the Board of Christian Education but elected by joint action of the two boards. It proposed, also, that the Board of Publication continue to negotiate the business contracts and determine the amount of salary to be paid editors and contributors, but that the ratification of these contracts be by joint action of the two boards.[71]

The Committee on Overtures, to which this particular question was referred, recommended that a joint committee composed of three members from each of the two boards be set up to make recommendations regarding the literature, including selection of editors and contributors. This committee's recommendations would then be acted on by the two boards in joint session. The report was amended, however, so as to limit the power of the joint committee to making recommendations to the two boards. The actual election of editors and contributors remained in the hands of the Board of Publication.[72]

During its first year of operation the Board of Christian Education formulated a leadership education curriculum known as "The Course of Study in Christian Education." In 1937, Morris Pepper was added to the staff as director of the Young People's Division, and the office of the Board was moved to the Administration Building of Bethel College where a room was provided.[73]

With this addition to the staff, the General Secretary was able to turn his attention more effectively to the development of Sunday schools. One of his first efforts was to attempt to obtain adequate statistics concerning the Sunday schools of the denomination. A Standard of Excellence for Sunday schools was developed, and a mimeographed publication known as the

*Sunday School Builder* was published at irregular intervals.[74] Later issues carried material designed to be of assistance to Workers' Conferences of local churches.

The observance of Denominational Week (the week including February 4), already begun by the Board of Young People's Work, was continued, and the observance of Christian Education Day in September was initiated. The Board also promoted local church institutes during Denominational Week, 1939, using as a basis for discussion a book entitled *The Purpose and Program of the Church,* which had been prepared cooperatively by several agencies of the Church.[75] The following year the local church institute was devoted to a study of evangelism using the booklet *Evangelism: A Study in Motive and Methods,* by Pepper and Williamson.[76]

The leadership education program continued to grow in its acceptance by the Church. During the year 1940 there were twenty-five summer camps, eleven schools conducted in local churches, eighteen classes in local churches, and twelve "Home Study" classes, in which a total of 1,858 credit certificates were earned. Up until that time a total of 7,269 individuals had taken one or more credits in the leadership education program of the Church.[77] This number represented approximately 10 per cent of the constituency of the Church. This degree of participation made its impact on the programs of the local churches, for there was a more widespread understanding of what the Church ought to be doing. Numbers of young people were led, through their participation in summer camps, to answer the call to the ministry or to other types of full-time Christian service.

In 1938, the Board of Publication and Sunday School Work elected O. A. Barbee general editor of the *Cumberland Presbyterian* and the Sunday school literature. Ky Curry was secured as his assistant. The Rev. W. H. McLeskey, who since 1919 had edited the Sunday school literature, was continued on a part-time basis as writer of the *Advanced Quarterly.*[78]

The question of millennialism caused some excitement during the latter part of this period. Several young men who were students in Dallas Theological Seminary, along with one professor in that institution, were received and ordained as ministers by Dallas Presbytery. Other ministers had attended Moody Bible Institute. In some areas the question proved to be a divisive one. Both in 1940 and in 1941 the General Assembly was asked to make a deliverance on this subject, but each time it declined to do so. The statement adopted in 1941 noted that "for 131 years the fathers of our Church have not deemed it wise to speak dogmatically on this subject, doubtless realizing the danger of disputes, controversies, and divisions which might be involved therein." [79]

One of the more significant actions taken by the General Assembly during this period had to do with the interpretation of requirements for ordination to the work of the ministry. In 1939, a committee of three was appointed to make a careful study of the ordination requirements and report to the next Assembly. The committee was also directed to work out educational requirements to which ministers coming into the Church from other communions should conform.[80] This committee, in its report to the General Assembly in 1940, recommended that the requirements set forth in Section 56 of the Constitution be interpreted as being equivalent to an acceptable college education as set forth by the American Association of Theological Schools. Presbyterial committees on literature and theology would be instructed to recommend for ordination only those candidates who had conformed to this standard. Exceptions were to be allowed only in cases where presbyteries had under their care "acceptable men with suitable gifts and capacities for a constructive service in the gospel ministry who because of their age or reasonable family obligations should not be able to conform completely" to the standard set forth.[81] Final action was postponed until the following year, and a committee was named to set up a three-year course of study for those who should not completely conform to the requirement of a college degree.

The special committee to which this matter was referred in 1941 noted that the subjects on which licentiates are to be examined, according to the Constitution, "are clearly college and seminary subjects." The adoption of the proposed interpretation was therefore recommended with no change. For those who could not be expected to conform completely to the recommended standard the "Standard Presbyterial Home Study Course for Ministers" was set up. Bethel College was requested to establish a lending library for the benefit of those who would not be in position to purchase the required textbooks.[82]

The total reported membership of the Cumberland Presbyterian Church, which had remained around 65,000 from 1916 to 1930, began to rise during the 1930s. The total in 1931 was 68,099, and the number further increased, with some fluctuations, to 72,951 in 1941. The number of "resident" members, however, which rose from 48,020 in 1930 to 50,612 in 1931, had decreased to 48,149 in 1940.

Collections of the Educational Endowment Commission as found in its "interest account" from year to year provide an index to economic conditions during this period in the area where the Cumberland Presbyterian Church had its greatest strength. This agency handled the largest endowment fund of the Church. Here, as will be seen from the accompanying

## CHART SHOWING CONVERSIONS, ADDITIONS, AND CERTAIN PHASES OF THE ECONOMIC PICTURE OF THE CUMBERLAND PRESBYTERIAN CHURCH DURING THE DEPRESSION

|         | Conversions | Additions | Interest Collections, Educ. End. | Contributions to Denom. Budget | Contributed to Woman's Bd. of Missions | Total Paid to Pastors |
|---------|-------------|-----------|----------------------------------|--------------------------------|----------------------------------------|-----------------------|
| 1930-31 | 4,343       | 3,947     | 19,076                           | 16,611                         | 30,912                                 | 259,876               |
| 1931-32 | 4,613       | 4,137     | 15,373                           | 12,794                         | N.A.                                   | 220,641               |
| 1932-33 | 3,993       | 3,952     | 13,462                           | 8,986                          | 20,884                                 | 185,205               |
| 1933-34 | 4,817       | 4,220     | 13,255                           | 12,597                         | 14,870                                 | 170,698               |
| 1934-35 | 4,424       | 4,348     | 14,395                           | 13,782                         | 16,140                                 | 177,295               |
| 1935-36 | 3,694       | 3,534     | 15,937                           | 15,749                         | 23,045                                 | 190,897               |
| 1936-37 | 3,521       | 3,420     | 16,239                           | 18,336                         | 24,460                                 | 204,560               |
| 1937-38 | 3,240       | 2,862     | 18,789*                          | 18,778                         | 30,744                                 | 203,967               |
| 1938-39 | 4,442       | 4,071     | 18,226                           | 18,644                         | 28,555                                 | 220,934               |
| 1939-40 | 4,062       | 3,892     | 18,271                           | 17,370                         | 30,953                                 | 224,238               |
| 1940-41 | 3,456       | 3,219     | 19,665                           | 20,783                         | 28,720                                 | 243,419               |

* During the year 1937-1938 the Educational Endowment Fund was increased by approximately $30,000 through settlement of the H. P. King estate.

Statistics are given as they appeared in General Assembly Minutes.

chart, there was a sharp drop in collections from 1930-1931 to 1931-1932. The decrease continued with the low point occurring in 1933-1934. Beginning in 1934-1935 and continuing to the end of the period there was a gradual upturn in collections. The total amount paid pastors, contributions of the churches to the denominational budget, and contributions to the Woman's Board of Missions followed a similar pattern.

Measured in terms of conversions and additions, it would appear that the "spiritual" life of the Church during the first half of the decade was in inverse proportion to the economic conditions; that is to say, the number of conversions reached its highest level in 1933-1934, the year in which economic conditions were at their lowest level. There was a decrease in the number of conversions as the economy recovered. There was, however, another upturn in the number of conversions and additions leading up to 1938-1939, while the state of the economy was rising.

The number of candidates for the ministry remained fairly constant, with the highest number reported in the years 1934 and 1936; however, a larger number of these were attending Bethel College than had been the case earlier, and more were remaining to complete their seminary education.

# 23

## WORLD WAR II AND POSTWAR FERMENT

*Although manifest progress was being made . . . there was serious question in the minds of some as to whether or not the Cumberland Presbyterian Church would respond to the challenge of the demands of the new order. Why did not the Church grow more rapidly?*

The effects of World War II, which already had begun to be felt by the Church before the official entrance of the United States into that conflict in December 1941, were greatly intensified thereafter.

In September 1940, the Selective Service Act was passed by the Congress of the United States, and a month later all men between the ages of eighteen and thirty-six were required to register. The drafting of young men into the armed services began at least a year before the Japanese attack on Pearl Harbor, and by the end of the war some ten million young Americans had been inducted. From the standpoint of the Church this meant the absence of these men from the services and activities of their local churches. The local youth work suffered not only because many young men were in the armed forces but also because many young people, men and women, were in government service or war work of some kind.

The Board of Christian Education sought to minister to the men in the armed forces by promoting a "Cumberland Service Fellowship." The *Upper Room,* daily devotional guide published by the Methodist Church, and a mimeographed paper, the *Torch,* were sent to them. In 1943 there were about 900 names on the list composing this fellowship.[1] The following year, however, the Cumberland Service Fellowship was discontinued because of the frequent movement of the men which made it impossible for the Board office to keep in touch with them.[2]

The degree of mobility of the population increased sharply during this period as men and women alike found employment in munition plants and aircraft factories. Many moved away from their home communities never to return as residents. The reported active membership of the Cumberland Presbyterian Church, which in the spring of 1941 stood at 45,842, was reduced to 43,378 in 1943. Sunday school enrollment dropped from 48,806 in 1941 to 43,210 in 1944.

Due to governmental restrictions on critical building materials, church building came to a virtual standstill. On the other hand, a wartime economy resulted in an increase in offerings for church purposes. Contributions to all church causes rose somewhat. The General Assembly's Budget Fund, which in 1941-1942 was $28,794.42, rose to $40,258.73 in 1944-1945. Offerings to the work of the Board of Foreign Missions increased from $30,725.36 in 1941-1942 to $62,990.67 in 1944-1945. (The name of this board, formerly the Woman's Board of Missions, had been changed in 1939 as the result of action taken by the Missionary Convention in 1938.) Easter offerings to the Board of Ministerial Relief rose from a figure of $6,213.57 in 1941-1942 to $13,130.45 in 1944-1945. Although few new churches could be built, this was a good time to pay off existing debts. In 1944, the Board of Trustees of the General Assembly, which had been lending money to churches for building purposes, reported that during the preceding year eight loans had been paid in full, while only two new loans had been made. One of these had been paid in full before the Board made its report.[3]

In 1942-1943 the enrollment in Bethel College totaled only 119 students, forty-six fewer than the preceding year.[4] In the fall of 1943 only fifty-seven students were enrolled, and the number continued at around sixty throughout the school years 1943-1944 and 1944-1945. These figures included the enrollment in the Cumberland Presbyterian Theological Seminary. Income from endowment tended to decrease due to the fact that interest rates were down. The Educational Endowment Commission had to invest in low-interest government bonds or make loans at a lower rate of interest than that to which it had been accustomed. Thus the income of Bethel College was reduced. During the year 1942 Dean H. B. Evans and A. S. Rudolph, both of whom had been professors at Bethel College for many years, left to accept positions elsewhere. Thus the faculty of the college was weakened.

The supply of ministerial students entering Bethel College was virtually cut off. Not one freshman ministerial student was enrolled in the fall of 1943, and only one the following fall. The enrollment in the Theological Seminary, which had been increasing in recent years, held its own, although the lack of ministerial students in the freshman and sophomore classes in college would soon take its toll in terms of the Seminary enrollment. In 1943, however, nine men received the Bachelor of Divinity degree.

Meanwhile, the shortage of pastors was made acute by the fact that a number of ministers were serving as chaplains in the armed forces. In 1945 twenty Cumberland Presbyterian chaplains were serving.[5] Fortunately none of these chaplains lost his life in the war.

Travel restrictions curtailed field work on the part of the boards and agencies of the Church. In 1945 the Missionary Convention did not meet, and attendance at the General Assembly was limited to commissioners and board representatives.

About the time that France fell to the German blitzkrieg in 1940, the General Assembly, meeting at Cookeville, Tennessee, passed two resolutions which reflected the ambivalent attitude which then prevailed toward the war. On the one hand, a resolution presented by I. M. Vaughn, of Jackson, Tennessee, was adopted calling upon the Church to pray for divine guidance and at the same time urging the President and Congress to "speed a program for adequate national defense," to take steps to insure against "fifth column'" activities, and to empower the President to take whatever steps were necessary "for the preservation, propagation, and the perpetuity of the principles upon which our great Republic was founded and for which it stands." [6] At the same meeting a resolution was adopted providing that conscientious objectors might register with the office of the Stated Clerk of the General Assembly in order that they might not be inducted into the armed services in the event of war.[7] It is not known whether any Cumberland Presbyterians registered as conscientious objectors. There is a notable absence of resolutions concerning the war in the records of the General Assembly thereafter. It appears that Cumberland Presbyterians, like the people of most other churches in the United States, regarded this war as a grim task which must be finished as soon as possible rather than as a crusade for righteousness.

While the United States became increasingly involved in the war, the Cumberland Presbyterian Church was not without internal troubles of its own. In the spring of 1942 a group of ministers and laymen in Cherokee Presbytery, in Oklahoma, undertook to warn the Church against what they mistakenly believed to be a movement to take the Cumberland Presbyterian Church into union with one or more of the larger Presbyterian bodies. This action was sparked in part by a news release which reported a service held at the Presbyterian Church, U. S. A., in McKenzie, Tennessee, in which the moderators of three Presbyterian bodies participated. This meeting was hailed as a prophecy of a union soon to be consummated. Meanwhile, the Rev. Leonard L. Thomas, formerly president of Bethel College and still teaching there, and Moderator of the Cumberland Presbyterian General Assembly, was serving as temporary supply of the Presbyterian Church, U. S. A., at Huntingdon, Tennessee, near McKenzie. Through a clerical oversight or a printer's error, the Minutes of the General Assembly of the Presbyterian Church, U. S. A., for 1941 failed to carry in connection with the name of Thomas as supply pastor for the Huntingdon church the symbol indicating that he was a minister of another denomination.[8] Thus the word got out that he was·no longer a Cumberland Presbyterian. A letter calling attention to these items and including also an attack on Bethel College, its president, and the Board of Education was sent by a group in Cherokee Presbytery to many of the presbyteries prior to their spring meetings in 1942. Copies of the news release above mentioned were included.

The response to these efforts was meager, however, for only two presbyteries other than Cherokee adopted memorials supporting its positions. Cherokee Presbytery itself asked for changes in the Board of Education and in the presidency of Bethel College.[9] Another memorial based its charge of "modernism" in Bethel College primarily upon the content of a promotional leaflet which had been sent out from the college.[10] The third dealt mostly with alleged doctrinal errors in textbooks recommended by various boards of the Church.[11] McMinnville Presbytery submitted a memorial defending the administration and faculty of Bethel College, although this memorial was vitiated by a reference of an unfavorable kind to an individual on the other side of the controversy.[12]

About the same time it was learned that the pastor of the Cumberland Presbyterian Church at Lakeland, Florida, had led that congregation into the Presbyterian Church, U. S. A. The loss of this church along with its valuable building so weakened Florida Presbytery as to bring about its eventual dissolution, though this dissolution was not to be permanent.

The special committee to which the memorials above mentioned were referred found no tangible evidence to support the accusations made against Bethel College. Not one textbook was cited, so the committee reported, which contained statements or theories which could be termed "modernistic or contrary to our system of doctrine."[13] The committee reported, also, that it had been unable to uncover any evidence of an existing group "who plan any effort looking toward union between our Church and any other."[14]

In 1943, the Rev. Ewell K. Reagin, president of Bethel, submitted to the General Assembly a resolution calling for the Cumberland Presbyterian Church to accept membership in the World Council of Churches, then in process of being formed.[15] The resolution was adopted. Before the next

General Assembly, however, two synods and three presbyteries passed memorials asking the General Assembly to sever all ties with the World Council. It was argued that the action of the preceding General Assembly was premature inasmuch as the people of the Church had not had opportunity to study the program and proposals of the World Council. It was also contended that the World Council was controlled by "modernists," and that its leaders were seeking to substitute a "Social Gospel" for evangelical Christianity.[16] After lengthy debate, the General Assembly in 1944 adopted a recommendation that the Church sever its relationship with the World Council.[17]

The following year McAdow Presbytery, in Texas, memorialized the General Assembly to apply again for membership in the World Council.[18] At this Assembly opponents of membership in the World Council procured the passage of a judicial deliverance to the effect that the General Assembly had no power, by its vote, to commit the Church to membership in any organization outside the Church itself.[19] Nevertheless, the Assembly appointed a commission of three members to gather information concerning the World Council of Churches to submit to the next General Assembly.[20]

The commission adopted the procedure of having one member present the advantages of membership in the World Council and another member the disadvantages, inasmuch as members of the commission were divided in their opinions as to the desirability of such membership. The former presented his case in three short paragraphs, the latter in four and one-half pages.[21] The General Assembly in 1946 adopted a recommendation "that the Cumberland Presbyterian Church shall not affiliate with the World Council of Churches by taking membership in it at the present time." [22]

An action taken by the General Assembly in 1942 concerning the rotation of board members was to have a profound effect upon the subsequent policies of the Church. There is little doubt that the intent of the "Lackey Law" passed in 1909 was that no board member should succeed himself.[23] The General Assembly on various occasions had ruled otherwise, however, with the result that in 1942 there was one board member who had served continuously for seventeen years, another who had served thirteen years, and at least two others who were in their fourth term, having served eleven years. In 1942 a memorial was addressed to the General Assembly by Lincoln-Decatur Presbytery asking

1. That no board member of the General Assembly be elected to succeed himself more than twice, thus giving him a term of office of not more than nine years, and

2. That a one-year period must elapse before being returned to any General Assembly board office after the nine-year period.[24]

The granting of this memorial by the General Assembly was interpreted to mean that the new regulation would go into effect immediately in the case of those whose terms expired at that Assembly.[25] The following year a memorial from Cookeville Presbytery asked that the action of the 1942 Assembly be rescinded and that certain members of the Board of Publication whose eligibility for reelection would be affected be continued as members.[26] This memorial, however, was not granted, and the nine-year limitation was permitted to stand.[27] The result was the election to board membership of a number of younger men.

The resignation of the Rev. O. A. Barbee as editor of the *Cumberland Presbyterian* and the death of the Rev. D. W. Fooks, Stated Clerk of the General Assembly, both of which occurred during the year 1944, were followed by the appointment of younger men to these positions. The Rev. Ky Curry, who since 1938 had been serving as assistant editor, was elected editor of the *Cumberland Presbyterian*. The Rev. Wayne Wiman was elected Stated Clerk.

The Rev. C. Ray Dobbins succeeded Curry in the office of the *Cumberland Presbyterian* in 1948. The first issue under his editorship was that of October 14.

The decrease in enrollment at Bethel College during the war has already been noted. The Church responded to the "Forward Movement," however, by contributions which were sufficient to pay off the more than $48,000 indebtedness which remained in 1941. Despite the response of the Church to this cause, the Committee on Education, in 1943, called attention to the fact that "conditions affecting the educational needs of our Church have been constantly changing" and noted that "in the minds of your committee there are some serious problems and deficiencies associated with the type of educational program we have been for some time trying to carry on." A special committee of eight men was therefore appointed

to make a careful study of the educational needs of our Church and report its findings together with recommendations for whatever changes may seem to be called for in adjusting the educational program to our practical situation and the long-range needs of our Church to the next meeting of the General Assembly.[28]

The special committee, in its report to the 1944 General Assembly, noted that Bethel College and the Cumberland Presbyterian Theological Seminary were greatly understaffed; that there had been a steady decrease in the enrollment during the six preceding years; that a high percentage of students attending during the three preceding years had been subsidized in some manner; and that although the school was now finally free of debt,

### The Changing Face of Publications

Representative front pages show the progressive modernization of the typography of the *Cumberland Presbyterian* over a period of more than fifty years. The *CP Pastor*, also pictured, was a separate publication for ministers, first issued in October 1947 and discontinued in June of the following year.

the buildings were greatly in need of repair, and both student body and faculty were depleted. A subsidy of at least $10,000 per year in addition to current income from endowment and denominational budget would be needed to keep the school operating in a manner which would reflect credit upon the Church. The committee reached the following conclusion:

It is our measured judgment that, unless the Church can, and will, provide Bethel College a minimum student body of 300 and an annual subsidy of at least $10,000.00 in addition to present endowment and budget income, the denomination's educational needs can best be filled by using the funds available to provide a thoroughly adequate theological training for our young ministers. . . . Since a program of providing facilities for literary courses for undergraduates is essential for these young ministers, it seems to us that it would be advantageous to make arrangements with some suitable liberal arts college to provide this instruction on a mutually satisfactory basis, and for the Church to operate its own theological seminary in the same locality.[29]

It would seem that during the war, when conditions everywhere were abnormal, was hardly the time to propose such drastic measures as the abandonment of Bethel College.

The Committee on Education, to which the report of the special committee was referred at the General Assembly, expressed the belief that "there is a future for our college and seminary" and a "definite need for the school." Its recommendation was "that we maintain a school to meet the educational needs of our Church."[30] Under pressure from the committee, Ewell K. Reagin consented to resign as president of Bethel College, and mention of this fact was made in the committee's report. The opposition to Reagin as president was spearheaded by the fundamentalists who had been responsible for the memorials attacking the college in 1942. Added to this opposition was the factor that over a period of several years the whole administration of the school had become concentrated in the hands of the president. When Reagin was elected president of Bethel College, he continued to carry on the functions he had previously performed as dean of the Theological Seminary. When H. B. Evans resigned as dean of the college, he was not replaced, but the duties of the dean were taken over by the president with the aid, in some instances, of faculty committees. Reagin had also served on the special committee appointed to study the educational needs of the Church. Consequently, when things did not go well at Bethel College, he was the one who was blamed.

The General Assembly amended the report of the Committee on Education by deleting the section which referred to Reagin's resignation, thus relieving him of the obligation of carrying out his intention to resign. The remainder of the report was adopted. Included was a recommendation that the estimated budget of $25,000 be supplemented so as to bring it up to $50,000, and that the Board of Education put on a campaign "to inform the Church fully of our condition and financial needs."

School opened in September 1944 with about sixty students, approximately the same enrollment as the year before. The term had been in progress only a few weeks, however, when President Reagin resigned to accept the pastorate of the church at Knoxville, Tennessee. On November 16, the Board of Education met in called session, accepted Reagin's resignation, and appointed the Rev. Thomas H. Campbell, who had joined the faculty in January of that year to teach Bible and theology in the Seminary, as acting administrator. Campbell was left as the only teacher in the Seminary, but the Rev. Morris Pepper and the Rev. O. T. Arnett, who were pastors in the area, and the Rev. Clark Williamson, general secretary of the Board of Christian Education, taught on a part-time basis. Despite the uncertainties under which the school was operating, the Church responded to the Board's appeal by special fund contributions in excess of $13,000. This indicated that the Church was interested in its school. With this fund some needed repairs were carried out by a committee of the Board.

In the spring of 1945 the Board of Education elected Roy N. Baker, a Cumberland Presbyterian ruling elder who was serving as superintendent of the city schools of Martin, Tennessee, as president, and Thomas H. Campbell as dean. Salaries, which had remained at depression levels until this time, were increased about 25 per cent. A budget of $38,850 was adopted for the year 1945-1946. Approval was also given to adding a department of commerce as a regular department of the college, and minimum equipment for such a department, which under wartime conditions was difficult to obtain, was purchased from a business college in Union City, Tennessee, which had been discontinued. The Board anticipated a deficit of $16,100 for the coming year and suggested that the General Assembly ask the Church to contribute $18,000 for the operation of Bethel College.[31]

Instead of granting the request for a special campaign for Bethel College, the General Assembly adopted a joint report submitted by the Committees on Education, Ministerial Relief, and Tithing and Budget calling for a denominational budget of $80,000, twice the amount raised the preceding year, for the year 1945-1946.[32] Bethel College was to receive 34 per cent of this budget. For the first time in its history the operation of Bethel College was to be subsidized through the denominational budget. Previously the percentage allotted for education had been designated for ministerial aid: that is, scholarships for ministerial students attending the college and seminary.

The Board of Education elected the Rev. Raymon Burroughs and the

Rev. John E. Gardner to teach in the Theological Seminary. These two men, together with Dean Campbell, constituted the faculty of the Seminary. In the fall of 1946, the Rev. William T. Ingram, Jr., upon his release from active duty as a chaplain in the United States Army, was added to the faculty of the Seminary to occupy the chair of missions which the Board of Foreign Missions had voted to provide.

In the fall of 1945, inasmuch as the war had ended, there was a slight increase in the enrollment at Bethel College. Eighty-five students were enrolled, of whom ten were in the Seminary. In the fall of 1946 a total of 228 students were enrolled. In 1948-1949 the number exceeded 300. Many of these students attended college under the G. I. Bill of Rights, which provided educational benefits for persons who had served in the armed forces during World War II (and later was extended). There was also a sharp upturn in the number of ministerial students. From an enrollment of twenty ministerial students (ten undergraduates and ten in the Seminary) in the fall of 1945, the number climbed to a total of sixty-nine ministerial students (fifty-nine of whom were Cumberland Presbyterians) in 1948-1949. During 1947-1948 and 1948-1949, however, there were very few students in the Seminary, since the scarcity of ministerial students entering college during the war years was now being felt at the graduate level.

Thomas H. Campbell served as dean of both Bethel College and the Seminary for two years. In 1947, Raymon Burroughs was named dean of Bethel College, and Campbell continued as dean of the Seminary. Meanwhile the number of full-time faculty members on the campus, in all departments, was increased from twelve in 1945-1946 to twenty for the year 1948-1949. The budget set for the year 1948-1949 was $91,650, more than double the budget for 1945-1946.

When the General Assembly in 1945 adopted a recommendation for a larger and more inclusive denominational budget it also directed that the Board of Tithing and Budget employ a full-time worker to promote the raising of the budget and that new quotas be set for each local church. Selected as field worker was the Rev. Hubert W. Morrow, of Batesville, Arkansas, a student in the Vanderbilt University School of Religion, who interrupted his theological education for a year to render this service. The office work continued to be done by the Rev. Thurman Levacy, assistant secretary, who had served in this capacity since January 1945. Although there were misgivings as to the ability of the Church to raise the anticipated budget, a vigorous campaign was carried on. The result was the raising of a denominational budget of $73,482.47. All boards received more money through the denominational budget than they had received the year before, and some received a great deal more.[33] Morrow was succeeded by the Rev. Lelon Looper, who was named executive secretary of the Board of Tithing and Budget. Contributions to the denominational budget continued to increase, and in 1948-1949 the goal of $100,000 was attained. During this year Looper also assisted ten churches in setting up a systematic plan of finance.[34]

In 1944, in response to a memorial from Corsicana Presbytery, the rule requiring that for admission to the Cumberland Presbyterian Orphans' Home one or both parents must have been members of the Cumberland Presbyterian Church was rescinded, with the provision that some space should always be reserved for children of Cumberland Presbyterian parentage who might be in need of a home.[35] Consequently, there was an increase in the number of children in the Home. In 1948, the Board of Ministerial Relief reported that there were twenty-nine children in the Home. It called attention to the fact, however, that the nature of the service rendered by the Home had changed in that most of the children now there were from homes broken by causes other than death.[36] Meanwhile the Rev. D. E. Williams and his wife succeeded Mr. and Mrs. L. J. Springer at the Home. In 1948, the Rev. J. W. Burgett was employed as superintendent. In 1949, there were twenty-five children in the Home.[37]

At the same time that Ky Curry became editor of the *Cumberland Presbyterian*, the Rev. J. W. Stiles was elected editor of the Sunday school literature. Under his editorship the *Cumberland Worker*, a monthly magazine for Sunday school teachers and other Christian workers, was begun.[38] O. A. Barbee was employed to write the *Advanced Quarterly* for adults,[39] in which capacity he served on a part-time basis as long as his health permitted. Because of his administrative duties at Bethel College, Thomas H. Campbell resigned in the spring of 1945 as editor of the *Cumberland Crusader,* and the Rev. Franklin Chesnut, secretary of the Young People's Division of the Board of Christian Education, became editor. This marked the beginning of a period of closer cooperation between the Board of Publication and the Board of Christian Education in the production of church school literature.

In 1947, the Board of Publication elected the Rev. Carl Ramsey, a member of the Board, as executive secretary on a part-time basis. The former manager, C. C. Brock, was appointed to continue as shop manager at the publishing house but declined to do so. The Rev. M. F. Allen, Jr., was elected editor of Sunday school literature, but a health condition prevented his assuming the responsibilities of this office.[40] For a time there was no general editor of Sunday school literature. Clark Williamson was chosen editor of the *Cumberland Worker,* and Miss Virginia Malcom, secretary of the Children's

Division of the Board of Christian Education, edited the *Junior Quarterly* and materials for the Children's Division in the *Cumberland Worker*.[41]

When the Board of Christian Education found its program of work with older youth curtailed because of the war, it gave increasing attention to the intermediate, or junior high, age group. To this group the name "Pioneers" was given.[42] As early as 1944 Miss Malcom, of Jefferson City, Tennessee, was employed as part-time secretary of the Children's Division.[43] Much of her attention was given to the promotion of vacation church schools and the selection and editing of materials for use in these schools.

In 1944, Morris Pepper resigned as secretary of the Young People's Division to accept a pastorate. He was succeeded by Franklin Chesnut. In April, 1947, Miss Sarah Cunningham, of Union City, Tennessee, was employed as assistant secretary of the Young People's Division. Along with other duties she became editor of the *Cumberland Crusader*.[44]

Although the number of young people actively involved in local church groups decreased during the war, the interest of youth in the mission projects continued. In 1942-1943 the foreign missions offerings of the young people were given toward the erection of a church building at Dagua, Colombia. The home missions project was that of assisting in the work being done among the Choctaw Indians, in southeastern Oklahoma.[45] In 1943-1944 mission offerings by the young people totaled more than $1,200. These offerings were given for the church at Dagua and for the erection of a church for Cumberland Presbyterian Negroes in Muskogee, Oklahoma.[46] During 1947-1948 and 1948-49 the foreign missions project was that of contributing to an orphanage which had been established by the Rev. Samuel

D. W. FOOKS
(1874-1944)

CLARK WILLIAMSON
(1891-1949)

King Gam in Canton, China. The church in Muskogee, Oklahoma, was continued as the home missions project until 1947 when final payment was made on the church building. The home missions project for the spring of 1948 was that of aiding in building a manse for the Mount Bethel-Steam Mill group of churches in Mississippi Presbytery.[47]

In 1944, the General Assembly received an appeal from the General Assembly of the Cumberland Presbyterian Church, Colored, asking that aid be given in establishing a chair of theology in some accredited college for Negroes, that the Home Study Course be made available to its ministers, and that the Board of Christian Education assist in the denomination's National Sunday School Convention and School of Methods held just preceding its General Assembly each year.[48] Partly because of the crisis which was facing Bethel College, the first two requests received little consideration.[49] The Assembly's Committee on Christian Education, however, was headed by the Rev. Alba H. Bates, of Texas, who had become intensely interested in the welfare of the Cumberland Presbyterian Church, Colored. The Committee recommended

that our General Assembly's Board of Christian Education be instructed to cooperate with the Colored Cumberland Presbyterian Church, both in finance and leadership, in promoting the Work of the National Sunday School Convention and School of Methods; also, in any other way in which it may be possible to assist them in preparing for greater Christian service.[50]

The Board of Christian Education appointed a committee to look into the leadership training needs of the Cumberland Presbyterian Church, Colored. A conference was held with representatives of that church and plans made to assist them in their work.[51] In 1947, Clark Williamson, the general secretary of the Board of Christian Education, along with Miss Malcom and the Rev. Davis O. Bryson and his wife, attended the Sunday School Convention and School of Methods of the Cumberland Presbyterian Church, Colored.[52] This marked the beginning of a cooperative program which was to continue through the years.

In the fall of 1946 the Board of Christian Education sponsored a Bible Conference for Ministers at Bethel College. Its purpose was to present approaches to Bible teaching which could be employed by ministers in conducting Bible conferences in their local churches.[53] In April 1948, a similar conference was held at the Rose City Church, North Little Rock, Arkansas, for ministers of the four synods west of the Mississippi River.[54] In the fall of 1948 conferences were held at Muskogee, Oklahoma, and at Bethel College.[55]

In September 1947, the first camp leaders' retreat was held at Bethel

College.[56] Those who were responsible for camping programs at the synodic and presbyterial levels were invited. Ideas regarding improvement of such programs were shared. In the fall of 1948 four regional camp leaders' retreats were held.[57]

In May 1947, the Board of Christian Education moved its offices to a building in downtown McKenzie. From this location the work of Christian education was directed until the completion of the Denominational Center in Memphis in the fall of 1951. Meanwhile, on April 28, 1949, Clark Williamson had died after nearly twenty-two years of service in planning and promoting the Christian education program of the Cumberland Presbyterian Church.

During the year 1943 the headquarters of the Board of Missions and Church Erection were established in Memphis, Tennessee, and the Rev. M. F. Allen was employed as its full-time secretary. The Board continued to give aid in small amounts to many fields. The Committee on Missions of the 1947 General Assembly questioned the advisability of so many small gifts and recommended that the Board "endeavor to invest their gifts in places that would be more apt to bring better returns than the many small gifts could possibly bring."[58] In reply to this criticism the Board, in its report to the General Assembly in 1948, pointed out that there are circumstances which make even a small gift of great importance. A specific case was cited of a gift of fifty dollars to the Holly Grove Church, near Brighton, Tennessee, in Memphis Presbytery. This rural church had employed a full-time pastor and had built a manse without board assistance. This program had taxed the membership heavily. A new piano was needed, and it was found that one could be purchased at a bargain price. The church lacked fifty dollars of having enough to pay for it and asked for assistance. The fifty dollars was given, and the Board felt that the gift was worthily bestowed.[59]

The employment of synodic field men was continued throughout the greater part of this period in at least five of the synods. In some instances it was through the efforts of these men that new churches in strategic areas were begun.

The Board gave aid in some fashion to at least a dozen churches which were organized during this period. These churches, with approximate dates of organization, were Booneville and Fort Smith, Arkansas (1941); Louisville, Kentucky (1942); Indianapolis, Indiana (1944); Houston, Texas (1945); Pine Bluff, Arkansas (1947); Cherokee, Alabama (1947); Clinton, Oklahoma (1948); Waverly, Tennessee (1948); Parsons, Tennessee (1948); Florence, Alabama (1948); and Madison, Tennessee. The last-named church first appears on the roll of churches in 1946 as Old Hickory but was moved to Madison about 1949. The church at Houston was organized by the Rev. O. N. Baucom, field worker for Texas Synod. The church at Parsons was organized by the Rev. J. T. Buck, field worker for West Tennessee Synod, on November 7, 1948, with 51 charter members. The church at Florence was organized with eleven members on October 31, 1948, by the Rev. E. W. Johnson, field worker for Alabama-Mississippi Synod.[60]

There was renewed interest during this period in improving the physical facilities and programs of the many rural churches of the denomination. One such instance was that of Young's Chapel, in Knoxville Presbytery. Here the men of the Knoxville church, the General Assembly's Board of Missions and Church Erection, and the local congregation pledged themselves to contribute $500 each, as groups, to make possible the calling of a full-time pastor for Young's Chapel. Aid in some amount was given many rural churches, and a number of such churches moved forward to having resident full-time ministers. In 1941, only about 120 Cumberland Presbyterian churches had the full-time service of a minister. Few of these were rural. By 1949 there were approximately 200 churches with full-time ministers, and many of these were rural.

Interest in making the rural church a more effective instrument for service took concrete form when at a Rural Life Conference held at Bethel College in 1946 a Christian Rural Fellowship in the Cumberland Presbyterian Church was organized. Hubert W. Morrow was chosen president, and Miss Lela Smartt, secretary. A planning committee of five was appointed, and this committee drafted a constitution which was approved by the Fellowship and by the General Assembly.[61] A second Rural Life Conference held at Jackson, Tennessee, February 11-13, 1947, was attended by some eighty ministers and laymen. For several years the rural life conference was an annual affair. A set of goals for local churches participating in the "More Abundant Rural Life Movement" was set up in the form of a score-sheet. A service of dedication of seed, soil, and sower was prepared for use by the churches during the month of March, and a service of dedication of the harvest was circulated for use in the Harvest Home Festival in November. In 1948 the General Assembly appropriated $500 for the use of the Christian Rural Fellowship. At the same time the Fellowship was placed under the supervision and sponsorship of the General Assembly's Board of Missions.[62]

After a temporary interruption at the time of the Japanese invasion, the missions in South China were able to function again. There were grave difficulties, of course, for much of the church property, including the church in Canton, had been destroyed, and there were many refugees to be fed.

When war between Japan and the United States became a reality, communications between the United States and the missions in China were cut off, since the missions were in territory occupied by the Japanese. Hong Kong also fell to the Japanese in December 1941.

In the summer of 1943, McAdow Gam, brother of Samuel King Gam, returned to China after having been in the United States as a student since 1938. Early in 1944 he became assistant to E. H. Lockwood, executive chairman of the Church Committee for China Relief, in Kwangtung province, which was within the area of Free China.[63]

Following the Japanese surrender in September 1945 communications between the Board of Foreign Missions and the missions in South China were resumed. By May 1946, Honam, Fat Shan, Shek Won, Shekki, Sha Kai, and Ti Won churches were functioning.[64] A new chapel built in Canton at a cost of $1,465—some 64 per cent of which was contributed by the Chinese themselves—was dedicated June 2, 1946.[65] In August 1946, Canton Presbytery met for the first time in several years. Church buildings were being repaired, new pastors were appointed, and three districts for evangelism were formed.[66] Repairs were made on the Boys' Home, and at least four schools were in operation.

Meanwhile, promotion of the Gam Sing Quah Memorial Fund to rebuild the work in China was resumed, and in the summer of 1947 the goal of $35,000 was reached.[67] Samuel King Gam attended the General Assembly which met at Knoxville, Tennessee, that year. When he returned to South China he found that refugees were coming in from the North where civil war was raging.[68]

By the fall of 1949 the communists had overrun most of China, and on October 1 of that year the communist state, officially styled "the People's Democratic Republic of China," was proclaimed at Peking. The Cumberland Presbyterian Church had to withdraw its Board's direction of the mission work in China. The Gam family had to leave the area because of their American associations. Other national pastors remained to carry on the work, which they could do only under severe restrictions.

In Colombia there was growth although changes in personnel were frequent. The Rev. Arleigh G. Matlock and his wife and the Rev. Emery Newman and his wife were sent to Colombia in 1942, but Mrs. Bernice Gonzalez returned to the United States that year. In 1944, the Rev. Vance Shultz and his wife went to Colombia, but the Rev. Plutarco Roa and his wife decided to live in the United States. The Rev. Paul F. Brown and his family returned to the United States and, after some months, he resigned. In the fall of 1944 Arleigh Matlock and his wife returned to the United States on account of his ill health. In 1945, the Rev. Edward W. Clyne and

MARTINIANO FAJARDO
(1897-1949)

ROY N. BAKER
(1906-1968)

his wife, who formerly had served in Colombia with the World-Wide Evangelistic Crusade, accepted work under the Cumberland Presbyterian Board. The Rev. Fred W. Bryson was commissioned in June 1945 to serve in Colombia; he returned to the United States in 1947. Miss Cassandra Stockburger, who was commissioned in 1947, served until 1950. In 1948, the Rev. James Kelso and his wife were commissioned. On December 26, 1949, the mission suffered the loss by death of the Rev. Martiniano Fajardo, whose years of effectual work caused him to be called "the Paul of Colombia."

In June 1946, at the Missionary Convention held at Birmingham, Alabama, more than $6,000 was given in the consecration offering for the completion of the Pereira building fund.[69] In 1948, the building at Pereira was completed under the direction of Emery Newman. During this year, also, a new church building was completed in the *barrio* of Alameda, in Cali, preparatory to organizing a church there. The eight organized churches in Cauca Valley Presbytery reported in 1949 a total membership of 627. A persecution of the evangelical churches in Colombia, which was to take its toll in terms of destruction of life and property and annoyance of the evangelicals, was just beginning.

Beginning in about 1946 there was a clamor on the part of some to open a mission work in Africa. A minister who had placed his membership in the Cumberland Presbyterian Church several years earlier and had formerly worked under the board of another Presbyterian body wished to be sent to Liberia. When the Board of Foreign Missions decided against opening such a mission, a group within the Cumberland Presbyterian Church formed an organization called "The Cumberland Missionary Fellowship." Early in 1947 a leaflet, the *Fellowship Herald,* was distributed. An appeal was made for $10,000 to open a mission in Liberia. Shortly before the meeting of the General Assembly the Board of Foreign Missions stated its position through the columns of the *Cumberland Presbyterian.* The Board stated that it felt that it would be "unethical and unwise" to start another mission in the small Republic of Liberia where at least three strong mission boards and a number of smaller ones were already operating.[70.]

A resolution passed by the Missionary Convention regarding this matter was presented to the General Assembly. The Committee on Missions and Church Erection, to which the resolution was referred, expressed the opinion, which was concurred in by the Assembly, that "all foreign mission work of and within the Cumberland Presbyterian Church should rightfully come under the supervision and direction of the Board of Foreign Missions," and that any solicitation of funds for any cause that rightfully comes under the supervision of any board but is being carried on independently of that board "is improper and should not be done." [71]

Although manifest progress was being made in some areas in the period following World War II, there was serious question in the minds of some as to whether or not the Cumberland Presbyterian Church would respond to the challenge to meet the demands of the new order. Why did not the Church grow more rapidly? Why were ministers leaving the denomination? It was such questions which led Morris Pepper, Moderator of the General Assembly in 1947, to call a churchwide "Conference on Policy and Program of Our Church." This conference was held on April 6 and 7, 1948, at the Central Cumberland Presbyterian Church in Memphis, Tennessee. The conference was well publicized and well attended. Ten states were represented. There was a registered attendance of 160 persons, including nine past moderators and forty-five board members and employees.

The Moderator presented a document setting forth the picture of the Church as he saw it. The counsel of those present was sought on various matters. The Moderator announced that those matters on which there was a consensus would be presented for the consideration of the General Assembly, and that those matters in which there was marked disagreement would be dropped.

In substance, he suggested a congregation-centered program rather than an institution-centered one. Standards were suggested as to what a congregation ought to be doing. On the other hand, questions were raised as to whether the institutions of the Church ought to be maintained. Should the Church, for example, continue to operate a printing plant? Or should it arrange to have its printing done elsewhere? On the matter of higher education three alternatives were suggested: (1) Should the Church continue to attempt to operate both a liberal arts college and a theological seminary? (2) Or should it close its college and concentrate its resources on operating a theological seminary, perhaps on the campus of some university? (3) Or should the Church dispense with its theological seminary and seek to strengthen Bethel College?

In full recognition of the need for much more money to operate its educational institutions, the conference group as a whole favored the continued operation of both Bethel College and the Theological Seminary. The Board of Publication was requested to submit figures to the General Assembly showing whether or not the printing shop was operating at a profit. The Board of Ministerial Relief was also asked to make a full report to the General Assembly on the nature of the work being done by the Children's Home.

The Moderator recommended that the General Assembly approve selling the existing publishing house and the erection of a publishing house and central office building at a new location; that the Board of Education and the Educational Endowment Commission meet together to attempt to secure a field representative to solicit students for Bethel College and raise money for the school; and that consideration be given to employing the services of a fund-raising firm to assist in raising money for the educational institutions of the Church. He also recommended the merger of certain of the General Assembly's boards and agencies.[72]

A special committee appointed at the General Assembly to deal with the proposed mergers of boards and agencies recommended that the Board of Publication and the Board of Christian Education be consolidated to form a Board of Publication and Christian Education.[73] A Board of Finance was created to be the legal successor of the Board of Trustees of the General Assembly, the Board of Tithing and Budget, the Board of Ministerial Relief, and the Educational Endowment Commission. To this Board was committed the responsibility of handling the endowment funds of other General Assembly boards and agencies as well. A Board of Trustees of the Cumberland Presbyterian Children's Home was also created, this board being composed of the members already serving on the Board of Ministerial Relief or their successors.[74] It was also recommended that the Board of Missions and Church Erection become the Board of Extension and Evangelism. (The name "Board of Missions and Evangelism" was subsequently chosen.) It was suggested that the Board of Foreign Missions confine its home mis-

CUMBERLAND PRESBYTERIAN PUBLISHING HOUSE, NASHVILLE, TENNESSEE

This building was "headquarters," in effect, of the denomination for a quarter century. The front portion, facing Eighth Avenue South, was previously the Tennessee Governor's Mansion. The addition at the rear housed a modern printing plant.

sions project to work among minority groups.[75] Thus six boards were set up to do the work which formerly had been committed to nine.

The same General Assembly directed that the publishing house in Nashville be sold and that an office building to house all the General Assembly boards and a publishing house be erected at a place to be chosen by a commission elected for that purpose.[76] The commission chose Memphis as the city where the headquarters of the Church would be established.[77]

Details of effecting the consolidation of the various boards and instructions regarding the procuring of charters were committed to a Charters Committee.[78] This committee made its report to the General Assembly which met at Muskogee, Oklahoma, in June 1949, and details necessary to making the transition to the new organizational setup were approved.[79]

During the year 1948-1949 the Board of Finance organized, employed Charles W. Hughes, of Union City, Tennessee, as executive secretary, and formulated plans for a financial campaign to raise $350,000: $150,000 to build a new Denominational Center, $100,000 endowment for Bethel College, and $100,000 for capital improvements at Bethel College.[80]

Meanwhile a site in Memphis was selected for the Denominational Center and a lot purchased at a cost of $22,750. The General Assembly directed that the Board of Publication contribute $25,000 to the Center project fom funds derived from the sale of the publishing house property in Nashville, a portion of which had already been sold. It was further recommended that the cost of the Denominational Center, including the lot, be not in excess of $175,000.[81] The remaining $150,000 was expected to come from proceeds of the proposed financial campaign.

Thus was launched the most ambitious program which the Cumberland Presbyterian Church had attempted since the campaign for educational endowment was launched in 1918. Although there were some who doubted, there were evidences of a new attitude of hope pulsating through the Church.

In 1940 the General Assembly changed the method of reporting membership from a classification of members as "resident" and "nonresident" to that of "active" and "inactive." [82] The new system was first reflected in the Minutes of the General Assembly for 1941. In that year the reported active membership was 45,842, and the total membership figure was 72,951. In 1949, the reported active membership was 53,047, a net increase of 7,205 for the eight-year period. The total membership figure was 79,453.

A large proportion of this increase was in the urban churches. In 1941, sixty-one churches were listed as being situated in cities of 10,000 or more people.[83] Of these, the fifty-nine churches which reported had a total active membership of 7,363, or slightly more than 16 per cent of the active membership of the denomination. In 1949, these same churches (fifty-five reporting) had 10,693 active members. By this time, however, there were seventy-seven churches in cities with a population of 10,000 or more.[84] Altogether these had a total active membership of 12,515, or approximately 23.5 per cent of the active membership of the denomination. The largest percentage of increase was in those presbyteries having an urban constituency.

Statistical reports indicate a marked increase in the number of conversions and additions to the churches of the denomination during the last four years of this period. In 1944-1945, there were 2,905 conversions and 3,497 additions reported. There was a gradual increase in the number of conversions and additions each year until 1948-1949, when 4,696 conversions and 5,595 additions were reported. This was a period when much emphasis was being given to visitation evangelism. Such was the emphasis that in planning the program for the General Assembly at Nashville in 1948 the program committee arranged to have a school of evangelism in conjunction with the General Assembly. This school was conducted by Dr. Guy H. Black, of Hollywood, Florida, a member of the Methodist Church and one of the leading advocates of visitation evangelism.

# 24

## ADVANCE IN THE MID-CENTURY

*A Church which always had been predominantly rural had to become involved in urban life if it were to serve its own constituency, not to mention persons of other backgrounds to whom it would be called to minister.*

The period following the year 1950 was characterized by the increasing urbanization of American culture. Although various government-sponsored farm programs after World War II encouraged some who were coming out of the armed forces to return to the farm, increased wages in industry and higher salaries in white-collar jobs soon pulled increasing numbers to the cities.

In Tennessee, where the Cumberland Presbyterian Church has always had its greatest numerical strength,[1] the urban population increased from 44.1 per cent of the total population in 1950 to 52.3 per cent in 1960. Fifty-six of the ninety-five counties in Tennessee lost population. For example, Carroll County, in which Bethel College is situated, lost 11.6 per cent of its population during that decade. In contrast, counties containing the large urban centers registered a marked increase in population. Shelby County (Memphis) showed an increase of 30 per cent.[2]

Meanwhile the United States Bureau of the Census recognized a new category, the urbanized area. An urbanized area was defined as one containing at least one city of 50,000 or more inhabitants together with the surrounding closely settled incorporated and unincorporated areas. Unincorporated areas containing as many as 1,000 inhabitants per square mile were considered

CUMBERLAND PRESBYTERIAN CENTER, MEMPHIS, TENNESSEE

part of the urbanized area.[3] Thus many Cumberland Presbyterian churches formerly counted as rural fell within such urbanized areas.

It was in such an environment that the Cumberland Presbyterian Church, as it emerged from its period of reorganization in the late 1940s, found itself. A Church which always had been predominantly rural had to become involved in urban life if it were to serve its own constituency, not to mention persons of other backgrounds to whom it would be called to minister. During this period the work of the Cumberland Presbyterian Church was characterized both by a closer correlation of the work of its various boards and agencies and by an increasing involvement in ecumenical concerns.

The location of the General Assembly office and the offices of four (later three) of the boards in the Denominational Center at Memphis made possible a correlation of the work of the various agencies which long had been needed. In 1950, the General Assembly took action to bring about such correlation in an official way when it created the General Assembly's Planning Committee.[4] This body was composed of the Moderator and Stated Clerk of the General Assembly, the two immediate past Moderators, three members-at-large elected by the Assembly, and one representative and one executive from each board. It was designed to make recommendations to the General Assembly concerning the denominational budget and its apportionment, denominational goals, plans for any promotional activities involving all or a majority of the General Assembly's boards and agencies, and the correlation of the work of any two or more boards or agencies. It replaced the Moderator's Council, which had been primarily an advisory body.

The ecumenical relations of the denomination were also the subject of much discussion. Traditionally the Cumberland Presbyterian Church had manifested a willingness to cooperate with other Christian churches in every good work. After the attempted union of 1906, however, many of those who remained Cumberland Presbyterian tended to be suspicious of participation involving close ties with other churches, especially at the denominational level. Despite some opposition, the denomination maintained its connection after 1906 with the United Society of Christian Endeavor,[5] and in 1913 the General Assembly, in response to an inquiry from the Rev. G. D. Matthews, of London, general secretary of the Alliance of the Reformed Churches Throughout the World Holding the Presbyterian System, voted to continue its membership in the Alliance.[6] A breakdown in communications occurred, however, due to the deaths of Matthews and Dr. J. L. Goodknight, Stated Clerk of the General Assembly, with the result that the matter went by default.[7] The Cumberland Presbyterian Church was in and out of the International Council of Religious Education twice prior to its becoming a member again in 1942.[8] The Board of Foreign Missions had become a member of the Foreign Missions Conference and the Missionary Education Movement prior to 1950.

In 1950, the Board of Missions and Evangelism reported that it had applied for membership in the Home Missions Council of North America and the Missionary Education Movement. In view of the General Assembly's deliverance in 1945 ruling that the Assembly had no power to vote the Church into membership in any organization outside the Church itself, the legality of the membership of boards and agencies of the General Assembly in such organizations was also questioned. Accordingly, the General Assembly referred this question to its Permanent Judiciary Committee.[9]

In November 1950, the International Council of Religious Education, the Foreign Missions Conference, the Home Missions Council of North America, and the Missionary Education Movement, together with several other interdenominational organizations, were merged to form the National Council of Churches in America. These organizations became divisions within the National Council.

Majority and minority reports were submitted by members of the Permanent Judiciary Committee to the next General Assembly. The majority held that if affiliation with some organization outside the denomination by either the General Assembly or one of its boards, agencies, or institutions was deemed necessary, proper, or helpful in carrying out any of the general powers and purposes of the General Assembly and did not involve the surrender of the autonomy of the General Assembly or the board or agency or any doctrinal change or commitment, the Assembly had the power to authorize or direct such membership or affiliation. The minority report emphasized that the jurisdiction of the various church courts was "limited by the express provisions of the Constitution" and held that the action taken in 1945 was sound.[10] After concurring in the majority report, the General Assembly took action authorizing the Board of Missions and Evangelism to hold membership in the Joint Commission on Missionary Education, the Home Missions Division of the National Council, and the Protestant Indian Council of Oklahoma.[11]

In 1952 the General Assembly received memorials from ten presbyteries and one synod asking that all relationships with the National Council of Churches be severed. The General Assembly, by a vote of approximately four to one, adopted a recommendation that the relationships of the various boards with divisions of the National Council "remain unsevered at present" and that a fact-finding committee of four be created "to assemble documentary facts on this entire question to be presented to the Presbyteries of this General Assembly for their study and guidance in future actions." [12]

Unwilling to await the findings of this committee, Springfield Presbytery, in the fall of 1952, directed its churches to withhold support from the denominational budget until the relationships of denominational boards with the National Council should be severed. This action was appealed to Missouri Synod, which directed the presbytery to rescind its action.[13]

The committee above mentioned submitted a lengthy report setting forth requirements for membership in the National Council of Churches, the American Council of Christian Churches, and the National Association of Evangelicals, all interdenominational councils but representing diverse points of view. Included also were statements from the various boards setting forth the advantages to be derived from affiliation with appropriate divisions of the National Council. It was recognized that the views of some leaders in the National Council were not pleasing to members of the committee and not in keeping with the doctrinal beliefs of the Cumberland Presbyterian Church. It was also recognized that some of these persons had been listed by the Committee on Un-American Activities of the United States House of Representatives as belonging to questionable organizations. The committee urged, however, that the National Council be judged on the basis of its constitution and other official statements rather than by the views of individuals connected with it.[14]

Meanwhile, in the fall of 1952, the Revised Standard Version of the Bible had appeared. The New Testament, which had been published in 1946 and bore the copyright of the International Council of Religious Education, had not provoked any formidable opposition. The new Bible, however, carried the copyright of the National Council of Churches. Furthermore, the use of the term "young woman" instead of "virgin" in Isaiah 7:14 provoked a fury of opposition, although the word "virgin" was retained in Matthew 1:23.[15]

Ten presbyteries memorialized the General Assembly meeting in 1953 to sever the relationships of its agencies with the National Council. Some of these also called for disapproval of the Revised Standard Version of the Bible. On the other hand, five presbyteries requested the General Assembly to approve the existing relationships. The General Assembly, meeting at Gadsden, Alabama, concurred in the report of its Committee on Overtures which noted that the Church was not a member of the National Council of Churches and was not seeking such membership, while reaffirming the privilege of the boards to hold membership in the divisions of the Council.[16]

Following adjournment of the General Assembly a group of commissioners and visitors who were displeased with the Assembly's actions met at the Walnut Park Church in Gadsden and formed a "Fellowship of Cumberland Presbyterian Conservatives." An affirmation was drawn up to be signed by those desiring to become members. Subsequently a monthly paper entitled *Cumberland Presbyterian Conservatives* was edited by the Rev. Ward Gately at Springfield, Missouri. In September, an "Assembly of the Cumberland Presbyterian Conservatives" was held at Huntsville, Alabama. This "Assembly" elected a moderator and a stated clerk. Plans were made to promote the organization of "Conservative Fellowships" on a presbyterial level. Meanwhile the Huntsville church had ceased contributing to the denominational budget, thus repudiating an agreement previously made as a condition to securing a loan. At that time the Huntsville church owed the Board of Finance about $17,000.

The next General Assembly had before it an opinion concerning the Fellowship of Cumberland Presbyterian Conservatives rendered by a majority of the Permanent Judiciary Committee at the request of the Moderator.[17] The Assembly's Committee on Judiciary concurred in the report of the Permanent Committee that the Fellowship was illegal. It pointed out that membership in the Fellowship involved the signing of a statement of beliefs which included elements not contained in the Confession of Faith of the Cumberland Presbyterian Church. It further noted that the Fellowship gave evidence of the influence of "independent, non-denominational groups" which were not primarily concerned with the welfare of the Cumberland Presbyterian Church. The opinion was expressed that the organization in question "endangers the spiritual welfare of the Cumberland Presbyterian Church." Presbyteries were directed to counsel with their ministers and churches regarding these matters.[18]

Extremists within the "Conservative" group persisted in their rebellion. The Rev. Charles Pruitt, who together with his church (Second Church, of Memphis), had been directed by Memphis Presbytery to withdraw an invitation for the second Assembly of Cumberland Presbyterian Conservatives to be held there, was suspended indefinitely for disobeying the presbytery's directive.[19] Approximately one hundred members of the church at Huntsville, Alabama, which meanwhile had called Pruitt as pastor, withdrew upon Robert Donnell Presbytery's refusal to approve the pastoral relationship and formed the "Huntsville Bible Church." Three churches in Missouri, including one which had been formed by a dissident group out of the Springfield church, withdrew from Springfield Presbytery and formed an "Association of Independent Presbyterian Churches." One of these was the historic Mount Comfort Church.

The Rev. Stephen B. Williams, who had come into Louisiana Presbytery from the Presbyterian Church, U. S., and was preaching to an independent church which had withdrawn from the Presbyterian Church, persuaded the majority in Louisiana Presbytery to incorporate under the laws of the state of Louisiana. He argued that this act would enable the presbytery to manage its own affairs without outside interference. A committee from Texas Synod which was sent to investigate conditions in the presbytery declared the corporation illegal because it provided for a manner of transacting business which was at variance with the Constitution of the Cumberland Presbyterian Church. The committee recommended that Louisiana Presbytery be directed to dissolve the corporation.[20] Williams published a paper, the *Kingdom Herald,* in which he threatened that if Texas Synod persisted in its course there would be a number of independent Cumberland Presbyterian churches in Louisiana. He did not have the support of the people in advocating such a step, however, for no church withdrew. Finding himself unable any longer to dictate the policies of the presbytery, Williams called for his letter.

In the fall of 1954 the Rev. H. C. Wakefield, pastor at Pleasant Shade, Tennessee, was deposed from the ministry by Cookeville Presbytery on account of his activities in the "Conservative" movement. In April 1955, he and the Rev. W. M. Dycus, who still held membership in Cookeville Presbytery, ordained Lum Oliver to the work of the ministry and formed what they called the Carthage Presbytery of the Upper Cumberland

Presbyterian Church. About half a dozen churches, or portions of churches, in Middle Tennessee joined this presbytery as did three churches in northern Alabama, a church at Rose, Oklahoma, and one of the Missouri churches above mentioned.

The number of persons involved in these various defections is not known but was probably about 600.

In 1951, the General Assembly received a communication from Dr. Ralph Waldo Lloyd, secretary of the Western Section of the Alliance of Reformed Churches Throughout the World Holding the Presbyterian Order (commonly known as the World Presbyterian Alliance) inviting the Cumberland Presbyterian Church to become a member. The Assembly requested the Moderator, the Rev. John E. Gardner, to attend the next meeting of the Western Section and to report to the next General Assembly concerning the purposes, benefits, and responsibilities of membership.[21] Although the Moderator reported favorably, the Assembly's decision was "that to make application for membership . . . is not advisable at this time." [22]

In 1956, however, in response to memorials from McAdow Presbytery and West Tennessee Synod, the General Assembly voted to accept the invitation to membership. The Moderator, the Rev. Hubert W. Morrow, and the Stated Clerk, the Rev. H. Shaw Scates (who had been elected to that office in 1955), were appointed to represent the denomination in the next area meeting.[23] Thus the Cumberland Presbyterian Church, after an interruption of fifty years, took its place again as a member of the Alliance. Scates served as recording clerk for the Eighteenth General Council of the Alliance at Sao Paulo, Brazil, July 26-August 6, 1959, at which six official delegates from the Cumberland Presbyterian Church were enrolled.[24]

The Church's membership has been continued in the subsequent years, and other delegates attended General Council meetings in Frankfurt, Germany, in 1964, and Nairobi, Kenya, in 1970. A Cumberland Presbyterian, Mrs. Wesley Mattonen, was named to the Executive Committee of the Alliance at the 1970 meeting.[25] Also, at that meeting, the Alliance was merged with the International Congregational Council to form the World Alliance of Reformed Churches (Presbyterian and Congregational).[26]

The relationship established with other Presbyterian churches within the Alliance was doubtless instrumental in bringing about the message of apology from the General Assembly of the United Presbyterian Church in the U. S. A. to the Cumberland Presbyterian General Assembly in

1962 for actions and attitudes manifested in the early 1800s and following 1906. The occasion of this message and the Cumberland Presbyterian response to it have been narrated in a previous chapter.[27]

Other, representative ecumenical involvements of the Cumberland Presbyterian Church included participation of the Board of Missions in the Presbyterian Appalachian Council,[28] adoption of the Covenant Life Curriculum (discussed in this chapter), and the production in 1970 of a book of worship forms and prayers (a later edition of which would include hymns) prepared by a Joint Committee on Worship made up of members from the Cumberland Presbyterian Church, the United Presbyterian Church in the U.S.A., and the Presbyterian Church, U. S., and intended for use in the three denominations.[29]

The question of organic union with some larger denomination was thrust upon the Cumberland Presbyterian Church when in the Denominational Day issue of the *Cumberland Presbyterian* in February 1962 there was published a sermon which had been preached a year earlier by the Rev. Turner N. Clinard, pastor at Greeneville, Tennessee. Emphasizing the problems and disadvantages of a small denomination, he expressed the belief that "the Cumberland Presbyterian Church in our generation can best fulfill her servant role, can most economically use her resources for the Kingdom of God, by losing herself." Joining a larger denomination, even though it may mean that "we shall have to become one lost drop in a great bucket to do it," was advocated.[30] Reactions to the sermon were varied,[31] but no presbytery sent a memorial to the General Assembly on this subject.

That same year, however, in response to a memorial from Knoxville Presbytery, the General Assembly appointed a Permanent Committee on Inter-Church Relations "to plan for a mutually closer working relationship between our Church and other members of the Presbyterian and Reformed family of churches."[32] Two years later the scope of the Committee's work was enlarged when it was authorized to communicate with other bodies "concerning the possibility of organic union with our denomination."[33] This action was in response to a memorial from South Texas Presbytery asking that a commission be appointed "to study the possibilities of inviting other communions of like faith to enter into organic union with the Cumberland Presbyterian Church." Specifically mentioned were the Moravian Church, Northern Province; the Moravian Church, Southern Province; and the Unity of the Brethren.[34] Subsequent contacts with those bodies revealed that none of them was ready to enter into union negotiations with the Cumberland Presbyterian Church.[35]

In 1966 the General Assembly received a memorial from Western Presbytery, Texas Synod, asking that the Assembly instruct the Permanent Committee on Inter-Church Relations that "our desire is for one General Assembly uniting the UPUSA and Cumberland Presbyterian Churches." It further requested that this Committee "engage in dialogue with representatives of the United Presbyterian Church in the United States in the interest of uniting our communions into one body in government, doctrine, and mission."[36] Memorials from three presbyteries expressed opposition to a consideration of organic union.[37]

Both the Permanent Committee and the Assembly's Committee on Judiciary noted that the General Assembly did not have the power of itself to make such a commitment.[38] The Assembly adopted a recommendation "that our denomination proceed no further at this time in conversations with any other denominations except the Second Cumberland Presbyterian Church concerning organic union."[39]

In three other actions this General Assembly expressed its unwillingness to seek organic union with other denominations. A memorial from South Texas Presbytery requested the General Assembly to hold its 1969 meeting in San Antonio. The General Assembly of the United Presbyterian Church in the U. S. A. was also scheduled to meet in San Antonio, and it was suggested that an overlapping date be selected, and that a joint worship and communion service and other joint meetings be arranged. The General Assembly granted the memorial, but with the understanding "that such simultaneous meetings and joint services shall not be connected with any merger proposals."[40] Two memorials requested that the action taken in 1964 enlarging the scope of work of the Inter-Church Relations Committee be rescinded.[41] While not granting the memorials, the General Assembly clarified the duties of the Committee by stating that "only by specific direction by the Assembly" was the Committee authorized to initiate conversations or respond to communications from other denominations concerning consultation on organic union.[42] The Committee on Inter-Church Relations had proposed a "Consultation on the Role and Future of the Cumberland Presbyterian Church."[43] Instead, the General Assembly made provision for a conference on "The Nature and Mission of the Church in the Contemporary World" to be planned by the Assembly's Program Council together with an elected representative from each of the ten synods. It was understood that this conference "should not be set in the context of organic union with other denominations."[44]

The next General Assembly, which met at Paducah, Kentucky, in 1967, relaxed its restrictions on the Inter-Church Relations Committee to some extent.[45] It also voted, in response to a memorial from Knoxville Presbytery, to name two observers to the Consultation on Church Union, which was working toward the unification of a number of denominations.[46] In 1969, the Committee reported that it was not carrying on conversations with any group concerning union.[47]

The most serious attempt at organic union since 1906 had to do with proposals for union with the Second Cumberland Presbyterian Church.[48] In 1957, the General Assembly, in response to a memorial from Cherokee Presbytery, in Oklahoma, set up a committee to work with a similar committee from the Cumberland Presbyterian Church, Colored (as the Negro denomination was then known) to study the possibility of organic union between the two Cumberland Presbyterian denominations. The committee was composed of the Moderator of the General Assembly together with one member to be elected by each of the Assembly's seven boards. The following year it was reported that the committees from the two churches had agreed "that church union is impractical at this time." The desire was expressed, however, that the possibility of union should not be abandoned.[49]

In 1959, the General Assembly suggested "that we take as our ultimate goal the formation of the Colored Churches in their various presbyteries into one synod and that this synod become a synod of the Cumberland Presbyterian Church." The following year the Joint Committee reported that this proposal was not feasible. It suggested rather the need for a program of education to convince the people of both churches that union was feasible.[50]

In 1963 the General Assembly of the Second Cumberland Presbyterian Church, meeting at Decatur, Alabama, took the initiative by appointing a Merger Commission of seven to meet with a similar commission from the Cumberland Presbyterian Church. This action was communicated to the General Assembly of the Cumberland Presbyterian Church which met that year at Austin, Texas.[51] This General Assembly dissolved the previously appointed Committee on Cooperation and Union and named a new committee of seven members to meet with representatives of the Second Cumberland Presbyterian Church.[52]

The plan finally submitted to the two Assemblies in 1966 called for the reunion of the two churches under the name and framework of the Cumberland Presbyterian Church. The General Assembly of the Cumberland Presbyterian Church would vote to receive the Second Cumberland Presbyterian Church under the provision in its Constitution giving the General Assembly the power "to receive under its jurisdiction other ecclesiastical bodies whose organization is conformed to the doctrine and order of this Church." [53] The Second Church, since it would be surrendering its name and separate identity, which would be in the nature of a constitutional

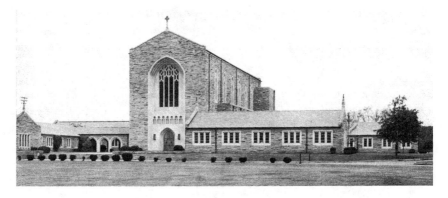

### First Church, Chattanooga, Tennessee

Representative of churches serving an urban population is the First Church of Chattanooga, the largest in the denomination for many years, with a membership in 1970 of 1,406. It was organized in 1841. The pictured physical plant was constructed in 1958, in the twenty-fifth year of the pastorate of the Rev. J. Fred Johnson, and in 1970 was valued at more than $1,500,000. The General Assembly convened there in 1964.

### Mount Sinai Church, Nashville, Tennessee

Another urban church of historic interest, though much younger in years, is Mount Sinai, which was organized in 1961 and was received into Nashville Presbytery in 1965 as the only black congregation in the predominantly white Cumberland Presbyterian denomination. The pictured building was completed in 1970 under the leadership of the Rev. James Price, the church's first pastor, and was dedicated in services held on May 10 of that year.

change, would submit the question to its presbyteries. The two Assemblies would be united to form one Assembly, but the synods and presbyteries would remain as they were except for some changes in names where the two churches had judicatories of the same name. The denominational boards would be united with the provision that in the beginning the ratio of membership would be in proportion to the membership ratio of the two churches. Provisions was made whereby overlapping presbyteries and synods might be merged at a later date.[54]

By the required three-fourths majority the General Assembly of the Second Church, meeting in Dallas, Texas, submitted the plan of union to its presbyteries. The General Assembly of the Cumberland Presbyterian Church, which met in Memphis, Tennessee, voted by a substantial majority for the plan of union which was, in effect, a vote to receive the synods and presbyteries of the Second Church. It was hoped that the two Assemblies, both of which would meet in Paducah, Kentucky, in 1967, would be reunited at that time. Nine of the sixteen presbyeries of the Second Church voted for reunification but this was three short of the three-fourths majority required. The time for approval of the plan was extended another year.[55] During the year 1967-1968, one additional presbytery voted for the plan, but the number approving was still short of the required three-fourths. The General Assembly of the Cumberland Presbyterian Church in its 1968 meeting dissolved its Committee on Unification but directed the Board of Missions to appoint five of its members as a subcommittee to work with a corresponding committee of the Second Church.[56] The size of the body, designated the Committee on Cooperative Activities and Unification, was increased later; in late 1970 the joint committee had fourteen members, seven from each denomination.[57]

In helping the Church to minister adequately in the new era the newly organized Board of Finance had a large function to perform. Originally charged with administering the endowment and trust funds of all General Assembly agencies and raising the denominational budget, its duties were soon expanded to include the raising and administering of a new church loan fund and development of a retirement program for ministers and other church employees. The Board of Finance, in its first twenty years of existence, also led in four major capital funds campaigns: the Program of Achievement (scheduled for 1949-1951), the Mid-Century Expansion and Development Program (scheduled for 1959-1961), the Seminary Development Program (scheduled for 1964-1966), and the Advance in Missions (scheduled for 1968-1970).

The campaign to raise $350,000 for Bethel College and for the erection of the proposed Denominational Center, approved by the General Assembly in 1949, was carried forward under the name of the "Program of Achievement." It was designed that $50,000 should be raised through individual gifts and $300,000 through the churches by an apportionment to each church of a quota of six dollars per active member. By April 1, 1950, a total of $198,615.56 was raised.[58] A year later the total was $266,051.42.[59] This amount was still more than $80,000 short of the goal. Also, low bids on construction of the two buildings (the Denominational Center and the Library-Seminary Building at Bethel College) were in excess of the original estimates. As the portion of the fund (two-sevenths of the total) allotted for endowment had pushed the Bethel College Endowment beyond the $500,000 goal projected in 1918, receipts after the General Assembly in 1951 were divided on the basis of two-fifths for the Library-Seminary Building and three-fifths for the Denominational Center. In order to complete the two buildings the Board of Finance borrowed $145,000. This amount was gradually repaid through Thanksgiving offerings received each year from 1951 through 1958; in 1955 and afterward, the Thanksgiving offerings went into the denominational budget, a percentage of which was assigned to retirement of the building debts. The necessity of borrowing money and repaying the notes, with more interest year by year, required more than the original amount of the goal which was part of the program in 1949. It required almost ten years to complete this program. Final payment on the building loans was made in February 1959.[60] The total amount raised was $450,386.66, including $180,539.44 received in the Thanksgiving offerings.

Charles W. Hughes, who served as executive secretary of the Board of Finance during the initial phase of the Program of Achievement, resigned early in 1951. He was succeeded by Eugene Warren.[61]

The next major capital funds campaign was known as the Mid-Century Expansion and Development Program. Plans for this campaign, designed to climax the Mid-Century Spiritual Advance Program (1955-1960), were first presented to and approved by the General Assembly in 1957. It was planned that $600,000 in capital funds would be raised for the following purposes: $100,000 for Bethel College, $100,000 for the Cumberland Presbyterian Theological Seminary, $100,000 for development of a denominational conference ground, $100,000 for the new church loan fund, $100,000 for foreign missions, $60,000 for expansion of the Denominational Center, $25,000 for erection of a chapel at the birthplace of the Cumberland Presbyterian Church in Dickson County, Tennessee, and $15,000 for the Cumberland Presbyterian Children's Home.[62]

It was planned that $300,000 would be obtained through individual gifts and $300,000 through shares apportioned to the churches. By the spring of 1961 shares accepted by the churches totaled $319,255.85 and personal pledges $251,094.55, making the total amount pledged to be $570,350.40.[63] By the conclusion of the campaign in 1964, the sum of $511,885.49 had been received: $295,783.09 from churches and $216,102.40 from individuals. Direct payments thus were less than had been pledged. However, in addition, earnings from the investment of the money received amounted to $60,015.54, giving a total in the fund resulting from the Mid-Century Expansion and Development Program of $571,901.03.[64]

The Seminary Development Fund campaign is described elsewhere in this chapter, as part of the history of the Seminary after 1950.

The Advance in Missions Program, presented to the General Assembly in 1967 at the call of the preceding year's General Assembly, was a three-year effort to raise money for missions—half for home ministries and half for world missions. The initially recommended goal was $500,000.[65] Through the end of December 1970, when promotion and emphasis of the program was concluded, a total of $338,686.85 had been received; some additional receipts would be recorded in 1971.[66]

In 1949, in response to a memorial from Austin Presbytery, the Board of Finance was directed to make a study of a system of retirement and group insurance for ministers and board employees.[67] In 1950, a voluntary plan was approved to be financed by contributions from the participating pastors and board employees of 5 per cent of their salaries, such contributions to be matched by the local church or employing board.[68] At the end of the year 1951 there were seventy-two individuals participating, and the total in the fund was $16,575.14.[69] At the end of the year 1970 there was in the retirement fund a total of $2,359,793.28.[70] The number of individuals participating had increased to 381.

The General Assembly in 1949 removed restrictions from its trust funds to enable the Board of Finance to make loans to churches for the building of churches, manses, and educational buildings and for repairs on such buildings.[71] The Board of Finance adopted a policy requiring, among other things, that no loan be made to any church in excess of 60 per cent of the appraised value of the property offered as security.[72] This policy was adequate to meet the needs of churches already established, but newly organized churches could not qualify. Consequently the Board, in its report to the General Assembly in 1952, requested the Assembly to establish a building loan fund for new churches in an amount not less than $75,000.[73] Gradually, such a fund was accumulated, and by the end of 1970 it totaled $362,739.38.[74] Principal sources included a gift from Mrs. Susie McKenzie, of Norris City, Illinois; a portion of the annual income from the "Tithing and Budget Account" derived from the estate of the late William T. Finley, of Springfield, Missouri; and the Mid-Century Expansion and Development Program. This fund proved to be of inestimable benefit to the missions program of the Church.

In 1950, the first year the Board of Finance reported on the funds under its care, endowment funds totaled $747,324.96.[75] At the end of 1970, the Board was handling endowments totaling $3,873,052.39 besides the retirement fund and church loan fund. The total of all funds—endowment, trust, and retirement—for the handling and investment of which the Board was responsible was $6,595,585.05.[76]

The denominational budget, which had reached $100,000 in 1948-1949, decreased to $93,682.54 in 1949-1950, the decrease being due to the emphasis on the Program of Achievement. In 1951, however, the figure was $118,718.26, and from then through 1970, when a total of $497,360.17 was received from all sources, an increase was registered annually with the exception of two years (1958 and 1968). Notable increases occurred when the denominational budget was broadened to include items which previously had been cared for through special offerings, as in 1955 when the Thanksgiving offering and the Easter offering were included with the denominational budget and in 1966—this being the year of the greatest single increase—when foreign missions was brought within the denominational budget and the total rose from $278,718.01 in 1965 to $481,832.25. In 1962 the denominational budget was given the name "Our United Outreach."

The increase in local and denominational giving, although due in part to inflation and the affluence which characterized the period, also reflected an improvement in the stewardship practices of Cumberland Presbyterians. In 1950, the total per capita giving of Cumberland Presbyterians was about twenty dollars annually.[77] In 1970, the per capita giving was $82.37.[78]

Strengthened by the benefits derived from the Program of Achievement, Bethel College continued to grow. During the year 1949 the Bethel Grill property adjoining the campus was purchased to be used by the music department and the college bookstore. The campus was enlarged by the purchase of an adjoining ten acres. On December 4, 1952, Bethel College became fully accredited by the Southern Association of Colleges and Secondary Schools.

The necessity of supplying the Southern Association with information relating solely to the college program made advisable the planning of separate budgets for the college and the Cumberland Presbyterian Theological

Seminary, the graduate department of theology of Bethel College. In 1951 a budget of $216,704.50 was planned for the college and a budget of $26,225 for the Seminary. Meanwhile, occupancy of the Library-Seminary Building, which was completed in the fall of 1951, gave to the Seminary an identity it had not enjoyed before. In 1950-1951 the enrollment in the Seminary had ranged from ten to fifteen students. In the fall of 1951, twenty-six students were enrolled. By the spring of 1952 the number had increased to thirty-two. In the fall of 1955 the enrollment reached a total of fifty-eight students.

At the General Assembly which met at Lubbock, Texas, in June 1955, considerable excitement was occasioned by the receipt of a memorial from Memphis Presbytery asking that the Assembly give consideration to relocating Bethel College at Memphis. The McKenzie Chamber of Commerce sent a delegation to the Assembly to express McKenzie's interest in retaining the college. The outcome was the appointment by the General Assembly of a committee of eleven, the Moderator of the Assembly and one person from each of the ten synods, to "study the location of the college and seminary and our total educational program, and accept overtures from any city interested in our college and seminary being located within its bounds." [79]

This committee reported to the General Assembly in 1956 that the costs of relocation of the college in a metropolitan area appeared to be prohibitive but recommended that the Theological Seminary be separated from Bethel College and relocated in Memphis, provided the sum of $500,000 be raised by the Memphis community to finance the relocation.[80] The General Assembly, meeting in Cookeville, Tennessee, approved the recommendation that the theological department be separated from Bethel College, and that the Cumberland Presbyterian Theological Seminary be governed by a Board of Trustees. It was recommended that the Seminary be relocated in a metropolitan area when two conditions should have been fulfilled: first, the planning of a curriculum, after thorough study, to "best fit our ministers and Christian education workers for the most effective work in our Church," and, second, when adequate financial resources should be available to provide for an effective program of theological education.[81]

During the Seminary's first year of operation as a separate institution a curriculum study was made by the faculty with the assistance of a committee of the Board of Trustees, and the curriculum was reorganized. Leaders in the Cumberland Presbyterian churches in both the Memphis and Nashville areas manifested an interest in having the Seminary located in their city. The Board of Trustees, after considering the advantages of the two locations, proposed a meeting with representatives of Memphis to lay before them the costs that would be involved in providing the necessary physical facilities for locating the Seminary in Memphis. Such a meeting was held in February 1957, at which time a representative group pledged its support to a campaign to provide a suitable site and a minimum of $500,000 for buildings. The Board of Trustees recommended to the General Assembly that the Seminary be moved to the Memphis area when this condition should be met. This recommendation was approved by the General Assembly in its meeting in Evansville, Indiana, in June 1957.[82]

A seven-acre site was purchased by G. H. Kensinger, a ruling elder in the East Side Church in Memphis, whose advocacy of relocating Bethel College had inspired the memorial from Memphis Presbytery in 1955. This site was deeded to the Board of Trustees of the Seminary with the stipulation that if the Seminary were not moved to Memphis the property would revert to him. A date was set for a financial campaign, and a contract was made with a fund-raising company to assist in organizing and directing the campaign. Arrangements for the campaign were left to a four-man commission of Memphis Presbytery headed by Kensinger. On April 1, 1958, the presbyterial commission notified the Board of Trustees that the campaign had been called off. The reasons given were the inability of the commission to enlist some top-level leaders for the campaign and the adverse economic conditions prevailing in Memphis at the time.[83] A nationwide economic recession had occurred. The site donated by Kensinger was returned to him. He paid the fund-raising company and other expenses which had been incurred.

The Board of Trustees reaffirmed its belief that Memphis was the best location for the Seminary, and the General Assembly recommended that the Board be authorized to proceed with the relocation of the Seminary in an urban area. Such location was to be declared and established only upon the commitment of sufficient funds to provide facilities for an improved seminary program. Sources for the needed funds would include the Seminary's portion of the Mid-Century Expansion and Development Fund, a community financial campaign, and receipts for the Seminary's equity in property which would be vacated in McKenzie.[84]

Early in 1961 the issue of relocation was revived when a group of interested persons in the Nashville area formed a committee in the interest of having the Seminary located in Nashville. It was believed by some that a location adjacent to the university center in that city would be advantageous. Tennessee Synod, in a called meeting, memorialized the General Assembly to locate the Seminary at Nashville. The Assembly, however, directed the Board of Trustees of the Seminary to "give consideration to McKenzie and to every possible urban area and make a selection for the location of the Seminary and present the same to the 132nd General Assembly."[85]

The same General Assembly approved a priority study suggested by the Board of Missions and Evangelism and recommended by the Planning Committee. All boards were asked to set forth their needs for the next several years. The Planning Committee in its spring meeting the following year would "approve and recommend a priority listing of needs, together with suggestions as to how and when they can be met." It was recognized that the Church had many needs, and that not all of them could be met immediately.[86]

As a result of this study, the Planning Committee recommended that the program of the Seminary be the first concern. Meanwhile, representatives of the Board of Trustees of the Seminary and of the Board of Finance conferred to determine what the minimum needs of the Seminary were, and what support could reasonably be expected from the denomination and from other sources. The Board of Trustees announced that it was ready to consider proposals from communities which might be interested in securing the location of the Seminary. Committees were appointed by the McKenzie Chamber of Commerce and by Memphis Presbytery in addition to the committee at Nashville already mentioned. Following an open meeting held at Memphis at which all parties were heard, the Board of Trustees of the Seminary recommended to the General Assembly that the Seminary be located at Memphis and requested the Memphis community to provide a site at East Parkway and Union Extended which had been inspected by representatives of the Board.[87] There was not another theological seminary within 200 miles of Memphis, and it was believed that a seminary located there could serve an area as well as serving the denomination.

The General Assembly which met in Little Rock, Arkansas, in June 1962, approved the recommendation relative to relocation of the Seminary in Memphis. A commission consisting of G. H. Kensinger, Joe H. Davis, and Charles I. Freeman, all of Memphis, was named to acquire suitable property for the Seminary and to supervise the making of the necessary improvements to put it in condition for occupancy. The Assembly also directed that a "thorough evaluation of the total work of the Cumberland Presbyterian Theological Seminary be made" and empowered the Moderator to appoint a committee for this purpose. The Assembly also concurred in the opinion of the Committee on Finance that at least $300,000 and a site would be needed to effect the relocation of the Seminary.[88]

On June 30, 1962, the Board of Finance, acting for the above mentioned commission, purchased for the sum of $95,000 the property previously selected. This property included a mansion of Italian Renaissance architecture built in 1912 and a three-car garage with apartment overhead of matching architecture. The buildings were easily adapted, with a minimum of remodeling, for the Seminary's use. A library wing was added to the main building.

The Moderator appointed three pastors and former Moderators, the Rev. Ewell K. Reagin, the Rev. Ernest C. Cross, and the Rev. Paul F. Brown, to constitute the committee to evaluate the program of the Seminary. Reagin had served as head of the theological department of Bethel College from 1931 until 1944. Cross had served on the Board of Trustees of the Seminary from its appointment in 1956 until 1962. Brown was a former missionary. The committee did its work thoroughly, and its recommendations were constructive. Emphasis was placed on the need for greater financial support and the need for administrative officers and professors to devote their full time to the work of the Seminary.[89] Prior to this time the majority of the faculty had been forced to accept part-time pastoral work for financial reasons.

In 1963 the General Assembly approved plans submitted by the Board of Finance for a financial campaign for the Seminary. This campaign, which was called the Seminary Development Program, was designed to raise $450,000 to be used as follows: $210,000 for endowment, $100,000 for purchase of property in Memphis, $60,000 for erection of a library wing, $40,000 for landscaping the grounds and redecorating the building, and $40,000 for student housing. It was planned that $125,000 of this amount would come from Memphis Presbytery and the city of Memphis, $125,000 from individual gifts outside Memphis Presbytery, and $200,000 from churches outside the Presbytery.[90] The campaign was scheduled to begin early in 1964 and to continue into 1966.

The Board of Trustees determined to open the Seminary in its new location in September 1964. The necessary renovation of existing buildings and erection of the library wing were carried forward, although much of the work had to be done with borrowed money, since the Seminary Development Program would not be launched until 1964. The building was ready for occupancy by the summer of 1964, and the removal of the Seminary's equipment, library, and faculty to Memphis was effected with a minimum of difficulty. In keeping with the desire of the Board of Trustees of the Seminary, the property occupied by the Seminary at McKenzie was made available to Bethel College without any payment therefor. Meanwhile the General Assembly in its 1964 meeting voted to change the name of the Seminary to Memphis Theological Seminary of the Cumberland Presbyterian Church.[91]

The chapel in the newly occupied Seminary building later was named in memory of the Rev. P. F. Johnson, dean from 1908 to 1925.

In June 1964, Dr. William T. Ingram, Jr., became president of the Seminary, succeeding Dr. Thomas H. Campbell. Campbell, who had been

MEMPHIS THEOLOGICAL SEMINARY

president since the Seminary was separated from Bethel College in 1956, again became dean.

Meanwhile the Seminary Development Program, although begun in the Memphis area somewhat earlier, was launched on a churchwide basis just prior to the General Assembly in 1964. The Board of Finance, in its report to the General Assembly in 1965, reported that the churches of Memphis Presbytery had accepted a quota of $25,000. Cumberland Presbyterian individuals in Memphis had pledged nearly $20,000, other individual gifts and pledges amounting to $17,650 had been received in the Memphis area, and individuals outside of Memphis had pledged $119,000. A total of $104,198.57 had been paid into the Seminary Development Fund during 1964, and more than $30,000 during the first three months of 1965.[92] As of March 18, 1968, when a concluding report was made, a total of $356,725.25 had been received, $220,929.69 from churches and $125,793.56 from individuals.[93] These figures include amounts given from within the Memphis area. The property in Memphis, valued at approximately $250,000, was paid for, but to the end of 1970 only $74,389.23 had been added to the endowment of the Seminary through this program.

The removal of the Seminary to Memphis made possible an enrichment of its offerings. The establishment of the Memphis Institute of Medicine and Religion brought to Memphis a program of clinical pastoral education approved by the Council for Clinical Education, an organization in which the

Seminary had held membership since 1962. The program of field education was enriched through contacts with welfare agencies operating in an urban center. Several part-time faculty members were added, and in 1967 a full-time professor of church history was employed. In the fall of 1970 the faculty consisted of eight full-time persons and five serving part-time.

Even before the decision was made to separate the Seminary from Bethel College the Board of Education projected a development program calling for the erection of half a dozen buildings at an estimated cost of some $785,000.[94] The General Assembly's Planning Committee gave its approval to the plan to erect a residence hall, a dining hall, and an infirmary to be financed by a loan from the Federal Housing Authority. It was noted, however, that any churchwide appeal for funds for other buildings would necessarily take its place in schedule behind other commitments already made by the Assembly.[95] In December 1958, a loan agreement with the FHA was signed for a loan in the amount of $285,000 to finance the erection of a girls' dormitory and a dining hall.[96] These buildings were completed in the summer of 1960 and were dedicated with appropriate ceremonies. The dormitory was named McDonald Hall in memory of Frank McDonald, of Knoxville, Tennessee, from whose estate came the funds for the purchase of furniture for the building. The cafeteria was named Moore Cafeteria in memory of Mrs. Fannye Baxter Moore, of McKenzie, who left a substantial portion of her estate to the college.

In 1964, a ten-year program of development for Bethel College was projected by the Board of Trustees. This program, to be known as "A Decade of Achievement for Bethel College" and scheduled to extend from 1965 to 1975, was approved in principle by the General Assembly.[97] Authorization was given for erection of a new library-classroom building, subsequently named the C. Raymon Burroughs Learning Center, in honor of the college's executive vice-president and academic dean, and for remodeling the Library-Seminary Building for use as a science building. These were financed through the use of Bethel's share of the Mid-Century Expansion and Development Program, sale of property derived from the Butler estate (a bequest) in Florida, use of a reserve account established by the McKenzie Chamber of Commerce, and a loan from the Federal Housing Authority. Other buildings added in the Decade of Achievement also were financed with a combination of institutional funds and government funds (grants and loans). Three of these—a college activities center, built as an addition to the cafeteria, and dormitories designated East Hall and West Hall—were completed in the late 1960s also.

In the latter part of 1970, two more buildings were ready for occupancy:

the Roy N. Baker Health and Physical Education Center and the Henry M. Dickey Fine Arts Center. The latter was named in memory of an alumnus, of Trenton, Tennessee, whose gifts to the college had included large tracts of land in Gibson and Benton counties. The gymnasium in the new health and physical education facility bore the name of the late Rev. John W. Dishman; a part of the older gymnasium, which had been named in his memory, was incorporated into the fine arts center.

The erection of these buildings in the Decade of Achievement program was planned and promoted under the direction of the Rev. John David Hall, vice-president in charge of development until his resignation in 1970.

Roy N. Baker, president of Bethel College since 1945, died October 29, 1968. James Alton Barksdale, professor of education at Bethel and a former state commissioner of education, was named as his successor in January 1969 and served on an interim basis the remainder of that year. In January 1970, James E. McKee, then residing in Martin, Tennessee, became president. Both Barksdale and McKee were Cumberland Presbyterian laymen, Bethel graduates, and former members of the college's Board of Trustees.

The enrollment of Bethel College, which at the beginning of the 1950s was slightly more than 400 students, passed the 500 mark in 1955. In the fall of 1965 there were 789 students, and in the fall of 1966, 812. Enrollment declined, toward the end of the decade, and in the fall of 1970 the figure was 549.

From the standpoint of the Church, one of the most discouraging factors in the life of Bethel College was the decrease in the number of ministerial students. For several years following the end of World War II there was a marked increase in the number of ministerial students. As late as the spring of 1957 there were eighty Cumberland Presbyterian ministerial students enrolled in the college. In the fall of 1966 there were only thirty-six ministerial students, including those of all denominations. In the fall of 1970 there were forty-one, thirty-two of whom were Cumberland Presbyterian.

The Cumberland Presbyterian Children's Home at Denton, Texas, experienced growth in terms of both physical facilities and number of children cared for. In 1955, a cottage for boys was built. In 1961, a director's residence was provided at a cost of $18,500. In 1965, a new cottage for boys was erected and the older cottage converted into administrative offices. The newest cottage was provided in part by the Children's Home's share of the Mid-Century Expansion and Development Program. In 1965, with the completion of the newest facility, the property of the Home was appraised at $210,275 including $130,200 land value.[98]

During the first decade of the period under consideration there were frequent changes in administration and personnel. In 1959, the Rev. J. C. Forester was employed as director with the Rev. James L. Bridges as co-director. Subsequently there was more continuity in personnel, although Forester resigned in 1964 on account of ill health and was succeeded by the Rev. James C. Gilbert, who became executive secretary and director. Bridges's title became "resident director."

From a dormitory type of living the home has been changed to provide cottage, or small unit, living as a step toward family living. In 1969 each of four living areas for younger boys, younger girls, older boys, and older girls respectively had a houseparent. The children through the years have attended the public schools and have thereby been brought in contact with the other children of the community. There has been a wholesome participation on the part of the residents of the Home in extracurricular activities.[99] The children also have participated in the life and work of the Denton Cumberland Presbyterian Church. In 1965, the Home became an associate member of the Child Welfare League of America.

As early as 1947 the Board of Christian Education had expressed the conviction that a permanent site to be owned by the denomination was needed for YPGA.[100] Subsequently the Board of Publication and Christian Education, formed by the merger of two boards in 1948, named a committee on camp site.[101] In this it had the encouragement of the General Assembly.[102] Early in 1950 a movement was initiated to raise $20,000 for a chapel to be erected at the projected permanent camp site in memory of the Rev. Clark Williamson, who had died in 1949.[103] He more than any other one man had furthered the camping program of the Cumberland Presbyterian Church, and such a memorial seemed fitting. From February 1 until April 30, 1950, $2,625.79 was received for this project.[104] A book of Williamson's poems, *He Threw the Pattern Away,* was published and sold to enhance the memorial fund, and there were gifts to the project. In September 1954, a request was made to the Planning Committee and General Assembly that the Board of Publication and Christian Education be permitted to plan for the securing of a YPGA camp site and conference ground and that the program of development of such site, which would require the raising of funds on a denominational level, "be placed on schedule in the denominational financial program as soon as possible."[105] It was, beyond doubt, in consideration of this request that in 1957 the sum of $100,000 was set into the Mid-Century Expansion and Development Program for "NACPYF and Denominational Conference Grounds."[106]

Meanwhile West Tennessee Synod purchased property near Jackson which it began to develop for its own use for camping purposes. A proposal was

made by the General Assembly's Board of Publication and Christian Education that the West Tennessee Camp Site be developed as the permanent
meeting place of NACPYF. The proposal was that the synod complete
payment for the property and for development of the lake, and that when
the title to the property was clear, it would be conveyed to the General
Assembly's Board with the understanding that West Tennessee Synod would
be given priority in the scheduling of summer camps and that long-range
plans called for the expansion of the site into a denominational conference
ground to serve the entire Church.[107] This proposal was recommended
to West Tennessee Synod by its Boards of Finance and Publication and
Christian Education. The plan broke down, however, when members of
the synod were insistent upon assurances that the synod would be granted
adequate time for the scheduling of its own camping needs which members
of the staff of the General Assembly's Board (who also were members of West
Tennessee Synod) were reluctant to give. Although the proposal was accepted by the synod by a small majority, the action was reconsidered (at the
suggestion of the Executive Secretary and Director of Youth Work of the
General Assembly's Board), and the proposal was rejected.[108]

In 1960, with the Mid-Century Expansion and Development Program
well on its way, plans were approved looking to the securing of a suitable
site for a denominational conference ground and the developing of a master
plan for the needed facilities.[109] The Conference Ground Committee of the
Board evaluated eight possible sites, and at a meeting held on February
28-March 1, 1961, the Board approved the purchase of a tract of 160 acres
located twenty miles west of Little Rock, Arkansas, at a cost of $16,000.[110]
Preparation of a master plan for the conference ground was authorized by
the General Assembly.[111]

That same year the General Assembly ordered the priority study heretofore mentioned. The result was that priority was given to the development of
the Seminary. Next in line there was to be a campaign for home and
foreign missions. This meant that probably ten years would elapse before a
campaign could be launched that would include additional funds for development of a conference ground. The Board of Publication and Christian Education estimated that at least $150,000 would be needed to develop minimum
facilities for NACPYF and that an eventual expenditure of $300,000 for
facilities and an annual budget of $10,000 to $12,000 for care and maintenance would be needed.[112]

In 1964 the Board asked that when the Conference Ground fund reached
a total of $100,000 (including the $16,000 invested in the site) earnings from
the fund be released to the Board for use in the program of the Division of
Christian Education.[113] The General Assembly, however, directed that the

fund together with its earnings be held intact "until such time as the General Assembly can proceed with development of the desired conference ground." [114] At the end of the year 1964, with the site paid for, there was a total of $82,283.74 in the Conference Ground fund. In 1965 the Board, which was now getting in desperate financial circumstances with its operational budget, asked that the fund be designated as Christian education endowment until such time as the General Assembly should authorize a campaign for additional funds.[115] Instead the Assembly authorized the use of the income from the fund for two years (1966 and 1967) for Christian education.[116]

In 1967 the Board expressed the opinion that it was no longer feasible to think in terms of conference ground development and recommended that the property purchased as a site be sold.[117] The General Assembly approved the recommendation and authorized the use of $10,000 to retire indebtedness the Board had incurred in its operation, designated $15,000 as a machinery replacement fund, and placed the remainder in a permanent Christian education endowment fund. The corpus of the Clark Williamson Memorial Fund, which had by this time reached a total of $14,205.92, was established at $15,000 with the earnings to be used for the support of youth work.[118] Thus ended the "dream" of developing a denominational conference ground.

Recognizing the need for a more adequate curriculum for the educational task of the Church and being conscious, at the same time, of the limitations of resources which seemed to make it impossible for a denomination the size of the Cumberland Presbyterian Church to produce all the curriculum materials needed, the Board of Publication and Christian Education accepted an invitation issued in 1957 by the Board of Christian Education of the Presbyterian Church, U. S., to join with it and the corresponding boards of several kindred denominations in a comprehensive curriculum study. The result was the development of the Covenant Life Curriculum, which was officially adopted by the General Assembly in 1962 as the curriculum of the Cumberland Presbyterian Church.[119] Other churches (besides the Presbyterian Church, U. S.) which adopted the Covenant Life Curriculum were the Reformed Church in America, the Associate Reformed Presbyterian Church, and the Moravian Church in America. At the same time, alternate materials were provided.

Undoubtedly the Covenant Life Curriculum provided a far more comprehensive program of Christian education than the piecemeal approach to Bible study which had characterized most Sunday school materials in the past; however, reception of the Covenant Life Curriculum within the Cumberland Presbyterian Church varied from wholehearted acceptance to complete rejection. By 1967, at the end of the first three-year cycle, of 736 Cumberland Presbyterian churches reporting on their use of curriculum materials, 190 were using CLC materials exclusively, 192 were using some CLC materials and some alternate materials, 199 were using recommended alternate materials exclusively, and 155 were not using recommended literature at all. Of a church school enrollment of 58,817, it was figured that 37,656 were in churches which were using CLC materials wholly or in part.[120] By 1970, however, the number using only CLC materials had dropped to 79, with a church school enrollment of 7,089, while 205 churches, with a church school enrollment of 21,228, were using a combination of CLC materials and recommended alternate materials. The number of churches reported as not using any of the recommended alternate materials remained about the same as in 1967.[121]

Covenant Life Curriculum materials were produced at Richmond, Virginia, by the CLC Press. The Cumberland Presbyterian Church's own publishing activities remained under the Board of Publication and Christian Education, which in 1961 chose "Frontier Press" as the new trade and business name for its Division of Publication and Distribution. The press would be managed by William E. Phalan, a Board employee since 1946.

The Rev. Harold Davis had succeeded the Rev. Morris Pepper as executive secretary of this Board in 1960.

On September 1, 1949, Hubert W. Morrow was employed as executive secretary of the Board of Missions and Evangelism. Under his leadership the Board launched out in several new directions.

The organization of Cumberland Men's Fellowships at the local and presbyterial levels was authorized in 1949. By the spring of 1950, charters had been issued to forty-six fellowships in twenty-eight presbyteries.[122] In August 1954, a Denominational Cumberland Men's Fellowship was organized. The DCMF would hold annual meetings. The one in 1970, at Bethel College, was attended by 159 men.

The Board's budget for 1951 provided for a short-term school for the in-service training of ministers who had not had the opportunity to obtain a college and seminary education.[123] The first such school was held in the summer of 1951 with fifteen ministers in attendance. The school was continued on an annual basis, and in 1957 the attendance reached a peak with forty ministers participating. In later years the enrollment waned, although the need for the program was still apparent. In 1970, ten men were enrolled.

The Board of Missions and Evangelism also became more active in the field of Indian missions. The Rev. Raymond Kinslow was employed as a full-

DINING HALL, CAMP ISRAEL FOLSOM

The presbyterial camp for Choctaw Presbytery, near Bethel, Oklahoma, was dedicated in June 1969 and was named for the first Indian Cumberland Presbyterian minister.

time worker in Choctaw Presbytery and began his work September 1, 1951. In 1953, the Rev. John Lovelace was added as a second missionary in this presbytery and became pastor of the Wright City and Honey Grove churches, which had been organized recently. Early in 1955, Kinslow resigned his work in Choctaw Presbytery, leaving Lovelace in full charge. Early in 1959, Lovelace resigned to become a missionary to Colombia, and the Rev. Charles Faith became the missionary in Choctaw Presbytery. He served until the end of 1964. He was succeeded by Claude Gilbert, then a licentiate in Choctaw Presbytery. In 1957 a manse was built at Idabel, Oklahoma, for the missionary, at a cost of $11,000. This amount included $4,798.21 from vacation church school offerings throughout the denomination, and $794 from offerings given in 1955 by the young people of the denomination. Besides providing leadership to the already existing Indian churches in the presbytery, the missionaries organized one additional Indian congregation (Wright City) and three congregations among the white people of the area. In 1968, the Rev. Randolph Jacobs, a young Choctaw who had attended Bethel College and Memphis Theological Seminary, returned to Choctaw Presbytery to assist in the work.

In 1951, the Board announced its plan to create a staff of qualified workers who would be available to serve in mission projects financed by denominational funds.[124] It was intended that such missionaries would be transferred to new projects when the churches where they were serving became self-sustaining. The first mission to be opened under this policy was in Oklahoma City where Paul F. Brown began serving as minister in December 1951.

In the summer of 1952, the Rev. Virgil Weeks was sent to Jackson, Mississippi, as a missionary. In its report in 1953 the Board mentioned the organization of churches in both cities.[125]

In December 1953, the Rev. J. P. Bright began work as a missionary at Oak Ridge, Tennessee, where a Sunday school had been begun under the direction of the Board of Missions and Evangelism of Knoxville Presbytery. Here a church was organized in February 1954. Meanwhile a church had been organized in May 1953 in the Meadowbrook subdivision of Fort Worth, Texas, with the Rev. H. O. Bennett as the missionary.[126]

In December 1954, the Rev. Dudley Condron and the Rev. Sidney Slaton were employed as missionaries and assigned to Tulsa, Oklahoma, and Wichita, Kansas, respectively. The work at Tulsa at that time was financed by the Synod of Oklahoma.

In 1955, the Board had nine missionaries in its employ.[127] These included, in addition to those assigned to the six urban projects already mentioned, the two missionaries in Choctaw Presbytery and one missionary, the Rev. Vernon Burrow, who was employed in a rural parish in the Parsons, Tennessee, area. In the fall of 1955, the Rev. O. H. Gibson was employed as a missionary and assigned to Raytown, Missouri, where property had been purchased and a first unit of a building erected under the joint sponsorship of Platte-Lexington Presbytery and Missouri Synod. During 1955, four churches were organized: Tuscaloosa, Alabama; Faith, Saint Clair Shores, Michigan; and those in Wichita and Tulsa, all of which were served by missionaries commissioned by the General Assembly's Board.[128]

In the fall of 1954, Hubert Morrow resigned as executive secretary, and the Rev. J. T. Buck was elected in his stead. On January 1, 1957, the Rev. Carl Ramsey succeeded him.

The new executive secretary encouraged the assumption of more responsibility by the synods and presbyteries for mission work within their bounds. In its report to the General Assembly in 1958, the General Assembly's Board expressed its intention of giving support to "fringe" areas in starting new urban mission work. Where the presbytery or synod was able to support the work, the financial program would be left to those judicatories through their boards of missions. The Board conceived of its work as being basically that of a service agency to give supervision, counsel, and assistance to presbyterial and synodic boards of missions.[129] Already it had been decided that no new work would be considered except that undertaken in cooperation with presbyterial boards of missions. During 1959 twenty urban mission projects and three town and country parishes were under the supervision of the General Assembly's Board.[130] In 1962, there were thirty-six projects under supervision.[131] Most of these were financed by presbyterial or synodic boards.

In 1970, presbyteries and synods raised and disbursed for mission projects within their bounds a total of $134,746.82.[132]

Under this program numerous projects were launched by presbyteries and synods, usually with the counsel of the General Assembly's Board. The presbytery took the initiative, since the presbytery alone has the power to form new churches. Synodic boards, however, gave substantial support in a number of instances.

Alabama-Florida-Mississippi Synod, which probably had the largest missions budget of any of the synods, gave substantial aid during the 1960s to new churches at Kosciusko, Mississippi; Columbus, Mississippi (Fairview); Tampa, Florida (University Heights); Sheffield, Alabama (Park Terrace); Tuscaloosa, Alabama; and Huntsville, Alabama (the Church of the Good Shepherd). From 1957 to 1969 Arkansas Synod gave substantial aid to new mission projects at El Dorado, Batesville, Mountain Home, and Little Rock, as well as Fayetteville, which involved the relocation of an already existing church. Kentucky Synod made substantial grants for buildings at Glasgow, Mayfield, Harrodsburg, and Leitchfield, as well as aiding on the operational budgets of these new churches. In 1966, the Lansdowne Fellowship, in Lexington, was begun. Here the synod paid $32,500 for land, moved a minister on the field, and voted to borrow $50,000 for the first unit of a building and to support an annual budget of $16,000.[133] Texas Synod, during the 1960s, gave support to the Hill County Cooperative Parish; Saint Andrew Church, Odessa, Texas; Heights Church, Albuquerque, New Mexico; the church at Trona, California; Faith Church, San Antonio, Texas; and Saint Paul Church, Austin, Texas. The General Assembly's Board also aided Trona and Saint Paul. Missouri Synod and the General Assembly's Board aided Faith Church, Independence, Missouri, where a fellowship was begun in the fall of 1964.

Several presbyteries provided the major support for new churches. As early as 1958, Chattanooga Presbytery voted to attempt to establish a church in the Atlanta, Georgia, area. This effort resulted in the building of the Church of the Three Crosses in Doraville, a suburb of Atlanta. North Central Texas Presbytery gave the major support toward the building program of the Saint Luke Church, in Fort Worth, Texas, where a fellowship was formed in 1964. The local group supplied the operating budget from the beginning. Memphis Presbytery (with assistance from West Tennessee Synod) sponsored four mission projects during the 1960s: Frayser, Whitehaven, Grace (which involved the relocation of the old Second Church), and Cromwell. In 1970, Grace and Whitehaven were combined into one church.

Not all mission projects were equally successful, and a few were closed during the latter half of the 1960s. Internal dissension, lack of adequate ministerial leadership, or involvement in building debts beyond the congregation's ability to pay were principal contributing factors.

The Board of Foreign Missions moved its offices to Memphis December 1, 1949. The Rev. Arleigh G. Matlock, who had served for a time as a missionary in Colombia, became executive secretary July 1, 1950. At that time the outlook for the future of the mission work in both China and Colombia was uncertain.

With the completion of the conquest of mainland China by the communist regime in 1949, new restrictions were imposed upon Christian work and workers. Members of the Gam family were marked for ill treatment because of their American connections. In October 1951, the Rev. Samuel King Gam and his family returned to the United States, where he served as pastor in San Francisco from 1952 till his death in 1955. McAdow Gam, youngest of the three sons whom Gam Sing Quah had named for the founders of the denomination, assumed charge of the work on the coast of Asia.

Already there was a gospel hall in Macau, a Portuguese colony off the Chinese mainland, and plans were made to establish a permanent mission in the nearby British colony of Hong Kong. In October 1952, a mission was organized on Cheung Chau island in Hong Kong, and in 1957 the Board authorized the purchase of property there. Many members from the churches on the mainland settled in Hong Kong. By 1959, church services were begun on the Kowloon peninsula, and a chapel at North Point was nearing completion. In June 1952, while on a visit to the United States, McAdow Gam was ordained to the work of the ministry by Lebanon Presbytery. He returned to continue supervision of the work at Macau and Hong Kong. In 1963, the Rev. Paul Hom, who came from the church in San Francisco and had just graduated from the Cumberland Presbyterian Theological Seminary, was sent as a missionary to Hong Kong, where he served until 1967. At the end of 1970 there were 194 active members in the four organized churches in Hong Kong and Macau. A rooftop school in Hong Kong conducted morning and afternoon sessions, and there were also schools at Macau and on Cheung Chau.[134]

A persecution of evangelicals in Colombia, which, although politically inspired, was often aided and abetted by the Roman Catholic hierarchy, reached its height in 1949 and 1950. On the night of October 16, 1949, the church at Restrepo was burned amid cries of *"Viva la Virgen del Carmen! Abajo los protestantes!"* On November 6 a young member of the Restrepo church, José Loaiza, was brutally murdered.[135] Members of the church at Dagua were forced to leave their homes under threat of violence. It became necessary to close the rural churches.

The churches in the cities of Cali, Pereira, Armenia, and Cartago continued to grow, although hostility continued. As late as the autumn of 1956, within a two-week period, an elder in the Cartago church was killed, another elder was severely wounded, and another member was killed. Many of the members from the rural churches moved into the cities where they could have a measure of police protection. A group who moved into Cali from Restrepo formed the nucleus of a new church known as La Floresta. In 1957 the dictatorship which had ruled Colombia was overthrown. A measure of relief came to the evangelicals.

In 1961 the Board reported that the Rev. Edward W. Clyne and his family had moved to Cali and that Clyne had been assigned to a task of evangelism in the Cauca Valley outside of Cali.[136] By 1962 several mission points had been opened between Cali and Pereira. From these beginnings came churches at Palmira and El Cerrito. A church at Guacari, which had been planted by the Gospel Missionary Union, had already been received. Approval was also given to establishing a mission in Manizales, capital of the department of Caldas and located some sixty miles north of Pereira,[137] and at Buenaventura, on the Pacific coast.

A fourth church in Cali, known as San Marcos, was organized in an economically destitute area of the city. The Alameda church, in the meantime, had been closed, and attempts were made unsuccessfully to sell the property. Later, however, the work at Alameda was revived, and on September 4, 1966, the church was reorganized with a membership of forty. Central Church of Cali, which had been meeting in the Colegio Americano, erected a new building which was dedicated in April 1962, the sum of $40,000 having been appropriated for this purpose from the proceeds of the Mid-Century Expansion and Development Program.

At the end of 1970 there were in Cauca Valley Presbytery ten organized churches and three missions with a total reported membership of 1,323 and a church school enrollment of 1,187. The Colegio Americano, which was accredited in 1961, had twenty full-time teachers and ten part-time teachers in 1970. Enrollment was 600 at the downtown school and about 300 at the San Marcos and Samaria branches.[138] The 1970 high school graduating class, with thirty-three members, was the largest in the Colegio's history.[139] In 1963 some forty acres of land located on a mountainside about six miles west of Cali on the highway toward Buenaventura was purchased for a camp site. This camp, known as El Coro, proved very useful not only for youth camps but also for retreats sponsored by the Colegio Americano and for various presbyterial functions. A seminary program for the education of ministers and other Christian workers was begun in the fall of

COLEGIO AMERICANO, CALI, COLOMBIA

KOZA CHURCH, JAPAN

1969 under the direction of the Rev. Boyce Wallace, who had been appointed as a missionary, with his wife, in 1963.

Other mission personnel who, with their wives (always commissioned also), began serving in Colombia during these decades include B. D. Mathias, who was commissioned in 1952 and returned to the United States in late 1953; the Rev. William D. Wood, who was commissioned in 1956 and returned in 1970; David Pierce, whose service on the field began in 1964 and ended in 1967; the Rev. Larry Acton, who went to Colombia in 1969; and John Lovelace, mentioned above, who was commissioned in 1960 and returned in 1968. Among missionaries who began serving earlier, these couples returned to the United States: the Rev. Emery Newman and his wife, in 1952; the Rev. Vance Shultz and his wife, in 1960; and the Rev. James Kelso and his wife, in 1957, although the Kelsos were in Colombia again from 1960 to 1963.

On April 14, 1950, the Board of Foreign Missions voted to open a mission in Japan, accepting as a mission the Koza Community Church, near Tokyo, which had received the encouragement of Chaplain Cleetis C. Clemens when he was stationed nearby following World War II. The Board assumed a balance of $1,400 on the building and the salary of the pastor, the Rev. Tadao Yoshizaki.[140] The Rev. Thomas Forester and his wife arrived in Japan as missionaries in 1953. By 1955 the Koza mission had established four other Sunday schools, and the enrollment of the schools, including the one at Koza, was 510. By 1957 a mission point had been established at Shibusawa, a town of some 12,000 people about twenty-five miles from the church at Koza. Shortly thereafter Yoshizaki was placed in charge of the work at Shibusawa. A commission from California Presbytery ordained the Rev. Michiobu Ikushima, who became pastor at Koza.

In 1961 the Rev. Tolbert Dill and his wife were commissioned as missionaries to Japan. During the same year property was purchased for missions in Kibo ga Oka, on the outskirts of Yokohama, and in the town of Kunitachi. During the following year a church building was erected at Kibo ga Oka with the help of men stationed at the United States Naval Air Station at Atsugi, who gave money and spent Saturdays in voluntary labor to finish the building.[141] The mission in Kunitachi was organized as the Nozomi Church.

In 1964 the Forester family returned to the United States, and the Rev. Melvin D. Stott, Jr., and his family went to Japan. In 1963 it was reported that a Bible class had been started at Higashi Koganei. The following year the Naruse mission, in Machida, in metropolitan Tokyo, was opened. At the end of the year 1970 the six churches in Japan had a combined church membership of 482, of whom 308 were reported as active, and a church school enrollment of 991.[142] In June 1967, by order of Texas Synod, a presbytery was organized in Japan. It was first known as Kanto Presbytery, but the name was changed soon afterward to Japan Presbytery. During this year, also, Tolbert Dill was employed as secretary of the Division of World Missions of the Cumberland Presbyterian Church's realigned missions board, thus leaving the Stott family as the only American missionary family on the Japanese field.

After several years had been given to a consideration of a realignment of the program of missions, the Board of Missions and Evangelism and the Board of Foreign Missions were combined in 1964 to form one board of fifteen members to be known as the Board of Missions. It was decided that this board should include not less than six nor more than nine women.[143] The Board organized its work under four divisions: Women's Work, Home Ministries, World Missions, and Education for Mission. The object of the realignment was to involve the whole Church in missions and at the same time to involve the women of the Church in its total program. Since 1907, Cumberland Presbyterian foreign missions had come to be considered primarily the work of the women of the Church.

The former Missionary Convention and the missionary auxiliaries on synodical, presbyterial, and local levels were succeeded by corresponding units of the new organization of Cumberland Presbyterian Women. The Convention of CPW continued to meet annually in conjunction with the General Assembly as the Missionary Convention had done for many years.

Among persons giving leadership in the period of transition were Carl Ramsey, executive secretary of the Board of Missions and secretary of the Division of Home Ministries; these other divisional secretaries: Mrs. William A. St. John in the Division of Women's Work, the Rev. O. T. Arnett in the Division of World Missions (succeeded by Dill), and the Rev. Roy Blakeburn in the Division of Education for Mission (the duties of whose office, to which Dudley Condron succeeded early in 1966, include editorship of the *Missionary Messenger*); Mrs. T. C. Stockton, editor of the *Missionary Messenger* from 1950 through 1965; the Rev. Eugene Leslie, associate secretary of the Division of Home Ministries; Miss Helen Deal, office executive; and Mrs. Floyd Leonhard, first president of the denominational CPW.

During the period from April 1, 1950, to December 31, 1960, the total membership of the Cumberland Presbyterian Church increased from 80,264 to 88,452, an increase of 8,188 members. The reported active membership increased from 51,822 to 60,088, and increase of 8,266. After 1961, however, and continuing through the remainder of the decade, there was a small decrease in the reported active membership each year except 1966 and

1970. The total reported membership at the end of 1970 was 87,823, of whom 57,147 were reported as active.

Eighty-six churches and missions (including sixteen in Hong Kong, Japan, and Colombia) listed in the 1971 Yearbook had been added since 1950; however, the total number of churches decreased from 1,035 in 1950 to 901 at the end of 1970. This meant that 220 churches had disappeared from the presbyterial rolls during the twenty-year period. The majority of the new churches were in urban areas or county seat towns, whereas most of the churches dropped from the rolls were rural or village churches. At the end of 1970, approximately 42 per cent of the active membership of the Cumberland Presbyterian Church within the United States belonged to churches situated in cities of 10,000 or more or in urbanized areas.

Signs of an awakening social conscience among Cumberland Presbyterians should also be mentioned. In a previous chapter the conclusion was reached that Cumberland Presbyterians did not differ significantly from the main body of American Protestants in the diversity and tendencies of their opinions on nineteenth century moral, social, and intellectual questions.[144] A study completed in 1940, however, concluded that the Cumberland Presbyterian Church had not played a positive role in social change. It had

evaded unpleasant reality in the social order by looking upon itself as an institution apart, not being charged with responsibility for taking action on social issues with regard to which specific instructions were not laid down in the Bible. . . . The denomination . . . has little realized that it is a social institution with social obligations and responsibilities to maintain and discharge.[145]

In 1954, the General Assembly set up a permanent committee to study the major moral and social issues confronting the Church and to work in cooperation with appropriate boards in preparing materials to aid the Church in meeting the moral and social problems of the day.[146] Listed in 1954 as the Committee on Moral and Social Welfare, the name was changed in 1955 to the Committee on Christian Social Relations. That year the committee made a comprehensive report pointing out areas of concern into which the Church should move. This report, with few alterations, was approved by the General Assembly.[147] In 1959, the Committee proposed a social creed dealing with these named topics: The Family; Civil Government; The Economic Order; Nationality, Class, and Race; Health; Education; Recreational and Social Activities; and Welfare Services. It was intended that through following the necessary procedures such a creed should be made a part of the Confession of Faith.[148] The General Assembly in 1960 adopted a Social Creed substantially as prepared by the Permanent Committee the preceding year but without making it a part of the Confession of Faith. Rather it was to be printed for distribution and used as a point of reference by the various boards and agencies in the formulation of their policies and programs.[149]

The Committee on Christian Social Relations was not given authority to speak for the denomination in matters referred to it between meetings of the General Assembly but was authorized and encouraged to speak its own convictions as a committee.[150] Its function was conceived as that of keeping the Church aware of the moral and social issues of the day, interpreting these issues in keeping with its understanding of the Scriptures, and providing materials for individual study and for study groups.

At the end of the decade, about 90 per cent of the active membership of the Cumberland Presbyterian Church was in churches located in Southern and border states. Its attitudes and actions on the race question will therefore be given special attention.

Prior to the decision of the United States Supreme Court in May 1954, outlawing racial segregation in the public schools, the General Assembly had taken action, in response to a memorial from Texas Synod, opening the Cumberland Presbyterian Theological Seminary to members of the Cumberland Presbyterian Church, Colored, who were preparing for the ministry or other types of full-time Christian service.[151] Only one black student enrolled under this program, however.

The General Assembly in 1954 went on record as approving the decision of the United States Supreme Court regarding racial segregation in the public schools.[152] It also voted to open the In-Service Training School to ministers of the Cumberland Presbyterian Church, Colored;[153] however, this directive was not implemented until 1956.

In 1957, the General Assembly adopted a recommendation "that the Assembly declare that its position, in principle, is that all facilities of higher education in our denomination should be open to all persons regardless of race"; however, the report as adopted went on to express the view "that the removal of discrimination from the program of higher education should be part of a larger decision to remove this barrier from the total life of the church." Plans for the elimination of this barrier, it was suggested, should be coupled with plans for the merger of the two Cumberland Presbyterian denominations as proposed by the memorial from Cherokee Presbytery addressed to that Assembly.[154]

The question of admitting black students to Bethel College was before the General Assembly several times, but it was not until the summer of 1961 that the Board of Trustees voted to open the college to ministerial students of the Second Cumberland Presbyterian Church. In the fall of 1961, one black student was enrolled; in 1962-1963, two black students; and in 1963-1964, four.

In 1964, resolutions were introduced in the General Assembly by the Rev. Thomas D. Campbell, then pastor of a mission church at Batesville, Arkansas, to instruct the Board of Trustees of the Seminary to open its doors to "all qualified persons, who are studying for full-time Christian service," and to instruct the Board of Trustees of Bethel College to open the doors of the college to all qualified persons "regardless of race, denomination, or choice of vocation." [155] These resolutions were adopted. The directive establishing an open door policy for the Seminary coincided with its relocation in Memphis. In 1968-1969, the institution's fifth year in the city, black students constituted about 15 per cent of the enrollment of Memphis Theological Seminary. Bethel College's enrollment of black students increased significantly; the figure in 1968-1969 was thirty-six, out of a total cumulative enrollment of 737 that year. Thus progress was made, although not without resistance, in breaking down the barrier of race.

Believing that reconciliation between man and man must have its basis in reconciliation of man to God, the Committee on Overtures and Resolutions of the 1968 General Assembly, headed by the Rev. Raymon Burroughs, was critical of certain studies in "Reconciliation" which had been proposed for 1970. The Committee expressed the opinion

that the studies on "Reconciliation" for the Spring of 1970 as now described do not take into account fully enough their principal dimension. It is our feeling that reconciliation on the horizontal plane, as here described, is impossible except in conjunction with real reconciliation between men and God.[156]

In adopting this statement the General Assembly was saying, in effect, that the primary responsibility of the Church is the proclamation of the evangelistic message, "Be ye reconciled to God," for only in Christ are the barriers which separate men from each other effectively broken down.

The apparent decrease over a period of years in the effectiveness of the Church in evangelism had become a matter of concern. The average number of conversions per year reported by Cumberland Presbyterian churches dropped from 3,705 in 1951-1955 to 2,982 in 1956-1960, and to a new low of 2,555 in 1961-1965. Beginning in 1966, the categories for reporting were changed, but during the five years from 1966 through 1970 the number of additions on profession of faith averaged only 1,937 per year, with a low of 1,831 being recorded for the year 1969. Such facts as these doubtless led Dr. Lyle E. Schaller, of the Center for Parish Development, Naperville,

Illinois, who conducted an In-Depth Study of the Cumberland Presbyterian Church during the years 1969 and 1970, for presentation to the General Assembly in 1971, to make the statement that "The most serious *religious* issue facing the Cumberland Presbyterian Church is the lack of an effective approach to evangelism." [157] A similar concern led some twelve commissioners to the General Assembly in 1970 to submit a resolution, which was adopted, asking that boards, agencies, and planning groups be instructed "to give high priority to an intensive and intense program of evangelism," this campaign to be conducted over a three-year period beginning in January 1972.[158]

Already, following the U. S. Congress on Evangelism held in Minneapolis, Minnesota, in 1969, plans were in the making for a meeting tentatively called "Presbyterian Congress on Evangelism" (later named "A Celebration of Evangelism") to be held in Cincinnati, Ohio, in September 1971, and the Board of Missions had looked with favor upon the prospect of the Cumberland Presbyterian Church's participation.[159] Two persons from the denomination were asked to serve on the steering committee.

Out of the In-Depth Study of the Church, by Schaller, came a recommendation that the 1971 General Assembly should direct that one person of the Board of Missions staff be assigned on at least a half-time basis responsibility for helping the churches strengthen their evangelistic efforts.[160] Thus there were evidences, as the denomination entered its seventeenth decade, of an awakening of the evangelistic concern which traditionally has characterized the Cumberland Presbyterian Church.

The interest of Cumberland Presbyterians in the history of their denomination has been apparent through the years. A focal point for expression of this interest has been the site of Samuel McAdow's home in Dickson County, Tennessee, where the independent Cumberland Presbytery was organized on February 4, 1810.

The site of the home was acquired by Charlotte Presbytery from W. L. Napier on July 21, 1856. In the latter part of that century a modest frame chapel was erected on the property, and for a number of years, until the state acquired the surrounding area for a state park, a congregation known as the McAdow Memorial Church worshiped there.

On three occasions the Cumberland Presbyterian Church, through its General Assembly, has returned to the place of its birth. The first of these occasions was in 1907. The continuing General Assembly at Decatur, Illinois, in 1906, had adjourned to meet at the birthplace site the following May, and there the 77th General Assembly was constituted, though the subsequent sessions were held in the town of Dickson, six miles away. Those

"THE OLD LOG HOUSE" (RECONSTRUCTED) AND THE CHAPEL AT THE BIRTHPLACE SHRINE, DICKSON COUNTY, TENNESSEE

attending the Assembly made pilgrimages to the birthplace site in numbers estimated at 250 daily during the Assembly's sessions.[161]

In 1910, the General Assembly again met in Dickson, in observance of the denomination's centennial. A number of historical papers were prepared to be read at this Assembly, and these were later published.[162] On this occasion a "multitude" went to the birthplace to worship on Sunday. [163]

Meanwhile the surrounding area was acquired by the State of Tennessee, and in the 1940s Montgomery Bell State Park was developed. In 1953, a resolution was adopted by the General Assembly in which it was noted that the birthplace site was in the midst of the park and was itself undeveloped. It provided for the creation of a Birthplace Shrine Commission with authority to solicit funds for the development of a shrine at the birthplace and to proceed with the project as funds would permit. It was also suggested that the presbytery then holding title to the property be asked to deed it to the Board of Finance. Named to the Commission were Joe M. Forbis, Paul Hampton, John B. Tally, Chester Parham, and the Rev. W. T. Ingram.[164]

On October 24, 1953, title to the birthplace site, consisting of about five acres, was conveyed to the Board of Finance by Clarksville Presbytery (successor to Charlotte Presbytery). Response to the effort for development was such that during the year 1956 an approximate replica of the McAdow log house was erected. The work was supervised by Robert Kaiser, Chief Ranger of Montgomery Bell State Park, for a set fee.[165] On Sunday, February 3, 1957, some 103 Cumberland Presbyterians assembled for an 11 o'clock worship service, "to sit before the two log fires, drink coffee and hot chocolate, eat cookies, look out the windows and imagine they could see King and Ewing riding horseback down the road to visit Samuel McAdow." [166]

In setting up plans for the Mid-Century Expansion and Development Program, $25,000 was designated for the Birthplace Shrine.[167] This was requested by the Commission for the building of a stone chapel.

In 1960, the sesquicentennial of the Church, the General Assembly met in Nashville. Although the Mid-Century Expansion and Development Program was in its early stages, money was advanced from proceeds of the fund to erect the chapel, which was completed just in time for the General Assembly. On Saturday, June 18, some 3,000 persons traveled to the birthplace and gathered on the hillside overlooking the log house and the chapel. Joe M. Forbis, chairman of the Birthplace Shrine Commission, presided. After the hills resounded with the singing of "Whosoever Will" and other songs, a pageant, "The Miracle of 1800," about the Great Revival and its aftermath, was dramatized by representatives of the Memphis churches.[168]

Beginning in 1961, Sunday services were conducted by various ministers during the months of June, July, and August. In later years a ministerial student was employed each summer to conduct the services and serve each day as host at the Shrine. Persons residing or visiting in Montgomery Bell State Park were invited to the services. Subsequently the Board of Missions was assigned the responsibility of arranging for this park ministry and subsidizing it as needed.[169]

Thus the role of the Birthplace Shrine came to be not only that of a memorial to the past but also a means of rendering service to the surrounding community, symbolizing the fact that the Cumberland Presbyterian Church, while mindful of its rich heritage, was continuing in its efforts "to serve the present age."

# Appendix

## ASSEMBLY MEETINGS AND OFFICERS

Historical Review of the Stated Meetings and Officers of the Cumberland Presbytery, the Cumberland Synod, and the General Assembly of the Cumberland Presbyterian Church.

### THE CUMBERLAND PRESBYTERY, 1810-1813

| Date | Place | Moderator | Clerk | Members |
|---|---|---|---|---|
| 1810, February 4... | Samuel McAdow's house, Dickson Co., Tenn...... | Samuel McAdow... | ...................... | 3 |
| 1810, March 20.... | Ridge Meetinghouse, Sumner Co., Tenn...... | Samuel McAdow... | Young Ewing.......... | 14 |
| 1810, October 23... | Lebanon Meetinghouse, Christian Co., Ky...... | Finis Ewing........ | Young Ewing.......... | 16 |
| 1811, March 19.... | Big Spring Meetinghouse, Wilson Co., Tenn...... | Robert Bell........ | Young Ewing.......... | 19 |
| 1811, October 9.... | Ridge Meetinghouse..... | Thomas Calhoun... | David Foster.......... | 23 |
| 1812, April 7....... | Suggs Creek Meetinghouse, Wilson Co., Tenn...... | Hugh Kirkpatrick.. | James B. Porter........ | 28 |
| 1812, November 3.. | Lebanon Meetinghouse.... | Finis Ewing........ | Hugh Kirkpatrick....... | 22 |
| 1813, April 6....... | Beech Meetinghouse, Sumner Co., Tenn...... | Robert Bell........ | James B. Porter........ | 34 |

### THE CUMBERLAND SYNOD, 1813-1828

| | | | | |
|---|---|---|---|---|
| 1813, October 5.... | Beech Meetinghouse...... | William McGee.... | Finis Ewing............ | 13 |
| 1814, April 5...... | Suggs Creek Meetinghouse. | David Foster....... | James B. Porter........ | 27 |
| 1815, October 17... | Beech Meetinghouse...... | William Barnett.... | David Foster.......... | 15 |
| 1816, October 15... | Free Meetinghouse, Maury Co., Tenn....... | Thomas Calhoun... | David Foster.......... | 22 |
| 1817, October 21... | Mt. Moriah Meetinghouse, Logan Co., Ky......... | Robert Donnell.... | Hugh Kirkpatrick....... | 27 |
| 1818, October 20... | Big Spring Meetinghouse.. | Finis Ewing....... | Robert Bell............. | 27 |
| 1819, October 19... | Suggs Creek Meetinghouse. | Samuel King....... | William Barnett........ | 24 |
| 1820, October 17... | Russellville, Ky.......... | Thomas Calhoun... | William Moore......... | 30 |
| 1821, Third Tues. in Oct...... | Russellville, Ky.......... | .................. | Minutes not on record...... | |
| 1822, October 15... | Beech Meetinghouse...... | James B. Porter.... | David Foster.......... | 47 |
| 1823, October 21... | Russellville, Ky.......... | John Barnett...... | Aaron Alexander........ | 48 |
| 1824, October 19... | Cane Creek Meetinghouse, Lincoln Co., Tenn...... | Samuel King....... | William Moore......... | 68 |
| 1825, October 18... | Princeton, Ky........... | William Barnett.... | Hiram McDaniel........ | 76 |
| 1826, Third Tues. in Oct...... | Russellville, Ky.......... | .................. | Minutes not on record...... | |
| 1827, November 20. | Russellville, Ky.......... | James S. Guthrie... | Laban Jones........... | 63 |
| 1828, October 21... | Franklin, Tenn.......... | Hiram A. Hunter... | Richard Beard......... | 94 |

### THE GENERAL ASSEMBLY, 1829-

| | | | | |
|---|---|---|---|---|
| 1829, May 19...... | Princeton, Ky........... | Thomas Calhoun... | F. R. Cossitt............ | 26 |
| 1830, May 18...... | Princeton, Ky........... | James B. Porter.... | F. R. Cossitt............ | 36 |
| 1831, May 17...... | Princeton, Ky........... | Alexander Chapman | F. R. Cossitt............ | 34 |
| 1832, May 15...... | Nashville, Tenn......... | Samuel King....... | F. R. Cossitt............ | 36 |
| 1833, May 21...... | Nashville, Tenn......... | Thomas Calhoun... | F. R. Cossitt............ | 35 |

| Date | Place | Moderator | Clerk | Members |
|------|-------|-----------|-------|---------|
| 1834, May 20..... | Nashville, Tenn.......... | F. R. Cossitt...... | James Smith............ 48 | |
| 1835, May 19..... | Princeton, Ky........... | Samuel King....... | James Smith............ 42 | |
| 1836, May 17..... | Nashville, Tenn.......... | Reuben Burrow.... | James Smith............ 43 | |
| 1837, May 16..... | Princeton, Ky........... | Robert Donnell.... | James Smith............ 49 | |
| 1838, May 15..... | Lebanon, Tenn........... | Hiram A. Hunter... | James Smith............ 47 | |
| 1840, May 19..... | Elkton, Ky............ | Reuben Burrow.... | James Smith............ 55 | |
| 1841, May 18..... | Owensboro, Ky.......... | William Ralston.... | C. G. McPherson........ 56 | |
| 1842, May 17..... | Owensboro, Ky.......... | Milton Bird....... | C. G. McPherson........ 57 | |
| 1843, May 16..... | Owensboro, Ky.......... | A. M. Bryan....... | C. G. McPherson........ 68 | |
| 1845, May 20..... | Lebanon, Ky........... | Richard Beard..... | C. G. McPherson........ 95 | |
| 1846, May 19..... | Owensboro, Ky.......... | M. H. Bone....... | C. G. McPherson........ 86 | |
| 1847, May 18..... | Lebanon, Ohio.......... | Hiram A. Hunter... | C. G. McPherson........ 71 | |
| 1848, May 16..... | Memphis, Tenn.......... | Milton Bird....... | C. G. McPherson........100 | |
| 1849, May 15..... | Princeton, Ky.......... | John L. Smith..... | C. G. McPherson........ 75 | |
| 1850, May 21..... | Clarksville, Tenn........ | Reuben Burrow.... | Milton Bird............102 | |
| 1851, May 20..... | Pittsburgh, Pa.......... | Milton Bird....... | Milton Bird............ 71 | |
| 1852, May 18..... | Nashville, Tenn.......... | David Lowry...... | Milton Bird............107 | |
| 1853, May 17..... | Princeton, Ky.......... | H. S. Porter...... | Milton Bird............108 | |
| 1854, May 16..... | Memphis, Tenn.......... | Isaac Shook....... | Milton Bird............112 | |
| 1855, May 15..... | Lebanon, Tenn........... | M. H. Bone....... | Milton Bird............101 | |
| 1856, May 15..... | Louisville, Ky.......... | Milton Bird....... | Milton Bird............ 99 | |
| 1857, May 21..... | Lexington, Mo.......... | Carson P. Reed.... | Milton Bird............106 | |
| 1858, May 20..... | Huntsville, Ala.......... | Felix Johnson...... | Milton Bird............124 | |
| 1859, May 19..... | Evansville, Ind.......... | T. B. Wilson....... | Milton Bird............131 | |
| 1860, May 17..... | Nashville, Tenn.......... | S. G. Burney...... | Milton Bird............168 | |
| 1861, May 16..... | St. Louis, Mo.......... | A. E. Cooper...... | Milton Bird............ 51 | |
| 1862, May 15..... | Owensboro, Ky.......... | P. G. Rea......... | Milton Bird............ 58 | |
| 1863, May 21..... | Alton, Ill............. | Milton Bird....... | Milton Bird............ 73 | |
| 1864, May 19..... | Lebanon, Ohio.......... | Jesse Anderson..... | Milton Bird............ 65 | |
| 1865, May 18..... | Evansville, Ind.......... | Hiram Douglas..... | Milton Bird............ 78 | |
| 1866, May 17..... | Owensboro, Ky.......... | Richard Beard..... | Milton Bird............155 | |
| 1867, May 16..... | Memphis, Tenn.......... | J. B. Mitchell..... | Milton Bird............176 | |
| 1868, May 21..... | Lincoln, Ill............ | G. W. Mitchell..... | Milton Bird............184 | |
| 1869, May 20..... | Murfreesboro, Tenn....... | S. T. Anderson..... | Milton Bird............173 | |
| 1870, May 19..... | Warrensburg, Mo......... | J. C. Provine...... | Milton Bird............167 | |
| 1871, May 18..... | Nashville, Tenn.......... | J. B. Logan....... | Milton Bird............173 | |
| 1872, May 16..... | Evansville, Ind.......... | C. H. Bell........ | Milton Bird............182 | |
| 1873, May 15..... | Huntsville, Ala.......... | J. W. Poindexter... | John Frizzell...........165 | |
| 1874, May 21..... | Springfield, Mo......... | T. C. Blake....... | John Frizzell...........185 | |
| 1875, May 20..... | Jefferson, Texas......... | W. S. Campbell.... | John Frizzell...........169 | |
| 1876, May 18..... | Bowling Green, Ky....... | J. M. Gill........ | John Frizzell...........184 | |
| 1877, May 17..... | Lincoln, Ill........... | A. B. Miller...... | John Frizzell...........171 | |
| 1878, May 16..... | Lebanon, Tenn........... | D. E. Bushnell..... | John Frizzell...........205 | |
| 1879, May 15..... | Memphis, Tenn.......... | J. S. Grider....... | John Frizzell...........143 | |
| 1880, May 20..... | Evansville, Ind.......... | A. Templeton...... | John Frizzell...........194 | |
| 1881, May 19..... | Austin, Texas.......... | W. J. Darby....... | John Frizzell...........187 | |
| 1882, May 18..... | Huntsville, Ala.......... | S. H. Buchanan.... | John Frizzell...........188 | |
| 1883, May 17..... | Nashville, Tenn.......... | A. J. McGlumphy.. | T. C. Blake............204 | |
| 1884, May 15..... | McKeesport, Pa.......... | John Frizzell...... | T. C. Blake............148 | |
| 1885, May 21..... | Bentonville, Ark......... | G. T. Stainback.... | T. C. Blake............185 | |
| 1886, May 20..... | Sedalia, Mo........... | E. B. Crisman..... | T. C. Blake............193 | |
| 1887, May 19..... | Covington, Ohio.......... | Nathan Green..... | T. C. Blake............187 | |
| 1888, May 17..... | Waco, Texas........... | W. H. Black...... | T. C. Blake............217 | |
| 1889, May 16..... | Kansas City, Mo........ | J. M. Hubbert..... | T. C. Blake............217 | |
| 1890, May 15..... | Union City, Tenn........ | E. G. McLean..... | T. C. Blake............220 | |
| 1891, May 21..... | Owensboro, Ky......... | E. E. Beard....... | T. C. Blake............213 | |
| 1892, May 19..... | Memphis, Tenn.......... | W. T. Danley...... | T. C. Blake............229 | |
| 1893, May 18..... | Little Rock, Ark........ | W. S. Ferguson.... | T. C. Blake............226 | |
| 1894, May 17..... | Eugene, Ore............ | F. R. Earle....... | T. C. Blake............167 | |
| 1895, May 16..... | Meridian, Miss.......... | M. B. DeWitt..... | T. C. Blake............208 | |
| 1896, May 21..... | Birmingham, Ala........ | A. W. Hawkins.... | J. M. Hubbert........200 | |
| 1897, May 20..... | Chicago, Ill........... | H. S. Williams..... | J. M. Hubbert........224 | |
| 1898, May 19..... | Marshall, Mo.......... | H. H. Norman..... | J. M. Hubbert........221 | |
| 1899, May 18..... | Denver, Colo.......... | J. M. Halsell...... | J. M. Hubbert........181 | |
| 1900, May 17..... | Chattanooga, Tenn....... | H. C. Bird....... | J. M. Hubbert........230 | |
| 1901, May 16..... | West Point, Miss........ | E. E. Morris....... | J. M. Hubbert........226 | |
| 1902, May 15..... | Springfield, Mo......... | S. M. Templeton... | J. M. Hubbert........255 | |
| 1903, May 21..... | Nashville, Tenn.......... | R. M. Tinnon...... | J. M. Hubbert........247 | |
| 1904, May 19..... | Dallas, Texas........... | W. E. Settle...... | J. M. Hubbert........251 | |
| 1905, May 18..... | Fresno, Calif.......... | J. B. Hail......... | J. M. Hubbert........249 | |
| 1906, May 17..... | Decatur, Ill........... | Ira Landrith...... | J. M. Hubbert........279 | |
| 1906, May 24..... | Decatur, Ill........... | J. L. Hudgins..... | T. H. Padgett........106 | |
| 1907, May 17..... | Dickson, Tenn.......... | A. N. Eshman..... | J. L. Goodknight.......140 | |
| 1908, May 21..... | Corsicana, Texas........ | F. H. Prendergast.. | J. L. Goodknight.......136 | |
| 1909, May 20..... | Bentonville, Ark........ | J. T. Barbee...... | J. L. Goodknight.......142 | |
| 1910, May 19..... | Dickson, Tenn.......... | J. H. Fussell...... | J. L. Goodknight.......144 | |
| 1911, May 18..... | Evansville, Ind.......... | J. W. Duvall...... | J. L. Goodknight.......105 | |
| 1912, May 16..... | Warrensburg, Mo........ | J. D. Lewis....... | J. L. Goodknight.......109 | |
| 1913, May 15..... | Bowling Green, Ky....... | J. H. Milholland... | J. L. Goodknight.......119 | |
| 1914, May 21..... | Wagoner, Okla.......... | F. A. Brown....... | J. L. Goodknight.......112 | |
| 1915, May 20..... | Memphis, Tenn.......... | William Clark...... | D. W. Fooks............116 | |

| Date | Place | Moderator | Clerk | Members |
|------|-------|-----------|-------|---------|
| 1916, May 18 | Birmingham, Ala. | J. L. Price | D. W. Fooks | 125 |
| 1917, May 17 | Lincoln, Ill. | F. A. Seagle | D. W. Fooks | 102 |
| 1918, May 16 | Dallas, Texas | C. H. Walton | D. W. Fooks | 117 |
| 1919, May 15 | Fayetteville, Ark. | J. H. Zwingle | D. W. Fooks | 101 |
| 1920, May 15 | McKenzie, Tenn. | J. E. Cortner | D. W. Fooks | 123 |
| 1921, May 19 | Greenfield, Mo. | John B. Tally | D. W. Fooks | 108 |
| 1922, May 18 | Greeneville, Tenn. | Hugh S. McCord | D. W. Fooks | 102 |
| 1923, May 17 | Fairfield, Ill. | P. F. Johnson | D. W. Fooks | 105 |
| 1924, May 15 | Austin, Texas | D. M. McAnulty | D. W. Fooks | 93 |
| 1925, May 21 | Nashville, Tenn. | W. E. Morrow | D. W. Fooks | 114 |
| 1926, May 20 | Columbus, Miss. | I. K. Floyd | D. W. Fooks | 111 |
| 1927, May 19 | Lakeland, Fla. | T. A. DeVore | D. W. Fooks | 97 |
| 1928, June 21 | Jackson, Tenn. | J. L. Hudgins | D. W. Fooks | 97 |
| 1929, May 16 | Princeton, Ky. | H. C. Walton | D. W. Fooks | 98 |
| 1930, May 15 | Olney, Texas | O. A. Barbee | D. W. Fooks | 92 |
| 1931, May 21 | Evansville, Ind. | J. L. Elliott | D. W. Fooks | 98 |
| 1932, May 19 | Chattanooga, Tenn. | G. G. Halliburton | D. W. Fooks | 104 |
| 1933, June 14 | Memphis, Tenn. | W. B. Cunningham | D. W. Fooks | 94 |
| 1934, June 14 | Springfield, Mo. | A. C. DeForest | D. W. Fooks | 103 |
| 1935, June 13 | McKenzie, Tenn. | C. A. Davis | D. W. Fooks | 104 |
| 1936, June 18 | San Antonio, Texas | E. K. Reagin | D. W. Fooks | 100 |
| 1937, June 16 | Knoxville, Tenn. | Geo. E. Coleman | D. W. Fooks | 109 |
| 1938, June 16 | Russellville, Ark. | D. D. Dowell | D. W. Fooks | 117 |
| 1939, June 15 | Marshall, Mo. | E. R. Ramer | D. W. Fooks | 126 |
| 1940, June 13 | Cookeville, Tenn. | Keith T. Postlethwaite | D. W. Fooks | 116 |
| 1941, June 19 | Denton, Texas | L. L. Thomas | D. W. Fooks | 120 |
| 1942, June 18 | McKenzie, Tenn. | Geo. W. Burroughs | D. W. Fooks | 108 |
| 1943, June 17 | Paducah, Ky. | A. A. Collins | D. W. Fooks | 94 |
| 1944, June 15 | Bowling Green, Ky. | I. M. Vaughn | D. W. Fooks | 94 |
| 1945, May 31 | Lewisburg, Tenn. | S. T. Byars | Wayne Wiman | 103 |
| 1946, June 13 | Birmingham, Ala. | C. R. Matlock | Wayne Wiman | 105 |
| 1947, June 12 | Knoxville, Tenn. | Morris Pepper | Wayne Wiman | 108 |
| 1948, June 17 | Nashville, Tenn. | Paul F. Brown | Wayne Wiman | 105 |
| 1949, June 16 | Muskogee, Okla. | Blake F. Warren | Wayne Wiman | 109 |
| 1950, June 15 | Los Angeles, Calif. | L. P. Turnbow | Wayne Wiman | 98 |
| 1951, June 14 | Longview, Texas | John E. Gardner | Wayne Wiman | 105 |
| 1952, June 18 | Memphis, Tenn. | Emery A. Newman | Wayne Wiman | 120 |
| 1953, June 18 | Gadsden, Ala. | Chas. L. Lehning, Jr. | Wayne Wiman | 107 |
| 1954, June 17 | Dyersburg, Tenn. | John S. Smith | Wayne Wiman | 124 |
| 1955, June 16 | Lubbock, Texas | Ernest C. Cross | Shaw Scates | 118 |
| 1956, June 21 | Cookeville, Tenn. | Hubert W. Morrow | Shaw Scates | 118 |
| 1957, June 21 | Evansville, Ind. | Wm. T. Ingram, Jr. | Shaw Scates | 119 |
| 1958, June 18 | Birmingham, Ala. | Wayne Wiman | Shaw Scates | 116 |
| 1959, June 17 | Springfield, Mo. | Virgil T. Weeks | Shaw Scates | 120 |
| 1960, June 15 | Nashville, Tenn. | Arleigh G. Matlock | Shaw Scates | 130 |
| 1961, June 21 | Florence, Ala. | Ollie W. McClung | Shaw Scates | 126 |
| 1962, June 20 | Little Rock, Ark. | Eugene L. Warren | Shaw Scates | 126 |
| 1963, June 19 | Austin, Texas | Franklin Chesnut | Shaw Scates | 117 |
| 1964, June 17 | Chattanooga, Tenn. | Vaughn Fults | Shaw Scates | 123 |
| 1965, June 16 | San Francisco, Calif. | Thomas Forester | Shaw Scates | 114 |
| 1966, June 15 | Memphis, Tenn. | John W. Sparks | Shaw Scates | 124 |
| 1967, June 21 | Paducah, Ky. | Raymon Burroughs | Shaw Scates | 123 |
| 1968, June 19 | Oklahoma City, Okla. | Loyce S. Estes | Shaw Scates | 115 |
| 1969, June 18 | San Antonio, Texas | J. David Hester | Shaw Scates | 116 |
| 1970, June 17 | Knoxville, Tenn. | L. C. Waddle | Shaw Scates | 116 |

# NOTES

## Introduction

[1] James Smith, *History of the Christian Church from Its Origin to the Present Time. Compiled from Various Authors: Including a History of the Cumberland Presbyterian Church, Drawn from Authentic Documents* (Nashville: Cumberland Presbyterian Office, 1835), p. 639.

[2] *A Circular Letter Addressed to the Societies and Brethren of the Late Cumberland Presbytery; in Which There Is a Correct Statement of the Origin, Progress, and Termination of the Differences between the Synod of Kentucky, and the Former Presbytery of Cumberland, 1810* (Russellville, Ky.: Matthew Duncan, 1810), p. 12.

## PART I

### Background and Formation of the Cumberland Presbyterian Church, Through 1829

#### Chapter 1

#### Born in Controversy: Early American Presbyterianism

[1] William B. Sprague, ed., *Presbyterians*, Vol. III of *Annals of the American Pulpit; or Commemorative Notices of Distinguished American Clergymen of Various Denominations, from the Early Settlements of the Country to the Close of the Year Eighteen Hundred and Fifty-five, with Historical Introductions* (New York: Robert Carter & Brothers, 1857-1869), p. x.

[2] Ezra H. Gillett, *History of the Presbyterian Church in the United States of America*, rev. ed. (Philadelphia: Board of Publication and Sabbath-School Work, 1873), I, 1.

[3] Vernon L. Parrington, *The Colonial Mind, 1620-1800*, Vol. I of *Main Currents in American Thought, an Interpretation of American Literature from the Beginnings to 1920* (New York: Harcourt, Brace and Company, 1927), pp. 62-75. Williams's principle of absolute religious freedom is set forth in Perry Miller, *Roger Williams: His Contribution to the American Tradition* (Indianapolis: Bobbs-Merrill, 1953). A candid portrayal of

Williams's opposition to civil magistrates having the authority to control the affairs of the church is given in R. E. E. Harkness, "Roger Williams—Prophet of Tomorrow," *Journal of Religion*, XV (October 1935), 400-425.

⁴ John Winthrop, *John Winthrop's Journal*, ed. James K. Hasmer (New York: Charles Scribner's Sons, 1908), I, 240-255, 263-265; Ernest S. Bates, *American Faith* (New York: W. W. Norton and Co., 1940), pp. 135-146; Edmund Morgan, "The Case Against Anne Hutchinson," *New England Quarterly*, X (December 1937), 635-649.

⁵ *Magnalia Christi Americana* (Hartford: S. Andrus, 1820), I, 72.

⁶ For details of this complicated phase of church history, see Theodore Hoyer, "The Historical Background of the Westminster Assembly," *Concordia Theological Monthly*, XVIII (August 1947), 572-591. The Westminster Assembly is discussed in detail in Philip Schaff, *The Creeds of Christendom, with a History and Critical Notes*, rev. ed. (New York: Harper & Brothers, 1931), I, 727-804. The conflict between the Independents and the Presbyterians is treated in Charles Firth, *Oliver Cromwell and the Rule of the Puritans in England* (London: Oxford University Press, 1900), Chap. VIII.

⁷ For the full text of the Platform, see Williston Walker, *The Creeds and Platforms of Congregationalism* (New York: Charles Scribner's Sons, 1893), pp. 156-237.

⁸ XI. 4, XVI. 1-4.

⁹ Herbert W. Schneider, *The Puritan Mind* (New York: Henry Holt and Co., 1930), pp. 86-87.

¹⁰ The statement of the synod in answer to the question: "Who are the Subjects of Baptism?" is contained in "The Answer of the Elders and Other Messengers of the Churches, Assembled at Boston in the Year 1662," reprinted in H. Shelton Smith, Robert T. Handy, and Lefferts A. Loetscher, *American Christianity, an Historical Interpretation with Representative Documents, 1607-1820* (New York: Charles Scribner's Sons, 1960), I, 203-204.

¹¹ *Ibid.*

¹² James H. Nichols, *Democracy and the Churches* (Philadelphia: Westminster Press, 1951), p. 33. Also, see Williston Walker, *A History of the Congregational Churches*, Vol. III of *The American Church History Series*, ed. Philip Schaff, et al. (New York: Christian Literature Co., 1894), pp. 170-182; Frank H. Foster, *A Genetic History of New England Theology* (Chicago: University of Chicago Press, 1907), pp. 31-43; Perry Miller, "The Half-Way Covenant," *New England Quarterly*, VI (1933), 676-715.

¹³ Solomon Stoddard, *The Doctrine of Instituted Churches, Explained and Proved from the Word of God* (London, 1700), reprinted in Smith, Handy, and Loetscher, *American Christianity*, I, 220-224; Perry Miller, "Solomon Stoddard, 1643-1729," *Harvard Theological Review*, XXXIV (October 1941), 298.

¹⁴ Articles II, XII, XIV, XV. For a comparison of the Articles and the *Massachusetts Proposals*, see Walker, *Creeds and Platforms*, pp. 503-506.

¹⁵ Jerald C. Brauer, *Protestantism in America* (Philadelphia: Westminster Press, 1953), p. 42.

¹⁶ William Warren Sweet, *Religion in Colonial America* (New York: Charles Scribner's Sons, 1942), pp. 113-115. See Walker, *Creeds and Platforms*, pp. 495-514, for documents relating to the Saybrook Synod.

¹⁷ Henry M. Dexter, *Congregationalism of the Last Three Hundred Years, as Seen in Its Literature: with Special Reference to Certain Recondite, Neglected, or Disputed Passages* (New York: Harper & Brothers, 1880), p. 463.

¹⁸ For the diverse views of Presbyterian historians, see Charles A. Briggs, *American Presbyterianism, Its Origins and Early History, Together with an Appendix of Letters and Documents, Many of Which Have Been Recently Discovered* (New York: Charles Scribner's Sons, 1885), pp. 87-131; Charles A. Hodge, *The Constitutional History of the Presbyterian Church in the United States of America* (Philadelphia: Presbyterian Board of Publication, 1857), I, 27-66; Leonard J. Trinterud, *The Forming of an American Tradition: A Re-examination of Colonial Presbyterianism* (Philadelphia: Westminster Press, 1949), 22-28; Gaius

J. Slosser, ed., *They Seek a Country: The American Presbyterians—Some Aspects* (New York: Macmillan Co., 1955), pp. 29-32; James H. Nichols, *Presbyterianism in New York State: A History of the Synod and Its Predecessors* (Philadelphia: Westminster Press, 1963), pp. 9-17; Henry D. Funk, "The Influence of the Presbyterian Church in Early American History," *Journal of the Presbyterian Historical Society*, XII (April 1924), 32-33; William P. Finney, "The Period of the Isolated Congregations and General Presbytery, 1614-1716," *Journal of the Department of History (The Presbyterian Historical Society) of the Presbyterian Church in the U. S. A.*, XV (March 1932), 8-17; Clifford M. Drury, "Presbyterian Beginnings in New England and the Middle Colonies," *Journal of the Presbyterian Historical Society*, XXXIV (March 1956), 19-35.

[19] Quoted in Leonard J. Trinterud, "The New England Contribution to Colonial American Presbyterianism," *Church History*, XVII (March 1948), 33.

[20] See "Letters to Increase Mather," reprinted in Richard Webster, *A History of the Presbyterian Church in America from Its Origins until the Year 1760, with Biographical Sketches of Its Early Ministers* (Philadelphia: Joseph M. Wilson, 1857), pp. 297-300.

[21] *Records of the Presbyterian Church in the United States of America: Embracing the Minutes of the Presbytery of Philadelphia, from A. D. 1706 to 1716: Minutes of the Synod of Philadelphia, from A. D. 1717 to 1758: Minutes of the Synod of New York, from A. D. 1745 to 1758: Minutes of the Synod of Philadelphia and New York, from 1758 to 1788* (Philadelphia: Presbyterian Board of Publication, 1841), p. 60; Hodge, *Constitutional History*, I, 76-77; Webster, *Presbyterian Church in America*, p. 90; Gillett, *Presbyterian Church in the United States of America*, I, 5.

[22] Francis Makemie, *A Narrative of a New and Unusual American Imprisonment of Two Presbyterian Ministers, and Prosecution of Mr. Francis Makemie, One of Them for Preaching One Sermon in the City of New York. By a Learner of Law and a Lover of Liberty*, reprinted in Smith, Handy, and Loetscher, *American Christianity*, I, 258-261.

[23] Webster, *Presbyterian Church in America*, p. 303.

[24] Letter of Edward Hyde, Viscount Cornbury to the Lords Commissioners for the Trades and Plantations, Oct. 14, 1706, reprinted in Webster, *Presbyterian Church in America*, pp. 307-309.

[25] Since the first page of the record book is missing, there has been much conjecture about the date of the first meeting and the constitution of the presbytery. For a study of this problem, see Benjamin L. Agnew, "When Was the First Presbytery of the Presbyterian Church in the United States of America Organized?" *Journal of the Presbyterian Historical Society*, III (March 1905), 9-24.

[26] *Records of the Presbyterian Church*, p. 8.

[27] *Records of the Presbyterian Church*, p. 79; Sprague, *Annals*, III, 2-3; Webster, *Presbyterian Church in America*, pp. 310-311, 358-361.

[28] Henry G. Ford, *The Scotch-Irish in America* (Princeton: Princeton University Press, 1915), pp. 11-20.

[29] Robert E. Thompson, *A History of the Presbyterian Churches in the United States*, Vol. VI of *The American Church History Series*, ed. Philip Schaff, *et al.* (New York: Christian Literature Co., 1893-1897), p. 13. The name "Scotch-Irish" is used for want of a better appellation. George S. Pride, a Scots historian, condemns the use of "Scotch-Irish" because it implies a mixture of races. The Scots refused to intermarry with the Irish. See "The Scots in East New Jersey," *Proceedings of the New Jersey Historical Society*, XV (1930), 3, n. 2; James G. Leyburn, *The Scotch-Irish: A Social History* (Chapel Hill: University of North Carolina Press, 1962), Chap. X discusses the problem of whether or not the Scots mixed racially, socially, and religiously with the inhabitants of Ireland. Also see Charles A. Hanna, *The Scotch-Irish, or the Scot in North Britain, North Ireland and North America* (New York: G. P. Putnam's Sons, 1902), I, 498-505; John W. Dinsmore, *The Scotch-Irish in America: Their History, Traits, Institutions and Influ-*

*ences, Especially as Illustrated in the Early Settlers of Western Pennsylvania, and Their Descendants* (Chicago: Winona Publishing Co., 1906), p. 16.

[30] Ford, *The Scotch-Irish in America*, pp. 167-177.

[31] Hanna, *The Scotch-Irish*, I, 57-61; James G. Craighead, *Scotch and Irish Seeds in American Soil: The Early History of the Scotch and Irish Churches, and Their Relations to the Presbyterian Church of America* (Philadelphia: Presbyterian Board of Publication, 1878), pp. 267-268.

[32] Ford, *The Scotch-Irish in America*, p. 188.

[33] Hanna, *The Scotch-Irish*, I, 16-22; Sweet, *Religion in Colonial America*, pp. 250-251.

[34] Quoted in Herbert S. Turner, *Church in the Old Fields: Hawfields Presbyterian Church and Community in North Carolina* (Chapel Hill: University of North Carolina Press, 1962), p. 30.

[35] Leyburn, *The Scotch-Irish*, p. 192.

[36] Donald McDougall, ed., *Scots and Scots' Descendants in America* (New York: Caledonian Publishing Co., 1917), I, 17-18; Clifton E. Olmstead, *History of Religion in the United States* (Englewood Cliffs, N. J.: Prentice-Hall, 1960), p. 46.

[37] Benjamin Franklin estimated their number to be 350,000. Ford, *The Scotch-Irish in America*, p. 265.

[38] These stern measures probably contributed much to the opposition of the Scotch-Irish to England in the struggle for independence. Hanna, *The Scotch-Irish*, I, 621; II, 15.

[39] Leyburn, *The Scotch-Irish*, p. 140.

[40] *Ibid.*, p. 323.

[41] Dinsmore, *The Scotch-Irish in America*, pp. 47-52.

[42] *Ibid.*, pp. 227-231.

[43] Walter Brownlow Posey, *The Presbyterian Church in the Old Southwest,* *1778-1838* (Richmond: John Knox Press, 1952), p. 11.

[44] William H. Foote, *Sketches of North Carolina, Historical and Biographical, Illustrative of the Principles of a Portion of Her Early Settlers* (New York: Robert Carter, 1846), Chaps. X-XII. John MacLean, *An Historical Account of the Settlements of Scotch Highlanders in America Prior to the Peace of 1783: Together with Notices of Highland Regiments and Biographical Sketches* (Cleveland: Holman-Taylor Co., 1900), *passim.*

[45] The "political exile" theory was first expounded by Foote, *Sketches of North Carolina*, pp. 129-130, and Foote served as the basis for subsequent historians who held to the same theory, such as Webster, *Presbyterian Church in America*, pp. 63, 531; Craighead, *Scotch and Irish Seeds*, p. 268; MacLean, *Scotch Highlanders in America*, p. 104; Hanna, *The Scotch-Irish*, II, 34; and Herbert L. Osgood, *The American Colonies in the Eighteenth Century* (New York: Columbia University Press, 1924), II, 522.

[46] Duane Meyer, *The Highland Scots of North Carolina, 1732-1776* (Chapel Hill: University of North Carolina Press, 1961), Chap. III, "Motives for Migration."

[47] Even John Witherspoon, who came directly from Scotland, has been referred to as Scotch-Irish by Carl Wittke in *We Who Built America: The Saga of the Immigrant* (New York: Prentice-Hall, 1948), p. 65. Wittke may have been influenced by the fact that Witherspoon was one of the few Scots who favored the cause for independence. See Ian C. C. Graham, *Colonists from Scotland: Immigration to North America, 1707-1783* (Ithaca: Cornell University Press, 1956), pp. 17-22, 177-183.

[48] *Records of the Presbyterian Church,* p. 17.

## Chapter 2

## The Right To Dissent

[1] *Records of the Presbyterian Church,* p. 66.

[2] *Ibid.,* pp. 61-62. Cross became the leader of the Old Side party during the schism of 1741-1758.

[3] *Records of the Presbyterian Church,* pp. 71-72.

[4] The Articles, adopted by the Irish Synod in 1720, declared: "If any person called to subscribe shall scruple any phrase or phrases in the Confession, he shall have leave to use his own expression, which the Presbytry [*sic*] shall accept of, Providing they judge such a person sound in the Faith, and that such expressions are consistent with the substance of the doctrine." *Records of the General Synod of Ulster,* quoted in Trinterud, *American Tradition,* pp. 42-43.

[5] "Records of Presbytery of New Castle," in *Journal of the Department of History (The Presbyterian Historical Society) of the Presbyterian Church in the U. S. A.,* XV (1932), 98, 207. The formula used by the Armagh Presbytery, in Ulster, was: "I do believe the Westminster Confession of Faith to be founded on and agreeable to the Word of God, and therefore as such, by this my subscription, do own it as the confession of my faith." Reprinted in Webster, *Presbyterian Church in America,* p. 102.

[6] The overture was not included in the minutes of the synod. The full text is reprinted in Hodge, *Constitutional History,* I, 136-141.

[7] The synod of 1724 had agreed to have a delegated synod meet for two years and a full synod every third year. Because of the distance involved, the delegated synods would consist of half of the members of the New Castle and Philadelphia presbyteries and two delegates from the Long Island Presbytery. *Records of the Presbyterian Church,* pp. 78, 89. Delegated synods convened in 1725 and 1726; a full synod convened in 1727. Another full synod was not to meet until 1730, but the subscription controversy forced a full synod in 1729. The synod never met again as a delegated body; it continued to meet as a presbytery of the whole. Trinterud, *American Tradition,* p. 45.

[8] Trinterud, *American Tradition,* p. 46.

[9] Dickinson's *Remarks* are reprinted in Smith, Handy, and Loetscher, *American Christianity,* I, 263-268.

[10] Andrews's letter to Colman is reprinted in Webster, *Presbyterian Church in America,* p. 105. The letter reveals two parties in the Presbyterian Church, but they were willing to compromise in order to prevent separation.

[11] Briggs, *American Presbyterianism,* pp. 214-215; Trinterud, *American Tradition,* pp. 47-48. The intensity of feelings is revealed in an article by Ezra H. Gillett, "The Men and Times of the Reunion of 1758," *American Presbyterian and Theological Review,* VI (July 1868), 414-443, and the answer by Charles Hodge, "Dr. Gillett and Liberal Presbyterianism," *Princeton Review,* XL (October 1868), 608-632. Gillett, a New School historian, defends the activities of the New Side party during the schism of 1741-1758; Hodge, an Old School historian, attempts to refute Gillett by presenting the Old Side version. This clearly indicates a continuation of the Old Side-Old School and the New Side-New School segments of American Presbyterianism.

[12] *Records of the Presbyterian Church,* pp. 94-95.

[13] The Four Articles of 1722 are quoted in this chapter. For a comparison of the Adopting Act and the Pacific Articles, see Briggs, *American Presbyterianism,* pp. 217-220.

[14] "Letter of Rev. Ebenezer Pemberton of New York, to Rev. Dr. Colman at Boston," New York, September 30, 1729, quoted in Jonathan F. Stearns, *First Church in Newark. Historical Discourse Relating to the First Presbyterian Church in Newark* (Newark, N. J.: privately printed, 1853), p. 138.

[15] The East Jersey and Long Island presbyteries were united in 1738 to form the Presbytery of New York. *Records of*

*the Presbyterian Church,* p. 134. See Nichols, *Presbyterianism in New York State,* pp. 30-37, for a discussion of the growth of the churches on Long Island and in East Jersey.

[16] *Records of the Presbyterian Church,* pp. 49-50.

[17] Tennent served as pastor at Bensalem, Pennsylvania, and Bedford, New Jersey, from 1721 to 1727. Briggs, *American Presbyterianism,* p. 186; Archibald Alexander, *Biographical Sketches of the Founders and Principal Alumni of the Log College, Together with an Account of the Revival of Religion under Their Ministry* (Philadelphia: Presbyterian Board of Publication, 1851), Chap. III.

[18] The autobiographical quotations are reprinted in Joseph Tracy, *The Great Awakening, A History of the Revival of Religion in the Time of Edwards and Whitefield* (Boston: Tappan & Dennent, 1842), pp. 31-34.

[19] *Journal,* Nov. 25, 1739, quoted in Stearns, *First Church in Newark,* p. 166.

[20] *Records of the Presbyterian Church,* p. 136. The Adopting Act of 1729 was reconfirmed by the Synod in 1730 and 1735. *Ibid.,* pp. 96, 107-108.

[21] *Ibid.,* pp. 132-140.

[22] The same issues—revivalism, subscription, educational qualifications, and ecclesiastical authority over a minister (synodical or presbyterial)—were involved in the controversies between the Synod of Kentucky and Cumberland Presbytery during the years 1803-1806, which resulted in the organization of the Cumberland Presbyterian Church.

[23] Sixty-seven years later, the older Presbyterian ministers of Cumberland Presbytery refused to allow the Synod of Kentucky to reexamine the men their presbytery had licensed and ordained.

[24] Hodge, *Constitutional History,* II, 109.

[25] Charles Maxson, *The Great Awakening in the Middle Colonies* (Chicago: University of Chicago Press, 1920), p. 38.

[26] *Records of the Presbyterian Church,* p. 187.

[27] Sweet, *Religion in Colonial America,* p. 284.

[28] Ola Elizabeth Winslow, *Jonathan Edwards, 1703-1758: A Biography* (New York: Macmillan Co., 1940), p. 166.

[29] Reprinted in Smith, Handy, and Loetscher, *American Christianity,* I, 321-328.

[30] According to rumor, Whitefield had plans to bring candidates from England, have them ordained by New Brunswick Presbytery, and use them to supplant the pastors who were lacking in piety and zeal. Stearns, *Historical Discourses,* p. 166.

[31] Tennent was probably referring to the Log College. Three months later, the Synod of Philadelphia declared its right to examine candidates who had received a "private education." This was obviously aimed at the Log College. *Records of the Presbyterian Church,* p. 152.

[32] "The Nottingham sermon, which was repeatedly published and widely circulated, was one of the causes of the disruption of the Presbyterian Church, but its ultimate effect was to make its doctrine dominant policy of that church." Maxson, *The Great Awakening in the Middle Colonies,* p. 56. The doctrine of a "divine call" to the ministry was one of the issues involved in the controversy over the examination of candidates for the ministry. The antirevivalists and Log College men differed on the doctrine of the call to the ministry. The Log College men distinguished between the divine call to the ministry and the act of ordination by the presbytery. The antirevival party asserted that every candidate ordained by the presbytery is called of God. Samuel Finley set forth the issue in an argument with John Thomson: "This is the Point at which Mr. Th. . .n and I do part asunder, viz. That the Call of God to the Office of the Ministry, is distinguished from, tho' not opposed unto, the Presbytery's Trying and Ordaining a Person to that Office. This he denies, and we affirm." Quoted in Trinterud, *American Tradition,* p. 92.

[33] *Records of the Presbyterian Church,* pp. 149-152.

[34] Trinterud, *American Tradition,* p. 97.

[35] "A Protestation Presented to the Synod, 1 June 1741"; in *Records of the Presbyterian Church,* pp. 155-158.

[36] Twelve ministers signed the protest, from the presbyteries of Philadelphia, New Castle, Donegal, and Lewes.

[37] *Records of the Presbyterian Church,* pp. 156-157.

[38] *Ibid.,* p. 160.

[39] *Ibid.,* p. 161.

[40] *Ibid.,* p. 163.

[41] *Ibid.,* pp. 164-166.

[42] *Ibid.,* pp. 166-167.

[43] *Ibid.,* p. 169.

[44] *Ibid.,* p. 232. The New York Synod was composed of the presbyteries of New York, New Brunswick, and New Castle. (The Synod of Philadelphia also had a New Castle Presbytery.)

[45] *Ibid.,* pp. 232-233.

[46] Nichols, *Presbyterianism in New York State,* p. 44.

[47] Alexander, *Log College,* pp. 215-223; Samuel Miller, *Memoirs of John Rodgers* (New York: Whiting and Watson, 1813), pp. 33-35.

[48] Letter of Samuel Morris to Samuel Davies in S. Miller, *John Rodgers,* pp. 42-43.

[49] *Records of the Presbyterian Church,* p. 292; T. Watson Street, *The Story of Southern Presbyterians* (Richmond: John Knox Press, 1961), pp. 14-16.

[50] Maxson, *The Great Awakening in the Middle Colonies,* pp. 113-114.

[51] *Records of the Presbyterian Church,* pp. 193-205, 237-245.

[52] *Ibid.,* pp. 221, 224, 230, 250-251, 267, 275, 279, 284. For a description of this continuing conflict, see Trinterud, *American Tradition,* Chap. IX, "Union Without Love."

[53] Trinterud, "New England Contribution," 34-35.

[54] Trinterud, *American Tradition,* pp. 31-33.

[55] Trinterud, "New England Contribution," 35.

[56] *Ibid.,* 38.

[57] *Records of the Presbyterian Church,* p. 127.

[58] Trinterud, "New England Contribution," 36-40.

[59] Trinterud, *American Tradition,* pp. 31-32.

## Chapter 3

### Presbyterianism on the Frontier: A New Awakening

[1] Frederick Jackson Turner, *The Frontier in American History* (New York: Henry Holt and Co., 1920), pp. 103-104.

[2] Guy S. Klett, *Presbyterians in Colonial Pennsylvania* (Philadelphia: University of Pennsylvania Press, 1937), p. 3.

[3] *Records of the Presbyterian Church,* p. 100.

[4] Trinterud, *American Tradition,* pp. 23-29.

[5] *Records of the Presbyterian Church,* pp. 325-326; Joseph Smith, *Old Redstone, or Historical Sketches of Western Presbyterianism, Its Early Ministers, Its Perilous Times and Its First Records* (Philadelphia: Lippincott, Grambo & Co., 1854), pp. 113-116.

[6] Charles Beatty, *Journal of a Two-Months Tour, with a View of Promoting Religion among the Frontier Inhabitants of Pennsylvania* (London: William Davenhill, 1768), p. 30; *Records of the Presbyterian Church,* p. 362. Beatty and Duffield were the first Presbyterian ministers to visit the Ohio Valley.

[7] *Records of the Presbyterian Church,* pp. 375-376.

[8] *Ibid.,* p. 417.

[9] *Ibid.,* p. 432; "Minutes of the Donegal Presbytery" in Thomas C. Pears, "The Foundations of Our Western Zion," *Journal of the Department of History (The Presbyterian Historical Society) of the Presbyterian Church in the U. S. A.,* XVI (December 1934), 145-162.

[10] David McClure, *Diary of David McClure, with Notes by Franklin B. Dexter* (New York: Knickerbocker Press, 1889), pp. 47-56, 100-112, 124.

[11] *Records of the Presbyterian Church,* p. 491.

[12] A biographical sketch of James Power is given in Smith, *Old Redstone,* pp. 225-250. Also see Sprague, *Annals,* III, 326-330.

[13] D. M. Bennett, "Life and Work of Reverend John McMillan," *Journal of the*

Department of History (*The Presbyterian Historical Society*) *of the Presbyterian Church in the U. S. A.*, XV (September 1932), 133-158; Sprague, *Annals*, III, 353-355; Dwight R. Guthrie, *John Mc-Millan, The Apostle of Presbyterianism in the West* (Pittsburgh: University of Pittsburgh Press, 1952), pp. 57 ff.

[14] Cephas Dodd, "Memoir of Dr. T. Dod," *Presbyterian Magazine*, IV (August-September, 1854), 368-378, 415-425. A sketch of Dod is given in Smith, *Old Redstone*, pp. 139-151. Also see Sprague, *Annals*, III, 356-359.

[15] William W. McKinney, ed., *The Presbyterian Valley: 200 Years of Presbyterianism in the Upper Ohio Valley* (Pittsburgh: Davis and Warde, 1958), p. 151; *Minutes of the Presbytery of Redstone of the Presbyterian Church, from September 1781 to December 1831* (Cincinnati: privately printed, 1878), pp. 3-4; Smith, *Old Redstone*, p. 62.

[16] *Minutes of Redstone Presbytery*, pp. 4-6.

[17] Dunlap served later as president of Jefferson College for eight years. Smith, *Old Redstone*, p. 302; *Records of the Presbyterian Church*, p. 493.

[18] *Minutes of Redstone Presbytery*, pp. 7-16; *Records of the Presbyterian Church*, pp. 498-507.

[19] McKinney, *Presbyterian Valley*, pp. 17-19; *Minutes of Redstone Presbytery*, pp. 25, 30, 46, 66-67, 87.

[20] Smith, *Old Redstone*, pp. 359-364.

[21] Samuel Eliot Morison and Henry Steele Commager, *The Growth of the American Republic*, 4th ed. (New York: Oxford University Press, 1956), I, 252-256.

[22] Thomas C. Pears, "First Formal History of Transylvania Presbytery," *Journal of the Department of History (The Presbyterian Historical Society) of the Presbyterian Church in the U. S. A.*, XIX (December 1940), 147-148; Robert Davidson, *History of the Presbyterian Church in the State of Kentucky with a Preliminary Sketch of the Churches in the Valley of Virginia* (Lexington, Ky.: Charles Marshall, 1847), pp. 58-63.

[23] Robert H. Bishop, *An Outline of the History of the Church in the State of Kentucky, during a Period of Forty Years: Containing the Memoirs of Rev. David Rice* (Lexington, Ky.: Thomas T. Skillman, 1824), pp. 64-67.

[24] Davidson, *Presbyterian Church in Kentucky*, pp. 73-74; Bishop, *Outline of the Church in Kentucky*, pp. 67-69.

[25] Minutes of Transylvania Presbytery, 1786-1829. Typed manuscript, Historical Foundation of the Presbyterian and Reformed Churches, Montreat, N. C., Oct. 17, 1786. The new presbytery listed six ministers: David Rice, Thomas Craighead, Adam Rankin, Andrew McClure, James Crawford, and Terah Templin.

[26] Theodore Roosevelt, *The Winning of the West* (New York: Current Literature Publishing Co., 1906), pp. 99-100; Sprague, *Annals*, III, 392-397; C. W. Sommerville, "Samuel Doak," *Union Seminary Review*, XL (1928-1929), 193-205.

[27] Gillett, *Presbyterian Church in the United States of America*, I, 426-427; Lucius S. Merriam, *Higher Education in Tennessee* (Washington, D.C.: Government Printing Office, 1893), p. 227.

[28] Stanley J. Folmsbee, "Blount College and East Tennessee College, 1794-1840," *East Tennessee Historical Society Publications*, No. 17 (1945), 22-50.

[29] John M. Bass, "Rev. Thomas Craighead," *American Historical Magazine*, VII (January 1901), 88-96.

[30] Leonard W. Bacon, *A History of American Christianity* (New York: Charles Scribner's Sons, 1901), p. 230.

[31] Bishop, *Outline of the Church in Kentucky*, pp. 67-69.

[32] Davidson, *Presbyterian Church in Kentucky*, p. 130.

[33] *Minutes of the General Assembly of the Presbyterian Church from Its Organization: A. D. 1789 to A. D. 1820, Inclusive* (Philadelphia: Presbyterian Board of Publication, 1847), pp. 152-153.

[34] Bishop, *Outline of the Church in Kentucky*, p. 79.

[35] Charles A. Johnson, *The Frontier Camp Meeting, Religion's Harvest Time* (Dallas: Southern Methodist University Press, 1955), pp. 11-13.

[36] Albert J. Beveridge, *Abraham Lincoln, 1809-1858* (Boston: Houghton Mifflin Co., 1928), I, 53-56.

[37] Francis Asbury, *The Journal of Rev. Francis Asbury* (New York: Lane & Scott, 1852), II, 342.

[38] Bacon, *American Christianity*, p. 230. For further descriptions of the spiritual climate preceding the revival in the West, see Johnson, *The Frontier Camp Meeting*, Chap. I; Davidson, *Presbyterian Church in Kentucky*, Chap. II; Catherine C. Cleveland, *The Great Revival in the West, 1797-1805* (Chicago: University of Chicago Press, 1916), Chap. I; Frederick M. Davenport, *Primitive Traits in Religious Revivals: A Study in Mental and Social Evolution* (New York: Macmillan Co., 1905), Chap. I.

[39] McGready left no memoirs, except for an account of the origin of the revival in his Kentucky churches. The account is found in the book titled *The Posthumous Works of the Reverend and Pious James M'Gready, Late Minister of the Gospel, in Henderson, Kentucky*, edited by James Smith (Louisville: W. W. Worsley, 1831-1833), I, ix-xvi. For brief sketches of his life, see Foote, *Sketches of North Carolina*, pp. 367-413; Sprague, *Annals*, III, 278 ff.; Smith, *History of the Christian Church*, pp. 565-579; *Dictionary of American Biography*, XII, 56-57; Richard Beard, *Brief Biographical Sketches of Some of the Early Ministers of the Cumberland Presbyterian Church* (Nashville: Southern Methodist Publishing House, 1869), pp. 7-17.

[40] *Diary of Joseph Badger*, quoted in McKinney, *Presbyterian Valley*, pp. 58-60. It is interesting to note that even as people "fell and cried out," the writer is careful to say that "order and decency were preserved." This is indicative of the fear among the Presbyterians of a recurrence of the emotionalism of the Great Awakening of 1740.

[41] Gillett, *Presbyterian Church in the United States of America*, II, 176-177. Also see Turner, *Hawfields Presbyterian Church*, Chap. VI.

[42] For a discussion of the sporadic awakenings in North Carolina prior to 1801, see Guion G. Johnson, "Revival Movements in Ante-Bellum North Carolina, 1856-1861," *North Carolina Historical Review*, X (January 1933), 21-43, and "The Camp Meeting in Ante-Bellum North Carolina," *North Carolina Historical Review*, X (April 1933), 95-100.

[43] Quoted in Turner, *Hawfields Presbyterian Church*, pp. 105-106.

[44] *New York Missionary Magazine, and Repository of Religious Intelligence*, III (1802), 176.

[45] *Acts and Proceedings of the General Association of Connecticut, 1800*, p. 205, quoted in Charles R. Keller, *The Second Awakening in Connecticut* (New Haven: Yale University Press, 1942), *passim*.

[46] Keller, *Second Awakening in Connecticut*, pp. 42-54. The following will be helpful for an understanding of the Second Great Awakening in the East: Keller, *Second Awakening in Connecticut*; Bernard A. Weisberger, *They Gathered at the River: The Story of the Great Revivalists and Their Impact upon Religion in America* (Boston: Little, Brown and Co., 1958), Chaps. I and II; Frank Beardsley, *A History of American Revivals* (New York: American Tract Society, 1904), Chaps. V and VI; Wesley Gewehr, *The Great Awakening in Virginia, 1740-1790* (Durham, N. C.: Duke University Press, 1930); Smith, Handy, and Loetscher, *American Christianity*, I, Chap. X.

[47] Foote, *Sketches of North Carolina*, p. 368; Cleveland, *The Great Revival in the West*, pp. 37-38.

[48] Cleveland, *The Great Revival in the West*, p. 38.

[49] *Ibid.*, p. 369; Davenport, *Primitive Traits*, pp. 66-67.

[50] When Cumberland Presbytery of the Synod of Kentucky divided into the prorevival and antirevival factions with five ministers on each side, the four who sided with McGready—John Rankin, William Hodge, William McGee, and Samuel McAdow—had been colaborers with him in Guilford County, North Carolina, and members of Orange Presbytery. Foote, *Sketches of North Carolina*, p. 376.

[51] John Rogers, *The Biography of Eld. Barton Warren Stone, Written by Himself: with Additions and Reflections by Elder John Rogers, Written in Part by John Rogers* (Cincinnati: J. A. & U. P. James, 1847), pp. 6-7.

[52] Smith, *History of the Christian Church*, pp. 563-564.

[53] Quoted in Foote, *Sketches of North Carolina,* pp. 10-11. For a psychological interpretation of the "law of expectancy," in connection with prayers for an outpouring of the Spirit, see Davenport, *Primitive Traits,* pp. 9-10.

[54] McGready, *Posthumous Works,* I, ix-xvi; Foote, *Sketches of North Carolina,* pp. 376-377.

[55] Minutes of the Synod of Kentucky, 1802-1829. Manuscript Record, Historical Foundation of the Presbyterian and Reformed Churches, Montreat, N. C., Oct. 26, 1807; Minutes of Transylvania Presbytery, Mar. 25, 1809, Oct. 5, 1809; George B. Hays, *Presbyterians: A Popular Narrative of Their Origin, Progress, Doctrines, and Achievements* (New York: J. A. Hill & Co., 1892), pp. 466-467; Beard, *Brief Biographical Sketches,* p. 13.

[56] Franceway R. Cossitt, *The Life and Times of Rev. Finis Ewing, One of the Fathers and Founders of the Cumberland Presbyterian Church. To Which Is Added Remarks on Davidson's History, or, a Review of His Chapters on the Revival of 1800 and His History of the Cumberland Presbyterians* (Louisville: Lee Roy Woods, Agent, for the Board of Publication of the Cumberland Presbyterian Church, 1853), p. 166; Davidson, *Presbyterian Church in Kentucky,* p. 261; Posey, *Presbyterian Church in the Old Southwest,* p. 38.

[57] James McGready, "A Short Narrative of the Revival of Religion in Logan County, in the State of Kentucky, and the Adjacent Settlements in the State of Tennessee, from May 1797, until September 1800," printed in the *New York Missionary Magazine, and Repository of Religious Intelligence,* IV (1803), 154.

[58] Johnson, *The Frontier Camp Meeting,* pp. 34-35.

[59] Peter Cartwright, *Autobiography of Peter Cartwright, the Backwoods Preacher,* ed. W. P. Strickland (New York: Calton & Porter, 1857), pp. 36-37. For a detailed account of the origins of the camp meeting, see Johnson, *The Frontier Camp Meeting,* Chap. II.

[60] McGready, "A Short Narrative of the Revival of Religion," p. 192. McGready counted thirteen wagons filled with people and provisions. For a description of the Gasper River meeting, see Johnson, *The Frontier Camp Meeting,* pp. 35-38; Davidson, *Presbyterian Church in Kentucky,* pp. 134 ff.; Cossitt, *Finis Ewing,* p. 66; Cleveland, *The Great Revival in the West,* pp. 56-57; William Warren Sweet, *The Presbyterians, 1783-1840.* Vol. II of *Religion on the American Frontier* (New York: Harper & Brothers, 1936), pp. 85-86.

[61] Davidson, *Presbyterian Church in Kentucky,* pp. 136-137.

[62] Davenport, *Primitive Traits,* pp. 66-67.

[63] McGready, *Posthumous Works,* II, 71-82.

[64] *Ibid.,* II, 82, 241.

[65] *Ibid.,* I, 63, 168.

[66] In an unindexed section added to his *Works,* II, 4.

[67] *Ibid.,* II, 22.

[68] Davidson, *Presbyterian Church in Kentucky,* p. 132.

[69] Rogers, *Barton Stone,* pp. 9-11, 36-37.

[70] *Ibid.,* p. 37.

[71] Letter of Colonel Robert Patterson to the Rev. John King, Lexington, Kentucky, September 25, 1801, quoted in Smith, Handy, and Loetscher, *American Christianity,* I, 566-567.

[72] Peter Cartwright, in his *Autobiography,* pp. 30-31, said that from 12,000 to 20,000 were present at different times during the meeting. William Burke, a Methodist, described the crowd to be as large as 20,000, having preached to 10,000 himself, and James Finley, a circuit rider present at the Cane Ridge meeting, increased the estimate to 25,000. See Finley, *Sketches of Western Methodism: Biographical, Historical, and Miscellaneous, Illustrative of Pioneer Life* (Cincinnati: Methodist Book Concern, 1855), pp. 77-79. Archibald Alexander, president of Hampden-Sydney College, supported the figure of 20,000. See *Connecticut Evangelical Magazine and Religious Intelligencer,* II (1801-1802), 354-360. Barton Stone accepted the estimate of experienced military men present "that there were between twenty and thirty thousand collected." See Rogers, *Barton Stone,* p. 38.

[73] See Johnson, *The Frontier Camp Meeting,* p. 51, and Patterson to King,

in Smith, Handy, and Loetscher, *American Christianity*, I, 568-569.

[74] Ray A. Billington and J. B. Hedges, *Westward Expansion: A History of the American Frontier* (New York: Macmillan Co., 1950), p. 250.

[75] Richard McNemar, *The Kentucky Revival: Or a Short History of the Late Outpouring of the Spirit of God in the Western States of America, with a Brief Account of the Entrance and Progress of What the World Called Shakerism, among Subjects of the Late Revival in Ohio and Kentucky* (Cincinnati: J. W. Brown, 1807), p. 23.

[76] Rogers, *Barton Stone*, p. 38.

[77] Finley, *Sketches of Western Methodism*, p. 78; Cartwright, *Autobiography*, p. 36; Cleveland, *The Great Revival in the West*, p. 79.

[78] Letter of Samuel Blair to Thomas Prince, 1744, quoted in McKinney, *Presbyterian Valley*, pp. 69-73.

[79] "Thoughts on Revival of Religion," in Carl J. C. Wolfe, ed., *Jonathan Edwards on Evangelism* (Grand Rapids, Mich.: Wm. B. Eerdmans Publishing Co., 1958), p. 55.

[80] Quoted in Briggs, *American Presbyterianism*, p. 318.

[81] McNemar, *The Kentucky Revival*, pp. 23 ff.

[82] Patterson to King, in Smith, Handy, and Loetscher, *American Christianity*, I, 568. Posey, *A Presbyterian History*, stresses the fact that the Revival reached only the lower strata of society, and the more sophisticated were untouched by the movement. See *The Presbyterian Church in the Old Southwest*, p. 28. Yet, a man in Kentucky wrote to his brother in Virginia that he had witnessed hundreds falling prostrate on the ground, people who were not "mere riffraff or hysterical children, but the learned pastor, the steady patriot, and the obedient son . . . the honorable matron and the virtuous maiden crying, Jesus, thou Son of the most high God, have mercy on us," quoted in the *Connecticut Evangelical Magazine*, II (1801-1802), 392-394.

[83] Patterson to King, in Smith, Handy, and Loetscher, *American Christianity*, I, 568.

[84] Rogers, *Barton Stone*, p. 34.

[85] James B. Finley, *Autobiography of Rev. James B. Finley; or, Pioneer Life in the West*, ed. W. P. Strickland (Cincinnati: Methodist Book Concern, 1853), p. 167.

[86] McNemar, *The Kentucky Revival*, p. 167.

[87] Patterson to King, in Smith, Handy, and Loetscher, *American Christianity*, I, 567-569; Cleveland, *The Great Revival in the West*, pp. 88-98.

[88] Joseph Badger, "Extract of a Letter from Joseph Badger, July 19, 1803," in *Connecticut Evangelical Magazine*, III (1803-1804), pp. 113-118.

[89] Rogers, *Barton Stone*, p. 40.

[90] *Autobiography of a Pioneer; or, the Nativity, Experience, Travels, and Ministerial Labors of Rev. Jacob Young, with Incidents, Observations, and Reflections* (Cincinnati: Cranston and Curts, 1857), pp. 135-137.

[91] Smith, *History of the Christian Church*, p. 590.

[92] Davidson, *Presbyterian Church in Kentucky*, p. 181.

[93] Cleveland, *The Great Revival in the West*, Chap. IV, vouches for the thesis that modern psychology and medical science have demonstrated the genuineness of the nervous disorders and bodily actions of the revival. Also see Davenport, *Primitive Traits*, pp. 74-81, and Johnson, *The Frontier Camp Meeting*, pp. 57-62.

[94] Cartwright, *Autobiography*, p. 364.

[95] Sweet, *Presbyterians*, p. 89. Part of Lyle's account of the Cane Ridge meeting is given in Appendix V, Cleveland, *The Great Revival in the West*, pp. 183-189.

[96] Johnson, *The Frontier Camp Meeting*, pp. 65-66; Weisberger, *They Gathered at the River*, pp. 35-36.

[97] Sidney E. Mead, *The Lively Experiment: The Shaping of Christianity in America* (New York: Harper and Row, 1963), p. 123; Henry C. Lay, "The Revival System: Its Good and Evil," *Church Review*, VII (October 1854), 356-375.

[98] See Schneider, *The Puritan Mind*, for a description of the attack on Calvinism.

[99] Mead, *The Lively Experiment*, pp. 123-128; William Mitchell, "An Enquiry into the Utility of Modern Evangelists and Their Measures," *Literary and Theo-*

logical Review, II (September 1835), 494-507; Edwin P. Pond, "Evangelists," *New Englander,* II (April 1844), 297-303.

[100] William Speer, *The Great Revival of 1800* (Philadelphia: Presbyterian Board of Publication, 1872), pp. 61-64.

[101] "Second Epistle to the Citizens of Kentucky," reprinted in Bishop, *Outline of the Church in Kentucky,* p. 367.

[102] Cossitt, *Finis Ewing,* pp. 409-416. Cossitt gives an interesting account of the use—or misuse—of Lyle's Diary by critics of the revival.

[103] Quoted in Posey, *Presbyterian Church in the Old Southwest,* p. 27.

[104] *Minutes of the General Assembly, 1789-1820,* pp. 223, 260, 274, 308-310, 315, 334, 364.

[105] Bacon, *American Christianity,* pp. 237-238.

[106] Gillett, *Presbyterian Church in the United States of America,* II, 196.

[107] Johnson, *The Frontier Camp Meeting,* p. 67; Cleveland, *The Great Revival in the West,* pp. 130-131.

[108] *Minutes of the General Assembly, 1789-1820,* p. 223.

## Chapter 4

### Pressure for Ministers: A Growing Dispute

[1] Minutes of Transylvania Presbytery, Oct. 6, 1792.

[2] Benjamin W. McDonnold, *History of the Cumberland Presbyterian Church* (Nashville: Board of Publication of the Cumberland Presbyterian Church, 1888), pp. 48-49; Minutes of Transylvania Presbytery, Oct. 9, 1801.

[3] Reprinted in John Knox, *The Works of John Knox* (Edinburgh: James Thin, 1895), II, 183-258. Also see William M. Hetherington, *History of the Church of Scotland* (New York: Robert Carter and Brothers, 1881), p. 54.

[4] Knox, *Works of John Knox,* II, 195-199. Only ordained ministers could "minister" the sacraments.

[5] *Ibid.,* II, 513; Janet MacGregor, *The Scottish Presbyterian Polity: A Study of Its Origins in the Sixteenth Century* (Edinburgh: Oliver and Boyd, 1926), pp. 48, 122.

[6] Minutes of Transylvania Presbytery, Oct. 9, 1796. This significant fact is overlooked by Sweet, in *The Presbyterians,* pp. 90-92.

[7] Hays, *Presbyterians,* p. 457; Smith, *History of the Christian Church,* pp. 580, 598; Davidson, *Presbyterian Church in Kentucky,* p. 224.

[8] Chap. XIV, Sec. III and VI.

[9] The antirevival group believed that it would have been better to acquire additional ministers from the East; the revival party felt that missionaries could not cope with the needs of the frontier. R. E. Thompson, *History of the Presbyterian Churches in the United States,* p. 74. For some reason, not explained in the Minutes, McLean was not licensed, but he continued in the capacity of exhorter. McDonnold states that McLean objected to being received with an exception made to the educational requirements: that he wanted to meet the required standards before being licensed. *C. P. Church,* pp. 55 ff. The evidence indicates, however, that he had wished to resolve a personal problem before he felt adequate to be set apart for the ministry. In 1804, McLean "came forward and confessed to presbytery that he had been guilty of intoxication, hoping to be restored upon his confession as he had voluntarily ceased from his public ministration since the crime was committed." McLean was restored in 1805, but he failed to attend any meetings of the presbytery after his confession in 1804. *Minutes of the "Original" Cumberland Presbytery, 1802-1806* (Louisville, 1906), Oct. 3, 1804, Apr. 4, 1805.

[10] Minutes of Transylvania Presbytery, Oct. 6-8, 1802.

[11] Minutes of the Synod of Kentucky, Oct. 15, 1802.

[12] Foote, *Sketches of North Carolina*, p. 376.

[13] The founder of the Republican Methodist Church was James O'Kelly, a Methodist presiding elder in Virginia. O'Kelly led a movement to restrict the appointive powers of the bishops. In 1792 he offered an amendment to the Discipline which would allow a preacher to appeal to the Conference if "any one think himself injured by the appointment . . . and if the conference approve his objections, the bishop shall appoint him to another circuit." The proposed amendment was defeated. O'Kelly and his supporters left the Conference and formed the Republican Methodist Church. See Jesse Lee, *A Short History of the Methodists in the United States of America: Beginning in 1766, and Continued till 1809* (Baltimore: McGill and Cline, 1810), p. 178.

[14] *Minutes of the Cumberland Presbytery, 1802-1806,* Apr. 6. 1803.

[15] Sweet in *Presbyterians*, p. 287, makes the following erroneous statement concerning Porter: "Note the absence of an examination on educational qualifications." The records actually declare that "Mr. Porter's examination on the languages was sustained." *Minutes of the Cumberland Presbytery, 1802-1806,* Oct. 7, 1803.

[16] The questions usually asked to both candidates and exhorters related to their personal experiences concerning salvation and the factors conducive to their offering themselves to preach or to exhort. The office of exhorter was terminal in nature, but a candidate for the regular ministry was expected to pass through a series of trials and examinations before he could be licensed as a probationer (i.e., licensed to preach), and, finally, be approved for ordination. Sometimes an exhorter would decide to pursue the regular ministry and seek licensure as a probationer.

[17] *Minutes of the Cumberland Presbytery, 1802-1806,* Oct. 5-7, 1803.

[18] John Hodge was licensed by Transylvania Presbytery. Minutes of Transylvania Presbytery, Oct. 8, 1802. He is not to be confused with another John Hodge who became a candidate under the care of Cumberland Presbytery in April 1804.

[19] *Minutes of the Cumberland Presbytery, 1802-1806,* Apr. 3, 1805.

[20] Not "James Farr and David Foster" as set forth by Smith, *History of the Christian Church,* p. 595, and Thomas J. Simpson, *History of the Cumberland Presbyterian Church, with Miscellaneous Thoughts on Several Subjects of Divinity So Much Controverted in the World* (Jefferson City: J. T. Quesenberry, 1844), p. 30.

[21] *Minutes of the Cumberland Presbytery, 1802-1806,* Apr. 3-4, 1804. Also see Hays, *Presbyterians,* pp. 457-458; Bishop, *Outline of the Church in Kentucky,* pp. 119-120.

[22] Minutes of Transylvania Presbytery, Apr. 12, 1804.

[23] *Minutes of the General Assembly, 1789-1820,* May 25, 1804, pp. 299-301. A letter was also received from the Presbytery of West Lexington signed by James Blythe, John Lyle, and Robert Stuart. They asked the intervention of the General Assembly in the "unhappy division which has taken place in the Synod of Kentucky." This division was not the trouble within the Cumberland Presbytery, but the "unhappy division" referred to the "New Light" group in northern Kentucky. *Ibid.*, pp. 293, 312.

[24] Minutes of the Synod of Kentucky, Sept. 10-13, 1803. See the *Last Will and Testament of the Springfield Presbytery,* reprinted in Smith, Handy, and Loetscher, *American Christianity,* I, 576-578.

[25] "An Address from the Synod of Kentucky, to the Churches under Their Care," reprinted in Samuel J. Baird, ed., *A Collection of the Acts and Deliverances, and Testimonies of the Supreme Judicatory of the Presbyterian Church, from Its Origin in America to the Present Time, with Notes and Documents, Explanatory and Historical: Constituting a Complete Illustration of Her Polity, Faith, and History* (Philadelphia: Presbyterian Board of Publication, 1856), pp. 622-625.

[26] Minutes of the Synod of Kentucky, Oct. 17-22, 1804.

[27] *Minutes of the General Assembly, 1789-1820,* pp. 311-325.

[28] E. B. Crisman, *Origin and Doctrines of the Cumberland Presbyterian*

*Church* (St. Louis: Perrin & Smith, 1877), p. 43.

[29] John Vant Stephens, *Genesis of the Cumberland Presbyterian Church* (Cincinnati: privately printed, 1941), p. 33.

[30] The correspondence between Miller and Ewing is reprinted by J. Berrien Lindsley in "Sources and Sketches of Cumberland Presbyterian History, No. IV," *Theological Medium and Cumberland Presbyterian Quarterly*, n.s. VII (January 1876), 12-27. Samuel Miller was a leader in the Old School Party which gained control of the General Assembly in 1837 and expelled forty presbyteries consisting of more than 1,300 churches and more than 100,000 members. At the same time that he misrepresented the Cumberland Presbyterians, he also gave a false picture of American Presbyterianism by ascribing it to Scotch and Scotch-Irish origins. "A later and better generation repudiated the Old School party's schismatic acts, but oddly enough the Old School enjoyed a certain triumph even in the grave, as its propaganda line gradually attained to the stature of historical fact." Trinterud, "New England Contribution to American Presbyterianism," 32-33.

[31] The most recently published history on Presbyterianism perpetuates the idea of the Cumberland ministers being suspended for licensing and ordaining uneducated men, by making generalizations, sometimes erroneous and without documentation. When documentation is used, it is Davidson's *Presbyterian Church in Kentucky* or Sweet's *Presbyterians*, a collection of eviscerated documents of the judicatories relative to the Presbyterian Church in Kentucky and Tennessee. Not once is a reference made to Cumberland Presbyterian writers in the documentation. See Ernest T. Thompson, *Presbyterians in the South, 1607-1861* (Richmond: John Knox Press, 1963), Chap. X, "Frontier Schisms."

[32] *Minutes of the Cumberland Presbytery, 1802-1806*, Oct. 2, 1804. The personal conflict between Craighead and Ewing represents a major factor in the suspension of the revival ministers. Previous investigations into the origin of the Cumberland Presbyterian Church refer to Craighead as the leader of the antirevival party. However, the evidence indicates that he did not oppose the revival; he opposed the excesses. He not only wrote the letter referred to above; he also presented a written protest against the licensure of Finis Ewing and Samuel King at the meeting of Transylvania Presbytery in October 1802. His opposition stemmed from personal feelings against Ewing and not from theological or ecclesiastical motives. Both Ewing and Craighead shared a New Side Presbyterian heritage.

[33] Minutes of the Synod of Kentucky, Oct. 22, 1804. The committee included David Rice, James Blythe, John Lyle, Archibald Cameron, and Samuel Rannels.

[34] Ewing and King were licensed in October 1802. See Minutes of Transylvania Presbytery, Oct. 8, 1802.

[35] The "Letter" is the reply to David Rice quoted above.

[36] Minutes of the Synod of Kentucky, Oct. 22, 1804.

[37] Smith, *History of the Christian Church*, p. 596. Also see Thomas H. Campbell, *Studies in Cumberland Presbyterian History* (Nashville: Cumberland Presbyterian Publishing House, 1944), pp. 67-68; Thaddeus C. Blake, *The Old Log House* (Nashville: Cumberland Presbyterian Publishing House, 1897), p. 42; Davidson, *Presbyterian Church in Kentucky*, p. 231.

[38] *Form of Government of the Constitution of the Presbyterian Church*, Chap. IX, Sec. V; Chap. X, Sec. IV.

[39] *Forms of Process*, Chap. II, Sec. I.

[40] Crisman, *Origins and Doctrine of the Cumberland Presbyterian Church*, p. 85; Campbell, *Studies in Cumberland Presbyterian History*, p. 67. The synod had directed that at least *two* were to attend. Minutes of the Synod of Kentucky, Oct. 22, 1804.

[41] *Minutes of the Cumberland Presbytery, 1802-1806*, Apr. 3, 1805; Cossitt, *Finis Ewing*, p. 123.

[42] It is to be noted that Nelson and Hodge were ordained with Dickey, an antirevivalist, and both Nelson and Hodge, along with William Hodge and James McGready, were reconciled to the Presbyterian Church just several months before Finis Ewing, Samuel King, and

Samuel McAdow organized the independent Cumberland Presbytery in February 1810. Minutes of Transylvania Presbytery, Dec. 6-7, 1809.

[43] It should be noted that no dissent was registered by any delegate attending the presbytery when Haw was received. Minutes of Transylvania Presbytery, Oct. 8, 1802, and *Minutes of the Cumberland Presbytery, 1802-1806,* Apr. 4, 1803.

[44] The Minutes of Cumberland Presbytery did not say "Finis Ewing's circuit." This phrase was a distortion of what the record book really said. It declared: "A written petition from the congregation of Spring Creek, McAdow and Clarksville praying the ordination of Finis Ewing, *in whose circuit* these congregations are included." *Minutes of the Cumberland Presbytery, 1802-1806,* Oct. 7, 1803. Italics not in the original.

[45] Minutes of the Synod of Kentucky, Oct. 17-18, 1805.

[46] Dickey favored the antirevival faction. Matthew Hall and Reuben Dooley are not referred to in the *Minutes of the Cumberland Presbytery* after April 1804.

[47] The Synod of Kentucky sent a committee to Logan County to investigate the activities of Barton Stone and others. Minutes of the Synod of Kentucky, Sept. 10-13, 1803. For the use of synodical commissions in general, and the commission of the Synod of Kentucky in particular, see *A Brief History of the Rise, Progress and Termination of the Synod of Kentucky, Relative to the Late Cumberland Presbytery: in Which is Brought to View a Brief Account of the Origin and Present Standing of the People Usually Denominated Cumberland Presbyterians* (Lexington, Ky.: Thomas T. Skillman, 1823), pp. 6-7.

[48] Davidson, *Presbyterian Church in Kentucky,* p. 242; Blake, *Log House,* p. 43; Campbell, *Studies in Cumberland Presbyterian History,* p. 69.

[49] Minutes of the Synod of Kentucky, Dec. 3, 1805.

[50] *Brief History of the Synod of Kentucky,* p. 7; McDonnold, *C. P. Church,* p. 81; Hays, *Presbyterians,* p. 461; Gillett, *History of the Presbyterian Church in the United States of America,* II, 181-185; Davidson, *Presbyterian Church in Ken-*

tucky, pp. 234-235; Bishop, *Outline of the Church in Kentucky,* pp. 120-124.

[51] Minutes of the Synod of Kentucky, Dec. 4, 1805; *Brief History of the Synod of Kentucky,* p. 7.

[52] Minutes of the Synod of Kentucky, Dec. 5-6, 1805; Davidson, *Presbyterian Church in Kentucky,* p. 236. McGready also cited the chapter on "Licensing Candidates or Probationers to Preach the Gospel" from the *Form of Government,* Chap. XIV, Sec. VI.

[53] See Jonathan Dickinson, "Remarks Upon a Discourse Intitled An Overture Presented to the Reverend Synod of Dissenting Ministers Sitting in Philadelphia, in the Month of September, 1728," reprinted in Smith, Handy, and Loetscher, *American Christianity,* I, 263-268. The full text of the Adopting Act is in the *Records of the Presbyterian Church,* pp. 92-95. John Thomson's *Overture* is reprinted in Charles Hodge, *Constitutional History,* I, 162-167.

[54] Minutes of the Synod of Kentucky, Dec. 6, 1805. The meeting began on Tuesday, December 3, and ended on Wednesday, December 11.

[55] Regardless of their ages, the Minutes refer to all the members of the revival group as "young men" with the exception of the five ministers who were ordained before the Cumberland Presbytery was constituted.

[56] Minutes of the Synod of Kentucky, Dec. 6, 1805.

[57] *Form of Government,* Chap. IX, Sec. V.

[58] Minutes of the Synod of Kentucky, Dec. 7, 1805.

[59] This latter account is recorded in Crisman, *Origin and Doctrines of the Cumberland Presbyterian Church,* p. 32. Crisman received it from a son-in-law of Samuel King. This incident illustrates the conflicting historical interpretation of the revival and the antirevival parties.

[60] Robert Bell and Samuel Blythe requested that they be given until Monday to give a reply. They refused to submit.

[61] Minutes of the Synod of Kentucky, Dec. 7-9, 1805.

[62] Minutes of Transylvania Presbytery, Oct. 8, 1802; *Minutes of the Cumberland*

Presbytery, 1802-1806, Oct. 7, 1803, Apr. 4, 1804.

[63] Minutes of Transylvania Presbytery, Oct. 8, 1802; Minutes of the Cumberland Presbytery, 1802-1806, Apr. 5, 1803.

[64] Minutes of the Cumberland Presbytery, 1802-1806, Apr. 6, 1803, Apr. 3, 1805.

[65] Ibid., Oct. 2-3, 1804, Apr. 3, 1805; Minutes of Transylvania Presbytery, Dec. 6-7, 1809.

[66] Minutes of Transylvania Presbytery, Oct. 4-8, 1801.

[67] Minutes of the Cumberland Presbytery, 1802-1806, Oct. 5, 1803, Apr. 4, 1804.

[68] Ibid., Oct. 5, 1804, Oct. 2, 1805.

[69] Minutes of Transylvania Presbytery, Oct. 8, 1802.

[70] Ibid., Oct. 9, 1802. Anderson died in 1803.

[71] Minutes of the Synod of Kentucky, Dec. 9, 1805.

[72] Ibid., Dec. 10, 1805.

[73] Minutes of the Synod of Kentucky, Oct. 22, 1804. The General Assembly referred to the action of the Commission as being of "questionable authority." Minutes of the General Assembly, 1789-1820, p. 389.

[74] Minutes of the Synod of Kentucky, Dec. 10, 1805. The synod gave him a warning after he appeared before an examining committee. He was deposed from the ministry in 1810, but the Presbyterian Church restored him to his ministerial status in 1824, one year before his death. Minutes of the Synod of Kentucky, Oct. 29, 1806; Minutes of the General Assembly, 1789-1820, pp. 481-482; Minutes of the General Assembly, from A. D. 1821 to A. D. 1835, Inclusive (Philadelphia: Presbyterian Board of Publication, n.d.), pp. 38, 48, 52.

[75] The trial of Balch is not recorded in the regular Minutes of Cumberland Presbytery. It was probably recorded in one of the intermediate meetings which James McGready, presbyterial clerk, failed to record. This omission covered the period from April 1805 to October 1805. This was the period immediately preceding the meeting of the Commission. McGready admits the omission in the Minutes of the Cumberland Presbytery, 1802-1806, Oct. 2, 1805.

[76] Minutes of the Synod of Kentucky, Dec. 10, 1805.

[77] Davidson, Presbyterian Church in Kentucky, p. 242.

[78] Minutes of the Synod of Kentucky, Oct. 18, 1805.

[79] Crisman, Origin and Doctrines of the Cumberland Presbyterian Church, pp. 33-35.

## Chapter 5
## Unresolved Differences: A New Church

[1] Smith, History of the Christian Church, pp. 614-616; Campbell, Studies in Cumberland Presbyterian History, p. 74.

[2] The members of Cumberland Presbytery were annexed to Transylvania Presbytery in the next regular meeting of the Synod of Kentucky following the convocation of the synodical Commission. Minutes of the Synod of Kentucky, Oct. 28, 1806. McGready later recognized that the members of the Council were following the right course, even if the outcome meant complete separation from the Presbyterian Church.

[3] The letter of Blythe to Hodge is included in A Pastoral Letter Addressed to the Churches under the Care of the Presbytery of West Tennessee (Nashville: Eastin & Gwin, 1812), pp. 9-10.

[4] The Constitution refers to the doctrine as the "High Mystery of Predestination," The Confession of Faith, Chap. III, Sec. VIII.

[5] Minutes of the Synod of Kentucky, Oct. 27-28, 1806; Cossitt, Finis Ewing, pp. 159-160; McDonnold, C. P. Church, p. 82; Campbell, Studies in Cumberland Presbyterian History, p. 74.

[6] Smith quotes a letter from the Stated Clerk of the General Assembly of the Presbyterian Church: "There can be no doubt now in the mind of any sound Presbyterian but that the *suspension* of the ministers above named [Hodge and Rankin] was wholly unconstitutional and ought to be held to be void." *History of the Christian Church,* pp. 616-617.

[7] Minutes of the Synod of Kentucky, Oct. 28, 1806.

[8] Quoted in *A Pastoral Letter . . . of the Presbytery of West Tennessee,* p. 10.

[9] *Minutes of the General Assembly, 1789-1820,* pp. 378, 384.

[10] The General Assembly had agreed to this in their reply to David Rice's letter in April 1804. *Minutes of the General Assembly, 1789-1820,* pp. 299-301.

[11] Minutes of Transylvania Presbytery, Oct. 8, 1802; *Minutes of the Cumberland Presbytery, 1802-1806,* Oct. 7, 1803, Apr. 3, 1805, Oct. 2, 1805.

[12] The complete text of the Letter is reprinted in Smith, *History of the Christian Church,* pp. 617-625.

[13] The following notation was appended to the Minutes of the Synod of Kentucky by the General Assembly: "Thus far examined and approved. A few inaccuracies, & obscurities excepted—and also some proceedings relative to the Cumberland Presbytery of at least questionable regularity—In Gen. Assembly at Philadelphia May 1807. Arch. I. Alexander, Modr."

[14] *Minutes of the General Assembly, 1789-1820,* pp. 389-393; Davidson, *Presbyterian Church in Kentucky,* p. 376; Crisman, *Origin and Doctrines of the Cumberland Presbyterian Church,* pp. 36-41; Hays, *Presbyterians,* p. 463; Gillett, *History of the Presbyterian Church in the United States of America,* II, 186-187; Posey, *Presbyterian Church in the Old Southwest,* pp. 34-36.

[15] The Trustee is identified by Finis Ewing as Mr. Jackson of Philadelphia. The Trustee's letter is reprinted in "A Series of Letters Containing a Reply to a Pastoral Letter of the West Tennessee Presbytery: To Which is Added an Address to the Congregations &c. under the Care of the Cumberland Presbytery." Typed Manuscript Copy, Foundation of the Presbyterian and Reformed Churches, Montreat, N. C.

[16] *Minutes of the General Assembly, 1789-1820,* pp. 406, 408-409; Stephens, *Genesis of the Cumberland Presbyterian Church,* p. 67.

[17] Wilson's letter is reprinted in Smith, *History of the Christian Church,* p. 628.

[18] Minutes of the Synod of Kentucky, Sept. 8, 1803, Oct. 17, 1804.

[19] Minutes of Transylvania Presbytery, Oct. 7, 1808.

[20] Minutes of Transylvania Presbytery, Mar. 25, 1809; Crisman, *Origin and Doctrines of the Cumberland Presbyterian Church,* pp. 66-67.

[21] Davidson, *Presbyterian Church in Kentucky,* pp. 119, 250.

[22] *Minutes of the General Assembly, 1789-1820,* p. 416; Stephens, *Genesis of the Cumberland Presbyterian Church,* p. 69.

[23] Quoted in *A Pastoral Letter . . . of the Presbytery of West Tennessee,* pp. 7-8.

[24] See the *Circular Letter,* p. 12; Robert Donnell, *Thoughts on Various Subjects* (Louisville: Cumberland Presbyterian Board of Publication, 1856), p. 233; McDonnold, *C. P. Church,* p. 84.

[25] Peter Cartwright, in his usual exaggerated literary style, states that the revival party attempted to join the Methodists, but the proposition was rejected by the Methodists. In October 1810, the new Cumberland Presbytery sent a letter to the Methodist Society about "an agreement of cooperation" between the two churches. The Methodists agreed to a "sacramental union." Cartwright, *Autobiography,* p. 47; "Minutes of the Cumberland Presbytery, 1810-1813." Reprinted in the *Theological Medium,* IX (April and October 1878), 209-224, 480-498; X (January 1879), 90-96; Oct. 25, 1810; Mar. 19, 1811.

[26] Letter from Finis Ewing to James Porter, Dec. 6, 1809, quoted in Cossitt, *Finis Ewing,* pp. 191-192.

[27] The compact is in the *Circular Letter.*

[28] McAdow never took an active part in the new Church. He attended only two meetings of the Cumberland Presbyterians after they organized in his home; he was

never a member of Cumberland Synod. Richard Beard, *Brief Biographical Sketches of Some of the Early Ministers of the Cumberland Presbyterian Church*, second series (Nashville: Cumberland Presbyterian Board of Publication, 1874), pp. 7-26.

[29] Brief biographical accounts of the founders (except Farr) are given in Beard, *Brief Biographical Sketches* and *Brief Biographical Sketches*, second series.

[30] "Minutes of the Cumberland Presbytery, 1810-1813," Mar. 20-22, 1810; Ewing, Reply to the Presbytery of West Tennessee, Letter II; John M. Gaut, *Patriotism and Presbyterianism: an Address before the Lebanon, Tennessee Bible Conference* (Nashville: Cumberland Press, 1908), pp. 40-41; Davidson, *Presbyterian Church in Kentucky*, p. 253.

[31] Minutes of West Tennessee Presbytery, 1810-1863. Manuscript Record, Historical Foundation of the Presbyterian and Reformed Churches, Montreat, N. C.

[32] The Letter to Stephenson is included in the Minutes of West Tennessee Presbytery, May 11, 1811. Also see the *Minutes of the General Assembly, 1789-1820*, p. 473.

[33] Minutes of West Tennessee Presbytery. Samuel Hodge, a former member of Cumberland Presbytery and one who had been described by a Presbyterian historian as having very little education, was a member of West Tennessee Presbytery. Davidson, *Presbyterian Church in Kentucky*, p. 256.

[34] "Minutes of the Cumberland Presbytery, 1810-1813," Oct. 11, 1811, Apr. 7, 1812; Minutes of West Tennessee Presbytery, Sept. 16-17, 1811, Apr. 7, 1812. The "Pastoral Letter" covers pp. 23-52 of the manuscript record.

[35] Along with Ewing's "Reply" is a "Pastoral Letter" to the churches served by the Cumberland ministers.

[36] Minutes of West Tennessee Presbytery, Sept. 22, 1812.

[37] "Minutes of the Cumberland Presbytery, 1810-1813," Nov. 5, 1812.

[38] *Ibid.*, Nov. 6, 1812.

[39] *Ibid.*, Apr. 8, 1813.

[40] The committee included William McGee, Robert Donnell, Thomas Calhoun, and Finis Ewing. "Minutes of the Cumberland Synod, 1813-1817." Reprinted in the *Theological Medium*, X (January 1879), 96-105.

[41] "Minutes of the Cumberland Synod," Oct. 6, 1813.

[42] *Brief History of the Synod of Kentucky*, p. 1.

[43] *Minutes of the General Assembly, 1821-1835*, pp. 145, 148, 155-156.

*Chapter 6*

Old Issues Revisited: An Interpretation

[1] *Minutes of the General Assembly of the Cumberland Presbyterian Church*, 1962, pp. 155, 176-177. The United Presbyterian Church in the U. S. A. was formed in 1958 by the merger of the Presbyterian Church, U. S. A., and the United Presbyterian Church of North America. Prior to this merger the two churches had ranked first and third, respectively, in membership among Presbyterian bodies in the country. The United Presbyterian Church of North America itself had been formed one hundred years earlier by a union of the Associate Reformed Presbyterian Church and the Associate Presbyterian Church, which shared a Scottish heritage. The present-day denomination known as the Associate Reformed Presbyterian Church (General Synod) continues the name of one of these bodies. *Yearbook of American Churches*, 1960 ed. (New York: National Council of the Churches of Christ in the U. S. A., 1959), pp. 89, 92, 95.

[2] Smith, *History of the Christian Church, passim*.

[3] Davidson, *Presbyterian Church in Kentucky*, p. 218.

[4] Cossitt, *Finis Ewing*, pp. 168-170, 331-478.

[5] Crisman, *Origin and Doctrines of the Cumberland Presbyterian Church.*

[6] McDonnold, *C. P. Church.* The most recently published work which treats the origins of the Cumberland Presbyterian Church falls into the trap laid by McDonnold. See Posey, *The Presbyterian Church in the Old Southwest,* Chap. III.

[7] "A Sketch of the History of the Cumberland Presbyterian Church," in Gross Alexander, *et al., A History of the Methodist Church, South, the United Presbyterian Church, the Cumberland Presbyterian Church, and the Presbyterian Church, South, in the United States,* Vol. XI of *The American Church History Series,* ed. Philip Schaff, *et al.* (New York: Christian Literature Co., 1894).

[8] Blake, *Old Log House,* Chap. VI.

[9] *Causes Leading to the Organization of the Cumberland Presbyterian Church* (Nashville: Cumberland Presbyterian Publishing House, 1898), pp. 61-113.

[10] Sara Belle Reeves, "The Origin of the Cumberland Presbyterian Church" (unpublished M.A. thesis, George Peabody College for Teachers, 1929).

[11] Haskell M. Miller, "Institutional Behavior of the Cumberland Presbyterian Church, an American Protestant Religious Denomination" (unpublished Ph.D. dissertation, New York University, 1940).

[12] Milton L. Baughn, "Social Views in Official Publications of the Cumberland Presbyterian Church, 1875-1900" (unpublished Ph.D. dissertation, Vanderbilt University, 1954).

[13] Even one of the most recently published accounts of the Cumberland Presbyterian Church follows James Smith and Franceway R. Cossitt in resolving the problem of the causes leading to the emergence of the Church. See T. H. Campbell, *Studies in Cumberland Presbyterian History,* pp. 86-92.

[14] Davidson, *Presbyterian Church in Kentucky,* p. 218.

[15] Baird, *Collection,* p. 626.

[16] John T. McNeill, *The History and Character of Calvinism* (New York: Oxford University Press, 1954), p. 366.

[17] Smith, Handy, and Loetscher, *American Christianity,* I, 562-563, 566-576.

[18] William Warren Sweet, *Religion in the Development of American Culture, 1765-1840* (New York: Charles Scribner's Sons, 1952), p. 22.

[19] Sweet, *Presbyterians.*

[20] E. T. Thompson, *Presbyterians in the South,* Chap. X.

[21] Elwyn A. Smith, *The Presbyterian Ministry in American Culture: A Study in Changing Concepts, 1700-1900* (Philadelphia: Westminster Press, 1962), pp. 195-196.

[22] For a less critical view see R. E. Thompson, *History of the Presbyterian Church in the United States,* pp. 74-75; Olmstead, *History of Religion in the United States,* pp. 304-306.

[23] Minutes of the Synod of Kentucky, Dec. 9, 1805.

[24] Minutes of Transylvania Presbytery, 1786-1829.

[25] Perry Miller, *The New England Mind: The Seventeenth Century* (New York: Macmillan Co., 1939), Chap. VI; Trinterud, *American Tradition,* p. 128; Smith, *The Presbyterian Ministry,* Chap. V.

[26] Beard, *Brief Biographical Sketches,* p. 32.

[27] Reply to West Tennessee Presbytery.

[28] Beard, *Brief Biographical Sketches,* second series, pp. 8-10.

[29] *Ibid.,* pp. 72-73; *Minutes of the Cumberland Presbytery, 1802-1806,* Oct. 7, 1803.

[30] Minutes of Transylvania Presbytery, Oct. 7-8, 1801.

[31] Sweet, *Presbyterians,* pp. 287-289.

[32] E. T. Thompson, *Presbyterians in the South,* p. 146.

[33] Trinterud, *American Tradition,* p. 307.

[34] Gillett, *History of the Presbyterian Church in the United States,* I, p. 70.

[35] *Ibid.,* pp. 403-404.

[35] Bacon, *History of American Christianity,* p. 332.

[37] *Records of the Presbyterian Church,* p. 476.

[38] *Ibid.,* p. 499.

[39] *Ibid.,* p. 512.

[40] *Ibid.,* p. 309.

[41] The Old Side Synod of Philadelphia and the New Side Synod of New York agreed to a "Plan of Union" and formed

the Synod of New York and Philadelphia.

[42] *Records of the Presbyterian Church,* pp. 289-290.

[43] Sprague, *Annals,* III, 361-362.

[44] *Ibid.,* III, 540.

[45] *Ibid.,* III, 554-555.

[46] *Ibid.,* III, 582.

[47] *Minutes of the General Assembly, 1789-1820,* pp. 299-301.

[48] See the *Circular Letter,* pp. 8-9.

[49] Posey, *Presbyterian Church in the Old Southwest,* p. 45.

[50] Davidson, *Presbyterian Church in Kentucky,* p. 229.

[51] *Ibid.,* p. 255.

[52] Minutes of the Synod of Kentucky, Dec. 9, 1805.

[53] Minutes of Transylvania Presbytery, Dec. 10, 1805.

[54] Davidson, *Presbyterian Church in Kentucky,* p. 242.

[55] *Minutes of the General Assembly, 1789-1820,* pp. 389-393.

[56] The "Letter" is reprinted in Ewing's Reply to West Tennessee Presbytery, Letter II.

[57] Letter of James Wilson to William Hodge, Philadelphia, 1808, reprinted in Smith, *History of the Christian Church,* p. 628.

[58] *Minutes of the General Assembly, 1789-1820,* p. 406.

[59] Minutes of Transylvania Presbytery, Mar. 25, 1809.

[60] *Ibid.,* Dec. 7, 1809.

[61] Minutes of West Tennessee Presbytery, Mar. 11, 1811; *Minutes of the General Assembly, 1789-1820,* p. 473.

[62] *Minutes of the General Assembly, 1789-1820,* p. 551.

[63] *Brief History of the Synod of Kentucky,* p. 17.

[64] Trinterud, "New England Contribution to Colonial American Presbyterianism," 35-38.

[65] Alexander, *Log College,* pp. 164-200; S. Miller, *John Rodgers,* pp. 17-22; Gillett, *Presbyterian Church in the United States of America,* I, 350-354; Foote, *Sketches of North Carolina,* p. 232.

[66] Alexander, *Log College,* p. 202.

[67] Foote, *Sketches of North Carolina,* pp. 232-233; David Caldwell married Rachel, the sister of Thomas Craighead. James G. Craighead, *The Craighead Family: A Genealogical Memoir of the Descendents of Rev. Thomas and Margaret Craighead, 1658-1876* (Philadelphia: Sherman & Co., 1876), p. 78.

[68] Turner, *Hawfields Presbyterian Church,* pp. 99-100; Beard, *Brief Biographical Sketches,* pp. 7-45; Beard, *Brief Biographical Sketches,* second series, pp. 7-27.

[69] Smith, *History of the Christian Church,* p. 594; T. C. Anderson, *Life of Rev. George Donnell: First Pastor of the Church in Lebanon; with a Sketch of the Scotch-Irish Race* (Nashville: privately printed, 1858), pp. 104-105; McDonnold, C. P. Church, p. 39; Campbell, *Studies in Cumberland Presbyterian History,* pp. 66-67.

[70] Alexander Craighead withdrew from the Synod of Philadelphia with the New Brunswick Presbytery (New Side) in 1741. He was one of the first members of Hanover Presbytery (New Side) in Virginia at its organization in 1755. From Virginia he moved to North Carolina and became pastor of the Sugar Creek Church in Orange Presbytery. After his death, his son Thomas served the Sugar Creek Church for about a year before he moved to Tennessee to become head of Davidson Academy. Foote, *Sketches of North Carolina,* pp. 184-193.

[71] John Brevard Alexander, *Biographical Sketches of the Hopewell Section and Reminiscences of the Pioneers* (Charlotte, N. C.: Observer Printing and Publishing House, 1897), p. 26.

[72] Minutes of the Synod of Kentucky, Dec. 9-10, 1805.

[73] Samuel J. Baird, *A History of the New School* (Philadelphia: Claxton, Remsen & Haffelfinger, 1868), pp. 133-136.

[74] Charles C. Ware, *Barton Warren Stone, Pathfinder of Christian Union: A Story of His Life and Times* (St. Louis: Bethany Press, 1932), p. 83.

[75] John P. Campbell, *The Pelagian Detected, or a Review of Mr. Craighead's Letters Addressed to the Public and the Author* (Lexington, Ky., 1811), pp. 21, 66, quoted in E. T. Thompson, *Presbyterians in the South,* p. 357.

[76] Minutes of Transylvania Presbytery, Oct. 5, 1810.

[77] *Ibid.*, Oct. 17, 1786, Oct. 11, 1794, Feb. 11, 1795.

[78] *Ibid.*, Mar. 8, 1797. A division was made in 1799, but Craighead and Rice were again placed in the same presbytery. Craighead would not be separated from Rice until 1803 when Cumberland Presbytery would be organized with Craighead as the senior member.

[79] Cossitt, *Finis Ewing*, pp. 23-30.

[80] Rice was followed at Peaks of Otter by James Mitchell. Gillett, *Presbyterian Church in the United States of America,* I, 342.

[81] Records of Davidson County Court, Sept. 4, 1797, Samuel Barton v. Robertson, Clarke, in Answer to the Suit of John Buchanon v. Samuel Barton and James Shaw, cited in C. R. Little, "The Coming of Presbyterianism to Tennessee." An Address Delivered at the One Hundred and Twenty-fifth Anniversary of the First Presbyterian Church, November 14, 1939. Typed Manuscript, Microfilm R-46, Joint University Libraries, Nashville, Tenn.

[82] Ewing's wife was one of the heirs of General Davidson, who in 1788 received 5,750 acres of land in the present Davidson County, Tennessee, from the state of North Carolina. Chalmers G. Davidson, *Piedmont Partisan: The Life and Times of Brigadier General William Lee Davidson* (Davidson, N. C.: Davidson College, 1951), p. 133.

[83] Ephraim McLean was the nephew of Ephraim McLean, Sr., and cousin by marriage to Andrew Ewing. Finis Ewing was a first cousin to Andrew Ewing and a nephew by marriage to Ephraim McLean, Sr.

[84] Bass, "Rev. Thomas Craighead," 88-96.

[85] *Ibid.*, 95; Cossitt, *Finis Ewing*, p. 279; Presley K. Ewing and Mary E. Ewing, *The Ewing Genealogy with Cognate Branches: A Summary of the Ewings and their Kin in America* (Houston: Hercules Book Co., 1919), pp. 58-59.

[86] Cossitt, *Finis Ewing*, p. 39.

[87] There was never any opposition to Anderson. He died in 1803 and therefore was not involved in the conflict that erupted within Cumberland Presbytery. King's sister married McGee, who was pastor of the Shiloh Church until opposition in his church to his emphasis on the necessity of a conversion "experience" for church membership forced him to leave in 1800. He was followed by William Hodge, who caused a division within the Shiloh Church on the same issue. One faction followed Hodge; the other faction called Craighead to be their pastor.

[88] Ephraim McLean did not complete the examinations. He gave a discourse as part of his trial for licensure, but when they were examined on divinity, the records simply state that "Pby. proceeded to judge of the examinations of . . . Anderson, Ewing, & King which were sustained as the last pieces of trial for licensure." Minutes of Transylvania Presbytery, Oct. 7-8, 1802.

[89] *Minutes of the Cumberland Presbytery, 1802-1806,* Apr. 5, 1803, Oct. 6-7, 1803, Apr. 3, 1804, Oct. 2, 1804.

[90] Minutes of the Synod of Kentucky, Oct. 16-22, 1804.

[91] *Minutes of the Cumberland Presbytery, 1802-1806,* Apr. 2, 1805. Cameron voted against the presbytery when the presbytery's case was carried to the General Assembly in 1809.

[92] *Ibid.*, Oct. 1-2, 1805.

[93] Minutes of the Synod of Kentucky, Oct. 17-19, 1805, Dec. 3, 1805.

[94] Minutes of Transylvania Presbytery, Apr. 5, 1810, Oct. 5, 1810; Minutes of the Synod of Kentucky, Oct. 12-13, 1810. Craighead was reinstated in 1824. Baird, *Collection,* pp. 638-644.

## Chapter 7

### Vast Fields To Cultivate

[1] The latter title appears in the minutes of the 1828 meeting without explanation. Prior to that time the Synod had been consistently called "Cumberland Synod."

[2] Minutes of Cumberland Synod, MS., p. 49.

[3] Ibid., pp. 51-53.

[4] McDonnold, C. P. Church, pp. 101-105.

[5] Minutes of Cumberland Synod, p. 53.

[6] McDonnold, C. P. Church, p. 111.

[7] Cossitt, Finis Ewing, pp. 200-201.

[8] Minutes of Cumberland Presbytery, MS., p. 36.

[9] McDonnold, C. P. Church, p. 164.

[10] Minute Book of Logan Presbytery, p. 26.

[11] W. J. Darby and J. E. Jenkins, comps. Cumberland Presbyterianism in Southern Indiana (Indianapolis: published by the presbytery, 1876), p. 52.

[12] J. B. Logan, History of the Cumberland Presbyterian Church in Illinois (Alton, Ill.: Perrin & Smith, 1878), pp. 13-14.

[13] R. C. Ewing, Historical Memoirs (Nashville: Cumberland Presbyterian Board of Publication, 1874), p. 11.

[14] Logan, Church in Illinois, p. 15.

[15] Ibid., p. 19.

[16] Ibid., pp. 23-24.

[17] Ibid., p. 28.

[18] R. C. Ewing, Historical Memoirs, pp. 11-12.

[19] Ibid., p. 12; Cossitt, Finis Ewing, pp. 261-262.

[20] R. C. Ewing, Historical Memoirs, p. 61.

[21] McDonnold, C. P. Church, pp. 143-145.

[22] Ibid., pp. 148-150.

[23] Minutes of Cumberland Synod, p. 60.

[24] Ibid., p. 62.

[25] Ibid., p. 65.

[26] Ibid., p. 62.

[27] Ibid., p. 63.

[28] Ibid., pp. 79-81.

[29] Cossitt, Finis Ewing, pp. 269-271.

[30] "Minutes of Cumberland Synod for 1823," typed copy, pp. 2-4.

[31] Minutes of Cumberland Synod, pp. 74-75.

[32] Records of McGee Presbytery, 1820-1878, p. 2.

[33] R. C. Ewing, Historical Memoirs, p. 65.

[34] Finis Ewing, A Series of Lectures on the Most Important Subjects in Divinity (Fayetteville, Tenn.: printed for the Cumberland Presbyterian Synod by E. and J. B. Hill, 1827); Beard, Brief Biographical Sketches, second series, pp. 210-211.

[35] Minutes of Cumberland Synod, pp. 84-85.

[36] Ibid., pp. 85-86.

[37] Logan, Church in Illinois, pp. 29-32.

[38] Carl Sandburg, Abraham Lincoln: The Prairie Years and The War Years, one-volume ed. (New York: Harcourt, Brace & World, 1966), pp. 23-24, 26-27.

[39] "Minutes of Cumberland Synod for 1823," p. 4.

[40] Minutes of Cumberland Synod, p. 90.

[41] Records of McGee Presbytery, 1820-1878, p. 13.

[42] "Auto-biographical Sketch of Rev. R. Burrow, Written Just Before His Death," Medium Theology (Nashville: Cumberland Presbyterian Publishing House, 1881), pp. 9-18.

[43] "Minutes of Cumberland Synod for 1823," p. 4.

[44] "Minutes of Arkansas Presbytery, 1823-1876," pp. 2-5.

[45] Minutes of Cumberland Synod, p. 104.

[46] James H. B. Hall, The History of the Cumberland Presbyterian Church in Alabama Prior to 1826 (Montgomery, 1904), pp. 28-29. From Transactions of the Alabama Historical Society, 1899-1903, Vol. IV, Reprint No. 18.

[47] Minutes of Cumberland Synod, p. 97.

[48] Ibid., pp. 97-98.

[49] *Ibid.*, p. 98.
[50] *Ibid.*, p. 103. As far as is known, there was no organized Cumberland Presbyterian work in Ohio at the time.
[51] *Ibid.*, pp. 114-115.
[52] *Ibid.*, p. 115.
[53] *Ibid.*, pp. 129-130.
[54] *Ibid.*, p. 132.
[55] *Ibid.*, p. 134. Cumberland College had been founded by the Synod in 1825. The story of its origin and development is told in a subsequent chapter.

[56] *Ibid.*, p. 99.
[57] *Ibid.*, p. 107.
[58] Cossitt, *Finis Ewing*, p. 282.
[59] Minutes of Cumberland Synod, p. 113.
[60] *Ibid.*, p. 135.
[61] *Ibid.*, pp. 135-136.
[62] Minutes of the Cumberland Presbyterian General Assembly, Vol. I, 1829-1840, p. 3.
[63] *Ibid.*, p. 9.

# PART II
## Growth and Development of the Cumberland Presbyterian Church, 1830-1900

### Chapter 8
### Answering the Macedonian Cry: Missions and Expansion to 1860

[1] David Lowry, *Life and Labors of Robert Donnell* (Alton, Ill.: S. V. Crossman, Printer, 1867), p. 204.
[2] Quoted in *ibid.*, p. 237.
[3] *Ibid.*
[4] H. M. Miller, "Institutional Behavior," pp. 93-95.
[5] McDonnold, *C. P. Church*, p. 370.
[6] Minutes of the General Assembly, May 27, 1834. Minutes for the years 1830-1835 and 1837-1848 are cited hereafter by date. Minutes for 1836 and 1849 and after are cited by page number.
[7] *Ibid.*, May 25, 1835.
[8] McDonnold, *C. P. Church*, pp. 251-252.
[9] *Ibid.*, p. 133.
[10] Minutes of the General Assembly, May 24, 1841.
[11] *Ibid.*, May 20, 1843.
[12] McDonnold, *C. P. Church*, p. 312.
[13] *Ibid.*, pp. 312-313.
[14] Minutes of the General Assembly, 1861, p. 18.
[15] T. C. Anderson, *Life of Rev. George Donnell, First Pastor of the Church in Lebanon: with a Sketch of the Scotch-Irish Race* (Nashville: privately printed, 1858), p. 219.
[16] Minutes of the General Assembly, 1845-1861, *passim;* McDonnold, *C. P. Church*, pp. 322-324.
[17] McDonnold, *C. P. Church*, pp. 116-117.

[18] H. M. Miller, "Institutional Behavior," p. 169.
[19] Minutes of the General Assembly, May 23, 1835.
[20] *Ibid.*, 1859, pp. 108-110.
[21] McDonnold, *C. P. Church*, pp. 143-147; Anderson, *Life of George Donnell*, pp. 157-209; Hiram Arnett Douglas, comp., "The Story Is Told: Rev. Hiram Douglas, D.D., a Biographical Sketch" (Minneapolis: mimeographed MS., 1940), p. 22.
[22] McDonnold, *C. P. Church*, pp. 148-150.
[23] *Ibid.*, pp. 155-163.
[24] *Ibid.*, pp. 253-261; Minutes of the General Assembly, 1830-1860, *passim.*
[25] McDonnold, *C. P. Church*, pp. 261-262; Minutes of the General Assembly, 1849, p. 26.
[26] Material on expansion in Kentucky, Illinois, and Indiana is from Sandburg, *Abraham Lincoln*, pp. 23-27; Beard, *Brief Biographical Sketches*, second series, pp. 210-211; Roy L. Smith, "The Influence of Cumberland Presbyterianism on Abraham Lincoln," *Cumberland Presbyterian*, July 1, 1952 (reprinted from *Christian Herald*, February 1952. Original title, "Lincoln's Alma Mater"); McDonnold, *C. P. Church*, pp. 150-154, 164-174; Darby and Jenkins, *Cumberland*

*Presbyterianism in Southern Indiana,* pp. 18-23; Logan, *Church in Illinois,* pp. 32-83, 207-209.

[27] R. C. Ewing, *Historical Memoirs,* pp. 11-13, 51-52; Cossitt, *Finis Ewing,* p. 293; Eva Wollard Hughs, "History of the Cumberland Presbyterian Church: North, Central, Southeast Missouri, Book I" (mimeographed MS., n.d.), pp. 20-22, 55; McDonnold, *C. P. Church,* pp. 175-188.

[28] Parks McCullah, "History of the Cumberland Presbyterian Church in Arkansas, White County, and Searcy" (mimeographed MS., 1964), p. 1; McDonnold, *C. P. Church,* pp. 188-200.

[29] McDonnold, *C. P. Church,* p. 357; *Banner of Peace,* Feb. 19, 1847, Mar. 26, 1847.

[30] McDonnold, *C. P. Church,* pp. 273-274.

[31] John Morgan, "History of the Cumberland Presbyterian Church in Western Pennsylvania and Ohio, No. 2," *Christian Messenger,* I (April 1873), 122-125 (reprinted from *Union Evangelist*); Milton Bird, *The Life of Rev. Alexander Chapman* (Nashville: published for the author by W. E. Dunaway, Agent, Cumberland Presbyterian Board of Publication, 1872), pp. 91-93; McDonnold, *C. P. Church,* pp. 276-277, 285-286.

[32] Bird, *Life of Chapman,* pp. 94, 126-128; Morgan, "History of the Cumberland Presbyterian Church in Western Pennsylvania and Ohio," (March 1873), 90; Lowry, *Life of Robert Donnell,* pp. 58-60; McDonnold, *C. P. Church,* pp. 276-282; Beard, *Brief Biographical Sketches,* second series, p. 259.

[33] Lowry, *Life of Robert Donnell,* pp. 61-62; McDonnold, *C. P. Church,* pp. 284-290; Morgan, "History of the Cumberland Presbyterian Church in Western Pennsylvania and Ohio" (March 1873), 90-91.

[34] E. B. Crisman, *Biographical Sketches of Living Old Men, of the Cumberland Presbyterian Church* (St. Louis: Perrin & Smith, 1877), I, pp. 24-28; McDonnold, *C. P. Church,* pp. 292-300; Minutes of the General Assembly, 1858, p. 38.

[35] William Ransom Hogan, *The Texas Republic: A Social and Economic History* (Norman: University of Oklahoma Press, 1946), pp. 191-192.

[36] Walter Brownlow Posey, *The Baptist Church in the Lower Mississippi Valley, 1776-1784* (Lexington: University of Kentucky Press), p. 148; Emory Stevens Bucke, ed., *The History of American Methodism* (New York: Abingdon Press, 1964), II, p. 424.

[37] McDonnold, *C. P. Church,* pp. 263-264.

[38] The material on the Church in Texas is from R. Douglas Brackenridge, *Voice in the Wilderness* (San Antonio: Trinity University Press, 1968), pp. 13-70; Thomas H. Campbell, *History of the Cumberland Presbyterian Church in Texas* (Nashville: Cumberland Presbyterian Publishing House, 1936), pp. 11-40; Hogan, *Texas Republic,* pp. 195-200; McDonnold, *C. P. Church,* pp. 263-269; Beard, *Brief Biographical Sketches,* second series, p. 376; J. J. A. Roach, "Cumberland Presbyterianism in Texas," *Cumberland Presbyterian Quarterly Review,* III (July 1882), 280; Minutes of the General Assembly, 1841-1854, *passim.*

[39] Charles M. Kennedy, "The Presbyterian Church on the Wisconsin Frontier," *Journal of the Department of History (The Presbyterian Historical Society) of the Presbyterian Church in the U. S. A.,* XVIII (March 1939), 187-194, note p. 209.

[40] Editorial, "Demand for the Home Missionary in Iowa," *Theological Medium,* II (October 1847), 569-570; McDonnold, *C. P. Church,* pp. 336-340; Minutes of the General Assembly, 1857, pp. 12-13; 1858, p. 58; 1859, p. 64.

[41] McDonnold, *C. P. Church,* pp. 359-361; Minutes of the General Assembly, 1858, p. 58; 1859, p. 64.

[42] Letter of Cornwall, Apr. 6, 1846, *Banner of Peace,* May 8, 1846; letter of Cornwall, June 27, 1846, *Banner of Peace,* Aug. 7, 1846; "Minutes of the Arkansas Presbytery of the Cumberland Presbyterian Church, 1824-1827," *Journal of the Presbyterian Historical Society,* XXXI (September 1953), 192; D. E. Bushnell, "Our Work at the Front," *Cumberland Presbyterian Quarterly,* I (July 1880), 344.

[43] Quoted in Clifford M. Drury, "Beginnings of the Synod of Oregon," *Journal of the Presbyterian Historical Society*, XXXVII (December 1959), 214-215.

[44] *Ibid.*, 214; Letter of Neill Johnson, *Banner of Peace*, Apr. 6, 1850; letter of Johnson, Oct. 10, 1851, *Banner of Peace*, Dec. 19, 1851; "Constitution of Oregon Presbytery—Extracts from the Minutes," *Banner of Peace*, Jan. 30, 1852; Minutes of the General Assembly, 1851, pp. 41-49.

[45] Letter of Ish, Mar. 25, 1850, *Banner of Peace*, May 31, 1850, reprinted from the *Cumberland Presbyterian;* McDonnold, *C. P. Church*, pp. 349-351; Bushnell, "Work at the Front," 346.

[46] Letter of Wesley Gallimore, Apr. 12, 1851, *Banner of Peace*, June 6, 1851; letter of John E. Braly, July 29, 1851, *Banner of Peace*, Sept. 19, 1851; Minutes of the General Assembly, 1851, pp. 49-54.

[47] John E. Braly to General Assembly, Apr. 11, 1851, *Banner of Peace*, July 13, 1851; Bushnell, "Work at the Front," 351; Minutes of the General Assembly, 1852, p. 25; 1860, p. 25.

[48] William Warren Sweet, *The Congregationalists*. Vol. III of *Religion on the American Frontier* (Chicago: University of Chicago Press, 1939), p. 52.

[49] Minutes of Cumberland Synod, MS., p. 71.

[50] Sweet, *Religion in the Development of American Culture*, p. 242.

[51] McDonnold, *C. P. Church*, pp. 128-141, and an autobiographical sketch by Robert Bell in *Banner of Peace*, Feb. 4, 1848.

[52] McDonnold, *C. P. Church*, pp. 328-332; Minutes of the General Assembly, 1858, p. 59; 1859, p. 66; 1860, p. 40.

[53] Kennedy, "Church on the Wisconsin Frontier," 189-192; Lindsley, "Sources and Sketches, No. IV," 10; McDonnold, *C. P. Church*, pp. 324-328; *Banner of Peace*, June 4, 1846, Aug. 4, 1846, Sept. 4, 1846, Sept. 15, 1848, Sept. 22, 1848, Sept. 29, 1848, Nov. 3, 1848, May 18, 1849, May 25, 1849; editorial, "Winnebago Indians—a Thought for Our Missionary Board," *Theological Medium*, II (July 1847), 495.

[54] McDonnold, *C. P. Church*, p. 333; *Banner of Peace*, Nov. 7, 1851; Minutes of the General Assembly, 1891, pp. 53-54.

[55] McDonnold, *C. P. Church*, pp. 443-447; Minutes of the General Assembly, 1863, pp. 95-96; 1866, pp. 55-59.

## Chapter 9

## Weathering the Storm over Slavery and Sectionalism

[1] For a rather detailed treatment of how the Presbyterian churches reacted to secession and war, see Lewis G. Vander Velde, *The Presbyterian Churches and the Federal Union, 1861-1869* (Cambridge, Mass.: Harvard University Press, 1932).

[2] Quoted in Lowry, *Life of Robert Donnell*, p. 47.

[3] *Ibid.*, pp. 209-210.

[4] Quoted in *ibid.*, p. 73.

[5] Cossitt, *Finis Ewing*, pp. 272-274. Italics Cossitt's.

[6] Beard, *Brief Biographical Sketches*, p. 66; McDonnold, *C. P. Church*, p. 411.

[7] Lindsley, "Sources and Sketches, No. IV," 10.

[8] McDonnold, *C. P. Church*, pp. 410-413, 432-434; T. H. Campbell, *Church in Texas*, p. 32; Logan, *Church in Illinois*, pp. 212-215; R. C. Ewing, *Historical Memoirs*, pp. 18-19; H. M. Miller, "Institutional Behavior," pp. 209-224; Vander Velde, *Presbyterian Churches*, p. 104, note 64; Brackenridge, *Voice in the Wilderness*, pp. 76-78.

[9] Minutes of the General Assembly, May 27, 1833.

[10] Brackenridge, *Voice in the Wilderness*, pp. 73-76.

[11] To Richard Beard, Nov. 25, 1844, quoted in Lowry, *Life of Donnell*, p. 147.

[12] Lindsley, "Sources and Sketches, No. IV," 11.

[13] Minutes of the General Assembly, May 20, 1848.

[14] *Ibid.*, 1850, p. 13.

[15] *Ibid.*, 1851, pp. 56-57.

[16] *Ibid.*, 1858, p. 76.

[17] Editorial, "Disease of the Times," *Cumberland Presbyterian Quarterly,* n. s. V (January 1861), 253-254. .

[18] McDonnold, *C. P. Church,* pp. 293-295.

[19] *Ibid.*, p. 295.

[20] Minutes of the General Assembly, 1861, pp. 21-22.

[21] *Ibid.*, 1862, pp. 45-47.

[22] Beard, *Brief Biographical Sketches,* second series, p. 343.

[23] James L. Riley, *Life Sketches of the Rev. James L. Riley, Beloved Cumberland Presbyterian Minister, Late of Cynthiana, Indiana, 1824-1911* (Carmi, Ill.: White County Tribune, 1911), pp. 25-27.

[24] *Ibid.*, pp. 27-28.

[25] Minutes of the General Assembly, 1863, pp. 88-90.

[26] Riley, *Life Sketches,* p. 28.

[27] Beard, *Brief Biographical Sketches,* second series, p. 343.

[28] Minutes of the General Assembly, 1864, p. 142.

[29] *Ibid.*, pp. 142-143.

[30] *Ibid.*, pp. 127-129.

[31] *Ibid.*, 1865, pp. 191-192.

[32] *Ibid.*, p. 171.

[33] McDonnold, *C. P. Church,* pp. 383-384, 404-405.

[34] *Ibid.*, p. 383; Brackenridge, *Voice in the Wilderness,* pp. 85-86.

[35] Minutes of the General Assembly, 1861-1865, Introduction, p. 2.

[36] Quoted in Eva Wollard Hughs, "History of the Cumberland Presbyterian Church within Southwest Missouri: Book II" (mimeographed MS., n. d.), p. 72.

[37] Beard, *Brief Biographical Sketches,* second series, p. 352.

[38] *Ibid.*

[39] Minutes of the General Assembly, 1866, pp. 16-31, 37-38, 45-49.

[40] *Ibid.*, 1867, p. 25.

[41] *Ibid.*, p. 104.

[42] Quoted in General Assembly Minutes, 1868, p. 18. This action led some historians to the erroneous conclusion that Pennsylvania Synod seceded from the Church.

[43] *Ibid.*, pp. 18, 27, 49.

[44] *Ibid.*, pp. 26-27.

[45] *Ibid.*, 1869, p. 33.

[46] *Ibid.*, 1877, pp. 69-70.

[47] *Ibid.*, 1868, p. 29. Italics not in the original. This account of the formation of the new church and relations of the two Cumberland Presbyterian churches is based on McDonnold, *C. P. Church,* pp. 434-439; David Wayne Wiman, "A History of the Colored Cumberland Presbyterian Church" (unpublished B.D. thesis, Cumberland Presbyterian Theological Seminary, 1936), *passim*; and General Assembly Minutes of the period.

[48] Minutes of the General Assembly, 1869, p. 24. Italics not in the original.

[49] *Ibid.*

[50] *Ibid.*, 1871, p. 28.

[51] McDonnold, *C. P. Church,* p. 438.

[52] Minutes of the General Assembly, 1886, p. 185.

[53] *Ibid.*, 1895, p. 347.

## Chapter 10

### Extending the Missionary Frontier, 1861-1900

[1] B. W. McDonnold, who was himself a chaplain in the C. S. A., has an excellent chapter on "Preaching to Soldiers," *C. P. Church,* pp. 420-431.

[2] Quoted in T. H. Campbell, *Church in Texas,* p. 82.

[3] Crisman, *Living Old Men,* I, p. 16; Beard, *Brief Biographical Sketches,* second series, p. 263.

[4] Quoted in T. H. Campbell, *Church in Texas,* p. 83.

[5] Darby and Jenkins, *Cumberland Presbyterianism in Southern Indiana,* p. 35.

[6] Except as otherwise noted, material on domestic missions and expansion in this chapter is from General Assembly Minutes, 1861-1900, especially Board of Missions annual reports. Specific references are given for quotations and statistical data.

[7] Minutes of the General Assembly, 1885, p. 17; 1899, p. 43a.

[8] *Missionary Record,* XVII (October 1891), 112.

[9] McDonnold, *C. P. Church,* p. 129.

[10] Quoted in Logan, *Church in Illinois,* pp. 136-137.

[11] McDonnold, *C. P. Church,* p. 457; Frances C. Maghee, comp., *History and Work of the Woman's Board of Missions of the Cumberland Presbyterian Church* (Evansville, Ind.: published by the Woman's Board of Missions, 1895), pp. 3-14.

[12] Minutes of the General Assembly, 1881, pp. 52-53.

[13] *Ibid.,* p. 53; 1899, pp. 53a-54a.

[14] Maghee, *Woman's Board,* p. 88.

[15] McDonnold, *C. P. Church,* pp. 618-619.

[16] Minutes of the General Assembly, 1870, pp. 63-65.

[17] McDonnold, *C. P. Church,* p. 436.

[18] Minutes of the General Assembly, 1876, p. 110; 1888, p. 195; 1895, p. 343; 1896, p. 283.

[19] *Ibid.,* 1898, pp. 270-271.

[20] *Ibid.,* 1899, p. 160a.

[21] *Ibid.,* 1887, p. 44.

[22] *Ibid.,* 1898, p. 116.

[23] *Ibid.,* 1871, p. 46.

[24] *Ibid.,* 1881, pp. 83-84.

[25] *Ibid.,* 1879, p. 18; McDonnold, *C. P. Church,* p. 477.

[26] Minutes of the General Assembly, 1897, p. 101; 1898, p. 88; 1899, pp. 9-10.

[27] *Ibid.,* 1886, p. 35; 1887, p. 84; 1894, p. 87; 1895, p. 78; Maghee, *Woman's Board,* pp. 35-36.

[28] McDonnold, *C. P. Church,* pp. 480-482.

[29] Except as otherwise noted, the information on the Japan and Mexico missions is from *ibid.,* pp. 480-504, and General Assembly Minutes. Specific references are given for quotations and statistical data.

[30] Mrs. J. H. Morton, *Hands at Rest, A Sequel to "Filled Hands": The Complete Story of Mrs. A. M. Drennan's Life and Work in Japan* (Nashville: Cumberland Presbyterian Publishing House, 1904), pp. 29-30.

[31] Minutes of the General Assembly, 1895, p. 83.

[32] *Ibid.,* 1889, p. 60.

[33] *Ibid.,* 1894, pp. 65-66.

[34] *Ibid.,* 1898, pp. 124-125.

[35] *Ibid.,* 1890, pp. 49-50.

[36] *Ibid.,* 1887, p. 43; 1888, pp. 50-51; McDonnold, *C. P. Church,* pp. 504-506.

[37] *Missionary Record,* XV (August 1889), 47.

[38] Maghee, *Woman's Board,* pp. 67-80; *Missionary Record,* XXII (November 1896), 134.

[39] Minutes of the General Assembly, 1897, p. 101.

## Chapter 11

## Preachers of the Gospel

[1] Joel Knight, "Success of Our Fathers," *Cumberland Presbyterian,* Feb. 11, 1875.

[2] Quoted in McDonnold, *C. P. Church,* p. 275. Italics not in the original.

[3] J. W. W., "What One of the Fathers Told Me," *Banner of Peace,* June 7, 1850.

[4] Nov. 23, 1852, to editor, *Banner of Peace,* Dec. 24, 1852.

[5] Knight, "Success of Our Fathers."

[6] F. G. Black, "Sermon at the Opening of Miami Presbytery, March 1850," *Theological Medium,* V (May 1850), 219.

[7] "Minutes of Arkansas Presbytery, 1823-1876," p. 187.

[8] Logan, *Church in Illinois,* p. 38.

[9] McDonnold, *C. P. Church,* p. 161.

[10] R. C. Ewing, *Historical Memoirs,* p. 47.

[11] Anderson, *Life of George Donnell,* p. 286.

[12] T. H. Campbell, *Church in Texas,* pp. 147-148.

[13] McDonnold, *C. P. Church,* pp. 57-58.

[14] Quoted in John Vant Stephens, *The Cumberland Presbyterian Digest (1899)* (Nashville: Cumberland Presbyterian Publishing House, 1899), p. 23.

Italics in Stephens.

[15] Lowry, *Life of Robert Donnell*, p. 205.

[16] Letter of B. H. Pierson to Mrs. Silas Newton Davis, in Beard, *Brief Biographical Sketches*, pp. 322-324, 333-335.

[17] McDonnold, *C. P. Church*, pp. 178-179; R. C. Ewing, *Historical Memoirs*, pp. 36-37, 67.

[18] Logan, *Church in Illinois*, p. 122.

[19] T. H. Campbell, *Church in Texas*, p. 96.

[20] April 10, 1833. Quoted in Lindsley, "Sources and Sketches, No. IV," 9.

[21] Minutes of the General Assembly, May 23, 1835.

[22] October 23, 1846.

[23] *Ibid.*

[24] *Banner of Peace*, Dec. 10, 1847.

[25] "On the Importance of a Well Trained Ministry," *Theological Medium*, IV (March 1849), 149.

[26] F. G. Black, "Sermon," 227.

[27] A. Templeton, "Connection between Learning and Religion," *Theological Medium and Quarterly Review*, n. s. II (January 1855), 113-121.

[28] "The Minister as Workman," *Theological Medium and Cumberland Presbyterian Quarterly*, n. s. III (September 1858), 30.

[29] Minutes of the General Assembly, 1865, p. 186.

[30] Quoted in Stephens, *C. P. Digest*, p. 130.

[31] W. S. Danley, "Ministerial Education," *Cumberland Presbyterian Review*, II (July 1890), 258.

[32] Minutes of the General Assembly, 1892, p. 37.

[33] *Ibid.*, 1896, pp. 21, 31-32; 1897, p. 36; 1898, p. 92; 1899, p. 42.

[34] Henry Bascom Evans, "History of the Organization and Administration of Cumberland Presbyterian Colleges" (unpublished Ph.D. dissertation, George Peabody College for Teachers, 1943), p. 17.

[35] Quoted in Darby and Jenkins, *Cumberland Presbyterianism in Southern Indiana*, p. 24.

[36] Minutes of the General Assembly, May 25, 1835; Richard Beard, "The Cumberland Presbyterian Church during the Last Half Century," *Theological Medium*

and *Cumberland Presbyterian Quarterly*, n. s. I (October 1870), 494-495.

[37] McDonnold, *C. P. Church*, p. 240; S. G. Burney, "Rev. John Miller and Some of His Books," *Cumberland Presbyterian Review*, II (October 1890), 415.

[38] John Vant Stephens, *The Story of the Founding of the Theological School in the Cumberland Presbyterian Church* (Cincinnati: privately printed, 1933), p. 9; Evans, "History of Cumberland Presbyterian Colleges," p. 191.

[39] Stephens, *Founding of Theological School*, p. 13.

[40] *Ibid.*, pp. 17-18; Minutes of the General Assembly, 1849, pp. 11, 14-15, 18, 20-21, 30-33; Evans, "History of Cumberland Presbyterian Colleges," pp. 184-186.

[41] Minutes of the General Assembly, 1850, pp. 12-13, 17, 41-43; Stephens, *Founding of Theological School*, pp. 18-20; Evans, "History of Cumberland Presbyterian Colleges," p. 186.

[42] McDonnold, *C. P. Church*, pp. 363-364; Stephens, *Founding of Theological School*, pp. 21-23.

[43] McDonnold, *C. P. Church*, p. 364.

[44] Minutes of the General Assembly, 1853, p. 39; 1854, pp. 64-65; Evans, "History of Cumberland Presbyterian Colleges," p. 191.

[45] Minutes of the General Assembly, 1860, pp. 90-92; Evans, "History of Cumberland Presbyterian Colleges," pp. 192-193; McDonnold, *C. P. Church*, p. 514.

[46] Minutes of the General Assembly, 1860, p. 67.

[47] McDonnold, *C. P. Church*, p. 511.

[48] *Ibid.*, pp. 515-524; Minutes of the General Assembly, 1870, p. 58; 1898, p. 102; 1899, p. 17a.

[49] Minutes of the General Assembly, 1878, p. 24; Bushnell, "Work at the Front," 350.

[50] Minutes of the General Assembly, 1892, pp. 32, 48, 53; 1893, pp. 121-122; 1895, p. 41.

[51] *Ibid.*, 1874, p. 68; McDonnold, *C. P. Church*, pp. 518-519.

[52] Minutes of the General Assembly, 1881, pp. 32-33; 1888, pp. 140-148; 1895, pp. 28-29; 1896, pp. 104-105.

[53] *Ibid.*, 1895, p. 118.

[54] H. M. Miller, "Institutional Be-

havior," p. 100; McDonnold, *C. P. Church*, p. 184.

[55] McDonnold, *C. P. Church*, p. 250.

[56] R. C. Ewing, *Historical Memoirs*, pp. 118-119.

[57] Quoted in Logan, *Church in Illinois*, p. 216.

[58] Beard, *Brief Biographical Sketches*, second series, p. 369.

[59] Logan, *Church in Illinois*, pp. 48-49.

[60] McDonnold, *C. P. Church*, pp. 182, 250.

[61] *Ibid.*, p. 242.

[62] *Ibid.*, pp. 243, 246; Minutes of the General Assembly, May 21, 1830.

[63] McDonnold, *C. P. Church*, p. 246.

[64] "On Supporting the Gospel," *Cumberland Magazine*, no. 1 (August, September, October 1836), pp. 7-14.

[65] Minutes of the General Assembly, 1836, p. 9.

[66] *Ibid.*, May 23, 1848.

[67] "Minutes of St. Louis Presbytery, September 6, 1877," *Cumberland Presbyterian*, Oct. 4, 1877.

[68] Minutes of the General Assembly, 1882, p. 17.

[69] McDonnold, *C. P. Church*, pp. 286-287, 290-291.

[70] Darby and Jenkins, *Cumberland Presbyterianism in Southern Indiana*, pp. 28, 31.

[71] Logan, *Church in Illinois*, pp. 65-66, 109, 167-170.

[72] "Extracts from Minutes of Oxford (Miss.) Presbytery, April, 1850," *Banner of Peace*, May 3, 1850.

[73] McDonnold, *C. P. Church*, pp. 250-251. The discrepancy in totals as in McDonnold.

[74] Beard, *Brief Biographical Sketches*, second series, p. 288.

[75] "Rev. Hiram A. Hunter," *Cumberland Presbyterian*, Nov. 29, 1883.

[76] Minutes of the General Assembly, May 25, 1833.

[77] McDonnold, *C. P. Church*, p. 460; various General Assembly Minutes.

[78] Minutes of the General Assembly, 1891, pp. 97, 100-102.

## Chapter 12

## The Handmaid of Religion

[1] Sweet, *Religion in the Development of American Culture*, p. 160.

[2] *Ibid.*, pp. 160-178; Donald G. Tewksbury, *The Founding of American Colleges and Universities before the Civil War* (Hamden, Conn.: Archon Books, 1965), *passim;* Walter Brownlow Posey, *Frontier Mission: A History of Religion West of the Southern Appalachians to 1861* (Lexington: University of Kentucky Press, 1966), pp. 257-293.

[3] Tewksbury, *American Colleges*, p. 90.

[4] Minutes of the General Assembly, 1851, pp. 37-38. Italics in Minutes.

[5] *Ibid.*, 1855, p. 55.

[6] *Ibid.*, 1859, pp. 102-103.

[7] "Substance of a Discourse on National Affairs," *Theological Medium*, VI (December 1850), 52-53.

[8] Minutes of the General Assembly, 1849, pp. 46-48. This report of the Com-

mittee on Education probably was written by its chairman, Milton Bird.

[9] "Education," *Theological Medium and Cumberland Presbyterian Quarterly*, IV (January 1860), 136-138.

[10] Minutes of the General Assembly, 1855, pp. 36-37. Italics in Minutes.

[11] The material on Cumberland College is from McDonnold, *C. P. Church*, pp. 214-228, and Evans, "History of Cumberland Presbyterian Colleges," pp. 70-139, except as otherwise indicated.

[12] *Brief Biographical Sketches*, p. 38.

[13] Beard, *Brief Biographical Sketches*, second series, pp. 254-257.

[14] Beard, "Church during the Last Half Century," 493.

[15] Minutes of the General Assembly, May 23, 1842.

[16] *Ibid.*, May 23, 1843.

[17] Beard, *Brief Biographical Sketches*, second series, pp. 248-249.

[18] Beard, *Brief Biographical Sketches*, p. 188.

[19] *C. P. Church*, p. 226.

[20] The material on Cumberland University is from McDonnold, *C. P. Church*, pp. 509-526; Evans, "History of Cumberland Presbyterian Colleges," pp. 140-206; and Winstead Paine Bone, *A History of Cumberland University, 1842-1935* (Lebanon, Tenn.: published for the author, 1935), *passim*, except as otherwise indicated.

[21] Anderson, *Life of George Donnell*, p. 305.

[22] *Ibid.*, p. 307.

[23] T. C. Anderson, "History of Cumberland University," *Theological Medium and Cumberland Presbyterian Quarterly*, III (December 1858), 192.

[24] Quoted in Evans, "History of Cumberland Presbyterian Colleges," p. 173.

[25] Minutes of the General Assembly, 1858, p. 73.

[26] McDonnold, *C. P. Church*, p. 515.

[27] Evans, "History of Cumberland Presbyterian Colleges," p. 107.

[28] This general information on Cumberland Presbyterian schools and colleges and on Waynesburg College is mostly from Evans, *passim*; McDonnold, *C. P. Church*, *passim*, but especially pp. 527-576; and various reports in General Assembly Minutes. Various other sources provided supplemental information.

[29] Minutes of the General Assembly, 1859, p. 103.

[30] "Historical Sketch of Waynesburg College, Waynesburg, Pennsylvania," number XII in J. Berrien Lindsley, "Sources and Sketches," *Theological Medium and Cumberland Presbyterian Quarterly*, n. s. IX (January 1878), 110-111. Italics Miller's.

[31] Evans, "History of Cumberland Presbyterian Colleges," pp. 212-227.

[32] Information on Lincoln University is from McDonnold, *C. P. Church*, pp. 541-551; Logan, *Church in Illinois*, pp. 127-131; Evans, "History of Cumberland Presbyterian Colleges," pp. 240-245; and various reports in General Assembly Minutes.

[33] Minutes of the General Assembly, 1898, p. 104.

[34] Material on Trinity University is from T. H. Campbell, *Church in Texas*, pp. 97-109; Evans, "History of Cumberland Presbyterian Colleges," pp. 245-256; Donald E. Everett, *Trinity University: A Record of 100 Years* (San Antonio: Trinity University Press, 1969), pp. 1-45; McDonnold, *C. P. Church*, pp. 551-554; and various reports in General Assembly Minutes.

[35] Minutes of the General Assembly, 1895, p. 137.

[36] Material on Missouri Valley College is from Evans, "History of Cumberland Presbyterian Colleges," pp. 257-263; Hughs, "History of Church in Missouri, Book I," pp. 146-158; and various reports in General Assembly Minutes.

[37] Sweet, *Religion in American Culture*, pp. 165-166.

## *Chapter 13*

## Problems with Publications

[1] Sweet, *Religion in American Culture*, p. 184.

[2] *Ibid.*, pp. 184-189; Posey, *Frontier Mission*, pp. 293-302.

[3] Henry C. McCook, "The Several Editions of the Constitution of the Cumberland Presbyterian Church," *Journal of the Presbyterian Historical Society*, I (December 1901), pp. 209-210.

[4] The material on publishing activities during the 1830s and early 1840s is from McDonnold, *C. P. Church*, pp. 229-241, and General Assembly Minutes of the period, supplemented by other sources as indicated in other notes.

[5] McDonnold, *C. P. Church*, p. 229. McDonnold, of course, was writing before the controversy over union in the early twentieth century.

[6] *Ibid.*, p. 230.

[7] Minutes of the General Assembly, May 22, 1835; 1836, p. 8.

[8] McDonnold, *C. P. Church*, p. 233.

[9] Anderson, *Life of George Donnell,* p. 288.

[10] *Minutes of the Convention of the Cumberland Presbyterian Church, Held in Nashville, on the 21st, 22nd, 23rd, 24th, and 25th Days of May 1839* (Lebanon, Tenn.: printed at the Chronicle Office, 1839), pp. 11-18.

[11] McDonnold, *C. P. Church,* p. 236.

[12] *Ibid.,* pp. 238-239.

[13] June 24, 1844, to M. H. Bone, in Lowry, *Life of Robert Donnell,* p. 146.

[14] Richard Beard, "Historical Sketch, Briefly Setting Forth the Early History and Progress of the Church," in the Minutes of the General Assembly, 1880, p. 59.

[15] This information on periodicals is drawn from the following sources: Brackenridge, *Voice in the Wilderness,* pp. 61-62; McDonnold, *C. P. Church,* pp. 590-597; Logan, *Church in Illinois,* pp. 116-117; *Banner of Peace,* Mar. 13, 1846, July 13, 1851, Oct. 10, 1851, June 11, 1852, July 1, 1853. Note that Smith's paper, the *Cumberland Presbyterian,* is not given since its history has been given in the text.

[16] Beard, *Brief Biographical Sketches,* second series, p. 128.

[17] Minutes of the General Assembly, 1854, p. 31.

[18] *Ibid.,* May 29, 1845.

[19] The material on publishing activities from 1847 to 1860 is based on McDonnold, *C. P. Church,* pp. 578-582, and numerous actions of and reports to the General Assembly as given in the Minutes.

[20] Minutes of the General Assembly, 1857, p. 24.

[21] The material on publishing activities from 1861 to 1900 is based on material from McDonnold, *C. P. Church,* pp. 582-597; Baughn, "Social Views," pp. 36-44; and numerous reports to and actions of the General Assembly as given in the Minutes.

[22] Minutes of the General Assembly, 1879, p. 71.

[23] R. L. Baskette, *History of Publication of the Cumberland Presbyterian Church* (Nashville: Cumberland Press, 1910), p. 18.

## Chapter 14

## The Church and the "World"

[1] For a treatment of Protestantism's relation to secular questions in the first half of the nineteenth century see John R. Bodo, *The Protestant Clergy and Public Issues, 1812-1848* (Princeton, N. J.: Princeton University Press, 1954).

[2] McDonnold, *C. P. Church,* p. 605.

[3] *Ibid.,* p. 261.

[4] Cossitt, *Finis Ewing,* p. 272.

[5] Beard, *Brief Biographical Sketches,* second series, pp. 367, 373.

[6] Beard, "Church during the Last Half Century," 491-492.

[7] "Minutes of Cumberland Synod," number XVIII in Lindsley, "Sources and Sketches," *Theological Medium and Cumberland Presbyterian Quarterly,* n. s. X (October 1879), 431.

[8] R. C. Ewing, *Historical Memoirs,* p. 16.

[9] Minutes of the General Assembly, 1836, p. 8.

[10] *Ibid.,* 1851, p. 13.

[11] *Ibid.,* 1855, pp. 34-35.

[12] *Ibid.,* 1873, p. 19.

[13] *Ibid.,* 1877, p. 34. Much of the material in this chapter on the period 1875-1900 has been drawn liberally from the author's "Social Views Reflected in Official Publications of the Cumberland Presbyterian Church."

[14] *Cumberland Presbyterian,* June 6, 1878.

[15] Minutes of the General Assembly, 1887, p. 31.

[16] *Ibid.,* 1889, pp. 36, 55.

[17] *Ibid.,* 1855, pp. 31-32.

[18] *Cumberland Presbyterian,* June 3, June 10, 1880.

[19] *Ibid.,* May 23, 1883.

[20] *Ibid.,* May 23, 1889.

[21] "My Five Reasons," *ibid.,* Aug. 20, 1891.

[22] Minutes of the General Assembly, 1852, p. 30.

[23] *Ibid.,* 1870, p. 31.

[24] W. H. Darnell, "The Christian Rule Governing Popular Amusements," *Theological Medium and Cumberland Presbyterian Quarterly*, n. s. III (January 1872), 55. Italics Darnell's.

[25] Minutes of the General Assembly, May 29, 1845.

[26] *Ibid.*, 1891, p. 36.

[27] *Ibid.*, May 29, 1845.

[28] Baughn, "Social Views," pp. 232-243.

[29] The material in this section on social questions is summarized from *ibid.*, pp. 101-161.

[30] The material in this section on science is summarized from *ibid.*, pp. 48-100.

[31] Minutes of the General Assembly, 1882, p. 36; 1883, pp. 10-11.

[32] S. L. Russell, "Revision," *Cumberland Presbyterian*, May 3, 1883.

[33] Baughn, "Social Views," pp. 203-213.

## Chapter 15

## "A Position of Usefulness and Respectability"

[1] Minutes of the General Assembly, 1850, pp. 7, 37-38.

[2] *Ibid.*, 1880, p. 20; 1881, p. 13.

[3] Beard, "Historical Sketch," p. 57.

[4] Minutes of the General Assembly, 1836, pp. 42-46.

[5] *Ibid.*, 1870, p. 23.

[6] *Ibid.*, 1859, pp. 92-93.

[7] "The Spiritual Life," *Cumberland Presbyterian*, Sept. 2, 1875.

[8] Logan, *Church in Illinois*, p. 8.

[9] *C. P. Church*, pp. 107-108.

[10] Minutes of the General Assembly, May 21, 1835. Except as otherwise noted, material on correspondence with other American churches is from proceedings and reports in General Assembly Minutes. Citations are given only for quoted or statistical material.

[11] Beard, "Historical Sketch," pp. 60-61; McDonnold, *C. P. Church*, pp. 316-318.

[12] Minutes of the General Assembly, May 22, 1848.

[13] McDonnold, *C. P. Church*, p. 318.

[14] *Ibid.*, p. 319.

[15] Minutes of the General Assembly of the Presbyterian Church in the United States, 1866, pp. 15, 30-32. Italics not in the original.

[16] Beard, *Brief Biographical Sketches*, second series, pp. 383-384; McDonnold, *C. P. Church*, pp. 385-387.

[17] Minutes of the General Assembly, 1874, pp. 57-64.

[18] Information on correspondence with the Evangelical Union of Scotland is from proceedings, reports, and other documents published in General Assembly Minutes, 1870-1890.

[19] Except as otherwise noted, material on the Pan-Presbyterian Alliance is from McDonnold, *C. P. Church*, pp. 461-467, from proceedings and reports in General Assembly Minutes, 1880-1899, and from numerous articles and editorials in *Cumberland Presbyterian* and other publications. Citations are given only for quoted or statistical material.

[20] " 'Pan-Presbyterian Council,' Etc.," *Cumberland Presbyterian*, Feb. 19, 1880.

[21] Quoted in McDonnold, *C. P. Church*, p. 463.

[22] "Honor to Whom Honor," *Cumberland Presbyterian*, Mar. 17, 1881.

[23] Minutes of the General Assembly, 1883, p. 40.

[24] Quoted in McDonnold, *C. P. Church*, p. 465.

[25] Quoted in *ibid.*, p. 466.

[26] *Ibid.*; Minutes of the General Assembly, 1885, p. 109.

[27] Minutes of the General Assembly, 1885, pp. 41-42.

[28] For the Cumberland Presbyterian Committee's report see General Assembly Minutes, 1883, pp. 30-32.

[29] *Ibid.*, May 21, 1830.

[30] Lindsley, "Sources and Sketches, No. IV," 6.

[31] Minutes of the General Assembly, 1876, p. 26.

[32] *Ibid.*, 1887, p. 18.

[33] *Ibid.*, 1895, p. 142.

[34] "Excerpts from Minutes of Pennsylvania Presbytery, August 28, 1877," *Cumberland Presbyterian*, Sept. 20, 1877.

[35] Minutes of the General Assembly, 1894, pp. 7-9, 22-29; 1895, pp. 34-37; 1898, pp. 19, 52; 1899, p. 21.

[36] "The Moderator Question," *Cumberland Presbyterian*, Nov. 4, 1880.

[37] Minutes of the General Assembly, 1880, p. 35; 1881, p. 22.

[38] A. J. Baird, "Our Rights and the Church," *Cumberland Presbyterian*, Oct. 7, 1879.

[39] *C. P. Church*, p. 365.

[40] Minutes of the General Assembly, 1894, p. 50.

## Chapter 16

## A Progressive Theology

[1] [Finis Ewing], *A Series of Letters Containing a Reply to a Pastoral Letter of West Tennessee Presbytery, to Which Is Added an Address to the Congregation, etc., under the Care of Cumberland Presbytery, by a Member of That Body* (Russellville, Ky.: Matthew Duncan, 1812), p. 19. Though this pamphlet was published anonymously, Finis Ewing is generally regarded as having been its author. See Cossitt, *Finis Ewing*, p. 203.

[2] *Ibid.*, p. 20.

[3] *Ibid.*, p. 22.

[4] Samuel Davies, *Charity and Truth United or the Way of the Multitude Exposed in Six Letters to the Rev. Mr. William Stith, A.M., President of William and Mary College*, ed. Thomas C. Pears, Jr. (Philadelphia: Department of History of the Office of the General Assembly of the Presbyterian Church in the U. S. A., 1941), p. 300.

[5] Samuel Davies, *Sermons on Important Subjects by the Reverend Samuel Davies, A.M., President of the College of New Jersey, with an Essay on the Life and Times of the Author, by Albert Barnes*, ed. Albert Barnes (New York: Robert Carter and Brothers, 1849), II, p. 277.

[6] *Ibid.*, p. 85.

[7] James McGready, *Posthumous Works*, I, p. 284.

[8] "Letter of the Council of Revival Ministers to the General Assembly of 1807," in James Smith, *History of the Christian Church*, p. 622.

[9] [Ewing], *A Series of Letters*, p. 12.

[10] *Ibid.*, p. 22.

[11] Finis Ewing and Robert Donnell, "Cumberland Presbyterians," *A Theological Dictionary Containing Definitions of All Religious Terms; a Comprehensive View of Every Article in the System of Divinity, and Impartial Account of All the Principal Denominations Which Have Subsisted in the Religious World from the Birth of Christ to the Present Days; Together with an Accurate Statement of the Most Remarkable Transactions and Events Recorded in Ecclesiastical History*, ed. Charles Buck, 3rd ed. (Philadelphia: W. W. Woodward, 1814), p. 388.

[12] David Rice, *A Lecture on the Divine Decrees, to Which Is Annexed a Few Observations on a Piece Lately Printed in Lexington, Entitled "The Principles of the Methodists or the Scripture Doctrines of Predestination, Election, and Reprobation"* (Lexington, Ky.: John Bradford, 1791), p. 7.

[13] Beard, *Brief Biographical Sketches*, p. 37.

[14] "Preface," *The Constitution of the Cumberland Presbyterian Church in the United States of America, Containing the Confession of Faith, a Catechism, the Government and Discipline, and the Directory for the Worship of God, Ratified and Adopted by the Synod of the Cumberland, Held at Sugg's Creek, in Tennessee State, April 5, 1814, and Continued by Adjournment until the 9th of the Same Month* (Russellville, Ky.: Charles Rhea, 1821), p. iv. Hereafter citations will be documented by means of a parenthesis immediately following the quotation and by use of the abbreviation "C.P.C., 1814."

[15] "The Confession of Faith," ix, 3,

The Constitution of the Presbyterian Church in the United States of America; Being Its Standards Subordinate to the Word of God, viz., the Confession of Faith, the Larger and Shorter Catechisms, the Form of Government, the Book of Discipline, and the Directory for the Worship of God, as Ratified and Adopted by the Synod of New York and Philadelphia in the Year of Our Lord, 1788; and as Amended in the Years 1805-1908, Together with the Constitutional Rules Adopted in 1893-1907, and Administrative Acts of the Assembly of a General Nature (Philadelphia: Presbyterian Board of Publication and Sabbath-School Work, 1909).

[16] Finis Ewing, Lectures on the Most Important Subjects in Divinity, [2nd ed.] (Louisville: Cumberland Presbyterian Board of Publication, 1849), p. 55.

[17] Ibid., p. 50.

[18] Ibid.

[19] Robert Donnell, Thoughts on Various Subjects (Louisville: Board of Publication of the Cumberland Presbyterian Church, 1856), pp. 16-17.

[20] Ibid., pp. 23-24.

[21] Ibid., p. 173.

[22] Minutes of the General Assembly, 1840.

[23] Reuben Burrow, Lectures of Reuben Burrow, D.D., Professor of Theology in Bethel College, from 1851 to 1860, with Autobiographical Sketch and Short Account of Funeral, ed. A. G. Burrow (Nashville: Cumberland Presbyterian Publishing House, 1881), p. 88.

[24] Reuben Burrow, "A Lecture on the Doctrine of Faith," Theological Medium, Vol. I, No. 7, 1846, p. 159.

[25] Milton Bird, "The Doctrine of Faith," Theological Medium, Vol. I, No. 7, 1846, p. 166.

[26] Ibid.

[27] Ibid., p. 170.

[28] Milton Bird, "Saving Faith," Theological Medium, Vol. I, No. 6, 1846, p. 142.

[29] Milton Bird, The Doctrine of Grace as Revealed in the Gospel, or Medium Theology in Familiar Lectures, Being a Revised and Enlarged Edition of "Error Unmasked," First Published at Pittsburg, Pa., in 1844, in Reply to Dr. A. G. Fairchild's "Great Supper" (Louisville: J. F. Brennan, 1856), p. 210.

[30] Ibid., p. 208.

[31] Minutes of the General Assembly, 1849, pp. 13-14, 36; 1852, p. 22.

[32] Ibid., 1852, p. 44.

[33] Ibid., 1854, pp. 15, 22, 34, 37, 39, 54.

[34] Richard Beard, Lectures on Theology (Nashville: Committee on Publication, 1860), I, p. 56.

[35] Ibid., p. 55.

[36] Minutes of the General Assembly, 1880, p. 58.

[37] Beard, Lectures on Theology, I, p. 9.

[38] Richard Beard, Lectures on Theology (Nashville: Board of Publication of the Cumberland Presbyterian Church, 1864), II, p. 49.

[39] Richard Beard, Lectures on Theology (Nashville: Board of Publication of the Cumberland Presbyterian Church, 1870), III, p. 102.

[40] Ibid., p. 503.

[41] Beard, Lectures on Theology, II, p. 211.

[42] Ibid.

[43] Ibid., p. 365.

[44] Ibid., p. 376.

[45] S. G. Burney, Studies in Psychology (Nashville: Cumberland Presbyterian Publishing House, 1890), p. 394.

[46] Ibid., p. 380.

[47] S. G. Burney, Studies in Moral Science (Nashville: Cumberland Presbyterian Publishing House, 1890), p. 30.

[48] S. G. Burney, Anthropology: A Discussion Chiefly of the Problem of Evil; of Man as a Sinner; the Relation of the First Man and His Posterity, Sin and Physical Evil, etc. (Nashville: Cumberland Presbyterian Publishing House, 1894), p. 64.

[49] Horace Bushnell, Christian Nurture (New Haven: Yale University Press, 1947), p. 40.

[50] Burney, Anthropology, p. 70.

[51] Ibid., pp. 63-64.

[52] F. Ewing, Lectures, p. 90.

[53] Minutes of the General Assembly, 1881, p. 14.

[54] "Report of the Committee on Revision," included in a preface to the revision of the Confession of Faith prepared and submitted to the General Assembly in 1882. *The Confession of Faith and Government of the Cumberland Presbyterian Church,* Proposed Revision (Nashville: Board of Publication of the Cumberland Presbyterian Church, 1882), p. 3.

[55] *Ibid.,* p. 5.

[56] *The Confession of Faith and Government of the Cumberland Presbyterian Church,* Revised, 1883 (Nashville: Cumberland Presbyterian Publishing House, 1885), Sections 11, 34. Hereafter citations will be documented by means of a parenthesis immediately following the quotation and by use of the abbreviation "C.P.C., 1883."

[57] *Cumberland Presbyterian Confession,* Proposed Revision, p. 6.

[58] William H. Black, "The New Theology," *Cumberland Presbyterian Quarterly Review,* II (October 1881), p. 430.

[59] A. B. Miller, *Doctrines and Genius of the Cumberland Presbyterian Church* (Nashville: Cumberland Presbyterian Publishing House, 1892), p. 13.

[60] *Ibid.,* p. 17.

[61] McDonnold, *C. P. Church,* p. 466.

[62] W. J. Darby, *Our Position, or Cumberland Presbyterians in Relation to the Presbyterian Family* (Nashville: Cumberland Presbyterian Publishing House, n.d.), p. 2.

[63] *Ibid.,* p. 15.

[64] J. M. Howard, "The New Confession," *Cumberland Presbyterian,* May 17, 1883, p. 4.

[65] The quotation is from an article entitled "Our Book" which appeared under the signature of N.W.M., *Cumberland Presbyterian,* Sept. 5, 1878, p. 2.

# PART III

## The Cumberland Presbyterian Church in the Twentieth Century, 1901-1970

### Chapter 17

### Moving In To Possess the Land

[1] William Warren Sweet, *Story of Religion in America* (New York: Harper & Brothers, 1950), pp. 345-346.

[2] *Ibid.,* pp. 347-348.

[3] Minutes of the General Assembly, 1904, p. 27.

[4] Sweet, *Story of Religion in America,* p. 348.

[5] *Ibid.,* pp. 355-357.

[6] *Ibid.,* pp. 357-358.

[7] *Cumberland Presbyterian,* Nov. 30, 1899, p. 687.

[8] Minutes of the General Assembly, 1901, p. 10a.

[9] *Ibid.,* 1900, p. 19a.

[10] *Ibid.,* 1901, pp. 7a-8a. Some of these churches had appeared in earlier lists. Apparently the Board found it necessary to take them under its care a second time.

[11] *Ibid.,* 1902, p. 28a.

[12] *Ibid.,* 1901, pp. 210a-211a.

[13] *Ibid.,* p. 205a.

[14] Frances C. Maghee *et al., History of the Woman's Board of Missions of the Cumberland Presbyterian Church, 1880-1933* (Nashville: Woman's Board of Missions, 1934), pp. 72-73.

[15] *Ibid.,* pp. 89-90.

[16] *Ibid.,* p. 130.

[17] Minutes of the General Assembly, 1900, pp. 18a-19a.

[18] *Ibid.,* 1902, p. 28a.

[19] Paul Hom, "Historical Survey of the First Chinese Cumberland Presbyterian Church" (unpublished term paper, Cumberland Presbyterian Theological Seminary, 1961), pp. 1-2. The author cites a letter from Miss Julia McCaslin dated Apr. 25, 1961, as his source of information.

[20] Maghee *et al., Woman's Board, 1880-1933,* p. 101.

[21] *Ibid.*, p. 89.

[22] *Ibid.*, p. 122.

[23] *Ibid.*, p. 89; Minutes of the General Assembly, 1901, p. 7a.

[24] Minutes of the General Assembly, 1897, pp. 104-105.

[25] *Cumberland Presbyterian*, June 2, 1897, p. 1543.

[26] Minutes of the General Assembly, 1899, p. 33.

[27] *Ibid.*, 1900, p. 17a.

[28] *Ibid.*, 1901, p. 4a.

[29] *Ibid.*, 1902, pp. 24a-25a.

[30] *Ibid.*, 1903, p. 25a.

[31] *Ibid.*, 1904, p. 21a.

[32] *Ibid.*, 1906, p. 23a.

[33] Counting Oklahoma and the Indian Territory as two separate entities, as they were at that time.

[34] Minutes of the General Assembly, 1900, pp. 255a-256a.

[35] *Ibid.*, 1903, p. 3a.

[36] Minutes of Porter Presbytery, 1891-1916, p. 111.

[37] Minutes of the General Assembly, 1902, p. 18.

[38] *Ibid.*, p. 72.

[39] Minutes of Porter Presbytery, 1891-1916, p. 115.

[40] *Ibid.*, pp. 122-124.

[41] *Ibid.*, pp. 127-128.

[42] According to the Preface of the Confession of Faith of the Reformed Cumberland Presbyterian Church. The minutes of this particular meeting of presbytery are not available.

[43] *Confession of Faith and Form of Government of the Reformed Cumberland Presbyterian Church*, Section 1.

[44] *Ibid.*, Section 12.

[45] *Ibid.*, Section 40.

[46] Constitution, Section 25.

[47] *Ibid.*, Sections 26, 27.

[48] *Ibid.*, Sections 31-37.

[49] Minutes of Porter Presbytery, 1891-1916, pp. 161-162.

[50] *Ibid.*, p. 170.

[51] *Ibid.*, p. 186.

[52] *Ibid.*, p. 192.

[53] Minutes of Arkansas Synod, 1906, p. 6.

[54] Minutes of the General Assembly, 1899, pp. 39-42.

[55] *Ibid.*, 1900, p. 67a.

[56] *Ibid.*, pp. 59a-61a.

[57] *Ibid.*, p. 55.

[58] *Ibid.*, p. 25; 1901, p. 27.

[59] *Ibid.*, 1901, p. 107.

[60] *Ibid.*, p. 105.

[61] "The Proposed Industrial College and Lincoln University," *Cumberland Presbyterian*, June 7, 1900, pp. 730-731.

[62] Minutes of the General Assembly, 1900, pp. 55-56.

[63] "A Great Day at Millikin University," *Cumberland Presbyterian*, June 11, 1903, pp. 754-755.

[64] Minutes of the General Assembly, 1901, p. 95a; 1902, p. 37.

[65] Minutes of Texas Synod, 1900, pp. 18-23.

[66] *Ibid.*, 1901, pp. 14-19.

[67] *Ibid.*, p. 23.

[68] Minutes of the General Assembly, 1904, pp. 49a-50a.

[69] Minutes of Texas Synod, 1899, p. 33.

[70] *Ibid.*, 1903, pp. 22-23.

[71] Minutes of the General Assembly, 1899, p. 47.

[72] *Ibid.*, 1900, p. 25.

[73] *Ibid.*, p. 48.

[74] *Ibid.*, pp. 26, 49; 1901, pp. 22-23, 54.

[75] *Ibid.*, 1902, p. 47.

[76] *Ibid.*, 1900, p. 88.

[77] *Ibid.*, 1901, p. 44.

[78] *Ibid.*, 1903, pp. 30, 58-59.

[79] *Ibid.*, p. 23.

## *Chapter 18*

## Enduring Through Crisis

[1] The Cumberland Presbyterian Church, in its revision of the Westminster Confession in 1814, had changed Chap. XVI, Sec. VII, to read that works done by unregenerate men "cannot merit the favor of God; yet their neglect of them is displeasing to God." In the Confession of 1814, Chap. XXII, Sec. III, and Chap.

XXV, Sec. VI, remained unchanged. In the Confession of 1883 there is no statement corresponding either to Chap. XVI, Sec. VII, or to Chap. XXII, Sec. III. Section 101, which takes the place of Chap. XXV, Sec. VI, in the older Confession, states only that "The Lord Jesus Christ is the only head of his Church on earth."

[2] Minutes of the General Assembly of the Presbyterian Church in the United States of America, 1902, pp. 91-97.

[3] See "Union of Churches Desired," *Cumberland Presbyterian*, Aug. 14, 1902, pp. 172-173; "The United Brethren Union Movement," Sept. 11, 1902, pp. 290-291; "That Other Proposition for Union," Oct. 2, 1902, pp. 385-386.

[4] J. L. Goodknight, "The Seed Thought of an Evolution," *Cumberland Banner*, Sept. 7, 1906, p. 1; "How It Was Done," *ibid.*, Sept. 14, 1906, p. 2.

[5] "Lebanon Presbytery's Action on Union," *Cumberland Presbyterian*, Sept. 18, 1902, p. 332.

[6] "Indiana Presbytery on Organic Union," *Ibid.*, pp. 332-333.

[7] "The Duty of the Hour: A Plain Talk about Denominational Conditions and Obligations," Sept. 25, 1902, pp. 353-354.

[8] Minutes of the General Assembly, 1903, p. 29.

[9] Minutes of Texas Synod, 1902, pp. 19-20.

[10] Minutes of the General Assembly, 1903, pp. 47-48.

[11] For text of dissenting statement see Minutes of the General Assembly, PCUSA, 1904, p. 140.

[12] *Cumberland Presbyterian*, Oct. 15, 1903, p. 1.

[13] Minutes of the General Assembly, 1904, pp. 61a-65a.

[14] Editorial, "Our Position on the Union Question," *Cumberland Presbyterian*, Feb. 25, 1904, pp. 227-228; S. P. Pryor, "Why Ask More?" *ibid.*, Mar. 24, 1904, pp. 360-361.

[15] R. V. F., "The Cumberland Presbyterian Confession," *ibid.*, May 5, 1904, pp. 348-349.

[16] John M. Gaut, "Why Unite?" *ibid.*, Apr. 14, 1904, p. 456.

[17] J. R. Sharp, "Not What We May, But What We Must," *ibid.*, Mar. 31, 1904, p. 394.

[18] J. R. Lamb, "Revision and Union as They Will Affect the Border Presbyteries and Synods," *ibid.*, May 12, 1904, p. 587.

[19] J. L. Hudgins, "Opposed to Union," *ibid.*, Mar. 3, 1904, p. 281.

[20] W. T. Dale, "The Difference," *ibid.*, Mar. 24, 1904, pp. 361-362; Mar. 31, 1904, pp. 393-394. See also J. L. Hudgins, "What It Means," *ibid.*, Apr. 7, 1904, pp. 423-424.

[21] W. P. Bone, "The Meaning of the Revision of 1903," *ibid.*, Mar. 10, 1904, p. 296; "Objections to the Joint Report on Union," *ibid.*, May 5, 1904, pp. 554-555.

[22] T. A. Havron, "Is Union Consistent? A Demurrer," *ibid.*, Apr. 14, 1904, p. 455.

[23] The reference is to the Form of Government of the Presbyterian Church, U. S. A., Chap. XIV, Sec. IV.

[24] J. P. McDonald, "Points of Difference," *Cumberland Presbyterian*, Apr. 21, 1904, p. 491.

[25] E. E. Beard, "Recommendation No. 1," *ibid.*, Mar. 17, 1904, p. 328; M. M. Smith, "Joint Report on Union," *ibid.*, p. 327.

[26] Minutes of Obion Presbytery, March 1904, p. 8; Minutes of the General Assembly, 1904, pp. 31, 37.

[27] Minutes of the General Assembly, 1904, pp. 25-30.

[28] Minutes of the General Assembly, PCUSA, 1904, pp. 129-140.

[29] *Ibid.*, pp. 141-147.

[30] Minutes of the General Assembly, 1904, p. 30.

[31] There was considerable discussion during the ensuing months as to how the two-thirds majority was obtained. The resolution did not unequivocally recommend the Basis of Union as the procedure for amending the Confession of Faith seemed to require, but recommended it to the presbyteries "for their approval or disapproval." Some who voted for submitting the Basis of Union to the presbyteries asserted that they did so believing that the object was simply to give the presbyteries

a chance to express themselves. At least three commissioners stated that they so understood the matter. See F. A. Seagle, "The Union Question Referred but Not Recommended," *Cumberland Presbyterian,* Dec. 15, 1904, pp. 751, 766; "Eight Votes That Were Cast for Submission," *Cumberland Banner,* Feb. 3, 1905, p. 1; T. C. Newman, "Did the Assembly Vote To Recommend?" *ibid.,* Feb. 10, 1905, p. 1. On the other hand, the unionists claimed that there were commissioners who voted against the Basis of Union who would have changed their votes to the affirmative had they been needed to carry the measure. See S. M. Templeton, "Valid Assembly Recommendation," *Cumberland Presbyterian,* Mar. 16, 1905, pp. 344-345.

[32] Minutes of the General Assembly, PCUSA, 1904, p. 119.

[33] "The 'Supplemental Report,'" *Herald and Presbyter,* June 29, 1904.

[34] *Cumberland Banner,* Oct. 14, 1904, p. 1.

[35] "A Plain Statement," *Cumberland Presbyterian,* Aug. 25, 1904, p. 235.

[36] "The Church Paper and the Union Question," *ibid.,* pp. 227-228; "The Church Paper and the Current Discussion," *ibid.,* Nov. 10, 1904, pp. 580-581.

[37] J. M. Hubbert, "The Vote of the Presbyteries on the Plan of Union," *ibid.,* June 23, 1904, p. 799.

[38] P. F. Johnson, "Why Wait until Spring To Vote on the Union?" *ibid.,* July 28, 1904, p. 107.

[39] "Marshall Presbytery," *ibid.,* pp. 126-127.

[40] For a copy of this letter see the *Cumberland Banner,* Jan. 12, 1905, p. 5. On the same page appears the letter of "Special Instructions" sent out by the steering committee of the opposition.

[41] Ira Landrith, "Opposition Arguments and Accusations," *Cumberland Presbyterian,* Oct. 14, 1904, pp. 457-458. The accusation is traceable to a private letter written by the Rev. A. M. Buchanan, of Moberly, Missouri, to a Presbyterian minister, which was published in the *Presbyterian,* of Philadelphia. See the *Cumberland Presbyterian,* Mar. 2, 1905, pp. 280-281, 284-286, for correspondence between the editor and Buchanan together with signed statements regarding arguments used by proponents of union on the floor of McGee Presbytery.

[42] W. P. Bone, "Why Cumberland Presbyterians Are Divided on the Union Question," *Cumberland Banner,* Apr. 7, 1905, p. 2.

[43] B. C. Scruggs, "Who Sprung the Union Question?" *Cumberland Banner,* Feb. 17, 1905, p. 1. The Minutes of Memphis Presbytery, Sept. 23-25, 1902, p. 4, state: "A Communication from Indiana Presbytery of the Cumberland Presbyterian Church was read and referred to a special committee consisting of Rev. John W. Hart, Rev. R. M. Neale and Elder G. L. Myers." In a later action (p. 10), "The Special Committee on Organic Union reported and the report was not adopted." The resolution and memorial of Indiana Presbytery favoring union were printed in pamphlet form, obviously for distribution. Apparently a copy reached Memphis Presbytery.

[44] Resolution adopted by Robert Donnell Presbytery at Athens, Alabama, Sept. 18, 1904, quoted in the *Cumberland Banner,* Mar. 3, 1905, p. 5.

[45] Editorial, "Should the Congregations Be Consulted?" *Cumberland Banner,* Oct. 14, 1904, p. 3; R. R. Kime, "Thoughts on Church Union," *ibid.,* Oct. 21, 1904, pp. 1, 3; J. H. Hughey, "Oligarchy versus Presbyterianism," *ibid.,* Nov. 25, 1904, p. 2.

[46] J. M. Gaut, "Legal Queries," *Cumberland Presbyterian,* Nov. 3, 1904, pp. 554-555.

[47] J. H. Milholland, "Presbyterianism versus Oligarchy," *ibid.,* Nov. 10, 1904, pp. 601-602.

[48] Landrith, "Opposition Arguments and Accusations," p. 458.

[49] A. T. Cory, "A Puzzling Question," *ibid.,* Mar. 16, 1905, pp. 345-346.

[50] T. Ashburn, "A Defense," *ibid.,* p. 346.

[51] F. H. Ford, "Significant Figures," *ibid.,* Feb. 16, 1905, p. 219. See also R. E. Chandler, "A Study in Figures," *ibid.,* Nov. 10, 1904, p. 601; George H. Silvius, "Look at the Record," *ibid.,* Jan.

5, 1905, p. 31; P. A. Rice, "An Open Letter to Rev. A. N. Eshman," *ibid.,* Jan. 26, 1905, pp. 126-127. For an antiunionist reply see J. D. Lewis, "Anti-Everything," *Cumberland Banner,* Mar. 10, 1905, p. 5.

[52] *Cumberland Presbyterian,* Feb. 9, 1905, p. 163.

[53] W. L. Livingston, "Some Interesting Phases of the Union Situation," *ibid.,* Jan. 19, 1905, p. 95.

[54] J. E. Martin, "An Old Question," *Cumberland Banner,* Dec. 8, 1904, p. 1.

[55] N. H. Murray, "What an Aged Elder Thinks of Union," *ibid.,* Nov. 11, 1904, p. 6. John J. Jenkins ("A Plea in Behalf of Colored Cumberland Presbyterians," *Cumberland Presbyterian,* Jan. 19, 1905, p. 91) estimated the strength of the Cumberland Presbyterian Church, Colored, at "probably 35,000 and possibly more communicants."

[56] W. B. Young, "Union and the Negro," *Cumberland Banner,* Feb. 24, 1905, p. 1.

[57] W. H. Berry, "Church Union," *ibid.,* Dec. 15, 1904, p. 6.

[58] J. J. McClellan, "Union and the Relation of Churches," *ibid.,* Feb. 24, 1905, p. 3.

[59] T. G. Randle, "Not Sectional Feeling," *ibid.,* p. 8.

[60] E. N. Allen, "A Plea from the West," *Cumberland Presbyterian,* Oct. 20, 1904, p. 510.

[61] R. L. Vannice, "Iowa and the Union Question," *ibid.,* July 14, 1904, p. 43. See also D. H. Barnwell, "On the Union Question," *ibid.,* July 28, 1904, p. 105.

[62] P. A. Rice, "An Open Letter to Rev. A. N. Eshman," p. 127.

[63] W. P. Thurston, "Some 'Clear-cut' Ideas," *Cumberland Presbyterian,* Aug. 4, 1904, pp. 13-14.

[64] R. A. D. Dunlap, "An Argument for Union," *ibid.,* Oct. 27, 1904, p. 521.

[65] Bone, "Why Cumberland Presbyterians Are Divided on the Union Question," p. 2.

[66] *Presbyterian,* June 8, 1904, p. 6.

[67] P. Robertson, "The Question of Reunion," *Herald and Presbyter,* Nov. 2, 1904, pp. 13-14.

[68] *The Interior,* June 23, 1904, p. 811.

[69] *Herald and Presbyter,* Dec. 7, 1904, p. 2.

[70] John Donnan Countermine, "Whence? What? Whither?" *Presbyterian Banner,* Nov. 10, 1904, p. 12.

[71] Rollin A. Sawyer, "The Cumberland Question," *Christian Work and Evangelist,* Dec. 3, 1904, p. 721.

[72] Minutes of the General Assembly, 1905, pp. 37-44.

[73] *Cumberland Banner,* June 1, 1905, p. 8. *The Cumberland Presbyterian* of the same date, p. 6, quotes Fussell as saying, "Remember that after we are gone, there will be living and working somewhere in the sunlight of God's own glory, a Cumberland Presbyterian Church."

[74] Minutes of the General Assembly, 1905, pp. 78-81.

[75] *Ibid.,* pp. 81-92.

[76] "Cumberland Union," *Herald and Presbyter,* May 3, 1905, pp. 1-2.

[77] Minutes of the General Assembly, 1906, pp. 52-58.

[78] *Ibid.,* pp. 61-77.

[79] *Ibid.,* pp. 79-80.

[80] Opinion of the Supreme Court of Tennessee by Judge M. M. Neil in Ira Landrith *et al.,* Complainants (Unionists) v. J. L. Hudgins *et al.,* Defendants (Cumberland Presbyterians). Delivered at Nashville, Apr. 3, 1909.

[81] One minister who went with the union in 1906 and later returned to the Cumberland Presbyterian Church expressed the view that many unionists "got their eyes fixed on the 'patch' put on the Westminster Confession in 1903, and the 'Brief Statement advertisement' " and failed to consider all the facts. He states that when he began to see the "old goods," the patch grew "exceedingly small." He found that he was in a Calvinistic church. See W. J. Walker, "The Facts, the Law and the Testimony," *Cumberland Presbyterian Banner,* Apr. 21, 1909, p. 6.

[82] Minutes of the General Assembly, 1906, pp. 107-112.

[83] The Minutes of this continued session were printed for distribution and were also bound with the printed Minutes of 1907.

## Chapter 19

## The Broken Body

[1] Editorials, "The New Situation" and "The 'Cumberland Presbyterian Assembly'," *Cumberland Presbyterian*, May 31, 1906, pp. 642-643.

[2] "Special Session of Obion Presbytery," *ibid.*, June 21, 1906, pp. 762-763.

[3] "Snyder Presbytery," *ibid.*, July 5, 1906, p. 23.

[4] Minutes of Austin Presbytery, 1906-1920, p. 1.

[5] *Cumberland Banner*, Sept. 21, 1906, p. 1. Thomas H. Buchanan was a son of former Governor J. P. Buchanan, who was a ruling elder in the Mount Tabor Church and spokesman for the majority of the session on this occasion.

[6] *Ibid.*, Sept. 28, 1906, p. 5; cf. *Cumberland Presbyterian*, Oct. 4, 1906, pp. 444-445.

[7] "Little Rock Presbytery," *Cumberland Presbyterian*, Aug. 2, 1906, p. 152; "Rev. J. Silvester Hall's Reply to The Little Rock Presbytery of the Presbyterian Church, U. S. A.," *Cumberland Banner*, Aug. 10, 1906, p. 3.

[8] John H. Hughey, *Lights and Shadows of the Cumberland Presbyterian Church* (Decatur, Ill.: privately printed, 1906), pp. 123-130.

[9] *Cumberland Banner*, Aug. 31, 1906, p. 1.

[10] Minutes of Mound Prairie Presbytery, PCUSA, contained in "Minutes of the Mound Prairie Presbytery of the Cumberland Presbyterian Church 1842-1910 with a few missing years. Copied and edited by Rev. Thomas S. Hickman, Mt. Pleasant, Ark., from the Original Records, 1842-1903, now in possession of the Presbyterian and Reformed Foundation, Montreat, N.C., and 1906-1910, now in possession of the Department of History, Witherspoon Bldg., Philadelphia, Penna.," pp. 326 ff.

[11] Minutes of White River Presbytery, July 1906.

[12] "Advice of Pastoral Committee," *Cumberland Presbyterian*, July 5, 1906, pp. 24-25.

[13] "The Tennessee Injunction Case," *Cumberland Banner*, Sept. 28, 1906, p. 4.

[14] *Cumberland Banner*, Aug. 31, 1906, p. 1.

[15] *Cumberland Presbyterian Banner*, July 12, 1907, p. 8. See also "The Tennessee Injunction Dismissed," *ibid.*, Aug. 9, 1907, pp. 3-4; J. B. Eshman, "The Cumberland Presbyterian Church," *ibid.*, Sept. 6, 1907, p. 6.

[16] *Cumberland Banner*, Sept. 28, 1906, p. 4.

[17] *Ibid.*, Aug. 10, 1906, p. 8.

[18] *Ibid.*, Feb. 8, 1907, p. 1.

[19] "The Indiana Decision—A General Review of the Rulings," *ibid.*, Mar. 15, 1907, p. 1.

[20] J. S. Groves, "Justice versus Legal Rights," *Cumberland Presbyterian*, Aug. 2, 1906.

[21] William Laurie, "Where Are We As to Reunion?" *Presbyterian*, Dec. 26, 1906, pp. 8-9.

[22] Senex Presbyterianus [pseud.], "The Property of the Cumberland Presbyterian Church—A Suggestion," *ibid.*, Mar. 6, 1907, p. 7.

[23] Minutes of the Synod of New Jersey, PCUSA, October 1906, p. 37.

[24] Minutes of the General Assembly, PCUSA, 1907, p. 39.

[25] Minutes of the General Assembly, 1907, pp. 18-22.

[26] Minutes of the General Assembly, PCUSA, 1907, p. 1. With reference to this sermon the editor of the *Cumberland Presbyterian Banner* (Oct. 11, 1907, p. 3) facetiously suggested Deut. 2:3, "Turn you northward," as a text for a sermon addressed to the Presbyterian Church, U. S., which had largely confined its activities to the South. He pointed out that although Landrith's text was addressed only to the tribe of Naphtali, Deut. 2:3 was addressed to all Israel.

[27] Minutes of the General Assembly, PCUSA, 1907, p. 66.

[28] *Ibid.*, p. 139.

[29] *Ibid.*, p. 256.

[30] *Ibid.*, pp. 279-280.

[31] *Ibid.*, p. 240.

[32] *Ibid.*, 1910, pp. 71-72.

[33] "Opinion of Appellate Court of Illi-

nois," *Cumberland Presbyterian,* June 13, 1907, pp. 764-765.

[34] Opinion of the Supreme Court of Illinois in Joe H. Fussell *et al.,* Appellants, v. J. B. Hail *et al.,* Appellees. [Delivered at Springfield], Feb. 20, 1908.

[35] Opinion of the Supreme Court of Georgia in George H. Mack *et al.,* Plaintiffs in Error, v. R. R. Kime *et al.,* Defendants in Error. [Delivered at Atlanta], Aug. 9, 1907.

[36] Opinion of the Court of Civil Appeals of the Sixth Supreme Judicial District of Texas by Judge W. Hodges in William Clark *et al.,* Appellants, v. G. W. Brown *et al.,* Appellees. Delivered at Texarkana, Feb. 27, 1908.

[37] Opinion of the Supreme Court of Tennessee by Judge M. M. Neil in Ira Landrith *et al.,* Complainants (Unionists), v. J. L. Hudgins *et al.,* Defendants (Cumberland Presbyterians). Delivered at Nashville, Apr. 3, 1909.

[38] Minutes of the General Assembly, PCUSA, 1909, p. 82.

[39] Opinion of the Supreme Court of Missouri by Judge W. W. Graves in Charles A. Boyles *et al.,* Complainants (Unionists), v. J. L. Roberts *et al.,* Defendants (Cumberland Presbyterians). Delivered at Jefferson City, June 8, 1909.

[40] J. L. Goodknight, "Lincoln Illinois Suit," *Cumberland Presbyterian Banner,* July 23, 1909, p. 9.

[41] "Another Federal Suit Dismissed," *Cumberland Presbyterian Banner,* Aug. 13, 1909, p. 5.

[42] The Bethel Church property, however, was awarded to the remaining Cumberland Presbyterians on the basis of the definition of a "particular Church" contained in Section 4 of the Constitution of the Cumberland Presbyterian Church: "A particular Church consists of a number of professing Christians voluntarily associated together for Divine worship and godly living. . . ." Persons living in distant states could hardly meet with the congregation for worship.

[43] *Cumberland Presbyterian Banner,* Aug. 29, 1913, p. 2.

[44] "Grace Church Awarded the Unionists," *ibid.,* Aug. 15, 1913, p. 9.

[45] "The Missouri Decision," *ibid.,* Aug. 29, 1913, p. 7. This decision involved both the Missouri "blanket" suit (James M. Barkley and William H. Roberts v. Hugh Hayes *et al.*) and the Missouri Valley College case (The Synod of Kansas of the Presbyterian Church, U. S. A., v. J. W. Duvall, *et al.*).

[46] "Wobbly Court Decisions," *ibid.,* Apr. 30, 1915, pp. 2-3.

[47] "Adverse Decision in Illinois," *ibid.,* Apr. 29, 1910, p. 5.

[48] Decisions favorable to the remaining Cumberland Presbyterians had been rendered in the Appellate Court of Indiana in the case of Ramsey v. Hicks, involving the church property at Washington, Indiana, and in Bentle v. Ulay, in the Monroe City case.

[49] "Refuses Jurisdiction," *ibid.,* June 23, 1911, p. 9.

[50] F. A. Brown Correspondence. Letter to J. S. Hall, Nov. 24, 1911.

[51] *Ibid.,* Letter to J. L. Hudgins, July 3, 1912.

[52] *Cumberland Presbyterian Banner,* Feb. 5, 1915, p. 7.

[53] *Supra,* Chap. 17.

[54] For the six General Assembly years 1900-1905, the average annual death rate per one hundred Cumberland Presbyterian ministers was 2.08. For the years 1907-1912, the annual average rose to 3.11. For the year 1907-1908; it was 4.05, and for 1912-1913, 3.79.

[55] Minutes of the General Assembly, 1907, p. 46.

[56] "Some Preliminary Suggestions," *Cumberland Banner,* June 22, 1906, p. 2; "Better Be Lost Than Listen to a Union Preacher," *Cumberland Presbyterian,* July 5, 1906, p. 24.

[57] "Another Confidential Union Circular," *Cumberland Banner,* July 20, 1906, p. 3.

[58] Minutes of the General Assembly, 1907, pp. 47-48.

[59] F. A. Brown Correspondence, 1911-1915.

[60] *Cumberland Banner,* Aug. 24, 1906, p. 8.

[61] *Cumberland Presbyterian Banner,* Feb. 28, 1908, p. 1; "Cumberland Presbyterianism in and around Nashville," *ibid.,* Oct. 9, 1908, pp. 2-3.

[62] "Addison Avenue Church," *Cumberland Banner,* Sept. 7, 1906, pp. 5, 8.

[63] "An Appeal for Cumberland Presbyterianism in Memphis," *ibid.*, Jan. 18, 1907, p. 6; "Memphis Presbytery," *ibid.*, Feb. 1, 1907, p. 8.

[64] "Unionism at the Present Stage," *Cumberland Presbyterian Banner*, Nov. 8, 1907, pp. 3-4.

[65] J. L. Stocking, "Jefferson Avenue Church," *ibid.*, Jan. 10, 1908, p. 8.

[66] *Age Herald*, quoted in *Cumberland Presbyterian Banner*, July 12, 1907, pp. 12, 16.

[67] "Notes from Alabama," *Cumberland Presbyterian Banner*, Oct. 30, 1908, pp. 8-9.

[68] *Cumberland Banner*, Aug. 10, 1906, p. 8.

[69] *Cumberland Presbyterian Banner*, July 19, 1907, p. 12; *ibid.*, Sept. 13, 1907, p. 11.

[70] "The Dallas Church," *ibid.*, Aug. 20, 1915.

[71] Minutes of the General Assembly, 1918, pp. 101-102.

[72] Session Records, Fort Worth Cumberland Presbyterian Church, 1908-1924, p. 7.

[73] *Cumberland Presbyterian Banner*, June 26, 1908, p. 14. Session records show that on a prior visit by the Rev. B. E. Bowmer, synodical missionary, on December 2, 1906, thirteen Cumberland Presbyterians met and elected four trustees and four elders. Apparently some eighteen months elapsed before these elders were installed.

[74] *Cumberland Presbyterian*, Apr. 9, 1914, pp. 12-13. Some of these members had continued for a while in the "Cumberland Presbyterian Church, U. S. A." as the former Cumberland Presbyterian congregation was called, until that congregation voted to unite with the First Presbyterian Church across the street in December 1908. All services at the former Cumberland Presbyterian church building were discontinued shortly thereafter.

[75] "A Letter from Austin, Texas," *ibid.*, July 16, 1914, p. 13.

[76] *Cumberland Banner*, June 15, 1906, p. 8.

[77] *Cumberland Presbyterian Banner*, May 24, 1907, p. 15; *ibid.*, June 3, 1910, p. 16.

[78] J. T. Barbee, "Field Work in Kentucky," *Cumberland Banner*, Mar. 29, 1907; "Notes from Mayfield Presbytery," *Cumberland Presbyterian Banner*, Aug. 7, 1908, p. 13.

[79] J. T. Barbee, "Cumberlands Marching On," *Cumberland Presbyterian Banner*, May 21, 1909, p. 8; A. D. Salisbury, Jr., "A History of the Churches of Owensboro Presbytery" (unpublished B. D. thesis, Cumberland Presbyterian Theological Seminary, 1947), pp. 33-35.

[80] *Cumberland Presbyterian Banner*, Aug. 14, 1908, p. 13; *ibid.*, Jan. 15, 1909, p. 6; *ibid.*, Feb. 25, 1909, p. 13.

[81] *Ibid.*, Feb. 18, 1910, p. 4.

[82] *Ibid.*, June 30, 1911, p. 7; "The Obligation of Missouri Synod," *ibid.*, June 26, 1914, p. 8.

[83] *Ibid.*, Nov. 21, 1913, p. 8.

[84] *Cumberland Presbyterian*, Apr. 16, 1914, p. 10; *ibid.*, June 25, 1914, p. 14.

[85] *Cumberland Banner*, July 6, 1906, p. 8; *ibid.*, Dec. 21, 1906, p. 8; *Cumberland Presbyterian Banner*, Dec. 13, 1907, p. 13.

[86] "Texas News and Notes," *Cumberland Presbyterian Banner*, Nov. 27, 1908, p. 13.

[87] *Ibid.*, May 31, 1907, p. 2.

[88] *Minutes of the General Assembly*, 1907, p. 19.

[89] *Cumberland Presbyterian*, Oct. 24, 1907, p. 532.

[90] R. L. Baskette, "Padded Reports," *Cumberland Presbyterian Banner*, Nov. 8, 1907, p. 7.

[91] "Figuring the Membership," *ibid.*, Oct. 8, 1909, p. 2.

[92] Minutes of the General Assembly, 1916, p. 174.

[93] Wilson Loran Waller, "Cumberland Presbyterian Evangelicalism Before and After Default in Ecumenical Union in 1906" (unpublished D.Div. thesis, Vanderbilt University Divinity School, 1971), p. 85.

[94] J. L. Goodknight, "The Works of a 'Dead' Denomination," *Cumberland Presbyterian Banner*, Apr. 10, 1914, p. 4.

[95] Waller, "Cumberland Presbyterian Evangelicalism," pp. 206-207.

[96] *Cumberland Presbyterian Banner*, Sept. 4, 1908, pp. 12-13.

[97] Minutes of the General Assembly, 1912, pp. 19, 125.

[98] *Ibid.,* 1913, p. 133.

[99] *Cumberland Presbyterian Banner,* Sept. 13, 1912, p. 8.

[100] "A New Presbytery Organized," *ibid.,* Jan. 31, 1913, p. 5.

[101] Minutes of the General Assembly, 1915, pp. 107-108.

[102] Minutes of Texas Synod, 1920, p. 12.

## Chapter 20

## Gathering Together the Pieces

[1] Minutes of the General Assembly, 1906, p. 10a.

[2] *Ibid.,* 1907, p. 45.

[3] *Ibid.,* 1911, pp. 37-49.

[4] *Ibid.,* 1913, pp. 63-128.

[5] *Ibid.,* 1905, p. 69.

[6] *Ibid.,* 1912, p. 66.

[7] *Ibid.,* 1913, pp. 68-69.

[8] *Ibid.,* 1912, p. 22.

[9] *Ibid.,* 1913, pp. 71-72.

[10] *Ibid.,* pp. 67-68.

[11] *Ibid.,* pp. 71-72.

[12] *Ibid.,* 1914, pp. 46-47; 1915, p. 63; 1916, p. 89; 1917, p. 53.

[13] *Ibid.,* 1915, p. 62.

[14] *Ibid.,* 1907, p. 47.

[15] *Ibid.,* 1908, pp. 54-58.

[16] *Ibid.,* 1909, p. 49.

[17] *Ibid.,* 1908, p. 82.

[18] *Ibid.,* 1909, p. 49.

[19] *Ibid.,* 1913, p. 130.

[20] *Ibid.,* p. 131.

[21] *Ibid.,* 1915, pp. 68-69.

[22] *Ibid.,* 1914, p. 83.

[23] *Ibid.,* 1910, pp. 25-28, 55.

[24] *Ibid.,* 1913, p. 132.

[25] *Ibid.,* 1914, p. 84.

[26] *Ibid.,* 1916, p. 59.

[27] *Ibid.,* 1914, p. 84.

[28] *Cumberland Presbyterian Banner,* June 13, 1913, p. 8; Minutes of the General Assembly, 1914, p. 82.

[29] Maghee *et al., Woman's Board,* 1880-1933, p. 144.

[30] *Ibid.,* p. 145.

[31] *Ibid.,* p. 146.

[32] *Ibid.,* p. 182.

[33] *Ibid.,* p. 171.

[34] *Ibid.,* pp. 164, 168, 170; Minutes of the General Assembly, 1912, p. 82.

[35] Minutes of the General Assembly, 1906 (Continued Session), p. 12.

[36] *Ibid.,* 1907, p. 83.

[37] *Ibid.,* 1908, p. 34.

[38] *Ibid.,* 1909, pp. 62, 64.

[39] *Ibid.,* 1915, p. 116.

[40] *Ibid.,* 1908, p. 84.

[41] *Ibid.,* 1909, pp. 62-63.

[42] *Cumberland Banner,* Oct. 26, 1906, p. 5.

[43] Minutes of the General Assembly, 1909, p. 58.

[44] *Ibid.,* 1910, p. 82.

[45] *Ibid.,* pp. 88-92.

[46] *Ibid.,* p. 86.

[47] *Ibid.,* 1912, pp. 95-99.

[48] *Ibid.,* 1909, p. 90.

[49] "Report of Rev. J. R. Goodpasture, as Editor of the Sunday School Literature," *Cumberland Presbyterian Banner,* May 23, 1913.

[50] Minutes of the General Assembly, 1911, p. 119.

[51] *Ibid.,* 1912, pp. 128-129.

[52] Editorial, "A Toast and a Roast," *Cumberland Presbyterian Banner,* Aug. 30, 1912, pp. 3-4.

[53] J. R. Goodpasture, "On Question of Personal Privilege," *ibid.,* Sept. 13, 1912, p. 6. A copy of the committee's report adopted by Lebanon Presbytery is printed on the same page.

[54] A. N. Eshman, "Pointers and Center Lights on the Question of the Hour" (a circular letter), *ibid.,* Apr. 4, 1913.

[55] J. L. Goodknight, "A Wrong Righted," *ibid.,* Sept. 26, 1913, p. 4.

[56] Minutes of the General Assembly, 1913, pp. 157-158.

[57] *Cumberland Presbyterian Banner,* May 23, 1913, pp. 6-9, 16. The editor states that Goodpasture's report was printed in pamphlet form for distribution prior to the Assembly.

[58] Minutes of the General Assembly, 1913, pp. 205-207.

[59] *Ibid.*, 1914, pp. 113-114.

[60] *Ibid.*, pp. 114-115.

[61] *Ibid.*, pp. 115-116.

[62] *Ibid.*, p. 158.

[63] *Ibid.*, p. 115.

[64] *Ibid.*, 1916, pp. 78-84.

[65] *Ibid.*, 1917, p. 95.

[66] *Ibid.*, pp. 113-114.

[67] *Ibid.*, 1917, p. 96. Specific reference was made to the *Banner* of Mar. 16 and 30; Apr. 6, 13, 20 and 27; and May 4, 1917.

[68] The *Banner's* position was set forth in an editorial, "Must Salute the Flag," in the issue of May 14, 1915. The letter in question was published in the *Cumberland Presbyterian*, Apr. 29, 1915.

[69] Minutes of the General Assembly, 1907, p. 63.

[70] *Cumberland Presbyterian Banner*, July 12, 1907, p. 5.

[71] Minutes of the General Assembly, 1908, p. 40.

[72] Minutes of West Tennessee Synod, 1908, pp. 15-17.

[73] *Ibid.*, 1910, pp. 9-10.

[74] *Ibid.*, 1909, p. 22.

[75] Minutes of the General Assembly, 1910, p. 41.

[76] Minutes of West Tennessee Synod, 1911, p. 9.

[77] *Ibid.*

[78] *Ibid.*, 1913, p. 12.

[79] *Ibid.*, 1914, pp. 30-31.

[80] *Ibid.*, 1917, p. 15.

[81] Minutes of Texas Synod, 1910, p. 25.

[82] *Ibid.*, called meeting, June 29, 1911 (typed copy of unpublished minutes of Texas Synod transcribed from the original records, 1939, in the Historical Library and Archives of the Cumberland Presbyterian Church, pp. 1-4).

[83] *Ibid.*, 1911 (typed copy, pp. 24-27).

[84] *Ibid.* (typed copy, pp. 27-29, 34).

[85] *Ibid.*, called meeting, Mar. 17-18, 1914 (typed copy, pp. 85-87).

[86] *Ibid.*, 1915 (typed copy, pp. 114-118).

[87] *Ibid.*, 1916, p. 5.

[88] *Ibid.*, called meeting, Dec. 28, 1917 (typed copy, pp. 126-128).

[89] *Ibid.*, 1918 (typed copy, pp. 130-137).

[90] *Ibid.*, 1919 (typed copy, pp. 185-188).

[91] Minutes of the General Assembly, 1907, p. 88.

[92] *Ibid.*, 1909, pp. 33-34.

[93] *Ibid.*, 1911, pp. 22-25.

[94] *Ibid.*, 1913, pp. 203-204.

[95] *Ibid.*, 1915, pp. 113-114.

[96] *Ibid.*, 1914, pp. 122-125, 163.

[97] *Ibid.*, 1916, pp. 91-94.

[98] *Ibid.*, 1917, p. 127.

[99] *Ibid.*, 1913, pp. 27, 200.

[100] *Ibid.*, 1914, p. 164.

[101] *Ibid.*, 1916, p. 128.

[102] *Ibid.*, 1917, pp. 20, 138.

## Chapter 21

### Broadening of Horizons

[1] Minutes of the General Assembly, 1917, p. 27.

[2] *Ibid.*, 1918, p. 16.

[3] *Ibid.*, pp. 19-20.

[4] *Ibid.*, p. 102.

[5] *Ibid.*, pp. 112-113.

[6] *Cumberland Presbyterian*, Sept. 12, 1918, p. 2. See also editorial of June 20, 1918, p. 1. For articles published in the *Cumberland Presbyterian Banner* see J. F. Jacobs, "For What Are We Fighting?" (Oct. 25, 1918, p. 5) and Newell Dwight Hillis, "The Hour Is Big with Destiny—Only Safe Word Is Unconditional Surrender" (Nov. 1, 1918, pp. 5-7).

[7] C. D. Cartner, "The War, When Will It Close, and Means To Bring It to a Close," *Cumberland Presbyterian Banner*, June 28, 1918, p. 8.

[8] C. R. Matlock, "Does a Heroic Death Save a Soldier?" *Cumberland Presbyterian*, Aug. 1, 1918, p. 8.

[9] Minutes of the General Assembly, 1920, pp. 112-113.

[10] *Ibid.*, 1916, pp. 129-130; 1917, pp. 108-109.

[11] *Ibid.*, 1924, p. 118.

[12] *Ibid.*, 1929, p. 105.

[13] *Ibid.*, 1927, p. 142.

[14] *Ibid.*, 1918, p. 92.

[15] *Ibid.*, pp. 27-28.
[16] *Ibid.*, 1919, pp. 88-91.
[17] *Ibid.*, pp. 108-109. See also p. 26.
[18] *Ibid.*, 1918, pp. 100-101.
[19] *Ibid.*, p. 28.
[20] *Ibid.*, 1919, pp. 87-88.
[21] *Ibid.*, 1918, pp. 82-85, 112.
[22] *Ibid.*, 1919, pp. 34-37.
[23] *Ibid.*, 1920, pp. 96-99.
[24] *Ibid.*, pp. 120-121.
[25] *Ibid.*, 1921, pp. 30-31.
[26] *Ibid.*, pp. 31-32.
[27] *Ibid.*, 1922, pp. 29-32.
[28] *Ibid.*, p. 169.
[29] *Ibid.*, 1920, p. 85.
[30] *Ibid.*, 1921, pp. 40-47.
[31] *Ibid.*, p. 209.
[32] *Ibid.*, 1923, p. 23.
[33] *Ibid.*, 1924, p. 43.
[34] *Ibid.*, 1925, pp. 116-118.
[35] *Ibid.*, 1926, pp. 47-48.
[36] George W. Burroughs, "A Personal Statement," *Cumberland Presbyterian,* May 13, 1926, pp. 4-6.
[37] Minutes of the General Assembly, 1926, pp. 48-49.
[38] Burroughs, "A Personal Statement," p. 5.
[39] Minutes of the General Assembly, 1926, p. 30.
[40] *Ibid.*, 1927, pp. 103-106.
[41] *Ibid.*, pp. 46-51; D. M. McAnulty, "Educational Food for Thought," *Cumberland Presbyterian,* Oct. 1, 1926, pp. 2-4.
[42] Minutes of the General Assembly, 1927, p. 20. For contents of some of the memorials see Minutes of West Tennessee Synod, 1926, p. 17; Minutes of the Synod of Arkansas, 1926, p. 7; Minutes of Elk Presbytery, 1916-1931, pp. 173-174; Minutes of New Hope Presbytery, 1915-1936, pp. 238-239; Minutes of White River Presbytery, Dec. 29-31, 1926.
[43] Minutes of the General Assembly, 1927, pp. 137-138.
[44] *Ibid.*, p. 141.
[45] *Ibid.*, 1919, pp. 99-100.
[46] *Ibid.*, 1920, p. 113.
[47] *Ibid.*, 1923, p. 167.
[48] *Ibid.*, 1924, pp. 91-92.
[49] *Ibid.*, 1927, pp. 114, 146.
[50] *Ibid.*, 1928, pp. 127-128.
[51] *Ibid.*, 1930, pp. 100-101.
[52] *Ibid.*, pp. 145-146.
[53] *Ibid.*, 1919, pp. 66-67.
[54] *Ibid.*, 1921, pp. 49-51. The lot in Highland Park was sold in 1923. *Ibid.*, 1924, p. 54.
[55] *Ibid.*, 1919, p. 66.
[56] *Ibid.*, 1921, p. 50.
[57] *Ibid.*, 1922, p. 51.
[58] *Ibid.*, 1925, p. 50.
[59] *Ibid.*, 1926, p. 59.
[60] *Cumberland Presbyterian,* Oct. 22, 1925, pp. 6-7.
[61] *Ibid.*, Sept. 6, 1923, p. 3; July 2, 1925, p. 15.
[62] Minutes of the General Assembly, 1928, p. 139.
[63] *Ibid.*, 1930, p. 55.
[64] *Cumberland Presbyterian,* Feb. 11, 1926, p. 14.
[65] Minutes of the General Assembly, 1927, p. 64.
[66] *Ibid.*, 1929, p. 130.
[67] B. O. Wolfe Correspondence; Minutes of the General Assembly, 1929, p. 22.
[68] Minutes of the General Assembly, 1929, p. 130.
[69] *Ibid.*, 1922, p. 56.
[70] *Ibid.*, 1925, p. 50.
[71] *Ibid.*, p. 114.
[72] *Ibid.*, 1926, p. 126.
[73] *Ibid.*, 1929, pp. 130-131.
[74] *Ibid.*, 1918, p. 23. In Maghee *et al., Woman's Board, 1880-1933,* pp. 187-188, the amount of the offering is given as $1,525.65 in cash and pledges.
[75] Maghee *et al., Woman's Board, 1880-1933,* pp. 195, 197.
[76] *Ibid.*, pp. 199, 202.
[77] *Ibid.*, p. 210.
[78] Minutes of the General Assembly, 1924, pp. 156-157.
[79] *Ibid.*, 1925, p. 82.
[80] Maghee *et al., Woman's Board, 1880-1933,* p. 167.
[81] *Ibid.*, p. 197.
[82] *Ibid.*, pp. 209-210.
[83] *Ibid.*, p. 227.
[84] *Ibid.*, pp. 242-243.
[85] Mrs. J. L. Mize and Annie McCroskey, "History of Knoxville Presbyterial Missionary Society of the Cumberland Presbyterian Church" (unpublished manuscript).
[86] Minutes of Knoxville Presbytery, 1907-1927, p. 311.

[87] *Ibid.*, p. 326.

[88] *Ibid.*, p. 365.

[89] *Ibid.*, pp. 384, 397.

[90] Maghee *et al.*, *Woman's Board, 1880-1933*, pp. 236-237.

[91] *Ibid.*, p. 249.

[92] *Ibid.*, p. 292.

[93] "Twelve Hundred in a Single Day for Ministerial Relief: How It Can Be Done," *Cumberland Presbyterian*, Apr. 3, 1919, p. 8.

[94] Minutes of the General Assembly, 1929, p. 121.

[95] *Ibid.*, 1921, p. 211.

[96] *Ibid.*, 1922, p. 63.

[97] *Ibid.*, 1929, pp. 120-121.

[98] *Ibid.*, 1930, pp. 64-65.

[99] *Ibid.*, p. 120.

[100] *Ibid.*, p. 129.

[101] *Ibid.*, 1931, p. 70.

[102] *Ibid.*, 1919, pp. 72-73.

[103] *Ibid.*, 1920, p. 52.

[104] *Ibid.*, 1922, p. 58.

[105] *Ibid.*, 1923, p. 57.

[106] *Ibid.*, 1924, pp. 55-56.

[107] *Ibid.*, 1925, p. 52.

[108] Maghee *et al.*, *Woman's Board, 1880-1933*, p. 230; "We Welcome the Woman's Board," *Cumberland Presbyterian*, Oct. 1, 1925, p. 2.

[109] Minutes of the General Assembly, 1926, p. 122.

[100] *Ibid.*, 1927, pp. 139-140.

[111] *Ibid.*, 1920, p. 116.

[112] *Ibid.*, p. 33.

[113] *Ibid.*, 1923, pp. 60-61.

[114] *Ibid.*, 1924, p. 148.

[115] *Ibid.*, p. 25.

[116] *Ibid.*, 1927, p. 139.

[117] *Ibid.*, 1928, pp. 115-116.

[118] *Ibid.*, 1930, p. 112.

[119] *Supra*, Chap. 19.

[120] Minutes of the General Assembly, 1924, pp. 139-141.

[121] *Ibid.*, 1928, pp. 128-129.

[122] *Ibid.*, 1925, p. 115.

[123] *Supra*, Chap. 15.

[124] Minutes of the General Assembly, 1920, pp. 114-115.

[125] *Ibid.*, 1921, p. 200. See also p. 33.

[126] The Presbyterian Church, U. S. A., authorized the ordination of women as ruling elders in 1930 and in 1955 made provision for the ordination of women as ministers. The Presbyterian Church, U. S., authorized the election and ordination of women as ruling elders and deacons in 1964 and the ordination of women as ministers in 1967.

[127] "Some Needed Amendments," *Cumberland Presbyterian*, Dec. 3, 1925, p. 2.

[128] Minutes of the General Assembly, 1927, pp. 39-40.

[129] The rumors concerned George W. Burroughs and Hugh S. McCord. Both emphatically denied the allegations (Burroughs, "A Personal Statement," p. 6; Minutes of the General Assembly, 1927, p. 32). Both were exonerated (*Ibid.*, pp. 32, 106).

[130] According to Mrs. Wolfe. Wolfe's correspondence reveals that he was very active in the effort to secure presbyterial approval of the amendment recommended in 1929. His activity may well account for the larger number of presbyteries which voted for this amendment as compared with the relative lack of interest in the amendment recommended in 1927.

[131] Minutes of the General Assembly, 1927, p. 31.

[132] *Ibid.*, 1928, pp. 132-133.

[133] *Ibid.*, 1929, p. 135.

[134] *Ibid.*, 1930, pp. 126-127.

## Chapter 22

### Pulling Through a Depression

[1] Minutes of the General Assembly, 1932, pp. 75-76. Partial payment was later made to the depositors.

[2] *Ibid.*, 1931, pp. 55-58.

[3] *Ibid.*, 1932, pp. 45-46.

[4] *Ibid.*, p. 126.

[5] *Ibid.*, 1933, pp. 45-46.

[6] *Ibid.*, 1939, pp. 45-46.

[7] *Ibid.*, 1937, p. 46.

[8] *Ibid.*, 1941, p. 37.

[9] *Ibid.*, 1940, p. 41; 1941, p. 39.

[10] *Ibid.*, 1939, pp. 44-45; 1940, p. 42.

[11] *Ibid.*, 1941, p. 144.

[12] *Ibid.*, 1931, pp. 99-100.

[13] *Ibid.*, 1932, pp. 85-96.

[14] *Ibid.*, 1934, p. 82.

[15] *Ibid.*, 1936, pp. 83-84.

[16] *Ibid.*, 1938, pp. 90-91.

[17] *Ibid.*, 1937, pp. 106-107.

[18] *Ibid.*, 1938, p. 91.

[19] *Ibid.*, 1939, p. 95.

[20] *Ibid.*, 1941, p. 96.

[21] *Ibid.*, 1931, pp. 113-114.

[22] *Ibid.*, pp. 129-130.

[23] Minutes of Texas Synod (called meeting), June 11, 1929.

[24] *Ibid.*, 1931, pp. 15-17.

[25] Minutes of the General Assembly, 1932, pp. 113-114.

[26] *Ibid.*, 1936, p. 55.

[27] *Ibid.*, 1939, pp. 63, 79.

[28] *Ibid.*, 1941, p. 25.

[29] *Ibid.*, 1934, p. 104.

[30] *Ibid.*, 1940, p. 82.

[31] *Ibid.*, 1931, p. 120.

[32] *Ibid.*, 1932, p. 50.

[33] *Ibid.*, p. 110.

[34] *Ibid.*, 1933, p. 131.

[35] *Ibid.*, 1932, p. 111.

[36] *Ibid.*, 1933, p. 121.

[37] *Ibid.*, 1934, p. 44.

[38] *Ibid.*, p. 45.

[39] *Ibid.*, 1935, pp. 116-117.

[40] *Ibid.*, 1936, pp. 44-45.

[41] *Ibid.*, p. 107.

[42] *Ibid.*, 1937, pp. 53-57.

[43] *Ibid*, pp. 156-157.

[44] *Ibid.*, 1938, pp. 49-51.

[45] *Ibid.*, p. 144.

[46] *Ibid.*, 1940, pp. 45-46; 1941, pp. 47-50.

[47] *Ibid.*, 1931, p. 86.

[48] *Cumberland Presbyterian*, Mar. 9, 1939, p. 11.

[49] *Ibid.*, Mar. 23, 1939, p. 11.

[50] Minutes of the General Assembly, 1941, p. 46.

[51] *Ibid.*, 1932, p. 115.

[52] *Ibid.*, 1938, p. 71.

[53] *Ibid.*, 1934, p. 39.

[54] Minutes of Texas Synod, 1934, pp. 14-15.

[55] *Missionary Messenger*, May 1935, pp. 15-18.

[56] *Ibid.*, December 1937, pp. 12-14.

[57] *Cumberland Presbyterian*, Aug. 10, 1939, p. 11.

[58] *Missionary Messenger*, September 1940, p. 9.

[59] Minutes of the General Assembly, 1935, pp. 95-96; 1936, p. 94.

[60] *Ibid.*, 1931, p. 110.

[61] *Ibid.*, 1935, p. 94.

[62] *Ibid.*, 1931, p. 109.

[63] *Ibid.*, 1935, p. 120.

[64] *Ibid.*, 1936, p. 41.

[65] *Ibid.*, pp. 39-40.

[66] *Ibid.*, p. 116.

[67] *Ibid.*, 1937, pp. 122-123.

[68] *Cumberland Presbyterian*, Nov. 26, 1936, p. 11.

[69] See editorial, "Who Is To Produce the S. S. Literature?" *ibid.*, Jan. 28, 1937; H. M. Guynn, "For What Did Assembly Create the New Board?" *ibid.*, Mar. 4, 1937, p. 2; C. A. Davis, "The Board of Christian Education," *ibid.*, Mar. 11, 1937, p. 2; J. P. McDonald, "Publishing House Should Produce Literature," and Lebanon Presbytery Preacher [pseud.], "More About the New Board," *ibid.*, Mar. 18, 1937, p. 2. For a different point of view see Hinkley Smartt, "Christian Education and S. S. Literature," *ibid.*, Feb. 18, 1937, p. 2; W. T. Ingram, Jr., "Facts About the Board of Christian Education," *ibid.*, Apr. 22, 1937, p. 2.

[70] *Ibid.*, May 13, 1937, p. 2.

[71] Minutes of the General Assembly, 1937, p. 123.

[72] *Ibid.*, p. 154.

[73] *Ibid.*, 1938, p. 107.

[74] *Ibid.*, pp. 107-111; 1939, pp. 110-111.

[75] *Ibid.*, 1939, pp. 112-113.

[76] *Ibid.*, 1940, p. 121.

[77] *Ibid.*, 1941, p. 114.

[78] *Ibid.*, 1938, pp. 51-52.

[79] *Ibid.*, 1941, p. 147.

[80] *Ibid.*, 1939, p. 145.

[81] *Ibid.*, 1940, pp. 131, 152.

[82] *Ibid.*, 1941, pp. 139-142.

## Chapter 23
### World War II and Postwar Ferment

[1] Minutes of the General Assembly, 1943, p. 135.

[2] *Ibid.*, 1944, p. 122.

[3] *Ibid.*, p. 89.

[4] *Ibid.*, 1943, p. 45.

[5] *Ibid.*, 1945, p. 138.

[6] *Ibid.*, 1940, p. 24.

[7] *Ibid.*, p. 31.

[8] Minutes of the General Assembly, PCUSA, 1941, p. 890.

[9] Preliminary Minutes, General Assembly of the Cumberland Presbyterian Church, 1942, pp. 28-29.

[10] *Ibid.*, pp. 31-32.

[11] *Ibid.*, pp. 29-31.

[12] *Ibid.*, pp. 27-28.

[13] Minutes of the General Assembly, 1944, p. 165.

[14] *Ibid.*, pp. 167-168.

[15] *Ibid.*, 1943, pp. 165-167.

[16] See especially the memorial from Memphis Presbytery, Preliminary Minutes, 1944, pp. 22-23.

[17] Minutes of the General Assembly, 1944, p. 149.

[18] Preliminary Minutes, 1945, p. 23.

[19] Minutes of the General Assembly, 1945, p. 155.

[20] *Ibid.*, p. 157.

[21] *Ibid.*, 1946, pp. 105-111.

[22] *Ibid.*, p. 126.

[23] *Supra*, Chap. 20.

[24] Minutes of the General Assembly, 1942, p. 45.

[25] *Ibid.*, p. 37.

[26] Preliminary Minutes, 1943, pp. 26-27.

[27] Minutes of the General Assembly, 1943, p. 152.

[28] *Ibid.*, p. 160.

[29] *Ibid.*, 1944, pp. 127-130.

[30] *Ibid.*, pp. 149-151.

[31] *Ibid.*, 1945, pp. 47-51.

[32] *Ibid.*, pp. 162-164.

[33] *Ibid.*, 1946, p. 88. Cf. *Ibid.*, 1945, p. 80.

[34] *Ibid.*, 1949, pp. 85 ff.

[35] *Ibid.*, 1944, pp. 143-144.

[36] *Ibid.*, 1948, p. 54.

[37] *Ibid.*, 1949, p. 60.

[38] *Ibid.*, 1944, pp. 57-59.

[39] *Ibid.*, p. 146.

[40] *Ibid.*, 1947, p. 58.

[41] *Ibid.*, 1948, p. 62. See also pp. 95 ff.

[42] *Ibid.*, 1945, p. 132.

[43] *Ibid.*, 1944, p. 122.

[44] *Ibid.*, 1947, p. 96.

[45] *Ibid.*, 1943, p. 135.

[46] *Ibid.*, 1944, p. 122.

[47] *Ibid.*, 1948, p. 96.

[48] *Ibid.*, 1944, pp. 131-132.

[49] *Ibid.*, p. 150.

[50] *Ibid.*, p. 140.

[51] *Ibid.*, 1945, p. 131.

[52] *Ibid.*, 1948, p. 97.

[53] *Ibid.*, 1947, p. 98.

[54] *Ibid.*, 1948, p. 97.

[55] *Ibid.*, 1949, p. 56.

[56] *Ibid.*, 1948, pp. 96-97.

[57] *Ibid.*, 1949, p. 135.

[58] *Ibid.*, 1947, p. 135.

[59] *Ibid.*, 1948, p. 50.

[60] *Ibid.*, 1949, p. 78.

[61] *Ibid.*, 1947, pp. 110 ff.

[62] *Ibid.*, 1948, p. 151.

[63] *Missionary Messenger,* July 1944, p. 27; August 1944, pp. 27-28; December 1944, p. 21.

[64] Samuel King Gam, ". . . Suffering for His Sake," *ibid.*, May 1946, pp. 9, 21.

[65] Samuel King Gam, "The New Canton Chapel," *ibid.*, September 1946, pp. 7-8.

[66] Samuel King Gam, "Canton Presbyterial Meeting," *ibid.*, November 1946, pp. 11, 32.

[67] Minutes of the General Assembly, 1947, p. 34.

[68] Samuel King Gam, "Forward in China," *Missionary Messenger,* June 1948, pp. 5-6.

[69] Minutes of the General Assembly, 1946, p. 36.

[70] "Concerning the Opening of a Mission in Africa," *Cumberland Presbyterian,* June 12, 1947, p. 10.

[71] Minutes of the General Assembly, 1947, p. 138.

[72] *Ibid.*, 1948, pp. 83-93.

[73] *Ibid.*, pp. 138-139.

[74] *Ibid.*, pp. 156-157.

[75] *Ibid.*, p. 155.

[76] *Ibid.*, p. 153.

[77] *Ibid.*, 1949, pp. 117-118.
[78] *Ibid.*, 1948, p. 158.
[79] *Ibid.*, 1949, pp. 104-113, 149.
[80] *Ibid.*, pp. 69, 161.

[81] *Ibid.*, p. 158.
[82] *Ibid.*, 1940, pp. 38-39, 149.
[83] *Ibid.*, 1941, pp. 260-261.
[84] *Ibid.*, 1949, pp. 266-270.

## Chapter 24

## Advance in the Mid-Century

[1] In 1950, approximately 42.76 per cent of the reported active membership of the Cumberland Presbyterian Church belonged to churches in Tennessee. In 1970, the approximate percentage was 44.48.

[2] U. S. Bureau of the Census, *U. S. Census of Population: 1960*, Vol. I, *Characteristics of the Population*, Part 44, Tennessee, pp. 44-12, 44-13.

[3] *Ibid.*, Introduction, p. xvii.

[4] Minutes of the General Assembly, 1950, p. 155.

[5] *Supra,* Chap. 20.

[6] Minutes of the General Assembly, 1913, pp. 170-171, 185-186.

[7] *Ibid.*, 1914, pp. 144-145; 1915, p. 41.

[8] *Ibid.*, 1926, p. 121; 1927, p. 140; 1928, p. 125; 1931, pp. 122-123; 1942, p. 164.

[9] *Ibid.*, 1950, p. 35.

[10] *Ibid.*, 1951, pp. 124-130.

[11] *Ibid.*, p. 179.

[12] *Ibid.*, 1952, p. 155.

[13] Minutes of the Synod of Missouri, 1952, p. 11.

[14] Minutes of the General Assembly, 1953, pp. 124-141.

[15] The quotation contained in Matt. 1:25 is from the Septuagint (Greek version of the Old Testament) rather than from the Hebrew text of Isa. 7:14. The editors of the RSV translated Isa. 7:14 directly from the Hebrew text.

[16] Minutes of the General Assembly, 1953, pp. 180-181.

[17] *Ibid.*, 1954, pp. 141-146. For a dissenting opinion see pp. 146-151.

[18] *Ibid.*, pp. 191-193.

[19] Minutes of Memphis Presbytery (adjourned session), Oct. 11, 1954. In 1958, Pruitt was restored by Memphis Presbytery upon the basis of satisfactory evidence of his repentance. *Ibid.*, Sept. 18, 1958, pp. 8, 10, 19, 27.

[20] Minutes of Texas Synod, 1954, pp. 51-52; 1955, pp. 8, 16-23.

[21] Minutes of the General Assembly, 1951, p. 182.

[22] *Ibid.*, 1952, p. 156.

[23] *Ibid.*, 1956, p. 188.

[24] *Cumberland Presbyterian,* July 21, 1959, pp. 3-4.

[25] Minutes of the General Assembly, 1971, p. 164.

[26] *Cumberland Presbyterian,* Sept. 15, 1970, p. 17.

[27] *Supra,* Chap. 6.

[28] The Presbyterian Appalachian Council was organized in the fall of 1964 to formulate a strategy to meet the total needs of the Appalachian region. Five presbyteries of the Cumberland Presbyterian Church were considered as lying in this region: East Tennessee, Chattanooga, Knoxville, Murfreesboro, and Robert Donnell.

[29] *Cumberland Presbyterian,* Dec. 8, 1970, pp. 6, 15.

[30] Turner N. Clinard, "The Church Losing Itself," *Cumberland Presbyterian,* Feb. 6, 1962, pp. 8-9, 12-13.

[31] Clinard indicated that the majority of letters directed to him in response to his published sermon were favorable. *Ibid.*, May 29, 1962, pp. 3, 12-13. Letters to the editor, on the other hand, were predominantly opposed to raising the question of organic union. *Ibid.*, Feb. 27, 1962, pp. 11-12; Mar. 6, 1962, pp. 11-13; May 1, 1962, p. 13.

[32] Minutes of the General Assembly, 1962, p. 181.

[33] *Ibid.*, 1964, p. 188.

[34] *Ibid.*, pp. 150-151.

[35] *Ibid.*, 1965, p. 135; 1968, p. 137.

[36] *Ibid.*, 1966, p. 162.

[37] *Ibid.*, pp. 158-163.

[38] *Ibid.*, p. 189.

[39] *Ibid.*, p. 194.

[40] *Ibid.*, p. 193.

[41] *Ibid.*, pp. 158-159, 162-163.

[42] *Ibid.*, p. 194.

[43] *Ibid.*, p. 120.

[44] *Ibid.*, p. 194.

[45] *Ibid.*, 1967, p. 213.

[46] *Ibid.*, p. 214.

[47] *Ibid.*, 1969, p. 150.

[48] In 1958 the General Assembly of the Colored Cumberland Presbyterian Church voted to drop the word "Colored" from the denomination's name, and the name "Cumberland Presbyterian Church in the United States and Liberia" was subsequently adopted. (A group of churches in Liberia had become affiliated with this denomination in 1940. By 1970 this affiliation was no longer actively in effect.) From 1960 onward, by further Assembly action, the official name was "Second Cumberland Presbyterian Church." However, some discontent with this name remained apparent at the end of the decade.

[49] Minutes of the General Assembly, 1957, pp. 130, 157; 1958, pp. 127-128.

[50] *Ibid.*, 1959, p. 177; 1960, pp. 130-131.

[51] *Ibid.*, 1963, pp. 172-173.

[52] *Ibid.*, pp. 200-201.

[53] Section 43 of Constitution, pp. 104-105 of the Confession of Faith.

[54] Minutes of the General Assembly, 1966, pp. 142-143.

[55] *Ibid.*, 1967, pp. 178, 222.

[56] *Ibid.*, 1968, p. 182.

[57] *Ibid.*, 1971, p. 53.

[58] *Ibid.*, 1950, p. 112.

[59] *Ibid.*, 1951, p. 43.

[60] *Ibid.*, 1959, p. 30.

[61] *Ibid.*, 1951, p. 161.

[62] *Ibid.*, 1957, pp. 162-163.

[63] *Ibid.*, 1961, p. 27.

[64] Eugene Warren, "A Special Summary on Capital Funds Campaigns," (Memphis: Mimeographed MS., 1968).

[65] Minutes of the General Assembly, 1967, p. 60.

[66] *Ibid.*, 1971, pp. 35-36.

[67] *Ibid.*, 1949, p. 38.

[68] *Ibid.*, 1950, p. 159.

[69] *Ibid.*, 1953, p. 82.

[70] *Ibid.*, 1971, p. 34.

[71] *Ibid.*, 1949, p. 161.

[72] *Ibid.*, 1950, p. 131.

[73] *Ibid.*, 1952, p. 101.

[74] *Ibid.*, 1971, p. 32.

[75] *Ibid.*, 1950, pp. 123-129.

[76] *Ibid.*, 1971, p. 32.

[77] Wilson Loran Waller, "Studies in Statistical Analysis of the Cumberland Presbyterian Church, 1931-1957" (unpublished B.D. thesis, Cumberland Presbyterian Theological Seminary, 1960), pp. 71-72.

[78] Yearbook of the General Assembly, 1971, pp. 70-71.

[79] Minutes of the General Assembly, 1955, pp. 159-160.

[80] *Ibid.*, 1956, pp. 152-156.

[81] *Ibid.*, pp. 196-199.

[82] *Ibid.*, 1957, pp. 33-37, 159.

[83] *Ibid.*, 1958, p. 97.

[84] *Ibid.*, p. 162.

[85] *Ibid.*, 1961, p. 187.

[86] *Ibid.*, pp. 142, 188.

[87] *Ibid.*, 1962, pp. 120-121.

[88] *Ibid.*, pp. 189-190.

[89] *Ibid.*, 1963, pp. 124-137.

[90] *Ibid.*, p. 201. The amount allotted for student housing was reallocated later, with the General Assembly's approval, to be used in the further development of the library. *Ibid.*, 1965, p. 183.

[91] *Ibid.*, 1964, p. 183.

[92] *Ibid.*, 1965, p. 32.

[93] *Ibid.*, 1968, p. 32.

[94] *Ibid.*, 1956, p. 26.

[95] *Ibid.*, p. 137.

[96] *Ibid.*, 1959, p. 89.

[97] *Ibid.*, 1964, pp. 184-185.

[98] *Ibid.*, 1965, pp. 93-94.

[99] *Ibid.*, 1969, p. 104.

[100] *Ibid.*, 1947, p. 99.

[101] *Ibid.*, 1950, p. 102.

[102] *Ibid.*, p. 157.

[103] *Ibid.*

[104] *Ibid.*, pp. 105-106.

[105] *Ibid.*, 1955, p. 47.

[106] *Ibid.*, 1957, pp. 162-163. In 1956 the name of the denominational youth convention was changed from Young People's General Assembly (YPGA) to National Assembly of Cumberland Presbyterian Youth Fellowships (NACPYF), and in 1970 the name became Cumberland Presbyterian Youth Conference (CPYC). The CPYC remained under the oversight of the Board of Publication and Christian

Education's Division of Christian Education. The Rev. Donald Carter became general secretary of this division in 1966.

[107] *Ibid.*, pp. 64-65.
[108] *Ibid.*, 1958, p. 66.
[109] *Ibid.*, 1960, pp. 188-189.
[110] *Ibid.*, 1961, pp. 80-81.
[111] *Ibid.*, p. 192.
[112] *Ibid.*, 1962, pp. 88-89.
[113] *Ibid.*, 1964, p. 64.
[114] *Ibid.*, p. 186.
[115] *Ibid.*, 1965, p. 76.
[116] *Ibid.*, pp. 153-154, 183.
[117] *Ibid.*, 1967, p. 129.
[118] *Ibid.*, p. 207.
[119] *Ibid.*, 1962, pp. 81-82, 178.
[120] *Ibid.*, 1967, pp. 65-66.
[121] *Ibid.*, 1970, p. 72.
[122] *Ibid.*, 1950, p. 51.
[123] *Ibid.*, p. 56.
[124] *Ibid.*, 1952, p. 42.
[125] *Ibid.*, 1953, p. 58.
[126] *Ibid.*, 1954, p. 33.
[127] *Ibid.*, 1955, p. 67.
[128] *Ibid.*, 1956, p. 81.
[129] *Ibid.*, 1958, pp. 53-54.
[130] *Ibid.*, 1960, p. 58.
[131] *Ibid.*, 1963, pp. 56-57.
[132] *Ibid.*, 1971, p. 50.
[133] *Ibid.*, 1967, p. 48.
[134] Yearbook of the General Assembly, 1971, p. 54.
[135] Francisco Ordóñez, *História del cristianismo evangélico en Colombia* (Cali, Colombia: Alianza Cristiana y Misionera, n.d.), pp. 229-230.
[136] Minutes of the General Assembly, 1961, p. 50.
[137] *Ibid.*, 1962, p. 54.
[138] William D. Wood, "Colombia Newsletter," *Cumberland Presbyterian,* Aug. 18, 1970, p. 4.
[139] "An Interview with Luciano Jaramillo," *Missionary Messenger,* April 1971, p. 11.
[140] Minutes of the General Assembly, 1950, p. 111.
[141] *Ibid.*, 1963, p. 48.
[142] Yearbook of the General Assembly, 1971, p. 56.
[143] Minutes of the General Assembly, 1964, p. 180.
[144] *Supra,* Chap. 14. For the study which led to this conclusion, see also Baughn, "Social Views."

[145] H. M. Miller, "Institutional Behavior," pp. 274-276.
[146] Minutes of the General Assembly, 1954, pp. 183-184.
[147] *Ibid.*, 1955, pp. 130-134.
[148] *Ibid.*, 1959, pp. 121-122.
[149] *Ibid.*, 1960, pp. 198-200.
[150] *Ibid.*, 1958, p. 161.
[151] *Ibid.*, 1953, pp. 184-185.
[152] *Ibid.*, 1954, pp. 183-184.
[153] *Ibid.*, p. 198.
[154] *Ibid.*, 1957, p. 132.
[155] *Ibid.*, 1964, pp. 154-155.
[156] *Ibid.*, 1968, p. 183.
[157] Lyle E. Schaller, *Report of the In-Depth Study of the Cumberland Presbyterian Church* (Naperville, Ill.: Center for Parish Development, 1971), p. 25. This Report is reprinted in the Minutes of the General Assembly, 1971, pp. 114-155.
[158] Minutes of the General Assembly, 1970, p. 209.
[159] *Ibid.*, p. 62; 1971, pp. 48-49.
[160] Schaller, *Report of the In-Depth Study,* p. 26.
[161] "Anti-Unionists at Dickson," *Cumberland Presbyterian,* May 23, 1907, pp. 664-665.
[162] R. L. Baskette, comp., *Centennial Sermons and Papers Delivered at the One Hundredth Anniversary of the Organization of the Cumberland Presbyterian Church Before the Eightieth General Assembly, Dickson, Tenn., May 19-24, 1910.* Nashville: Cumberland Press, 1911.
[163] "Sunday at Dickson," *Cumberland Presbyterian Banner,* May 27, 1910, p. 5.
[164] Minutes of the General Assembly, 1953, pp. 176-177.
[165] *Ibid.*, 1956, p. 140.
[166] *Ibid.*, 1957, pp. 111-112.
[167] *Ibid.*, pp. 162-163.
[168] *Ibid.*, 1960, pp. 171-172.
[169] *Ibid.*, 1966, pp. 113, 188.

Unless otherwise identified, references to General Assembly Minutes in the Notes to Part I are to those of the Presbyterian Church, and references to General Assembly Minutes in the Notes to Part II and Part III are to those of the Cumberland Presbyterian Church.

# *Bibliography*

## OFFICIAL CHURCH RECORDS

The official records of a church's courts on every level are primary sources for a history of that church. In the case of the Cumberland Presbyterian Church and the Presbyterian Church in the United States of America, from which it sprang, these records have been set down and transcribed in various physical forms and are housed in many places. Much material, particularly on the local level, remains uncollected and unexamined. Listed here are only those Minutes and other records to which reference is made in this history or which an author has designated as representative and readily accessible sources of background information. The physical form may be assumed to be printed books or booklets, unless otherwise stated, and regardless of whether the title appears in italics. The location of church records cited, and of unpublished materials listed in the next section of this bibliography, may be assumed to be the Historical Library and Archives of the Cumberland Presbyterian Church, housed at Memphis Theological Seminary, Memphis, Tennessee, or the general collection of the Seminary's Library (cited jointly as "Memphis" where citation is necessary)—again, unless otherwise noted. Other major depositories of source materials, with the citations used, are the Historical Foundation of the Presbyterian and Reformed Churches, Montreat, North Carolina ("Montreat"); the Archives of the Presbyterian Historical Society, Philadelphia, Pennsylvania ("Phila."); and the Trinity University Archives, San Antonio, Texas ("Trinity"). An asterisk indicates the location of a microfilm copy.

## RECORDS OF THE CUMBERLAND PRESBYTERIAN CHURCH

Minutes of Cumberland Presbytery, 1810-1813, MS. Phila.; *Memphis. Also in Lindsley, J. Berrien, "Sources and Sketches of Cumberland Presbyterian History," *Theological Medium and Cumberland Presbyterian Quarterly,* n. s. IX (April and October 1878), 209-224, 480-498; n. s. X (January 1879), 90-96.

Minutes of Cumberland Synod, 1813-1828, MS. Phila.; *Memphis. Also in Lindsley, "Sources and Sketches," *Theological Medium and Cumber-*

*land Presbyterian Quarterly,* n. s. X (January and October 1879), 96-105, 425-443. (Minutes for 1821 and 1826 are not on record.)

Minutes of the General Assembly of the Cumberland Presbyterian Church, 1829-1855, MS. Phila.; *Memphis. (The General Assembly did not meet in 1839 and 1844.)

———, 1847-1971.

Minutes of the Convention of the Cumberland Presbyterian Church, 1839. "Held in Nashville on the 21st, 22nd, 23rd, 24th, and 25th Days of May, 1839." Typed copy.

Preliminary Minutes of the General Assembly of the Cumberland Presbyterian Church, 1942-1945.

Yearbook of the General Assembly of the Cumberland Presbyterian Church, 1958-1971.

SYNODS AND PRESBYTERIES (SELECTED):

In this list the words "Minutes of" and the name of the denomination, which appear as part of the title of each set of records, have been omitted from each entry after the first.

Minutes of Abilene Presbytery of the Cumberland Presbyterian Church, 1895-1905. Trinity; *Memphis.

———, 1902.

. . . Alabama Presbytery, 1885-1890.

. . . Alabama Synod, 1923.

. . . Alabama-Florida-Mississippi Synod, 1965-1966, 1968, 1970.

. . . Alabama-Mississippi Synod, 1937-1941, 1943-1953, 1955-1956.

. . . Amarillo Presbytery, 1903-1907 (PCUSA after 1906). Trinity, *Memphis.

———, 1907-1913, MS.; 1947-1949, typed.

. . . Arkansas Presbytery, 1823-1846, 1865-1876, MS.; 1876-1881, 1885, 1888-1896, 1898-1902, typed copy. University of Arkansas Library, Fayetteville. Minutes for 1824-1827 are also in *Journal of the Presbyterian Historical Society,* XXXI (September 1953) 181-203.

. . . Arkansas Synod, 1884, 1886, 1889-1890, 1904, 1906, 1908, 1911-1917, 1920, 1922, 1926-1927, 1929, 1931, 1933-1969.

. . . Austin Presbytery, 1906-1920, MS.; 1921-1929, 1953-1958, typed copy.

. . . Bacon Presbytery, 1904-1907 (PCUSA after 1906). Trinity, *Memphis.

. . . Bartholomew Presbytery, 1851-1858, 1887-1937, MS.; 1938, 1951-1952, 1964-1966, 1968.

. . . Birmingham Presbytery, 1906-1907, MS.; 1908-1931, 1948-1950, 1952-1954, 1957-1965.

. . . Bosque Presbytery, 1874-1875. Trinity; *Memphis.

. . . Brazos Synod, 1849-1887. Trinity; *Memphis.

. . . Brownwood Presbytery, 1902-1912 (PCUSA after August 1906). Trinity; *Memphis.

————, 1902-1933.

. . . Buffalo Gap Presbytery, 1884-1895. Trinity; *Memphis.

. . . Burrow Presbytery, March 1907. Montreat; *Memphis.

. . . California Presbytery, 1897, 1899, 1901-1903, 1931, 1935. Montreat; *Memphis.

————, 1930-1931, 1935-1953.

. . . Cauca Valley, 1935-1940. Montreat; *Memphis.

————, 1938, 1966.

. . . Chattanooga Presbytery, 1924-1926, 1937-1965, 1967-1970.

. . . Cherokee Presbytery, 1916-1932, MS.; 1932-1935, typed copy; 1936-1938, MS.; 1956, 1961.

. . . Chickasaw Presbytery, 1890-1899, 1901-1905, 1913, 1937, 1939-1945, 1958, 1962.

. . . Chillicothe Presbytery, 1895-1899. Trinity; *Memphis.

. . . Choctaw Presbytery, 1955, 1957, 1959-1962, 1964.

. . . Clarksville Presbytery, March 1900, March 1904, 1908-1911, 1913-1915, 1917-1941, 1945-1950, 1952-1956, 1959-1962.

. . . Clinton Presbytery, 1900-1901, typed copy.

. . . Colorado Synod, 1854-1878. Montreat.

. . . Columbia Presbytery, 1903-1908, MS.; 1963-1970.

. . . Cookeville Presbytery, April 1934, April 1942, April 1950, April 1951, 1952-1957, 1959-1962.

. . . Corsicana Presbytery, November 1893, 1900-1903, 1905-1907 (PCUSA after June 1906). Trinity, *Memphis.

————, 1907-1949, MS. (some missing); 1953-1958, mimeographed.

. . . Cullman Presbytery, 1952-1954.

. . . Cumberland Presbytery, 1844-1937, MS.; 1937-1939, 1941, 1944-1945, 1947, 1952-1970.

. . . Dallas Presbytery, 1893-1911 (PCUSA after October 1906). Trinity; *Memphis.

————, 1941-1958.

. . . Dallas-Bonham Presbytery, December 1915.

. . . Decatur Presbytery, 1906-1908, MS.

. . . Denton Presbytery, 1906-1926, MS.

. . . East Tennessee Presbytery, 1891-1928, MS.; October 1970.

. . . East Tennessee Synod, 1928-1929, 1932, 1934-1943, 1945-1955, 1958-1962, 1966-1967.

. . . East Texas Presbytery, April 1959, 1961-1962, September 1963-April 1964, 1965.

. . . Elk Presbytery, 1850-1862, 1892-1899, MS.; 1900-1902; 1904-1905, MS.; 1906-1908, typed copy; 1908-1911, MS.; 1911-1962.

. . . Elyton Presbytery, 1880.

. . . Ewing Presbytery, 1926-1935, typed copy; 1936-1952, MS.; 1955-1968.

. . . Ewing-Burrow Presbytery, 1967-1970.

. . . Ewing-McLin Presbytery, 1916-1930, MS.; 1930-1938, 1950-1966, typed copy; 1967-1970.

. . . Florida Presbytery, 1934-1940, typed copy.

. . . Foster Presbytery, 1903, 1917-1960, MS.; 1960-1965, typed copy; 1966-1970.

. . . Gadsden Presbytery, 1948-1960, 1962-1965, 1967-1968.

. . . Greenville Presbytery, 1872-1907 (PCUSA after June 1906). Trinity; *Memphis.

. . . Greer Presbytery, 1955-1957, fall 1958, fall 1961.

. . . Gregory Presbytery, 1883-1943, MS.

. . . Guadalupe Presbytery, 1867-1888. Trinity; *Memphis.

. . . Hernando Synod, 1855-1861, 1865, 1867, 1869-1870, MS.; 1868.

. . . Hiwassee Presbytery, 1856-1880, 1882-1890.

. . . Hopewell Presbytery, 1825-1880, MS.; March 1891, March 1910, September 1916, September 1921, 1924-1970 (some issues missing).

. . . Illinois Presbytery, 1950-1963, 1965.

. . . Illinois Synod, 1927-1963.

. . . Indiana Presbytery, March 1913, September 1915, September 1917, September 1918. Montreat; *Memphis.

————, fall 1930, fall 1931, spring 1937, fall 1941, fall 1943, spring 1945, 1946-1950, fall 1951-1962, 1964-1968, fall 1970.

. . . Indiana Synod, 1861, 1897, 1901. Montreat; *Memphis.

. . . Indianola Synod, 1937-1940, 1942, 1944.

. . . John Buchanan Presbytery, 1891-1899, MS.

. . . Kentucky Synod, 1899, 1905, 1907, 1911-1956, 1961-1970.

. . . King Presbytery, 1843-1844, MS.

. . . Kirkpatrick Presbytery, 1889-1890. Trinity; *Memphis.

. . . Knoxville Presbytery, 1873-1927, MS.; 1936-1968.

. . . LaCrosse Presbytery, 1880, 1882-1887, MS.

. . . Lebanon Presbytery, October 1884, March 1900, March 1909. Montreat; *Memphis.

————, 1930-1933, 1935-1936, 1938, 1940-1941, 1943-1958, 1961.

. . . Lexington Presbytery, 1932, 1937-1945.

. . . Lincoln Presbytery, 1901-1910, MS.

. . . Lincoln-Decatur Presbytery, 1911-1962, MS.

. . Little River Presbytery, fall 1883, spring 1895.

. . . Little Rock Presbytery, 1906-1914, MS.

. . . Little Rock-Burrow Presbytery, 1914-1929, MS.; 1954-1967, typed copy.

. . . Logan Presbytery, 1813-1845, typed copy; 1938-1940, fall 1942, fall 1943, 1945, 1949-1964, 1966-1967, 1969-1970.

. . . Louisiana Presbytery, 1905-1918, 1921-1968, MS.

. . . Lubbock Presbytery, 1950-1954.

. . . McAdow Presbytery, 1930-1958.

. . . McGee Presbytery, 1820-1878, typed copy; 1880-1935.

. . . McGee-New Lebanon Presbytery, 1941-1942, 1945-1949, 1951-1955, 1961-1963.

. . . McGready Presbytery, 1951-1957, 1959-1969.

. . . McMinnville Presbytery, fall 1945, spring 1954.

. . . Madison Presbytery, September 1872. Montreat; *Memphis.

————, fall 1927, 1931-1970.

. . . Marshall Presbytery, November 1892, June 1893, October 1895, March 1896, December 1896, July 1898, April 1899, 1900-1902, October 1908, October 1909, September 1915, September 1916. Montreat; *Memphis.

. . . Marshall-Greenville Presbytery, September 1926. Montreat; *Memphis.

. . . Mayfield Presbytery, 1882-1902, MS.; 1902-1970.

. . . Memphis Presbytery, 1872-February 1873. Montreat; *Memphis.

————, 1897-1903, April 1927, September 1928, 1943-1952, 1961-1968.

. . . Miami Presbytery, 1943-1949.

. . . Middle Tennessee Synod, 1884-1885. Montreat; *Memphis.

. . . Mississippi Presbytery, fall 1964.

. . . Mississippi Synod, 1856, 1894-1901, MS.; 1902-1905.

. . . Missouri Synod, 1829 (part), 1830. Montreat; *Memphis.

————, 1894-1901, 1910-1911, 1917-1938, 1940-1970.

. . . Morrilton Presbytery, 1902-1935, MS.

. . . Mound Prairie Presbytery, 1842-1903. Montreat.

————, 1906-1910. Phila.

————, 1903-1919, MS.; 1931-1970, typed copy.

. . . Murfreesboro Presbytery, 1963-spring 1965, fall 1966-1967.

. . . Nashville Presbytery, 1961, fall 1962-1965.

. . . New Hope Presbytery, 1864-1949, MS.; 1950-1970 (some mimeographed).

. . . New Lebanon Presbytery, spring 1873.

. . . Nolin Presbytery, 1873-1897, MS.

. . . North Central Synod, 1964-1968.

. . . North Central Texas Presbytery, 1959-1970.

. . . Northeast Oklahoma Presbytery, spring 1962.

. . . Obion Presbytery, 1833, 1885, typed copy; September 1892-1970 (some issues missing).

. . . Ohio Presbytery, 1949-1953.

. . . Oklahoma Presbytery, 1899-1922, MS.

. . . Oklahoma Synod, 1941-1943, 1945-1954, 1956-1963, 1965-1968.

. . . Oklahoma Western Presbytery, 1962-1963, fall 1967, 1969, fall 1970.

. . . Oregon Synod, 1897. Montreat; *Memphis.

. . . Ouachita Presbytery, 1849-1894, MS.

. . . Owensboro Presbytery, spring 1898, fall 1899, spring 1907, spring 1911, fall 1914-spring 1917, spring 1920, 1921-1924, 1928-1930, 1932-1940, fall 1944-1948, 1951, 1961-1967.

. . . Oxford Presbytery, fall 1901, fall 1904.

. . . Ozark Presbytery, fall 1893, 1942-1950, 1952, 1961-1963, 1966.

. . . Pacific Presbytery, October 1873-1874, September 1875-1876, September 1879. Montreat; *Memphis.

————, September 1924, September 1929.

. . . Pacific Synod, 1873, 1880, 1882-1884, 1887, 1889-1890, 1892-1900, 1902, 1904, 1906-1910, 1914-1923.

. . . Parsons Presbytery, fall 1885, fall 1887.

. . . Pease River Presbytery, 1890-1902. Trinity; *Memphis.

. . . Platte Presbytery, 1917, 1923, 1925-1927, 1930-1934, 1937, 1945.

. . . Platte-Lexington Presbytery, 1945-1948, 1951, 1953-1963, 1965-1966, 1968, 1970.

. . . Porter Presbytery, 1891-1955, typed; 1955-1971, mimeographed.

. . . Princeton Presbytery, fall 1888, spring 1897-1898, 1900-1970.

. . . Red Oak Presbytery, 1875 (called sessions), 1896-1902.

. . . Red River Presbytery, 1842-1873. Trinity; *Memphis.

. . . Richland Presbytery, 1835-1852, MS.; 1853-April 1856. Montreat; *Memphis.

————, 1863-1875, 1889-1897, 1909-1925, MS.; 1933-1962, typed copy.

. . . Robert Donnell Presbytery, April 1890, September 1892-April 1893, 1906-1911, 1918-1927, September 1952-1970.

. . . Sacramento Presbytery, 1890, 1895, 1898 (special session), 1899-1900. Montreat; *Memphis.

. . . Salt River Presbytery, August 1900, March-April 1903. Montreat, *Memphis.

. . . San Antonio Presbytery, 1900-1910 (PCUSA after June 1906). Trinity; *Memphis.

. . . San Saba Presbytery, 1937-1942, MS.

. . . Scioto Presbytery, 1948-1949.

. . . Searcy Presbytery, 1872-1893. *Memphis.

. . . South Texas Presbytery, 1959-1966, 1968-1970.

. . . Springfield Presbytery, 1947-spring 1950, fall 1951, 1953, 1957-1970 (some issues missing).

. . . Sweetwater Presbytery, fall 1907, fall 1908.

. . . Tehuacana Presbytery, April 1901. Montreat; *Memphis.

————, fall 1901.

. . . Tennessee Presbytery, September 1869. Montreat; *Memphis.

————, 1886-1891, MS.

. . . Tennessee Synod, 1888-1903. Montreat; *Memphis.

————, 1888, 1891, 1893-1900, 1902; 1913, MS.; 1916-1917; 1919, MS.; 1920-1962, 1964, 1966-1968.

. . . Texas Presbytery, 1837-1907 (PCUSA after July 1906). Phila.; *Memphis.

————, 1905; 1906-1917, MS.

. . . Texas Synod, 1869-1888. Trinity; *Memphis.

————, printed: 1888, 1890-1897, 1899-1910, 1913, 1916, 1920, 1922-1970; typed copy: 1911-1912, March 1914 (called meeting), 1915, December 1917 (called meeting), 1918-1919, 1921, June 1929 (called meeting), July 1932 (called meeting).

. . . Tulare Presbytery, spring 1900.

. . . Tulsa-Muskogee Presbytery, fall 1945.

. . . Waco Presbytery, 1875-1907 (PCUSA after June 1906). Trinity; *Memphis.

. . . Washington Presbytery, fall 1891.

. . . Weatherford Presbytery, 1906-1916, MS.; 1917-1926, typed.

. . . West Prairie Presbytery, fall 1891, winter 1900.

————, March 1915. Montreat; *Memphis.

. . . West Tennessee Synod, 1905-1970.

. . . West Texas and New Mexico Synod, 1915-1918.

. . . White River Presbytery, 1849-1943, typed copy.

Local churches (selected):

Microfilm copies of the records listed are in the Memphis Theological Seminary Library.

Session Records, First Cumberland Presbyterian Church, Austin, Texas,

1869-1940 (including records of the Cumberland Presbyterian Church, U. S. A., 1906-1909).

Session Records, Fort Worth Cumberland Presbyterian Church (Saint Mark Church after 1955), Fort Worth, Texas, 1908-1966.

Session Records, Shiloh Cumberland Presbyterian Church, Ellis County, Texas, 1847-1958.

## RECORDS OF THE PRESBYTERIAN CHURCH

*Records of the Presbyterian Church in the United States of America: Embracing the Minutes of the Presbytery of Philadelphia, from A.D. 1706 to 1716: Minutes of the Synod of Philadelphia, from A.D. 1717 to 1758: Minutes of the Synod of New York, from A.D. 1745 to 1758: Minutes of the Synod of Philadelphia and New York, from 1758 to 1788.* Philadelphia: Presbyterian Board of Publication, 1841.

*Minutes of the General Assembly of the Presbyterian Church from Its Organization: A.D. 1787 to 1820, Inclusive.* Philadelphia: Presbyterian Board of Publication, 1847.

*Minutes of the General Assembly, from A.D. 1821 to A.D. 1835, Inclusive.* Philadelphia: Presbyterian Board of Publication, n.d.

*Minutes of the General Assembly of the Presbyterian Church in the United States of America, 1901-1910,* 1941.

SYNODS AND PRESBYTERIES (SELECTED):

*Minutes of the "Original" Cumberland Presbytery, 1802-1806 of the Presbyterian Church, U. S. A.* Louisville: Office of the Stated Clerk, 1906.

*Minutes of the Presbytery of Redstone of the Presbyterian Church, from September 1781 to December 1831.* Cincinnati, 1878.

Minutes of the Synod of Kentucky, 1802-1829, MS. Montreat.

Minutes of the Synod of New Jersey, 1906. Montreat.

Minutes of Transylvania Presbytery, 1786-1829, MS. Montreat.

Minutes of West Tennessee Presbytery, 1810-1863, typed copy. Montreat.

Records of the Presbytery of New Castle upon Delaware, published in *Journal of the Department of History (The Presbyterian Historical Society) of the Presbyterian Church in the U. S. A.,* XIV (September, December 1931) 239-308, 377-384; XV (June, September, December 1932) 73-120, 159-168, 174-207.

## UNPUBLISHED MATERIALS

Alexander, Don Charles. "A Historical Study of the Cumberland Presbyterian Church in Upper East Tennessee." B. D. thesis, Cumberland Presbyterian Theological Seminary, 1958.

Baughn, Milton L. "Social Views Reflected in Official Publications of the Cumberland Presbyterian Church, 1875-1900." Ph. D. dissertation, Vanderbilt University, 1954.

Blain, Frank Thomas. "A History of the Existing Churches of Illinois Presbytery of the Cumberland Presbyterian Church." B. D. thesis, Cumberland Presbyterian Theological Seminary, 1957.

Brown, F. A. Correspondence, 1911-1915.

Campbell, Thomas Dishman. "The Cumberland Presbyterian Church and the Negro." B. D. thesis, Cumberland Presbyterian Theological Seminary, 1964. (Published in part as *Brothers of the Faith*.)

————. "The Upward Call: Memphis Theological Seminary, 1908-1968." Th. M. thesis, Brite Divinity School, Texas Christian University, 1969.

Chesnut, Franklin G. "Christian Education in the Cumberland Presbyterian Church: A Study of Its Development, 1860-1942." B. D. thesis, Cumberland Presbyterian Theological Seminary, 1943.

Douglas, Hiram Arnett, comp. "The Story Is Told: Rev. Hiram Douglas, D. D.; A Biographical Sketch." Mimeographed. Minneapolis, 1940.

Durham, J. L. "A Short Account of the Origin of the Reformed Cumberland Presbyterian Church." Manuscript, n. p., n. d. Speer Library, Princeton Theological Seminary, Princeton, N. J.; photocopy at Memphis.

Esch, Robert E. "Actions Taken by the Cumberland Presbyterian Church on Social Problems, 1906-1940." B. D. thesis, Cumberland Presbyterian Theological Seminary, 1947.

Evans, Henry Bascom. "History of the Organization and Administration of Cumberland Presbyterian Colleges." Ph. D. dissertation, George Peabody College for Teachers, 1943.

Forester, J. C. "A History of the Cumberland Presbyterian Church in Arkansas from Its Beginning to the Consolidation of Synods in 1884 as Revealed by the Available Minutes of the Presbyteries, Synods, and the General Assembly." B. D. thesis, Cumberland Presbyterian Theological Seminary, 1952.

Forester, Robert G. "A History of the Development of Youth Camp Work in the Cumberland Presbyterian Church." B. D. thesis, Cumberland Presbyterian Theological Seminary, 1952.

Harvey, Ollie Newsome. "A History of the Existing Churches of Clarksville

Presbytery of the Cumberland Presbyterian Church." B. D. thesis, Cumberland Presbyterian Theological Seminary, 1956.

Hendershot, Charles A. "The History of the Cumberland Presbyterian Church in Oklahoma Synod." B. D. thesis, Cumberland Presbyterian Theological Seminary, 1952.

Hom, Paul. "Historical Survey of the First Chinese Cumberland Presbyterian Church." Term paper, Cumberland Presbyterian Theological Seminary, 1961.

Hughs, Eva Wollard. "History of the Cumberland Presbyterian Church": Book I, "North, Central, Southeast Missouri"; Book II, "Within Southwest Missouri." Mimeographed, n. p., n. d.

Little, C. R. "The Coming of Presbyterianism to Tennessee." Typed manuscript; Microfilm R-46, Joint University Libraries, Nashville, Tennessee.

McCaskey, Charles. "A History of the Cumberland Presbyterian Church in Arkansas from the Consolidation of Synods in 1884 to the Organic Union of the Cumberland Presbyterian Church and the Presbyterian Church, U. S. A., in 1906." B. D. thesis, Memphis Theological Seminary, 1966.

McCullah, Parks. "History of the Cumberland Presbyterian Church in Arkansas, White County, and Searcy." Mimeographed, n. p., 1964.

Miller, Haskell M. "Institutional Behavior of the Cumberland Presbyterian Church, an American Protestant Religious Denomination." Ph. D. dissertation, New York University, 1940.

Mize, Mrs. J. L., and McCroskey, Annie. "History of Knoxville Presbyterial Missionary Society of the Cumberland Presbyterian Church." Manuscript, n. p., n. d.

Norman, Maury A. "A History of the Churches of Obion Presbytery, Cumberland Presbyterian Church." B. D. thesis, Cumberland Presbyterian Theological Seminary, 1955.

Nugent, S. Ellis. "A History of the Cumberland Presbyterian Church, 1895-1905." B. D. thesis, Cumberland Presbyterian Theological Seminary, 1958.

Reeves, Sara Belle. "The Origin of the Cumberland Presbyterian Church." M. A. thesis, George Peabody College for Teachers, 1929.

Salisbury, A. D., Jr. "A History of the Churches of Owensboro Presbytery." B. D. thesis, Cumberland Presbyterian Theological Seminary, 1947.

"A Series of Letters Containing a Reply to a Pastoral Letter of the West Tennessee Presbytery: To Which Is Added an Address to the Congregations &c. under the Care of the Cumberland Presbytery." Typed manuscript copy. Montreat.

Slaton, Sidney. "The History of the Cumberland Presbyterian Church in

Louisiana." B. D. thesis, Cumberland Presbyterian Theological Seminary, 1943.

Smartt, Charles Hinkley, and Smith, Archie D. "The First One Hundred Years of the History of Bethel College." B. D. thesis, Cumberland Presbyterian Theological Seminary, 1944.

Waller, Wilson Loran. "Cumberland Presbyterian Evangelicalism Before and After Default in Ecumenical Union in 1906." D. Div. thesis, Vanderbilt University Divinity School, 1971.

_____. "Studies in Statistical Analysis of the Cumberland Presbyterian Church, 1931-1957." B. D. thesis, Cumberland Presbyterian Theological Seminary, 1960.

Warren, Eugene. "A Special Summary on Capital Funds Campaigns." Mimeographed. [Memphis], 1968.

Weeks, Virgil T. "A History of the Churches of Mayfield Presbytery." B. D. thesis, Cumberland Presbyterian Theological Seminary, 1943.

Wiman, David Wayne. "A History of the Colored Cumberland Presbyterian Church." B. D. thesis, Cumberland Presbyterian Theological Seminary, 1936.

Wolfe, B. O. Correspondence.

## CHURCH PERIODICALS

Available issues of publications listed are at Memphis, in the original or on microfilm, unless otherwise noted.

*Banner of Peace,* 1843-1853.

*Christian Work and Evangelist,* Dec. 3, 1904. Speer Library, Princeton Theological Seminary, Princeton, New Jersey.

*Conservative Cumberland Presbyterian,* June 1954, February 1955. (A continuation of *Cumberland Presbyterian Conservatives.*)

*Cumberland Banner,* April-September 1904.

*Cumberland Presbyterian,* 1874-1971.

*Cumberland Presbyterian Banner,* 1904-1919.

*Cumberland Presbyterian Conservatives,* July 1953-April 1954. (Sponsored by the Cumberland Presbyterian Conservatives Fellowship.)

*Cumberland Presbyterian Missionary,* 1854-1855.

*Herald and Presbyter,* 1904-1905. Montreat.

*Interior,* June 2, 1904, July 28, 1904. Montreat.

*Jubilee Journal,* 1930.

*Missionary Messenger,* 1931-1971.

*Missionary Record,* 1889-1907.

*Presbyterian,* 1904-1907. Phila.

*Presbyterian Banner,* Nov. 10, 1904. Montreat.
*St. Louis Observer,* 1882-1899.

## ARTICLES

Agnew, Benjamin L. "When Was the First Presbytery of the Presbyterian Church in the United States of America Organized?" *Journal of the Presbyterian Historical Society,* III (March 1905), 9-24.

Anderson, T. C. "History of Cumberland University," *Theological Medium and Cumberland Presbyterian Quarterly,* III (December 1858), 190-197.

Badger, Joseph. "Extract of a Letter from Joseph Badger, 19 July 1803," *Connecticut Evangelical Magazine,* III (1803-1804), 113-118.

Bass, John M. "Rev. Thomas Craighead," *American Historical Magazine,* VII (January 1901), 88-96.

Beard, Richard. "The Cumberland Presbyterian Church During the Last Half Century," *Theological Medium and Cumberland Presbyterian Quarterly,* n. s. I (October 1870), 486-504.

Bennett, D. M. "Life and Work of Reverend John McMillan," *Journal of the Department of History (The Presbyterian Historical Society) of the Presbyterian Church in the U. S. A.,* XV (September 1932), 133-158.

[Bird, Milton]. "Education," *Theological Medium and Cumberland Presbyterian Review,* IV (January 1860), 129-161.

Bird, Milton. "The Minister a Workman," *Theological Medium and Cumberland Presbyterian Review,* n. s. III (September 1858), 28-59.

————. "Saving Faith," *Theological Medium,* I (February 1846), 142-143.

Black, F. G. "Sermon at the Opening of Miami Presbytery, March 1850," *Theological Medium,* V (June 1850), 225-235.

Black, William H. "The New Theology," *Cumberland Presbyterian Quarterly Review,* II (October 1881), 424-435.

Burney, S. G. "Rev. John Miller and Some of His Books," *Cumberland Presbyterian Review,* II (October 1890), 415-429.

Burrow, Reuben. "A Lecture on the Doctrine of Faith," *Theological Medium,* I (March 1846), 145-161.

Bushnell, D. E. "Our Work at the Front," *Cumberland Presbyterian Quarterly,* I (July 1880), 333-353.

Danley, W. S. "Ministerial Education," *Cumberland Presbyterian Quarterly,* II (July 1890), 257-269.

Darnell, W. H. "The Christian Rule Governing Popular Amusements," *Theological Medium and Cumberland Presbyterian Quarterly,* n. s. III (January 1872), 55-62.

"Demand for the Home Missionary in Iowa," *Theological Medium,* II (October 1847), 569-570.

Dodd, Cephas. "Memoir of Dr. T. Dod," *Presbyterian Magazine,* IV (August-September 1854), 368-378, 415-425.

Drury, Clifford M. "Beginnings of the Synod of Oregon," *Journal of the Presbyterian Historical Society,* XXXVII (December 1959), 208-231.

————. "Presbyterian Beginnings in New England and the Middle Colonies," *Journal of the Presbyterian Historical Society,* XXXIV (March 1956), 19-35.

Ewing, Finis. "On Supporting the Gospel," *Cumberland Magazine,* no. 1 (August, September, October 1836), 7-14.

————. "Substance of a Discourse on National Affairs," *Theological Medium,* VI (December 1850), 40-64.

Finney, William P. "The Period of the Isolated Congregations and General Presbytery, 1614-1716," *Journal of the Department of History (The Presbyterian Historical Society) of the Presbyterian Church in the U. S. A.,* XV (March 1932), 8-17.

Folmsbee, Stanley J. "Blount College and East Tennessee College, 1794-1840," *East Tennessee Historical Society Publications,* No. 17 (1945), 22-50.

Funk, Henry D. "The Influence of the Presbyterian Church in Early American History," *Journal of the Presbyterian Historical Society,* XII (April 1924), 32-33.

Gillett, Ezra H. "The Men and Times of the Reunion of 1758," *American Presbyterian and Theological Review,* VI (July 1868), 414-443.

Harkness, R. E. E. "Roger Williams—Prophet of Tomorrow," *Journal of Religion,* XV (October 1935), 400-425.

Hodge, Charles. "Dr. Gillett and Liberal Presbyterianism," *Princeton Review,* XL (October 1868), 608-632.

Howard, J. M. "The New Confession," *Cumberland Presbyterian* (May 17, 1883), 4.

Hoyer, Theodore. "The Historical Background of the Westminster Assembly," *Concordia Theological Monthly,* XVIII (August 1947), 572-591.

Johnson, Guion G. "The Camp Meeting in Ante-Bellum North Carolina," *North Carolina Historical Review,* X (April 1933), 95-100.

————. "Revival Movements in Ante-Bellum North Carolina, 1856-1861," *North Carolina Historical Review,* X (January 1933), 21-43.

Kennedy, Charles M. "The Presbyterian Church on the Wisconsin Frontier," *Journal of the Department of History (The Presbyterian Historical Society) of the Presbyterian Church in the U. S. A.,* XVIII (March 1939), 186-210.

Lay, Henry C. "The Revival System: Its Good and Evil," *Church Review,* VII (October 1854), 356-375.

Lindsley, J. Berrien. "Sources and Sketches of Cumberland Presbyterian History," *Theological Medium and Cumberland Presbyterian Quarterly,* n. s. VII (January-April 1876), 1-36, 129-172.

Lowry, David. "On the Importance of a Well Trained Ministry," *Theological Medium,* IV (March 1849), 148-154.

McCook, Henry C. "The Several Editions of the Constitution of the Cumberland Presbyterian Church," *Journal of the Presbyterian Historical Society,* I (December 1901), 209-211.

McGready, James. "A Short Narrative of the Revival of Religion in Logan County, in the State of Kentucky, and the Adjacent Settlements in the State of Tennessee, from May 1797, until September 1800," *New York Missionary Magazine, and Repository of Religious Intelligence,* IV (1803), 154.

Miller, A. B. "Historical Sketch of Waynesburg College, Waynesburg, Pennsylvania," No. XII of J. Berrien Lindsley, "Sources and Sketches of Cumberland Presbyterian History," *Theological Medium and Cumberland Presbyterian Quarterly,* n. s. IX (January 1878), 63-117.

Miller, Perry. "The Half-Way Covenant," *New England Quarterly,* VI (1933), 676-715.

———. "Solomon Stoddard, 1643-1729," *Harvard Theological Review,* XXXIV (October 1941), 298.

Mitchell, William. "An Enquiry into the Utility of Modern Evangelists and Their Measures," *Literary and Theological Review,* II (September 1835), 494-507.

Morgan, Edmund. "The Case Against Anne Hutchinson," *New England Quarterly,* X (December 1937), 635-649.

Morgan, John. "History of the Cumberland Presbyterian Church in Western Pennsylvania and Ohio," *Christian Messenger,* I (March-April 1873), 88-91, 122-125. Reprinted from *Union Evangelist* (1840).

Pears, Thomas C. "First Formal History of Transylvania Presbytery," *Journal of the Presbyterian Historical Society,* XIX (December 1940), 147-148.

———. "The Foundations of Our Western Zion," *Journal of the Department of History (The Presbyterian Historical Society) of the Presbyterian Church in the U. S. A.,* XVI (December 1934), 145-162.

Pond, Edwin P. "Evangelists," *New Englander,* II (April 1844), 297-303.

Roach, J. J. A. "Cumberland Presbyterianism in Texas," *Cumberland Presbyterian Review,* III (July 1882), 276-284.

"The Scots in East New Jersey," *Proceedings of the New Jersey Historical Society,* XV (1930).

Smith, Roy L. "The Influence of Cumberland Presbyterianism on Abraham

Lincoln," *Cumberland Presbyterian* (July 1, 1952). Originally published as "Lincoln's Alma Mater," *Christian Herald* (February 1952).

Sommerville, C. W. "Samuel Doak," *Union Seminary Review*, XL (1928-1929), 193-205.

Templeton, A. "Connection between Learning and Religion," *Theological Medium and Quarterly Review*, n. s. II (January 1855), 113-127.

## COURT DECISIONS

These opinions, separately printed, are at Memphis in a collection of opinions and briefs from court actions related to the attempted union of denominations in 1906.

William Bentle, Sr., *et al.* v. Jerome Ulay *et al.*, appealed from the Vanderburgh Superior Court. Opinion of the Appellate Court of Indiana, by Chief Justice Frank S. Roby, delivered at Indianapolis, n. d.

Charles A. Boyles *et al.*, Plaintiffs, Respondents v. J. L. Roberts *et al.*, Defendants, Appellants. Opinion of the Supreme Court of Missouri (in Banc), by Judge W. W. Graves, delivered at Jefferson City, June 8, 1909. Printed at Jackson, Tenn., by McCowat-Mercer Printing Co.

William Clark *et al.*, Appellants, v. G. W. Brown *et al.*, Appellees, appealed from the District Court of Marion County. Opinion of the Court of Civil Appeals for the Sixth Supreme Judicial District of Texas, by Judge W. Hodges, delivered at Texarkana, Feb. 27, 1908.

First Cumberland Presbyterian Church, of Jackson, Tenn., W. E. Dunaway *et al.*, Complainants, v. John Y. Keith, S. A. Mitchell *et al.*, Defendants. Opinion of Chancellor E. L. Bullock, in the Chancery Court of Madison County, Tennessee, delivered at Jackson, Feb. 5, 1908. Printed at Jackson by McCowat-Mercer Printing Co.

Joe H. Fussell *et al.*, Appellants v. J. B. Hail *et al.*, Appellees, appealed from the Circuit Court at Macon. Opinion of the Supreme Court of Illinois, delivered at Springfield, Feb. 20, 1908.

Ira Landrith *et al.*, Complainants, v. J. L. Hudgins *et al.*, Defendants, appealed from the Chancery Court of Lincoln County. Opinion of the Supreme Court of Tennessee, by Judge M. M. Neil, delivered at Nashville, Apr. 3, 1909. Printed at Jackson, Tenn., by McCowat-Mercer Printing Co.

George H. Mack *et al.* Plaintiffs in Error, v. R. R. Kime *et al.*, Defendants in Error. Opinion of the Supreme Court of Georgia, delivered at Atlanta, Aug. 19, 1907.

James W. Ramsey *et al.*, Appellants, v. Joseph Hicks *et al.*, Appellees, appealed from Vanderburgh Superior Court. Opinion of the Appellate

Court of Indiana, by Judge Frank S. Roby, delivered at Indianapolis, Apr. 23, 1909. Printed at Jackson, Tenn., by McCowat-Mercer Printing Co.

William Westfall *et al.,* Plaintiffs, v. James A. Myers *et al.,* Defendants. Opinion of Judge G. W. Buff, in the Knox County Court, delivered at Vincennes, Ind., June 15, 1908. Printed at Trenton, Tenn., by the *Herald-Democrat.*

## BOOKS AND PAMPHLETS

*Action of Indiana Presbytery on Union with the Presbyterian Church, Adopted by Unanimous Vote of the Presbytery in Session at Newburgh, Ind., Sept. 11, 1902.* N. p.: printed by order of the presbytery.

Alexander, Archibald. *Biographical Sketches of the Founders and Principal Alumni of the Log College, Together with an Account of the Revival of Religion under Their Ministry.* Philadelphia: Presbyterian Board of Publication, 1851.

Alexander, Gross, *et al. A History of the Methodist Church, South, the United Presbyterian Church, the Cumberland Presbyterian Church, and the Presbyterian Church, South, in the United States.* Vol. XI of *The American Church History Series,* ed. Philip Schaff, *et al.* New York: Christian Literature Co., 1894.

Alexander, John Brevard. *Biographical Sketches of the Hopewell Section and Reminiscences of the Pioneers.* Charlotte, N. C.: Observer Printing and Publishing House, 1897.

Anderson, T. C. *Life of Rev. George Donnell: First Pastor of the Church in Lebanon; with a Sketch of the Scotch-Irish Race.* Nashville: privately printed, 1858.

Asbury, Francis. *The Journal of Rev. Francis Asbury.* New York: Lane & Scott, 1852.

Bacon, Leonard W. *A History of American Christianity.* New York: Charles Scribner's Sons, 1901.

Baird, Samuel J. *A History of the New School.* Philadelphia: Claxton, Remsen & Haffelfinger, 1868.

————, ed. *A Collection of the Acts and Deliverances, and Testimonies of the Supreme Judicatory of the Presbyterian Church from Its Origin in America to the Present Time, with Notes and Documents, Explanatory and Historical: Constituting a Complete Illustration of Her Polity, Faith, and History.* Philadelphia: Presbyterian Board of Publication, 1856.

Baskette, R. L. *History of Publication of the Cumberland Presbyterian Church.* Nashville: Cumberland Press, 1910.

Bates, Ernest S. *American Faith*. New York: W. W. Norton and Co., 1940.

Beard, Richard. *Brief Biographical Sketches of Some of the Early Ministers of the Cumberland Presbyterian Church*. Nashville: published for the author by Southern Methodist Publishing House, 1867.

_____. *Brief Biographical Sketches of Some of the Early Ministers of the Cumberland Presbyterian Church*. Second Series. Nashville: Cumberland Presbyterian Board of Publication, 1874.

_____. *Lectures on Theology*. Vol. I. Nashville: Committee on Publication, 1860. Vols. II, III. Nashville: Board of Publication of the Cumberland Presbyterian Church, 1864-1870.

Beardsley, Frank. *A History of American Revivals*. New York: American Tract Society, 1904.

Beatty, Charles. *Journal of a Two-Months Tour, with a View of Promoting Religion among the Frontier Inhabitants of Pennsylvania*. London: William Davenhill, 1768.

Beveridge, Albert J. *Abraham Lincoln, 1809-1858*. Boston: Houghton Mifflin Co., 1928.

Billington, Ray A. *Westward Expansion: A History of the American Frontier*. New York: Macmillan Co., 1950.

Bird, Milton. *The Doctrine of Grace as Revealed in the Gospel, or Medium Theology in Familiar Lectures, Being a Revised and Enlarged Edition of "Error Unmasked," First Published at Pittsburg, Pa., in 1844, in Reply to Dr. A. G. Fairchild's "Great Supper."* Louisville: J. F. Brennan, 1856.

_____. *The Life of Rev. Alexander Chapman*. Nashville: published for the author by W. E. Dunaway, Agent, Cumberland Presbyterian Board of Publication, 1872.

Bishop, Robert H. *An Outline of the History of the Church in the State of Kentucky, during a Period of Forty Years: Containing the Memoirs of Rev. David Rice*. Lexington, Ky.: Thomas T. Skillman, 1824.

Blake, Thaddeus C. *The Old Log House*. Nashville: Cumberland Presbyterian Publishing House, 1897.

Bodo, John R. *The Protestant Clergy and Public Issues, 1812-1848*. Princeton, N. J.: Princeton University Press, 1954.

Bone, Winstead Paine. *A History of Cumberland University, 1842-1935*. Lebanon, Tenn.: published by the author, 1935.

Brackenridge, R. Douglas. *Voice in the Wilderness: A History of the Cumberland Presbyterian Church in Texas*. San Antonio: Trinity University Press, 1968.

Brauer, Jerald C. *Protestantism in America*. Philadelphia: Westminster Press, 1953.

*A Brief History of the Rise, Progress and Termination of the Synod of Kentucky, Relative to the Late Cumberland Presbytery; In Which Is Brought to View a Brief Account of the Origin and Present Standing of the People Usually Denominated Cumberland Presbyterians.* Lexington, Ky.: Thomas T. Skillman, 1823.

Briggs, Charles A. *American Presbyterianism, Its Origins and Early History, Together with an Appendix of Letters and Documents, Many of Which Have Been Recently Discovered.* New York: Charles Scribner's Sons, 1885.

Buck, Charles, ed. *A Theological Dictionary Containing Definitions of All Religious Terms; A Comprehensive View of Every Article in the System of Divinity, and Impartial Account of All the Principal Denominations Which Have Subsisted in the Religious World from the Birth of Christ to the Present Days; Together with an Accurate Statement of the Most Remarkable Transactions and Events Recorded in Ecclesiastical History.* 3rd ed. Philadelphia: W. W. Woodward, 1814.

Bucke, Emory Stevens, ed. *The History of American Methodism.* Vol. II. New York: Abingdon Press, 1964.

Burney, S. G. *Anthropology: A Discussion Chiefly of the Problem of Evil; of Man as a Sinner; the Relation of the First Man and His Posterity, Sin and Physical Evil, etc.* Nashville: Cumberland Presbyterian Publishing House, 1894.

————. *Studies in Moral Science.* Nashville: Cumberland Presbyterian Publishing House, 1890.

————. *Studies in Psychology.* Nashville: Cumberland Presbyterian Publishing House, 1890.

Burrow, Reuben. *Medium Theology; Lectures of Rev. Reuben Burrow, D. D., Professor of Theology in Bethel College from 1851 to 1860, with Autobiographical Sketch and Short Account of Funeral,* ed. A. G. Burrow. Nashville: Cumberland Presbyterian Publishing House, 1881.

Bushnell, Horace. *Christian Nurture.* New Haven: Yale University Press, 1947.

Campbell, Thomas Dishman. *Brothers of the Faith: A Study of the History of a Relationship.* [Memphis: Frontier Press], 1965.

Campbell, Thomas H. *Good News on the Frontier; A History of the Cumberland Presbyterian Church.* Richmond: CLC Press, 1965.

————. *History of the Cumberland Presbyterian Church in Texas.* Nashville: Cumberland Presbyterian Publishing House, 1936.

————. *Studies in Cumberland Presbyterian History.* Nashville: Cumberland Presbyterian Publishing House, 1944.

Cartwright, Peter. *Autobiography of Peter Cartwright, the Backwoods Preacher*, ed. W. P. Strickland. New York: Calton & Porter, 1857.

*A Circular Letter Addressed to the Societies and Brethren of the Late Cumberland Presbytery; in Which There Is a Correct Statement of the Origin, Progress, and Termination of the Differences between the Synod of Kentucky, and the Former Presbytery of Cumberland, 1810*. Russellville, Ky.: Matthew Duncan, 1810.

Cleveland, Catherine C. *The Great Revival in the West, 1797-1805*. Chicago: University of Chicago Press, 1916.

*The Confession of Faith and Government of the Cumberland Presbyterian Church*. Revised 1883. Nashville: Cumberland Presbyterian Publishing House, 1885.

*The Confession of Faith and Government of the Cumberland Presbyterian Church; Proposed Revision*. Nashville: Board of Publication of the Cumberland Presbyterian Church, 1882.

*The Confession of Faith and Form of Government of the Reformed Cumberland Presbyterian Church*. Paris, Ark.: Wagner Printery, 1903.

*The Constitution of the Cumberland Presbyterian Church in the United States of America, Containing the Confession of Faith, a Catechism, the Government and Discipline, and the Directory for the Worship of God. Ratified and Adopted by the Synod of Cumberland, Held at Sugg's Creek, in Tennessee State, April the 5th, 1814, and Continued by Adjournments, until the 9th of the Same Month*. Nashville: printed by M. & J. Norvell, for the publishers, 1815.

*The Constitution of the Presbyterian Church in the United States of America; Being Its Standards Subordinate to the Word of God, viz., the Confession of Faith, the Larger and Shorter Catechisms, the Form of Government, the Book of Discipline, and the Directory for the Worship of God, as Ratified and Adopted by the Synod of New York and Philadelphia in the Year of Our Lord 1788; and as Amended in the Years 1805-1905, Together with the Constitutional Rules Adopted in 1893-1901, and Administrative Acts of the Assembly of a General Nature*. Philadelphia: Presbyterian Board of Publication and Sabbath-School Work, 1906.

*The Constitution of the Presbyterian Church in the United States of America; Being Its Standards Subordinate to the Word of God, viz., the Confession of Faith, the Larger and Shorter Catechisms, the Form of Government, the Book of Discipline, and the Directory for the Worship of God, as Ratified and Adopted by the Synod of New York and Philadelphia in the Year of Our Lord, 1778; and as Amended in the Years 1805-1908, Together with the Constitutional Rules Adopted in 1893-1907, and Administrative Acts of the Assembly of a General Nature.* Philadelphia: Presbyterian Board of Publication and Sabbath-School Work, 1909.

Cossitt, F. R. *The Life and Times of Rev. Finis Ewing, One of the Fathers and Founders of the Cumberland Presbyterian Church. To Which Is Added Remarks on Davidson's History, or, a Review of His Chapters on the Revival of 1800, and His History of the Cumberland Presbyterians.* Louisville: Lee Roy Woods, Agent, for the Board of Publication of the Cumberland Presbyterian Church, 1853.

Craighead, James G. *The Craighead Family: A Genealogical Memoir of the Descendents of Rev. Thomas and Margaret Craighead, 1658-1876.* Philadelphia: Sherman & Co., 1876.

_____. *Scotch and Irish Seeds in American Soil: The Early History of the Scotch and Irish Churches, and Their Relations to the Presbyterian Church of America.* Philadelphia: Presbyterian Board of Publication, 1878.

Crisman, E. B. *Biographical Sketches of Living Old Men, of the Cumberland Presbyterian Church.* Vol. I. St. Louis: Perrin & Smith, 1877.

_____. *Origin and Doctrines of the Cumberland Presbyterian Church.* Nashville: Cumberland Presbyterian Publishing House, 1856.

_____. *Origin and Doctrines of the Cumberland Presbyterian Church.* Enl. ed. St. Louis: Perrin & Smith, 1877.

Darby, W. J. *Our Position, or Cumberland Presbyterians in Relation to the Presbyterian Family.* Nashville: Cumberland Presbyterian Publishing House, n. d.

_____, and Jenkins, J. E., comps. *Cumberland Presbyterianism in Southern Indiana; Being a History of Indiana Presbytery and an Account of the Proceedings of Its Fiftieth Anniversary Held at Princeton, Indiana, April 13-18, 1876, Together with Various Addresses and Communications, and a Sermon on the Doctrines of the Church.* Indianapolis: published by the presbytery, 1876.

Davenport, Frederick M. *Primitive Traits in Religious Revivals: A Study in Mental and Social Evolution.* New York: Macmillan Co., 1905.

Davidson, Chalmers G. *Piedmont Partisan: The Life and Times of Brigadier General William Lee Davidson.* Davidson, N. C.: Davidson College, 1951.

Davidson, Robert. *History of the Presbyterian Church in the State of Kentucky with a Preliminary Sketch of the Churches in the Valley of Virginia.* Lexington, Ky.: Charles Marshall, 1847.

Davies, Samuel. *Clarity and Truth United or the Way of the Multitude Exposed in Six Letters to the Rev. M. William Stith, A. M., President of William and Mary College,* ed. Thomas C. Pears, Jr. Philadelphia:

Department of History of the Office of the General Assembly of the Presbyterian Church in the U. S. A., 1941.

_____. *Sermons on Important Subjects by the Reverend Samuel Davies, A. M., President of the College of New Jersey, with an Essay on the Life and Times of the Author, by Albert Barnes,* ed. Albert Barnes. New York: Robert Carter and Brothers, 1849.

Dexter, Henry M. *Congregationalism of the Last Three Hundred Years, as Seen in Its Literature: with Special Reference to Certain Recondite, Neglected, or Disputed Passages.* New York: Harper & Brothers, 1880.

Dinsmore, John W. *The Scotch-Irish in America: Their History, Traits, Institutions and Influences, Especially as Illustrated in the Early Settlers of Western Pennsylvania, and Their Descendents.* Chicago: Winona Publishing Co., 1906.

Donnell, Robert. *Thoughts on Various Subjects.* Louisville: Board of Publication of the Cumberland Presbyterian Church, 1856.

Everett, Donald E., with Reiwald, Eugenia DeB.; Mason, Blanche M., and Prassel, Ann Hetherington. *Trinity University: A Record of One Hundred Years.* San Antonio: Trinity University Press, 1968.

[Ewing, Finis]. *A Series of Letters Containing a Reply to a Pastoral Letter of West Tennessee Presbytery, to Which Is Added an Address to the Congregation, etc., under the Care of Cumberland Presbytery, by a Member of That Body.* Russellville, Ky.: Matthew Duncan, 1812.

Ewing, Finis. *A Series of Lectures on the Most Important Subjects in Divinity.* Fayetteville, Tenn.: printed by E. and J. B. Hill for the Cumberland Presbyterian Synod, 1827.

_____. *Lectures on the Most Important Subjects in Divinity.* [2nd ed.] Louisville: Cumberland Presbyterian Board of Publication, 1849.

Ewing, Presley K., and Ewing, Mary E. *The Ewing Genealogy with Cognate Branches: A Summary of the Ewings and Their Kin in America.* Houston: Hercules Book Co., 1919.

Ewing, R. C. *Historical Memoirs: Containing a Brief History of the Cumberland Presbyterian Church in Missouri, and Biographical Sketches of a Number of Those Ministers Who Contributed to the Organization and the Establishment of That Church in the Country West of the Mississippi River.* Nashville: Cumberland Presbyterian Board of Publication, 1874.

Finley, James B. *Autobiography of Rev. James B. Finley; or, Pioneer Life in the West,* ed. W. P. Strickland. Cincinnati: Methodist Book Concern, 1853.

Firth, Charles. *Oliver Cromwell and the Rule of the Puritans in England.* London: Oxford University Press, 1900.

Fly, J. B., and Dunlap, L. A. *Life and Labors of the Late Alexander Anderson Young.* St. Louis: Perrin & Smith, 1881.

Foote, William H. *Sketches of North Carolina, Historical and Biographical, Illustrative of the Principles of a Portion of Her Early Settlers.* New York: Robert Carter, 1846.

Ford, Henry G. *The Scotch-Irish in America.* Princeton, N. J.: Princeton University Press, 1915.

Foster, Frank H. *A Genetic History of New England Theology.* Chicago: University of Chicago Press, 1907.

Foster, Robert V. *Systematic Theology.* Nashville: Cumberland Presbyterian Publishing House, 1898.

Gaut, John M. *Patriotism and Presbyterianism: An Address before the Lebanon, Tennessee, Bible Conference.* Nashville: Cumberland Press, 1908.

Gewehr, Wesley. *The Great Awakening in Virginia, 1740-1790.* Durham, N. C.: Duke University Press, 1930.

Gillett, Ezra H. *History of the Presbyterian Church in the United States of America.* Rev. ed. Philadelphia: Board of Publication and Sabbath-School Work, 1873.

Graham, Ian C. C. *Colonists from Scotland: Immigration to North America, 1707-1783.* Ithaca, N. Y.: Cornell University Press, 1956.

Guthrie, Dwight R. *John McMillan, the Apostle of Presbyterianism in the West.* Pittsburgh: University of Pittsburgh Press, 1952.

Hall, James H. B. *The History of the Cumberland Presbyterian Church in Alabama Prior to 1826.* From the *Transactions of the Alabama Historical Society, 1899-1903,* Vol. IV, Reprint No. 18. Montgomery, 1904.

Hanna, Charles A. *The Scotch-Irish, or the Scot in North Britain, North Ireland and North America.* New York: G. P. Putnam's Sons, 1902.

Hays, George B. *Presbyterians: A Popular Narrative of Their Origin, Progress, Doctrines, and Achievements.* New York: J. A. Hill & Co., 1892.

Hetherington, William M. *History of the Church of Scotland.* New York: Robert Carter and Brothers, 1881.

Hodge, Charles A. *The Constitutional History of the Presbyterian Church in the United States of America.* Vol. I. Philadelphia: Presbyterian Board of Publication, 1857.

Hogan, William Ransom. *The Texas Republic: A Social and Economic History.* Norman: University of Oklahoma Press, 1946.

Hughey, John R. *Lights and Shadows of the Cumberland Presbyterian Church.* Decatur, Ill.: privately printed, 1906.

*Inventory of the Church Archives of Illinois: Cumberland Presbyterian Church.* Prepared by Illinois Historical Records Survey, Division of Community Service Programs, Work Projects Administration. Chicago: Illinois Historical Records Survey, Illinois Records Project, 1942.

Johnson, Charles A. *The Frontier Camp Meeting, Religion's Harvest Time.* Dallas: Southern Methodist University Press, 1955.

Keller, Charles R. *The Second Awakening in Connecticut.* New Haven: Yale University Press, 1942.

Klett, Guy S. *Presbyterians in Colonial Pennsylvania.* Philadelphia: University of Pennsylvania Press, 1937.

Knox, John. *The Works of John Knox.* Vol. II. Edinburgh: James Thin, 1895.

Lee, Jesse. *A Short History of the Methodists in the United States of America: Beginning in 1766, and Continued till 1809.* Baltimore: McGill and Cline, 1810.

Leyburn, James G. *The Scotch-Irish: A Social History.* Chapel Hill: University of North Carolina Press, 1962.

Logan, J. B. *History of the Cumberland Presbyterian Church in Illinois, Containing Sketches of the First Ministers, Churches, Presbyteries and Synods; also a History of Missions, Publication and Education.* Alton, Ill.: Perrin & Smith, 1878.

Lowry, David. *Life and Labors of the Late Rev. Robert Donnell, of Alabama, Minister of the Gospel in the Cumberland Presbyterian Church, with an Appendix containing a Sketch of the Life of the Late Hugh Bone, Esq., of Kentucky.* Alton, Ill.: S. V. Crossman, Printer, 1867.

McClure, David. *Dairy of David McClure,* with Notes by Franklin B. Dexter. New York: Knickerbocker Press, 1889.

McDonnold, B. W. *History of the Cumberland Presbyterian Church.* Nashville: Board of Publication of Cumberland Presbyterian Church, 1888.

McDougall, Donald, ed. *Scots and Scots' Descendants in America.* New York: Caledonian Publishing Co., 1917.

McGready, James. *The Posthumous Works of the Reverend and Pious James M'Gready, Late Minister of the Gospel, in Henderson, Kentucky,* ed. James Smith. Louisville: W. W. Worsley, 1831-1833.

MacGregor, Janet. *The Scottish Presbyterian Polity: A Study of Its Origins in the Sixteenth Century.* Edinburgh: Oliver and Boyd, 1926.

McKinney, William W., ed. *The Presbyterian Valley: 200 Years of Presbyterianism in the Upper Ohio Valley.* Pittsburgh: Davis and Warde, 1958.

MacLean, John. *An Historical Account of the Settlements of Scotch Highlanders in America Prior to the Peace of 1783: Together with Notices of Highland Regiments and Biographical Sketches.* Cleveland: Holman-Taylor Co., 1900.

McNeil, John T. *The History and Character of Calvinism.* New York: Oxford University Press, 1954.

McNemar, Richard. *The Kentucky Revival: Or a Short History of the Late Outpouring of the Spirit of God in the Western States of America, with a Brief Account of the Entrance and Progress of What the World Called Shakerism, among Subjects of the Late Revival in Ohio and Kentucky.* Cincinnati: J. W. Brown, 1807.

Maghee, Frances C., comp. *History and Work of the Woman's Board of Missions of the Cumberland Presbyterian Church.* Evansville, Ind.: Woman's Board of Missions of the Cumberland Presbyterian Church, 1895.

————; Graf, Mary M.; Burchett, Mrs. R. E.; Wilson, Mamie. *History of the Woman's Board of Missions of the Cumberland Presbyterian Church, 1880-1933.* Nashville: Woman's Board of Missions of the Cumberland Presbyterian Church, 1934.

*Magnalia Christi Americana.* Vol. I. Hartford: S. Andrus, 1820.

Maxson, Charles. *The Great Awakening in the Middle Colonies.* Chicago: University of Chicago Press, 1920.

Mead, Sidney E. *The Lively Experiment: The Shaping of Christianity in America.* New York: Harper and Row, 1963.

Merriam, Lucius S. *Higher Education in Tennessee.* Washington, D. C.: Government Printing Office, 1893.

Meyer, Duane. *The Highland Scots of North Carolina, 1732-1776.* Chapel Hill: University of North Carolina Press, 1961.

Miller, A. B. *Doctrines and Genius of the Cumberland Presbyterian Church.* Nashville: Cumberland Presbyterian Publishing House, 1892.

Miller, Perry. *The New England Mind: The Seventeenth Century.* New York: Macmillan Co., 1939.

————. *Roger Williams: His Contribution to the American Tradition.* Indianapolis: Bobbs-Merrill, 1953.

Miller, Samuel. *Memoirs of John Rodgers.* New York: Whiting and Watson, 1813.

Morison, Samuel Eliot, and Commager, Henry Steele. *The Growth of the American Republic.* 4th ed., Vol. I. New York: Oxford University Press, 1956.

Morton, Mrs. J. H. *Hands at Rest: A Sequel to "Filled Hands": The Complete Story of Mrs. A. M. Drennan's Life and Work in Japan.* Nashville: Cumberland Presbyterian Publishing House, 1904.

Nichols, James H. *Democracy and the Churches.* Philadelphia: Westminster Press, 1951.

Nichols, Robert H. *Presbyterianism in New York State: A History of the Synod and Its Predecessors*. Philadelphia: Westminster Press, 1963.

Olmstead, Clifton E. *History of Religion in the United States*. Englewood Cliffs, N. J.: Prentice-Hall, 1960.

Ordóñez, Francisco. *História del cristianismo evangélico en Colombia*. [Cali, Colombia: Alianza Cristiana y Misionera], n. d.

Osgood, Herbert L. *The American Colonies in the Eighteenth Century*. New York: Columbia University Press, 1924.

*Our Senior Soldiers: The Biographies and Autobiographies of Eighty Cumberland Presbyterian Preachers*. Compiled by the Cumberland Presbyterian Board of Publication. Nashville, 1915.

Parrington, Vernon L. *The Colonial Mind, 1620-1800*. Vol. I of *Main Currents in American Thought, and Interpretation of American Literature from the Beginnings to 1920*. New York: Harcourt, Brace and Co., 1927.

*A Pastoral Letter Addressed to the Churches under the Care of the Presbytery of West Tennessee*. Nashville: Eastin & Gwin, 1812.

Posey, Walter Brownlow. *The Baptist Church in the Lower Mississippi Valley, 1776-1845*. Lexington: University of Kentucky Press, 1957.

————. *Frontier Mission: A History of Religion West of the Southern Appalachians to 1861*. Lexington: University of Kentucky Press, 1966.

————. *The Presbyterian Church in the Old Southwest, 1778-1838*. Richmond: John Knox Press, 1952.

Rice, David. *A Lecture on the Divine Decrees, to Which Is Annexed a Few Observations on a Piece Lately Printed in Lexington, Entitled "The Principles of the Methodists or the Scripture Doctrines of Predestination, Election, and Reprobation."* Lexington, Ky.: John Bradford, 1791.

Riley, James L. *Life Sketches of the Rev. James L. Riley, Beloved Cumberland Presbyterian Minister, Late of Cynthiana, Indiana, 1824-1911*. Carmi, Ill.: White County Tribune, 1911.

Rogers, John. *The Biography of Eld. Barton Stone, Written by Himself: with Additions and Reflections by Elder John Rogers, Written in Part by John Rogers*. Cincinnati: J. A. & U. P. James, 1847.

Roosevelt, Theodore. *The Winning of the West*. New York: Current Literature Publishing Co., 1906.

Sandburg, Carl. *Abraham Lincoln: The Prairie Years and the War Years*. One-volume ed. New York: Harcourt, Brace & World, 1966.

Schaff, Philip. *The Creeds of Christendom, with a History and Critical Notes*. Rev. ed. New York: Harper & Brothers, 1931.

Schaller, Lyle E. *Report of the In-Depth Study of the Cumberland Presbyterian Church*. Naperville, Ill.: Center for Parish Development, 1971.

Schneider, Herbert W. *The Puritan Mind*. New York: Henry Holt and Co., 1930.

Simpson, Thomas J. *History of the Cumberland Presbyterian Church, with Miscellaneous Thoughts on Several Subjects of Divinity So Much Controverted in the World*. Jefferson City: J. T. Quesenberry, 1844.

Slosser, Gaius J., ed. *They Seek a Country: The American Presbyterians— Some Aspects*. New York: Macmillan Co., 1955.

Smith, Elwyn A. *The Presbyterian Ministry in American Culture: A Study in Changing Concepts, 1700-1900*. Philadelphia: Westminster Press, 1962.

Smith, H. Shelton; Handy, Robert T.; and Loetscher, Lefferts A. *American Christianity, an Historical Interpretation with Representative Documents, 1607-1820*. Vol. I. New York: Charles Scribner's Sons, 1960.

Smith, James. *History of the Christian Church from Its Origin to the Present Time. Compiled from Various Authors: Including a History of the Cumberland Presbyterian Church, Drawn from Authentic Documents*. Nashville: Cumberland Presbyterian Office, 1835.

Smith, Joseph. *Old Redstone, or Historical Sketches of Western Presbyterianism, Its Early Ministers, Its Perilous Times and Its First Records*. Philadelphia: Lippincott, Grambo and Co., 1854.

Speer, William. *The Great Revival of 1800*. Philadelphia: Presbyterian Board of Publication, 1872.

Sprague, William B., ed. *Presbyterians*. Vol. III of *Annals of the American Pulpit; or Commemorative Notices of Distinguished American Clergymen of Various Denominations, from the Early Settlements of the Country to the Close of the Year Eighteen Hundred and Fifty-Five, with Historical Introductions*. New York: Robert Carter and Brothers, 1858.

Stearns, Jonathan F. *First Church in Newark. Historical Discourse Relating to the First Presbyterian Church in Newark*. Newark, N. J.: privately printed, 1853.

Stephens, John Vant. *Causes Leading to the Organization of the Cumberland Presbyterian Church*. Nashville: Cumberland Presbyterian Publishing House, 1898.

————. *Genesis of the Cumberland Presbyterian Church*. Cincinnati: privately printed, 1941.

————. *The Story of the Founding of the Theological School in the Cumberland Presbyterian Church*. Cincinnati: privately printed, 1933.

————, ed. *The Cumberland Presbyterian Digest (1899)*. Nashville: Cumberland Presbyterian Publishing House, 1899.

Street, T. Watson. *The Story of Southern Presbyterians*. Richmond: John Knox Press, 1961.

Stringfield, E. E. *Presbyterianism in the Ozarks: A History of the Work of the Various Branches of the Presbyterian Church in Southwest Missouri, 1834-1907.* N. p.: published at the request of the Presbytery of Ozark, U. S. A., 1909.

Sweet, William Warren. *The Congregationalists.* Vol. III of *Religion on the American Frontier.* Chicago: University of Chicago Press, 1939.

_____. *The Presbyterians, 1783-1840.* Vol. II of *Religion on the American Frontier.* New York: Harper & Brothers, 1936.

_____. *Religion in Colonial America.* New York: Charles Scribner's Sons, 1942.

_____. *Religion in the Development of American Culture, 1765-1840.* New York: Charles Scribner's Sons, 1952.

_____. *The Story of Religion in America.* Rev. and enl. ed. New York: Harper & Brothers, 1950.

Tewksbury, Donald G. *The Founding of American Colleges and Universities before the Civil War.* Hamden, Conn.: Archon Books, 1965.

Thompson, Ernest T. *Presbyterians in the South, 1607-1861.* Richmond: John Knox Press, 1963.

Thompson, Robert E. *A History of the Presbyterian Churches in the United States.* Vol. VI of *The American Church History Series,* ed. Philip Schaff *et al.* New York: Christian Literature Co., 1895.

Tracy, Joseph. *The Great Awakening; A History of the Revival of Religion in the Time of Edwards and Whitefield.* Boston: Tappan and Dennent, 1842.

Trinterud, Leonard J. *The Forming of an American Tradition: A Reexamination of Colonial Presbyterianism.* Philadelphia: Westminster Press, 1949.

Turner, Frederick Jackson. *The Frontier in American History.* New York: Henry Holt and Co., 1920.

Turner, Herbert S. *Church in the Old Fields: Hawfields Presbyterian Church and Community in North Carolina.* Chapel Hill: University of North Carolina Press, 1962.

Vander Velde, Lewis G. *The Presbyterian Churches and the Federal Union, 1861-1869.* Cambridge, Mass.: Harvard University Press, 1932.

Walker, Williston. *The Creeds and Platforms of Congregationalism.* New York: Charles Scribner's Sons, 1893.

_____. *A History of the Congregational Churches.* Vol. III of *The American Church History Series,* ed. Philip Schaff *et al.* New York: Christian Literature Co., 1894.

Ware, C. W. *Barton Warren Stone, Pathfinder of Christian Union: A Story of His Life and Times.* St. Louis: Bethany Press, 1932.

Webster, Richard. *A History of the Presbyterian Church in America from*

*Its Origins until the Year 1760, with Biographical Sketches of Its Early Ministers.* Philadelphia: Joseph M. Wilson, 1857.

Weisberger, Bernard A. *They Gathered at the River: The Story of the Great Revivalists and Their Impact upon Religion in America.* Boston: Little, Brown and Co., 1958.

Winslow, Ola Elizabeth. *Jonathan Edwards, 1703-1758: A Biography.* New York: Macmillan Co., 1940.

Winthrop, John. *John Winthrop's Journal,* ed. James K. Hasmer. New York: Charles Scribner's Sons, 1908.

Wittke, Carl. *We Who Built America: The Saga of the Immigrant.* New York: Prentice-Hall, 1948.

Wolfe, Carl J. C., ed. *Jonathan Edwards on Evangelism.* Grand Rapids, Mich.: Wm. B. Eerdmans Publishing Co., 1958.

Young, Jacob. *Autobiography of a Pioneer; or, the Nativity, Experience, Travels, and Ministerial Labors of Rev. Jacob Young, with Incidents, Observations, and Reflections.* Cincinnati: Cranston and Curts, 1857.

# INDEX